Schools and Society

Mayfield Publishing Company
Palo Alto and London

Schools and Society

A Reader in Education and Sociology

JEANNE H. BALLANTINE
Wright State University

Manufactured in the United States of America
10 9 8 7 6 5 4 3 2 1

Mayfield Publishing Company
285 Hamilton Avenue
Palo Alto, California 94301

Sponsoring editor: Susan Elliott Loring
Manuscript editor: Victoria Nelson
Managing editor: Pat Herbst
Production editor: Jan deProsse
Art director and designer: Nancy Sears
Cover designer: Ellen Schmutz
Illustrator: Mary Burkhardt
Production manager: Cathy Willkie
Compositor: Publisher's Typography
Printer and binder: Malloy Lithographing

To Hardy:
for helping me
see what education
can be

Contents

Preface

This text/reader presents an overview of the sociology of education. After many years of teaching courses in the field and assigning students reading materials to give some notion of the scope, perspectives, and issues of the field, I decided to compile a set of representative readings. The selections cover those major topics most discussed by instructors, according to survey data, and are tied together by introductions that summarize the contributions each article makes to its subject area. My main challenge was to include a balance of material that would effectively present a well-rounded and interest-provoking summary of the fields of sociology of education and social foundations of education. I selected a group of readings, connected by the introductions and a systematic framework, designed to appeal to both graduate and undergraduate students and to present major theoretical perspectives, a sample of classic studies, current issues in the field, and applications of knowledge to educational issues and problems.

As explained in the Introduction, the framework for this text is the open systems model. Sociology of education is sometimes presented as a disparate group of topics grouped together under one heading; the open systems model, however, allows students to fully understand the scope of the field, the interconnections among topics, and the varied applications of the material.

According to a survey of instructors, the most frequently covered topics in the field of sociology of education include stratification, school and classroom as social systems, historical background, schools as organizations and bureaucracies, socialization, and theory.[1] All these major topics are covered in this text. In addition to the introductions and articles examining these topics, other issues of current interest are included: control of edu-

---

1. American Sociological Association, *Teaching Sociology of Education* (Washington, D.C.: ASA Teaching Resources Center, 1984).

cation, higher education, cross-cultural models, role expectations, sex roles, peer influence, achievement, school climate, school environments, the informal system, and change.

This reader can be used alone, with a text, or with other readings. Discussion and study questions are included to connect each article to the field and to other sections and articles in the text.

Several criteria were used for selecting articles for this text. I attempted to choose readings that

1. Illustrate major concepts, theoretical perspectives, and issues in sociology of education
2. Are written at a level of sophistication appropriate to students in advanced undergraduate or graduate courses
3. Are applicable to sociology, education, or "general" majors (students most likely to take the course)
4. Cover a variety of topics in the field—scientific studies, issues, commentaries, popular articles—selected from a range of respected sources but always relevant to sociology of education
5. Carry through the "open systems" approach of the text and provide unity to an often disparate group of topics

All the selections except the most recent ones have been tested for readability and interest level with graduate and undergraduate students; all were seen as useful and important contributions to understanding the field.

A number of colleagues have also served as reviewers. I would like to thank the following for their invaluable suggestions and comments on both the introductory material and the selections: David E. Olday, Moorhead State University; Mark O. Rousseau, University of Nebraska at Omaha; Ronald W. Smith, University of Nevada at Las Vegas; Jean Stockard, University of Oregon; and Theodore C. Wagenaar, Miami University (Ohio).

Jeanne Ballantine

Schools and Society

Introduction

Have you ever asked yourself what would happen if there were no schools, why there is controversy over what to teach in schools, or even when children should start school? Why do some children do better in school than others? Or why has busing become such a heated topic? Sociologists of education address a range of issues concerning schools, including these. This text will acquaint you with several of the primary sociological perspectives on educational systems as well as some major studies addressing these and other issues. To give you an idea of the variety of topics covered in sociology of education, here are some examples of questions addressed by recent research:

1. How do the physical setup and program of an educational organization affect such variables as learning, communication between faculty and students, and subject areas taught?
2. How effective are different teaching techniques, styles of learning, and classroom organizations in teaching students of various types and ability levels?
3. What are some community influences on schools? How do these affect their decision making, especially as related to socialization of the young?
4. How do professionalization of teachers and teacher militancy affect the school system?
5. How do issues such as equal opportunity and integration affect schools? Can minority students learn better in an integrated school?

As students, parents, taxpayers, and perhaps educators, you can make more effective decisions concerning schools if you have knowledge about these and other educational issues.

When you have read this text, you should have gained some understanding of the field of sociology of education, what it contributes to the study of educational systems, and some specific issues that concern sociologists of education.

WHAT DO SOCIOLOGISTS OF EDUCATION STUDY?

Sociologists study people interacting in groups, organizations, and institutions of society, family, education, religion, economics, and politics. Institutions constitute the major structural parts of any society. Sociologists of education focus on the *institution of education and the structure, processes, and interaction patterns within it.* These aspects of education vary greatly across societies. In some societies, children learn their proper roles and adult traits by observing their elders and imitating or modeling after adult behavior. In others, children attend formal schools from a young age and learn skills and knowledge necessary for survival. The kind of knowledge passed on through schools may be a matter of disagreement, but regardless of who controls decisions on the content of knowledge, educational institutions are the vehicle for passing on this information.

Education and other institutions are interdependent within a society. Change in one brings change in others. For instance, a family's attitudes toward education will affect the child's school experience. Many of these interrelationships fall within the parameters of sociology of education, including

1. Teacher-student interactions
2. Group dynamics in classrooms or teachers' organizations
3. The structure and functioning of educational systems
4. Societal and world systems of education

You will note as you read the selections that each focuses on one or more of these *levels of analysis,* from interaction between teachers and students to international influences on national educational systems.

THE EDUCATIONAL SYSTEM

At whatever level of analysis we study the system, *processes* are at work. These are the action part of the system, bringing the structure alive. Examples of processes include teaching, learning, communication, decision making, socialization, and stratification. They are essential dynamic parts of the educational system.

The *structure* of a system includes the hierarchy and roles people play—administrators, teachers, staff, and students—as well as the physical structure—classroom and school layout. Nor can we ignore the school's *environment,* which consists of individuals, groups, organizations, other institutions, and even world systems outside the school that influence its functioning. For instance, the Parent-Teachers Association (PTA) may put pressure on schools to revise the curriculum; other schools provide competition in academic achievement and sports; families influence their children's success in school; and the political-economic system determines funding available to schools. In short, no school exists in a vacuum. This *open systems* perspective will be the uniting theme in your text-reader.

PERSPECTIVES

Since the origins of sociology as a discipline, sociologists have provided valuable insights into how society works. The major perspectives used by sociologists to study society are also used by sociologists of education. Chapter 2 outlines several of these perspectives, which help us understand educational systems as well.

Sociology of education has a recent origin as a distinct field. The nineteenth-century French educator Emile Durkheim was the first to apply the sociological approach to the study of education. Many of his ideas centered on the contribution the educational institution makes to societal cohesion and order. Society and the institutions in it are intertwined, each reflecting the changes in the other. Durkheim wrote about a number of areas that influence sociologists of education today, and his work laid the foundation for the structural-functional perspective in sociology of education. Several brief excerpts from his works included in Chapter 1 illustrate Durkheim's contributions.

The writings of Karl Marx and Max Weber laid the groundwork for conflict theory and its applications to sociology of education. Whereas Durkheim assumed that education would contribute to societal cohesion by teaching a culture's shared values, Marx argued that institutions, including education, were controlled by the economically powerful and served to perpetuate the class structure. The "haves" control power, wealth, material goods, privilege, and influence; the "have nots" constantly present a challenge to those in power as they seek a larger share of society's wealth. This struggle for power influences the structures of institutions. Power is used to control knowledge taught at various levels of education as well as access to elite education; in classrooms, power systems between teacher and students prevail. This approach, which implies a volatile, changing situation in schools and society, is reflected in several readings in the text.

In the United States, the first interest in sociology of education took a problems approach. This early work, which was stimulated by efforts to reform society, including educational systems, was supplanted by the view that educational systems were sources of scientific data. Today, sociologists of education combine both approaches; they study systems and make practical policy recommendations. Recent theoretical approaches, such as interaction theories, as well as substantive areas of interest are equally influenced by societal trends (as the articles in Chapter 2 illustrate).

FUNCTIONS OF EDUCATION

Defining the main purposes or functions of educational systems in society provides the foundation for much sociological work, both classical and modern. These *functions* are the important roles played by education in society, especially in preparing its young to become members of society; they are at the root of functional discussions of education. Sociologists using the functional approach see the survival of society at stake; if a society fails to train its members in the skills and knowledge necessary for contributing to society, order and social control will be lowered.

Each function of education has generated controversy. Conflict theorists, for instance, point out problems in the functionalists' interpretation of each function, a debate you will observe throughout the text. The following are some functions identified by sociologists. As you read the selections in this text, you will be able to associate many of the issues discussed with one of these functions.

1. *Socialization.* Society provides the mechanism for teaching each new generation the "three Rs"—their rights, roles and responsibilities— so that initiates will understand and accept society's expectations. Through this process, young people learn to be productive members of society and teachers pass on its culture. Socialization continues throughout the life cycle, taking many forms both formal and informal: early childhood education; public schooling; university education; technical schooling; adult education; advanced training; workshop training; learning from observation, criticism, and peer interaction. How this socialization function is carried out varies from society to society, as the examples on cross-cultural education in Chapter 9 will show. In some societies learning by imitating elders is a primary mode of education, whereas formal classroom settings take precedence in others.

   Socialization is not always a smooth process. What to teach, whom to teach, and how to teach are worrisome questions to educators, societal leaders, and community members. Where several interest groups (racial, religious, socioeconomic) coexist, conflicts over control of educational systems can create schisms in communities, as exemplified in the Kanawha County textbook controversy described in Chapter 10.

2. *Selection, training, and allocation.* In this function, positions in society are filled through selection and placement of individuals. Education prepares, sorts, and places people. It prepares by teaching needed skills and knowledge. It sorts by testing and controlling. It places by tracking, credentialing, grading, and ultimately filling positions in society.

   The controversies surrounding equality of educational opportunity are closely related to this function. Do all groups of children receive the same educational opportunities? What are long-term job placement results if they do not? Conflict theorists are concerned with the results of testing, tracking, and placement for children from various backgrounds; a clear example of this position is presented in the Samuel Bowles article in Chapter 6.

3. *Change and innovation.* This is the function of expanding knowledge frontiers and adapting to changing environments. Culture accumulates; it builds on itself. Individuals in educational systems, especially those in institutions of higher education, research, write, create new technology, help set social policy, and contribute ideas for the advancement of knowledge. In addition, citizens expect schools to solve many societal problems: In our society, assimilation of immigrants has rested largely with schools, which were expected to create a "melting pot" and prepare newcomers to take a productive role in the society. This plan was abandoned in favor of cultural pluralism, allowing each group to maintain its heritage. With cultural pluralism, however, comes the distinct possibility of differential treatment of groups, a fact experienced by racial and religious minorities.

   When change is introduced, it threatens existing patterns. Moreover, the nature of the change may itself be controversial. Consider busing to achieve integration and facilitate equal opportunity, for example; the article by Ray C. Rist in Chapter 6 addresses this issue.

4. *Social and personal development.* This function of education introduces young people to expectations of the world outside the family. Children learn quickly that teachers accept, reject, reward, or punish by judging them in relation to other children and to a set of standards and expectations. This transition from the family world, where the child is accepted and belongs, to the outside world, where more formal, judgmental secondary relationships govern interactions, forces painful assessments of one's strengths and weaknesses. We all learn techniques for coping with the expectations of schools and the bigger community, some of which are discussed in Paul Willis's article in Chapter 6.

PERSPECTIVE OF YOUR TEXT

Theoretical perspectives are based on differing assumptions about interaction and societal order. Each perspective contributes to our understanding
of issues in sociology of education. To present only one perspective, however, would be limiting your knowledge base and the value of sociology
for understanding current educational issues.

Therefore, this book uses the *open systems* approach to present sociology
of education as a coherent, integrated field in which each topic relates to
a larger whole. Several theoretical perspectives are discussed in Chapters
1 and 2 to acquaint you with alternative ways of understanding and interpreting issues in sociology of education.

Each of these perspectives is useful for understanding some aspect of
the open system of education. The following discussion explains this approach in detail.

The Open Systems Approach*

Suppose that we want to understand an educational system as a whole,
integrated, dynamic entity. We are faced with a problem. Most research
studies focus on parts of the whole system, and most theoretical approaches
have biases or limitations. An open systems approach is not a panacea for
all the problems we face when trying to get the total picture, but it can
help us conceptualize a whole system and understand how the small pieces
fit together into a working unity. A model provides a useful way of visu-
alizing the many elements in the system; it helps order observations and
data, and represents a generalized picture of complex interacting elements
and sets of relationships.[1] The model given in Figure 1 refers to no one
particular organization or theoretical approach, but rather to the common
characteristics of many educational settings.

While this model indicates the component parts of a total system, it
does not imply that one theory is better than another for explaining situations or events in the system. Neither does it suggest which is the best
methodology to use in studying any part of the system. It does allow us
to visualize the parts we may read about or study in relation to the whole
system—to see where they fit and what relationship they bear to the whole.

In describing a systems model, Marvin Olsen has said:

*From Jeanne H. Ballantine, *The Sociology of Education: A Systematic Analysis*, pp. 16–22.
Copyright © 1983 by Prentice-Hall, Inc., Englewood Cliffs, N.J. Reprinted by permission of
the publisher.

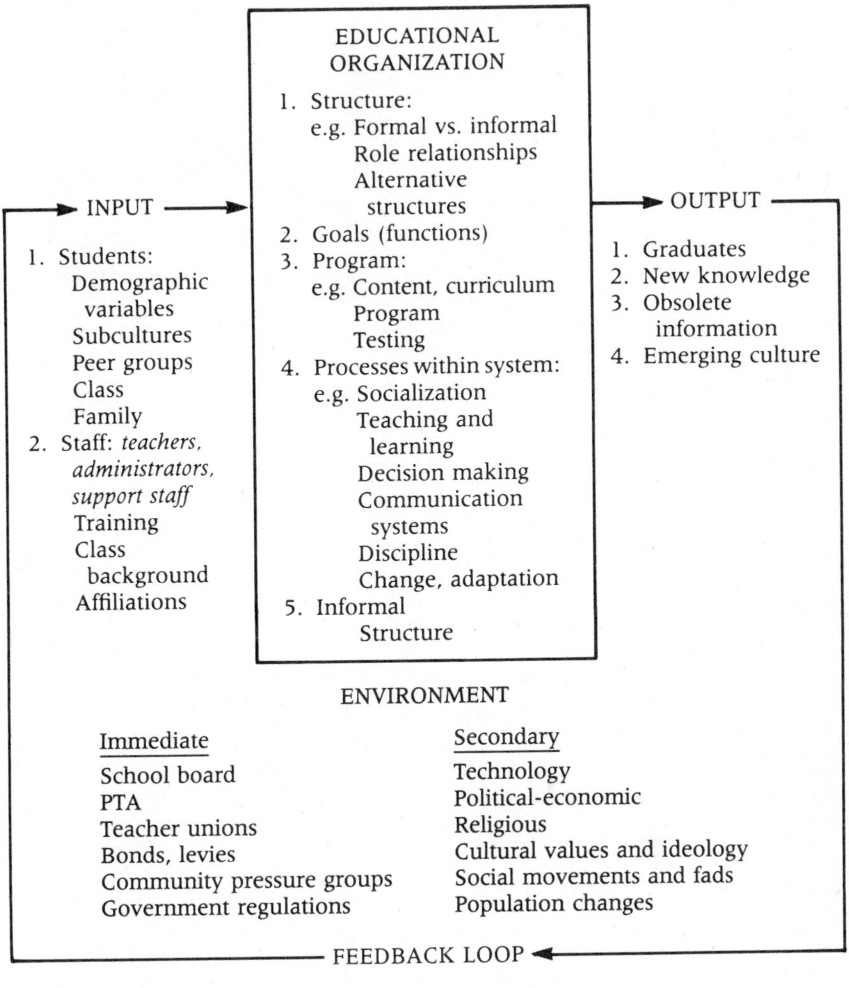

```
                    ┌─────────────────────────────┐
                    │    EDUCATIONAL              │
                    │    ORGANIZATION            │
                    │                            │
                    │  1. Structure:             │
                    │     e.g. Formal vs. informal│
                    │         Role relationships  │
                    │         Alternative        │
   ► INPUT ───────► │           structures       │    ► OUTPUT ──┐
                    │  2. Goals (functions)       │
  1. Students:      │  3. Program:               │   1. Graduates
     Demographic    │     e.g. Content, curriculum│   2. New knowledge
     variables      │         Program            │   3. Obsolete
     Subcultures    │         Testing            │      information
     Peer groups    │  4. Processes within system:│   4. Emerging culture
     Class          │     e.g. Socialization     │
     Family         │         Teaching and       │
  2. Staff: teachers,│        learning           │
     administrators,│         Decision making    │
     support staff  │         Communication      │
     Training       │           systems          │
     Class          │         Discipline         │
       background   │         Change, adaptation  │
     Affiliations   │  5. Informal               │
                    │       Structure            │
                    └─────────────────────────────┘
```

ENVIRONMENT

Immediate	Secondary
School board	Technology
PTA	Political-economic
Teacher unions	Religious
Bonds, levies	Cultural values and ideology
Community pressure groups	Social movements and fads
Government regulations	Population changes

──────── FEEDBACK LOOP ◄─────────

FIGURE 1
Systems Model of Education

It is not a particular kind of social organization. It is an analytical model that can be applied to any instance of the process of social organization, from families to nation. . . . Nor is [it] a substantive theory—though it is sometimes spoken of as a theory in sociological literature. This model is a highly general, content-free conceptual framework within which any number of different substantive theories of social organization can be constructed.[2]

Figure 1 shows the basic components of any social system. These components are the organization, the environment, input, output, and feedback. We will discuss each of these by following five steps.

Step 1. Focus your attention on the center box, *the organization*. This refers to the center of activity and the central concern for the researcher. This box can represent a society (such as the United States), an institution (such as education or family), an organization (such as a particular school or church), or a subsystem (such as a classroom). For purposes of discussion, we shall refer to this as "the organization." It is in the organization that action takes place, illustrating that the organization is more than structure, positions, roles, and functions. Within the organizational boundaries is a *structure* consisting of parts and subparts, positions and roles. Though we speak of the organization as though it were a living entity, we are really referring to the personnel who carry out the activities of the organization and make decisions about organizational action. The *processes* in the system bring the organization alive. Decision making by key personnel, communication between members of the organization, socialization into positions in the organization—these are among the many activities that are constantly taking place.

These processes do not take place in a vacuum. The decision makers holding positions and carrying out roles in the organization are constantly responding to demands from both inside and outside of the organization. The boundaries of the organization are not solid, but rather remain flexible and pliable in most systems to allow system needs to be met. We call this "open boundaries" or an *open system*.

Capturing the informal relationships in the school—who eats lunch with whom, who cuts classes, what subtle cues teachers transmit to students, what is the gossip in the teachers' lounge—can tell us as much about its functioning as observing formal roles and structure.

Step 2. An open system implies that there is interaction between the organization and the environment outside of the organization.

Focus now on the *environment*. This includes everything which surrounds the organization and influences it in some way. Typically, the environment includes other surrounding systems. For a country, these would be all other countries of the world; for an organization, they would be other competing or cooperating organizations. In addition, there is the *technological environment* with new developments which affect the operation of the system; the *political environment* which affects the system through legal controls; the *economic environment* from which the system gets its financing; the *surrounding community* and its prevailing attitudes; the values, norms, and changes in society which are often reflected in *social movements* or fads; *population changes;* and so forth.

For each organization, the crucial environment will differ; its importance, however, does not. The organization depends on the environment to meet many of its resource requirements and to obtain information.

Every school and school district faces a different set of challenges from the environment. There are necessary and desired interactions with the environment, and some that are not so pleasant. The interaction of the school with the environment takes place in our systems model in the form of input and output.

Step 3. The organization receives *input* from the environment in such forms as information, raw materials, personnel, finances and new ideas. Furthermore, the persons who are members of the organization are also part of its environment and bring into the organization influences from the environment.

Some of the environmental inputs are mandatory for the organization's survival; others vary in degree of importance. For most organizations, some inputs are undesirable, but unavoidable: new legal restrictions, competition, or financial pressures. The organization can exert some control over the inputs. For instance, schools have selection processes for new teachers; textbooks, and other curricular materials. Certain positions in the organization are held by personnel who act as *buffers* between the organization and its environment. The secretary who answers the phone, for example, has a major controlling function.

Step 4. *Output* refers to the material items and the non-material ideas which leave the organization: completed products, wastes, information, evolving culture, new technology. There may be personnel in *boundary spanning* positions, bridging the gap between organization and environment. Personnel with responsibility for selling the organization's product, whether they work in a manufacturing organization or in a placement office for college graduates, serve this function.

Step 5. A key aspect of a systems model is the process of *feedback*. This implies an organization constantly adapting to changes and demands in the environment as a result of new information it receives. For instance, the organizational personnel compare the current state of affairs with desired goals and environmental feedback to determine new courses of action. The feedback may be positive or negative, requiring differing responses.

The basic model of Figure 1 can serve us in many ways. It is used as a framework for organizing content in this book. It can help promote interdisciplinary study. Consider, for example, Kenneth Boulding's statement:

> An interdisciplinary movement has been abroad for some time. The first signs of this are usually the development of hybrid disciplines. . . . It is one of the main objectives of General Systems Theory to develop these generalized ears, and by developing a framework of general theory to enable one specialist to catch relevant communications from others.[4]

Sociology of education cannot be discussed within the fields of education and sociology alone. Examples of related fields are numerous: economics and school financing; political science, power and policy issues; the family and the child; church-state separation controversies; health fields and medical care for children; humanities and the arts; and the school's role in early childhood training.

Several social scientists[5] have pointed to the value of an open systems approach in organizational analysis. David Easton, for example, writes:

> A systems analysis promises a more expansive, more inclusive, and more flexible theoretical structure than is available even in a thoroughly self-conscious and well-developed equilibrium approach.[6]

For our purposes, this approach not only serves the above functions but also helps to give unity to a complex field.

ORGANIZATION OF THE TEXT

Using the open systems model as a framework, the chapters of this text are organized within three sections. Section One presents historical roots and an overview of the field. Section Two focuses on internal organization—roles, structure, and what takes place inside the school. Section Three includes discussions of the processes of change and stratification as well as examples of the system of higher education and the world system of education. The following outline of the ten chapters of the text will serve as a further orientation.

SECTION ONE: What Can Sociology of Education Contribute to Our Understanding of Schools?

1. An overview of sociology of education, defining the parameters of the field. Several "classical" contributions show the origins of the field and early issues that stimulated its development.

2. Current theoretical perspectives: functionalism, conflict theory, and interaction theory, along with other directions presented in this and later chapters.

SECTION TWO: What Goes on Inside the School System? Structure, Roles, and Processes

3. Formal organization, or the structure of the educational system, with the typical focus on hierarchy and organizational structure and features. Some authors point to problems with bureaucratic structure in facilitating the process of learning and community participation; conflicts may arise over control held at each level of the system, as illustrated in the readings.

4. Hierarchies of positions—administrators, teachers, students, staff—present within most organizational structures. What these roles entail, how they are executed, and problems encountered by role holders in interaction with others in the system are the focus of the chapter. Particular emphasis is placed on student roles.

5. The informal system, or the unofficial activities and processes that influence how the system works: the school's "climate," which affects students' achievements, the "hidden curriculum," the self-concepts of children, peer group influences, teacher-student interactions, power dynamics in the school, and all parts of the system that defy neat categorization.

SECTION THREE: The Relationship Between Educational Systems and Society

6. Stratification, also discussed in Chapter 3, and other major controversial processes in educational systems such as equal educational opportunity, busing, testing, public versus private schools, and sex role socialization, are discussed in these selections.

7. The social environment surrounding the school, perhaps as important as internal structure and processes in determining what goes on in schools: the importance of family background and attitudes toward education for student achievement; public attitudes because they influence curriculum, funding, and decision making; government legislation and funding because they can limit or expand school programs. The articles illustrate some of these influences on schools.

8. Higher education as a specific level in the educational system, sharing some features of schools at lower levels and possessing some unique issues of its own: affirmative action, open admis-

sions, professional identity, quality control, and shrinking enrollments.

9. Educational systems around the world, viewed as individual case studies or seen as part of the global system of education. Inter-relationships among countries, analysis of world environmental influences that contribute to the structure and processes in each individual country's educational system.

10. Change, ever-present in educational systems, reflects the influence of societal and educational movements on schools; in recent years, these trends include stress on basic education, competency testing, and accountability, in contrast to a previous emphasis on open classrooms and humanistic education. The issues in Chapter 10 illustrate the way the pendulum has swung from decade to decade as well as what may be in store for the future.

Reading the chapter introductions first will help you put the articles into the open systems perspective and measure their importance to the topic being discussed. Make note of the questions preceding each article *before* you read the article and again afterwards. The questions will help point out (1) the main point of the article, (2) its relationship to other articles in the chapter, (3) how it fits into the total picture, and (4) its relevance to you.

Now proceed to study an institution that touches all of us many times during our lives—education.

NOTES

1. D. Griffiths, "Systems Theory and School Districts," *Ontario Journal of Educational Research*, Vol. 8, 1965, 24.

2. Marvin Olsen, *The Process of Social Organization: Power in Social Systems* (2nd ed.), New York: Holt, Rinehart, & Winston, 1978, p. 228.

3. Adapted from Ludwig von Bertalanfly, "General Systems Theory—A Critical Review," *General Systems*, Vol. 7, 1962, 1–20.

4. Kenneth E. Boulding, "GST—The Skeleton of Science," *Management Science*, Vol. 2, 1956, 197–208.

5. W. G. Scott, "Organization Theory: An Overview and an Appraisal," in J. A. Litterer (Ed.), *Organizations: Structure and Behavior*, New York: John Wiley & Sons, 1963.

6. David Easton, *A Systems Analysis of Political Life*, New York: John Wiley & Sons, 1965, p. 20.

SECTION ONE

What Can Sociology of Education Contribute to Our Understanding of Schools?

To understand any *system*—ourselves, our family, school, community, or country—certain information is important. First, a picture of that system—what it includes and its boundaries; second, its purpose in the larger system—what it accomplishes and how; third, interpretations or perspectives on the system—how it is studied and explained; fourth, processes taking place in the system—key issues it faces.

A system is composed of an internal organization and an environment, as discussed and diagrammed in the Introduction. Certain theories and explanations presented here relate primarily to the internal structure and processes of the system, while others take into account its environment. Note the differences among these theoretical perspectives and when each might be appropriate as a framework for studying problems in educational systems.

The first two chapters provide an introduction to the field of sociology of education. Its scope, diversity, and target issues are represented in the selections, along with some historical and recent perspectives on the field.

CHAPTER 1

The Sociology of Education: Where We Are and How We Got Here

Every discipline has roots; the sociology of education as a subfield of sociology is no exception. Before the articles in this text can be properly understood, they need to be placed in a historical context. Hence, this chapter presents both descriptions of the field as it exists today and the historical foundations on which current interpretations are based. The open systems framework further helps us to place current issues in the field within the context of broader societal environmental influences and trends, allowing us to discriminate among theoretical perspectives and methodological approaches. How the sociology of education evolved as a discipline and its current status is the topic of our first chapter.

SOME CLASSICAL CONTRIBUTIONS

The origins of our field can be traced to the earliest educational philosophers. For the purposes of this book, however, we will limit our examination to those roots directly within the field of sociology. Emile Durkheim (1858–1917), who taught pedagogy (education) at the Sorbonne in Paris, voiced many of the same concerns about education that we share today: how to maintain discipline in schools; what should be taught in the classroom and how; and what role government should play in educational policy. In his lectures Durkheim expressed concern regarding the relationships among education, other institutions, and society itself, all of which he saw as interdependent, and advocated the use of sociological perspective and methods to study education. In his major works—*Moral Education, The Evolution of Educational Thought,* and *Education and Sociology*—he applied a sociological approach to the understanding of educational systems, laying the foundation for sociologists to come by stressing, for example, the relationship between educational systems and larger societal trends. Through his studies of the history of education, he showed that changes in educational practice correlate with changes in societal beliefs and practices.

For Durkheim, moral values were the foundation of the social order. He believed that it was the duty of education to make responsible, reliable citizens out of schoolchildren. This in turn would ensure a society in which members shared common goals and supported the culture's moral standards. Because of his emphasis on social control and transmission of knowledge functions, Durkheim is usually considered a conservative defender of the societal status quo. He saw education as crucial to the integration of society, believing the State should control education and in that way train children to support the system. There is a flaw in this reasoning, however, for not all citizens agree with the actions of the State or with the goals of those in power at any given time. Governments, moreover, are likely to represent the interests of those who have power in society.

The Evolution of Educational Thought, a history of French education, is taken from a series of lectures given by Durkheim in 1904 and 1905 and was only recently translated into English. Notably, Durkheim discusses not only the structure of education and curriculum but also the transmission of knowledge, ideas that lay the foundation for much current research. Several interesting points about Durkheim's perspective at the time, just one hundred years ago, should be noted. First, he defends the physical sciences, arguing that although the humanities have long been with us, the study of nature has intrinsic value as well, not just practical value for industry-centered professions. This view seems strange today but illustrates how rapidly our educational values have changed. Second, he argues that teaching is educational only if it exerts moral influence on our thinking.

The first excerpt from Durkheim's *Education and Sociology* outlines what he saw as important features of educational systems: two generations, adults and students, with one influencing the other; and those factors common to all educational systems.

In the next excerpt, Durkheim discusses aspects of *moral education,* pointing out that classrooms are like small societies with rules and obligations; it is here that young people begin to learn the importance of group life, moving away from the intimate bonds of family life and toward the collective life of society.

Durkheim's contributions to the sociology of education have stimulated sociologists to do research in a number of areas including functions of education, relationships of education to societal change, cross-cultural research, social systems of schools and classrooms, and content of educational knowledge.

Max Weber, a contemporary of Durkheim, worked less directly in the field of education but contributed general sociological knowledge important in our study of education today. Noted for his discussions of bureaucracy and status group relationships, Weber argued that the interests of the dominant groups, or *insiders*, in society shape the schools; *outsiders* such as minority group members often face barriers in educational systems because they lack power. He believed that schools educate young into *status cultures* based on student wealth, power, and prestige. Some research today picks up on these issues, emphasizing experience in classrooms and results of schooling for insiders and outsiders.

Using historical, cross-cultural data, Weber developed a typology of authority styles: *charismatic*, based on an individual's ability to inspire others and gain a following; *traditional*, usually inherited authority, as in a chiefdom; and *rational-legal*, based on rules and merit, usually including examination systems. Education plays different roles depending on the type of leadership system. In a discussion of Chinese education, Weber points out opposing goals of education: those related to charismatic leadership structure and those preparing individuals for rational bureaucratic structures. The group with power will shape the educational system to its needs, as exemplified in this case study; they extend their ideal of culture and education to the general population. That ideal may be either a *cultivated* or *specialist* type of education, depending on the structure of domination. Groups lacking power are less likely to meet their educational ideal.

OVERVIEW OF THE FIELD

The last two articles in Chapter 1 provide an overview of sociology of education today. Maureen Hallinan, editor of the journal *Sociology of Education*, discusses the current state of the art, including important developments in the field, theoretical and methodological concerns, major studies and research stimulated by these studies, and where we need to go from here. Hallinan draws examples from an area that has received much research attention in recent years, namely, those factors affecting the academic productivity of students in school and their future educational and occupational attainment. Her summary of two studies illustrates the directions of some major current research in sociology of education.

Sociology of education and educational sociology are related, overlapping terms, but, as Donald Hansen points out, they need to be distinguished. The implications of each for research orientation, focus of interest, extent of interests, approaches, perspective, objectivity, and involvement are not necessarily the same. Though they have different missions, these two disciplines each contribute to the other; both are important fields today.

EMILE DURKHEIM

Definition of Education

Questions to think about

1 *According to Durkheim, what purpose does education serve for society?*
2 *Describe the interrelationship between society and education in the United States.*
3 *Is inequality of educational outcome inevitable, according to Durkheim?*

To define education we must . . . consider educational systems, present and past, put them together, and abstract the characteristics which are common to them. These characteristics will constitute the definition that we seek.

We have already determined, along the way, two elements. In order that there be education, there must be a generation of adults and one of youth, in interaction, and an influence exercised by the first on the second. It remains for us to define the nature of this influence.

There is, so to speak, no society in which the system of education does not present a twofold aspect: it is at the same time one and manifold.

It is manifold. Indeed, in one sense, it can be said that there are as many different kinds of education as there are different milieux in a given society. Is such a society formed of castes? Education varies from one caste to another; that of the patricians was not that of the plebeians; that of the Brahman was not that of the Sudra. Similarly, in the Middle Ages, what a difference between the culture that the young page received, instructed in all the arts of chivalry, and that of the villein, who learned in his parish school a smattering of arithmetic, song and grammar! Even today, do we not see education vary with social class, or even with locality? That of the city is not that of the country, that of the middle class is not that of the worker. Would one say that this organization is not morally justifiable, that one can see in it only a survival destined to disappear? This proposition is easy to defend. It is evident that the education of our children should not depend upon the chance of their having been born here or there, of some parents rather than others. But even though the moral conscience of our time would have received, on this point, the satisfaction that it expects, education would not, for all that, become more uniform. Even though the career of each child would, in large part, no longer be predetermined by a blind heredity, occupational specialization would not fail to result in a great pedagogical diversity. Each occupation, indeed, constitutes a milieu *sui generis* which requires particular aptitudes and specialized knowledge, in which certain ideas, certain practices, certain modes of viewing things, prevail: and as the child must be prepared for the function that he will be called upon to fulfill, education, beyond a certain age, can no longer remain the same for all those to whom it applies. That is why we see it, in all civilized countries, tending more and more to become diversified and specialized; and this specialization becomes more advanced daily. The heterogeneity which is thus created does not rest, as does that which we were just discussing, on unjust inequalities; but it is not less. To find an absolutely homogeneous and egalitarian education, it would be necessary to go back to prehistoric societies, in the structure of which there is no differentiation; and yet these kinds of societies represent hardly more than one logical stage in the history of humanity.

But, whatever may be the importance of these special educations, they are not all of education. It may even be said that they are not sufficient unto themselves; everywhere that one observes them, they vary from one another only beyond a certain point, up to which they are not differentiated. They all rest upon a common base. There is no people among whom there is not a certain number of ideas, sentiments and practices which education must inculcate in all children indiscriminately, to whatever social category they belong. Even in a society which is divided into closed castes, there is always a religion common to all, and, consequently, the principles of the religious culture, which is, then, fundamental, are the same throughout the population. If each caste, each family, has its special gods, there are general divinities that are recognized by everyone and which all children learn to worship. And as these divinities symbolize and personify certain sentiments, certain ways of conceiving the world and life, one cannot be initiated into their cult without acquiring, at the same time, all sorts of thought patterns which go beyond the sphere of the purely religious life. Similarly, in the Middle Ages, serfs, villeins, burghers and nobles received, equally, a common Christian education. If it is thus in societies where intellectual and moral diversity reach this degree of contrast, with how much more reason is it so among more advanced peoples where classes, while remaining distinct, are, however, separated by a less profound cleavage! Where these common elements of all education are not expressed in the form of religious symbols, they do not, however, cease to exist. In the course of our history, there has been established a whole set of ideas on human nature, on the respective importance of our different faculties, on right and duty, on society, on the individual, on progress, on science, on art, etc., which are the very basis of our national spirit; all education, that of the rich as well as that of the poor, that which leads to professional careers as well as that which prepares for industrial functions, has as its object to fix them in our minds.

From these facts it follows that each society sets up a certain idea of man, of what he should be, as much from the intellectual point of view as the physical and moral; that this ideal is, to a degree, the same for all the citizens; that beyond a certain point it becomes differentiated according to the particular milieux that every society contains in its structure. It is this ideal, at the same time one and various, that is the focus of education. Its function, then, is to arouse in the child: (1) a certain number of physical and mental states that the society to which he belongs considers should not be lacking in any of its members; (2) certain physical and mental states that the particular social group (caste, class, family, profession) considers, equally, ought to be found among all those who make it up. Thus, it is society as a whole and each particular social milieu that determine the ideal that education realizes. Society can survive only if there exists among its members a sufficient degree of homogeneity; education perpetuates and reinforces this homogeneity by fixing in the child, from the beginning, the essential similarities that collective life demands. But on the other hand, without a certain diversity all co-operation would be impossible; education assures the persistence of this necessary diversity by being itself diversified and specialized. If the society has reached a degree of development such that the old divisions into castes and classes can no longer be maintained, it will prescribe an education more uniform at its base. If at the same time there is more division of labor, it will arouse among children, on the underlying basic set of common ideas and sentiments, a richer diversity of occupational aptitudes. If it lives in a state of war with the surrounding societies, it tries to shape people according to a strongly nationalistic model; if international competition takes a more peaceful form, the type that it tries to realize is more general and more humanistic. Education is, then, only the means by which society prepares, within the children, the essential conditions of its very existence. We shall see later how the individual himself has an interest in submitting to these requirements.

We come, then, to the following formula: *Education is the influence exercised by adult generations on those that are not yet ready for social life. Its object is to arouse and to develop in the child a certain number of physical, intellectual and moral states which are demanded of him by both the political society as a whole and the special milieu for which he is specifically destined.* . . .

EMILE DURKHEIM

Moral Education

Questions to think about

1 *What is the role of discipline in schools, according to Durkheim? Does discipline serve the same function today? Explain.*
2 *How can schools instill collective conscience? Give an example.*
3 *What does Durkheim mean when he says we must make a "habit" of social life? Give an example.*

There is a whole system of rules in the school that predetermine the child's conduct. He must come to class regularly, he must arrive at a specified time and with an appropriate bearing and attitude. He must not disrupt things in class. He must have learned his lessons, done his homework, and have done so reasonably well, etc. There are, therefore, a host of obligations that the child is required to shoulder. Together they constitute the discipline of the school. It is through the practice of school discipline that we can inculcate the spirit of discipline in the child.

Too often, it is true, people conceive of school discipline so as to preclude endowing it with such an important moral function. Some see in it a simple way of guaranteeing superficial peace and order in the class. Under such conditions, one can quite reasonably come to view these imperative requirements as barbarous—as a tyranny of complicated rules. We protest against this kind of regulation, which is apparently imposed on the child for the sole purpose of easing the teacher's task in inducing uniformity. Does not such a system evoke feelings of hostility in the student

From Emile Durkheim, *Moral Education: A Study in the Theory and Application of the Sociology of Education,* translated by Everett K. Wilson. Copyright © 1961 by The Free Press, a division of Macmillan Publishing Company. Reprinted by permission of the publisher.

toward the teacher, rather than the affectionate confidence that should characterize their relationship?

In reality, however, the nature and function of school discipline is something altogether different. It is not a simple device for securing superficial peace in the classroom—a device allowing the work to roll on tranquilly. It is the morality of the classroom, just as the discipline of the social body is morality properly speaking. Each social group, each type of society, has and could not fail to have its own morality, which expresses its own make-up.

Now, the class is a small society. It is therefore both natural and necessary that it have its own morality corresponding to its size, the character of its elements, and its function. Discipline is this morality. The obligations we shall presently enumerate are the student's duties, just as the civic or professional obligations imposed by state or corporation are the duties of the adult. On the other hand, the schoolroom society is much closer to the society of adults than it is to that of the family. For aside from the fact that it is larger, the individuals—teachers and students—who make it up are not brought together by personal feelings or preferences but for altogether general and abstract reasons, that is to say, because of the social function to be performed by the teacher, and the immature mental condition of the students. For all these reasons, the rule of the classroom cannot bend or give with the same flexibility as that of the family in all kinds and combinations of circumstances. It cannot accommodate itself to given temperaments. There is already something colder and more impersonal about the obligations imposed by the school: they are now concerned with reason and less with feelings; they require more effort and greater application. And although—as we have previously said—we must guard against overdoing it, it is nevertheless indispensable in order that school discipline be everything that it should be and fulfil its function completely. For only on this condition will it be able to serve as intermediary between the affective morality of the family and the more rigorous morality of civil life. It is by respecting the school rules that the child learns to respect rules in general, that he develops the habit of self-control and restraint simply because he should control and restrain himself. It is a first initiation into the austerity of duty. Serious life has now begun.

This, then, is the true function of discipline. It is not a simple procedure aimed at making the child work, stimulating his desire for instruction, or husbanding the energies of the teacher. It is essentially an instrument—difficult to duplicate—of moral education. The teacher to whom it is entrusted cannot guard it too conscientiously. It is not only a matter of his own interest and peace of mind; one can say without exaggeration that the morality of the classroom rests upon his resolution. Indeed, it is certain that an undisciplined class lacks morality. When children no longer feel restrained, they are in a state of ferment that makes them impatient of all curbs, and their behavior shows it—even outside the classroom. One can see analogous situations in the family when domestic education is overly relaxed. In school, this unwholesome ferment of excitement, the result of a failure of discipline, constitutes a more serious moral danger because the agitation is collective. We must never lose sight of the fact that the class is a small society. Thus, no member of this small group acts as though he were alone; each is subject to the influence of the group, and this we must consider most carefully.

A class without discipline is like a mob. Because a given number of children are brought together in the same class, there is a kind of general stimulation deriving from the common life and imparted to all the individual activities—a stimulation that, when everything goes along normally and is well directed, emerges as more enthusiasm, more concern about doing things well than if each student were working individually. But if the teacher has not developed the necessary authority then this hyperactivity degenerates into an unwholesome ferment, and a genuine demoralization sets in, the more serious as the class is larger. This demoralization becomes obvious in that those elements of least moral value in the class come to have a preponderant place in the common life; just as in political societies during periods of great flux, one sees hosts of harmful elements come to the surface of public life, while in normal times they would be hidden in the shadows.

It is important, therefore, to react against the discredit into which, for a number of years, discipline has tended to fall. Doubtless when one examines the rules of conduct that the teacher must enforce, in themselves and in detail, one is inclined to judge them as useless vexations; and the benevolent feelings, which childhood quite naturally inspires in us, prompt us to feel that they are excessively demanding. Is it not possible for a child to be good and yet fail to be punctual, to be unprepared at the specified time for his lesson or other responsibilities, etc.? If, however, instead of examining these school rules in detail, we consider them as a whole, as the student's code of duty, the matter takes on a different aspect. Then conscientiousness in fulfilling all these petty obligations appears as a virtue. It is the virtue of childhood, the only one in accord with the kind of life the child leads at that age, and consequently the only one that can be asked of him. This is why one cannot cultivate it too conscientiously. . . .

GENERAL INFLUENCE OF THE SCHOOL ENVIRONMENT

To understand clearly the important role that the school environment can and should play in moral education we must first realize what the child faces when he comes to school. Up to that point he has only been acquainted with two kinds of groups. In the family the sentiment of solidarity is derived from blood relationships; and the moral bonds that result from such relationships are further re-enforced by intimate and constant contact of all the associated minds and by a mutual interpenetration of their lives. Then there are little groups of friends and companions—groups that have taken shape outside the family through free selection. Now, political society presents neither of these two characteristics. The bonds uniting the citizens of a given country have nothing to do with relationships or personal inclinations. There is therefore a great distance between the moral state in which the child finds himself as he leaves the family and the one towards which he must strive. This road cannot be travelled in a single stage. Intermediaries are necessary. The school environment is the most desirable. It is a more extensive association than the family or the little societies of friends. It results neither from blood relationships nor from free choice, but from a fortuitous and inevitable meeting among subjects brought together on the basis of similar age and social conditions. In that respect it resembles political society. On the other hand, it is limited enough so that personal relations can crystallize. The horizon is not too vast; the consciousness of the child can easily embrace it. The habit of common life in the class and attachment to the class and even to the school constitute an altogether natural preparation for the more elevated sentiments that we wish to develop in the child. We have here a precious instrument, which is used all too little and which can be of the greatest service.

It is the more natural to use the school to this end since it is precisely groups of young persons, more or less like those constituting the social system of the school, which have enabled the formation of societies larger than the family. With respect to animals, Espinas has already demonstrated that groupings of birds and mammals could not have taken shape if, at a certain moment in their lives, the young had not been induced to separate from their parents and formed societies of a new type, which no longer have domestic characteristics. Indeed, wherever the family keeps its members to itself it is easily self-sufficient; each particular family tends to live its own life, an autonomous life—tends to isolate itself from other families so as to provide more easily for itself; under these conditions, it is clearly impossible for another society to be formed. The small group appears only where the new generation, once it has been brought up, is induced to free itself from the family setting to lead a collective life of a new sort. Similarly, if, from the very beginning, inferior human societies are not limited to one household, if they comprise even in their humblest form a number of families, it is largely because the moral education of children is not undertaken by their parents, but by the elders of the clan. The elders would assemble the young, after they had reached a given age, to initiate them collectively into the religious beliefs, rites, traditions—in a word, to everything constituting the intellectual and moral patrimony of the group. Because of this gathering of the young into special groups, determined by age and not by blood, extrafamilial societies have been able to come into being and perpetuate themselves. The school is precisely a group of this kind; it is recruited according to the same principle. The gatherings of young neophytes, directed and taught by the elders, which we can observe in primitive societies, are already actual school societies and may be considered as the first form of the school. In asking the school to prepare children for a higher social life than that of the family, we are only asking something that is quite in accord with its character.

Furthermore, if there is a country in which the role of the school is particularly important and necessary, it is ours. In this respect, we are living under quite special conditions. Indeed, with the exception of the school, there is no longer in this country any society intermediate between the family and the state—that is to say, a society that is not merely artificial or superficial. All the groups of this kind, which at one time ranged between domestic and political society—provinces, communes, guilds—have been totally abolished or at least survive only in very attenuated form. The province and the guild are only memories; communal life is very impoverished and now holds a very secondary place in our consciousness. . . .

For morality to have a sound basis, the citizen must have an inclination toward collective life. It is only on this condition that he can become attached, as he should, to collective aims that are moral aims *par excellence*. This does not happen automatically; above all, this inclination toward collective life can only become strong enough to shape behavior by the most continuous practice. To appreciate social life to the point where one cannot do without it, one must have developed the habit of acting and thinking in common. We must learn to cherish these social bonds that for the unsocial being are heavy chains. We must learn through experience how cold and pale the pleasures of solitary life are in comparison. The development of such a temperament, such a mental outlook, can only be formed through repeated practice, through perpetual conditioning. If, on the contrary, we are invited only infrequently to act like social beings, it is impossible to be very interested in an existence to which we can only adapt ourselves imperfectly.

If, then, with the exception of the family, there is no collective life in which we participate, if in all the forms of human activity—scientific, artistic, professional, and so on—in other words, in all that constitutes the core of our existence, we are in the habit of acting like lone wolves, our social temperament has only rare opportunities to strengthen and develop itself. Consequently, we are inevitably inclined to a more or less suspicious isolation, at least in regard to everything concerning life outside the family. Indeed, the weakness of the spirit of association is one of the characteristics of our national temperament. We have a marked inclination toward a fierce individualism, which makes the obligations of social life appear intolerable to us and which prevents us from experiencing its joys.

The school is a real group, of which the child is naturally and necessarily a part. It is a group other than the family. Its principal function is not, as in the case of the family, that of emotional release and the sharing of affections. Every form of intellectual activity finds scope in it, in embryonic form. Consequently, we have through the school the means of training the child in a collective life different from home life. We can give him habits that, once developed, will survive beyond school years and demand the satisfaction that is their due. We have here a unique and irreplaceable opportunity to take hold of the child at a time when the gaps in our social organization have not yet been able to alter his nature profoundly, or to arouse in him feelings that make him partially rebellious to common life. This is virgin territory in which we can sow seeds that, once taken root, will grow by themselves. Of course, I do not mean that education alone can remedy the evil—that institutions are not necessary demanding legislative action. But that action can only be fruitful if it is rooted in a state of opinion, if it is an answer to needs that are really felt. Thus, although we could not at any time do without the school to instil in the child a social sense, although we have here a natural function from which the school should never withdraw, today, because of the critical situation in which we find ourselves, the services that the school can render are of incomparable importance. . . .

To bind the child to the social group of which he is a part, it is not enough to make him feel the reality of it. He must be attached to it with his whole being. There is only one effective way of doing this, and that is by making his society an integral part of him, so that he can no more separate himself from it than from himself. Society is not the work of the individuals that compose it at a given stage of history, nor is it a given place. It is a complex of ideas and sentiments, of ways of seeing and of feeling, a certain intellectual and moral framework distinctive of the entire group. Society is above all a consciousness of the whole. It is, therefore, this collective consciousness that we must instil in the child.

Of course, this penetration of the child's consciousness is effected in part by the mere fact of living, by the autonomous play of human relations. These ideas and sentiments are all around the child, and he is immersed in them by living. But there is another operation much too important to leave to chance. It is the business of the school to organize it methodically. An enlightened mind must select from among the welter of confused and often contradictory states of mind that constitute the social consciousness; it must set off what is essential and vital; and play down the trivial and the secondary. The teacher must bring this about and here again history will furnish him the means to this end.

The point is that to imbue children with the collective spirit it is useless to analyze it abstractly. On the contrary, they must be put in direct contact with this collective spirit. Now, what is the history of a people if not the genius of that people developing through time? By making the history of their country come alive for the children, we can at the same time make them live in close intimacy with the collective consciousness. Is it not through intimate and prolonged contact with a man that we finally get to know him? In this respect, a history lesson is the lesson of experience. But since our national character is immanent in historical events, the child would neither see nor feel them if the teacher did not try to set them off in bold relief, especially highlighting those events that merit it. Once again, the point is not to give a course on the French character. All that is needed is a knowledge of what it is and how to disentangle it from the welter of facts.

MAX WEBER

The Typological Position of
Confucian Education

Questions to think about

1 *How does Weber relate authority styles to types of
   education? What "authority style" is predominant in
   the United States and other Western societies? Does
   Weber's analysis hold true?*
2 *What are the characteristics of Chinese education?*
3 *What can we learn from this discussion about our
   educational systems today?*

We shall now discuss the position of this educational
system among the great types of education. To be sure, we cannot here,
in passing, give a sociological typology of pedagogical ends and means,
but perhaps some comments may be in place.

Historically, the two polar opposites in the field of educational ends
are: to awaken charisma, that is, heroic qualities or magical gifts; and, to
impart specialized expert training. The first type corresponds to the charismatic structure of domination; the latter type corresponds to the *rational*
and bureaucratic (modern) structure of domination. The two types do not
stand opposed, with no connections or transitions between them. The
warrior hero or the magician also needs special training, and the expert
official is generally not trained exclusively for knowledge. However, they
are polar opposites of types of education and they form the most radical
contrasts. Between them are found all those types which aim at cultivating
the pupil for a *conduct of life,* whether it is of a mundane or of a religious
character. In either case, the life conduct is the conduct of a status group.

From *From Max Weber: Essays in Sociology,* edited and translated by H. H. Gerth and C. Wright
Mills. Copyright © 1946 by Oxford University Press, Inc.; renewed 1973 by Dr. Hans H.
Gerth. Reprinted with permission.

The charismatic procedure of ancient magical asceticism and the hero trials, which sorcerers and warrior heroes have applied to boys, tried to aid the novice to acquire a "new soul," in the animist sense, and hence, to be reborn. Expressed in our language, this means that they merely wished to *awaken* and to test a capacity which was considered a purely personal gift of grace. For one can neither teach nor train for charisma. Either it exists *in nuce,* or it is infiltrated through a miracle of magical rebirth—otherwise it cannot be attained.

Specialized and expert schooling attempts to *train* the pupil for practical usefulness for administrative purposes—in the organization of public authorities, business offices, workshops, scientific or industrial laboratories, disciplined armies. In principle, this can be accomplished with anybody, though to varying extent.

The pedagogy of cultivation, finally, attempts to *educate* a cultivated type of man, whose nature depends on the decisive stratum's respective ideal of cultivation. And this means to educate a man for a certain internal and external deportment in life. In principle this can be done with everybody, only the goal differs. If a separate stratum of warriors form the decisive status group—as in Japan—education will aim at making the pupil a stylized knight and courtier, who despises the pen-pushers as the Japanese Samurai have despised them. In particular cases, the stratum may display great variations of type. If a priestly stratum is decisive, it will aim at making the disciple a scribe, or at least an intellectual, likewise of greatly varying character. In reality, none of these types ever occurs in pure form. The numerous combinations and intermediary links cannot be discussed in this context. What is important here is to define the position of Chinese education in terms of these forms.

The holdovers of the primeval charismatic training for regeneration, the milk name, the previously discussed initiation rites of youth, the bridegroom's change of name, and so on, have for a long time in China been a formula (in the manner of the Protestant confirmation) standing beside the testing of educational qualifications. Such tests have been monopolized by the political authorities. The educational qualification, however, in view of the educational means employed, has been a "cultural" qualification, in the sense of a general education. It was of a similar, yet of a more specific nature than, for instance, the *humanist* educational qualification of the Occident.

In Germany, such an education, until recently and almost exclusively, was a prerequisite for the official career leading to positions of command in civil and military administration. At the same time this *humanist* education has stamped the pupils who were to be prepared for such careers as belonging socially to the *cultured* status group. In Germany, however—

and this is a very important difference between China and the Occident—rational and specialized *expert* training has been added to, and in part has displaced, this educational status qualification.

The Chinese examinations did not test any special skills, as do our modern rational and bureaucratic examination regulations for jurists, medical doctors, or technicians. Nor did the Chinese examinations test the possession of charisma, as do the typical "trials" of magicians and bachelor leagues. To be sure, we shall presently see the qualifications which this statement requires. Yet it holds at least for the technique of the examinations.

The examinations of China tested whether or not the candidate's mind was thoroughly steeped in literature and whether or not he possessed the *ways of thought* suitable to a cultured man and resulting from cultivation in literature. These qualifications held far more specifically with China than with the German humanist gymnasium. Today one is used to justifying the gymnasium by pointing to the practical value of formal education through the study of Antiquity. As far as one may judge from the assignments given to the pupils of the lower grades in China, they were rather similar to the essay topics assigned to the top grades of a German gymnasium, or perhaps better still, to the select class of a German girls' college. All the grades were intended as tests in penmanship, style, mastery of classic writings, and finally—similar to our lessons in religion, history, and German—in conformity with the prescribed mental outlook. In our context it is decisive that this education was on the one hand purely secular in nature, but, on the other, was bound to the fixed norm of the orthodox interpretation of the classic authors. It was a highly exclusive and bookish literary education.

MAUREEN T. HALLINAN

Sociology of Education:
The State of the Art

Questions to think about

1 *What is the state of theory in sociology of education? What is the relationship between theory and empirical findings?*
2 *What needs to be done to advance the field of sociology of education? How do these ideas relate to the other articles on theory in this chapter?*
3 *How do theories relate to the open systems framework?*
4 *What are some policy implications of the Coleman Report for the educational system discussed here?*

The number of topics that could be included in a description of sociology of education as a field is legion, as is the number of ways one could organize and categorize the area. Yet despite its breadth, sociology of education has fairly clear boundaries. It includes the study of all aspects of education ranging from schools themselves to the determinants and consequences of schooling and the relationship between education and persons, groups and institutions in society. *Sociology of learning* is a subarea within sociology of education that focuses on the factors that influence educational aspirations and achievement (see Boocock, 1972).

Questions about schools can be asked at all levels of abstraction and from several ideological perspectives. In more abstract analyses, general theories from sociology are applied to educational issues. The role of the school in society, for example, has been analyzed both from a consensus or structural-functionalist perspective and from a conflict perspective. Consensus theorists see schools as the means through which students learn to take their place in society and contribute to the interdependence required to maintain the social order and satisfy the needs of its members. Schools are seen as the transmitters of traditional values and as instruments of societal stability and the maintenance of the existing social order. Elaboration of this perspective is found in Durkheim (1956) and Parsons (1959). Consensus theory is implicit in the recent report of the National Commission on Excellence in Education (1983), in which the authors criticize the schools for not challenging students to attain their intellectual potential in order to make the greatest possible contribution to society.

From a conflict perspective, schools are seen as agents of conflict and change. When applied to schools, Dahrendorf's (1959) conflict theory focuses on dominance and subordination in schools and conflicting goals of students, parents, educators, the community, and society at large. The power struggle that exists in and about schools leads to upheaval and change. When power has been assumed by a particular group, it is maintained through coercion. Class analysts, such as Bowles and Gintis (1976) and Carnoy (1972), look at schools from this perspective and interpret the status quo, including unequal educational opportunities for minorities and women, as efforts of the privileged class in American society to maintain their power and superiority over the underprivileged.

Other aspects of schools have been analyzed through an application of general sociological theory. Organization theorists describe schools as bureaucracies and semiprofessional organizations. Social psychologists rely on theories of attitude formation, norms, and values to study classroom processes as well as cognitive and social development. Demographic and ecological theories have informed school policy decisions, and theories of social stratification and social mobility have been used to explain educational and occupational attainment.

Sociological theories are fairly well formulated in the general sociological literature. Despite this, their application in sociology of education has not been very fruitful. One problem is that the theories are often applied without modification to a school setting or problem. Little effort has been made to adapt the theories to the specific circumstances of the school and its unique environment and population. Consequently, theoretical formulations in sociology of education are often weak in predictive power and provide incomplete explanations of school-related phenomena.

In contrast to the slow and discouraging development of theory in sociology of education, advances in empirical research have been impressive. Both basic and applied studies are numerous, though they vary in quality. Most empirical studies in sociology of education are grounded in low-level theory and many are narrow in scope. Nevertheless, the field has reached a point where researchers can build on previous work to refine, modify, and advance empirical findings. As a result, empirical research in sociology of education is more integrated than it was previously. Impressive research programs exist at many universities. Centers for research and development and the educational laboratories in the United States, Canada, and other countries have accelerated this development by bringing together researchers from sociology and other social science disciplines to study a single major area. For example, the Center for the Social Organization of Schools at Johns Hopkins University has for many years examined how school and classroom organization affects student achievement and other student outcomes as well as their future educational and occupational success. Within the rubric defined by each center, these research programs have produced a large number of studies that provide systematic examination of important problems in sociology of education.

One area of sociology of education that has commanded considerable attention over the past two decades is *educational productivity*. The use of this term and its associated *input-output model* shows the influence of economists on research on schools. The study of educational productivity is the investigation of factors that affect the academic productivity of students in schools and its effects on their future educational and occupational attainment. In this article I will rely on this body of research to illustrate three points: (1) that historical and political factors influence the development of large systematic bodies of empirical research in sociology of education; (2) that low-level theory characterizes much of the empirical work in sociology of education; and (3) that inconsistent findings as well as alternate interpretations of results make policy decisions based on research in sociology of education difficult.

Interest in educational productivity is motivated by a number of pressing societal concerns: the quality of schooling as reflected in level of competence of high school graduates (National Commission on Excellence in Education, 1983), the extent of our nation's monetary investment in education (1.8% of the federal budget was allotted to education in 1983), the relationship between education and employment or occupational attainment, the disparity between educational achievement and occupational attainment for minorities and women. Underlying these concerns is the basic belief that schools should equalize opportunities for learning and attainment for all students, regardless of race, ethnicity, social class, religion, or other family background characteristics. In addition, these public concerns reveal the expectation that schools be a wise societal investment and play a major role in the preparation of future citizens for their roles in a well-functioning society.

The study of educational productivity has evolved as two main lines of research. The first is the study of school effects, that is, the relationship between school characteristics and student outcomes. The most important early study in this tradition was the Coleman Report, now sometimes referred to as the *first* Coleman Report upon publication of Coleman, Hoffer and Kilgore's recent study *High School Achievement* (1982). The second line of research investigates how schooling affects change in achievement, aspirations, and educational or occupational attainment. The Wisconsin social psychological model of status attainment (Sewell, Haller and Portes, 1969) is at the center of this tradition.

SCHOOL EFFECTS STUDIES

The purpose of the landmark study by James Coleman and his colleagues, *Equality of Educational Opportunity* (known as the EEO or the Coleman Report), mandated by the U.S. President and Congress in 1964, was to investigate "the lack of availability of equal educational opportunity for individuals by reason of race, color, religion or national origin in public educational institutions . . ." (Coleman et al., 1966, iii). It was believed that the schools attended by racial and ethnic minority groups were inferior to white schools in resources and student characteristics and that these school differences explained the lower academic achievement of minority pupils. The sample for the EEO study consisted of over 645,000 students in grades 1, 3, 6, 9, and 12, randomly selected from 3000 elementary and 1180 high schools by means of stratified, two-stage probability sampling.

The Coleman Report concluded that family background accounts for a large proportion of the variation in student achievement and that controlling for background, variance across schools in resources, including facilities and curriculum, has little effect on academic achievement. The report also concluded that controlling for student background, the social composition of the student body is a stronger predictor of achievement than other school factors. Facilities and curriculum variables in the report include school size and location, systemwide per pupil expenditure, number of library volumes per student, and number of science laboratories and guidance counselors, as well as the comprehensiveness of curriculum offerings and tracking policies.

The Coleman Report was vigorously criticized on methodological grounds and stimulated countless reanalyses over the subsequent decade. Nevertheless, although reanalyses slightly modified some of the findings, they generally supported the conclusions reached by Coleman and his colleagues. The results of the EEO study surprised the academic community, generated heated debate on the topic, and led to a plethora of school effects studies.

One area of research stimulated by the Coleman Report was school resources studies. Although researchers had been examining the relationship between school resources and student achievement since the 1950s, the Coleman Report renewed interest in this relationship partly because it contradicted the persistent belief that school resources affect educational outcomes and because school resources constitute a manipulable policy-relevant variable of considerable interest to school personnel. Reviews of some of the larger school resource studies that followed the Coleman Report are found in Guthrie, Kleindorfer, Levin and Stout (1971), Averch, Carroll, Donaldson, Kiesling and Pincus (1972); some of the more methodologically sophisticated studies are reviewed by Spady (1973). Large data sets such as Project Talent were analyzed, and reanalyses of the EEO data were conducted. Some of these studies show a stronger relationship between selected school variables and student achievement (net of family background) than found in the Coleman Report, where class size, student-teacher ratio, and number of specialized staff and expenditure levels shared the strongest influence.

In general, however, these studies continue to show that the impact of school resources, net of background factors and characteristics, is small. Hanushek concludes that "almost uniformly, educational production models show no consistent or significant relationship between achievement and expenditures per pupil (either instructional expenditure or total expenditures). Analyses of specific purchased inputs (teacher experience, teacher education, class size and administrative/supervisory expenditures) show a similar lack of relationship" (1978, p. 47). Similarly, Lau states that there is "no consistent observed relationship between cognitive achievement and school resources" (1978, p. 13).

One shortcoming of this large body of research on school resources is the absence of outcome measures other than cognitive skills, such as other learning measures and noncognitive outcomes. There are substantive and analytical reasons to believe that a model with a single outcome measure such as standardized achievement is misspecified. Moreover, existing models fail to depict the interrelationships among outcomes, that is, the complex way in which production of one outcome can affect the production of other related outcomes. The most recent research on school resources has focused on developing better analytical tools to examine the effect of school resources on student variables and in particular on modifying the simple economic production model to portray the educational process more accurately (Brown and Saks, 1980; Levin, 1974; Schmidt, Aigner and Lowell, 1977). The goal of this research is to depict multiple outcomes and joint production as typical features of the educational productivity model. This work is more promising than earlier studies because reliance on a more powerful analytical device should allow a more rigorous analysis of the effects of school resources. In particular, these models can be estimated at the individual level and take into account individual differences in exposure to school or classroom resources. More importantly, they can perhaps portray other outcomes in addition to achievement. The resulting improved theoretical model of educational productivity is likely to provide a more accurate assessment of the effects of school inputs on a number of student outputs.

Another line of research influenced by the Coleman Report is the study of the effects of compositional or contextual variables on student outcomes. Since Coleman and colleagues (1966) concluded that controlling for student background, the social class composition of a student body has a stronger impact than any other school level variable on student achievement, the EEO study redirected the attention of researchers and policy makers to the socioeconomic composition of a school. Moreover, since race is strongly related to social class, the racial composition of the school received even more attention. Several large research studies examined the effects of school, and later classroom, racial composition on student achievement and aspirations. A fairly consistent finding of this research is a positive effect of being in a majority white school on the achievement of blacks. Some evidence supports the conclusion that being in a totally segregated black school is more conducive to growth in achievement for blacks than being in a majority black school. Similarly, black aspirations were found to increase in majority white schools for blacks with close white friends, whereas the educational aspirations of blacks with no close white friends is not affected by the school context. These results are generally interpreted as revealing a normative or comparative reference group influence, role modeling, or interpersonal influences.

In response to these studies, several researchers, including Hauser (1970); Campbell and Alexander (1965); and McDill, Meyers and Rigsby (1967), argued that the amount of variance in achievement explained by compositional or contextual variables was too small to have any substantive meaning and that compositional effects result from failing to specify, on an individual level, the social psychological processes involved in growth in achievement and in the development of educational aspirations.

The major policy issue that was affected by the Coleman Report's finding on school compositional effects was how to provide equality of educational opportunity for all students. The immediate implication of the Coleman Report findings is that desegregating the schools is a more preferred approach to increasing educational opportunities for blacks than increasing school resources and improving facilities. This was consistent with growing judicial advisement in the matter. In 1954, the Supreme Court had handed down the landmark *Brown* v. *the Board of Education* decision, which ruled that separate but equal schools were unconstitutional and that legally enforced school segregation must be abolished. The notion of equal protection under the law, articulated in the Fourteenth Amendment, was translated by the courts into the need for racially desegregated, if not racially balanced, schools. Since this decision, the judicial system had been pressuring American schools to desegregate. The findings of Coleman and others gave impetus to the policy of busing students in order to achieve racial desegregation and the practice received support in the courts. Opponents of busing, however, argued against it on many grounds. Some research showed little or no positive effect of busing on the achievement of black students. For example, utilizing data from Boston, New York City, Ann Arbor, Riverside (California), and Hartford and New Haven (Connecticut), Armor (1972) showed that whites in desegregated schools continued to outgain blacks in academic achievement, with the difference increasing over time, and that in integrated schools blacks on the average gained only two months over those in segregated schools. At the same time, Pettigrew, Useem, Normand and Smith (1973), analyzing the same data, showed that compared to national norms, the gain of black students in desegregated schools was much greater than in segregated schools.

Adding to the desegregation controversy, in the mid 1970s Coleman, Kelly and Moore (1975) reported results of a new study which they interpreted as showing that school desegregation contributes to white flight from large urban cities to the suburbs, leading to conclusions that desegregation was proceeding too rapidly. This "reversal" of Coleman's position helped to slow the movement toward school integration and remove some pressure from school districts to establish desegregation programs. Subsequent analyses by several researchers such as Rossell (1975), Giles (1978), and Erber (1979) contradicted the white flight thesis and identified other factors that could account for the phenomenon. Nevertheless, the fear of residential segregation resulting from school desegregation efforts and the establishment of a conservative Republican administration in Washington weakened the momentum in the school desegregation effort.

The most recent major study by Coleman and his colleagues also speaks to the issue of school desegregation, although this was not the major focus of the study. Coleman, Hoffer and Kilgore (1982) analyzed the first wave of data from "High School and Beyond" (HSB), a longitudinal study sponsored by the National Center for Education Statistics to investigate academic achievement and other student outcomes and to replicate the National Longitudinal Survey of the Class of 1972. The sample includes over 58,000 students in 874 public, 84 Catholic, and 27 other private schools. Coleman and his colleagues concluded from their analyses that private high schools promote academic achievement more than public high schools and, more relevant to the present discussion, that private schools in the United States do not intensify racial segregation. Rather, they claim, private schools have a lower level of segregation that counterbalances the small proportion of blacks in private schools, resulting in a net integrative rather than segregative effect. This research has evoked considerable debate and controversy among research scientists and policy makers. It has been criticized on methodological grounds, and the validity of the conclusions are being called into question. Taeuber and James (1982) challenge Coleman, Hoffer and Kilgore's conclusion that greater integration exists in the private schools and argue that the segregation index they employ is inappropriate to answer the questions they are asking. Through a series of reanalyses of the data, Taeuber and James conclude that private schools do contribute to racial segregation. These recent studies broaden and complexify the volatile issue of school desegregation. At a time when a conservative national mood provides an atmosphere in which federal support for private schools through tuition tax credits, voucher plans, and other financial schemes is being seriously considered, scientific evidence about the role of private schools in maintaining or increasing existing levels of racial segregation in the public schools is of considerable importance. Heated debate over this issue is expected to continue as the other waves of the HSB data become available and longitudinal analyses are possible. The importance of this issue and the nature of the empirical evidence to date is likely to elicit federal monies to support this line of research and ensure that it remains one of the more important research endeavors in the field.

STATUS ATTAINMENT STUDIES

The second body of research related to educational productivity is the study of status attainment. This research addresses a number of questions about how ascribed and achieved characteristics of students and characteristics of their schools influence their educational aspirations and attainment and, in turn, their occupational status and earnings. These questions are of considerable importance within the context of social stratification and social mobility. They address the fundamental concern of the extent to which our society is meritocratic, and whether it provides equality of opportunity for all its members, regardless of background characteristics such as gender, race, ethnicity, socioeconomic status, and religion.

The Wisconsin social psychological model of status attainment has undoubtedly had the strongest impact on this area of research in sociology of education. The model, first developed in 1969 (Sewell, Haller and Portes, 1969) and later expanded (Sewell, Haller and Ohlendorf, 1970; Sewell and Hauser, 1975) posits that the effects of social background on occupational status and income are mediated first by students' measured ability and then by grades. The effects of these variables are then transmitted through significant other influence, educational aspirations, and finally educational attainment. Thus the model links the ascribed and achieved characteristics of students to their status attainment by social psychological processes that occur at home and in school.

The Wisconsin model was originally tested on a sample of 10,317 farm boys who graduated from Wisconsin high schools in 1957. The model explained 50 percent of the variance in educational attainment and 34 percent of the variance in occupational status. The results showed that socioeconomic status has no effect on high school performance (rank in class) independent of measured ability. It does have strong direct and indirect effects on significant other's influence and on educational and occupational aspirations and, through these variables, on educational attainment and occupational status. Ability is seen to have strong effects on high school performance, independent of socioeconomic status; ability also has direct and indirect effects on significant other influence and on educational and occupational aspirations and, through these three variables, on educational attainment and occupational status. These results suggest that deficiencies in family background can be overcome through schooling; the findings have been interpreted as indicating that the process of social mobility and status attainment in America is indeed a meritocratic one.

Follow-up data were collected from the Wisconsin high school sample in 1964 and again in 1975. This made possible not only replications and extensions of the original model but longitudinal analyses of the effects of the exogenous and endogenous variables on the attainment process. Replications or near replications were conducted to compare status attainment processes on national samples of American youth, and on youth from other states, regions and nations. Moreover, the status attainment model was compared for different groups such as men and women, blacks and whites, and urban and rural persons.

One of the first major replications of the Wisconsin model was conducted by Alexander, Eckland and Griffin (1975) using a fifteen-year national longitudinal sample of U.S. males. The results showed substantial support for the Wisconsin model. Most recently, Jencks, Crouse and Mueser (1983) replicated the model using a 1972 follow-up of the eleventh-grade boys in the Project Talent data. The results were basically the same as Sewell and Hauser's follow-up analyses as well as those of Alexander and colleagues and supported the Wisconsin model. The Jencks study showed that conclusions based on tests of the model on the Wisconsin data were not significantly biased by geographic or educational limitations of the Wisconsin data or the low response rate of the EEO study.

Extensions of the Wisconsin model have included adding school characteristics to establish school effects on educational and occupational aspirations and to specify more fully the social psychological processes linking student characteristics to outcome measures (Alexander and Eckland, 1975; Alwin and Otto, 1977). Several other studies alter the model by deleting one or more variables, such as significant other influence (Kerckoff and Campbell, 1977) or by altering the structure of the model (Porter, 1974).

The Wisconsin model has been criticized on both substantive and methodological grounds. The most persistent theoretical criticism is that it focuses primarily on social psychological variables and omits structural factors such as the community, neighborhood, and school contexts. More specifically, the model fails to take into account selection and assignment processes that could influence how background variables affect student outcomes. For example, socioeconomic status could affect curriculum placement or tracking, which in turn could have a marked effect on aspirations and attainment. Sewell and Hauser (1980) counter this criticism by pointing to the small amount of variance explained by these allocation variables in other studies in the literature.

The model has also been criticized for the ordering of the variables and for the absence of reciprocal relationships or feedback mechanisms for how the variables were measured. Evidence countering each of these criticisms is also found in the literature.

RELATED HISTORICAL AND POLITICAL DEVELOPMENTS

These research developments in the areas of school effects and status attainment illustrate the way in which empirical studies in sociology of education are often a response on one hand to political realities on the national level and an influence on attitudes and opinions about these issues and legislation governing schools on the other. This is particularly true of the Coleman Report. As described earlier, the study, funded by the U.S. Office of Education, was conducted in response to a congressional mandate to examine the extent to which black students were afforded equality of educational opportunities. The mandate itself, a response to the national mood in the late 1950s, was the product of a liberal administration and

Congress. The results of the study acted as a catalyst to the research community to examine these issues more closely and stimulated ongoing debates about school expenditures and school desegregation. The Coleman Report influenced the formation of compensatory educational programs such as Head Start to reduce the negative impact of low socioeconomic background on children's chances to succeed in school. It was also used to promote school integration efforts and to support court decisions governing desegregation and busing. Interestingly, from a historical point of view, Coleman's subsequent research associating desegregation with white flight hindered desegregation efforts, and the conclusions from his most recent study on public and private schools may be a further setback to this effort.

Research on the Wisconsin status attainment model was supported from 1962 to the present primarily by funding from the National Institute of Mental Health, with occasional assistance from the Social Security Administration and other public and private agencies. The interest of policy makers in this basic research program stems from the importance of understanding the impact of family on educational, occupational, and economic attainment. The nature of the relationships among these variables has numerous implications for schooling and school policy. Moreover, this body of research has the potential to inform labor market theory and analysis, and to explicate social mobility processes and the processes underlying social stratification. It may be that definitive statements cannot be made about determinants of occupational status and income, and that the direct policy implications of the study will not be manifest before the project and related studies are completed. To date, the study and numerous related ones have continued to receive federal support and to attract the interest and involvement of the research community, partly in anticipation of answers to the policy-related questions it addresses.

EMPIRICAL RESEARCH AND THEORY IN SOCIOLOGY OF EDUCATION

Much of the empirical work in sociology of education is policy-relevant, and some of the research addresses problems of considerable social significance. In general, the work, however, is either atheoretical or based on low-level theory. Both school effects and status attainment studies can be characterized in this way.

The EEO study is a large survey analysis with a specific, well-defined purpose. The research was done hurriedly to meet deadlines set by the project sponsors. The absence of much conceptualization in the report and the emphasis on policy issues is not surprising, given the nature of the task and the constraints under which the researchers were operating. What is more significant is that the same lack of integrative theory is apparent in the subsequent studies on the effects of school resources and school context on student outcomes. The school resource literature is a stark example of efforts to relate independent and dependent variables with little attention to explaining why they might be associated. Every imaginable school characteristic has been correlated with, or regressed on, mean academic achievement. Discussions of the mechanisms that would transmit the effects of school resources are frequently absent. This is probably the reason that this body of research persisted until very recently in focusing on aggregate school characteristics and student outcomes without taking into account differences in the allocation of school resources across students within schools. The more recent approach, which looks at the effects of classroom resources and estimates models at the individual level, should generate testable hypotheses about how and why school characteristics affect student learning and other student outcomes.

Studies of contextual effects on student achievement and aspirations have been somewhat more concerned about the mechanisms through which school characteristics influence students. These studies generally rely on social psychological theories of normative and comparative reference groups, interpersonal influence, and role modeling to explain the effects of school social or racial composition on student outcomes. For example, to explain the observed increase in black achievement in majority white schools, it is often claimed that in these schools the large number of academically oriented whites creates an environment that is conducive to learning. Further, the white students serve as role models to blacks. When blacks choose white academic role models as friends, the positive influence of the latter on black achievement is greater. Conceptual paradigms such as this are rarely tested, however; they are merely invoked as post hoc explanations of observed results. One exception to this criticism is a study by Campbell and Alexander (1965) which proposes a two-step model that uses school status to predict features of a student's environment and then explain student behavior in terms of social psychological processes occurring in that environment. In general, however, this research, like the school resources studies, is usually based on survey analyses with limited information on the subjects in the study. It fails to formulate, in any kind of systematic way, a conceptual or theoretical statement about how differences in racial or class composition impact on student outcomes, aspirations, learning, and achievement.

Similarly, the status attainment research in the Wisconsin tradition has not been guided by a well-formulated theoretical or conceptual framework.

The model itself identifies background variables, ascribed characteristics of students, and characteristics of their environment that impact on their aspirations and achievements. The nature of the relationships are clearly established in the extensive literature, but the reasons for the linkages and the conditions under which one would expect to find the associations have received scant attention. For example, under what conditions would pupils' friends be a negative rather than positive influence on their educational aspirations? Why do father's and mother's education and occupation have similar effects on offsprings' aspirations? How does ability affect significant other influence? Why do characteristics of schools not affect the way in which the influence of socioeconomic status and ability are transmitted to achievement, aspirations, and earnings? Again, in this research, post hoc explanations for observed relationships are provided, but there exists no theoretical formation, either borrowed from the general sociological literature or developed specifically, to address these questions about schools and schooling that either generates or justifies the model. Clearly, the next step in this area of research needs to be on the conceptual level—without, of course, deflecting from the impressive progress that is being made in developing sophisticated analytical and measurement models to study status attainment.

POLICY IMPLICATIONS OF EMPIRICAL RESEARCH IN SOCIOLOGY OF EDUCATION

Although the policy implications of school productivity research may, at first, seem obvious, in actuality they are not at all straightforward. The nature of social science research in general and research in sociology of education in particular is such that making policy decisions based on research findings is, at best, challenging. The reason that policy implications do not follow directly from the basic and applied research in sociology of education is that many studies are not comparable, some findings are inconsistent across studies, and some results are subject to different interpretations. Moreover, the research designs of many studies are inappropriate to answer some of the important questions posed of school personnel.

A substantial number of educational productivity studies, including EEO, show a positive relationship between school resources and student achievement. Most of these studies are not directly comparable because they include different exogenous variables or different measures of the same variable. Some of the studies include only human resources, such as teacher-pupil ratio or teacher qualifications, whereas others include only expenditure measures, such as number of library books and per pupil expenditure. These studies fail to provide information about the differential impact of various school resources on learning.

Even when school resource studies are comparable, the findings are often inconsistent across samples. For example, contrary to some EEO results, some studies show a strong effect of expenditure levels on achievement (Mollenkopf and Melville, 1956; Kiesling, 1969; Bowles, 1970). In this case, policy makers have empirical studies available to support diametrically opposed policy decisions. Some comparable school resource studies report results that are consistent across samples, such as the finding that school characteristics have a stronger effect on the achievement of blacks than of whites (see Spady, 1973, for a review of these studies). One limitation of these studies from the policy maker's point of view is that they fail to include both school resource and school context variables and therefore preclude comparing the effects of other school characteristics, such as social or racial composition, on achievement. There are only a few large-scale survey analyses in the literature that include both the resource and context variables as well as the student background characteristics needed to evaluate the relative magnitude of the different effects. EEO is one of these, but its measures of school resources are limited and socio-economic status composition may merely be a proxy for racial composition. Other studies have similar shortcomings.

As a result of these limitations, the policy implications of school resource research are not clear. The findings could be interpreted as implying that school resources do make a difference and should be maximized. This interpretation would suggest establishing compensatory education and teacher training programs as well as promoting an increase in school budgets. On the other hand, one could conclude from the literature that school resources make little difference in academic achievement because school composition and family background have considerably stronger effects. This interpretation would support cutbacks in school budgets and the curtailment of special staff and special programs in the schools. Consequently, the school resource studies to date have not been very helpful to policy makers in reaching decisions about the allocation of school budgets and about the relative merits of school expenditures on school facilities or personnel.

Even if the research were clearer in terms of identifying school resources that have a significant impact on learning, it would still not be able, at least at present, to answer such questions as: Under what conditions does a particular resource have its effect? How do resource variables interact with school composition to affect learning? Are school expenditures linearly related to achievement and if so, is there a ceiling effect? Moreover, the school resource studies seldom look at the allocation of resources within the school. It is likely that resources are differentially allocated across students, possibly by race or age, so that a school level test of the effectiveness of different school resources would fail to find effects where they may exist. Classroom or individual level analyses are preferable to address this question.

The policy implications of the EEO study and other studies of the effects of school racial composition on achievement may also seem obvious. Since school resources had a small effect on achievement, compared to school social class composition and family background, school authorities may conclude that their efforts should be directed less toward increasing expenditures for special programs for disadvantaged students and more toward establishing programs to desegregate the schools. The research suggests that the effects of compensatory education programs is negligible compared to the effects of placing students with low socioeconomic status in schools with a majority of high socioeconomic status peers and that compensatory education cannot be expected to solve the serious problem of the differential achievement between blacks and whites.

On the other hand, studies stemming from the Wisconsin status attainment model indicate that family background is related to outcome measures through its direct effect on measured ability. This suggests the need for special programs to overcome the negative effects of background by increasing ability. Compensatory education is an obvious way of responding to this need. Hence the two research programs have quite different policy implications with respect to the importance of compensatory education and school desegregation for student achievement.

Studies such as the Coleman Report and other subsequent research seem to show the greater impact of desegregation over school resources for promoting student learning, but differences in interpretation are still prevalent. Here the atheoretical nature of this body of research is at fault, because it fails to specify the mechanisms through which racial composition affects achievement. Even after being officially desegregated, many schools remain effectively segregated through assignment processes within the school, but early research in this area did not alert us to this possible outcome. Moreover, the studies illustrate the difficulty in measuring the effects of desegregation and interpreting their meaning. The debate between Armor (1972) and Pettigrew and colleagues (1973) concerning Armor's interpretation of his analysis of desegregated schools in six major cities demonstrates the problem. The same data and same results were interpreted by the two researchers as having diametrically opposed implications for desegregation efforts and for busing in particular. Armor claimed that "mandatory busing for purposes of improving student achievement and interracial harmony is not effective and should not be adopted at this time"

(1972, p. 125). Pettigrew and colleagues concluded that "the academic achievement of both white and black children is not lowered by the types of racial desegregation studied so far" and that "the achievement of white and especially of black children in desegregated schools is generally higher when some of the following critical conditions are met: equal racial access to the school's resources, classroom not just school desegregation, the initiation of desegregation in the early grades, interracial staffs, substantial rather than token desegregation, the maintenance of our increase in school services and remedial retraining and the avoidance of strict ability grouping" (1973, p. 114). The reason for this difference in interpretation of the research results is that different standards of evaluation are being used, with Armor expecting an increase in the growth in achievement relative to whites and Pettigrew looking for accelerated black gain relative to their gain before desegregation.

CONCLUSIONS

The two areas of research discussed in this chapter—school effects and status attainment—are both distinctive and, at the same time, typical of research in sociology of education. These are distinctive because, along with a few other areas including organizational analyses of higher education and the study of teacher effects, they are characterized by a fairly systematic program of research that has built upon itself and progressed toward a better understanding of how schools influence students. Empirical research in these two traditions is among the best in the field in terms of scope and rigor. Researchers have mapped out well-defined areas of study, responded to a specific set of questions about schooling, raised new questions based on prior findings, and generated testable hypotheses for future work. Considerable progress has been made in methodology and statistical analysis and the work has been a focal point for the development of sophisticated modeling techniques. Moreover, the research is conducted on large cross-sectional and longitudinal data sets that include the best survey data on schools available to social scientists to date.

On the other hand, research in educational productivity and status attainment is typical of most of the empirical work in sociology of education in that it is fairly atheoretical and the results are not easily translated into policy recommendations. The research has often been a response to, or at least constrained by, historical and political factors such as funding opportunities rather than being guided by theory. The absence of a strong theoretical framework to guide and integrate the area leaves unanswered several important questions about the mechanisms through which schooling affects student cognitive and noncognitive outcomes. Moreover, the theoretical weaknesses of the research make it extremely difficult to interpret the results in a consistent way so as to infer policy decisions about schools and schooling. The state of the research is such that empirical results can be used to support whatever political position is being espoused by persons making decisions about schools.

The field of sociology of education in the mid-1980s is at an important juncture. Dreeban and Thomas recently claimed that the set of papers they were editing represented "the emerging second generation of investigations in education effects" (1980, p. 1). Current research in educational productivity and status attainment has indeed moved beyond the kinds of cross-sectional analyses that originally characterized it to rigorous longitudinal analyses of the educational process. It will probably take other areas in the field considerably longer to reach this level of sophistication and rigor. Nevertheless, the availability of research models and a growing interest in the field stimulated by concern about the quality of American schools may act as a catalyst to more productive research in these areas as well.

Ultimately, however, the field of sociology of education will thrive only if more serious efforts are made to provide a better conceptualization of the problems being studied and to develop rigorous theoretical underpinnings for future empirical studies. Grounding empirical work in theory can be done either by directly applying existing sociological theories to the problems being investigated or by constructing new theories to explain educational processes. Some progress is being made in this direction in ethnographic and observational studies of school and classroom processes. Yet even here, outstanding theoretical contributions are rare. Thus, even though sociology of education ranks high among other subdisciplines in sociology in terms of the quality of its empirical work and particularly of its quantitative studies, its greatest potential contribution has not yet been made—namely, the formulation of theories of the schooling process. The challenge of the future is to specify and explain, on a conceptual level, the processes that link institutional and interactional factors to student outcomes.

REFERENCES

Alexander, Karl, and Bruce K. Eckland. "Contextual Effects in the High School Attainment Process." *American Sociological Review* 40 (June 1975): 402–416.

Alexander, Karl L., B. K. Eckland, and L. J. Griffin. "The Wisconsin Model of Socioeconomic Achievement: A Replication." *American Journal of Sociology* 81 (1975): 324–342.

Alwin, Duane, and Luther B. Otto. "High School Context Effects on Aspirations." *Sociology of Education* 50 (October 1977): 259–273.

Armor, David. "The Evidence on Busing." *The Public Interest* 28 (Summer 1972): 90–126.

Averch, H. A., S. J. Carroll, T. S. Donaldson, H. J. Kiesling, and J. Pincus. *How Effective Is Schooling? A Critical Review and Synthesis of Research Findings.* Santa Monica, Calif.: Rand Corporation, 1972.

Boocock, Sarane S. *An Introduction to the Sociology of Learning.* Boston: Houghton Mifflin, 1972.

Bowles, S. "Toward an Educational Production Function." In W. L. Hansen (Ed.), *Education, Income and Human Capital.* New York: National Bureau of Economic Research, Columbia University Press, 1970.

Bowles, Samuel, and Herbert Gintis. *Schooling in Capitalist America: Educational Reform and the Contradictions of Economic Life.* New York: Basic Books, 1976.

Brown, Bryon W., and Daniel H. Saks. "Production Technologies and Resource Allocations within Classrooms and Schools: Theory and Measurement." In Robert Dreeban and J. Alan Thomas (Eds.), *The Analysis of Educational Productivity, Volume 1: Issues in Microanalysis.* Cambridge, Mass.: Ballinger, 1980.

Campbell, Ernest Q., and C. Norman Alexander. "Structural Effects and Interpersonal Relationships." *American Journal of Sociology* 71: 3 (November 1965): 284–289.

Carnoy, Martin (Ed.). *Schooling in a Corporate Society.* New York: David McKay, 1972.

Coleman, James S., with E. Q. Campbell, C. J. Hobson, J. McPartland, A. M. Mood, F. Weinfield and R. L. York. *Equality of Educational Opportunity.* Washington, D.C.: U.S Government Printing Office, 1966.

Coleman, James S., T. Hoffer, and S. Kilgore. *High School Achievement: Public, Catholic and Other Private Schools Compared.* New York: Basic Books, 1982.

Coleman, James, Sara D. Kelly, and John A. Moore. "Recent Trends in School Integration." Paper presented at the the annual meeting of the American Educational Research Association, Washington, D.C., April 2, 1975.

Dahrendorf, Ralf. *Class and Class Conflict in Industrial Society.* Stanford, Calif.: Stanford University Press, 1959.

Dreeben, Robert, and J. Alan Thomas. "Introduction." In Robert Dreeban and J. Alan Thomas (Eds.), *The Analysis of Educational Productivity, Volume 1: Issues in Microanalysis.* Cambridge, Mass.: Ballinger, 1980.

Durkheim, Emile. *Education and Sociology.* Trans. Sherwood D. Fox. Glencoe, Ill.: The Free Press, 1956.

Erber, Ernest. "White Flight and Political Retreat." *Dissent* 26 (1979): 53–58.

Giles, Michael W. "White Enrollment Stability and School Desegregation: A Two Level Analysis." *American Sociological Review* 43 (1978): 848–864.

Guthrie, J. W., G. Kleindorfer, H. M. Levin, and R. T. Stout. *Schools and Inequality.* Cambridge, Mass.: MIT Press, 1971.

Hanushek, Eric A. "A Reader's Guide to Educational Production Functions." Paper presented at the National Invitational Conference on School Organization and Effects, San Diego, Calif., January 27–29, 1978.

Hauser, Robert M. "Context and Consex: A Cautionary Tale." *American Journal of Sociology* 75 (January 1970): 645–664.

Jencks, Christopher, James Crouse, and Peter Mueser. "The Wisconsin Model of Status Attainment: A National Replication with Improved Measures of Ability and Aspiration." *Sociology of Education* 56 (1983): 3–19.

Kerckoff, A. C., and R. T. Campbell. "Black-White Differences in the Educational Attainment Process." *Sociology of Education* 50 (1977): 15–27.

Kiesling, H. J. *The Relationship of School Inputs to Public School Performance in New York State.* Santa Monica, Calif.: Rand Corporation, 1969.

Lau, Lawrence J. "Educational Production Functions." Paper presented at the National Institutional Conference on School Organization and Effects, San Diego, Calif., January 27–29, 1978.

Levin, Henry M. "Measuring Efficiency in Educational Production." *Public Finance Quarterly* 2:1 (January 1974): 3–23.

McDill, Edward, E. Meyers, Jr., and L. C. Rigsby. "Institutional Effects on the Academic Behavior of High School Students." *Sociology of Education* 40 (Winter 1967): 181–199.

Mollenkopf, W. G., and D. S. Melville. "A Study of Secondary School Characteristics as Related to Test Scores." *Research Bulletin* 56–6. Princeton, N.J.: Educational Testing Service, 1956.

National Commission on Excellence in Education. "A Nation at Risk: The Imperative for Educational Reform." Final report. *Education Week,* April 27, 1983.

Parsons, Talcott. "The School Class as a Social System." *Harvard Educational Review* 29 (Fall 1959): 297–313.

Pettigrew, Thomas F., Elizabeth Useem, Clarence Normand, and Marshall S. Smith. "Busing: A Review of 'the Evidence.'" *The Public Interest* 30 (Winter 1973): 88–118.

Porter, J. N. "Race, Socialization and Mobility in Education and Early Occupational Attainment." *American Sociological Review* 39 (1974): 303–316.

Rossell, Christine. "School Desegregation and White Flight." *Political Science Quarterly* 90 (1975): 675–699.

Schmidt, Peter, Dennis Aigner, and C. A. Knox Lowell. "Formulation and Estimation of Stochastic Frontier Production Function Models." *Journal of Econometrics* 5 (July 1977): 21–38.

Sewell, William H., A. O. Haller, and G. W. Ohlendorf. "The Educational and Early Occupational Status Attainment Process: Replication and Revision." *American Sociological Review* 35 (1970): 1014–1027.

Sewell, William H., A. O. Haller, and A. Portes. "The Educational and Early Occupational Attainment Process." *American Sociological Review* 34 (1969): 82–92.

Sewell, William H., and Robert Hauser. *Occupation and Earnings: Achievement in the Early Career.* New York: Academic Press, 1975.

Sewell, William H., and Robert Hauser. "The Wisconsin Longitudinal Study of Social and Psychological Factors in Aspirations and Achievements." *Research in Sociology of Education and Socialization* 1 (1980): 59–99.

Spady, William. "The Impact of School Resources on Students." In Fred N. Kerlinger (Ed.), *Review of Research in Education.* Itasca, Ill.: F. E. Peacock, 1973.

Taeuber, Karl E., and David R. James. "Racial Segregation among Public and Private Schools." *Sociology of Education* 55: 213 (April/July 1982): 133–143.

DONALD A. HANSEN and
JOEL E. GERSTL

The Uncomfortable Relation of Society and Education

Questions to think about

1 *What are the research implications of the distinction between educational sociology and sociology of education?*
2 *Would a sociologist of education ask different questions than an educational sociologist? Explain and give an example.*

How does the term "sociology of education" differ from the more traditional term "educational sociology"? Often the two are used interchangeably, the implication being that the user may employ the one which best suits his mood or taste. In this perspective, it is interesting that the sociologist active in the study of education will often insist that his specialty be called a sociology of education (and that when the American Sociological Association adopted the *Journal of Educational Sociology,* it changed the name to *The Sociology of Education*). It appears that often (though certainly not always) the intent is to set up a contrast with counterparts in education departments, that the terms are used in a sort of academic one-upmanship, in which the sociologist may not be attempting to one-up the educator so much as to protect himself from onedownery at the hands of his colleagues.

At times, the terms are better rationalized to imply a difference in research operation or in research sophistication, or to designate a difference

Reprinted from Donald A. Hansen and Joel E. Gerstl, *On Education: Sociological Perspectives* (New York: John Wiley & Sons, 1967), pp. 21–24.

in focus of interest, indicating that the sociology of education is more global. At other times, the terms are used to distinguish between the perspective employed by the investigator, for example:

> From one perspective, sociology can focus *within* education, examining educational theory, practices, and processes. With such a focus, sociology performs much as does educational psychology and this approach is labelled "educational sociology." From another perspective, sociology can focus *on* education and attempt to understand educators, schools, and other educational institutions in their social and cultural contexts. This "sociology of education" is concerned with the relationship between education and society. In brutally simple terms, sociology from the one perspective might ask education, "What can I do to serve you?" From the other perspective it might ask, "What, in the name of society, *are* you and what in the world are you doing?" (Hansen, 1963, 313)

Whatever the merits of such arguments, they add up to confusion. Methods are but supplements to investigation. Though at any time the methods employed by one field may differ from those employed in another, in following years these tools may be exchanged. Is the sociology of education of today to be the educational sociology of tomorrow—or vice versa? The argument that the terms should designate differences in subject matter is similarly faulty: though the distinction may serve at any one time, it is inadequate to cope with exchange of foci, for example, if those who call themselves "sociologists of education" are sensitized by and adopt a current focus of "educational sociologists," say, on the social contexts and consequences of curricular innovation.

Such confusion is avoided and more critical gains promised if the term "educational sociology" is used to refer to the pursuit of a normative theory of education and to research that is primarily directed to furthering that normative theory or to direct application. "Sociology of education" would then refer to the pursuit of empirical theory and to research that is essentially directed toward furthering it.

The distinction between the efforts has little to do with methods employed (both certainly require objective research), or the subject matter, or even the "scope" of the perspective. Either empirical or normative inquiry can focus on the individual or on the entire society; indeed, any pretense to adequacy in theory of either type requires individual-societal breadth. (Worthy investigations and attempts to establish components of each type of theory on both individual and societal scales are already developed.) Similarly, either type of theory can be served by historical or comparative analysis, or by any useful research methodology extant; obviously, it is possible that any given project will contribute to both.

The distinction does not necessarily separate the research of sociology from that of education. Although sociology may be, grossly, characterized as empirical, and education as normative, it is clear that neither sociology nor education can claim sole proprietorship of either mode of inquiry; it may even be that neither field can effectively develop without both.

The essential distinction is between the effort to develop knowledge and the effort to develop a base for effective action. A sociology of education, that is, would be an essential component of the effort toward general empirical theory, an educational sociology an essential part of the effort to establish action prescriptions and normative theory.

In educational sociology, then, inquiry is necessarily relative to some conception of present conditions to be improved. It follows that an adequate normative theory is served by an adequate conception of the current state and potentials of education and society; thus that an adequate normative theory requires an adequate sociology of education. But this is not to say that the normative educational sociology will be *based* on the empirical sociology of education. For empirical theory, no matter how adequate, can only tell the reformer what can be changed *from,* to help to make him aware of the special problems that might be faced in change, and assess the probabilities of consequences. The conception of what should be established, of what education should become, must be erected from a conception of the ideal. From where is this conception to come? Faced with pressing demands and plagued with egocentrism, reformers and educators have traditionally attempted to articulate a conception of the good society or the good education, resorting, where articulation was either impossible or obviously vulnerable to objective analysis, to "intuition" or "conscience." Although such makeshift criteria will likely continue to guide educational decisions and actions, ideally an adequate educational sociology would require a valid base in a cogent ethical theory from which constructive prescriptions might develop.

Educational sociology, then, is revealed as far more than an assemblage of investigations, responses to immediate, practical problems, or attempts to remove inadequacies in existing practice. Although today much, perhaps most, existing research that might be categorized as educational sociology is of this muddling-through, problem-oriented research type, educational sociology can be seen to be part of a larger enterprise to establish more adequate education in the society of today and tomorrow. But this statement may hide its own essential implication: the pursuit of an adequate normative theory of education, to which educational sociology might be an essential contributor, could be one of the most urgent efforts of our time. It can be argued readily and convincingly that in contemporary society as never before, exhaustive effort must be turned to establishing valid educational goals and programs.

It is apparent that the preceding discussion deals with ideals; that such adequacy in normative theory is at least equally beyond current capabilities as is adequate empirical theory. The discussion is of practical importance, however, in two critical points. *First, the task of an educational sociology is far broader than current research and discussion even vaguely imply. Second, an educational sociology is not but a simple extension of a sociology of education; normative inquiry cannot be validated simply through the application of empirical methods or empirical theory and knowledge.*

In summary, both empirical and normative enterprises—both sociology of education and educational sociology—are important today, and if they are to effectively develop, they must be carefully and explicitly distinguished as independent enterprises. But this is not to say that they cannot and should not contribute to one another. For in fact . . . the two may be in many ways closely compatible.

To state that a mutually productive relation is possible, however, is not to prove it practicable. Among the most tenacious barriers to realization of potentials, and even to their explicit identification, are the perennial questions:

1. What is the nature of "objectivity"—does it allow any conception of the empirical enterprise as anything but "value-free"?
2. Does "involvement in human life" by the researcher and theorist add to, or detract from, the empirical enterprise?

The potential relation of educational sociology and a sociology of education may be in large part determined by the answers to these questions. . . .

REFERENCE

Hansen, Donald A. (1963). "The Responsibility of the Sociologist to Education." *Harvard Educational Review* 33 (Summer): 312–325.

CHAPTER 2

Theoretical Perspectives: Understanding Educational Systems

Each of us is constantly interpreting our world. This is necessary for living, even survival. One reason we have differing opinions is because our interpretations of the world differ, influenced by our personal experiences and our social backgrounds: family, religion, sex, race, age, and other aspects of the social world. Sociologists also interpret the social world, using theoretical perspectives. For instance, a sociologist might ask why some people "get ahead," while others do not. You might say it is because some are smarter than others, some try harder than others, or some have more chances than others. In attempting to understand such issues, sociologists look at the society in which people live and the structure of that society. They look at the interrelationships, interactions, and conflicts among members of society.

Theoretical perspectives help sociologists in various ways: among others, to interpret empirical data; to focus attention on important problems; to understand why actions occur; and to guide research. Selection of a theoretical perspective by a sociological researcher represents a value statement or commitment because each theory carries with it certain assumptions about the social system and the place and purpose of education within it. Although underlying assumptions and propositions of theories differ, they share a common purpose of helping us understand and interpret facts, and even design policies and programs.

Topics falling anywhere within the open systems framework may be interpreted by one theory if it proves most useful, or by several theories if they help to shed light on the issue and if the theoretical assumptions are compatible with interpretation of the problem. The open systems framework helps us to locate the parts of the system involved in the issue or problem, identify the level of analysis, and narrow the range of applicable theories.

Supposing, for instance, we wish to study the relationship between stratification and the educational systems in a society. We would locate the problem in our systems framework—that is, determine which parts of the system will enter into the analysis. Then we would select an appropriate theoretical approach to study this broad topic with. If we wish to study student-teacher interactions in classrooms and their impact on student learning, different theoretical approaches would be in order.

Several major theoretical perspectives are used in sociology of education to guide research studies (see Table 1). Some of these approaches focus on large-scale problems in institutions or society. These we call *macro-level theories;* the major ones reviewed in this chapter are the structural-functional theory and conflict theory. If we wish to focus on interactions between individuals or small groups, these are *micro-level theories*. Inter-action theories, labeling theory, and the "new" sociology of education are examples of micro-level theories. Since studies have been conducted using these and many other theoretical approaches, it is important to know something about them as you read the selections in this text.

Valuable data and analyses have been contributed to the field of sociology of education by sociologists using the functionalist perspective. This theory, which reached its peak in the 1950s, remains an important perspective for understanding educational systems. Collins summarizes some key elements of the functional perspective in the first article. This perspective also appears in articles by Clark, Parsons, and Dreeben in other chapters of the text. The functional approach, however, has been criticized as supporting the educational status quo in countries while not recognizing alternative systems that might provide more equality of opportunity. By stressing the role of technology in guiding educational change, and by focusing on the selection and allocation function discussed in Chapter 1, this approach neglects the disagreements that exist in society over ways of attaining equality, concerns about content in educational programs, and ideologies that guide systems. It assumes a degree of consensus among societal members that conflict theorists argue is unrealistic.

Reflecting the social moods of the 1960s and 1970s, conflict theory has become an influential theoretical perspective for studying educational systems. Collins uses Weber's concept of *status groups* to argue that edu-

T A B L E   1
Theoretical Perspectives Used to Guide Research

Levels of analysis	Theoretical approaches
Macro	
Society	Conflict theory
Institutions	Structural-functional
Organizations	
Micro	
Small groups	Ethnomethodology
Interaction	Interaction theories
	Labeling
	"New" sociology of education

cational systems are shaped more by competition for wealth, power, and prestige than by the technological needs and growth of the societal economy. Schools teach *status culture,* which has the effect of perpetuating class distinctions between groups. In his article Collins evaluates functional and conflict theories as they deal with the process of stratification.

Two of the articles in this section describe theories that fall into the micro-level of analysis. Both examples focus on interaction dynamics within the classroom, but the "new" sociology of education considers how broader societal issues of control are reflected in classroom dynamics.

Ray C. Rist describes the role *labeling theory* can play in helping us understand interaction within educational systems such as student-teacher relationships and teacher expectations. Debate over how teachers develop expectations of students and the effect of self-fulfilling prophecy, and how students come to see their own role as students, has been extensive. Labeling theory provides a framework for study of the internal dynamics of the school and classroom: interpersonal dynamics, evaluation of students, and resulting student self-concept. Rist mentions several important studies that have used the interaction level of analysis. Note the differences in the subject matter of primary concern in the Collins and Rist articles: One focuses primarily on stratification systems, the other on classroom interaction dynamics.

Hugh Mehan presents an argument for a new approach to the study of schooling that he calls *constitutive ethnography.* Based on ethnomethodological theoretical and methodological approaches, this approach stresses the importance of examining the processes by which school structures are created instead of taking existing structures for granted. In this excerpt

Mehan explains constitutive ethnography; in the complete article he presents extended discussion of research using this approach in the areas of classroom organization, testing encounters, and counseling sessions.

The fourth selection, excerpted from Jerome Karabel and A. H. Halsey's discussion of educational research and theory, describes an approach to sociology of education that has attracted attention in Europe and is influencing many American sociologists of education—the so-called "new" sociology of education. Focusing on the use and control of knowledge to hold power in the school, this perspective concerns student-teacher interactions, the categories or concepts used by educators to evaluate systems and the educational curriculum.

Each of these approaches can be useful depending upon the problem to be researched. The open systems framework provides an organizational framework within which explanatory theories such as these can operate. For instance, when we wish to focus on the internal processes and interaction dynamics of student and teacher in classrooms and schools, labeling theory or the "new" sociology of education are two of the most useful theories that help to explain our research problems. If we are concerned with issues of educational systems in relation to the wider society, conflict or functional theory are appropriate.

The contents of this book are organized in such a way that each chapter represents a part of the total system—from the internal structure, roles, and informal organization to the processes, social movements, and changes that influence it, to examples of systems of higher education and world educational systems. As you read the articles gathered in these chapters, be aware of the theoretical perspectives that are explicitly or implicitly expressed.

RANDALL COLLINS

Functional and Conflict Theories of Educational Stratification

Questions to think about

1 *What are the outcomes of the author's comparison between functional and conflict theory for studying the link between education and stratification systems?*

2 *What different approaches are used in the technical-functional and conflict theories? Which do you consider the better approach and why?*

3 *Comparing these two approaches, what are the implications for changes in educational systems? How does each interrelate with the open systems framework?*

4 *Select an educational issue of interest to you. Explain how each theory discussed in this article might be applied to the issue.*

Education has become highly important in occupational attainment in modern America, and thus occupies a central place in the analysis of stratification and of social mobility. This paper attempts to assess the adequacy of two theories in accounting for available evidence on the link between education and stratification: a functional theory concerning trends in technical skill requirements in industrial societies; and a conflict theory derived from the approach of Max Weber, stating the determinants of various outcomes in the struggles among status groups. It will be argued that the evidence best supports the conflict theory, although

From *American Sociological Review* 36 (1971): 1002–1019. Reprinted with permission.

technical requirements have important effects in particular contexts. It will be further argued that the construction of a general theory of the determinants of stratification in its varying forms is best advanced by incorporating elements of the functional analysis of technical requirements of specific jobs at appropriate points within the conflict model. The conclusion offers an interpretation of historical change in education and stratification in industrial America, and suggests where further evidence is required for more precise tests and for further development of a comprehensive explanatory theory.

THE IMPORTANCE OF EDUCATION

A number of studies have shown that the number of years of education is a strong determinant of occupational achievement in America with social origins constant. They also show that social origins affect educational attainment, and also occupational attainment after the completion of education (Blau and Duncan, 1967: 163–205; Eckland, 1965; Sewell *et al.*, 1969; Duncan and Hodge, 1963; Lipset and Bendix, 1959: 189–192). There are differences in occupational attainment independent of social origins between the graduates of more prominent and less prominent secondary schools, colleges, graduate schools, and law schools (Smigel, 1964: 39, 73–74, 117; Havemann and West, 1952: 179–181; Ladinsky, 1967; Hargens and Hagstrom, 1967).

Educational requirements for employment have become increasingly widespread, not only in elite occupations but also at the bottom of the occupational hierarchy (see Table 1). In a 1967 survey of the San Francisco, Oakland, and San Jose areas (Collins, 1969), 17% of the employers surveyed required at least a high school diploma for employment in even unskilled positions;[1] a national survey (Bell, 1940) in 1937–1938 found a comparable figure of 1%. At the same time, educational requirements appear to have become more specialized, with 38% of the organizations in the 1967 survey which required college degrees of managers preferring business administration training, and an additional 15% preferring engineering training; such requirements appear to have been virtually unknown in the 1920s (Pierson, 1959: 34–54). At the same time, the proportions of the American population attending schools through the completion of high school and advanced levels have risen sharply during the last century (Table 2). Careers are thus increasingly shaped within the educational system.

TABLE 1
Percent of Employers Requiring Various Minimum Educational Levels of Employees, by Occupational Level

	National Survey, 1937–38					
	Unskilled	Semi-skilled	Skilled	Clerical	Managerial	Professional
Less than high school	99%	97%	89%	33%	32%	9%
High school diploma	1	3	11	63	54	16
Some college				1	2	23
College degree				3	12	52
	100%	100%	100%	100%	100%	100%
San Francisco Bay Area, 1967						
Less than high school	83%	76%	62%	29%	27%	10%
High school diploma	16	24	28	68	14	4
Vocational training beyond high school	1	1	10	2	2	4
Some college				2	12	7
College degree					41	70
Graduate degree					3	5
	100%	100%	100%	101%	99%	100%
	(244)	(237)	(245)	(306)	(288)	(240)

Sources: H.M. Bell, *Matching Youth and Jobs* (Washington: American Council on Education, 1940), p. 264, as analyzed in Lawrence Thomas, *The Occupational Structure and Education* (Englewood Cliffs: Prentice-Hall, 1956), p. 346; and Randall Collins, "Education and Employment," unpublished Ph.D. dissertation, University of California at Berkeley, 1969, Table III-I. Bell does not report the number of employers in the sample, but it was apparently large.

TABLE 2
Percentage Educational Attainment in the United States, 1869–1965

Period	High School Graduates/ Pop. 17 yrs. Old	Resident College Students/ Pop. 18–21	B.A.'s or 1st Prof. Degrees/1/10 of Pop. 15–24	M.A.'s or 2nd Prof. Degrees/1/10 of Pop. 25–34	Ph.D.'s 1/10 of Pop. 25–34
1869–1870	2.0	1.7			
1879–1880	2.5	2.7			
1889–1890	3.3	3.0			
1899–1900	6.4	4.0	1.66	0.12	0.03
1909–1910	8.8	5.1	1.85	0.13	0.02
1919–1920	16.8	8.9	2.33	0.24	0.03
1929–1930	29.0	12.4	4.90	0.78	0.12
1939–1940	50.8	15.6	7.05	1.24	0.15
1949–1950	59.0	29.6	17.66	2.43	0.27
1959–1960	65.1	34.9	17.72	3.25	0.42
1963	76.3	38.0			
1965			19.71	5.02	0.73

Sources: *Historical Statistics of the United States*, Series A-28-29, H 327-338; *Statistical Abstract of the United States 1966*, Tables 3 and 194; *Digest of Educational Statistics* (U. S. Office of Education, 1967), Tables 66 and 88.

THE TECHNICAL-FUNCTION THEORY OF EDUCATION

A common explanation of the importance of education in modern society may be termed the technical-function theory. Its basic propositions, found in a number of sources (see, for example, B. Clark, 1962; Kerr *et al.*, 1960), may be stated as follows: (1) the skill requirements of jobs in industrial society constantly increase because of technological change. Two processes are involved: (a) the proportion of jobs requiring low skill decreases and the proportion requiring high skill increases; and (b) the same jobs are upgraded in skill requirements. (2) Formal education provides the training, either in specific skills or in general capacities, necessary for the more highly skilled jobs. (3) Therefore, educational requirements for employment constantly rise, and increasingly larger proportions of the population are required to spend longer and longer periods in school.

The technical-function theory of education may be seen as a particular application of a more general functional approach. The functional theory of stratification (Davis and Moore, 1945) rests on the premises (A) that occupational positions require particular kinds of skilled performance; and (B) that positions must be filled with persons who have either the native ability, or who have acquired the training, necessary for the performance of the given occupational role.[2] The technical-function theory of education may be viewed as a subtype of this form of analysis, since it shares the premises that the occupational structure creates demands for particular kinds of performance, and that training is one way of filling these demands. In addition, it includes the more restrictive premises (1 and 2 above) concerning the way in which skill requirements of jobs change with industrialization, and concerning the content of school experiences.

The technical-function theory of education may be tested by reviewing the evidence for each of its propositions (1a, 1b, and 2).[3] As will be seen, these propositions do not adequately account for the evidence. In order to generate a more complete explanation, it will be necessary to examine the evidence for the underlying functional propositions, (A) and (B). This analysis leads to a focus on the processes of stratification—notably group conflict—not expressed in the functional theory, and to the formalization of a conflict theory to account for the evidence.

Proposition (1a): *Educational requirements of jobs in industrial society increase because the proportion of jobs requiring low skill decreases and the proportion requiring high skill increases.* Available evidence suggests that this process accounts for only a minor part of educational upgrading, at least in a society that has passed the point of initial industrialization. Fifteen percent of the increase in education of the U.S. labor force during the twentieth century may be attributed to shifts in the occupational structure—a decrease in the proportion of jobs with low skill requirements and an increase in proportion of jobs with high skill requirements (Folger and Nam, 1964). The bulk of educational upgrading (85%) has occurred *within* job categories.

Proposition (1b): *Educational requirements of jobs in industrial society rise because the same jobs are upgraded in skill requirements.* The only available evidence on this point consists of data collected by the U.S. Department of Labor in 1950 and 1960, which indicate the amount of change in skill requirements of specific jobs. Under the most plausible assumptions as to the skills provided by various levels of education, it appears that the educational level of the U.S. labor force has changed in excess of that which is necessary to keep up with skill requirements of jobs (Berg, 1970: 38–60). Over-education for available jobs is found particularly among males who have graduated from college and females with high school degrees or some college, and appears to have increased between 1950 and 1960.

Proposition (2): *Formal education provides required job skills.* This proposition may be tested in two ways: (a) Are better educated employees more productive than less educated employees? (b) Are vocational skills learned in schools, or elsewhere?

(a) *Are better educated employees more productive?* The evidence most often cited for the productive effects of education is indirect, consisting of relationships between *aggregate* levels of education in a society and its overall economic productivity. These are of three types:

(i) The national growth approach involves calculating the proportion of growth in the U.S. Gross National Product attributable to conventional inputs of capital and labor; these leave a large residual, which is attributed to improvements in skill of the labor force based on increased education (Schultz, 1961; Denison, 1965). This approach suffers from difficulty in clearly distinguishing among technological change affecting productive arrangements, changes in the abilities of workers acquired by experience at work with new technologies, and changes in skills due to formal education and motivational factors associated with a competitive or achievement-oriented society. The assignment of a large proportion of the residual category to education is arbitrary. Denison (1965) makes this attribution on the basis of the increased income to persons with higher levels of education interpreted as rewards for their contributions to productivity. Although it is a common assumption in economic argument that wage returns reflect output value, wage returns cannot be used to prove the productive contribution of education without circular reasoning.

(ii) Correlations of education and level of economic development for nations show that the higher the level of economic development of a country, the higher the proportion of its population in elementary, secondary, and higher education (Harbison and Myers, 1964). Such correlations beg the question of causality. There are considerable variations in school enrollments among countries at the same economic level, and many of these variations are explicable in terms of political demands for access to education (Ben-David, 1963–64). Also, the over-production of educated personnel in countries whose level of economic development cannot absorb them suggests the demand for education need not come directly from the economy, and may run counter to economic needs (Hoselitz, 1965).

(iii) Time-lag correlations of education and economic development show that increases in the proportion of population in elementary school precede increases in economic development after a takeoff point at approximately 30–50% of the 7–14 years old age-group in school. Similar anticipations of economic development are suggested for increases in secondary and higher education enrollment, although the data do not clearly support this conclusion (Peaslee, 1969). A pattern of advances in secondary school enrollments preceding advances in economic development is found only in a small number of cases (12 of 37 examined in Peaslee, 1969). A pattern of growth of university enrollments and subsequent economic development is found in 21 of 37 cases, but the exceptions (including the United States, France, Sweden, Russia, and Japan) are of such importance as to throw serious doubt on any *necessary* contribution of higher education to economic development. The main contribution of education to economic productivity, then, appears to occur at the level of the transition to mass literacy, and not significantly beyond this level.

Direct evidence of the contribution of education to *individual* productivity is summarized by Berg (1970:85–104, 143–176). It indicates that the better educated employees are not generally more productive, and in some cases are less productive, among samples of factory workers, maintenance men, department store clerks, technicians, secretaries, bank tellers, engineers, industrial research scientists, military personnel, and federal civil service employees.

(b) *Are vocational skills learned in school, or elsewhere?* Specifically vocational education in the schools for manual positions is virtually independent of job fate, as graduates of vocational programs are not more likely to be employed than high school dropouts (Plunkett, 1960; Duncan, 1964). Most skilled manual workers acquire their skills on the job or casually (Clark and Sloan, 1966:73). Retraining for important technological changes in industry has been carried out largely informally on-the-job; in only a very small proportion of jobs affected by technological change is formal retraining in educational institutions used (Collins, 1969:147–158; Bright, 1958).

The relevance of education for non-manual occupational skills is more difficult to evaluate. Training in specific professions, such as medicine, engineering, scientific or scholarly research, teaching, and law can plausibly be considered vocationally relevant, and possibly essential. Evidences comparing particular degrees of educational success with particular kinds of occupational performance or success are not available, except for a few occupations. For engineers, high college grades and degree levels generally predict high levels of technical responsibility and high participation in professional activities, but not necessarily high salary or supervisory responsibility (Perrucci and Perrucci, 1970). At the same time, a number of practicing engineers lack college degrees (about 40% of engineers in the early 1950s; see Soderberg, 1963:213), suggesting that even such highly technical skills may be acquired on the job. For academic research scientists, educational quality has little effect on subsequent productivity (Hagstrom and Hargens, 1968). For other professions, evidence is not available on the degree to which actual skills are learned in school rather than in practice. In professions such as medicine and law, where education is a legal requirement for admission to practice, a comparison group of non-educated practitioners is not available, at least in the modern era.

Outside of the traditional learned professions, the plausibility of the vocational importance of education is more questionable. Comparisons of the efforts of different occupations to achieve "professionalization" suggest that setting educational requirements and bolstering them through licensing laws is a common tactic in raising an occupation's prestige and autonomy (Wilensky, 1964). The result has been the proliferation of numerous pseudo-professions in modern society; nevertheless these fail to achieve strong professional organization through lack of a monopolizable (and hence teachable) skill base. Business administration schools represent such an effort. (See Pierson, 1959:9, 55–95, 140; Gordon and Howell, 1959: 1–18, 40, 324–337.) Descriptions of general, nonvocational education do not support the image of schools as places where skills are widely learned. Scattered studies suggest that the knowledge imparted in particular courses is retained only in small part through the next few years (Learned and Wood, 1938:28), and indicate a dominant student culture concerned with nonacademic interests or with achieving grades with a minimum of learning (Coleman, 1961, Becker et al., 1968).

The technical-function theory of education, then, does not give an adequate account of the evidence. Economic evidence indicates no clear contributions of education to economic development, beyond the provisions of mass literacy. Shifts in the proportions of more skilled and less skilled jobs do not account for the observed increase in education of the American labor force. Education is often irrelevant to on-the-job productivity and is sometimes counter-productive; specifically vocational training seems to be derived more from work experience than from formal school training. The quality of schools themselves, and the nature of dominant student cultures suggest that schooling is very inefficient as a means of training for work skills.

FUNCTIONAL AND CONFLICT PERSPECTIVES

It may be suggested that the inadequacies of the technical-function theory of education derive from a more basic source: the functional approach to stratification. A fundamental assumption is that there is a generally fixed set of positions, whose various requirements the labor force must satisfy. The fixed demand for skills of various types, at any given time, is the basic determinant of who will be selected for what positions. Social change may then be explained by specifying how these functional demands change with the process of modernization. In keeping with the functional perspective in general, the needs of society are seen as determining the behavior and the rewards of the individuals within it.

However, this premise may be questioned as an adequate picture of the fundamental processes of social organization. It may be suggested that the "demands" of any occupational position are not fixed, but represent whatever behavior is settled upon in bargaining between the persons who fill the positions and those who attempt to control them. Individuals want jobs primarily for the rewards to themselves in material goods, power, and prestige. The amount of productive skill they must demonstrate to hold their positions depends on how much clients, customers, or employers can successfully demand of them, and this in turn depends on the balance of power between workers and their employers.

Employers tend to have quite imprecise conceptions of the skill requirements of most jobs, and operate on a strategy of "satisficing" rather than optimizing—that is, setting average levels of performance as satisfactory, and making changes in procedures or personnel only when performance falls noticeably below minimum standards (Dill *et al.*, 1962; March and Simon, 1958:140–141). Efforts to predict work performance by objective tests have foundered due to difficulties in measuring performance (except on specific mechanical tasks) and the lack of control groups to validate the tests (Anastasi, 1967). Organizations do not force their employees to work at maximum efficiency; there is considerable insulation of workers at all levels from demands for full use of their skills and efforts. Informal controls over output are found not only among production workers in manufacturing but also among sales and clerical personnel (Roy, 1952; Blau, 1955; Lombard, 1955). The existence of informal organization at the managerial level, the widespread existence of bureaucratic pathologies such as evasion of responsibility, empire-building, and displacement of means by ends ("red tape"), and the fact that administrative work is only indirectly related to the output of the organization, suggest that managers, too, are insulated from strong technological pressures for use of technical skills. On all levels, wherever informal organization exists, it appears that standards of performance reflect the power of the groups involved.

In this light, it is possible to reinterpret the body of evidence that ascriptive factors continue to be important in occupational success even in advanced industrial society. The social mobility data summarized at the onset of this paper show that social origins have a direct effect on occupational success, even after the completion of education. Both case studies and cross-sectional samples amply document widespread discrimination against Negroes. Case studies show that the operation of ethnic and class standards in employment based not merely on skin color but on name, accent, style of dress, manners, and conversational abilities (Noland and Bakke, 1949; Turner, 1952; Taeuber et al., 1966; Nosow, 1956). Cross-sectional studies, based on both biographical and survey data, show that approximately 60 to 70% of the American business elite come from upper-class and upper-middle-class families, and fewer than 15% from working-class families (Taussig and Joselyn, 1932:97; Warner and Abegglen, 1955:37–68; Newcomer, 1955:53; Bendix, 1956:198–253; Mills, 1963:110–139). These proportions are fairly constant from the early 1800's through the 1950's. The business elite is overwhelmingly Protestant, male, and completely white, although there are some indications of a mild trend toward declining social origins and an increase of Catholics and Jews. Ethnic and class background have been found crucial for career advancement in the professions as well (Ladinsky, 1963; Hall, 1946). Sexual stereotyping of jobs is extremely widespread (Collins, 1969:234–238).

In the traditional functionalist approach, these forms of ascription are treated as residual categories: carry-overs from a less advanced period, or marks of the imperfections of the functional mechanism of placement. Yet available trend data suggest that the link between social class origins and occupational attainment has remained constant during the twentieth century in America (Blau and Duncan, 1967:81–113); the proportion of women in higher occupational levels has changed little since the late nineteenth century (Epstein, 1970:7); and the few available comparisons between elite groups in traditional and modern societies suggest comparable levels of mobility (Marsh, 1963). Declines in racial and ethnic discrimination that appear to have occurred at periods in twentieth-century America may be plausibly explained as results of political mobilization of particular minority groups rather than by an increased economic need to select by achievement criteria.

Goode (1967) has offered a modified functional model to account for these disparities: that work groups always organize to protect their inept members from being judged by outsiders' standards of productivity, and that this self-protection is functional to the organizations, preventing a Hobbesian competitiveness and distrust of all against all. This argument re-establishes a functional explanation, but only at the cost of undermining the technological view of functional requirements. Further, Goode's conclusions can be put in other terms: it is to the advantage of groups of employees to organize so that they will not be judged by strict performance standards; and it is at least minimally to the advantage of the employer to let them do so, for if he presses them harder he creates dissension and alienation. Just how hard an employer *can* press his employees is not given in Goode's functional model. That is, his model has the disadvantage, common to functional analysis in its most general form, of covering too many alternative possibilities to provide testable explanations of specific outcomes. Functional analysis too easily operates as a justification for whatever particular pattern exists, asserting in effect that there is a proper reason for it to be so, but failing to state the conditions under which a particular pattern will hold rather than another. The technical version of job requirements has the advantage of specifying patterns, but it is this specific form of functional explanation that is jettisoned by a return to a more abstract functional analysis.

A second hypothesis may be suggested: the power of "ascribed" groups may be the *prime* basis of selection in all organizations, and technical skills are secondary considerations depending on the balance of power. Education may thus be regarded as a mark of membership in a particular group (possibly at times its defining characteristic), not a mark of technical skills or achievement. Educational requirements may thus reflect the interests of whichever groups have power to set them. Weber (1968:1000) interpreted educational requirements in bureaucracies, drawing especially on the history of public administration in Prussia, as the result of efforts by university graduates to monopolize positions, raise their corporate status, and thereby increase their own security and power vis-à-vis both higher authorities and clients. Gusfield (1958) has shown that educational requirements in the British Civil Service were set as the result of a power struggle between a victorious educated upper-middle-class and the traditional aristocracy.

To summarize the argument to this point: available evidence suggests that the technical-functional view of educational requirements for jobs leaves a large number of facts unexplained. Functional analysis on the more abstract level does not provide a testable explanation of which ascribed groups will be able to dominate which positions. To answer this question, one must leave the functional frame of reference and examine the conditions of relative power of each group.

A CONFLICT THEORY OF STRATIFICATION

The conditions under which educational requirements will be set and changed may be stated more generally, on the basis of a conflict theory of stratification derived from Weber (1968:926–939; see also Collins, 1968), and from advances in modern organization theory fitting the spirit of this approach.

A. Status Groups

The basic units of society are associational groups sharing common cultures (or "subcultures"). The core of such groups is families and friends, but they may be extended to religious, educational,or ethnic communities. In general, they comprise all persons who share a sense of status equality based on participation in a common culture; styles of language, tastes in clothing and decor, manners and other ritual observances, conversational topics and styles, opinions and values, and preferences in sports, arts, and media. Participation in such cultural groups gives individuals their fundamental sense of identity, especially in contrast with members of other associational groups in whose everyday culture they cannot participate comfortably. Subjectively, status groups distinguish themselves from others in terms of categories of *moral evaluation* such as "honor," "taste," "breeding," "respectability," "propriety," "cultivation," "good fellows," "plain folks," etc. Thus the exclusion of persons who lack the ingroup culture is felt to be normatively legitimated.

There is no *a priori* determination of the number of status groups in a particular society, nor can the degree to which there is consensus on a rank order among them be stated in advance. These are not matters of definition, but empirical variations, the causes of which are subjects of other developments of the conflict theory of stratification. Status groups should be regarded as ideal types, without implication of *necessarily distinct* boundaries; the concepts remain useful even in the case where associational groupings and their status cultures are fluid and overlapping, as hypotheses about the conflicts among status groups may remain fruitful even under these circumstances.

Status groups may be derived from a number of sources. Weber outlines three: (a) differences in life style based on economic situation (i.e., class); (b) differences in life situation based on power position; (c) differences in life situation deriving directly from cultural conditions or institutions, such as geographical origin, ethnicity, religion, education, or intellectual or aesthetic cultures.

B. Struggle for Advantage

There is a continual struggle in society for various "goods"—wealth, power, or prestige. We need make no assumption that every individual is motivated to maximize his rewards; however, since power and prestige are inherently scarce commodities, and wealth is often contingent upon them, the ambition of even a small proportion of persons for more than equal shares of these goods sets up an implicit counter-struggle on the part of others to avoid subjection and disesteem. Individuals may struggle with each other, but since individual identity is derived primarily from membership in a status group, and because the cohesion of status groups is a key resource in the struggle against others, the primary focus of struggle is between status groups rather than within them.

The struggle for wealth, power, and prestige is carried out primarily through organizations. There have been struggles throughout history among organizations controlled by different status groups, for military conquest, business advantage, or cultural (e.g., religious) hegemony, and intricate sorts of interorganizational alliances are possible. In the more complex societies, struggle between status groups is carried on in large part *within* organizations, as the status groups controlling an organization coerce, hire, or culturally manipulate others to carry out their wishes (as in, respectively, a conscript army, a business, or a church). Organizational research shows that the success of organizational elites in controlling their subordinates is quite variable. Under particular conditions, lower or middle members have considerable *de facto* power to avoid compliance, and even to change the course of the organizations (see Etzioni, 1961).

This opposing power from below is strengthened when subordinate members constitute a cohesive status group of their own; it is weakened when subordinates acquiesce in the values of the organization elite. Coincidence of ethnic and class boundaries produces the sharpest cultural distinctions. Thus, Catholics of immigrant origins have been the bulwarks of informal norms restricting work output in American firms run by WASPs, whereas Protestants of native rural backgrounds are the main "rate-busters" (O. Collins *et al.*, 1946). Selection and manipulation of members in terms of status groups is thus a key weapon in intraorganizational struggles. In general, the organization elite selects its new members and key assistants from its own status group and makes an effort to secure lower-level employees who are at least indoctrinated to respect the cultural superiority of their status culture.[4]

Once groups of employees of different status groups are formed at various positions (middle, lower, or laterally differentiated) in the organization, each of these groups may be expected to launch efforts to recruit more members of their own status group. This process is illustrated by conflicts among whites and blacks, Protestants and Catholics and Jews, Yankee, Irish and Italian, etc. found in American occupational life (Hughes, 1949; Dalton, 1951). These conflicts are based on ethnically or religiously founded status cultures; their intensity rises and falls with processes increasing or decreasing the cultural distinctiveness of these groups, and with the succession of advantages and disadvantages set by previous outcomes of these struggles which determine the organizational resources available for further struggle. Parallel processes of cultural conflict may be based on distinctive class as well as ethnic cultures.

C. Education as Status Culture

The main activity of schools is to teach particular status cultures, both in and outside the classroom. In this light, any failure of schools to impart technical knowledge (although it may also be successful in this) is not important; schools primarily teach vocabulary and inflection, styles of dress, aesthetic tastes, values and manners. The emphasis on sociability and athletics found in many schools is not extraneous but may be at the core of the status culture propagated by the schools. Where schools have a more academic or vocational emphasis, this emphasis may itself be the content of a particular status culture, providing sets of values, materials for conversation, and shared activities for an associational group making claims to a particular basis for status.

Insofar as a particular status group controls education, it may use it to foster control within work organizations. Educational requirements for employment can serve both to select new members for elite positions who share the elite culture and, at a lower level of education, to hire lower and middle employees who have acquired a general respect for these elite values and styles.

TESTS OF THE CONFLICT THEORY OF
EDUCATIONAL STRATIFICATION

The conflict theory in its general form is supported by evidence (1) that there are distinctions among status group cultures—based on both class and on ethnicity—in modern societies (Kahl, 1957:127–156, 184–220); (2) that status groups tend to occupy different occupational positions within organizations (see data on ascription cited above); and (3) that occupants of different organizational positions struggle over power (Dalton, 1959; Crozier, 1964). The more specific tests called for here, however, are of the adequacy of conflict theory to explain the link between education and occupational stratification. Such tests may focus either on the proposed mechanism of occupational placement, or on the conditions for strong or weak links between education and occupation.

Education as a Mechanism of Occupational Placement

The mechanism proposed is that employers use education to select persons who have been socialized into the dominant status culture: for entrants to their own managerial ranks, into elite culture; for lower-level employees, into an attitude of respect for the dominant culture and the elite which carries it. This requires evidence that: (a) schools provide either training for the elite culture, or respect for it; and (b) employers use education as a means of selection for cultural attributes.

(a) Historical and descriptive studies of schools support the generalization that they are places where particular status cultures are acquired, either from the teachers, from other students, or both. Schools are usually founded by powerful or autonomous status groups, either to provide an exclusive education for their own children, or to propagate respect for their cultural values. Until recently most schools were founded by religions, often in opposition to those founded by rival religions; throughout the 19th century, this rivalry was an important basis for the founding of large numbers of colleges in the U.S., and of the Catholic and Lutheran school systems. The public school system in the U.S. was founded mainly under the impetus of WASP elites with the purpose of teaching respect for Protestant and middle-class standards of cultural and religious propriety, especially in the face of Catholic, working-class immigration from Europe (Cremin, 1961; Curti, 1935). The content of public school education has consisted especially of middle-class, WASP culture (Waller, 1932:15–131; Becker, 1961; Hess and Torney, 1967).

At the elite level, private secondary schools for children of the WASP upper class were founded from the 1880s, when the mass indoctrination function of the growing public schools made them unsuitable as means of maintaining cohesion of the elite culture itself (Baltzell, 1958:327–372). These elite schools produce a distinctive personality type, characterized by adherence to a distinctive set of upper-class values and manners (McArthur, 1955). The cultural role of schools has been more closely studied in Britain (Bernstein, 1961; Weinberg, 1967) and in France (Bourdieu and Passeron, 1964), although Riesman and his colleagues (Riesman, 1958; Jencks and Riesman, 1968) have shown some of the cultural differences among prestige levels of colleges and universities in the United States.

(b) Evidence that education has been used as a means of cultural selection may be found in several sources. Hollingshead's (1949:360–388) study of Elmtown school children, school dropouts, and community attitudes toward them suggests that employers use education as a means of selecting employees with middle-class attributes. A 1945–1946 survey of 240 employers in New Haven and Charlotte, N.C., indicated that they regarded education as a screening device for employees with desirable (middle-class) character and demeanor; white-collar positions particularly emphasized educational selection because these employees were considered most visible to outsiders (Noland and Bakke, 1949:20–63).

A survey of employers in nationally prominent corporations indicated that they regarded college degrees as important in hiring potential managers, not because they were thought to ensure technical skills, but rather to indicate "motivation" and "social experience" (Gordon and Howell, 1959:121). Business school training is similarly regarded, less as evidence of necessary training (as employers have been widely skeptical of the utility of this curriculum for most positions) than as an indication that the college graduate is committed to business attitudes. Thus, employers are more likely to refuse to hire liberal arts graduates if they come from a college which has a business school than if their college is without a business school (Gordon and Howell, 1959:84–87; see also Pierson, 1959:90–99). In the latter case, the students could be said not to have had a choice; but when both business and liberal arts courses are offered and the student chooses liberal arts, employers appear to take this as a rejection of business values.

Finally, a 1967 survey of 309 California organizations (Collins, 1971) found that educational requirements for white-collar workers were highest in organizations which placed the strongest emphasis on normative control over their employees.[5] Normative control emphasis was indicated by (i) relative emphasis on the absence of police record for job applicants, (ii) relative emphasis on a record of job loyalty, (iii) Etzioni's (1961) classification of organizations into those with high normative control emphasis (financial, professional services, government, and other public service organizations) and those with remunerative control emphasis (manufacturing, construction, and trade). These three indicators are highly interrelated, thus mutually validating their conceptualization as indicators of normative control emphasis. The relationship between normative control emphasis and educational requirements holds for managerial requirements and white-collar requirements generally, both including and excluding professional and technical positions. Normative control emphasis does not affect blue-collar education requirements.

VARIATIONS IN LINKAGE BETWEEN EDUCATION AND OCCUPATION

The conflict model may also be tested by examining the cases in which it predicts education will be relatively important or unimportant in occupational attainment. Education should be most important where two conditions hold simultaneously: (1) the type of education most closely reflects membership in a particular status group, and (2) that group controls employment in particular organizational contexts. Thus, education will be most important where the fit is greatest between the culture of the status groups emerging from schools, and the status group doing the hiring; it will be least important where there is the greatest disparity between the culture of the school and of the employers.

This fit between school-group culture and employer culture may be conceptualized as a continuum. The importance of elite education is highest where it is involved in selection of new members of organizational elites, and should fade off where jobs are less elite (either lower level jobs in these organizations, or jobs in other organizations not controlled by the cultural elite). Similarly, schools which produce the most elite graduates will be most closely linked to elite occupations; schools whose products are less well socialized into elite culture are selected for jobs correspondingly less close to elite organizational levels.

In the United States, the schools which produce culturally elite groups, either by virtue of explicit training or by selection of students from elite backgrounds, or both, are the private prep schools at the secondary level; at the higher level, the elite colleges (the Ivy League, and to a lesser degree the major state universities); at the professional training level, those professional schools attached to the elite colleges and universities. At the secondary level, schools which produce respectably socialized, non-elite persons are the public high schools (especially those in middle-class residential areas); from the point of view of the culture of WASP employers, Catholic schools (and all-black schools) are less acceptable. At the level of higher education, Catholic and black colleges and professional schools are less elite, and commercial training schools are the least elite form of education.

In the United States, the organizations most clearly dominated by the WASP upper class are large, nationally organized business corporations, and the largest law firms (Domhoff, 1967:38–62). Those organizations more likely to be dominated by members of minority ethnic cultures are the smaller and local businesses in manufacturing, construction, and retail trade; in legal practice, solo rather than firm employment. In government employment, local governments appear to be more heavily dominated by ethnic groups, whereas particular branches of the national government (notably the State Department and the Treasury) are dominated by WASP elites (Domhoff, 1967:84–114, 132–137).

Evidence on the fit between education and employment is available for only some of these organizations. In a broad sample of organizational types (Collins, 1971) educational requirements were higher in the bigger organizations, which also tended to be organized on a national scale, than in smaller and more localistic organizations.[6] The findings of Perrucci and Perrucci (1970) that upper-class social origins were important in career success precisely within the group of engineers who graduated from the most prestigious engineering schools with the highest grades may also bear on this question; since the big national corporations are most likely to hire this academically elite group, the importance of social origins within this group tends to corroborate the interpretation of education as part of a process of elite cultural selection in those organizations.

Among lawyers, the predicted differences are clear: graduates of the law schools attached to elite colleges and universities are more likely to be employed in firms, whereas graduates of Catholic or commercial law schools are more likely to be found in solo practice (Ladinsky, 1967). The elite Wall Street law firms are most educationally selective in this regard, choosing not only from Ivy League law schools but from a group whose background includes attendance at elite prep schools and colleges (Smigel, 1964:39, 73–74, 117). There are also indications that graduates of ethnically-dominated professional schools are most likely to practice within the ethnic community; this is clearly the case among black professionals. In general, the evidence that graduates of black colleges (Sharp, 1970:64–67) and of Catholic colleges (Jencks and Riesman, 1968:357–366) have attained lower occupational positions in business than graduates of white Protestant schools (at least until recent years) also bolsters this interpretation.[7]

It is possible to interpret this evidence according to the technical-function theory of education, arguing that the elite schools provide the best technical training, and that the major national organizations require the greatest degree of technical talent. What is necessary is to test simultaneously for technical and status-conflict conditions. The most direct evidence on this point is the California employer study (Collins, 1971), which examined the effects of normative control emphasis and of organizational prominence, while holding constant the organization's technological modernity, as measured by the number of technological and organizational changes in the previous six years. Technological change was found to affect educational requirements at managerial and white-collar (but not blue-collar) levels, thus giving some support to the technical-function theory of education. The three variables—normative control emphasis, organizational prominence, and technological change—each independently affected educational requirements, in particular contexts. Technological change produced significantly higher educational requirements only in smaller, localistic organizations, and in organizational sectors not emphasizing normative control. Organizational prominence produced significantly higher educational requirements in organizations with low technological change, and in sectors de-emphasizing normative control. Normative control emphasis produced significantly higher educational requirements in organizations with low technological change, and in less prominent organizations. Thus, technical and normative status conditions all affect educational requirements; measures of association indicated that the latter conditions were stronger in this sample.

Other evidence bearing on this point concerns business executives only. A study of the top executives in nationally prominent businesses indicated that the most highly educated managers were not found in most rapidly developing companies, but rather in the least economically vigorous ones, with highest education found in the traditionalistic financial and utility firms (Warner and Abegglen, 1955:141–143,148). The business elite has always been highly educated in relation to the American populace, but education seems to be a correlate of their social origins rather than the determinant of their success (Mills, 1963:128); Taussig and Joslyn, 1932:200; Newcomer, 1955:76). Those members of the business elite who entered its ranks from lower social origins had less education than the businessmen of upper and upper-middle-class origins, and those businessmen who inherited their companies were much more likely to be college educated than those who achieved their positions by entrepreneurship (Bendix, 1956:230; Newcomer, 1955:80).

In general, the evidence indicates that educational requirements for employment reflect employers' concerns for acquiring respectable and well-socialized employees; their concern for the provision of technical skills through education enters to a lesser degree. The higher the normative control concerns of the employer, and the more elite the organization's status, the higher his educational requirements.

HISTORICAL CHANGE

The rise in educational requirements for employment throughout the last century may be explained using the conflict theory, and incorporating elements of the technical-functional theory into it at appropriate points. The principal dynamic has centered on changes in the supply of educated persons caused by the expansion of the school system, which was in turn shaped by three conditions:

(1) Education has been associated with high economic and status position from the colonial period on through the twentieth century. The result was a popular demand for education as mobility opportunity. This demand has not been for vocational education at a terminal or commercial level, short of full university certification; the demand has rather focused on education giving entry into the elite status culture, and usually only those technically-oriented schools have prospered which have most closely associated themselves with the sequence of education leading to (or from) the classical Bachelor's degree (Collins, 1969:68–70, 86–87, 89, 96–101).

(2) Political decentralization, separation of church and state, and competition among religious denominations have made founding schools and colleges in America relatively easy, and provided initial motivations of competition among communities and religious groups that moved them to do so. As a result, education at all levels expanded faster in America than anywhere else in the world. At the time of the Revolution, there were nine colleges in the colonies; in all of Europe, with a population forty times that of America, there were approximately sixty colleges. By 1880 there were 811 American colleges and universities; by 1966, there were 2,337. The United States not only began with the highest ratio of institutions of higher education to population in the world, but increased this lead steadily, for the number of European universities was not much greater by the twentieth century than in the eighteenth (Ben-David and Zloezower, 1962).

(3) Technical changes also entered into the expansion of American education. As the evidence summarized above indicates: (a) mass literacy is crucial for beginnings of full-scale industrialization, although demand for literacy could not have been important in the expansion of education

beyond elementary levels. More importantly, (b) there is a mild trend toward the reduction in the proportion of unskilled jobs and an increase in the promotion of highly skilled (professional and technical) jobs as industrialism proceeds, accounting for 15% of the shift in educational levels in the twentieth century (Folger and Nam, 1964). (c) Technological change also brings about some upgrading in skill requirements of some continuing job positions, although the available evidence (Berg, 1970:38–60) refers only to the decade 1950–1960. Nevertheless, as Wilensky (1964) points out, there is no "professionalization of everyone," as most jobs do not require considerable technical knowledge on the order of that required of the engineer or the research scientist.

The existence of a relatively small group of experts in high-status positions, however, can have important effects on the structure of competition for mobility chances. In the United States, where democratic decentralization favors the use of schools (as well as government employment) as a kind of patronage for voter interests, the existence of even a small number of elite jobs fosters a demand for *large-scale* opportunities to acquire these positions. We thus have a "contest mobility" school system (Turner, 1960); it produced a widely educated populace because of the many dropouts who never achieve the elite level of schooling at which expert skills and/or high cultural status are acquired. In the process, the status value of American education has become diluted. Standards of respectability are always relative to the existing range of cultural differences. Once higher levels of education become recognized as an objective mark of elite status, and a moderate level of education as a mark of respectable middle-level status, increases in the supply of educated persons at given levels result in yet higher levels becoming recognized as superior, and previously superior levels become only average.

Thus, before the end of the nineteenth century, an elementary school or home education was no longer satisfactory for a middle-class gentleman; by the 1930s, a college degree was displacing the high school degree as the minimal standard of respectability; in the late 1960s, graduate school or specialized professional degrees were becoming necessary for initial entry to many middle-class positions, and high school graduation was becoming a standard for entry to manual laboring positions. Education has thus gradually become part of the status culture of classes far below the level of the original business and professional elites.

The increasing supply of educated persons (Table 2) has made education a rising requirement of jobs (Table 1). Led by the biggest and most prestigious organizations, employers have raised their educational requirements to maintain both the relative prestige of their own managerial ranks and the relative respectability of middle ranks.[8] Education has become a legitimate standard in terms of which employers select employees, and employees compete with each other for promotion opportunities or for raised prestige in their continuing positions. With the attainment of a mass (now approaching universal) higher education system in modern America, the ideal or image of technical skill becomes the legitimating culture in terms of which the struggle for position goes on.

Higher educational requirements, and the higher level of educational credentials offered by individuals competing for position in organizations, have in turn increased the demand for education by populace. The inter-action between formal job requirements and informal status cultures has resulted in a spiral in which educational requirements and educational attainments become ever higher. As the struggle for mass educational op-portunities enters new phases in the universities of today and perhaps in the graduate schools of the future, we may expect a further upgrading of educational requirements for employment. The mobilization of demands by minority groups for mobility opportunities through schooling can only contribute an extension of the prevailing pattern.

CONCLUSION

It has been argued that conflict theory provides an explanation of the principal dynamics of rising educational requirements for employment in America. Changes in the technical requirements of jobs have caused more limited changes in particular jobs. The conditions of the interaction of these two determinants may be more closely studied.

Precise measures of changes in the actual technical skill requirements of jobs are as yet available only in rudimentary form. Few systematic studies show how much of particular job skills may be learned in practice, and how much must be acquired through school background. Close studies of what is actually learned in school, and how long it is retained, are rare. Organizational studies of how employers rate performance and decide upon promotions give a picture of relatively loose controls over the tech-nical quality of employee performance, but this no doubt varies in partic-ular types of jobs.

The most central line of analysis for assessing the joint effects of status group conflict and technical requirements are those which compare the relative importance of education in different contexts. One such approach may take organization as the unit of analysis, comparing the educational requirements of organizations both to organizational technologies and to the status (including educational) background of organizational elites. Such analysis may also be applied to surveys of individual mobility, comparing the effects of education on mobility in different employment contexts, where the status group (and educational) background of employers varies in its fit with the educational culture of prospective employees. Such analysis of "old school tie" networks may also simultaneously test for the independent effect of the technical requirements of different sorts of jobs on the importance of education. Inter-nation comparisons provide variations here in the fit between types of education and particular kinds of jobs which may not be available within any particular country.

The full elaboration of such analysis would give a more precise answer to the historical question of assigning weight to various factors in the changing place of education in the stratification of modern societies. At the same time, to state the conditions under which status groups vary in organizational power, including the power to emphasize or limit the importance of technical skills, would be to state the basis elements of a comprehensive explanatory theory of the forms of stratification.

NOTES

I am indebted to Joseph Ben-David, Bennett Berger, Reinhard Bendix, Margaret S. Gordon, Joseph R. Gusfield, Stanford M. Lyman, Martin A. Trow, and Harold L. Wilensky for advice and comment; and to Margaret S. Gordon for making available data collected by the Institute of Industrial Relations of the University of California at Berkeley, under grants from the U.S. Office of Education and the U.S. Department of Labor. Their endorsement of the views expressed here is not implied.

1. This survey covered 309 establishments with 100 or more employees, representing all major industry groups.

2. The concern here is with these basic premises rather than with the theory elaborated by Davis and Moore to account for the universality of stratification. This theory involves a few further propositions: (C) in any particular form of society certain occupational positions are functionally most central to the operation of the social system; (D) the ability to fill these positions, and/or the motivation to acquire the necessary training, is unequally distributed in the population; (E) inequalities of rewards in wealth and prestige evolve to ensure that the supply of persons with the necessary ability or training meshes with the structure of demands for skilled performance. The problems of stating functional centrality in empirical terms have been subjects of much debate.

3. Proposition 3 is supported by Tables 1 and 2. The issue here is whether this can be explained by the previous propositions and premises.

4. It might be argued that the ethnic cultures may differ in their functionality: that middle-class Protestant culture provides the self-discipline and other attributes necessary for higher organizational positions in modern society. This version of functional theory is specific enough to be subject to empirical test: are middle-class WASPs in fact better businessmen or government administrators than Italians, Irishmen, or Jews of patrimonial or working class cultural backgrounds? Weber suggested that they were in the initial construction of the capitalist economy within the confines of traditional society; he also argued that once the new economic system was established, the original ethic was no longer necessary to run it

(Weber, 1930:180–183). Moreover, the functional explanation also requires some feedback mechanism whereby organizations with more efficient managers are selected for survival. The oligopolistic situation in large-scale American business since the late 19th century does not seem to provide such a mechanism; nor does government employment. Schumpeter (1951), the leading expositor of the importance of managerial talent in business, confined his emphasis to the formative period of business expansion, and regarded the large, oligopolistic corporation as an arena where advancement came to be based on skills in organizational politics (1951:122–124); these personalistic skills are arguably more characteristic of the patrimonial cultures than of WASP culture.

5. Sample consisted of approximately one-third of all organizations with 100 or more employees in the San Francisco, Oakland, and San Jose metropolitan areas. See Gordon and Thal-Larsen (1969) for a description of procedures and other findings.

6. Again, these relationships hold for managerial requirements and white-collar requirements generally, both including and excluding professional and technical positions, but not for blue-collar requirements. Noland and Bakke (1949:78) also report that larger organizations have higher educational requirements for administrative positions than smaller organizations.

7. Similar processes may be found in other societies, where the kinds of organizations linked to particular types of schools may differ. In England, the elite "public schools" are linked especially to the higher levels of the national civil service (Weinberg, 1967:139–143). In France, the elite École Polytechnique is linked to both government and industrial administrative positions (Crozier, 1964:238–244). In Germany, universities have been linked principally with government administration, and business executives are drawn from elsewhere (Ben-David and Zloczower, 1962). Comparative analysis of the kinds of education of government officials, business executives, and other groups in contexts where the status group links of schools differ is a promising area for further tests of conflict and technical-functional explanations.

8. It appears that employers may have raised their wage costs in the process. Their behavior is nevertheless plausible, in view of these considerations: (a) the thrust of organizational research since Mayo and Barnard has indicated that questions of internal organizational power and control, of which cultural dominance is a main feature, take precedence over purely economic considerations; (b) the large American corporations, which have led in educational requirements, have held positions of oligopolistic advantage since the late 19th century, and thus could afford a large internal "welfare" cost of maintaining a well-socialized work force; (c) there are inter-organizational wage differentials in local labor markets, corresponding to relative organizational prestige, and a "wage-escalator" process by which the wages of the leading organizations are gradually emulated by others according to their rank (Reynolds, 1951); a parallel structure of "educational status escalators" could plausibly be expected to operate.

REFERENCES

Anastasi, Anne (1967) "Psychology, psychologists, and psychological testing." *American Psychologist* 22 (April):297–306.

Baltzell, E. Digby (1958) *An American Business Aristocracy.* New York: Macmillan.

Becker, Howard S. (1961) "Schools and systems of stratification." Pp. 93–104 in A. H. Halsey, Jean Floud, and C. Arnold Anderson (eds.), *Education, Economy, and Society.* New York: Free Press.

Becker, Howard S., Blanche Geer, and Everett C. Hughes (1968) *Making the Grade: The Academic Side of College Life*. New York: Wiley.

Bell, H. M. (1940) *Matching Youth and Jobs*. Washington: American Council on Education.

Ben-David, Joseph (1963–64) "Professions in the class systems of present-day societies." *Current Sociology* 12:247–330.

Ben-David, Joseph; and Awraham Zloczower (1962) "Universities and academic systems in modern societies." *European Journal of Sociology* 31:45–85.

Bendix, Reinhard (1956) *Work and Authority in Industry*. New York: Wiley.

Berg, Ivar (1970) *Education and Jobs*. New York: Praeger.

Bernstein, Basil (1961) "Social class and linguistic development." Pp. 288–314 in A. H. Halsey, Jean Floud, and C. Arnold Anderson (eds.), *Education, Economy, and Society*. New York: Free Press.

Blau, Peter M. (1955). *The Dynamics of Bureaucracy*. Chicago: University of Chicago Press.

Blau, Peter M., and Otis Dudley Duncan (1967) *The American Occupational Structure*. New York: Wiley.

Bourdieu, Pierre, and Jean-Claude Passeron (1964) *Les Heritiers: Les Etudiants et la Culture*. Paris: Les Editions de Minuit.

Bright, James R. (1958) "Does automation raise skill requirements?" *Harvard Business Review* 36 (July–August):85–97.

Clark, Burton R. (1962). *Educating the Expert Society*. San Francisco: Chandler.

Clark, Harold F., and Harold S. Sloan (1966) *Classrooms on Main Street*. New York: Teachers College Press.

Coleman, James S. (1961) *The Adolescent Society*. New York: Free Press.

Collins, Orvis, Melville Dalton, and Donald Roy (1946) "Restriction of output and social cleavage in industry." *Applied Anthropology* 5 (Summer):1–14.

Collins, Randall (1968) "A comparative approach to political sociology." Pp. 42–67 in Reinhard Bendix *et al.* (eds.). *State and Society*. Boston: Little, Brown.
(1969) Education and employment. Unpublished Ph.D. dissertation. University of California at Berkeley.
(1971) "Educational requirements for employment: A comparative organizational study." Unpublished manuscript.

Cremin, Lawrence A. (1961) *The Transformation of the School*. New York: Knopf.

Crozier, Michel (1964) *The Bureaucratic Phenomenon*. Chicago: University of Chicago Press.

Curti, Merle (1935) *The Social Ideas of American Educators*. New York: Scribners.

Dalton, Melville (1951) "Informal factors in career achievement." *American Journal of Sociology* 56 (March):407–415.
(1959) *Men Who Manage*. New York: Wiley.

Davis, Kingsley, and Wilbert Moore (1945) "Some principles of stratification." *American Sociological Review* 10:242–249.

Denison, Edward F. (1965) "Education and economic productivity." Pp. 328–340 in Seymour Harris (ed.), *Education and Public Policy*. Berkeley: McCutchen.

Dill, William R., Thomas L. Hilton, and Walter R. Reitman (1962) *The New Managers*. Englewood Cliffs, N. J.: Prentice-Hall.

Domhoff, G. William (1967) *Who Rules America?* Englewood Cliffs, N. J.: Prentice-Hall.

Duncan, Beverly (1964) "Dropouts and the unemployed." *Journal of Political Economy* 73 (April):121–134.

Duncan, Otis Dudley, and Robert W. Hodge (1963) "Education and occupational mobility: A regression analysis." *American Journal of Sociology* 68:629–644.

Eckland, Bruce K. (1965) "Academic ability, higher education, and occupational mobility." *American Sociological Review* 30:735–746.

Epstein, Cynthia Fuchs (1970) *Woman's Place: Options and Limits in Professional Careers*. Berkeley: University of California Press.

Etzioni, Amitai (1961) *A Comparative Analysis of Complex Organizations*. New York: Free Press.

Folger, John K., and Charles B. Nam (1964) "Trends in education in relation to the occupational structure." *Sociology of Education* 38:19–33.

Goode, William J. (1967) "The protection of the inept." *American Sociological Review* 32:5–19.

Gordon, Margaret S., and Margaret Thal-Larsen (1969) *Employer Policies in a Changing Labor Market*. Berkeley: Institute of Industrial Relations, University of California.

Gordon, Robert A., and James E. Howell (1959) *Higher Education for Business*. New York: Columbia University Press.

Gusfield, Joseph R. (1958) "Equalitarianism and bureaucratic recruitment." *Administrative Science Quarterly* 2 (March):521–541.

Hagstrom, Warren O., and Lowell L. Hargens (1968) "Mobility theory in the sociology of science." Paper delivered at Cornell Conference on Human Mobility, Ithaca, N.Y. (October 31).

Hall, Oswald (1946) "The informal organization of the medical profession." *Canadian Journal of Economic and Political Science* 12 (February):30–44.

Harbison, Frederick, and Charles A. Myers (1964) *Education, Manpower, and Economic Growth*. New York: McGraw-Hill.

Hargens, Lowell, and Warren O. Hagstrom (1967) "Sponsored and contest mobility of American academic scientists." *Sociology of Education* 40:24–38.

Havemann, Ernest, and Patricia Salter West (1952) *They Went to College*. New York: Harcourt, Brace.

Hess, Robert D., and Judith V. Torney (1967) *The Development of Political Attitudes in Children*. Chicago: Aldine.

Hollingshead, August B. (1949) *Elmtown's Youth*. New York: Wiley.

Hoselitz, Bert F. (1965) "Investment in education and its political impact." Pp. 541–565 in James S. Coleman (ed.), *Education and Political Development*. Princeton, N.J.: Princeton University Press.

Hughes, Everett C. (1949) "Queries concerning industry and society growing out of the study of ethnic relations in industry." *American Sociological Review* 14:211–220.

Jencks, Christopher, and David Riesman (1968) *The Academic Revolution*. New York: Doubleday.

Kahl, Joseph A. (1957) *The American Class Structure*. New York: Rinehart.

Kerr, Clark, John T. Dunlop, Frederick H. Harbison and Charles A. Myers (1960) *Industrialism and Industrial Man*. Cambridge: Harvard University Press.

Ladinsky, Jack (1963) "Careers of lawyers, law practice, and legal institutions." *American Sociological Review* 28 (February):47–54.
(1967) "Higher education and work achievement among lawyers." *Sociological Quarterly* 8 (Spring):222–232.

Learned, W. S., and B. D. Wood (1938) *The Student and His Knowledge*. New York: Carnegie Foundation for the Advancement of Teaching.

Lipset, Seymour Martin, and Reinhard Bendix (1959) *Social Mobility in Industrial Society.* Berkeley: University of California Press.

Lombard, George F. (1955) *Behavior in a Selling Group.* Cambridge: Harvard University Press.

March, James G., and Herbert A. Simon (1958) *Organizations.* New York: Wiley.

Marsh, Robert M. (1963) "Values, demand, and social mobility." *American Sociological Review* 28 (August):567–575.

McArthur, C. (1955) "Personality differences between middle and upper classes." *Journal of Abnormal and Social Psychology* 50:247–254.

Mills, C. Wright (1963) *Power, Politics, and People.* New York: Oxford University Press.

Newcomer, Mabel (1955) *The Big Business Executive.* New York: Columbia University Press.

Noland, E. William, and E. Wight Bakke (1949) *Workers Wanted.* New York: Harper.

Nosow, Sigmund (1956) "Labor distribution and the normative system." *Social Forces* 30: 25–33.

Peaslee, Alexander L. (1969) "Education's role in development." *Economic Development and Cultural Change* 17 (April):293–318.

Perrucci, Carolyn Cummings, and Robert Perrucci (1970) "Social origins, educational contexts, and career mobility." *American Sociological Review* 35 (June):451–463.

Pierson, Frank C. (1959) *The Education of American Businessmen.* New York: McGraw-Hill.

Plunkett, M. (1960) "School and early work experience of youth." *Occupational Outlook Quarterly* 4:22–27.

Reynolds, Lloyd (1951) *The Structure of Labor Markets.* New York: Harper.

Riesman, David (1958) *Constraint and Variety in American Education.* New York: Doubleday.

Roy, Donald (1952) "Quota restriction and goldbricking in a machine shop." *American Journal of Sociology* 57 (March):427–442.

Schultz, Theodore W. (1961) "Investment in human capital." *American Economic Review* 51 (March):1–16.

Schumpeter, Joseph (1951) *Imperialism and Social Classes.* New York: Augustus M. Kelley.

Sewell, William H., Archibald O. Haller, and Alejandro Portes (1969) "The educational and early occupational attainment process." *American Sociological Review* 34 (February):82–92.

Sharp, Laure M. (1970) *Education and Employment: The Early Careers of College Graduates.* Baltimore: Johns Hopkins Press.

Smigel, Erwin O. (1964) *The Wall Street Lawyer.* New York: Free Press.

Soderberg, C. Richard (1963) "The American engineer." Pp. 203–230 in Kenneth S. Lynn, *The Professions in America.* Boston: Beacon Press.

Taeuber, Alma F., Karl E. Taeuber, and Glen G. Cain (1966) "Occupational assimilation and the competitive process: A reanalysis." *American Journal of Sociology* 72:278–285.

Taussig, Frank W., and C. S. Joslyn (1932) *American Business Leaders.* New York: Macmillan.

Turner, Ralph H. (1952) "Foci of discrimination in the employment of nonwhites." *American Journal of Sociology* 58:247–256.

———— (1960) "Sponsored and contest mobility and the school system." *American Sociological Review* 25 (October):855–867.

Waller, Willard (1932) *The Sociology of Teaching.* New York: Russell and Russell.

Warner, W. Lloyd, and James C. Abegglen (1955) *Occupational Mobility in American Business and Industry, 1928–1952.* Minneapolis: University of Minnesota Press.

Weber, Max (1930) *The Protestant Ethic and the Spirit of Capitalism.* New York: Scribner's.
  (1968) *Economy and Society.* New York: Bedminster Press.
Weinberg, Ian (1967) *The English Public Schools: The Sociology of Elite Education.* New York:
  Atherton Press.
Wilensky, Harold L. (1964) "The professionalization of everyone?" *American Journal of Sociology* 70 (September):137–158.

RAY C. RIST

On Understanding the Processes of Schooling: The Contributions of Labeling Theory

Questions to think about

1 *How can the labeling perspective help us understand interactions in classrooms?*

2 *What problems would you study using labeling theory? Functional theory? Conflict theory? Why?*

3 *Identify and diagram the part of the open systems model on which labeling theory would focus.*

4 *What questions might you research using the labeling theory and concept of teacher expectations?*

There have been few debates within American education which have been argued with such passion and intensity as that of positing causal explanations of success or failure in schools.[1] One explanation which has had considerable support in the past few years, particularly since the publication of *Pygmalion in the Classroom* by Rosenthal and Jacobson (1968), has been that of the "self-fulfilling prophecy." Numerous studies have appeared seeking to explicate the mechanisms by which the teacher comes to hold certain expectations of the students and how these are then operationalized within the classroom so as to produce

From *Power and Ideology in Education,* edited by Jerome Karabel and A. H. Halsey. Copyright © 1977 by Oxford University Press, Inc. Reprinted with permission.

what the teacher had initially assumed. The origins of teacher expectations have been attributed to such diverse variables as social class, physical appearance, contrived test scores, sex, race, language patterns, and school records. But in the flurry of recent research endeavors, there has emerged a hiatus between this growing body of data and any larger theoretical framework. The concept of the self-fulfilling prophecy has remained simply that—a concept. The lack of a broader conceptual scheme has meant that research in this area has become theoretically stymied. Consequently, there has evolved instead a growing concern over the refinement of minute methodological nuances.

The thrust of this paper is to argue that there is a theoretical perspective developing in the social sciences which can break the conceptual and methodological logjam building up on the self-fulfilling prophecy. Specifically, the emergence of *labeling theory* as an explanatory framework for the study of social deviance appears to be applicable to the study of education as well. Among the major contributions to the development of labeling theory are Becker, 1963, 1964; Broadhead, 1974; Lemert, 1951, 1972, 1974; Douglas, 1971, 1972; Kitsuse, 1964; Lofland, 1969; Matza, 1964, 1969; Scheff, 1966; Schur, 1971; Scott and Douglas, 1972; and Rubington and Weinberg, 1973.

If the labeling perspective can be shown to be a legitimate framework from which to analyze social processes influencing the educational experience and the contributions of such processes to success or failure in school, there would then be a viable *interactionist* perspective to counter both biological and cultural determinists' theories of educational outcomes. While the latter two positions both place ultimate causality for success or failure *outside* the school, the labeling approach allows for an examination of what, in fact, is happening *within* schools. Thus, labeling theory would call our attention, for example, to the various evaluative mechanisms (both formal and informal) operant in schools, the ways in which schools nurture and support such mechanisms, how students react, what the outcomes are for interpersonal interaction based on how these mechanisms have evaluated individual students, and how, *over time*, the consequences of having a certain evaluative tag influence the options available to a student within a school. What follows first is a summary of a number of the key aspects of labeling theory as it has been most fully developed in the sociological literature; second is an attempt to integrate the research on the self-fulfilling prophecy with the conceptual framework of labeling theory. Finally, the implications of this synthesis are explored for both future research and theoretical development.

I. BECOMING DEVIANT: THE LABELING PERSPECTIVE

Those who have used labeling theory have been concerned with the study of *why* people are labeled, and *who* it is that labels them as someone who has committed one form or another of deviant behavior. In sharp contrast to the predominant approaches for the study of deviance, there is little concern in labeling theory with the motivational and characterological nature of the person who committed the act.

Deviance is understood, not as a quality of the person or as created by his actions, but instead as created by group definitions and reactions. It is a social judgment imposed by a social audience. As Becker (1963:9) has argued:

> The central fact of deviance is that it is created by society. I do not mean this in the way it is ordinarily understood, in which the causes of deviance are located in the social situation of the deviant, or the social factors, which prompted his action. I mean, rather, that social groups create deviants by making the rules whose infraction constitute deviance, and by applying those rules to particular people and labeling them as outsiders. From this point of view, *deviance is not the quality of the act the person commits, but rather a consequence of the application by others of rules and sanctions to an "offender." The deviant is one to whom the label has been successfully applied. Deviant behavior is behavior that people so label.* (emphasis added)

The labeling approach is insistent on the need for a shift in attention from an exclusive concern with the deviant individual to a major concern with the *process* by which the deviant label is applied. Again citing Becker (1964:2):

> The labeling approach sees deviance always and everywhere as a process and interaction between at least two kinds of people: those who commit (or who are said to have committed) a deviant act, and the rest of the society, perhaps divided into several groups itself. . . . One consequence is that we become much more interested in the process by which deviants are defined by the rest of the society, than in the nature of the deviant act itself.

The important questions, then, for Becker and others, are not of the genre to include, for example: Why do some individuals come to act out norm-violating behavior? Rather, the questions are of the following sort: Who applied the deviant label to whom? Whose rules shall prevail and be enforced? Under what circumstances is the deviant label successfully and unsuccessfully applied? How does a community decide what forms of conduct should be singled out for this kind of attention? What forms of behavior do persons in the social system consider deviant, how do they interpret such behavior, and what are the consequences of these interpretations for their reactions to individuals who are seen as manifesting such behavior? (See Akers, 1973.)

The labeling perspective rejects any assumption that a clear consensus exists as to what constitutes a norm violation—or for that matter, what constitutes a norm—within a complex and highly heterogeneous society. What comes to be determined as deviance and who comes to be determined as a deviant is the result of a variety of social contingencies influenced by who has the power to enforce such determinations. Deviance is thus problematic and subjectively given. The case for making the societal reaction to rule-breaking a major independent variable in studies of deviant behavior has been succinctly stated by Kitsuse (1964:101):

> A sociological theory of deviance must focus specifically upon the interactions which not only define behaviors as deviant, but also organize and activate the application of sanctions by individuals, groups, or agencies. For in modern society, the socially significant differentiation of deviants from the nondeviant population is increasingly contingent upon circumstances of situation, place, social and personal biography, and the bureaucratically organized activities of agencies of social control.

Traditional notions of who is a deviant and what are the causes for such deviance are necessarily reworked. By emphasizing the processual nature of deviance, any particular deviant is seen to be a product of being caught, defined, segregated, labeled, and stigmatized. *This is one of the major thrusts of the labeling perspective—that forces of social control often produce the unintended consequence of making some persons defined as deviant even more confirmed as deviant because of the stigmatization of labeling. Thus, social reactions to deviance further deviant careers.* Erikson (1966) has even gone so far as to argue that a society will strive to maintain a certain level of deviance within itself as deviance is functional to clarifying group boundaries, providing scapegoats, creating out-groups who can be the source of furthering in-group solidarity, and the like.

The idea that social control may have the paradoxical effect of generating more of the very behavior it is designed to eradicate was first elaborated upon by Tannenbaum. He noted (1938:21):

> The first dramatization of the "evil" which separates the child out of his group . . . plays a greater role in making the criminal than perhaps any other experience. . . . He now lives in a different world. He has been tagged. . . . The person becomes the thing he is described as being.

Likewise, Schur (1965:4) writes:

> The societal reaction to the deviant, then, is vital to an
> understanding of the deviance itself and a major element in—
> if not the cause of—the deviant behavior.

The focus on outcomes of social control mechanisms has led labeling theorists to devote considerable attention to the workings of organizations and agencies which function ostensibly to rehabilitate the violator or in other ways draw him back into conformity. Their critiques of prisons, mental hospitals, training schools, and other people-changing institutions suggest that the results of such institutions are frequently nearly the opposite of what they were theoretically designed to produce. These institutions are seen as mechanisms by which opportunities to withdraw from deviance are sealed off from the deviant, stigmatization occurs, and a new identity as a social "outsider" is generated. There thus emerges on the part of the person so labeled a new view of himself which is one of being irrevocably deviant.

This movement from one who has violated a norm to one who sees himself as a habitual norm violator is what Lemert (1972:62) terms the transition from a primary to a secondary deviant. A primary deviant is one who holds to socially accepted roles, views himself as a nondeviant, and believes himself to be an insider. A primary deviant does not deny that he has violated some norm, and claims only that it is not characteristic of him as a person. A secondary deviant, on the other hand, is one who has reorganized his social-psychological characteristics around the deviant role. Lemert (1972:62) writes:

> Secondary deviation refers to a special class of socially defined
> responses which people make to problems created by the societal
> reaction to their deviance. These problems . . . become central facts
> of existence for those experiencing them. . . . Actions, which have
> these roles and self-attitudes as their referents make up secondary
> deviance. The secondary deviant . . . is a person whose life and
> identity are organized around the facts of deviance.

A person can commit repeated acts of primary deviation and never come to view himself or have others come to view him as a secondary deviant. Secondary deviation arises from the feedback whereby misconduct or deviation initiates social reaction to the behavior which then triggers further misconduct. Lemert (1951:77) first described this process as follows:

> The sequence of interaction leading to secondary deviation is
> roughly as follows: (1) primary deviation; (2) societal penalties;
> (3) further primary deviation; (4) stronger penalties and rejections;

(5) further deviations, perhaps with hostilities and resentments beginning to focus upon those doing the penalizing; (6) crisis reached in the tolerance quotient, expressed in formal action by the community stigmatizing of the deviant; (7) strengthening of the deviant conduct as a reaction to the stigmatizing and penalties; and (8) ultimate acceptance of deviant social status and efforts at adjustment on the basis of the associated role.

Thus, when persons engage in deviant behavior they would not otherwise participate in and when they develop social roles they would not have developed save for the application of social control measures, the outcome is the emergence of secondary deviance. The fact of having been apprehended and labeled is the critical element in the subsequent construction of a deviant identity and pursuit of a deviant career.

II. THE ORIGINS OF LABELING: TEACHER EXPECTATIONS

Labeling theory has significantly enhanced our understanding of the process of becoming deviant by shifting our attention from the deviant to the judges of deviance and the forces that affect their judgment. Such judgments are critical, for a recurrent decision made in all societies, and particularly frequent in advanced industrial societies, is that an individual has or has not mastered some body of information, or perhaps more basically, has or has not the capacity to master that information. These evaluations are made periodically as one moves through the institution of school and the consequences directly affect the opportunities to remain for an additional period. To be able to remain provides an option for mastering yet another body of information, and to be certified as having done so. As Ivan Illich (1971) has noted, it is in industrial societies that being perceived as a legitimate judge of such mastery has become restricted to those who carry the occupational role of "teacher." A major consequence of the professionalization of the role of teacher has been the ability to claim as a near exclusive decision whether mastery of material has occurred. Such exclusionary decision-making enhances those in the role of "teacher" as they alone come to possess the authority to provide certification for credentials (Edgar, 1974).

Labeling theorists report that in making judgments of deviance, persons may employ information drawn from a variety of sources. Further, even persons within the same profession (therapists, for example) may make divergent use of the same material in arriving at an evaluative decision on the behavior of an individual. Among the sources of information available to labelers, two appear primary: first-hand information obtained from face-to-face interaction with the person they may ultimately label, and second-hand information obtained from other than direct interaction.

The corollary here to the activities of teachers should be apparent. Oftentimes, the evaluation by teachers (which may lead to the label of "bright," "slow," etc.) is based on first-hand information gained through face-to-face interaction during the course of the time the teacher and student spent together in the classroom. But a goodly amount of information about the student which informs the teacher's evaluation is second-hand information. For·instance, comments from other teachers, test scores, prior report cards, permanent records, meetings with the parents, or evaluations from welfare agencies and psychological clinics are all potential informational sources. In a variation of the division between first-hand and second-hand sources of information, Johnson (1973) has suggested that there are three key determinants of teacher evaluations: student's prior performance, social status characteristics, and present performance. Prior performance would include information from cumulative records (grades, test scores, notes from past teachers or counselors, and outside evaluators) while social status and performance would be inferred and observed in the on-going context of the classroom.

What has been particularly captivating about the work of Rosenthal and Jacobson (1968) in this regard is their attempt to provide empirical justification for a truism considered self-evident by many in education: School achievement is not simply a matter of a child's native ability, but involves directly and inextricably the teacher as well. Described succinctly, their research involved a situation where, at the end of a school year, more than 500 students in a single elementary school were administered the "Harvard Test of Inflected Acquisition." In actuality this test was a standardized, relatively nonverbal test of intelligence, Flanagan's (1960) Test of General Ability (TOGA). The teachers were told that such a test would, with high predictive reliability, sort out those students who gave strong indication of being intellectual "spurters" or "bloomers" during the following academic year. Just before the beginning of school the following fall, the teachers were given lists with the names of between one and nine of their students. They were told that these students scored in the top twenty percent of the school on the test, though, of course, no factual basis for such determinations existed. A twenty percent subsample of the "special" students was selected for intensive analysis. Testing of the students at the end of the school year offered some evidence that these selected children did perform better than the nonselected. The ensuing debate as to the validity and implications of the findings from the study will be discussed in the next section.

The findings of Deutsch, Fishman, Kogan, North, and Whiteman (1964); Gibson (1965); Goslin and Glass (1967); McPherson (1966); and Pequignot (1966) all demonstrate the influence of standardized tests of intelligence and achievement on teacher's expectations. Goaldman (1971), in a review of the literature on the use of tests as a second-hand source of information for teachers, noted: "Although some of the research has been challenged, there is a basis for the belief that teachers at all levels are prejudiced by information they receive about a student's ability or character." Mehan (1971, 1974) has been concerned with the interaction between children who take tests and the teachers who administer them. He posits that testing is not the objective use of a measurement instrument, but the outcome of a set of interactional activities which are influenced by a variety of contingencies which ultimately manifest themselves in a reified "test score." Mehan suggests (1971):

> Standardized test performances are taken as an unquestioned, nonproblematic reflection of the child's underlying ability. The authority of the test to measure the child's real ability is accepted by both teachers and other school officials. Test results are accepted without doubt as the correct and valid document of the child's ability.

Characteristics of children such as sex and race are immediately apparent to teachers. Likewise, indications of status can be quickly inferred from grooming, style of dress, need for free lunches, information on enrollment cards, discussion of family activities by children, and visits to the school by parents. One intriguing study recently reported in this area is that by two sociologists, Clifford and Walster (1973:249). The substance of their study was described as follows:

> Our experiment was designed to determine what effect a student's physical attractiveness has on a teacher's expectations of the child's intellectual and social behavior. Our hypothesis was that a child's attractiveness strongly influences his teachers' judgments; the more attractive the child, the more biased in his favor we expect the teachers to be. The design required to test this hypothesis is a simple one: Teachers are given a standardized report card and an attached photograph. The report card includes an assessment of the child's academic performance as well as of his general social behavior. The attractiveness of the photos is experimentally varied. On the basis of this information, teachers are asked to state their expectations of the child's educational and social potential.

Based on the responses of 404 fifth grade teachers within the state of Missouri, Clifford and Walster concluded (1973:255):

> There is little question but that the physical appearance of a student affected the expectations of the teachers we studied. Regardless of whether the pupil is a boy or girl, the child's physical attractiveness has an equally strong association with his teacher's reactions to him.

The variables of race and ethnicity have been documented, by Brown (1968), Davidson and Lang (1960), Jackson and Cosca (1974), and Rubovits and Maehr (1973), among others, as powerful factors in generating the expectations teachers hold of children. It has also been documented that teachers expect less of lower-class children than they do of middle-class children (cf. Becker, 1952; Deutsch, 1963; Leacock, 1969; Rist, 1970, 1973; Stein, 1971; Warner, Havighurst, and Loeb, 1944; and Wilson, 1963). Douglas (1964), in a large scale study of the tracking system used in British schools, found that children who were clean and neatly dressed in nice clothing, and who came from what the teachers preceived as "better" homes, tended to be placed in higher tracks than their measured ability would predict. Further, when placed there they tended to stay and perform acceptably. Mackler (1969) studied schools in Harlem and found that children tended to stay in the tracks in which they were initially placed and that such placement was based on a variety of social considerations independent of measured ability. Doyle, Hancock, and Kifer (1971) and Palardy (1969) have shown teacher expectations for high performance in elementary grades to be stronger for girls than boys.

The on-going academic and interpersonal performance of the children may also serve as a potent source of expectations for teachers. Rowe (1969) found that teachers would wait longer for an answer from a student they believed to be a high achiever than for one from a student they believed to be a low achiever. Brophy and Good (1970) found that teachers were more likely to give perceived high achieving students a second chance to respond to an initial incorrect answer, and further, that high achievers were praised more frequently for success and criticized less for failure.

There is evidence that the expectations teachers hold for their students can be generated as early as the first few days of the school year and then remain stable over the months to follow (Rist, 1970, 1972, 1973; Willis, 1972). For example, I found during my three-year longitudinal and ethnographic study of a single, *de facto* segregated elementary school in the black community of St. Louis, that after only eight days of kindergarten, the teacher made permanent seating arrangements based on what she assumed were variations in academic capability. But no formal evaluation of the children had taken place. Instead, the assignments to the three tables were based on a number of socio-economic criteria as well as on early interaction patterns in the classroom. Thus, the placement of the children came to reflect the social class distinctions in the room—the poor children from public welfare families all sat at one table, the working class children sat at another and the middle class at the third. I demonstrated how the teacher operationalized her expectations of these different groups of children in terms of her differentials of teaching time, her use of praise and control, and the extent of autonomy within the classroom. By following the same children through first and second grade as well, I was able to show that the initial patterns established by the kindergarten teacher came to be perpetuated year after year. By second grade, labels given by another teacher clearly reflected the reality each of the three groups experienced in the school. The top group was called the "Tigers," the middle group the "Cardinals," and the lowest group, the "Clowns." What had begun as a subjective evaluation and labeling by the teacher took on objective dimensions as the school proceeded to process the children on the basis of the distinctions made when they first began.

Taken together, these studies strongly imply that the notion of "teacher expectations" is multi-faceted and multi-dimensional. It appears that when teachers generate expectations about their students, they do so not only for reasons of academic or cognitive performance, but for their classroom interactional patterns as well. Furthermore, not only ascribed characteristics such as race, sex, class, or ethnicity are highly salient, interpersonal traits are also. Thus, the interrelatedness of the various attributes which ultimately blend together to generate the evaluation a teacher makes as to what can be expected from a particular student suggests the strength and tenacity of such subsequent labels as "bright" or "slow" or "trouble-maker" or "teacher's little helper." It is to the outcomes of the student's having one or another of these labels that we now turn.

III. AN OUTCOME OF LABELING: THE SELF-FULFILLING PROPHECY

W. I. Thomas, many years ago, set forth what has become a basic dictum of the social sciences when he observed, "If men define situations as real, they are real in their consequences." This is at the core of the self-fulfilling prophecy. An expectation which defines a situation comes to influence the actual behavior within the situation so as to produce what was initially assumed to be there. Merton (1968:477) has elaborated on this concept and noted: "The self-fulfilling prophecy is, in the beginning, a *false* definition of the situation evoking a new behavior which makes the originally false conception come true." (emphasis in the original)

Here it is important to recall a basic tenet of labeling theory—that an individual does not become deviant simply by the commission of some act. As Becker (1963) stressed, deviance is not inherent in behavior *per se,* but in the application by others of rules and sanctions against one perceived as being an "offender." Thus, the only time one can accurately be termed a "deviant" is after the successful application of a label by a social audience. Thus, though many persons may commit norm violations, only select ones are subsequently labeled. The contingencies of race, class, sex, visibility of behavior, age, occupation, and who one's friends are all influence the outcome as to whether one is or is not labeled. Scheff (1966), for example, demonstrated the impact of these contingencies upon the diagnosis as to the severity of a patient's mental illness. The higher one's social status, the less the willingness to diagnose the same behavioral traits as indicative of serious illness in comparison to the diagnosis given to low status persons.

The crux of the labeling perspective lies not in whether one's norm violating behavior is known, but in whether others decide to do something about it. Further, if a label is applied to the individual, it is posited that this in fact causes the individual to become that which he is labeled as being. Due to the reaction of society, the change in the individual involves the development of a new socialized self-concept and social career centered around the deviant behavior. As Rubington and Weinberg (1973:7) have written:

> The person who has been typed, in turn, becomes aware of the new definition that has been placed upon him by members of his groups. He, too, takes this new understanding of himself into account when dealing with them. . . . When this happens, a social type has been ratified, and a person has been socially reconstructed.

As noted, Rosenthal and Jacobson's *Pygmalion in the Classroom* (1968) created wide interest in the notion of the self-fulfilling prophecy as a concept to explain differential performance by children in classrooms. Their findings suggested that the expectations teachers created about the children randomly selected as "intellectual bloomers" somehow caused the teachers to treat them differently, with the result that the children really did perform better by the end of the year. Though the critics of this particular research (Snow, 1969; Taylor, 1970; Thorndike, 1968, 1969) and those who have been unsuccessful in replicating the findings (Claiborn, 1969) have leveled strong challenges to Rosenthal and Jacobson, the disagreements are typically related to methodology, procedure, and analysis rather than to the proposition that relations exist between expectations and behavior.

The current status of the debate and the evidence accumulated in relation to it imply that teacher expectations are *sometimes* self-fulfilling. The early and, I think, over-enthusiastic accounts of Rosenthal and Jacobson have obscured the issue. The gist of such accounts have left the impression, as Good and Brophy (1973:73) have noted, that the mere existence of an expectation will automatically guarantee its fulfillment. Rather, as they suggest:

> The fact that teachers' expectations can be self-fulfilling is simply a special case of the principle that any expectations can be self-fulfilling. This process is not confined to classrooms. Although it is not true that "wishing can make it so," our expectations do affect the way we behave in situations, and the way we behave affects how other people respond. In some instances, our expectations about people cause us to treat them in a way that makes them respond just as we expect they would.

Such a position would be borne out by social psychologists who have demonstrated that an individual's first impressions of another person do influence subsequent interactions (Dailey, 1952; Newcomb, 1947) and that one's self-expectations influence one's subsequent behavior (Aronson and Carlsmith, 1962; Brock and Edelman, 1965; and Zajonc and Brinkman, 1969).

The conditionality of expectations related to their fulfillment is strongly emphasized by labeling theorists as well. Their emphasis upon the influence of social contingencies on whether one is labeled, how strong the label, and if it can be made to stick at all, points to a recognition that there is a social process involved where individuals are negotiating, rejecting, accepting, modifying, and reinterpreting the attempts at labeling. Such interaction is apparent in the eight stages of the development of secondary deviance outlined above by Lemert. Likewise, Erikson (1964:17), in his comments on the act of labeling as a rite of passage from one side of the group boundary to the other, has noted:

> The common assumption that deviants are not often cured or reformed, then, may be based on a faulty premise, but this assumption is stated so frequently and with such conviction that it often creates the facts which later "prove" it to be correct. If the returning deviant has to face the community's apprehensions often enough, it is understandable that he, too, may begin to wonder whether he has graduated from the deviant role—and *so respond to the uncertainty by resuming deviant activity*. In some respects, this may be the only way for the individual and his community to agree as to what kind of person he really is, for it often happens that the

community is only able to perceive his "true colors" when he lapses momentarily into some form of deviant performance. (emphasis added)

Explicit in Erikson's quote is the fact of the individual's being in interaction with the "community" to achieve some sort of agreement on what the person is "really" like. Though Erikson did not, in this instance, elaborate upon what he meant by "community," it can be inferred from elsewhere in his work that he sees "community" as manifesting itself in the institutions persons create in order to help organize and structure their lives. Such a perspective is clearly within the framework of labeling theory, where a major emphasis has been placed upon the role of institutions in sorting, labeling, tracking, and channeling persons along various routes depending upon the assessment the institution has made of the individual.

One pertinent example of the manner in which labeling theory has been applied to the study of social institutions and their impact upon participants has been in an analysis of the relation of schooling to juvenile delinquency. There have been several works which suggest as a major line of argument that schools, through and because of the manner in which they label students, serve as a chief instrument in the creation of delinquency (Hirschi, 1969; Noblit and Polk, 1975; Polk, 1969; Polk and Schafer, 1972; Schafer and Olexa, 1971). For example, Noblit and Polk (1975:3) have noted:

> In as much as the school is the primary institution in the adolescent experience—one that promises not only the future status available to the adolescent, but also that gives or denies status in adolescence itself—it can be expected that its definitions are of particular significance for the actions of youth. That is, the student who has been sorted from success via the school has little reason to conform to the often arbitrary and paternalistic regulations and rules of the school. In a very real sense, this student has no "rational constraints" against deviance. It is through the sorting mechanisms of the school, which are demanded by institutions of higher education and the world of work, that youth are labeled and thus sorted into the situation where deviant behavior threatens little while providing some alternative forms of status.

It is well to reiterate the point—interaction implies behavior and choices being made by both parties. The person facing the prospect of receiving a new label imputing a systemic change in the definition of his selfhood may respond in any of a myriad number of ways to this situation. Likewise, the institutional definition of the person is neither finalized nor solidified until the end of the negotiation as to what precisely that label should be.

But, in the context of a single student facing the authority and vested interests of a school administration and staff, the most likely outcome is that over time, the student will increasingly move towards conformity with the label the institution seeks to establish. Good and Brophy (1973:75) have elaborated upon this process within the classroom as follows:

1. The teacher expects specific behavior and achievement from particular students.
2. Because of these different expectations, the teacher behaves differently toward the different students.
3. This teacher treatment tells each student what behavior and achievement the teacher expects from him and affects his self-concept, achievement motivation, and level of aspiration.
4. If this teacher treatment is consistent over time, and if the student does not actively resist or change it in some way, it will tend to shape his achievement and behavior. High-expectation students will be led to achieve at high levels, while the achievement of low-expectation students will decline.
5. With time, the student's achievement and behavior will conform more and more closely to that originally expected of him.

The fourth point in this sequence makes the crucial observation that teacher expectations are not automatically self-fulfilling. For the expectations of the teacher to become realized, both the teacher and the student must move toward a pattern of interaction where expectations are clearly communicated and the behavioral response is consonant with the expected patterns. But as Good and Brophy (1973:75) also note:

This does not always happen. The teacher may not have clear-cut expectations about a particular student, or his expectations may continually change. Even when he has consistent expectations, he may not necessarily communicate them to the student through consistent behavior. In this case, the expectation would not be self-fulfilling even if it turned out to be correct. Finally, the student himself might prevent expectations from becoming self-fulfilling by overcoming them or by resisting them in a way that makes the teacher change them.

Yet, the critique of American education offered by such scholars as Henry (1963), Katz (1971), Goodman (1964), or Reimer (1971), suggests the struggle is unequal between the teacher (and the institution a teacher represents) and the student. The vulnerability of children to the dictates of adults in positions of power over them leaves the negotiations as to what evaluative definition will be tagged on the children more often than not in the hands of the powerful. As Max Weber himself stated, to have power is to be able to achieve one's ends, even in the face of resistance from others. When that resistance is manifested in school by children and is defined by teachers and administrators as truancy, recalcitrance, unruliness, and hostility, or conversely defined as a lack of motivation, intellectual apathy, sullenness, passivity, or withdrawal, the process is ready to be repeated and the options to escape further teacher definitions are increasingly removed.

POSTSCRIPT: BEYOND THE LOGJAM

This paper has argued that a fruitful convergence can be effected between the research being conducted on the self-fulfilling prophecy as a consequence of teacher expectations and the conceptual framework of labeling theory. The analysis of the outcomes of teacher expectations produces results highly similar to those found in the study of social deviance. Labels are applied to individuals which fundamentally shift their definitions of self and which further reinforce the behavior which had initially prompted the social reaction. The impact of the self-fulfilling prophecy in educational research is comparable to that found in the analysis of mental health clinics, asylums, prisons, juvenile homes, and other people-changing organizations. What the labeling perspective can provide to the study of educational outcomes as a result of the operationalization of teacher expectations is a model for the study of the *processes* by which the outcomes are produced. The detailing over time of the interactional patterns which lead to changes in self-definition and behavior within classrooms is sadly lacking in almost all of the expectation research to date. A most glaring example of this omission is the study by Rosenthal and Jacobson themselves. Their conclusions are based only on the analysis of a pre- and post-test. To posit that teacher expectations were the causal variable that produced changes in student performances was a leap from the data to speculation. They could offer only suggestions as to how the measured changes in the children's performance came about, since they were not in the classrooms to observe how assumed teacher attitudes were translated into subsequent actual student behavior.

To extend the research on the educational experiences of those students who are differentially labeled by teachers, what is needed is a theoretical framework which can clearly isolate the influences and effects of certain kinds of teacher reactions on certain types of students, producing certain typical outcomes. The labeling perspective appears particularly well-suited for this expansion of both research and theoretical development on teacher expectations by offering the basis for analysis at either a specific or a more general level. With the former, for example, there are areas of investigation related to 1) types of students perceived by teachers as prone to success or failure; 2) the kinds of reactions, based on their expectations, teachers have to different students; and 3) the effects of specific teacher reactions on specific student outcomes. At a more general level, fruitful lines of inquiry might include 1) the outcomes in the post-school world of having received a negative vs. a positive label within the school; 2) the influences of factors such as social class and race on the categories of expectations teachers hold; 3) how and why labels do emerge in schools as well as the phenomenological and structural meanings that are attached to them; and 4) whether there are means by which to modify or minimize the effects of school labeling processes on students.

Labeling theory provides a conceptual framework by which to understand the processes of transforming attitudes into behavior and the outcomes of having done so. To be able to detail the dynamics and influences within schools by which some children come to see themselves as successful and act as though they were, and to detail how others come to see themselves as failures and act accordingly, provides in the final analysis an opportunity to intervene so as to expand the numbers of winners and diminish the numbers of losers. For that reason above all others, labeling theory merits our attention.

NOTE

1. The preparation of this paper has been aided by a grant (GS–41522) from the National Science Foundation—Sociology Program. The views expressed here are solely those of the author and no official endorsement by either the National Science Foundation or the National Institute of Education is to be inferred.

REFERENCES

Akers, R. L. *Deviant Behavior: A Social Learning Approach.* Belmont, Calif.: Wadsworth, 1973.

Aronson, E., and Carlsmith, J. M. "Performance Expectancy as a Determinant of Actual Performance." *Journal of Abnormal and Social Psychology* 65 (1962): 179–182.

Becker, H. S. "Social Class Variations in the Teacher-Pupil Relationship." *Journal of Educational Sociology* 25 (1952):451–465.

Becker, H. S. *Outsiders.* New York: The Free Press, 1963.

Becker, H. S. *The Other Side.* New York: The Free Press, 1964.

Broadhead, R. S. "A Theoretical Critique of the Societal Reaction Approach to Deviance." *Pacific Sociological Review* 17 (1974):287–312.

Brock, T. C., and Edelman, H. "Seven Studies of Performance Expectancy as a Determinant of Actual Performance." *Journal of Experimental Social Psychology* 1 (1965):295–310.

Brophy, J., and Good, T. "Teachers' Communications of Differential Expectations for Children's Classroom Performance: Some Behavioral Data." *Journal of Educational Psychology* 61 (1970):365–374.

Brown, B. *The Assessment of Self-Concept among Four Year Old Negro and White Children: A Comparative Study Using the Brown IDS Self-Concept Reference Test.* New York: Institute for Developmental Studies, 1968.

Claiborn, W. L. "Expectancy Effects in the Classroom: A Failure to Replicate." *Journal of Educational Psychology* 60 (1969):377–383.

Clifford, M. M., and Walster, E. "The Effect of Physical Attractiveness on Teacher Expectations." *Sociology of Education* 46 (1973):248–258.

Dailey, C. A. "The Effects of Premature Conclusion upon the Acquisition of Understanding of a Person." *Journal of Psychology* 33 (1952):133–152.

Davidson, H. H., and Lang, G. "Children's Perceptions of Teachers' Feelings toward Them." *Journal of Experimental Education* 29 (1960):107–118.

Deutsch, M. "The Disadvantaged Child and the Learning Process," in *Education in Depressed Areas,* edited by H. Passow. New York: Teachers College Press, 1963.

Deutsch, M.; Fishman, J. A.; Kogan, L.; North, R.; and Whiteman, M. "Guidelines for Testing Minority Group Children." *Journal of Social Issues* 20 (1964):129–145.

Douglas, J. *The Home and the School.* London: MacGibbon and Kee, 1964.

Douglas, J. *The American Social Order.* New York: The Free Press, 1971.

Douglas, J. (ed.). *Deviance and Respectability.* New York: Basic Books, 1972.

Doyle, W.; Hancock, G.; and Kifer, E. "Teachers' Perceptions: Do They Make a Difference?" Paper presented at the meeting of the American Educational Research Association, 1971.

Edgar, D. E. *The Competent Teacher.* Sydney, Australia: Angus & Robertson, 1974.

Erikson, K. T. "Note on the Sociology of Deviance," in *The Other Side,* edited by H. S. Becker. New York: The Free Press, 1964.

Erikson, K. T. *Wayward Puritans.* New York: Wiley, 1966.

Flanagan, J. C. *Test of General Ability: Technical Report.* Chicago: Science Research Associates, 1960.

Gibson, G. "Aptitude Tests." *Science* 149 (1965):583.

Goaldman, L. "Counseling Methods and Techniques: The Use of Tests," in *The Encyclopedia of Education,* edited by L. C. Deighton. New York: MacMillan, 1971.

Good, T ., and Brophy, J. *Looking in Classrooms.* New York: Harper and Row, 1973.

Goodman, P. *Compulsory Mis-Education.* New York: Random House, 1964.

Goslin, D. A., and Glass, D. C. "The Social Effects of Standardized Testing on American Elementary Schools." *Sociology of Education* 40 (1967):115–131.

Henry, J. *Culture Against Man.* New York: Random House, 1963.

Hirschi, T. *Causes of Delinquency.* Berkeley: University of California Press, 1969.

Illich, I. *Deschooling Society.* New York: Harper & Row, 1971.

Jackson, G., and Cosca, C. "The Inequality of Educational Opportunity in the Southwest: An Observational Study of Ethnically Mixed Classrooms." *American Educational Research Journal* 11 (1974):219–229.

Johnson, J. *On the Interface between Low-income Urban Black Children and Their Teachers during the Early School Years: A Position Paper.* San Francisco: Far West Laboratory for Educational Research and Development, 1973.

Katz, M. *Class, Bureaucracy and Schools.* New York: Praeger, 1971.

Kitsuse, J. "Societal Reaction to Deviant Behavior: Problems of Theory and Method," in *The Other Side,* edited by H. S. Becker. New York: The Free Press, 1964.

Leacock, E. *Teaching and Learning in City Schools.* New York: Basic Books, 1969.

Lemert, E. *Social Pathology.* New York: McGraw-Hill, 1951.

Lemert, E. *Human Deviance, Social Problems and Social Control.* Englewood Cliffs, N.J.: Prentice-Hall, 1972.

Lemert, E. "Beyond Mead: The Societal Reaction to Deviance." *Social Problems* 21 (1974):457–468.

Lofland, J. *Deviance and Identity.* Englewood Cliffs, N.J.: Prentice-Hall, 1969.

Mackler, B. "Grouping in the Ghetto." *Education and Urban Society* 2 (1969):80–95.

Matza, D. *Delinquency and Drift.* New York: Wiley, 1964.

Matza, D. *Becoming Deviant.* Englewood Cliffs, N.J.: Prentice-Hall, 1969.

McPherson, G. H. *The Role-set of the Elementary School Teacher: A case study.* Unpublished Ph.D. dissertation, Columbia University, New York, 1966.

Mehan, H. B. *Accomplishing Understanding in Educational Settings.* Unpublished Ph.D. dissertation, University of California, Santa Barbara, 1971.

Mehan, H. B. *Ethnomethodology and Education.* Paper presented to the Sociology of Education Association conference, Pacific Grove, California, 1974.

Merton, R. K. "Social Problems and Social Theory," in *Contemporary Social Problems,* edited by R. Merton and R. Nisbet. New York: Harcourt, Brace and World, 1968.

Newcomb, T. M. "Autistic Hostility and Social Reality." *Human Relations* 1 (1947):69–86.

Noblit, G. W., and Polk, K. *Institutional Constraints and Labeling.* Paper presented to the Southern Sociological Association meetings, Washington, D .C., 1975.

Palardy, J. M. "What Teachers Believe—What Children Achieve." *Elementary School Journal,* 1969, pp. 168–169 and 370–374.

Pequignot, H. "L'équation personnelle du juge." In *Semaine des Hopitaux* (Paris), 1966.

Polk, K. "Class, Strain, and Rebellion and Adolescents." *Social Problems* 17 (1969):214–224.

Polk, K., and Schafer, W. E. *Schools and Delinquency.* Englewood Cliffs, N.J.: Prentice-Hall, 1972.

Reimer, E. *School is Dead.* New York: Doubleday, 1971.

Rist, R. C. "Student Social Class and Teachers' Expectations: The Self-fulfilling Prophecy in Ghetto Education." *Harvard Educational Review* 40 (1970):411–450.

Rist, R. C. "Social Distance and Social Inequality in a Kindergarten Classroom: An Examination of the 'Cultural Gap' Hypothesis." *Urban Education* 7 (1972):241–260.

Rist, R. C. *The Urban School: A Factory for Failure.* Cambridge, Mass.: The M. I. T. Press, 1973.

Rosenthal, R., and Jacobson, L. "Teachers' Expectancies: Determinants of Pupils' IQ Gains." *Psychology Reports* 19 (1966):115–118.

Rosenthal, R., and Jacobson, L. *Pygmalion in the Classroom.* New York: Holt, Rinehart, & Winston, 1968.

Rowe, M. "Science, Silence and Sanctions." *Science and Children* 6 (1969):11–13.

Rubington, E., and Weinberg, M. S. *Deviance: The Interactionist Perspective.* New York: Macmillan, 1973.

Rubovits, P., and Maehr, M. L. "Pygmalion Black and White." *Journal of Personality and Social Psychology* 2 (1973):210–218.

Schafer, W. E., and Olexa, C. *Tracking and Opportunity.* Scranton, Pa.: Chandler, 1971.

Scheff, T. *Being Mentally Ill.* Chicago: Aldine, 1966.

Schur, E. *Crimes without Victims.* Englewood Cliffs, N.J.: Prentice-Hall, 1965.

Schur, E. *Labeling Deviant Behavior.* New York: Harper & Row, 1971.

Scott, R. A., and Douglas, J. C. (eds.). *Theoretical Perspectives on Deviance.* New York: Basic Books, 1972.

Snow, R. E. "Unfinished Pygmalion." *Contemporary Psychology* 14 (1969):197–199.

Stein, A. "Strategies for Failure." *Harvard Educational Review* 41 (1971):158–204.

Tannenbaum, F. *Crime and the Community.* New York: Columbia University Press, 1938.

Taylor, C. "The Expectations of Pygmalion's Creators." *Educational Leadership* 28 (1970):161–164.

Thorndike, R. L. "Review of *Pygmalion in the Classroom.*" *Educational Research Journal* 5 (1968):708–711.

Thorndike, R. L. "But Do You Have to Know How to Tell Time?" *Educational Research Journal* 6 (1969):692.

Warner, W. L.; Havighurst, R.; and Loeb, M. B. *Who Shall be Educated?* New York: Harper & Row, 1944.

Willis, S. *Formation of Teachers' Expectations of Student Academic Performance.* Unpublished Ph.D. dissertation, University of Texas at Austin, 1972.

Wilson, A. B. "Social Stratification and Academic Achievement," in *Education in Depressed Areas,* edited by H. Passow. New York: Teachers College Press, 1963.

Zajonc, R. B., and Brinkman, P. "Expectancy and Feedback as Independent Factors in Task Performance." *Journal of Personality and Social Psychology* 11 (1969):148–150.

HUGH MEHAN

Structuring School Structure

Questions to think about

1 *How would you plan a research study in a school, using the author's approach? Give an example.*

2 *How does Mehan's approach differ from the other theories discussed in this chapter?*

3 *With what aspects of the open system would Mehan be most concerned? Therefore, how would his approach be most useful?*

4 *Using his approach, write a description of your own college experience.*

Most sociological studies of education treat social structures as objective and constraining "social facts." In seeking statistical relationships among these structures, such studies typically fail to consider the ways in which these social facts are produced. Recently, however, a number of researchers have been working to counter this omission by studying the structuring activities that assemble the social structures of education. In this paper I attempt to demonstrate the potential of this new approach, which I call "constitutive ethnography." As I review the work that has been conducted under this rubric to date, my purpose is as much to display the method of analysis as it is to report the findings.

I begin by placing constitutive ethnography in the context of the dominant research strategies and theoretical positions that have been adopted to investigate the influence of schools on students' careers. Because careful

Reprinted from *Harvard Educational Review* 48:1 (February 1978), 32–63. Copyright © 1978 by the President and Fellows of Harvard College. All rights reserved.

description of the processes occurring within educational environments has been neglected, constitutive enthnography is recommended as necessary for understanding the relationship between schooling and life chances. I then review representative examples of constitutive studies of educational processes. Finally, I discuss the implications of this approach for future sociological studies of schooling.

RESEARCH METHODS IN THE STUDY OF THE SCHOOL

Correlational Studies

Correlational research, the predominant approach used in the study of the school, has been especially concerned with the effects of schools on students. Typically these effects have been conceptualized in terms of an input-output model that treats aspects of people's lives, as well as their social and historical contexts, as "factors" or "variables." The input factors, or independent variables, usually include the social class, age, sex, and ability of students and teachers, the attitudes of teachers, and the size of classrooms. The output factors, or dependent variables, include students' cognitive achievement, their subsequent career plans, actual occupational attainment, and job earnings. The basic task in this model is to test the strength of the relationships among the input and output variables.

A number of positions have been taken with regard to the relative influence of schooling on later-life outcomes. The most prevalent view in this country is that differences in scholastic and economic success are primarily the result of environmental influence rather than genetic endowment. . . .

Faith in the environmentalist position has been shaken recently. One challenge has come from those who contend that schooling merely reproduces the existing system of class relationships (Bourdieu & Passeron, 1977; Bowles & Gintis, 1976). A second challenge has come from a group of researchers who assign greater weight to heredity than to environment in determining life chances. Proponents of this position (Herrnstein, 1973; Jensen, 1969) argue that, as in a hothouse, enrichment of the environment may speed the rate of intellectual growth, but adult ability will not exceed genetically programmed limits. A third challenge has come from those educational researchers (notably Coleman, Campbell, Hobson, McPartland, Mood, Weinfeld, & York, 1966) who emphasize the role of the social background of students, especially their early-childhood experiences, in determining life chances. "Home environment" researchers conclude that the quality of schools has little influence on students' achievement.

Each of these three positions minimizes the role of the school in affecting life chances, albeit for different reasons. The geneticist position is the most extreme on this point; its proponents claim that no environmental intervention, in or out of school, will make a significant difference in status attainment. Although less extreme, the early-childhood position advocated by proponents of programs like "Homestart" still minimizes the capacity of school experiences to equalize educational and economic opportunities. Finally, the radical economic position also minimizes the role of the school, but argues in favor of economic redistribution and social reorganization as the only sure means of achieving equality.

Caution must be exercised, however, before we dismiss the influence of schooling, blame schools for reproducing the class structure, or congratulate them for opening up opportunities for social mobility. There is a methodological irony in the work of researchers who have debated the influence of schools on students. Although "schooling" is a major variable in the equation that links people's backgrounds and their success in later life, these researchers have not directly examined the process of education. They have examined indices of schooling—the number of books in school libraries, the amount of equipment in science laboratories, the opinions of teachers and administrators toward their schools—but what actually happens inside schools on a practical daily basis—in classrooms, in testing encounters, at recess, in teachers' lounges—has not been examined directly by researchers who use the correlational method to debate the influence of schooling on people's subsequent life outcomes. The school has, in effect, been treated as a "black box" between input and output factors.

This point can be made even more clearly by referring specifically to the work of Jencks and his associates (Jencks, Smith, Acland, Bane, Cohen, Gintis, Heyns, & Michelson, 1972). They report a counterintuitive finding: although "everybody knows" that lowering teacher-student ratios and providing better books, teachers, and laboratory equipment should improve the quality of education, these researchers found that increased expenditures for educational facilities did not improve educational outcomes. The question that arises is why Jencks and his associates were unable to find a relationship between the quality of education and educational attainment. I suggest that the answer can be found in the nature of their methodology.

Because Jencks and his colleagues gathered data through large-scale surveys, they could not directly measure the influence of teacher-student ratios, classroom organization, and other factors associated with educational quality. As a result, people who fear the consequences of Jencks's arguments (and Jencks himself, for that matter) either try to manipulate the same indices of educational quality in different ways or fall back on personal experiences, anecdotes, and intuitions to counter his arguments.

What is lacking in most discussions of the influence of schooling is a solid foundation of evidence based on examinations of the actual processes of education. If we want to know whether teacher-student ratios, classroom size, teaching styles, and all the rest actually influence the quality of education, then we must show how these factors operate in practical educational situations. Likewise, if we are to determine whether input factors like "social class," "ethnicity," or "teachers' attitudes" influence such educational outcomes as "scholastic achievement" or "students' careers," then the processes denoted by these factors must be located in the interaction among participants in educational environments. Even Jencks recognized this limitation in large-scale surveys of schooling:

> We have ignored not only attitudes and values but the internal life
> of schools. We hve been preoccupied with the *effects* of schooling,
> especially those effects that might be expected to persist into
> adulthood. This has led us to adopt a "factory" metaphor, in which
> schools are seen primarily as places that alter the characteristics of
> their alumni. Our research has convinced us that this is the wrong
> way to think about schools. The long-term effects of schooling seem
> much less significant to us than they did when we began our work,
> and the internal life of the schools seems correspondingly more
> important. (Jencks et al., 1972, p. 13)

Conventional Field Studies

A second major research strategy that has been applied to examinations of the influence of schools is the "field-study" approach. Researchers from this perspective have examined the "internal life of the school" that has been left untouched by correlational research designs. Field studies are characterized by detailed descriptions of a small number of school events. Field researchers adopt some version of a participant-observer role in order to document the systematic patterns of routine behaviors that occur in the social situations they study. Examples of their research are found in investigations of schooling in other societies (Moore, 1973; Redfield, 1943; Warren, 1967; Wylie, 1957), studies of routine classroom events in this society (Jackson, 1968; Rist, 1970; Smith & Geoffrey, 1968), and natural histories of school activities (Burnett, 1972; Wolcott, 1973).

Field studies have a number of positive features. Typically, researchers describe their experiences in vivid prose. After reading a report of field research I often feel as if I have been there. Furnished with rich details about the setting, I find myself nodding in vague affirmation of the descriptions; I can often smell the smells and hear the sounds that the researchers experienced.

But there are also a number of difficulties in field studies of the schools. And as is so often the case, the strengths of an enterprise are also its weaknesses. First, conventional field reports tend to have an anecdotal quality. Researchers cull a few exemplary instances of behavior from field notes, but they seldom provide the criteria used to include certain instances and not others. As a result, it is difficult to determine the representativeness of the events described and, therefore, the generality of findings derived from them. Second, research reports presented in summary form often do not preserve the materials analyzed. Therefore, it is impossible to derive alternative interpretations, and one must accept the summary findings that field researchers have abstracted.

Constitutive Ethnography

In seeking correlations or simply describing recurrent patterns, educational researchers of the two most common methodological persuasions have ignored the social structuring activities that create the objective and constraining "social facts" of the educational world. A third research perspective, which only recently has been applied to education, seeks to counter this omission by studying the social structuring activities that assemble social structures in educational settings. . . .

Constitutive studies operate on the interactional premise that social structures are social accomplishments (Cicourel, 1974; Garfinkel, 1967; Garfinkel & Sacks, 1970; Scheflen, 1972). The central tenet of constitutive studies of the school is that "objective social facts," such as students' intelligence, scholastic achievement, or career patterns, and "routine patterns of behavior," such as classroom organization, are accomplished in the interaction between teachers and students, testers and students, principals and teachers. Rather than merely describe recurrent patterns of behavior or seek correlations among variables, constitutive analysts study the structuring activities that construct the social facts of education.

In addition to its theoretical interest in the structuring of school structure, there are several methodological features that distinguish constitutive studies from other research strategies used to examine the process of schooling. These include an emphasis on retrievability of data, exhaustiveness of data treatment, convergence between researchers' and participants' perspectives on events, and analysis at the interactional level.

In conventional research reports the materials upon which the analysis was conducted are not usually included. As researchers move from raw materials to coded data to summarized findings, the materials become increasingly abstracted from their original form. Thus, the opportunity to consider alternative interpretations of the same materials is lost.

In contrast, constitutive studies stress the importance of retrievable data, employing videotape or film for both data gathering and data display. Events depicted on videotape and film are not equivalent to school events per se, but audiovisual materials do preserve events in close to their original form. They thus serve as an external memory that allows researchers to examine interactions extensively and repeatedly, often frame by frame (McDermott, 1976; Erickson et al., Note 1). In some constitutive studies, these materials are transcribed. Some reports of constitutive studies include transcripts and audiovisual materials as support for their interpretations (see Cicourel, Jennings, Jennings, Leiter, MacKay, Mehan, & Roth, 1974; Mehan, Cazden, Coles, Fisher, & Maroules, Note 3).

For constitutive ethnographers, exhaustive data treatment is a necessary check against the tendency to seek only evidence that supports the researchers' orienting hypotheses or domain assumptions (Campbell & Fiske, 1959). When they include only a few exemplary instances that support the researchers' claims, research reports have a self-validating quality. They cannot be examined for disconfirming evidence, and alternative interpretations of the data cannot be entertained. Constitutive studies therefore attempt an exhaustive analysis of behavior in the flow of events. This policy represents a shift from a search for the most frequently occurring or dominant pattern of behavior to an analysis of the entire course of interaction among participants in social events. The continuous flow of activity depicted on videotape or film is segmented into sequential phases and hierarchical components. This analysis continues until the researchers have derived a small set of recursive rules that completely describes the structure and structuring of events (McDermott, 1976). . . .

A third feature of constitutive ethnography is interactional analysis. Since the organization of events is socially constructed, researchers attempt to locate this structuring in the words or gestures of the participants as a "cohort's situated accomplishment" (Garfinkel & Sacks, 1970, p. 396; see also Mehan & Wood, 1975). By confining analysis to the behavior displayed among participants, unfounded inferences are not made about the mental states of participants, and the researchers avoid both psychological reduction and sociological reification.

The fourth characteristic of constitutive analysis is the attempt to obtain convergence between researchers' and participants' perspectives. Constitutive ethnographers seek to insure that the structure they see in events is the same as the structure that orients the participants in those events (Garfinkel & Sacks, 1970; Mehan & Wood, 1975). One way in which the "psychological reality" of ethnographic findings has been tested is through the use of "elicitation frames." After ethnographers have constructed a model, such as a genealogical taxonomy, of some aspect of a group's culture, they ask group members questions about the scheme. If the group members' answers to the elicitation questions confirm the tentative analysis, then the ethnographers can have some confidence in the validity of their findings (Tylor, 1972).

However, as Frake (1977) reminds us, "plying frames can be dangerous," because the process of eliciting information structures respondents' answers (cf. Cicourel, 1964, 1974; Mehan & Wood, 1975). Thus, information from elicitation frames may provide convergent validation (Campbell & Fiske, 1959), but not independent verification, that group members are oriented to the researchers' model of the phenomenon. The test of members' orientation toward the researchers' model cannot be passed, therefore, by exclusive reliance on polling, naming, or other elicitation devices. If the researchers' phenomenon is also the participants' phenomenon, the participants in an event must be oriented to its structural features during the course of the event. The researchers' tentative model will thus be tested by participants' actions, especially in the absence of expected forms of interaction.

In the events described below, the participants continually indicate to each other that they are engaged in interaction. They mark the sequential and hierarchical organization of events by displaying distinctive verbal, paralinguistic, and kinesic behavior at significant junctures in the organization of events. In this manner the participants' orientation to the organization of events makes visible structures that are normally unnoticed. Thus, in contrast to correlational studies, which seek relationships among social structures treated as variables, and participant-observation studies, which look for systematic patterns of routine social behaviors, constitutive studies attempt to describe the interactional work that assembles systematic patterns and social structures.

Having contrasted constitutive ethnography with correlational and field studies and having outlined the policies guiding constitutive analysis, I will now review research that has been conducted under this rubric, placing constitutive studies in the context of students' career patterns in schools.

STUDENTS' CAREER PATTERNS

Although all children in the United States must enter school in the primary grades, they follow different paths and leave at different points (see Figure 1). The existence of different career paths raises important questions: How

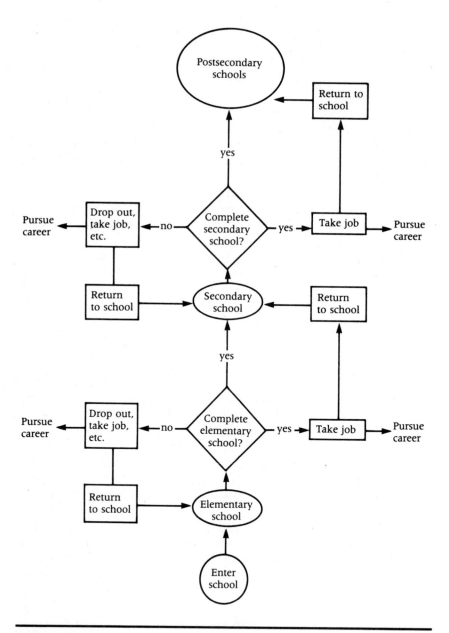

FIGURE 1
Educational Career Plans

do some students wind up following one path and not another? How is it that some students continue through the system while others, for example, drop out?

The "geneticist" position discussed in the previous section would suggest that differential career patterns are the result of individual differences in students' hereditary characteristics. The "home environment" position would account for differential school performance in terms of the effects of early-childhood experiences associated with the social class of students. The constitutive study of school settings suggests an alternate explanation: students' careers emerge from the interactional work of educators with students. Students' performance in school is not independent of the assessment procedures that produce accounts of students' successes, abilities, and progress.

The constitutive analysis of the structuring of school structure has been conducted in school settings that typically have consequences for students' careers: classrooms, educational-testing encounters, and counseling sessions. In each case researchers have demonstrated that the educational facts peculiar to the setting are assembled in the interaction among the participants. Constitutive studies of the classroom have been concerned with how participants organize events like lessons, reading groups, and "circles," and with the implications these processes have for the evaluation of students' performance. Constitutive studies of educational testing have been concerned with the processes by which individual and group test scores are assembled in the interaction between testers and students. Constitutive studies of counseling sessions have examined how students' career choices are structured in the interaction between counselors and students during guidance interviews.

. . . In recommending constitutive ethnography as a research strategy, I am not claiming that (the studies reviewed here) actually resolve the questions raised about the long-term effects of schooling. My concern here is less to provide a specific catalogue of findings than to suggest a means for finding answers in the process of educational interaction. This essay, then, is as much a recommendation about how to proceed as a report about what will be found at the end of the journey. When this journey is completed, I believe that we will be able to specify the interactional work in classrooms and other educational environments that does make a difference.

CONSTITUTIVE STUDIES OF CLASSROOM EVENTS

When classrooms are observed, they appear to be organized; teachers and students talk, read, and play in certain times and in certain places and not in others. At times the whole class acts in unison, as when students take notes on what the teacher is saying; while, at other times, small groups engage in different activities simultaneously, as when group of students conducts experiments at a "science learning center," another group does silent reading, and a third studies math with the teacher. How does this social organization come about? How do teachers and students know when to move and when to speak? How do they know if it is the right time or place to act in a certain way?

Constitutive analysis of the classroom addresses these questions by examining the social structuring of classroom events (Bremme & Erickson, 1977; McDermott, 1976; Shultz, Note 2; Mehan et al., Note 3). . . .

CONSTITUTIVE STUDIES OF EDUCATIONAL TESTING

Since educational tests play such a crucial role in the judgments made about students in United States schools, constitutive analysts have given them a great deal of attention. School officials use intelligence tests, reading tests, and other measures of achievement to assess students' abilities and to inform the placement decisions that lead to various career patterns (see Figure 1). The constitutive study of these tests begins with an analysis of testers' assumptions about the nature of mental abilities, the measurement of ability, the answers to test questions, the meaning of test items, the influence of the testing situation, and the role of the tester (Mehan, 1973).

Test takers are asumed to have underlying mental abilities that are defined as previously learned experiences. These experiences are generally concerned with substantive matters, like names, dates, and other factual information. Another assumption is that the tests actually measure abilities. In sampling previously learned experiences, test questions are supposed to elicit responses that index the test takers' underlying abilities. In order to answer questions correctly, respondents must make the appropriate link between the question asked and the test materials. Another testing assumption is that correct answers to test questions signal the presence of underlying abilities while incorrect answers indicate their absence. A fourth assumption is that the meaning of test items, instructions, questions, and answers is shared by testers and respondents; that is, that they share a "common culture." The influence of the testing situation is also assumed to be minimal, with respondents' behavior considered to be solely the result of their underlying abilities and the stimulus questions asked. Other factors that might be influential are either standardized or controlled for by testers. Finally, it is assumed that testers play a passive role, merely recording the behavior of respondents.

Test results based on these assumptions are treated as social facts by members of the educational community. Only the products of testing—either in the form of individual students' scores or group aggregates—are reported and employed. This practice, however, reveals neither the constitutive process by which students arrive at answers in group tests nor the constitutive process by which testers and students jointly produce answers in individualized tests. As a result, when using test scores, educators and researchers do not have access to students' actual reasoning processes, even though reasoning ability is the very thing most educational tests were set up to measure.

Constitutive studies of educational testing have followed three avenues of investigation that are related to the test assumptions outlined above: studies of item meaning, studies of the negotiation of measurement, and studies of answer assembly. . . .

CONSTITUTIVE STUDIES OF COUNSELING SESSIONS

General-education requirements, for which students take a specified number of courses in English, social studies, mathematics, and science, are an explicit and ubiquitous feature of schooling in the United States. Less explicit features of schooling are the facts that these courses are often stratified according to difficulty, with the most difficult courses reserved for the "best" students, and that counselors play an important role in channeling students. By assessing students' abilities, helping them decide which classes to take, advising them about their academic progress, and providing them with information on postsecondary-education options, counselors are in a position to influence students in a number of ways that help to determine their future career possibilities.

The question thus becomes: what are the grounds upon which counselors and other school officials make educational decisions? Cicourel and Kitsuse (1963) interviewed high-school counselors to determine how they advised black and white students from varying socioeconomic backgrounds about whether or not they should apply to college—and consequently whether they should anticipate professional or nonprofessional occupations. Black students who had average-to-high academic performance were consistently dissuaded from attending college, while white students with mediocre-to-low academic performance (but high socioeconomic status) were consistently encouraged to attend college. This study suggests that students' careers are not the direct result of genetic or environmental factors (cf. Rosenbaum, 1976) but are instead constituted by socially organized decision making (Leiter, 1974). To climb the career ladder, students must pass through a series of educational decision-making encounters.

Constitutive analysts have examined these situations in order to discover how the decisions that have so much influence on student careers are made. Erickson (1975; Erickson et al., Note 1) has analyzed the structure of interaction between junior-college students and counselors. His work provides a description of some of the interactional practices that assemble key choices in students' careers. According to Erickson, counselors perform several roles, and these are sometimes at odds. As advisers, they are supposed to act on behalf of students—as advocates. As officers of a formal institution, they are supposed to act on behalf of the school— as judges. Depending on which role they take with students, counselors can and do influence students' careers in different ways. . . .

. . . Studies demonstrate that the interactional work of participants structures the educational facts of these school settings. This constitutive work appears in the minute detail of each question-answer exchange in lessons and tests. It is visible as teachers' and students' procedures assemble the organized character of classroom events like lessons, and as testers aggregate series of answers-to-questions to produce students' overall test scores. Finally, it is evident in the strategies educators employ to open or close the gates to potential paths in students' careers. Thus, the interactional machinery that assembles the social facts of education can be seen to operate at increasing levels of generality.

Constitutive ethnographers contend that this interactional machinery is not just the researcher's analytic device but also the mechanism that guides participants in the course of their interaction. Participants display their orientation to the sequential and hierarchical organization of school events by marking the boundaries of interactional sequences and event phases with distinctive verbal, paralinguistic, and kinesic shifts. The presence of these markers demonstrates that teacher-student and counselor-student interactions—like mother-infant (Brazelton, Koslowski, & Main, 1973) and psychiatrist-patient (Condon, 1966; Scheflen, 1972) interactions—are rhythmic, cooperative activities, involving the complex coordination of speech and gesture. These studies consistently find that successful interaction occurs when participants synchronize the rhythm of speech and gesture, while breakdowns occur in the absence of synchrony. Interaction is segmented, and to some extent controlled, by systematic shifts in participants' postures, conversational rhythms, and prosody. These changing arrays of postural configurations demarcate the division of the continuous flow of interaction into discrete segments. By indicating that something new is happening, these changes have profound effects on what is communicated. In the classroom, for example, proxemic shifts, tempo changes, and unique lexical entries signal changes in lesson content.

Constitutive Ethnography, Ethnomethodology, and the Sociological Tradition

Ethnomethodology has been characterized by Mehan and Wood (1975) as derived from two intellectual traditions that are commonly held to be mutually exclusive: the "hermeneutic-dialectic" and the "logico-analytic" (Radnitsky, 1973). Ethnomethodology has borrowed many of its theoretical notions from the former and its methodological concerns from the latter. The presence of terms like "reflexivity," "retrospective-prospective relations," "indexical expressions," and "hermeneutic spirals" in the ethnomethodological literature reveals the influence of the hermeneutic-dialectic tradition. One need look no further than the conversational analysis of Sacks and his colleagues (Sacks et al., 1974) and the studies of language, cognition, and social organization of Cicourel (1964, 1974) for a reminder of the empiricist influence of the logico-analytic tradition. And I think that one of Garfinkel's (1967) seminal contributions was to translate the idealistic and subjectivistic notions associated with the phenomenological branch of the hermeneutic-dialectic tradition into the realm of the social by exhorting researchers to find in the interaction between people, not in their subjective states, the processes that assemble the concerted activities of everyday life.

But there was an unfortunate consequence fostered by the exuberance of this position. Early ethnomethodologists claimed that sociologists, in their search for regularities in social structures, had ignored participants' structuring activities. In so arguing, they swung the pendulum of social theory the other way, shifting from an exclusive concern with social facts to an equally exclusive concern for "members' methods," "practices," and "constitutive presuppositions."

The current approach to the ethnography of school settings is overcoming this early "constitutive bias" (Mehan & Wood, 1975) by not treating structuring separately from structures. Constitutive ethnographers neither deny the objective reality of the social world nor focus exclusively on social process; instead, they put structures and structuring on an equal footing by showing how the social facts of the educational world emerge from structuring activities to become external and constraining, as part of a world that is both of our making and beyond our making (Mehan & Wood, 1975).

Structuring Inequality

There is a more pragmatic analogue to this theoretical discussion. While inequality is a social fact in the United States, the contribution of schools to inequality is a matter of continuing debate. Central to this debate is the question of whether schools "make a difference." The survey research by Coleman et al. (1966) and Jencks et al. (1972) has been interpreted as implying that differences *between* schools do not affect social equality. Whether or not that conclusion is accurate, such research does not tell us whether processes *within* schools make a difference (Rosenbaum, 1976). Large-scale surveys may be appropriate for studying gross differences between schools, but they are not helpful in determining whether there are social processes operating there that contribute to inequality. When the practical daily work of educators with students is examined closely and rigorously, as the constitutive studies reviewed in this paper have done, it is clear that school and, to be more specific, the organized character of interaction in school, does make a difference in educational outcomes. Taken together, then, these constitutive studies point to stratifying practices within schools that produce differential treatment and may result in differences in later life.

Until now, constitutive-ethnographic research has been conducted on a series of classroom events and a number of counseling and testing sessions. Since these studies were conducted in different schools, with different participants, these events have been examined separately. The next step would be to conduct a constitutive-ethnographic study of school events that would relate each of them to the total school context. What I have in mind is a "constitutive career study."

During the course of their daily lives in schools, students come in contact with teachers, nurses, principals, testers, and counselors. Each of these educators makes educational decisions about students. While constitutive studies in discrete educational settings provide substantial evidence that educational outcomes are structured in interaction, we do not yet know how the same students are treated in different, though interlinked, school events. We need to follow the same group of students through decision-making situations in the school, videotaping their interactions with teachers, testers, counselors, and other educational decision makers.

In each setting, researchers would focus attention on the reflexive interconnections among interactional processes, students' displays, and educational outcomes as a means of determining whether interactional processes affect students differentially. To guard against unwarranted claims about the linear influence of presupposed input factors (like students' background characteristics or educators' predispositions toward students), the grounds of any differential treatment would have to be located in interaction among participants. By observing a broad range of these encounters and analyzing them together, we will be better able to display the interactional mechanisms in schools that operate to create inequality.

Restructuring School Structure

Behind questions about the structuring of school structure lie equally important questions about its restructuring. In addressing these questions, constitutive ethnography again contrasts with other methodologies. Rosenbaum (1976), for example, explains why few practical policies result from large-scale survey research in education:

> Even when agreeing on methodological issues, and using the same data, researchers can arrive at contradictory interpretations (compare Bowles and Gintis with Jencks). Furthermore, even if clear results were produced, reformers would have difficulty in implementing them in their communities. Because the findings would be probabilistic, one could not be certain that they applied to a particular community; because they would be static, one might not understand what actions to take to change the situation; because they would be abstract, one would have difficulty in motivating community concern. (p. 49)

Because it can address these problems, constitutive ethnography provides a rigorous methodological alternative to large-scale surveys as a means of guiding educational reform. Because the findings of constitutive ethnography are exhaustive rather than probabilistic, they can apply to particular educational circumstances. Because constitutive ethnographies reveal the machinery that structures school structure, they can suggest specific actions to change the structuring apparatus in specific educational situations. Because the findings of constitutive ethnographies are concrete, not abstract, they can motivate educators and communities to act in ways that make a difference.

NOTES

1. Erickson, F., Shultz, J., Leonard-Dolan, C., Pariser, D., Erder, M., Marchese, J., & Jean, C. *Inter-ethnic relations in urban institutional settings* (Final Technical Report, Projects MH 18230, MH 21460, National Institute of Mental Health). Cambridge, Mass.: Harvard University, Graduate School of Education, December 1973.

2. Shultz, J. *It's not whether you win or lose, but how you play the game* (Working Paper 1). Cambridge, Mass.: Harvard University, Graduate School of Education, Newton Classroom Interaction Project, 1976.

3. Mehan, H., Cazden, C. B., Coles, L., Fisher, S., & Maroules, N. *The social organization of classroom lessons* (CHIP Report 67). La Jolla, Calif.: University of California, San Diego, Center for Human Information Processing, December 1976.

REFERENCES

Blau, P. B., & Duncan, O. D. *The American occupational structure.* New York: Wiley, 1967.

Bourdieu, P., & Passeron, J. C. *Reproduction: In education, society and culture.* Beverly Hills, Calif.: Sage, 1977.

Bowles, S., & Gintis, H. *Schooling in capitalist America.* New York: Basic Books, 1976.

Brazelton, T. B., Koslowski, B., & Main, M. The origins of reciprocity. In M. Lewis & L. Rosenblum (Eds.), *The effect of the infant on its caregiver.* New York: Wiley, 1973.

Bremme, D. W., & Erickson, F. Relations among verbal and nonverbal classroom behaviors. *Theory into Practice,* 1977, 16, 153–161.

Burnett, J. Event description and analysis in the microethnography of urban classrooms. In F. Ianni & E. Storey (Eds.), *Cultural relevance and educational issues.* Boston: Little, Brown, 1972.

Campbell, D. J., & Fiske, D. W. Convergent and discriminant validation by the multitrait-multimethod matrix. *Psychological Bulletin,* 1959, 56, 81–105.

Cazden, C. B., John, V. P., & Hymes, D. (Eds.). *Functions of language in the classroom.* New York: Teachers College Press, 1972.

Chomsky, N. *Aspects of the theory of syntax.* Cambridge, Mass.: M.I.T. Press, 1965.

Cicourel, A. V. *Method and measurement in sociology.* New York: Free Press, 1964.

Cicourel, A. V. *The social organization of juvenile justice.* New York: Wiley, 1968.

Cicourel, A. V. *Theory and method in a study of Argentine fertility.* New York: Wiley, 1974.

Cicourel, A. V., Jennings, S. H. M., Jennings, K. H., Leiter, K. C. W., MacKay, R., Mehan, H., & Roth, D. R. *Language use and school performance.* New York: Academic Press, 1974.

Cicourel, A. V., & Kitsuse, J. I. *The educational decision makers.* Indianapolis: Bobbs-Merrill, 1963.

Coleman, J. S., Campbell, E. Q., Hobson, C. J., McPartland, J., Mood, A., Weinfeld, F. D., & York, R. L. *Equality of educational opportunity.* Washington, D.C.: U.S. Government Printing Office, 1966.

Condon, W. The sound-film analysis of normal and pathological behavior patterns. *Journal of Nervous and Mental Disease,* 1966, 143, 338–347.

Dreeben, R. *On what is learned in school.* Reading, Mass.: Addison-Wesley, 1968.

Duncan, O. D., Featherman, D. C., & Duncan, B. *Socioeconomic background and achievement.* New York: Seminar Press, 1972.

Dunkin, M. J., & Biddle, B. J. *The study of teaching.* New York: Holt, Rinehart & Winston, 1974.

Erickson, F. Gatekeeping and the melting pot: Interaction in counseling encounters. *Harvard Educational Review,* 1975, 45, 44–70.

Ervin-Tripp, S. *Language acquisition and communication choice.* Palo Alto, Calif.: Stanford University Press, 1972.

Feldman, C. F. Two functions of language. *Harvard Educational Review,* 1977, 47, 282–293.

Frake, C. O. Plying frames can be dangerous: Some reflections on methodology in cognitive anthropology. *The Quarterly Newsletter of the Institute for Comparative Human Development, The Rockefeller University,* 1977, 1(3), 1–7.

Garfinkel, H. *Studies in ethnomethodology.* Englewood Cliffs, N.J.: Prentice-Hall, 1967.

Garfinkel, H., & Sacks, H. The formal properties of practical actions. In J. C. McKinney & E. Tiryakian (Eds.), *Theoretical sociology.* New York: Appleton-Century-Crofts, 1970.

Goffman, E. Replies and responses. *Internazionale di Semiotica e di Linguistica,* 1975, 46–47, 1–42.

Gumperz, J. J. Linguistic and social interaction in two communities. *American Anthropologist,* 1964, 66 (6, Pt. 2), 137–153.

Herrnstein, R. J. *IQ in the meritocracy.* Boston: Little, Brown, 1973.

Hymes, D. Models of the interaction of language and social life. In J. J. Gumperz & D. Hymes (Eds.), *Directions in sociolinguistics.* New York: Holt, Rinehart & Winston, 1972.

Jackson, P. *Life in classrooms.* New York: Holt, Rinehart & Winston, 1968.

Jencks, C., Smith, M., Acland, H., Bane, M., Cohen, D., Gintis, H., Heyns, B., & Michelson, S. *Inequality: A reassessment of the effect of family and schooling in America.* New York: Basic Books, 1972.

Jensen, A. R. How much can we boost IQ and scholastic achievement? *Harvard Educational Review,* 1969, 39, 1–123.

Leiter, K. C. W. Ad hocing in the schools. In A. V. Cicourel et al., *Language use and school performance.* New York: Academic Press, 1974.

MacKay, R. Conceptions of children and models of socialization. In P. P. Dreitzel (Ed.), *Childhood and socialization.* New York: Macmillan, 1973.

MacKay, R. Standardized tests: Objective and objectivized measures. In A. V. Cicourel et al., *Language use and school performance.* New York: Academic Press, 1974.

McDermott, R. P. *Kids make sense.* Unpublished doctoral dissertation, Stanford University, 1976.

Mehan, H. Assessing children's language using abilities. In J. M. Armer & A. D. Grimshaw (Eds.), *Methodological issues in comparative sociological research.* New York: Wiley, 1973.

Mehan, H. Accomplishing classroom lessons. In A. V. Cicourel et al., *Language use and school performance.* New York: Academic Press, 1974. (a)

Mehan, H. Ethnomethodology and education. In D. O'Shea (Ed.), *Sociology of the school and schooling.* Washington, D.C.: National Institute of Education, 1974. (b)

Mehan, H., & Wood, H. *The reality of ethnomethodology.* New York: Wiley-Interscience, 1975.

Mishler, E. G. Studies in dialogue and discourse: An exponential law of successive questioning. *Language in Society,* 1975, 4, 31–52. (a)

Mishler, E. G. Studies in dialogue and discourse II: Types of discourse initiated by and sustained through questioning. *Journal of Psycholinguistic Research,* 1975, 4, 99–121. (b)

Moore, G. *Life cycles in Atchalan.* New York: Teachers College Press, 1973.

Parsons, T. The school as a social system. *Harvard Educational Review,* 1959, 29, 297–318.

Philips, S. Some sources of cultural variables in the regulation of talk. *Language in Society,* 1976, 5, 81–96.

Radnitsky, G. *Contemporary schools of metascience.* Chicago: Henry Regnery, 1973.

Redfield, R. Culture and education in the midwestern highlands of Guatemala. *American Journal of Sociology,* 1943, 48, 128–142.

Rist, R. *The urban school: Factory for failure.* Cambridge, Mass.: M.I.T. Press, 1974.

Rosenbaum, J. *Making inequality.* New York: Wiley, 1976.

Roth, D. R. Intelligence testing as a social activity. In A. V. Cicourel et al., *Language use and school performance.* New York: Academic Press, 1974.

Sacks, H., Schegloff, E., & Jefferson, G. A simplest systematics for the organization of turn-taking in conversation. *Language,* 1974, 50, 696–735.

Scheflen, A. E. *Communicational structure.* Bloomington: Indiana University Press, 1972.

Sewell, W. H., Haller, A., & Portes, A. The educational and early occupational attainment process. *American Sociological Review,* 1969, 34, 82–92.

Sinclair, J. M., & Coulthard, R. M. *Toward an analysis of discourse.* New York: Oxford University Press, 1975.

Smith, L., & Geoffrey, W. *Complexities of an urban classroom.* New York: Holt, Rinehart & Winston, 1968.

Tylor, S. *Cognitive anthropology.* New York: Holt, Rinehart & Winston, 1972.

Warren, C. *Education in Rebhausen, a German village.* New York: Holt, Rinehart & Winston, 1967.

Wechsler, D. I. *Examiner's manual: Wechsler Intelligence Scale for Children.* New York: The Psychological Corporation, 1949.

Wolcott, H. F. *The man in the principal's office.* New York: Holt, Rinehart & Winston, 1973.

Wylie, L. *Village in the Vaucluse.* Cambridge, Mass.: Harvard University Press, 1957.

JEROME KARABEL and
A. H. HALSEY

The "New" Sociology
of Education

Questions to think about

1 *What is the "new" sociology of education? How is it similar to and different from the other theories discussed in this chapter?*

2 *What research questions might a sociologist using the "new" sociology of education perspective ask?*

3 *What parts of the open systems framework are relevant to the "new" sociology of education?*

4 *Select an educational problem of interest to you. Which of the theories discussed in this chapter would be most useful in studying the problem and why?*

Political and ideological events, including the intensification of struggles for educational reform and the recrudescence of racially linked genetic theories of intelligence in the 1960s, added urgency to the problem of explaining differential academic achievement. By and large, the macrosociological approaches, whatever their political and ideological correlates, had proved inadequate to the task, and the time was thus opportune for analytical invention. In Europe, the major promise lay in the attempts of Bernstein in England and Bourdieu in France to relate the problem of educability to that of socially controlled cultural transmission. Bernstein's arrival in 1963 at the London Institute of Education, in particular, played an especially crucial role in stimulating the emergence of a new approach focusing directly on the content of education and the internal operation of schools, which has come to be called the "new" sociology of education.

At the end of the 1960s, Berger and Luckman (1967), whose theory of the "social construction of reality" was already exerting a widespread influence on the large discipline of sociology, seemed to offer promising lines of inquiry. Variously calling themselves ethnomethodologists, phenomenologists, and symbolic interactionists, a network of research workers sharing a common suspicion of macrosociological analysis and a diffuse commitment to studies of educational content appeared on the scene. Some heralds (Young, 1971a; Gorbutt, 1972) announced the beginning of a revolution and the birth of a new sociology of education. This is a claim worthy of serious attention. . . .

By the early 1970s, a school of thought stressing the significance of the content of education had formed, and one of its members (Gorbutt, 1972) was describing it as "the new sociology of education"—an emergent "alternative paradigm." Previous work was dismissed as a "positivistic" version of structural functionalism using "input-output models" and a "normative paradigm." The "old" sociology of education was soon to be transcended. Davies, in his critique of Hopper's (1968:29–44) typology of educational systems, dismissed research on educational selection with the cavalier remark that while it had been very important for collecting data, "one may wonder whether it has done much more than improve our knowledge of social stratification and raise uncomfortable questions about the consequences of public policy" (1971:117). Organizational studies, on the other hand, though "superior to what normally passes for the sociology of education," have the defect of not "necessarily contributing to a sociology of knowledge," and any comparative study which ignores the analysis of education as culture is "in danger of trivializing the entire subject" (1971:124). Davies goes on to state explicitly that "the management of knowledge" should be the central concern of the sociology of education (1971:133).

M. F. D. Young, the editor of the first reader in the sociology of education devoted to the "interpretative paradigm," was also harshly critical of previous educational research. Even at its best, as in Westergaard and Little's study (1964) on educational opportunity and Lacey's (1970) investigation of grouping and selection procedures, the old sociology of education, "by treating as unproblematic what it is to be educated," does "little more than provide what is often a somewhat questionable legitimacy to the various pressures for administrative and curricular 'reform'" (Young, 1971a:2). In general, sociologists have taken educators' definitions of problems as given and have neglected the task of formulating their own problems. For the sociologist who undertakes this task, however, the "problems" identified by educators (e.g., the "below average child") are themselves phenomena to be explained. With "what counts as educational knowledge" highly problematic, the structural issues that dominated the normative paradigm recede into the background, and the microlevel problems of the "curricular, pedagogic and assessment categories held by school personnel," teacher-student interaction, and above all the curriculum become the dominant concerns of educational research. From this perspective, "the sociology of education is no longer conceived as an area of enquiry distinct from the sociology of knowledge" (Young, 1971a:3–5).

(a) THE SOCIAL ORIGINS OF THE INTERPRETATIVE CRITIQUE

Without judging the accuracy of these pronouncements about the history of educational research, and before embarking on a critical assessment of the new approach, it may be helpful to examine the context in which they emerged. Perhaps the most striking feature of the "new" sociology of education is that it is almost entirely a British creation and has so far made few inroads into American educational research. At first glance this is somewhat surprising, given the long and impressive tradition in the United States of classroom observation going back to Waller's 1932 classic, *The Sociology of Teaching*, and extending through Becker's (1952;1953) studies of the Chicago school teacher to Rist's (1970;1973) recent investigations of ghetto schools. Moreover, sociologists like Everett Hughes and others connected with the Chicago school of sociology have taught and written about phenomenology since before World War II. Nevertheless, the "new" sociology of education is a lively focus of debate in Britain and remains essentially unknown in the United States. . . .

The intellectual context of specialist work on education within the wider discipline of sociology also differed between the two countries. In America, the main candidate for new leadership after the disarray of the 1960s was conflict theory (Friedrichs, 1970:45–61). In Britain, however, the challenge came much more from the new interpretative approaches.

. . . The question still remains why interpretative approaches were so warmly received in Britain. One factor, it may be suggested, was that the "new" sociology of education identified itself with the sociology of knowledge. Always considered a rather marginal, continental pursuit by American sociologists, the sociology of knowledge has roots in Britain at least as far back as the arrival of Karl Mannheim in the 1930s. The growing interest of recent years may also reflect the closer proximity of British sociologists to their German and French colleagues and in part their relatively greater philosophical sophistication in comparison to American sociologists. Although only vaguely familiar with continental philosophy, British sociologists tend to be aware of the epistemological problems raised by logical positivism. This greater familiarity with analytic philosophy makes them more receptive to approaches that raise questions about the social and philosophical basis of knowledge. . . .

In attempting to understand the origins and development of the "new" sociology of education, it is important to realize that it emerged less in university departments of sociology than in institutes and colleges of education. The University of London's Institute of Education, where in 1963 Basil Bernstein developed the first program to give higher degrees in the sociology of education, seems to have played a particularly important role in the development of the interpretative approach, and the Open University, an institution that by its nature is much concerned with problems of pedagogy and curriculum, has been instrumental in disseminating its perspective to the academic public. When one considers the substantive concerns of the "new" sociology of education, it seems quite fitting that its institutional incubator was the institute of education. For unlike the functionalist and conflict theories of education, both of which are essentially concerned with the macrosociological question of the structure of the relationships between schools and other social institutions, the interpretative approach focuses directly on the internal operations of the schools themselves. The preoccupations of the "new" sociology of education—above all, classroom interaction and the sociology of the curriculum—correspond quite strikingly to the professional interests of students in institutions primarily devoted to training school-teachers. Proponents of the interpretative approach (Esland, 1971:111; Gorbutt, 1972:9–10) have, indeed, explicitly cited its relevance to teacher training as one of its virtues, and the effort of the "new" sociology of education to illuminate what goes on in the classroom is doubtless one of the sources of its appeal not only to students in schools of education but also to those sociologists whose job it is to teach them.

Having embarked upon their new course, advocates of the "new" sociology of education faced the formidable problem of legitimating their approach. Their difficulties resided not only in the newness of their formulation, but also in the fragility of the institutional base from which they operated. For if the sociology of education has relatively low status among the sub-disciplines of sociology, colleges and institutes of education also have low status as institutions for the aspiring sociologist. The "old" sociology of education dealt with the legitimation problem posed by the questionable character of its subject matter by attaching itself to the larger framework of the respected sub-discipline of social stratification. It was also assisted by its location within university departments of sociology. The new approach, with its main social base outside the universities, had no equally prestigious source of institutional support. Despite efforts to borrow status from the increasingly prominent but still marginal ethnomethodological and phenomenological approaches and from the rather esoteric sub-discipline of the sociology of knowledge, the "new" sociology of education still faced considerable legitimation problems.

Foremost among the tactics of proponents of the "interpretative paradigm" was the drawing of exceedingly sharp lines between "old" and "new" sociology of education. Through a series of bold attacks (Davies, 1969; Young, 1971b; Davies, 1971; Gorbutt, 1972) on the so-called normative (or "conventional") paradigm, the advocates of the interpretative approach offered an explicit challenge to the established sociology of education that could hardly be ignored. If the loudness with which they announced an impending revolution in educational research caused skepticism in some quarters, the promise of "new directions for the sociology of education" (the subtitle of Young's reader) aroused eager anticipation in others. Throughout, they strongly emphasized the innovative character of the ethnomethodological approach and its incompatibility with the "old" sociology of education. Indeed, their criticisms of traditional educational research raised a number of important issues, and their own formulation was a strikingly novel one. Though holding only a tiny base in the universities and possessing no serious body of empirical research derived from its theoretical framework, the "new" sociology of education was, by 1972, able to present itself plausibly as an "emergent paradigm" constituting a comprehensive alternative to the approach that had dominated the discipline for two decades.

(b) THE "NEW" SOCIOLOGY OF EDUCATION: AN EARLY ASSESSMENT

The interpretative approach has had a generally salutary effect on the sociology of education in Great Britain. Bernstein (1974:149) has recently noted that the traditional sociology of education in Great Britain "bore the hallmarks of British applied sociology; atheoretical, pragmatic, descriptive and policy focused." Primarily concerned with the structural problem of the relation between the educational system and the system of social stratification, research in the postwar years had had little to say about the content of education and had carried out few classroom studies. Emerging within a discipline that despite impressive accomplishments had seemingly lost its forward momentum, the challenge raised by the interpretative school has infused new life into the sociology of education by pointing not only to crucial theoretical problems, but also to new areas of research.

The "new" sociology of education is too new to permit a confident assessment of its contribution. Its influence so far derives less from research findings than from the distinctively different research priorities it proposes. If the concerns of the traditional sociology of education, most notably selection and socialization, are not quite relegated to the historical dustbin, it is nevertheless clear that they are now to be considered marginal to a discipline that looks upon the "management of knowledge" (Davies, 1971) as its central problem. With the "interpretative paradigm," itself deeply influenced by the sociology of knowledge, providing the theoretical framework of the "new" sociology of education, three related problem areas emerge as the key concerns of the field: teacher-student interaction, the categories or concepts used by educators, and the curriculum.

The problem of classroom interaction, a subject already treated in some detail by American symbolic interactionists, has excited considerable interest among those British sociologists of education influenced by the work of the ethnomethodologists. As yet, however, the excitement accompanying the identification of a neglected problem has not so far been followed by much empirical research. One notable exception is Keddie's (1971) article, "Classroom Knowledge." A study of the teaching of a course in the humanities at a large and heterogeneous comprehensive school, it is concerned with the knowledge teachers have of pupils and with what counts as knowledge suitable for discussion and evaluation in the classroom.

Keddie's study is an excellent expression of the interests of the "new" sociology of education, for in its search for the processes involved in the production of academic "failures" it looks simultaneously at teacher-student interaction, the categories used by educators, and the organization of the curriculum. Careful observation of teachers both inside and outside the classroom reveals that the concepts they hold, though often in contradiction with their aims as "educationalists," influence their relations with pupils in the classroom. The teacher will, for example, vigorously deny that ability is associated with social class and then proceed in concrete cases to suggest the most intimate relationship between social background and academic capacity. The concept of the "normal pupil" in a given ability category enables the teacher to categorize students about whom he has little direct knowledge and, accordingly, to treat identical student behavior in a radically different fashion, depending upon the category in which the student is placed. What counts as knowledge when suggested by an A (high ability) pupil may be dismissed as error or incomprehension in the case of a C (low ability) pupil. The differential treatment of pupils in different ability categories is, in turn, facilitated by a system of streaming that provides students with readily available labels. The internal structure of the school is thus shown to be closely related to a process of categorizing pupils that itself conditions interaction between student and teacher. Through the use of the interpretative approach, Keddie is able to show how the educators' socially constructed concepts systematically influence their behavior in the classroom. The outcome is "the differentiation of an undifferentiated curriculum" (1971:143), and it is clear from Keddie's account that the nature of this differentiation impedes the academic achievement of lower-stream and lower-class students.

In an appeal for sociologists to look at the curriculum as an expression of the principles governing the organization and selection of knowledge, M. F. D. Young (1971b) points to an important subject that had been largely ignored by the traditional sociology of education and makes a number of suggestions about the relationship between the stratification of knowledge and the distribution of values and rewards in society. However, Young has not attempted to apply his suggestions to the analysis of a specific problem, and few followers of the interpretative approach have engaged in systematic studies of the curriculum. Here, as in many other areas of educational research, the new sociology of education has identified an interesting problem and suggested a possible way of tackling it, but it has not yet produced either close ethnographic descriptions (Bernstein, 1974:152) or a serious body of empirical literature based on its theoretical framework. Unlike the conflict theory of education, which is well established in the United States, the "interpretative paradigm" has produced many new departures but disturbingly few arrivals.

The reasons for this failure are not immediately apparent, but the reluctance of the critic to offer his own positive formulation of a problem, thereby putting forward propositions that would themselves be subject to refutation, is a well-known phenomenon. Ethnomethodologists may have felt particularly vulnerable on this issue, for it is in the nature of their approach to be acutely aware of the methodological difficulties involved in social research.

Two of the key research issues identified by the interpretative approach—the curriculum and the concepts of educators—posed particular problems for the prospective researcher, for the novelty of the subject matter called for the creation of new methods. Even the more familiar problem of student-teacher interaction, already treated by symbolic interactionists, posed at every turn the thorny question of what counts as valid knowledge. Clearly, empirical investigation of the problems raised by the interpretative approach could not proceed with the type of "rigor" demanded by a discipline that accords scientific status only to those propositions that are replicable and falsifiable. Equally clearly, the "new" sociology of education would never generate data as tidy as the quantitative figures on social stratification produced in the political arithmetic tradition. Furthermore, careful and long-term classroom observation called for an enormous investment of time and energy. Faced with these formidable obstacles, it is quite understandable that proponents of the "new" sociology of education should have been more successful in criticizing existing research than in producing their own body of substantive propositions.

It would be misleading, however, to convey the impression that supporters of an ethnomethodological approach to the sociology of education have undertaken no systematic empirical research. An ambitious field study in Southern California public schools, for example, has been led by one of the founders of ethnomethodology itself—Aaron V. Cicourel—and published as a series of articles under the title *Language Use and School Performance* (1974).

Sensitive, as ethnomethodologists are, to the fragility of "commonsense constructs," the authors investigate some of the assumptions implicit in the evaluation of the academic "performance" of school children. Their focus is on the test situation itself as a socially constructed phenomenon, and they pay particular attention to the interaction between the examiner and the examinee. They take nothing for granted—neither the concepts and procedures of the tester nor the linguistic comprehension and performance levels of the tested. The study is based on careful classroom observation, and its detailed analysis of the testing process constitutes a rebuke to those who would reify the results of ostensibly scientific scholastic examinations.

Yet despite the relative novelty of the ethnomethodological approach and the freshness of some of its insights, the most striking thing about the study led by Cicourel is its frequent banality. Roth (1974), for example, demonstrates in considerable detail that the cognitive operations leading to an answer marked as incorrect are often more complex than those which result in an acceptable response. Cicourel (1974:331) finds it necessary to reiterate the study's finding that bilingual children have particularly acute problems in understanding test instructions. In article after article, the authors advance the well-worn idea that the social setting in which a test takes place influences student performance. When one compares the self-consciously innovative work presented in *Language Use and School Performance* with the research of such representatives of the "traditional" sociology of education as Strodtbeck (1961) or Kahl (1961), it is hard to see how the interpretative approach has advanced understanding of a problem for which it seems eminently apt—that of educability.

Sociologists of diverse theoretical and methodological persuasions are vulnerable to the charge that they spend much of their time documenting the obvious. The ethnomethodologists, however, are distinctive in presenting their empirical analysis of the well-known distortions of test performance introduced by social context and linguistic misunderstanding within a framework of extreme relativism. Reading the studies reported in Cicourel (1974), for example, one is left with the impression that the tests used to measure reading commprehension are arbitrary human constructs laden with so many class-linked measurement problems that they are essentially unrelated to the student's actual capacity to understand written material.

There is an obvious egalitarian appeal in the notion that recorded differences in reading level between rich and poor children would disappear if one were able to measure their academic performance accurately, but such a formulation strains the limits of credibility. Yet the ideological impetus behind ultra-relativism is a powerful one, for if sociologists cannot eradicate glaring inequalities in the real world, they can perhaps do away with them on the conceptual level by denying that they are, appearances to the contrary notwithstanding, inequalities after all. What would seem to be racial and class differences in the distribution of knowledge are, instead, figments of a positivistic imagination.

This reluctance to recognize visible differences in knowledge is, in part, a product of ethnomethodological epistemology; Gorbutt (1972:7) states the position succinctly when he writes that "knowledge . . . becomes thoroughly relativized and the possibility of absolute knowledge is denied." As a consequence of their belief that all knowledge is ideological (Gorbutt, 1972:7), ethnomethodologists find themselves in an awkward position when the subordinate social groups with whom they sympathize set out to diminish inequalities in the social distribution of knowledge which, were one to take seriously the semantic and conceptual acrobatics of the "new" sociology of education, do not exist. Ultra-relativism is a double-edged sword; while useful in denouncing such intellectually problematic and politically retrograde concepts as the "problem child," it can easily degenerate into what Goody and Watt (1963:344), referring to a similar tendency among their colleagues in anthropology, have called "sentimental egalitarianism." When it takes this form, relativism is of service neither to academic social science nor to the poor and minority groups it wishes to defend.

Perhaps the most powerful weapon wielded by ethnomethodologists in their assault on their archenemy—"positivistic" social science—is their critique of measurement techniques in conventional empirical research. The issues raised by Cicourel in *Method and Measurement in Sociology* (1964) have been familiar ones in sociology for over a decade, but only recently have they begun to penetrate educational research. Here the raising of basic problems about the collection and interpretation of data has proved extremely useful, for there has been a tendency over the years for sociologists of education to assume that evidence that is quantitative is automatically "scientific" in character. Ethnomethodologists have effectively deflated this myth, but their own criticism of measurement techniques often becomes a critique of the use of all statistical data.

Interpretative sociologists hold that social reality, which is "constantly in a state of becoming rather than being . . . is such as to preclude conventional social science approaches to data" (Gorbutt, 1972:6). In practice, this suspicion of quantitative evidence, coupled with a commitment to relativism, often leads ethnomethodologists to move from valid criticisms of measurement error to a wholesale dismissal of attempts to measure phenomena as diverse as academic performance and educational aspirations. If the ethnomethodologist's *bête noire*, the methodological empiricist, can be faulted for tending to believe that relationships that are not readily measurable are not quite real, the ethnomethodologist is guilty of concluding that relationships that *are* measurable, but imperfectly, are equally unreal. Opposites here converge. If the pure methodological empiricist characteristically avoids those phenomena that are difficult to quantify while the ethnomethodologist wages a relentless campaign of criticism against such efforts at measurement as have been made, there is a very real sense in which the one approach is the converse of the other. Their common coin is that of the obsessive search for rigor, and it is only an apparent paradox that they unite in their failure to observe C. Wright Mills's (1959) injunction against allowing the question of method to take precedence over the need to investigate pressing substantive problems.

The preferred method of the "new" sociology of education is that of participant observation (Gorbutt, 1972:7), though direct observation without participation is also looked upon with favor. These two research techniques require an intimate social setting, and they are well-suited to classroom investigations. Depending upon whether researchers draw their theoretical cues from ethnomethodology or from symbolic interactionism, they may speak of the "social construction of reality" or of the "definition of the situation," but their closely related concerns come together in sociological analysis of the process of "negotiation" over meanings. Above all, their careful observation of face-to-face relationships is designed to show that "everyday social interaction is a creative activity" (Cicourel, 1974:348) that enables man to make sense of his world.

Stress on the fact that relations in educational institutions are humanly constructed products is a welcome antidote to the deterministic and reifying tendencies of some of the "old" sociology of education. But emphasis on "man the creator" often fails to take adequate account of the social constraints on human actors in everyday life. There is, to be sure, a considerable latitude available to those engaged in struggles over the "definition of the situation," but the question of whose definition will ultimately prevail is preeminently one of *power*. Battles between students and teachers as to who will define the situation, for example, clearly illustrate this principle; teachers, by virtue of their powerful institutional positions, wield sanctions that not only delimit the boundaries of what may be "negotiated" but also give them a crucial advantage in determining whose "definitions" will prevail. The teachers themselves, however, also operate under external constraints; they may be prohibited by law from giving corporal punishment, and it is likely that they will lose their jobs if they do not follow prescribed evaluative procedures and curricular programs. There is, without doubt, an important element of creativity in student-teacher interaction; but there are also limits to the extent to which "definitions of the situation" may be negotiated.

The notion that "meanings" are created anew in every encounter in an educational institution contains an important element of truth, but it also diverts attention away from the tendency of interactions to occur in repetitive patterns. Teachers and children do not come together in a historical vacuum; the weight of precedent conditions the outcome of "negotiation" over meaning at every turn. If empirical work is confined to obeservation of classroom interaction, it may miss the process by which political and economic power sets sharp bounds to what is "negotiable." The classroom analyses of the "new" sociology of education are not, in short, related to *social structure,* and therefore tend to ignore the constraints under which human actors operate and so to exaggerate the fragility of the daily routine of school life.

Though a preference for microcosmic studies is at times elevated into a general principle, most proponents of the "new" sociology of education affirm the necessity of integrating structural and interactional levels of analysis. Keddie (1971:156), for example, points to a need to understand both "the linkages between schools and other institutions" and "the relationship between the social distribution of power and the distribution of knowledge." And M. F. D. Young (1971b:24) declares that "it is or should be the central task of the sociology of education to relate" the "principles of selection and organization that underlay curricula to their institutional and interactional setting in schools and classrooms to the wider social structure." To carry out such studies would be difficult, and the hostility of followers of the interpretative approach to structural analysis (extending, at times, to the suggestion that social structures exist only in the minds of human actors) suggests that the absence of serious attempts by them to articulate micro- and macrolevels of analysis is not purely a result of technical barriers. Indeed, acceptance of the idea that analyses of the structure and content of education must be integrated would give dramatic testimony to the complementarity of the methods and concerns of the "old" and "new" sociology of education.

What, then, is one to make of the claim that the "interpretative paradigm" marks the beginning of a "scientific revolution" in educational research? The careful reader of Kuhn (1970), from whom the model of a scientific revolution is derived, would be likely to react with skepticism, for one of the distinctive features of a true scientific revolution is its invisibility. When the transformation of a discipline is announced *before* the event, there is reason to suspect that one is witnessing not a scientific revolution but a more familiar phenomenon—an attempt by an emergent school of thought to legitimate its approach. According to Kuhn, scientific revolutions have historically entailed the restructuring of existing knowledge, *not,* as has been implied by proponents of the interpretative school, its dismissal (Eggleston, 1973). Only if the "new" sociology of education were able to incorporate into its framework the contribution of "traditional" educational research could it lay claim to scientific revolution. This it has been unable to do.

Instead of building incrementally on previous work, the "new" sociology of education has generally engaged in an adversary relationship to it. Davies (1971), for example, conveys the impression that those interested in the "management of knowledge" have little to learn from previous research, but loses sight of the fact that the studies of educational selection are, in a fundamental sense, about the distribution of knowledge (Smith, 1971:146). Eager to distance themselves from the "old" sociology of education, interpretative sociologists are slow to attend to the implications of the fact that much of the work of such researchers as Bernstein and Bourdieu, whose interests they cite as converging with their own, is rooted in the "normative paradigm." The research of Bernstein and Bourdieu, as well as that of Becker, Clark, and many others, suggests that the discontinuities between "old" and "new" sociology of education are not as dramatic as proponents of the "interpretative paradigm" would like to believe.

The skepticism with which sociologists working within the interpretative framework treat administrative definitions of educational problems would seem to give them an important degree of intellectual autonomy not present among many "traditional" educational researchers, but a situation may well develop in which followers of the "new" sociology of education would have an even more intimate relationship with the state than their more "conventional" colleagues ever enjoyed. The microcosmic analyses favored by interpretative sociologists are potentially more useful to educational policy-makers than any of the macrostructural research carried out by functionalists. Even methodological empiricism, said by Gouldner to be particularly well-suited to the research needs of the Welfare State, is only of limited usefulness to those who would solve the "official" educational problems of the day, for it, too, typically avoids the "black box" of schooling. Interpretative sociology, however, focuses precisely on those classroom processes that must be understood if there is to be any chance of reducing the class and racial differentials in academic achievement that concern the administrators of the Welfare State. The structural reforms of the educational system that were derived in part from macroscopic research have left behavior inside the school substantially unchanged; even such apparently radical structural reforms as abolishing streaming and establishing a common curriculum would, as Keddie (1971:156,158) has pointed out, have little effect on the hierarchical categories of ability and knowledge that are so damaging to the scholastic performance of the "low-ability" working-class student.

The possibility of an interpretative sociology of education aligned with the interests of educational policy-makers is thus apparent. Impelled by the problems raised by recent structural reforms in the educational system and by the intensity of debate, particularly in Great Britain, over what is to be learned in school, government administrators have recently developed a strong interest in the content of the educational process; for them, followers of the interpretative approach promise to deliver sociologically informed studies of the consequences of given types of curricular offerings. The continued existence of massive group differences in academic achievement is increasingly unacceptable both politically and ideologically. For officials in private and public bureaucracies who would like to see these inequalities diminished, the "new" sociology of education offers detailed investigations of student-teacher interaction that promise to identify the process by which such factors as the "self-fulfilling prophecy" (Rosenthal and Jacobson, 1968) influence student performance. If the sociology of education is ever to provide a basis for an applied sociology which effectively meets the needs of the Welfare State, it may come, paradoxically, neither from the functionalists nor from the conflict theorists, but from the "new" sociology of education whose point of departure was a criticism of the tendency of previous researchers to take the "official" educational problems of the day as their own.

For the moment, however, the interpretative approach does not offer a viable alternative for either the policy concerns of the Welfare State or the research needs of the sociology of education. Yet even though the promise of a "scientific revolution" has been, and is likely to remain, unfulfilled, the interpretative perspective on educational research has stimulated controversy in the field and has generated a number of new ideas. What is now needed is a concerted effort by adherents of the interpretative school to carry out the program of empirical research it implies and to link its findings with the structural studies that have traditionally dominated the sociology of education and that continue to move the subject forward. For despite the existence of important differences between the interpretative and normative approaches to the sociology of education, it would be deplorable if the heat of polemic made it impossible for advocates of each of the two perspectives to recognize the light a considered appraisal of their opponents' position could shed on the problems that now face educational research.

REFERENCES

Becker, Howard S. "Social-Class Variations in the Teacher-Pupil Relationship." *Journal of Educational Sociology* 25 (April 1952):451–465.

Becker, Howard S. "The Teacher in the Authority System of the Public School." *Journal of Educational Sociology* 26 (November 1953):128–141.

Berger, Peter L., and Thomas Luckman. *The Social Construction of Reality.* Harmondsworth, Middlesex: Allen Lane, 1967.

Bernbaum, Gerald. *Knowledge and Ideology in the Sociology of Education.* London: Macmillan, 1976.

Bernstein, Basil. "Social Class and Linguistic Development: A Theory of Social Learning." In *Education, Economy, and Society,* edited by A. H. Halsey et al., pp. 288–314. New York: Free Press, 1961.

Bernstein, Basil. "Education Cannot Compensate for Society." *New Society* 387 (February 26, 1970):344–347.

Bernstein, Basil. *Class, Codes and Control,* Volume One. London: Paladin, 1973a.

Bernstein, Basil, ed. *Class, Codes and Control,* Volume Two. London: Routledge and Kegan Paul, 1973b.

Bernstein, Basil. *Class, Codes and Control,* Volume Three. London: Routledge and Kegan Paul, 1975.

Bernstein, Basil. "Sociology and the Sociology of Education: A Brief Account." In *Approaches to Sociology,* edited by John Rex, pp. 145–159. London: Routledge and Kegan Paul, 1974.

Bourdieu, Pierre. "Cultural Reproduction and Social Reproduction." In *Knowledge, Education, and Cultural Change,* edited by Richard Brown, pp. 71–112. London: Tavistock, 1973.

Bourdieu, Pierre, and Jean-Claude Passeron. *La reproduction.* Paris: Les Éditions de Minuit, 1970.

Cicourel, Aaron V. *Method and Measurement in Sociology.* New York: Free Press, 1964.

Cicourel, Aaron V., et al. *Language Use and School Performance.* New York: Academic Press, 1974.

Clark, Burton R. "The 'Cooling-Out' Function in Higher Education." *American Journal of Sociology* 65 (May 1960):569–576.

Clark, Burton R. *Educating the Expert Society.* San Francisco: Chandler, 1962.

Davies, Ioan. "Education and Social Science." *New Society* 345 (May 8, 1969):710–711.

Davies, Ioan. "The Management of Knowledge: A Critique of the Use of Typologies in Educational Sociology." In *Readings in the Theory of Educational Systems*, edited by Earl Hopper, pp. 111–138. London: Hutchinson University Library, 1971.

Eggleston, John. "Knowledge and the School Curriculum." *Education for Teaching* 91 (Summer 1973):12–18.

Esland, Geoffrey M. "Teaching and Learning as the Organization of Knowledge." In *Knowledge and Control*, edited by Michael F. D. Young, pp. 70–117. London: Collier-Macmillan, 1971.

Friedrichs, Robert W. *A Sociology of Sociology.* New York: The Free Press, 1970.

Goody, Jack, and Ian Watt. "The Consequences of Literacy." *Comparative Studies in Society and History* 5 (July 1963):304–345.

Gorbutt, David. "The New Sociology of Education." *Education for Teaching* 89 (Autumn 1972): 3–11.

Gouldner, Alvin W. *The Coming Crisis of Western Sociology.* New York: Avon Books, 1971.

Hopper, Earl. "A Typology for the Classification of Educational Systems." *Sociology* 2 (January 1968):29–44.

Kahl, Joseph A. " 'Common Man' Boys." In *Education, Economy, and Society*, edited by A. H. Halsey et al., pp. 348–366. New York: Free Press, 1961.

Keddie, Nell. "Classroom Knowledge." In *Knowledge and Control*, edited by Michael F. D. Young, pp. 133–160. London: Collier Macmillan, 1971.

Kuhn, Thomas S. *The Structure of Scientific Revolutions*, 2nd ed. Chicago: The University of Chicago Press, 1970.

Lacey, Colin. *Hightown Grammar: The School as a Social System.* Manchester: Manchester University Press, 1970.

Mannheim, Karl. *Ideology and Utopia.* New York: Harcourt, Brace and World, 1936.

Mannheim, Karl. *Essays on the Sociology of Knowledge.* London: Routledge and Kegan Paul, 1952.

Mills, C. Wright. *The Sociological Imagination.* New York: Oxford University Press, 1959.

Rist, Ray C. "Student Social Class and Teacher Expectations: The Self-Fulfilling Prophecy in Ghetto Education." *Harvard Educational Review* 40 (August 1970):411–450.

Rist, Ray C. *The Urban School: Factory for Failure.* Cambridge, Mass.: The M.I.T. Press, 1973.

Rosenthal, Robert, and Lenore Jacobson. *Pygmalion in the Classroom.* New York: Holt, Rinehart and Winston, 1968.

Roth, David R. "Intelligence Testing as a Social Activity." In *Language Use and School Performance*, edited by Aaron V. Cicourel et al., pp. 143–217. New York: Academic Press, 1974.

Smith, Dennis. "Selection and Knowledge Management in Education Systems." In *Readings in the Theory of Educational Systems*, edited by Earl Hopper, pp. 139–158. London: Hutchinson University Library, 1971.

Strodtbeck, Fred L. "Family Integration, Values, and Achievement." In *Education, Economy, and Society*, edited by A. H. Halsey et al., pp. 315–347. New York: Free Press, 1961.

Waller, Willard. *The Sociology of Teaching*. New York: John Wiley and Sons, 1967.

Westergaard, John, and Alan Little. "The Trend of Class Differentials in Educational Opportunity in England and Wales." *British Journal of Sociology* 15 (December 1964):301–316.

Young, Michael. *The Rise of the Meritocracy*. London: Thames and Hudson, 1958.

Young, Michael F. D., ed. *Knowledge and Control*. London: Collier-Macmillan, 1971a.

Young, Michael F. D. "An Approach to the Study of Curricula as Socially Organized Knowledge." In *Knowledge and Control*, edited by Michael F. D. Young, pp. 19–47. London: Collier-Macmillan, 1971b.

SECTION TWO

What Goes on Inside the School System? Structure, Roles, and Processes

Schools usually produce the impression of a controlled situation in which people know where they fit and who is in charge. In the next three chapters we will look inside this organization and examine the structure, roles, and processes that constitute a school's internal system. To complete the picture, Section Three will focus on the external environment of schools.

CHAPTER 3

The School as an Organization

T hink about the organizations you belong to. They probably have constitutions, stated formal goals, criteria for membership, a hierarchy of officers, and a number of informal goals such as friendship and sharing of interests. Educational systems are the same. If we drew up a list of formal goals held by schools, we would find a great deal of overlap among them—the desire to educate pupils in basic skills, for instance. Variations exist as well, however, because goals must include not only those of general education but also those of the individual school, the community and family, the region and state, and the national system.

Like other formal organizations, schools also have membership; usually all children of certain ages in a geographical area are required to attend public schools. The hierarchy consists of administrators, teachers, staff, students, and often some breakdown within the major categories. Because schools also provide a gathering place for young people of similar ages, peer group formation is a latent function of schools as well.

This chapter will examine the internal organization of educational systems: structure, functions, and bureaucratic influences. It is important to realize, however, that no system exists in a vacuum. Although we can isolate a part of the system for examination, we must never lose sight of the importance of environmental influences, or that the organization exists within a larger system.

The articles in this chapter discuss educational organization levels from school districts to classrooms. Educational systems share characteristics with organizations in other sectors of society such as business and government. But they also have significant differences that can cause stresses for educational systems run on bureaucratic models, as David Rogers points out in his article. A clear description of the concept of bureaucracy applied to schools, using elements from Max Weber's "ideal-type bureaucracy" as a model, is found in David Goslin's account:

> (1) an increasingly fine division of labor, both at the administrative and teaching levels, together with a concern for allocating personnel to those positions for which they are best suited and a formalization of recruitment and promotion policies; (2) the development of an administrative hierarchy incorporating a specified chain of command and designated channels of communications; (3) the gradual accumulation of specific rules of procedure that cover everything from counseling and guidance to school-wide or system-wide testing programs and requirements concerning topics to be covered in many subjects such as history, civics, and social studies; (4) a de-emphasis of personal relationships between students and teachers and betweeen teachers and administrators, and a consequent reorientation towards more formalized and affectively (emotionally) neutral role relationships; and finally (5) an emphasis on the rationality of the total organization and the processes going on within the organization. In general the movement, particularly at the secondary school level, has been in the direction of the rational bureaucratic organization that is typified by most government agencies and many business and industrial firms.[1]

The educational system in our country has expanded dramatically from the early 1800s, when many small schools were scattered about the country, to today's extensive national system of schools. In the early industrial period, the level of economic and technological development in the United States demanded primarily unskilled workers; as industries expanded and more sophisticated technology was employed, however, laborers needed more training to run the machinery. Although it is desirable to have a perfect fit between the work force skill level and industrial needs, this has not always occurred. A lag often develops between the increasingly advanced technology and the educational system. Changes in one system (here economics) influence others (here education).

Educational goals of early settlers and the colonies centered on biblical literacy, and the content of education was similarly moralistic. Gradually states took an interest in education, and the Massachusetts Bay Colony passed the first compulsory education acts in 1647, requiring reading and learning of a trade. The various types of education available included apprenticeships, vocational training, and private schooling for wealthy children. As more education was needed, private and public high schools and colleges developed.

By 1865, common schooling was established in the United States, but there was no standardization of size, organization, or curriculum. From the turn of the century until today, public schooling has expanded rapidly to the point where centralized bureaucracies became necessary to coordinate school organization. Today 85 percent of students are taught in 20 percent of the school districts.

Typically, large school systems are structured within a hierarchy that extends from the board of education down to students:

Board of education

Superintendent

Principal

Teachers

Staff and aides

Students

Bureaucracies are common in large city school systems, but trying to meet the needs of diverse population groups is a nearly impossible goal.

The original concept of lay control has kept a foothold in the form of boards of education. Some large centralized educational bureaucracies, however, have become insulated and unresponsive to community needs. This circumstance has created demands for local autonomy, with each area controlling its own schools to meet local needs most effectively.

The issue of centralization versus decentralization of decision making is important at the local school district level. Large cities have diverse subcultures representing different educational needs; community, subculture, school, family, and individual goals may conflict. In his book *110 Livingston Street,* David Rogers addresses problems in the New York City Board of Education offices; he presents a view of professionalism undermined by centralized bureaucracy, individual and local needs frustrated and unmet. The New York City board has made revisions in its method of selecting board members and has given some local schools more autonomy, but the problems are mammoth and not easily solved.

A further examination of the school system as bureaucracy is presented by Phillip Schlechty, who points out the dilemma of professionals working in bureaucracies, hampered by rules and red tape in their efforts to make decisions. Schlechty compares bureaucratic and professional models of school organizations, and suggests that to understand schools, researchers should look at the degree of autonomy, student positions, and commitment and involvement in schools.

The individual school and classroom represent another level in the organizational structure. This is the place where the business of schools is carried on. Willard Waller's classic book *The Sociology of Teaching* describes the school as a unit: its organizational structure, political order, and authority structure; what distinguishes a school as a "cultural entity"; and the "we" feeling that develops in schools.

In the introduction to your text, several functions of education were discussed. *Functions* refer to the purposes and importance of educational systems for society; they are reflected in the goals of educational systems. In his article, Talcott Parsons uses a functional theoretical perspective to analyze the structure and functions of classrooms. This is a classic discussion of the school class as a social system. From elementary school (discussed here; the secondary school discussion is not included in this excerpt) throughout the pupil's experience, dual processes are taking place: socialization for adult roles and a selection-allocation process based on success in this socialization process. Parsons points out that social status derived from family background is important in this process, and schools tend to institutionalize differences brought to school from home. Families and schools share general values related to education, but attitudes toward means for achieving goals differ. Those children who experience high achievement in schools come selectively from higher social status groups; other groups would like to share in the success. (In Chapter 4, which discusses roles, we will explore why class and achievement are closely related.)

NOTE

1. David Goslin, *The School in Contemporary Society* (Glenview, Ill.: Scott, Foresman, 1965), p. 133.

DAVID ROGERS

The Professional
Bureaucracy

Questions to think about

1 *What does Rogers mean when he calls the school system a "sick" bureaucracy? How did the New York City school systems become this way?*

2 *Do you think the political hierarchy of schools is different from that of other organizations? Explain.*

3 *What are some implications of viewing the school as a closed system?*

4 *What are some possibilities for change that might reduce the problems in large, centralized school districts? Can any of these be applied to your school district?*

A MODEL OF BUREAUCRATIC PATHOLOGY

The New York City school system is typical of what social scientists call a "sick" bureaucracy—a term for organizations whose traditions, structure, and operations subvert their stated missions and prevent any flexible accommodation to changing client demands. It has all those characteristics that every large bureaucratic organization has, but they have been instituted and followed to such a degree that they no longer serve their original purpose. Such characteristics as (1) overcentralization, the development of many levels in the chain of command, and an upward orientation of anxious subordinates; (2) vertical and horizontal fragmentation, isolating units from one another and limiting communication and coordination of functions; (3) the consequent development of chauvinism

From David Rogers, *110 Livingston Street*, pp. 267–274. Copyright © 1968 by David Rogers. Reprinted by permission of Random House, Inc.

within particular units, reflected in actions to protect and expand their power; (4) the exercise of strong, informal pressure from peers within units to conform to their codes, geared toward political protection and expansion and ignoring the organization's wider goals; (5) compulsive rule following and rule enforcing; (6) the rebellion of lower-level supervisors against headquarters directives, alternating at times with overconformity, as they develop concerns about ratings and promotions; (7) increasing insulation from clients, as internal politics and personal career interests override interests in serving various publics; and (8) the tendency to make decisions in committees, making it difficult to pinpoint responsibility and authority are the institution's main pathologies.[1]

Such characteristics are exaggerations of a number of administrative patterns that may not be bad if they are not carried too far. In the New York City school system, however, they are carried to the point where they paralyze the system in the face of rapid social changes that demand new administrative arrangements and programs.

Though the term "bureaucracy" usually has negative connotations in popular usage, I am using it here in a neutral sense, referring simply to social patterns associated with large scale organizations. There can be "good" and "bad" bureaucracy, and much of my analysis of the New York City school system, using the social science model of bureaucratic pathology, will include examples of "bad" bureaucracy.

The school system is set up to function as a "professional" bureaucracy, manned by more than 59,000 teachers and several thousand administrators and technicians. But the term "professionalism" has been given so many meanings, especially in school-community controversies, that little meaningful communication any longer occurs when school officials and community groups try to resolve their differences.* If we use the term in its conventional sense to refer to a combination of expertise and service to clients, the bureaucratic structure of the New York City school system clearly undermines the professionalism of its personnel. Service to clients and to the community are often secondary considerations for school officials who are more preoccupied with their own careers.†

---

*The term has been used as a slogan by school officials to defend themselves against outside attack ("We are professionals, and you, as laymen, have no right to tell us what to do").

†Political scientist Victor Thompson observes in his *Modern Organizations:* "When officials are caught between demands or 'rights' of clients and tight administrative controls from above, dissociation from the clients and disinterest in their problems may seem to be the only way out of the dilemma. Client hostility, generated by what appears to be official emphasis on the wrong goals, creates tension. Inconsiderate treatment of the clients may become a device for reducing tensions and maintaining the cohesion of the officials." *Modern Organization,* New York: Knopf, 1961, p. 162.

This is to suggest, then, that "bad" bureaucracy is often associated with "bad" professionalism in the New York City school system, as, indeed, it is in many large civil service bureaucracies.[2] While it may be appropriate for teachers and supervisors to want a degree of autonomy from client pressures, as many professionals do, on grounds that they are better equipped to do the job of educating than laymen, they may use their autonomy for personal ends that do not include service to the community. Further, professionals who are protected from their clients are likely to be unaware of changes in their clients' needs. And bureaucratic pressures to follow particular curricula, texts, instructional methods, and administrative procedures, may prevent teachers and principals from actually educating. Bureaucracy and professionalism may be incompatible in the New York City schools.

If arresting the failure of the schools were just a question of revamping the bureaucracy, there might be more hope for improvement than there really is. But the situation is much more complex. The entire institution of public education, including teacher training, the professional associations, and the technology of teaching, contribute to the schools' failures. While teachers and principals may know more about education than most laymen, they don't know very much. There is no codified body of knowledge that educators can learn and apply, as there is in medicine and law. Teacher training institutions reflect this in their curriculum, which is based on questionable and unvalidated principles of education, learning, and child development. The fact that these institutions often disregard the rapid demographic and social changes of the city, incapacitates their graduates further. There is little expertise to apply, despite any myths to the contrary.

Furthermore, the quality of people who go into public education careers is not very high. The situation may well be changing, but traditionally education has attracted the mediocre students in the colleges, often of provincial, lower middle class outlook, a large proportion of whom were women marking time before getting married.*[3]

This combination of poor training and personal mediocrity is reflected in the limited confidence that many college educated, upper middle class people have in the public schools. Many regard Board of Education personnel as culturally and intellectually inferior, and send their children to private schools.

One has only to review the frustrating and tragic experiences of the system's many victims to realize how bad it is. Consider the case of a Puerto

---

*It is unlikely, however, that the situation will change that much, given the irrelevant and tedious education courses that are required for licensing and later promotions, and given the fact that New York City school teachers are at the mercy of the bureaucracy and given little autonomy and responsibility.

Rican mother with two children in schools on Manhattan's West Side.[4] Anyone who cares to can collect hundreds of case histories like this one:

> In the 5th grade, Billy did not seem to me to be reading as well as he should. In the Spanish Mothers Club at the school, we asked if remedial help could be given. There was only one remedial reading teacher so that only a few children could be helped. Then the Club asked if Columbia students could help. In the meantime I took Billy to Columbia myself for reading assistance. In March I went to see the teacher to find out how Billy was doing. The teacher said "very well." He will soon be reading a 5th grade book. In May I received a letter from the Assistant Principal asking me to come to school about Billy. I was told that Billy could not go to the 6th grade because he was reading on a 3.0 level. I was very upset and angry because it seemed to me that the school had done nothing for Billy. He stayed in the 5th grade for another six months. We continued the tutoring but the school gave him no additional help. If I had not found a way to help him, nobody else would have helped him. He is now in 10th grade and still has a reading problem which hurts his other studies.
>
> When he went into the New York School of Printing, he needed algebra and science in order to take an academic program. The junior high school had told him that he would have an academic program. But when he got to high school, they refused to give it to him because he did not have these subjects. It was only through his and my persistence that they finally permitted him to take the academic program.
>
> In kindergarten, Grace could read Billy's first grade reader. When she went to the first grade, she never received a reader. When I asked the teacher why, she said that Grace wasn't ready yet. In the first half of second grade, she had a good teacher and books. In the second half, a new teacher came in. She did not give her much work. In the third grade, the teacher told me that she was a brilliant child and warned me to be careful. She feared that Grace might be hurt by other teachers. She tried to help her and told me to get her help at Columbia. . . . For 4th grade the teacher tried to have Grace put into a "good" class. She was not successful. Instead, she was put into a class where she fell behind—she read the same books she had read in the 3rd grade. When the 3rd grade teacher asked the 4th grade teacher why she was using the same books, the 4th grade teacher became angry with Grace. In the 5th grade Grace seemed to do better. She had a teacher of Puerto Rican background and read 5th grade books. But in the 6th grade she tested at 4.6. The teacher did not give too much work. When I saw the teacher, he said Grace was "blocked." He seemed to feel it was because we spoke Spanish

at home. In February, I noticed that Grace had nothing written in her notebook. She said that they were doing nothing in class. I spoke to the Assistant Principal about it. He looked at two notebooks from the class and saw that I was right. He was sorry about it but seemed to have no reason for it. I asked to have Grace's class changed. They asked me which class I wanted her in. I said a "good class" and they transferred her to a class with a teacher who taught. But this teacher told Grace that she didn't belong in her class. I told her not to worry and she remained in the class, where she did well. In March, the teacher in charge of a new program of teaching Spanish, asked Grace to take the program. Her 6th grade teachers said Grace could never make it. Grace insisted upon taking the program because she reads Spanish. She took the test for the program and passed it. She went on to the 7th grade even though her reading test showed a 4th grade level. She was never given any remedial reading in school.

She is now in the 9th grade and studies Spanish. Grace wants to be a teacher. We've been struggling not to make any mistakes so that she will be able to go to an academic high school. The junior high school wanted her to take General Math. She had to fight to get algebra. We knew enough to fight because of what happened to Billy and we won the fight.

WHY HAVE I HAD TO TAKE MY CHILDREN FOR OUTSIDE HELP? AND WHY DO THEY HAVE TO FIGHT TO GET THE KIND OF EDUCATION THEY WANT? I HAVE LEARNED HOW TO PROTECT MY CHILDREN AND IT IS STILL BAD. BUT WHAT ABOUT THE THOUSANDS OF MOTHERS WHO DON'T KNOW WHAT IS HAPPENING TO THEIR CHILDREN IN THE SCHOOLS?

BUREAUCRATIC CENTRALISM

Many of the pathologies of the New York City school system can be traced to the overcentralization of decisions, combined with the proliferation of specialized administrative units. Most decisions on such matters as curriculum, staffing, budgeting, supplies, construction, and maintenance are made by professionals at central headquarters, several layers removed from the schools themselves.[5] The headquarters personnel who make decisions do not know the problems directly, while district superintendents, principals, and teachers who do have some direct knowledge have never had the authority to adjust, experiment, and innovate, though a few adventurous types have taken it upon themselves to run their schools or classrooms as they see fit, without reference to headquarters.

Like any large bureaucracy that has to establish generalized rules for its field units, the Board of Education has a system of formulas and applies programs to schools as the schools fit into particular classifications—special service, transitional, segregated Negro–Puerto Rican, mid-range, segregated white. The system does not take into account gradations within each category, and so it minimizes its flexibility and effective use and distribution of supplies and personnel. While it may be important for large bureaucracies like this one with so many field offices and operating units to categorize and generalize about situations, they do so here with disastrous results. The categorizations are too gross, and many local variations and problems are overlooked.[6]

The NYC Board of Education is thus the prototype of what students of administration call "top down" rather than "bottom up" management.[7] Instead of looking at the particular school and community (with particular ethnic, socio-economic groups, local resources and institutions) and saying "here is a school and community, now let's work with parent and community groups to set up an appropriate program," they say "here is a program, now let's see where it can go." Too many schools and communities have their own particular problems that do not fit into standard formulas and programs.

Originally there were valid administrative reasons for centralization— to guarantee uniform standards across the city, to preserve professional autonomy from outside political interference at the local level, to prevent ethnic separatism, and to maintain headquarters control over field officials.[8] Also, the sheer size and geographic spread of the system contributed to centralization. Many headquarters officials distrust field personnel and hesitate to delegate authority.

Another reason for centralization was the complexity of the social and psychological problems the system faced. Numerous agencies have been formed over the years—such as the Bureau of Child Guidance, the Bureau for Children with Retarded Mental Development, the Bureau of Physically Handicapped, the Bureau of Socially Maladjusted Children, the Bureau of Speech Improvement, the Bureau of Visually Handicapped, the Bureau of Community Education, the More Effective Schools Program, the Bureau of In-Service Training, the Offices of Zoning, Integration, and Human Relations to deal with these problems. These bureaus in themselves may be necessary, although they often may obstruct education.

The school budget has also led to increased centralization. The difficulties of getting allocations in the budget for more staff led to the practice of transferring more and more teachers to headquarters. Many were eager to escape the trials and stresses of the classroom and, in some cases, the authoritarian rule of the principal. This practice is now reportedly being reversed, but the net effect of the policy change is still limited. There are still nearly 700 teachers on assignment at headquarters, and federal programs will add to the number.[9] Many teachers at headquarters are engaged in tasks for which they are not trained, in auditing, business affairs, programming, human relations, and demographic analysis. There are also cases of teachers at headquarters who direct and monitor research studies, and some teachers perform jobs that could be done by a lower level clerical person. The existence of such headquarters positions helped drain away many competent people from the classroom, while contributing to incompetent and inefficient administration.*

The centralized set-up created other obstacles to efficient administration too. The grouping of units and personnel at headquarters violates many basic principles of rational administration, creating little unity of command, much duplication and overlapping of responsibilities, and confusion on who should report to whom.

Positions and tasks were simultaneously grouped along both divisional (elementary, junior high, high) and functional (curriculum, instruction, staffing) lines.[10] Field officials often receive numerous directives, some of them contradictory, from different sources. A publisher finds, for example, that his curriculum materials are welcomed by the board, the superintendent, and the divisions, yet they are not acceptable to some curriculum official who invokes a state education law to justify his authority. A music teacher wants to serve in a ghetto school, but instead gets assigned to a white, middle class school in Queens. When an opening appears in a southeast Bronx school, the Queens principal will not let her go, threatening to give her a bad rating if she leaves. When she goes to headquarters to plead her case before the deputy superintendent in charge of personnel, it takes her a day before she can reach his secretary, and she never does get to see him. Parents who go to headquarters to inquire about zoning regulations are often shunted from office to office without getting any clear answer to their requests.[11]

This pattern of multiple authority hampers the efforts of field personnel to integrate various programs, confronted as they often are with buckpassing when making requests at headquarters for information, facilities, and support. It results in considerable frustration in securing services and much resentment among community groups, local school board members and field officials.

*It may also be true, however, as many informants in the system suggested, that putting teachers into headquarters jobs was one of the few ways to unburden the classrooms of incompetents.

NOTES

1. See Victor Thompson, *Modern Organizations*, New York: Knopf, 1961; Michel Crozier, *The Bureaucratic Phenomenon*, Chicago: University of Chicago Press, 1964; Robert K. Merton, "Bureaucratic Structure and Personality," in his *Social Theory and Social Structure*, Glencoe, Ill.: The Free Press, 1957, pp. 195–207; Chester I. Barnard, "The Functions and Pathologies of Status Systems," in William F. Whyte, ed., *Industry and Society*, New York: McGraw-Hill, 1946, pp. 46–83; James Worthy, "Organizational Structure and Employee Morale," *American Sociological Review*, April, 1950, pp. 169–79; F. L. W. Richardson and Charles Walker, *Human Relations in an Expanding Company*, New Haven: Labor and Management Center, 1948; and Warren G. Bennis, *Changing Organizations*, New York: McGraw-Hill, 1966. My "sick bureaucracy" model was derived from these works.

2. For social science writings on "bureaucracy" and "professionalism," see Howard M. Vollmer and Donald L. Mills, eds., *Professionalization*, Englewood Cliffs, N. J.: Prentice-Hall, 1966.

3. W. W. Charters, Jr., "The Social Background of Teaching," in N. L. Gage, ed., *Handbook of Research on Teaching*, Chicago, Rand McNally, 1963, pp. 718–723.

4. A case study written up for civil rights groups.

5. Marilyn Gittell, *Participants and Participation*, Center for Urban Education, 1967, chapters 4–6; and *Reconnection for Learning: Report of the Mayor's Advisory Board on Decentralization of the New York City Schools*, 1967; Cresap, McCormick, and Paget, *The New York City Board of Education, Organization of the School System*, August 1962; George Strayer and Louis Yavner, *Administrative Management of the School System of New York City*, 1951.

6. Inteviews with school officials, principals.

7. See Eliot D. Chapple and Leonard R. Sayles, *The Measure of Management*, New York: Macmillan, 1961. The term "bottom-up" management was originally coined by a business executive, William B. Given, Jr., of the American Brake Shoe Company, in his book, *Bottom-up Management*, New York: Harper & Brothers, 1949.

8. Interviews with school officials.

9. Interviews with headquarters officials.

10. See Cresap, McCormick, and Paget, *op. cit.*, chapter 2, p. 18; and Strayer and Yavner, *op. cit.*

11. These are not hypothetical examples, but come from many actual situations.

PHILLIP C. SCHLECHTY

Teaching and
Social Behavior

Questions to think about

1 *What are some conflicts for students in the school organization? For teachers? What structural factors contribute to these conflicts?*

2 *Relate what you have learned from this article to Rogers' discussion of the New York City school system.*

3 *What kinds of role expectations do teachers and students have from within the school system? From the environment?*

4 *Describe your position and the position of teachers in the organizational typology described by Schlechty.*

DEVELOPING A TYPOLOGY OF SCHOOLS

Schools can be usefully categorized in terms of two broad features of the school organization: the mode of organization that prevails in the school and the position students occupy *vis-à-vis* the boundaries of the schools.

Mode of organization[1] may be thought of as consisting of two elements: (1) the degree to which bureaucratic and professional expectations are present and effective and (2) the degree to which classrooms reflect structural looseness or structural tightness. The *position of students* in the school can be conceptualized in terms of (1) the degree to which students are identified as products, clients, and members and (2) the extent to which students are alienative, calculative, or moral in their involvement. Placing

From Phillip C. Schlechty, *Teaching and Social Behavior: Toward an Organizational Theory of Instruction* (Boston: Allyn & Bacon, 1976), pp. 84–100. Reprinted by permission of the author.

these variables on a two-dimensional matrix results in thirty-six distinct cells, each cell reflecting a different combination of boundary and expectational variance (see Table 1). For example, cell 1 is a school (or subunit in a school) characterized by bureaucratic expectations, structural tightness, and a morally involved student body who are defined as members. Cell 36 suggests a school (or subunit in a school) characterized by professional expectations, structural looseness, and an alienated student body identified as products.

EMPLOYEE EXPECTATIONS— BUREAUCRATS AND PROFESSIONALS

The nature of teachers' roles in school and in society has had considerable discussion in past years; but much of the discussion has lacked precision and clarity. Some, for example, do not distinguish between teacher role expectations that have their locus in the larger society and those role expectations that more clearly have their locus in the organizational structure of the school.[2] Unfortunately, many who study teachers' classroom roles disregard the fact that the teachers' role performance in the classroom may be interpretable only if one refers to the expectation structure within the school building or school district.[3]

The typology developed in the present chapter leans heavily on Corwin's[4] conceptualization of the differences between bureaucratic and professional modes of school organizations (see Table 2). The framework provided by Corwin assumes that whatever else the teacher is, the teacher is an employee of the school system. Teachers are not individual entrepreneurs, nor do they engage in private practice, although there is a compelling set of norms to uphold the teachers' freedom of action and freedom of decision making.[5] In school there is considerable allegiance to the idea that the teacher, by virtue of training and calling, should behave as and be treated as a professional. However, if the teacher is a professional, he is a professional in a bureaucratic setting. Expectations of the teacher as a professional have considerable significance in some schools and with some teachers, but in other schools and with other teachers it is clear that the dominant expectations are those of the teacher as bureaucrat.[6] Corwin notes, however, "An association (school) may be simultaneously organized around contradictory employee and professional principles. . . ."[7]

By way of example, consider the expectation of loyalty to one's superiors as compared with loyalty to clients. According to Corwin, a professional mode of organization would be high on loyalty to clients, but a bureaucratic organization would be high on loyalty to superiors.[8] In the short run it may be possible to uphold both sets of expectations. So long

TABLE 1
A Typology of Schools Based on Variance in Social Boundaries and Mode of Organization

POSITION OF STUDENT			MODE OF ORGANIZATION			
			Bureaucratic		Professional	
			Tight	*Loose*	*Tight*	*Loose*
Member		*Moral*	1	2	3	4
		Calculative	5	6	7	8
		Alienative	9	10	11	12
Client		*Moral*	13	14	15	16
		Calculative	17	18	19	20
		Alienative	21	22	23	24
Product		*Moral*	25	26	27	28
		Calculative	29	30	31	32
		Alienative	33	34	35	36

T A B L E 2
Contrasting Characteristics of Professional and Employee Modes of Organization

Continuum	Bureaucratic-Employee Expectations		Professional Expectations	
	High	*Low*	*High*	*Low*
Standardization	Stress on uniformity of clients' problems		Stress on uniqueness of clients' problems	
	Routine of Work			
	Stress on records and files		Stress on research and change	
	Continuity of Procedure			
	Rules stated as universals or rules specific		Rules stated as alternatives or rules diffuse	
	Specificity of Rules			
Specialization	Stress on efficiency of technique / Task orientation		Stress on achievement of goals / Client orientation	
	Specialization on the Basis of Function			
	Skill based primarily on practice		Skill based primarily on knowledge	
	Monopoly of Knowledge			
	Decisions concerning application of rules to routine problems		Decisions concerning professional policy and unique problems	
	Responsibility for Decision Making			
Authority	Punishment-centered administration		Representative administration	
	Centralization of Authority			
	Rules sanctioned by the public		Rules sanctioned by powerful and legally sanctioned professions	
	Loyalty to the organization and to superiors; authority from office		Loyalty to professional associations and clients; authority from personal competence	
	BASIS OF AUTHORITY			

Adapted from Ronald G. Corwin, *A Sociology of Education: Emerging Patterns of Class, Status, and Power in the Public Schools* (New York: Appleton-Century-Crofts, 1965), p. 232.

as administrators do not require actions that violate the teacher's view of what is "good for students," there is no reason for the teacher to behave in a way that is "disloyal" to superiors.

The question, therefore, is not simply one of whether the teacher is more or less loyal to superiors or students. It is also a question of whether those in authority hold the same expectation for students as does the teacher; what will happen if the teacher acts in a way that contradicts the commands of the principal; and how one comes to know which orientation is the appropriate one to apply in a given situation. In the situation where teachers hold the expectation that they should be loyal to their students and systematically behave in a manner that reflects this loyalty, the critical question of whether—on the dimension of loyalty—the school is bureaucratic or professional hinges on three facts. (1) Do administrative superiors of the teacher share the teacher's definition of the situation? (2) If they do not, do they attempt to enforce their own expectations through the systematic application of sanctions? (3) If they do apply sanctions, are they successful in inducing more conformity to their (the administrators') expectations? Schools in which administrators have bureaucratic expectations and are successful in gaining conformity to them are best typified as bureaucratic. Where administrators hold the view that teachers should be expected to behave as professionals, the key lies in the degree to which teachers conform to these expectations. If teachers insist on bureaucratic performance and are successful in their resistance to professional demands, the school continues to be best typified as a bureaucracy. On the other hand, if teachers share professional expectations with the administration, the school would be more appropriately categorized as professional.

Critical to the distinction of the school as a bureaucracy or a professional organization is the degree to which bureaucratic and professional expectations effectively regulate the school and classroom behavior of teachers. Schools can be typified as bureaucratic even when administrators make sincere efforts to create an environment in which the teachers will uphold professional expectations.[9] Conversely, teachers may well perceive themselves as professionals, develop elaborate evasion strategies to avoid bureaucratic expectations, perhaps engage in systematic and extreme forms of nonconformity (e.g., strikes), yet continue to behave as and be treated as bureaucratic employees.

STRUCTURAL LOOSENESS AND TIGHTNESS

The concept of structural looseness, as it is used here, means the degree to which the social unit under consideration (e.g., classroom or building) is characterized by autonomy of action.

Elementary school classrooms evidence a great deal more "structural looseness"[10] than do high school classrooms, or so it seems. But the degree to which classrooms are autonomous units within schools and school buildings varies not only with grade levels but from school to school. Some high schools may be more like some elementary schools (in terms of structural tightness and looseness) than they are like other high schools.

Bureaucratic modes of organization probably create conditions that are more conducive to structural tightness than structural looseness; however, the fact that a school is bureaucratic in its organizational form does not predetermine the existence of a structurally tight arrangement. Bidwell, for example, points out three ways in which routinization can be accomplished, only one of which necessarily results in a structurally tight bureaucratic arrangement. The first means identified by Bidwell is "the interweaving of staff orientations with professional norms and local school system policies, thus maximizing the commitment of teachers and school principals with such commitments."[11]

In this case the situation suggested here could be either "loose" or "tight," depending upon the degree to which professional norms were upheld by external as opposed to internalized sources of control. In some schools, the orientation of teachers may be such that they seek out bureaucratic authority and react with frustration when they do not feel that it is sufficiently present.[12] In these situations, whatever professional expectations permeate the classroom are more likely to be the result of outside enforcement of professional norms than the internalization of those norms within the classroom.

Because the concept of autonomy is so often used in conjunction with the idea of professionalism, it may be difficult to imagine a situation in which a professional mode of organization could exist in conjunction with structural tightness. On the surface, at least, the idea of structural tightness seems antithetical to professionalism. Yet, there is a sense in which this is not so.

Professionalism is not necessarily synonymous with "every one doing his own thing." Professionalism does not mean the absence of rules, sanctions, and norms for performance. Rather, it means that the rules, sanctions, and norms derive from some assumed basis of knowledge and expertise instead of being allocated to particular positions within the organization. The professional is autonomous only insofar as the norms, values, and performance standards of the profession are not violated. For example, a modern physician who insisted on continuing the practice of "bleeding" patients would—hopefully—quickly lose the right to practice.

In the school setting it is possible to conceive of situations in which the activities of any particular classroom might be carefully monitored and regulated by "outsiders," yet in which professional norms were rigorously upheld. Such a situation would be most likely to arise when a pattern of differentiated staffing had developed as a result of genuine and demonstrable differences in competence and training. In such a situation it would be likely that paraprofessionals might carry the bulk of the responsibility for implementing decisions at the classroom level, but at the same time these individuals would be only peripherally involved in making the critical decisions concerning what actions should be taken. Such situations—though probably rare—would fall into the professional-structurally tight category.

The second and third means identified by Bidwell by which schools can establish and maintain routine performance are more typically bureaucratic in nature. These are the following:

(a) the establishment of standards of student accomplishment prerequisite to movement from grade to grade, that is examinations which constrain the performance of teachers as well as of students;

(b) and the bureaucratization of school and classroom activities by rules of procedure which restrict the discretionary autonomy of classroom teachers or school staffs.[13]

Clearly, when bureaucratization of routines proceeds to the point that the discretionary autonomy of classroom teachers or school staffs is severely limited, the situation is best described as structurally tight. Yet, it is possible to bureaucratize most of the activities of schools without directly intervening in the activities of the classroom. Perhaps the most common way of bureaucratizing routines and maintaining structural looseness is by giving careful and systematic attention to "output" measures such as standardized examination scores and routine promotion policies. Bureaucratization probably tends to push schools toward structural tightness, but there are many other factors in schools (e.g., the professional orientations of teachers) that work to maintain structural looseness, even in bureaucratic environments.

STUDENTS—PRODUCTS, CLIENTS, AND MEMBERS

The position the student holds in relation to the organizational boundaries of the school is frequently discussed as a matter of philosophic preference or categorical definition. The present discussion proceeds from the assumption that students' boundary positions are determined by social definitions that obtain in the classroom, the school building, and/or the school district. Few schools consider very young children to be members of the school organization. The idea of membership carries with it some recognition of moral commitment, reciprocal obligations, shared goals, and a sense of belonging or community. (Very young children do not belong to the school; they belong to their family.) Very soon, often on the first day of school, some of the child's loyalty to the family is shifted to the teacher.[14] Indeed, some families begin the process of transferring the loyalties of children to school authorities, particularly teachers, long before children enter school. The process by which this is accomplished varies, but many have observed the tendency of middle class parents to take opportunities to point out to preschool children how nice, how good, and how right teachers are. "In a sense, parents are particularly occupied with forcing the child to develop so that he can leave the family."[15] The process that families start (shifting loyalties from home) is continued by the teacher. Using the loyalty students come to feel toward them as adult authorities, primary school teachers set about the delicate task of encouraging children to become loyal to ever more abstract symbols, beliefs, and customs.[16]

Student *membership* in school organizations is symbolized quite early in the lives of school children. Some children are given positions of "responsibility" (e.g., hall monitors, school patrol, and lunch money collection); others are not. As time goes on, some students become more and more integrated into the grain and fiber of the school, and they come to be viewed as members of the school community. However, many students never really become morally committed to the school and are therefore unwilling to take up the responsibility and obligations of membership.[17] Furthermore, in later school years schools become increasingly task and performance oriented, and the inclusion of all students as members may have dysfunctional consequences. Thus, both students and schools differentiate between students who are members and those who are not.

Membership is a reciprocal notion. The member accepts obligations and responsibilities to be sure, but the group also has obligations and responsibilities to the member. Students, as members of the school or the class, are in a position to make demands on the system, and they are also in a position of moral obligation to the system. Membership provides privileges as well as obligations. Privilege subverts control. Thus, as the control needs of the school increase and as the personal authority of teachers diminishes, the definition of student membership in school becomes increasingly restrictive. Students who were treated as members of their third grade class (and thus indirectly as members of the school) find themselves defined by the school as "outsiders." Certainly, some students retain their membership rights very late in their school careers. In most schools, however, the student position as member becomes an increasingly restricted category and significantly more demanding on those who would occupy it.

For example, in early school years about all that membership requires is that one passively submit to the teacher's authority and where the larger school intervenes, one must recognize the authority of those in charge (e.g., the principal). By junior high school, passive submission is not enough. Active performance and supporting actions are required. Students who do only that which is expected or required of all students are seldom seen as members of schools. To qualify for membership in later school years, students must show more than routine performance in academic matters. Students must also be actively involved in functions the school provides, such as clubs, athletics, and perhaps student government, and they must indicate a willingness to serve the interest of the school *even at some personal sacrifice.*[18]

Among the things students may be called on to sacrifice are the allegiances, friendships, and loyalties developed in earlier school years. As performance and task become more important, so does impersonal and objective evaluation. For example, the boy who, in the sixth grade, could well be designated a school boy patrolman because he was mature and responsible—even if only a C student—may, in high school, be excluded from office in student government because his grade point does not meet the required 2.5 average. It is not improbable that this young man (and there are many such) will see a friend[19] (perhaps from his old neighborhood elementary school) encouraged to seek student office while he (the C student) is discouraged or prohibited from doing so. Eventually, those who are members of the school organization will find themselves in the same clubs, the same classes—indeed at the same parties and in the same student hangouts.[20] Those who are not members may also find a common base of group action, and most will come to accept the fact that they are "outsiders."

The idea of the student as client of the school has almost as much support in the ideology and traditions of educators as does the idea of student as member. The need for teachers to identify themselves as professionals makes a client's view a comfortable one. However, whether one is a client of an organization is not determined by one's own definition of reality or even one's commitment to the organization. Rather, clientship has to do with the way categories of participants are defined by the organization. Members are inside the organization and clients are outside, but clients can and do have claims on the organization.

The basic distinctions between students as members and students as clients are to be found in differences on the boundary dimensions of scope, pervasiveness, permeability, and cohesiveness. In relative terms, for students who are members, the scope of the organization is likely to be wide. The number of social actions over which the school exercises some control—or attempts to exercise some control—will be relatively great. For the client, the scope of the organization will be more restricted. For example, athletic squad members often find that their dating, eating, and sleeping habits are regulated by the school; students who are not involved in athletics are not likely to be so regulated. For the client, the pervasiveness of the school organization is likely to be low. The client is unlikely to be given much direction about how to proceed to use the services extended. Rather, the services will be offered, and it is up to the client to use them. For members, on the other hand, performance expectations are more likely to be specified. It is accepted that members should do certain things in certain ways, and it is the responsibility of the organization to assure that this is done. If a member's performance falls below the expected level, it is a reflection on the organization as well as the member. On the other hand, students classified as clients are often told that "an education is here for you if you want to do what we suggest, but we cannot make you do it." Members are likely to get more positive direction. If a client fails, it is likely to be considered the fault of the client; if a member fails, *particularly if a significant number of members fail,* the teacher or school may begin serious appraisal to locate the organizational source of the problem. Furthermore, members, even low-level members, are likely to have more impact on the behavioral expectations applied in a given situation than are clients. School boundaries and classroom boundaries are more permeable through students considered as members than through students considered as clients. When students who are defined as clients attempt to influence areas the school considers within its boundaries, the matter is likely to be treated as a boundary threat and counteraction will be taken. When student members attempt to influence or change policy, the action is more likely to be considered a legitimate part of the organizational process. For example, the student council—with the approval of the advisor—may make recommendations about dress codes that will be positively received by the administration. (The students may indeed be congratulated and assured that this is the way democracy really works.) On the other hand, students identified as clients would probably be less likely to receive positive responses from "insiders." More likely, their suggestions would be treated as unwarranted invasions of boundaries.

The degree to which student members are likely to interact with each other outside school (a measure of cohesiveness) probably will be higher than is the case for clients. Clients are likely to have more diffuse peer groups, at least diffuse in terms of the particular population from which membership is drawn. Almost by definition, members will have more task-related interactions than will clients.

In addition to the student as member and client, there is a third category into which schools sometimes place students. That is the category of product. The most significant boundary dimension for distinguishing products from clients and members is pervasiveness. The degree to which the behavior of student *as product* is monitored, checked, and controlled is very high. Students as products find that those areas considered within the scope of the school are narrowly proscribed and prescribed. The range of deviation tolerated is small, the standards are explicit, and the performance required is generally known throughout the system. Frequently, a product orientation is reflected in the attention to individualization of instruction, diagnostic testing, and reliance on behavior modification techniques. Indeed, the language of behavior modification (reinforcement schedules, contingency plans, and criterion referenced instruction) gives attention to the uniformity of the end result.[21] For example, in addressing themselves to the utility of defining teachers in training as products, Howsam and Houston write:

> In a competency-based program, the emphasis is placed on exit rather than entrance requirements. With this approach, the possibility is opened for admitting a wider variety of persons to the group entering the program. Continual assessment of progress, optional choices of learning experiences and performance criteria within the program make entrance requirements far less crucial than they are in traditional programs. Many who previously would have been precluded from entrance by their cultural development or by their previous educational choices and performance safely can be admitted to the competency-based program. Many of these students may be expected to enter and to complete successfully such a program. The result can be a wholesome diversity of backgrounds in the teaching profession.[22]

Though contradictions and paradoxes are apparent in such thinking, Houston and Howsam's statement represents a mode of thought that is coming to dominate teacher education. Whether these human engineers will supplant diversity of means as they have already supplanted diversity of ends is a subject that needs to be given serious thought by educators who value democracy as much as efficiency and accountability. It is difficult to understand how treating students as products and people as things can be nearly as humanizing and liberating as those like Houston and Howsam claim it to be.

STUDENT COMMITMENT—ALIENATIVE, CALCULATIVE, AND MORAL

Involvement or commitment reflects the degree to which participants in the life of organizations define their position *vis-à-vis* the organization in terms of a positive affinity toward the organization or a negative orientation toward it.

In regard to involvement Etzioni writes: "The intensity of involvement ranges from high to low. The direction is either positive or negative."[23] Etzioni then goes on to define three types of involvement, each type representing a zone on a continuum from high-positive to low-negative involvement. Etzioni writes:

> Alienative involvement designates an intense negative orientation; it is predominant in relations among hostile foreigners. . . . Inmates in prisons, prisoners of war, people in concentration camps, enlisted men in basic training, all tend to be alienated from their respective organizations. . . .
>
> Calculative involvement designates either a negative or a positive orientation of low intensity. Calculative orientations are predominant in relationships of merchants who have continuous business contracts. . . .
>
> Moral involvement designates a positive orientation of high intensity. The involvement of the parishioner in his church, the devoted member to his party, and the loyal follower in his leader are all "moral." . . .
>
> . . . Pure moral commitments are based on internalization of norms and identification with authority (like Riesman's inner-directed "mode of conformity").[24]

Student commitment to the school organization and to subunits within the school (e.g., classrooms, athletic teams, and so on) can be characterized as alienative, calculative, and moral. There is, furthermore, considerable utility in such a classification of students. This classification permits one to consider student orientation toward school as a significant independent variable. It also opens up new avenues through which motivation and control may be studied, for as Etzioni makes clear, the type of involvement participants have in an organization is directly related to the kinds of power and authority that will be effective with them. In later chapters this will be explored in detail.

USING THE TYPOLOGY: HOW AND WHERE IT MIGHT BE APPLIED

Rather than precise descriptions of reality, typologies are ways of organizing reality into manageable proportions. Typologies necessarily ignore some differences in order to point up selected common features. Those who employ typologies must be conscious of what is being looked at and what is being ignored. Two considerations are paramount in the use of any typology: (1) the level at which the typology is to be applied, and (2) the criterion or criteria appropriate to inclusions or exclusion from any of the categories upon which the typology is based.

The typology suggested here lends itself to application at the building level and at the district level. With some modification and cautions, it can also be applied to units within school buildings, such as classrooms and student organizations. When the building level is the unit of analysis, the determination of structural tightness and looseness is made with reference to the degree of automony of action at the classroom level. If school units other than classrooms are of interest, then determinations about structural tightness are made in terms of the units under study. For example, if the interest is to compare behavior in various student government arrangements, one might characterize the student government in terms of structural looseness and tightness in much the same way as the classroom is characterized. For example, to what extent is the decision making within the governmental framework autonomous from other parts of the school structure, and to what extent is it dependent on the approval of "outside" authority?

The determination of participants would be all of those who are high on at least one of three dimensions—commitment, performance, and subordination.[25] Students, by definition, are always participants in the life of the school and the classroom, for they will always be high on subordination if not on the other two variables. Whether students are best categorized as products, clients, or members is determined by the way in which students are related to the social boundaries of the unit under study. As elementary classrooms take on social system characteristics, some students will clearly be "within" that system, and others outside, perhaps either as an audience or as potentially interfering groups. In classrooms with system qualities, all students who are defined as in the system are also members of the school.

At the high school level, however, the situation may be quite different. Students in a particular classroom may reflect relational patterns that characterize the group as having distinct and separate qualities from the school. Indeed, the student group may be related to the school in a way that suggests either a client or a product orientation. For example, students in a special education class may come to develop recognizable in-group loyalties, and relate to other students in the school in terms of those loyalties. But *as a group*, the special education students might be systematically defined as "nonmembers" of the school organization, at least as indicated by measures of scope, pervasiveness, cohesiveness, and permeability. Thus, if the unit of analysis is a classroom, it might be well to include some students as members who would not be viewed as members at the school or district level.

Alienative, calculative, and moral involvement has to do with the degree of commitment of students to the behavioral expectations that have their locus at the organizational level under study. For example, students committed to school organizations like athletic squads would, by definition, be less alienated from school (more positively committed) than students who have no unit in the school system to which they feel a positive commitment. Highly committed students would be characterized as morally involved while mildly alienated, or mildly committed, students would be categorized as calculative.

In general, then, determinations about the boundary dimensions of the typology are measured in terms of scope, pervasiveness, permeability, and cohesiveness. Indicators of expectational dimensions (e.g., bureaucratic or professional) are measures of variance in distribution, enforcement transmission, and conformity.

PLACING SCHOOLS

Making determinations about the correct placement of empirical illustrations of each of the thirty-six types of schools is a matter that stands in need of considerable attention. At present all that exists are some commonsense guidelines. (1) Whatever determination is made, judgments about the placement of the school unit must be made in terms of all the participants of the unit being studied (e.g., one could not use the typology at the building level and then exclude, *a priori,* some students who attend the school). (2) Most schools will represent "mixed" types rather than pure reflections of the typology. For example, schools where most students could be categorized as members will be likely to have some student participants who are alienated. (3) Alternative measures should be employed, depending on the purposes of using the category system. For example, in regard to student involvement, it may be useful to consider categorization from several perspectives. One means of categorizing students would be to develop a measure of involvement that would run from alienation to strong positive (moral) commitment. All student participants could be assessed in terms of commitment and the school judged to be alienative, calculative, or moral on the basis of some mean score of "involvement." An alternative means would be to categorize students into one of the three groups (alienative, calculative, and moral) and consider the category with the greatest participant representation to be the category that best typifies the organizational mode of the school.

Perhaps the most important guideline to placing schools is to remember that the function of ideal types and typologies is to illuminate reality and to facilitate generalization. It is neither useful nor necessary that a typology describe *precisely* any single occurrence.

NOTES

1. The basic concepts upon which the typology is based (i.e., the ideas of bureaucratic and professional expectations, structural tightness and looseness, the student as product, client, and member and the student as alienative, calculative, or morally involved) will be elaborated and developed in the pages that follow.

2. Robert J. Havighurst and Bernice L. Neugarten, *Society and Education*, ed. 4 (Boston: Allyn & Bacon, Inc., 1975), chapters 19 and 20. Havighurst and Neugarten present one of the more useful discussions of teacher roles, but their discussion is limited to description and does not move to a level of precise analysis.

3. One of the limitations of most of the work done by Flanders and those who have followed his lead is that little attention has been given to factors outside the classroom—but within the school—that might account for some of the variances he has reported in teacher classroom behavior. See, for example, E. J. Amidon and N. A. Flanders, *The Role of the Teacher in the Classroom* (Minneapolis: Paul Amidon and Associates, 1963).

4. Ronald G. Corwin, *A Sociology of Education: Emerging Patterns of Class, Status, and Power in the Public Schools* (New York: Appleton-Century-Crofts, 1965).

5. See Charles E. Bidwell, "The School as a Formal Organization," in *Handbook of Organizations*, ed. James G. March (Chicago: Rand McNally & Company, 1965), especially pp. 972–978.

6. Ibid.

7. Corwin, *A Sociology of Education*, p. 230.

8. Ibid.

9. On the basis of some research findings one could reasonably infer that some teachers might resist professional expectations on the grounds that the latitude of decision making creates too much ambiguity and thus a feeling of powerlessness and frustration. See, for example, Gerald H. Moeller, "Bureaucracy and Teachers' Sense of Power," *Administrators Notebook*, November 11, 1962.

10. Bidwell, "The School as a Formal Organization," develops the concept of structural looseness and applies it to schools (pp. 972–1022).

11. Ibid, p. 976.

12. See the earlier reference to Moeller, "Bureaucracy and Teachers' Sense of Power."

13. Bidwell, "The School as a Formal Organization."

14. See Robert S. Dreeben, *On What Is Learned in School* (Reading, Mass.: Addison-Wesley Publishing Co., 1968).

15. William J. Goode, *The Family* (Englewood Cliffs, N. J.: Prentice-Hall, Inc., 1964), p. 73.

16. Dreeben, *On What Is Learned in School*.

17. Dreeben (see preceding note) suggests that teachers often overestimate the extent to which students have internalized the reward structure of the school.

18. Waller's discussion of the role of martyrs in the life of schools, though perhaps overdrawn, is instructive. See Willard Waller, *The Sociology of Teaching* (New York: John Wiley & Sons, Inc., 1932, reprinted 1967), p. 129.

19. There is something quite sad about the ways school organizations disrupt loyalties and friendships established in the neighborhood school. Perhaps such disruptions are necessary to the socialization and educative process, but it is only the callous who fail to see pathos in the plight of the child who finds a friend moving away from him simply because one is a C student. Yet, C students do not participate in the organizational life of the school the way A students do. Perhaps "hard nosed" educators are correct when they say "that's the way it is in real life," but that is a debatable point.

20. David H. Hargreaves, *Social Relations in a Secondary School* (New York: Humanities Publishing Company, 1967).

21. The "systems approach" to school administration and curriculum development, with emphasis on input, output, and throughput, is often found in conjunction with performance contracting, competency-based programs, and behavior modification techniques.

22. Robert B. Howsam and W. Robert Houston, "Change and Challenge," in *Competency-Based Teacher Education: Progress, Problems and Prospects*, ed. Houston and Howsam (Chicago: Science Research Associates, Inc., 1972), p. 9.

23. Amitai Etzioni, *A Comparative Analysis of Complex Organizations: On Power, Involvement, and Their Correlates*. Copyright © 1961 by The Free Press of Glencoe, Inc., p. 9.

24. Ibid., pp. 10–11. Etzioni makes a distinction between pure moral commitment and social moral commitment. The distinction is not made here, as much of the distinction is picked up in the discussion of social exchange strategies and psychological strategies, which follows shortly.

25. This closely parallels Etzioni, *Comparative Analysis of Complex Organizations*.

WILLARD WALLER

The School as a
Social Organism

Questions to think about

1 *How does Waller describe the political structure of the school? Do you think this political structure is different from that of other organizations?*

2 *What theoretical perspective do you consider most closely related to Waller's discussion?*

3 *Compare Waller's description with those of Parsons and Rogers. Why are schools likely to be small "cultures"?*

4 *Why can a school be viewed as a closed system? What are the implications of viewing schools as closed systems?*

The school is a unity of interacting personalities. The personalities of all who meet in the school are bound together in an organic relation. The life of the whole is in all its parts, yet the whole could not exist without any of its parts. The school is a social organism[1]; it is this first and most general aspect of the social life of the schools which we propose to deal with in this chapter. As a social organism the school shows an organismic interdependence of its parts; it is not possible to affect a part of it without affecting the whole. As a social organism the school displays a differentiation of parts and a specialization of function. The organism as an entirety is nourished by the community.

Changing the figure slightly, the school is a closed system of social interaction. Without pedantry, we may point out that this fact is of importance, for if we are to study the school as a social entity, we must be able to distinguish clearly between school and not-school. The school is

Reprinted from Willard Waller, *The Sociology of Teaching* (New York: Russell & Russell, 1961), pp. 6–13; originally published in 1932. Copyright © John Wiley & Sons, Inc.

in fact clearly differentiated from its social milieu. The existence of a school is established by the emergence of a characteristic mode of social interaction. A school exists wherever and whenever teachers and students meet for the purpose of giving and receiving instruction. The instruction which is given is usually formal classroom instruction, but this need not be true. The giving and receiving of instruction constitutes the nucleus of the school as we now think of it. About this nucleus are clustered a great many less relevant activities.

When we analyze existing schools, we find that they have the following characteristics which enable us to set them apart and study them as social unities:

1. They have a definite population.
2. They have a clearly defined political structure, arising from the mode of social interaction characteristic of the school, and influenced by numerous minor processes of interaction.
3. They represent the nexus of a compact network of social relationships.
4. They are pervaded by a we-feeling.
5. They have a culture that is definitely their own.

Schools differ widely in the degree to which they show these traits and in the manner in which they are combined. Private boarding schools exemplify them all in the highest degree. They have a stable and homogeneous population; the original homogeneity, produced by economic and social selection, has been enhanced by intimate association and common experiences. They have a clear and explicit political organization, sometimes expressed in a book of rules and a long line of precedents. The persons of the school live very close to each other, and are bound each to each by an intricate maze of crisscrossing social relationships. Intimacy of association, stability of the group, the setting apart of the group by a distinctive dress and its isolation from other cultural influences, combine to make possible a strong feeling of unity in such a school; it has often been remarked that a private school has something of the solidarity of the family. The isolation of the school from the remainder of the community, and the richness of the life which its members lead in their close-packed association, make the culture developed in such a school pronounced and distinctive.

The private day school sometimes represents such a closed corporation, and shows up very clearly as a social unit. It may not, for the day school is sometimes nothing more than a painless substitute for public school for the children of wealthy parents. But in the ideal case the private day school may be a functioning unity much more clearly marked off from the rest of the world than is the public school.

The various kinds and conditions of public schools differ in the degree to which they are recognizable and delimitable social units. The one-room country school is obviously such a unit. So likewise is the great suburban high school, and the high school of the small city described in *Middletown*. Sometimes, however, the public school is so split into divergent social groups that the underlying unity is somewhat obscured. This is possible where the school population is drawn from several sources and where there is no school program capable of welding these groups together.

The school has, as we have said, a definite population, composed of those who are engaged in the giving or receiving of instruction, who "teach" or "are in school." It is a relatively stable population and one whose depletion and replacement occur slowly. Population movements go according to plan and can be predicted and charted in advance. A bimodal age distribution marks off teachers from students. This is the most significant cleavage in the school.

The young in the school population are likely to have been subjected to some sifting and sorting according to the economic status and social classification of their parents. The private schools select out a certain group, and there are specializations within the private schools, some being in fact reformatories for the children of the well-to-do, and some being very exacting as to the character and scholastic qualifications of their students. The public schools of the exclusive residence district are usually peopled by students of a limited range of social types. Slum schools are for slum children. Country schools serve the children of farmers. In undifferentiated residence districts and in small towns which have but one school the student population is least homogeneous and most representative of the entire community.

The teaching population is probably less differentiated. In part, this is because the variation from the teacher type must be limited if one is to teach successfully. There is nevertheless considerable variation in the training and ability of teachers from one school to another and one part of the country to another. Teachers the country over and in all schools tend to be predominantly selected from the rural districts and from the sons and daughters of the lower middle classes. The teaching population is in some schools more permanent than the student population. There is nevertheless a large turnover among the teachers.

The characteristic mode of social interaction of the school, an interaction centered about the giving and receiving of instruction, determines the political order of the school. The instruction which is given consists largely of facts and skills, and of other matter for which the spontaneous interests of students do not usually furnish a sufficient motivation. Yet teachers wish students to attain a certain mastery of these subjects, a much higher degree of mastery than they would attain, it is thought, if they were quite free in their choices. And teachers are responsible to the community for the mastery of these subjects by their students. The political organization of the school, therefore, is one which makes the teacher dominant, and it is the business of the teacher to use his dominance to further the process of teaching and learning which is central in the social interaction of the school.

Typically the school is organized on some variant of the autocratic principle. Details of organization show the greatest diversity. Intra-faculty relations greatly affect the relations between teachers and students. Where there is a favorable rapport between the teachers and the administrative authorities, this autocracy becomes an oligarchy with the teacher group as a solid and well-organized ruling class. It appears that the best practice extends the membership in this oligarchy as much as possible without making it unwieldy or losing control of it. In the most happily conducted institutions all the teachers and some of the leading students feel that they have a very real voice in the conduct of school affairs.

Where there is not a cordial rapport between school executives and teachers, control becomes more autocratic. A despotic system apparently becomes necessary when the teaching staff has increased in size beyond a certain limit. Weakness of the school executive may lead him to become arbitrary, or it may in the extreme case lead some other person to assume his authority. The relationship between students and teachers is in part determined by intra-faculty relationships; the social necessity of subordination as a condition of student achievement, and the general tradition governing the attitudes of students and teachers toward each other, set the limits of variation. But this variation is never sufficient to destroy the fact that the schools are organized on the authority principle, with power theoretically vested in the school superintendent and radiating from him down to the lowest substitute teacher in the system. This authority which pervades the school furnishes the best practical means of distinguishing school from not-school. Where the authority of the faculty and school board extends is the school. If it covers children on the way to and from school, at school parties, and on trips, then those children are in school at such times.

The generalization that the schools have a despotic political structure seems to hold true for nearly all types of schools, and for all about equally, without very much difference in fact to correspond to radical differences in theory. Self-government is rarely real. Usually it is but a mask for the rule of the teacher oligarchy, in its most liberal form the rule of a student oligarchy carefully selected and supervised by the faculty. The experimental school which wishes to do away with authority continually finds that in order to maintain requisite standards of achievement in imparting certain basic skills it has to introduce some variant of the authority principle, or it finds that it must select and employ teachers who can be in fact despotic without seeming to be so. Experimental schools, too, have great difficulty in finding teachers who are quite free from the authoritarian bias of other schools and able to treat children as independent human beings. Military schools, standing apparently at the most rigid pole of authority, may learn to conceal their despotism, or, discipline established, may furnish moments of relaxation and intimate association between faculty and students, and they may delegate much power and responsibility to student officers; thus they may be not very much more arbitrary than schools quite differently organized, and sometimes they are very much less arbitrary than schools with a less rigid formal structure. The manifestations of the authority principle vary somewhat. The one-room country school must have a different social structure from the city high school with five thousand students, but the basic fact of authority, of dominance and subordination, remains a fact in both.

It is not enough to point out that the school is a despotism. It is a despotism in a state of perilous equilibrium. It is a despotism threatened from within and exposed to regulation and interference from without. It is a despotism capable of being overturned in a moment, exposed to the instant loss of its stability and its prestige. It is a despotism demanded by the community of parents, but specially limited by them as to the techniques which it may use for the maintenance of a stable social order. It is a despotism resting upon children, at once the most tractable and the most unstable members of the community.

There may be some who, seeing the solid brick of school buildings, the rows of nicely regimented children sitting stiff and well-behaved in the classroom or marching briskly through the halls, will doubt that the school is in a state of unstable equilibrium. A school may in fact maintain a high morale through a period of years, so that its record in the eyes of the community is marred by no untoward incident. But how many schools are there with a teaching body of more than—let us say—ten teachers, in which there is not one teacher who is in imminent danger of losing his position because of poor discipline? How many such schools in which no teacher's discipline has broken down within the last three years? How many school executives would dare to plan a great mass meeting of students at which no teachers would be present or easily available in case of disorder?

To understand the political structure of the school we must know that the school is organized on the authority principle and that that authority is constantly threatened. The authority of the school executives and the teachers is in unremitting danger from: (1) The students. (2) Parents.

(3) The school board. (4) Each other. (5) Hangers-on and marginal members of the group. (6) Alumni. The members of these groups, since they threaten his authority, are to some extent the natural enemies of the person who represents and lives by authority. The difficulties of the teacher or school executive in maintaining authority are greatly increased by the low social standing of the teaching profession and its general disrepute in the community at large. There is a constant interaction between the elements of the authoritative system; the school is continually threatened because it is autocratic, and it has to be autocratic because it is threatened. The antagonistic forces are balanced in that ever-fickle equibrium which is discipline.

Within the larger political order of the school are many subsidiary institutions designed to supplement, correct, or support the parent institution, drawing their life from it and contributing in turn to its continued existence. These institutions are less definitely a part of the political structure, and they mitigate somewhat the rigidity of that structure by furnishing to students an opportunity for a freer sort of social expression. These ancillary institutions are organizations of extra-curricular activities, and comprise such groups as debating societies, glee clubs, choral societies, literary societies, theatrical groups, athletic teams, the staff of a school paper, social clubs, honorary societies, fraternities, etc. They are never entirely spontaneous social groupings but have rather the character of planned organizations for which the major impetus comes from the faculty, generally from some one member of the faculty delegated to act as "faculty adviser." These "activities" are part of that culture which springs up in the school from the life of students or is created by teachers for the edification of students. Such groups are often hardly less pervaded by faculty control than classroom activities, and there seems a tendency for the work of such institutions to be taken over by the larger social structure, made into courses and incorporated into the curriculum. Perhaps the worst that can happen to such organizations, if they are viewed as opportunities for the spontaneous self-expression of students, is that they shall be made over into classes. But the school administrator often thinks differently; from his point of view, the worst that can happen to such groups is that they shall become live and spontaneous groups, for such groups have a way of declaring their independence, much to the detriment of school discipline.

The political order of the school is characterized by control on three levels. Roughly, these are:

1. Theoretical. The control of the school by the school board, board of trustees, etc.
2. Actual. The control of school affairs by school executives as exerted through the teaching force or directly.

3. Ultimate. The control of school affairs by students, government resting upon the consent, mostly silent, of the governed.

The school is the meeting-point of a large number of intertangled social relationships. These social relationships are the paths pursued by social interaction, the channels in which social influences run. The crisscrossing and interaction of these groups make the school what it is. The social relationships centering in the school may be analyzed in terms of the interacting groups in the school. The two most important groups are the teacher-group and the pupil-group, each of which has its own moral and ethical code and its customary attitudes toward members of the other groups. There is a marked tendency for these groups to turn into conflict groups. Within the teacher-group are divisions according to rank and position, schismatic and conspirital groups, congenial groups, and cliques centering around different personalities. Within the student-groups are various divisions representing groups in the larger community, unplanned primary groups stair-stepped according to age, cliques, political organizations, and specialized groups such as teams and gangs. The social influence of the school is a result of the action of such groups upon the individual and of the organization of individual lives out of the materials furnished by such groups.

A rough idea of some of the more important social relationships arising in the school may be derived from the following schema:

I. Community-school relationships
   1. Relation of community to school in general. (Mediated through tradition and the political order of the community.)
   2. Relation of community to students individually and in groups. The parental relation and the general relation of the elders of the community to the young.
   3. Relation of community to teachers.
   4. Relation of special groups in the community to the school. (The school board, parent-teacher clubs, alumni, self-constituted advisory groups, etc.)
   5. Relation of special individuals to the school. (Patrons, ex-teachers, patriarchs, hangers-on, etc.)
II. Pupil to pupil relationships as not affected by the presence of teachers.
   1. Pupil to pupil relationships.
   2. Pupil to pupil-group relationships.
   3. Pupil-group to pupil-group relationships.
III. Teacher-pupil relationships. (Including also pupil to pupil relationships as affected by the presence of teachers.)

    1. Teacher to pupil-group relationship. (The customary classroom situation.)
    2. Teacher to pupil relationship.
    3. Pupil to pupil relationship as affected by the presence of the teacher.
IV. Teacher to teacher relationships.
    1. Relation of teacher to teacher.
        a. Teacher to teacher relationship as not affected by the presence of students.
        b. Teacher to teacher relationship as affected by the presence of students.
    2. Relation of teacher to teacher groups.
    3. Relation of teacher groups to teacher groups.
    4. Relation of teaching force to administrative officers.

Note: All these relationships are reciprocal.

The school is further marked off from the world that surrounds it by the spirit which pervades it. Feeling makes the school a social unity. The *we*-feeling of the school is in part a spontaneous creation in the minds of those who identify themselves with the school and in part a carefully nurtured and sensitive growth. In this latter aspect it is regarded as more or less the property of the department of athletics. Certainly the spirit of the group reaches its highest point in those ecstatic ceremonials which attend athletic spectacles. The group spirit extends itself also to parents and alumni.

A separate culture, we have indicated, grows up within the school. This is a culture which is in part the creation of children of different age levels, arising from the breakdown of adult culture into simpler configurations or from the survival of an older culture in the play group of children, and in part devised by teachers in order to canalize the activities of children passing through certain ages. The whole complex set of ceremonies centering around the school may be considered a part of the culture indigenous to the school. "Activities," which many youngsters consider by far the most important part of school life, are culture patterns. The specialized culture of the young is very real and satisfying for those who live within it. And this specialized culture is perhaps the agency most effective in binding personalities together to form a school.

TALCOTT PARSONS

The School Class as a Social System: Some of Its Functions in American Society

Questions to think about

1 *What functions of schooling are carried out in the classroom? How are they carried out?*

2 *How do family and family background interact with a child's school experience? What aspects of educational organizations account for the split between school and family?*

3 *What factors affect the elementary child's achievement in school? How does achievement relate to future chances?*

This essay will attempt to outline, if only sketchily, an analysis of the elementary and secondary school class as a social system, and the relation of its structure to its primary functions in the society as an agency of socialization and allocation. While it is important that the school class is normally part of the larger organization of a school, the class rather than the whole school will be the unit of analysis here, for it is recognized both by the school system and by the individual pupil as the place where the "business" of formal education actually takes place. In elementary schools, pupils of one grade are typically placed in a single "class" under one main teacher, but in the secondary school, and sometimes in the upper elementary grades, the pupil works on different subjects under different teachers; here the complex of classes participated in by the same pupil is the significant unit for our purposes.

From *Harvard Educational Review* 29 (1959), 297–313. Copyright © 1959 by the President and Fellows of Harvard College. All rights reserved.

THE PROBLEM: SOCIALIZATION AND SELECTION

Our main interest, then, is in a dual problem: first of how the school class functions to internalize in its pupils both the commitments and capacities for successful performance of their future adult roles, and second of how it functions to allocate these human resources within the role-structure of the adult society. The primary ways in which these two problems are interrelated will provide our main points of reference.

First, from the functional point of view the school class can be treated as an agency of socialization. That is to say, it is an agency through which individual personalities are trained to be motivationally and technically adequate to the performance of adult roles. It is not the sole such agency; the family, informal "peer groups," churches, and sundry voluntary organizations all play a part, as does actual on-the-job training. But, in the period extending from entry into first grade until entry into the labor force or marriage, the school class may be regarded as the focal socializing agency.

The socialization function may be summed up as the development in individuals of the commitments and capacities which are essential prerequisites of their future role-performance. Commitments may be broken down in turn into two components: commitment to the implementation of the broad *values* of society, and commitment to the performance of a specific type of role within the *structure* of society. Thus a person in a relatively humble occupation may be a "solid citizen" in the sense of commitment to honest work in that occupation, without an intensive and sophisticated concern with the implementation of society's higher-level values. Or conversely, someone else might object to the anchorage of the feminine role in marriage and the family on the grounds that such anchorage keeps society's total talent resources from being distributed equitably to business, government, and so on. Capacities can also be broken down into two components, the first being competence or the skill to perform the tasks involved in the individual's roles, and the second being "role-responsibility" or the capacity to live up to other people's expectations of the interpersonal behavior appropriate to these roles. Thus a mechanic as well as a doctor needs to have not only the basic "skills of his trade," but also the ability to behave responsibly toward those people with whom he is brought into contact in his work.

While on the one hand, the school class may be regarded as a primary agency by which these different components of commitments and capacities are generated, on the other hand, it is, from the point of view of the society, an agency of "manpower" allocation. It is well known that in American society there is a very high, and probably increasing, correlation between one's status level in the society and one's level of educational attainment. Both social status and educational level are obviously related to the occupational status which is attained. Now, as a result of the general process of both educational and occupational upgrading, completion of high school is increasingly coming to be the norm for minimum satisfactory educational attainment, and the most significant line for future occupational status has come to be drawn between members of an age-cohort who do and do not go to college.

We are interested, then, in what it is about the school class in our society that determines the distinction between the contingents of the age-cohort which do and do not go to college. Because of a tradition of localism and a rather pragmatic pluralism, there is apparently considerable variety among school systems of various cities and states. Although the situation in metropolitan Boston probably represents a more highly structured pattern than in many other parts of the country, it is probably not so extreme as to be misleading in its main features. There, though of course actual entry into college does not come until after graduation from high school, the main dividing line is between those who are and are not enrolled in the college preparatory course in high school; there is only a small amount of shifting either way after about the ninth grade when the decision is normally made. Furthermore, the evidence seems to be that by far the most important criterion of selection is the record of school performance in elementary school. These records are evaluated by teachers and principals, and there are few cases of entering the college preparatory course against their advice. It is therefore not stretching the evidence too far to say broadly that the primary selective process occurs through differential school performance in elementary school, and that the "seal" is put on it in junior high school.[1]

The evidence also is that the selective process is genuinely assortative. As in virtually all comparable processes, ascriptive as well as achieved factors influence the outcome. In this case, the ascriptive factor is the socio-economic status of the child's family, and the factor underlying his opportunity for achievement is his individual ability. In the study of 3,348 Boston high school boys on which these generalizations are based, each of these factors was quite highly correlated with planning college. For example, the percentages planning college, by father's occupation, were: 12 per cent for semi-skilled and unskilled, 19 per cent for skilled, 26 per cent for minor white collar, 52 per cent for middle white collar, and 80 per cent for major white collar. Likewise, intentions varied by ability (as measured by IQ), namely, 11 per cent for the lowest quintile, 17 per cent for the next, 24 per cent for the middle, 30 per cent for the next to the top, and 52 per cent for the highest. It should be noted also that within any ability quintile, the relationship of plans to father's occupation is seen.

For example, within the very important top quintile in ability as measured, the range in college intentions was from 29 per cent for sons of laborers to 89 per cent for sons of major white collar persons.[2]

The essential points here seem to be that there is a relatively uniform criterion of selection operating to differentiate between the college and the non-college contingents, and that for a very important part of the cohort the operation of this criterion is not a "put-up job"—it is not simply a way of affirming a previously determined ascriptive status. To be sure, the high-status, high-ability boy is very likely indeed to go to college, and the low-status, low-ability boy is very unlikely to go. But the "cross-pressured" group for whom these two factors do not coincide[3] is of considerable importance.

Considerations like these lead me to conclude that the main process of differentiation (which from another point of view is selection) that occurs during elementary school takes place on a single main axis of *achievement*. Broadly, moreover, the differentiation leads up through high school to a bifurcation into college-goers and non-college-goers.

To assess the significance of this pattern, let us look at its place in the socialization of the individual. Entering the system of formal education is the child's first major step out of primary involvement in his family of orientation. Within the family certain foundations of his motivational system have been laid down. But the only characteristic fundamental to later roles which has clearly been "determined" and psychologically stamped in by that time is sex role. The postoedipal child enters the system of formal education clearly categorized as boy or girl, but beyond that his *role* is not yet differentiated. The process of selection, by which persons will select and be selected for categories of roles, is yet to take place.

On grounds which cannot be gone into here, it may be said that the most important single predispositional factor with which the child enters the school is his level of *independence*. By this is meant his level of self-sufficiency relative to guidance by adults, his capacity to take responsibility and to make his own decisions in coping with new and varying situations. This, like his sex role, he has as a function of his experience in the family.

The family is a collectivity within which the basic status-structure is ascribed in terms of biological position, that is, by generation, sex, and age. There are inevitably differences of performance relative to these, and they are rewarded and punished in ways that contribute to differential character formation. But these differences are not given the sanction of institutionalized social status. The school is the first socializing agency in the child's experience which institutionalizes a differentiation of status on nonbiological bases. Moreover, this is not an ascribed but an achieved status; it is the status "earned" by differential performance of the tasks set by the teacher, who is acting as an agent of the community's school system. Let us look at the structure of this situation.

THE STRUCTURE OF THE ELEMENTARY SCHOOL CLASS

In accord with the generally wide variability of American institutions, and of course the basically local control of school systems, there is considerable variability of school situations, but broadly they have a single relatively well-marked framework.[4] Particularly in the primary part of the elementary grades, i.e., the first three grades, the basic pattern includes one main teacher for the class, who teaches all subjects and who is in charge of the class generally. Sometimes this early, and frequently in later grades, other teachers are brought in for a few special subjects, particularly gym, music, and art, but this does not alter the central position of the main teacher. This teacher is usually a woman.[5] The class is with this one teacher for the school year, but usually no longer.

The class, then, is composed of about 25 age-peers of both sexes drawn from a relatively small geographical area—the neighborhood. Except for sex in certain respects, there is initially no formal basis for differentiation of status within the school class. The main structural differentiation develops gradually, on the single main axis indicated above as achievement. That the differentiation should occur on a single main axis is insured by four primary features of the situation. The first is the initial equalization of the "contestants'" status by age and by "family background," the neighborhood being typically much more homogeneous than is the whole society. The second circumstance is the imposition of a common set of tasks which is, compared to most other task-areas, strikingly undifferentiated. The school situation is far more like a race in this respect than most role-performance situations. Third, there is the sharp polarization between the pupils in their initial equality and the *single* teacher who is an adult and "represents" the adult world. And fourth, there is a relatively systematic process of evaluation of the pupils' performances. From the point of view of a pupil, this evaluation, particularly (though not exclusively) in the form of report card marks, constitutes reward and/or punishment for past performance; from the viewpoint of the school system acting as an allocating agency, it is a basis of *selection* for future status in society.

Two important sets of qualifications need to be kept in mind in interpreting this structural pattern, but I think these do not destroy the significance of its main outline. The first qualification is for variations in the formal organization and procedures of the school class itself. Here the most important kind of variation is that between relatively "traditional" schools and relatively "progressive" schools. The more traditional schools put more emphasis on discrete units of subject-matter, whereas the progressive type allows more "indirect" teaching through "projects" and broader topical interests where more than one bird can be killed with a stone. In progressive schools there is more emphasis on groups of pupils working together, compared to the traditional direct relation of the individual pupil to the teacher. This is related to the progressive emphasis on co-operation among the pupils rather than direct competition, to greater permissiveness as opposed to strictness of discipline, and to a de-emphasis on formal marking.[6] In some schools one of these components will be more prominent, and in others, another. That it is, however, an important range of variation is clear. It has to do, I think, very largely with the independence-dependence training which is so important to early socialization in the family. My broad interpretation is that those people who emphasize independence training will tend to be those who favor relatively progressive education. The relation of support for progressive education to relatively high socioeconomic status and to "intellectual" interests and the like is well known. There is no contradiction between these emphases both on independence and on co-operation and group solidarity among pupils. In the first instance this is because the main focus of the independence problem at these ages is vis-à-vis adults. However, it can also be said that the peer group, which here is built into the school class, is an indirect field of expression of dependency needs, displaced from adults.

The second set of qualifications concerns the "informal" aspects of the school class, which are always somewhat at variance with the formal expectations. For instance, the formal pattern of nondifferentiation between the sexes may be modified informally, for the very salience of the one-sex peer group at this age period means that there is bound to be considerable implicit recognition of it—for example, in the form of teachers' encouraging group competition between boys and girls. Still, the fact of coeducation and the attempt to treat both sexes alike in all the crucial formal respects remain the most important. Another problem raised by informal organization is the question of how far teachers can and do treat pupils particularistically in violation of the universalistic expectations of the school. When compared with other types of formal organizations, however, I think the extent of this discrepancy in elementary schools is seen to be not unusual. The school class is structured so that opportunity for particularistic treatment is severely limited. Because there are so many more children in a school class than in a family and they are concentrated in a much narrower age range, the teacher has much less chance than does a parent to grant particularistic favors.

Bearing in mind these two sets of qualifications, it is still fair, I think, to conclude that the major characteristics of the elementary school class in this country are such as have been outlined. It should be especially emphasized that more or less progressive schools, even with their relative lack of emphasis on formal marking, do not constitute a separate pattern, but rather a variant tendency within the same pattern. A progressive teacher, like any other, will form opinions about the different merits of her pupils relative to the values and goals of the class and will communicate these evaluations to them, informally if not formally. It is my impression that the extremer cases of playing down relative evaluation are confined to those upper-status schools where going to a "good" college is so fully taken for granted that for practical purposes it is an ascribed status. In other words, in interpreting these facts the selective function of the school class should be kept continually in the forefront of attention. Quite clearly its importance has not been decreasing; rather the contrary.

THE NATURE OF SCHOOL ACHIEVEMENT

What, now, of the content of the "achievement" expected of elementary school children? Perhaps the best broad characterization which can be given is that it involves the types of performance which are, on the one hand, appropriate to the school situation and, on the other hand, are felt by adults to be important in themselves. This vague and somewhat circular characterization may, as was mentioned earlier, be broken down into two main components. One of these is the more purely "cognitive" learning of information, skills, and frames of reference associated with empirical knowledge and technological mastery. The *written* language and the early phases of mathematical thinking are clearly vital; they involve cognitive skills at altogether new levels of generality and abstraction compared to those commanded by the pre-school child. With these basic skills goes assimilation of much factual information about the world.

The second main component is what may broadly be called a "moral" one. In earlier generations of schooling this was known as "deportment." Somewhat more generally it might be called responsible citizenship in the school community. Such things as respect for the teacher, consideration and co-operativeness in relation to fellow-pupils, and good "work-habits" are the fundamentals, leading on to capacity for "leadership" and "initiative."

The striking fact about this achievement content is that in the elementary grades these two primary components are not clearly differentiated from each other. Rather, the pupil is evaluated in diffusely general terms; a *good* pupil is defined in terms of a fusion of the cognitive and the moral components, in which varying weight is given to one or the other. Broadly speaking, then, we may say that the "high achievers" of the elementary school are both the "bright" pupils, who catch on easily to their more strictly intellectual tasks, and the more "responsible" pupils, who "behave well" and on whom the teacher can "count" in her difficult problems of managing the class. One indication that this is the case is the fact that in elementary school the purely intellectual tasks are relatively easy for the pupil of high intellectual ability. In many such cases, it can be presumed that the primary challenge to the pupil is not to his intellectual, but to his "moral," capacities. On the whole, the progressive movement seems to have leaned in the direction of giving enhanced emphasis to this component, suggesting that of the two, it has tended to become the more problematical.[7]

The essential point, then, seems to be that the elementary school, regarded in the light of its socialization function, is an agency which differentiates the school class broadly along a single continuum of achievement, the content of which is relative excellence in living up to the expectations imposed by the teacher as an agent of the adult society. The criteria of this achievement are, generally speaking, undifferentiated into the cognitive or technical component and the moral or "social" component. But with respect to its bearing on societal values, it is broadly a differentiation of *levels* of capacity to act in accord with these values. Though the relation is far from neatly uniform, this differentiation underlies the processes of selection for levels of status and role in the adult society.

Next, a few words should be said about the out-of-school context in which this process goes on. Besides the school class, there are clearly two primary social structures in which the child participates: the family and the child's informal "peer group."

FAMILY AND PEER GROUP IN RELATION TO THE SCHOOL CLASS

The school age child, of course, continues to live in the parental household and to be highly dependent, emotionally as well as instrumentally, on his parents. But he is now spending several hours a day away from home, subject to a discipline and a reward system which are essentially independent of that administered by the parents. Moreover, the range of this independence gradually increases. As he grows older, he is permitted to range further territorially with neither parental nor school supervision, and to do an increasing range of things. He often gets an allowance for personal spending and begins to earn some money of his own. Generally, however, the emotional problem of dependence-independence continues to be a very salient one through this period, frequently with manifestations by the child of compulsive independence.

Concomitantly with this, the area for association with age-peers without detailed adult supervision expands. These associations are tied to the family, on the one hand, in that the home and yards of children who are neighbors and the adjacent streets serve as locations for their activities; and to the school, on the other hand, in that play periods and going to and from school provide occasions for informal association, even though organized extracurricular activities are introduced only later. Ways of bringing some of this activity under another sort of adult supervision are found in such organizations as the boy and girl scouts.

Two sociological characteristics of peer groups at this age are particularly striking. One is the fluidity of their boundaries, with individual children drifting into and out of associations. This element of "voluntary association" contrasts strikingly with the child's ascribed membership in the family and the school class, over which he has no control. The second characteristic is the peer group's sharp segregation by sex. To a striking degree this is enforced by the children themselves rather than by adults.

The psychological functions of peer association are suggested by these two characteristics. On the one hand, the peer group may be regarded as a field for the exercise of independence from adult control; hence it is not surprising that it is often a focus of behavior which goes beyond independence from adults to the range of adult-*disapproved* behavior; when this happens, it is the seed bed from which the extremists go over into delinquency. But another very important function is to provide the child a source of non-adult approval and acceptance. These depend on "technical" and "moral" criteria as diffuse as those required in the school situation. On the one hand, the peer group is a field for acquiring and displaying various types of "prowess"; for boys this is especially the physical prowess which may later ripen into athletic achievement. On the other hand, it is a matter of gaining acceptance from desirable peers as "belonging" in the group, which later ripens into the conception of the popular teen-ager, the "right guy." Thus the adult parents are augmented by age-peers as a source of rewards for performance and of security in acceptance.

The importance of the peer group for socialization in our type of society should be clear. The motivational foundations of character are inevitably first laid down through identification with parents, who are generation-superiors, and the generation difference is a type example of a hierarchical status difference. But an immense part of the individual's adult role performance will have to be in association with status-equals or near-equals. In this situation it is important to have a reorganization of the motivational structure so that the original dominance of the hierarchical axis is modified to strengthen the egalitarian components. The peer group plays a prominent part in this process.

Sex segregation of latency period peer groups may be regarded as a process of reinforcement of sex-role identification. Through intensive association with sex-peers and involvement in sex-typed activities, they strongly reinforce belongingness with other members of the same sex and contrast with the opposite sex. This is the more important because in the coeducational school a set of forces operates which specifically plays down sex-role differentiation.

It is notable that the latency period sex-role pattern, instead of institutionalizing relations to members of the opposite sex, is characterized by an avoidance of such relations, which only in adolescence gives way to dating. This avoidance is clearly associated with the process of reorganization of the erotic components of motivational structure. The pre-oedipal objects of erotic attachment were both intra-familial and generation-superior. In both respects there must be a fundamental shift by the time the child reaches adulthood. I would suggest that one of the main functions of the avoidance pattern is to help cope with the psychological difficulty of overcoming the earlier incestuous attachments, and hence to prepare the child for assuming an attachment to an age-mate of opposite sex later.

Seen in this perspective, the socialization function of the school class assumes a particular significance. The socialization functions of the family by this time are relatively residual, though their importance should not be underestimated. But the school remains adult-controlled and, moreover, induces basically the same kind of identification as was induced by the family in the child's pre-oedipal stage. This is to say that the learning of achievement-motivation is, psychologically speaking, a process of identification with the teacher, of doing well in school in order to please the teacher (often backed by the parents) in the same sense in which a pre-oedipal child learns new skills in order to please his mother.

In this connection I maintain that what is internalized through the process of identification is a reciprocal pattern of role-relationships.[8] Unless there is a drastic failure of internalization altogether, not just one, but both sides of the interaction will be internalized. There will, however, be an emphasis on one or the other, so that some children will more nearly identify with the socializing agent, and others will more nearly identify with the opposite role. Thus, in the pre-oedipal stage, the "independent" child has identified more with the parent, and the "dependent" one with the child-role vis-à-vis the parent.

In school the teacher is institutionally defined as superior to any pupil in knowledge of curriculum subject-matter and in responsibility as a good citizen of the school. In so far as the school class tends to be bifurcated (and of course the dichotomization is far from absolute), it will broadly be on the basis, on the one hand, of identification with the teacher, or acceptance of her role as a model; and, on the other hand, of identification with the pupil peer group. This bifurcation of the class on the basis of identification with teacher or with peer group so strikingly corresponds with the bifurcation into college-goers and non-college-goers that it would be hard to avoid the hypothesis that this structural dichotomization in the school system is the primary source of the selective dichotomization. Of course in detail the relationship is blurred, but certainly not more so than in a great many other fields of comparable analytical complexity.

These considerations suggest an interpretation of some features of the elementary teacher role in American society. The first major step in socialization, beyond that in the family, takes place in the elementary school, so it seems reasonable to expect that the teacher-figure should be characterized by a combination of similarities to and differences from parental figures. The teacher, then, is an adult, characterized by the generalized superiority, which a parent also has, of adult status relative to children. She is not, however, ascriptively related to her pupils, but is performing an occupational role—a role, however, in which the recipients of her services are tightly bound in solidarity to her and to each other. Furthermore, compared to a parent's, her responsibility to them is much more universalistic, this being reinforced, as we saw, by the size of the class; it is also much more oriented to performance rather than to solicitude for the emotional "needs" of the children. She is not entitled to suppress the distinction between high and low achievers, just because not being able to be included among the high group would be too hard on little Johnny— however much tendencies in this direction appear as deviant patterns. A mother, on the other hand, must give *first* priority to the needs of her child, regardless of his capacities to achieve.

It is also significant for the parallel of the elementary school class with the family that the teacher is normally a woman. As background it should be noted that in most European systems until recently, and often today in our private parochial and non-sectarian schools, the sexes have been segregated and each sex group has been taught by teachers of their own sex.

Given coeducation, however, the woman teacher represents continuity with the role of the mother. Precisely the lack of differentiation in the elementary school "curriculum" between the components of subject-matter competence and social responsibility fits in with the greater diffuseness of the feminine role.

But at the same time, it is essential that the teacher is not a mother to her pupils, but must insist on universalistic norms and the differential reward of achievement. Above all she must be the agent of bringing about and legitimizing a differentiation of the school class on an achievement axis. This aspect of her role is furthered by the fact that in American society the feminine role is less confined to the familial context than in most other societies, but joins the masculine in occupational and associational concerns, though still with a greater relative emphasis on the family. Through identification with their teacher, children of both sexes learn that the category "woman" is not co-extensive with "mother" (and future wife), but that the feminine role-personality is more complex than that.

In this connection it may well be that there is a relation to the once-controversial issue of the marriage of women teachers. If the differentiation between what may be called the maternal and the occupational components of the feminine role is incomplete and insecure, confusion between them may be avoided by insuring that both are not performed by the same persons. The "old maid" teacher of American tradition may thus be thought of as having renounced the maternal role in favor of the occupational.[9] Recently, however, the highly affective concern over the issue of married women's teaching has conspicuously abated, and their actual participation has greatly increased. It may be suggested that this change is associated with a change in the feminine role, the most conspicuous feature of which is the general social sanctioning of participation of women in the labor force, not only prior to marriage, but also after marriage. This I should interpret as a process of structural differentiation in that the same category of persons is permitted and even expected to engage in a more complex set of role-functions than before.

The process of identification with the teacher which has been postulated here is furthered by the fact that in the elementary grades the child typically has one teacher, just as in the pre-oedipal period he had one parent, the mother, who was the focus of his object-relations. The continuity between the two phases is also favored by the fact that the teacher, like the mother, is a woman. But, if she acted only like a mother, there would be no genuine reorganization of the pupil's personality system. This reorganization is furthered by the features of the teacher role which differentiate it from the maternal. One further point is that while a child has one main teacher in each grade, he will usually have a new teacher when he progresses to the next higher grade. He is thus accustomed to the fact that teachers are, unlike mothers, "interchangeable" in a certain sense. The school year is long enough to form an important relationship to a particular teacher, but not long enough for a highly particularistic attachment to crystallize. More than in the parent-child relationship, in school the child must internalize his relation to the teacher's *role* rather than her particular personality; this is a major step in the internalization of universalistic patterns.

SOCIALIZATION AND SELECTION IN THE ELEMENTARY SCHOOL

To conclude this discussion of the elementary school class, something should be said about the fundamental conditions underlying the process which is, as we have seen, simultaneously (1) an emancipation of the child from primary emotional attachment to his family, (2) an internalization of a level of societal values and norms that is a step higher than those he can learn in his family alone, (3) a differentiation of the school class in terms both of actual achievement and of differential *valuation* of achievement, and (4) from society's point of view, a selection and allocation of its human resources relative to the adult role system.[10]

Probably the most fundamental condition underlying this process is the sharing of common values by the two adult agencies involved—the family and the school. In this case the core is the shared valuation of *achievement*. It includes, above all, recognition that it is fair to give differential rewards for different levels of achievement, so long as there has been fair access to opportunity, and fair that these rewards lead on to higher-order opportunities for the successful. There is thus a basic sense in which the elementary school class is an embodiment of the fundamental American value of equality of opportunity, in that it places value *both* on initial equality and on differential achievement.

As a second condition, however, the rigor of this valuational pattern must be tempered by allowance for the difficulties and needs of the young child. Here the quasi-motherliness of the woman teacher plays an important part. Through her the school system, assisted by other agencies, attempts to minimize the insecurity resulting from the pressures to learn, by providing a certain amount of emotional support defined in terms of what is due to a child of a given age level. In this respect, however, the role of the school is relatively small. The underlying foundation of support is given in the home, and as we have seen, an important supplement to it can be provided by the informal peer associations of the child. It may be suggested that the development of extreme patterns of alienation from the school is often related to inadequate support in these respects.

Third, there must be a process of selective rewarding of valued performance. Here the teacher is clearly the primary agent, though the more progressive modes of education attempt to enlist classmates more systematically than in the traditional pattern. This is the process that is the direct source of intra-class differentiation along the achievement axis.

The final condition is that this initial differentiation tends to bring about a status system in the class, in which not only the immediate results of school work, but a whole series of influences, converge to consolidate different expectations which may be thought of as the children's "levels of aspiration." Generally some differentiation of friendship groups along this line occurs, though it is important that it is by no means complete, and that children are sensitive to the attitudes not only of their own friends, but of others.

Within this general discussion of processes and conditions, it is important to distinguish, as I have attempted to do all along, the socialization of the individual from the selective allocation of contingents to future roles. For the individual, the old familial identification is broken up (the family of orientation becomes, in Freudian terms, a "lost object") and a new identification is gradually built up, providing the first-order structure of the child's identity apart from his originally ascribed identity as son or daughter of the "Joneses." He both transcends his familial identification in favor of a more independent one and comes to occupy a differentiated status within the new system. His personal status is inevitably a direct function of the position he achieves, primarily in the formal school class and secondarily in the informal peer group structure. In spite of the sense in which achievement-ranking takes place along a continuum, I have put forward reasons to suggest that, with respect to this status, there is an important differentiation into two broad, relatively distinct levels, and that his position on one or the other enters into the individual's definition of his own identity. To an important degree this process of differentiation is independent of the socio-economic status of his family in the community, which to the child is a prior ascribed status.

When we look at the same system as a selective mechanism from the societal point of view, some further considerations become important. First, it may be noted that the valuation of achievement and its sharing by family and school not only provides the appropriate values for internalization by individuals, but also performs a crucial integrative function for the system. Differentiation of the class along the achievement axis is inevitably a source of strain, because it confers higher rewards and privileges on one contingent than on another within the same system. This common valuation helps make possible the acceptance of the crucial differentiation, especially by the losers in the competition. Here it is an essential point that this *common* value on achievement is shared by units with different statuses in the system. It cuts across the differentiation of families by socio-economic status. It is necessary that there be realistic opportunity and that the teacher can be relied on to implement it by being "fair" and rewarding achievement by whoever shows capacity for it. The fact is crucial that the distribution of abilities, though correlated with family status, clearly does not coincide with it. There can then be a genuine selective process within a set of "rules of the game."

This commitment to common values is not, however, the sole integrative mechanism counteracting the strain imposed by differentiation. Not only does the individual pupil enjoy familial support, but teachers also like and indeed "respect" pupils on bases independent of achievement-status, and peer-group friendship lines, though correlated with position on the achievement scale, again by no means coincide with it, but cross-cut it. Thus there are cross-cutting lines of solidarity which mitigate the strains generated by rewarding achievement differentially.[11]

It is only *within* this framework of institutionalized solidarity that the crucial selective process goes on through selective rewarding and the consolidation of its results into a status-differentiation within the school class. We have called special attention to the impact of the selective process on the children of relatively high ability but low family status. Precisely in this group, but pervading school classes generally, is another parallel to what was found in the studies of voting behavior.[12] In the voting studies it was found that the "shifters"—those voters who were transferring their allegiance from one major party to the other—tended, on the one hand, to be the "cross-pressured" people, who had multiple status characteristics and group allegiances which predisposed them simultaneously to vote in opposite directions. The analogy in the school class is clearly to the children for whom ability and family status do not coincide. On the other hand, it was precisely in this group of cross-pressured voters that political "indifference" was most conspicuous. Non-voting was particularly prevalent in this group, as was a generally cool emotional tone toward a campaign. The suggestion is that some of the pupil "indifference" to school performance may have a similar origin. This is clearly a complex phenomenon and cannot be further analyzed here. But rather than suggesting, as is usual on common sense grounds, that indifference to school work represents an "alienation" from cultural and intellectual values, I would suggest exactly the opposite: that an important component of such indifference, including in extreme cases overt revolt against school discipline, is connected with the fact that the stakes, as in politics, are very high indeed. Those pupils who are exposed to contradictory pressures are likely to be ambivalent; at the same time, the personal stakes for them are higher than for the others, because what happens in school may make much more of a difference for their futures than for the others, in whom ability and family status point to the same expectations for the future. In particular for the upwardly mobile pupils, too much emphasis on school success would pointedly suggest "burning their bridges" of association with their families and status peers. This phenomenon seems to operate even in elementary school, although it grows somewhat more conspicuous later. In general I think that an important part of the anti-intellectualism in American youth culture stems from the *importance* of the selective process through the educational system rather than the opposite.

One further major point should be made in this analysis. As we have noted, the general trend of American society has been toward a rapid upgrading in the educational status of the population. This means that, relative to past expectations, with each generation there is increased pressure to educational achievement, often associated with parents' occupational ambitions for their children.[13] To a sociologist this is a more or less classical situation of anomic strain, and the youth-culture ideology which plays down intellectual interests and school performance seems to fit in this context. The orientation of the youth culture is, in the nature of the case, ambivalent, but for the reasons suggested, the anti-intellectual side of the ambivalence tends to be overtly stressed. One of the reasons for the dominance of the anti-school side of the ideology is that it provides a means of protest against adults, who are at the opposite pole in the socialization situation. In certain respects one would expect that the trend toward greater emphasis on independence, which we have associated with progressive education, would accentuate the strain in this area and hence the tendency to decry adult expectations. The whole problem should be subjected to a thorough analysis in the light of what we know about ideologies more generally.

The same general considerations are relevant to the much-discussed problem of juvenile delinquency. Both the general upgrading process and the pressure to enhanced independence should be expected to increase strain on the lower, most marginal groups. The analysis of this paper has been concerned with the line between college and non-college contingents; there is, however, another line between those who achieve solid non-college educational status and those for whom adaptation to educational expectations at *any* level is difficult. As the acceptable minimum of educational qualification rises, persons near and below the margin will tend to be pushed into an attitude of repudiation of these expectations. Truancy and delinquency are ways of expressing this repudiation. Thus the very *improvement* of educational standards in the society at large may well be a major factor in the failure of the educational process for a growing number at the lower end of the status and ability distribution. It should therefore not be too easily assumed that delinquency is a symptom of a *general* failure of the educational process.

CONCLUSION

With the general cultural upgrading process in American society which has been going on for more than a century, the educational system has come to play an increasingly vital role. That this should be the case is, in my opinion, a consequence of the general trend to structural differentiation in the society. Relatively speaking, the school is a specialized agency. That it should increasingly have become the principal channel of selection as well as agency of socialization is in line with what one would expect in an increasingly differentiated and progressively more upgraded society. The legend of the "self-made man" has an element of nostalgic romanticism and is destined to become increasingly mythical, if by it is meant not just mobility from humble origins to high status, which does indeed continue to occur, but that the high status was attained through the "school of hard knocks" without the aid of formal education.

The structure of the public school system and the analysis of the ways in which it contributes both to the socialization of individuals and to their allocation to roles in society is, I feel, of vital concern to all students of American society. Nothwithstanding the variegated elements in the situation, I think it has been possible to sketch out a few major structural patterns of the public school system and at least to suggest some ways in which they serve these important functions. What could be presented in this paper is the merest outline of such an analysis. It is, however, hoped that it has been carried far enough to suggest a field of vital mutual interest for social scientists on the one hand and those concerned with the actual operation of the schools on the other.

NOTES

I am indebted to Mrs. Carolyn Cooper for research assistance in the relevant literature and for editorial work on the first draft of this paper.

1. The principal source for these statements is a study of social mobility among boys in ten public high schools in the Boston metropolitan area, conducted by Samual A. Stouffer, Florence R. Kluckhohn, and the present author. Unfortunately the material is not available in published form.

2. See table from this study in J. A. Kahl, *The American Class Structure* (New York: Rinehart & Co., 1953), p. 283. Data from a nationwide sample of high school students, published by the Educational Testing Service, show similar patterns of relationships. For example, the ETS study shows variation, by father's occupation, in proportion of high school seniors planning college, of from 35 per cent to 80 per cent for boys and 27 per cent to 79 per cent for girls. (From *Background Factors Related to College Plans and College Enrollment among High School Students* [Princeton, N.J.: Educational Testing Service, 1957]).

3. There seem to be two main reasons why the high-status, low-ability group is not so important as its obverse. The first is that in a society of expanding educational and occupational opportunity the general trend is one of upgrading, and the social pressures to downward mobility are not as great as they would otherwise be. The second is that there are cushioning mechanisms which tend to protect the high status boy who has difficulty "making the grade." He may be sent to a college with low academic standards, he may go to schools where the line between ability levels is not rigorously drawn, etc.

4. This discussion refers to public schools. Only about 13 per cent of all elementary and secondary school pupils attend non-public schools, with this proportion ranging from about 22 per cent in the Northeast to about 6 per cent in the South. U.S. Office of Education, *Biennial Survey of Education in the United States, 1954–56* (Washington: U.S. Government Printing Office, 1959), chap. ii, "Statistics of State School Systems, 1955–56." Table 44, p. 114.

5. In 1955–56, 13 per cent of the public elementary school instructional staff in the United States were men. *Ibid.*, p. 7.

6. This summary of some contrasts between traditional and progressive patterns is derived from general reading in the literature rather than any single authoritative account.

7. This account of the two components of elementary school achievement and their relation summarizes impressions gained from the literature, rather than being based on the opinions of particular authorities. I have the impression that achievement in this sense corresponds closely to what is meant by the term as used by McClelland and his associates. Cf. D. C. McClelland *et al., The Achievement Motive* (New York: Appleton-Century-Crofts, Inc., 1953).

8. On the identification process in the family see my paper, "Social Structure and the Development of Personality," *Psychiatry,* XXI (November, 1958), pp. 321–40.

9. It is worth noting that the Catholic parochial school system is in line with the more general older American tradition, in that the typical teacher is a nun. The only difference in this respect is the sharp religious symbolization of the difference between mother and teacher.

10. The following summary is adapted from T. Parsons, R. F. Bales, *et al., Family, Socialization and Interaction Process* (Glencoe, Ill.: The Free Press, 1955), esp. chap. iv.

11. In this, as in several other respects, there is a parallel to other important allocative processes in the society. A striking example is the voting process by which political support is allocated between party candidates. Here, the strain arises from the fact that one candidate and his party will come to enjoy all the perquisites—above all the power—of office, while the other will be excluded for the time being from these. This strain is mitigated, on the one hand, by the common commitment to constitutional procedure, and, on the other hand, by the fact that the nonpolitical bases of social solidarity, which figure so prominently as determinants of voting behavior, still cut across party lines. The average person is, in various of his roles, associated with people whose political preference is different from his own; he therefore could not regard the opposite party as composed of unmitigated scoundrels without introducing a rift within the groups to which he is attached. This feature of the electorate's structure is brought out strongly in B. R. Berelson, P. F. Lazarsfeld and W. N. McPhee, *Voting* (Chicago: University of Chicago Press, 1954). The conceptual analysis of it is developed in my own paper, "'Voting' and the Equilibrium of the American Political System" in E. Burdick and A. J. Brodbeck (eds.), *American Voting Behavior* (Glencoe, Ill.: The Free Press, 1959).

12. *Ibid.*

13. J. A. Kahl, "Educational and Occupational Aspirations of 'Common Man' Boys," *Harvard Educational Review*, XXIII (Summer, 1953), pp. 186–203.

CHAPTER 4

Learning and Performing Student and Teacher Roles

Why can't Johnny read? This familiar question pertains to the many students who are not meeting the expectations adults have placed on them. "Johnny" represents the millions of kids who for various reasons have problems fitting into the role that defines what, when, and how the average student should learn. In this chapter we will consider (1) the socialization process that teaches Johnny the proper student role, (2) attitudes of students who leave the system, (3) the process of learning to be a teacher and the status of teachers, and (4) problems faced by teachers in socializing Johnny.

Student roles can be located in the open systems framework, where they provide the positions through which individuals carry out their activities and duties, forming the action part or *processes* of the system. *Students* study and learn roles. *Teachers* teach, socialize students, and manage classes. *Administrators* make decisions and implement policy. *Staff* carry out school business and routines. When studying role structures, we must be aware of reciprocal roles, those that work together and influence each other, such as student-teacher roles, organizational demands and constraints on roles, and environmental factors influencing the performance of roles.

An organizational chart of the internal educational system will tell us what positions fit where, but the individuals filling those positions bring the organization to life with their actions and words. They learn the parameters of their positions through the process of socialization (here the parameters are the range of behaviors and responsibilities that compose those roles). The archetypal "Johnny" poses a problem for educational systems because he is not meeting the role expectations for the position of student. Misfits divert organizations from their main tasks, take extra energy and resources, and are therefore hard to tolerate.

Every organization's membership is made up of interrelated positions; each person has a role to play within the system to keep it functioning. In educational systems these positions include administrators, teachers, students, and support staff. Sometimes role responsibilities are clearly defined, but there is often a great deal of leeway, allowing individuals to bring their own interpretations and personalities into carrying out the role; this is especially true as an individual gains more responsibility in the organizational hierarchy. The less clearly defined the role, however, the more possibility for *role ambiguity,* or lack of clarity in what is expected, thus leaving open the possibility of not meeting others' expectations. This in turn can cause *role conflict,* or differing expectations of role performance. A student, for instance, may feel he/she is performing adequately based on an interpretation of vaguely stated expectations. The teacher, with different expectations, may disagree, surprising the student with a poor evaluation. In this chapter we focus on the reciprocal roles of student and teacher.

Students learn school roles through the process of socialization. You are currently being socialized into a college major and an occupation; for some of you, this occupational role is teacher. Learning school roles begins early, in most countries between the fifth and seventh year. Young children in American society have their first experience in socialization into school, a secondary organization, when they enter kindergarten. In the primary organization, family, children are generally accepted for what they are, but in school they begin to be judged in relation to others; this is part of the formal selection process. Even in kindergarten children are labeled on scales of good–bad, cooperative–troublemaker, smart–dumb, and may learn to accept and act out that label. Such labels have a way of influencing children's self-perceptions and teacher expectations. Thus we find students acting out a variety of roles—clown, brain, jock, loser—and not always by choice. If labeled early in their school years, they may retain that label for the rest of their secondary school career.

The socialization process can be functional or dysfunctional for school role holders. Students bring with them environmental influences from home, peer group, and community, including perceptions of their ability, values concerning education and what it can do for them, and a notion of where education fits into their overall life plan.

School experiences and peer groups further influence these perceptions. David Johnson's article shows the importance of the peer group in determining student attitudes toward self and school. (The Paul Willis article in Chapter 6 also addresses this point.) Johnson points to the importance of student-student interactions in the formation of attitudes toward schooling and self-adjustment. Peer groups provide opportunities for students to develop leadership skills, learn to manage aggression, see problems from other than their own egocentric position, and practice future roles.

By the time that most students are seniors in high school, they have achieved some degree of success in mastering their roles as students. What are some outcomes of this role, especially as it relates to their preparation for adulthood? Theodore Wagenaar addresses these questions in his comparison of data from 1972 and 1980 high school surveys. Wagenaar compares students' academic success, future expectations, values, and attitudes toward school experiences, and he notes major trends in their views.

Student roles cannot be fully understood without viewing the reciprocal teacher role, the topic of the Lortie and *Newsweek* articles. Students are more familiar with this role than most other adult occupational roles because they spend six hours a day for twelve or more years in classrooms. Most, however, have not been behind the *big* desk. Dan Lortie points out that the majority of teachers really form their teaching styles once they get into the classroom from the other end. Lortie discusses teaching as a profession and a subculture, and some of the factors that separate teaching from other professions.

The view from the opposite side of the desk is also the topic of a 1981 *Newsweek* series on education. The article points out frustrations experienced by teachers, problems in teacher training, some responses of communities and states to perceived poor teaching, and methods for helping teachers to improve.

Role expectations are often formally defined in student handbooks or teacher job descriptions. Roles, however, also possess latent aspects that are part of the informal system. These will be discussed in Chapter 5.

DAVID W. JOHNSON

Group Processes: Influences of Student-Student Interaction on School Outcomes

Questions to think about

1 *What functions in the socialization process do peer groups serve that schools cannot or do not provide?*
2 *From your own experience and other articles in this chapter, list some basic school goals. How might peer groups support and/or detract from these school goals?*
3 *Consider the various role relationships possible for students. Draw a diagram showing student role sets in the open system.*
4 *Thinking about your own experiences in school, document the importance of peers on your school outcomes at different levels of schooling.*

QUALITY OF STUDENT-STUDENT RELATIONSHIPS

Interpersonal interaction is the basis for learning, socialization, and development. While there has been considerable emphasis on teacher-student interaction, the educational value of student-student interaction has been largely ignored. There is evidence indicating that among other things student-student interaction will contribute to general socialization, future psychological health, acquisition of social com-

From *The Social Psychology of School Learning,* edited by James H. McMillan (New York: Academic Press, 1980), pp. 123–140. Reprinted with permission.

petencies, avoidance of engaging in antisocial or problem behaviors, mastery and control of impulses such as aggression, development of a sex-role identity, emergence of perspective-taking ability, and development of high educational aspirations and achievement. *Simply placing students near each other and allowing interaction to take place does not mean, however, that these outcomes will appear.* The nature of the interaction is important. Some interaction leads to students rejecting each other and defensively avoiding being influenced by peers. When student-student interaction leads to relationships characterized by perceived support and acceptance, then the potential beneficial effects are likely to be found.

In order for peer relationships to be constructive influences, they must promote feelings of belonging, acceptance, support, and caring, rather than feelings of hostility and rejection. Perceptions of being accepted by peers affect the following aspects of classroom life:

1. Peer acceptance is positively correlated with willingness to engage in social interaction (Furman, 1977; Johnson & Ahlgren, 1976; Johnson, Johnson, & Anderson, 1978).

2. Peer acceptance is positively correlated with the extent to which students provide positive social rewards for peers (Hartup, Glazer, & Charlesworth, 1967).

3. Isolation in the classroom is associated with high anxiety, low self-esteem, poor interpersonal skills, emotional handicaps, and psychological pathology (Bower, 1960; Gronlund, 1959; Horowitz, 1962; Johnson & Norem-Hebeisen, 1977; Mensh & Glidewell, 1958; Schmuck, 1963, 1966; Smith, 1958; Van Egmond, 1960).

4. Rejection by peers is related to disruptive classroom behavior (Lorber, 1966), hostile behavior and negative affect (Lippitt & Gold, 1959), and negative attitudes toward other students and school (Schmuck, 1966).

5. Acceptance by peers is related to utilization of abilities in achievement situations (Schmuck, 1963, 1966; Van Egmond, 1960).

On the basis of this evidence it may be concluded that peer relationships will have constructive effects only when student-student interaction is characterized by support and acceptance. In order to promote constructive peer influences, therefore, teachers must first ensure that students interact with each other and, second, must ensure that the interaction takes place within a supportive and accepting context. In other words, teachers must control the group dynamics affecting student-student interaction.

When teachers promote student-student interaction in the classroom there are several dynamics of groups that should be taken into account.

These include the way in which learning goals are structured, the way in which conflicts among ideas are managed, the composition of the group, the norms instituted within the group, and the size of the group.

GROUP GOALS AND GOAL STRUCTURE

All groups have goals, and one of the most important aspects of group effectiveness is the group's ability to define its goals and achieve them successfully. The essence of a goal is that it is an ideal. It is a desired place toward which people are working, a state of affairs that people value. A *group goal* is a future state of affairs desired by enough members of the group to motivate efforts to achieve it. In order to teach successfully, teachers need to know what outcomes they hope to achieve. After their instructional goals are formulated appropriately, a decision must be made as to the type of goal interdependence to be structured among students as they learn.

There are three types of goal interdependence that teachers may structure during instruction (Deutsch, 1962; Johnson & Johnson, 1975): cooperative (positive goal interdependence), competitive (negative goal interdependence), and individualistic (no goal interdependence). A *cooperative* goal structure exists when students perceive that they can obtain their goal if and only if the other students with whom they are linked obtain their goals. A *competitive* goal structure exists when students perceive that they can obtain their goal if and only if the other students with whom they are linked fail to obtain their goals. An *individualistic* goal structure exists when students perceive that obtaining their goal is unrelated to the goal achievement of other students.

In the ideal classroom all three goal structures would be appropriately used. All students would learn how to work cooperatively with other students, compete for fun and enjoyment, and work autonomously on their own. Most of the time, however, students would work on instructional tasks within the goal structure that is the most productive for the type of task to be done and for the cognitive and affective outcomes desired. It is the teacher who decides which goal structure to implement within each instructional activity. The way in which teachers structure learning goals determines how students interact with each other and with the teacher. The interaction patterns, in turn, determine the cognitive and affective outcomes of instruction. There is no aspect of teaching more important than the appropriate use of goal structures.

Student-Student Interaction

Each goal structure will promote a different pattern of interaction among students. Aspects of student-student interaction important for learning include (Johnson & Johnson, 1975): accurate communication and exchange of information, facilitation of each other's efforts to achieve, constructive conflict management, peer pressures toward achievement, decreased fear of failure, divergent thinking, acceptance and support by peers, utilization of other's resources, trust, and emotional involvement in and commitment to learning. A summary of the research findings on the relationships among the three goal structures and these aspects of student-student interaction is presented in Table 1 (for specific references, see Johnson & Johnson, 1975, 1978). Cooperation provides opportunities for positive interaction among students, whereas competition promotes cautious and defensive student-student interaction (except under very limited conditions). When students are in an individualistic goal structure, they work by themselves to master the skill or knowledge assigned, without interacting with other students. When teachers wish to promote positive interaction among students, a cooperative goal structure should be used, and competitive and individualistic goal structures should be avoided.

Of special importance for students influencing each other in regard to achievement, appropriate social behavior, cognitive and social development, and general socialization is the degree to which each goal structure affects (a) students' perceptions that they are accepted, supported, and liked by their peers; (b) students' exchange of information; (c) students' motivation to learn; and (d) students' emotional involvement in learning.

Acceptance, support, liking   Cooperative learning experiences, compared with competitive and individualistic ones, have been found to result in stronger beliefs that one is liked, supported, and accepted by other students, and that other students care about how much one learns and want to help one learn (Cooper, Johnson, Johnson, & Wilderson, 1980; Gunderson & Johnson, 1980; Johnson, Johnson, & Tauer, 1979; Johnson, Johnson, Johnson, & Anderson, 1976; Tjosvold, Marino, & Johnson, 1977). Furthermore, cooperative attitudes are related to the belief that one is liked by other students and wants to listen to, help, and do schoolwork with other students (Johnson & Ahlgren, 1976; Johnson, Johnson, & Anderson, 1978). Individualistic attitudes are related to *not* wanting to do schoolwork with other students, *not* wanting to help other students learn, *not* valuing being liked by other students, and *not* wanting to participate in social interaction (Johnson, Johnson, & Anderson, 1978; Johnson & Norem-

T A B L E 1
Goal Structures and Interpersonal Processes that Affect Learning

Cooperative	Competitive	Individualistic
High interaction	Low interaction	No interaction
Effective communication	No, misleading, or threatening communication	No interaction
Facilitation of other's achievement: helping, sharing, tutoring	Obstruction of other's achievement	No interaction
Peer influence toward achievement	Peer influence against achievement	No interaction
Problem-solving conflict management	Win-lose conflict management	No interaction
High divergent and risk-taking thinking	Low divergent and risk-taking thinking	No interaction
High trust	Low trust	No interaction
High acceptance and support by peers	Low acceptance and support by peers	No interaction
High emotional involvement in and commitment to learning by almost all students	High emotional involvement in and commitment to learning by the few students who have a chance to win	No interaction
High utilization of resources of other students	No utilization of resources of other students	No interaction
Division of labor possible	Division of labor impossible	No interaction
Decreased fear of failure	Increased fear of failure	No interaction

Hebeisen, 1977). Furthermore, Deutsch (1962) and other researchers (Johnson, 1974a) found that trust is built through cooperative interaction and is destroyed through competitive interaction.

Exchange of information   The seeking of information, and utilizing it in one's learning, is essential for academic achievement. Moreover, there is evidence that in problem-solving situations, students working within a cooperative goal structure will seek significantly more information from each other than will students working within a competitive goal structure (Crawford & Haaland, 1972). There is also evidence that students working within a cooperative goal structure will make optimal use of the information provided by other students, whereas students working within a competitive goal structure will fail to do so (Laughlin & McGlynn, 1967). Blake and Mouton (1961) provide evidence that competition biases a person's perceptions and the comprehension of viewpoints and positions of other individuals. A cooperative context, compared with a competitive one, promotes more accurate communication of information, more verbalization of ideas and information, more attentiveness to others' statements, and more acceptance of and willingness to be influenced by others' ideas and information. Furthermore, a cooperative context results in fewer difficulties in communicating with and understanding others, more confidence in one's own ideas and in the value that others attach to one's ideas, more frequent open and honest communication, and greater feelings of agreement between oneself and others (Johnson, 1974a; Johnson & R. Johnson, 1975).

Motivation   Motivation is most commonly viewed as a combination of the perceived likelihood of success and the perceived incentive for success. The greater the likelihood of success and the more important it is to succeed, the higher the motivation. Success that is intrinsically rewarding is usually seen as being more desirable for learning than is having students believe that only extrinsic rewards are worthwhile. There is a greater perceived likelihood of success and success is viewed as more important in a cooperative than in a competitive or individualistic learning situation (Johnson & R. Johnson, 1975).

The more cooperative students' attitudes, the more they see themselves as being intrinsically motivated: They persevere in pursuit of clearly defined learning goals; believe that it is their own efforts that determine their school success; want to be good students and get good grades; and believe that ideas, feelings, and learning new ideas are important and enjoyable (Johnson & Ahlgren, 1976; Johnson, Johnson, & Anderson, 1978). These studies also indicate that the more competitive students' attitudes are, the more they see themselves as being extrinsically motivated in elementary and junior high schools. Competitive attitudes are, however, somewhat related to intrinsic motivation, to being a good student, and to getting good marks in senior high school. Individualistic attitudes tend to be unrelated to all measured aspects of the motivation to learn. Being part of a cooperative learning group has been found to be related to a high subjective probability of academic success and continuing motivation for further learning by taking more advanced courses in the subject area studied (Gunderson & Johnson, 1980). There is also experimental evidence which indicates that cooperative learning experiences, compared with individualistic ones, will result in more intrinsic motivation, less extrinsic motivation, and less need for teachers to set clear goals for the students (Johnson, Johnson, & Anderson, 1976).

Emotional involvement in learning   Students are expected to become involved in instructional activities and to benefit from them as much as possible. There is evidence that the more cooperative students' attitudes are, the more they express their ideas and feelings in large and small classes and listen to the teacher, whereas competitive and individualistic attitudes are unrelated to indices of emotional involvement in instructional activities (Johnson & Ahlgren, 1976; Johnson, Johnson, & Anderson, 1978). There is evidence that cooperative learning experiences, compared with competitive and individualistic ones, result in a greater desire to express one's ideas to the class (Johnson, Johnson, Johnson, & Anderson, 1976; Wheeler & Ryan, 1973). Cooperative learning experiences, compared with competitive and individualistic ones, promote greater willingness to present one's answers and thus create more positive feelings toward one's answers and the instructional experience (Garibaldi, 1976; Gunderson & Johnson, 1980), as well as more positive attitudes toward the instructional tasks and subject areas (Garibaldi, 1976; Gunderson & Johnson, 1980; R. Johnson & Johnson, 1979; Johnson, Johnson, & Skon, 1979; Wheeler & Ryan, 1973).

Instructional Outcomes

There has been a great deal of research on the relationship among cooperative, competitive, and individualistic efforts and the cognitive and affective outcomes of instruction (Johnson & R. Johnson, 1975, 1978). According to hundreds of research studies that have been conducted, dramatically different learning outcomes will result from the use of the different goal structures. While space is too short in this chapter to review all of the research, the evidence concerning achievement, perspective-taking, self-esteem, psychological health, liking for other students, and positive attitudes toward school personnel such as teachers and principals will be discussed.

Achievement   Johnson, Maruyama, Johnson, Nelson, and Skon (1980) recently completed a meta-analysis of 108 studies comparing the relative effects of cooperative, competitive, and individualistic learning situations on achievement. The results strongly indicate that cooperative learning promotes higher achievement than do competitive and individualistic instruction. These results hold for all age levels, for all subject areas, and for tasks involving concept attainment, verbal problem-solving, categorizing, spatial problem-solving, retention and memory, motor performance, and guessing-judging-predicting. For rote-decoding and correcting tasks, cooperation does not seem to be superior. The average student in a cooperative situation performs at approximately the eightieth percentile of students in competitive and individualistic situations.

Perspective-taking   An important instructional question is, "Which goal structure is most conducive to promoting the emergence of social perspective-taking abilities?" A series of studies have found that cooperativeness is positively related to the ability to take the emotional perspective of others, and that competitiveness is related to egocentrism (Johnson, 1980; Barnett, Matthews, & Howard, 1979). Cooperative learning experiences, furthermore, have been found to promote greater cognitive and emotional perspective-taking abilities than either competitive or individualistic learning experiences (Bridgeman, 1977; Johnson, Johnson, Johnson, & Anderson, 1976).

Self-esteem   Schools are concerned with promoting student self-esteem for a variety of reasons, including school and postschool achievement and general psychological health and well-being. There is correlational evidence that cooperativeness is positively related to self-esteem in students throughout elementary, junior, and senior high school in rural, urban, and suburban settings; competitiveness is generally unrelated to self-esteem; and individualistic attitudes tend to be related to feelings of worthlessness and self-rejection (Gunderson & Johnson, 1980; Johnson & Ahlgren, 1976; Johnson, Johnson, & Anderson, 1978; Johnson & Norem-Hebeisen, 1977; Norem-Hebeisen & Johnson, 1980). There is experimental evidence indicating that cooperative learning experiences, compared with individualistic ones, result in higher self-esteem (Johnson, Johnson, & Scott, 1978); that cooperative learning experiences promote higher self-esteem than does learning in a traditional classroom (Blaney, et al., 1977; Geffner, 1978); and that failure in competitive situations promotes increased self-derogation (Ames, Ames, & Felker, 1977).

In a series of studies with suburban junior and senior high school students Norem-Hebeisen and Johnson (1980) examined the relationship among cooperative, competitive, and individualistic attitudes and ways of conceptualizing one's worth from the information that is available about oneself. Four primary ways of deriving self-esteem are: *(a)* basic self-acceptance (a belief in the intrinsic acceptability of oneself); *(b)* conditional self-acceptance (acceptance contingent on meeting external standards and expectations); *(c)* self-evaluation (one's estimate of how one compares with one's peers); and *(d)* real-ideal congruence (correspondence between what one thinks one is and what one thinks one should be). Attitudes toward cooperation are related to basic self-acceptance and positive self-evaluation compared to peers, whereas attitudes toward competition are related to conditional self-acceptance, and individualistic attitudes are related to basic self-rejection.

Psychological health The ability to build and maintain cooperative relationships is a primary manifestation of psychological health. Johnson and Norem-Hebeisen (1977) compared the attitudes of high school seniors toward cooperation, competition, and individualism with their responses on the Minnesota Multiphasic Personality Inventory (MMPI). They found that attitudes toward cooperation were significantly negatively correlated with 9 of the 10 scales indicating psychological pathology. Attitudes toward competition were significantly negatively correlated with 7 of the 10 psychological pathology scales. Attitudes toward individualism were significantly positively related to 9 of the 10 pathology scales. Both cooperation and competition involve relationships with other people, whereas individualistic activities involve isolation from other people. These findings indicate that an emphasis on cooperative involvement with other people and on appropriate competition during socialization may promote psychological health and well-being, whereas social isolation may promote psychological illness.

In addition, cooperative attitudes were significantly positively related to emotional maturity, well adjusted social relations, strong personal identity, the ability to resolve conflicts between self-perceptions and adverse information about oneself, amount of social participation, and basic trust and optimism. Attitudes toward competition were significantly related to emotional maturity, lack of a need for affection, the ability to resolve conflicts between self-perceptions and adverse information about oneself, social participation, and basic trust and optimism. Individualistic attitudes were significantly related to delinquency, emotional immaturity, social maladjustment, self-alienation, inability to resolve conflicts between self-perceptions and adverse information about oneself, self-rejection, lack of social participation, and basic distrust and pessimism.

Liking for other students   There is considerable evidence that cooperative experiences, compared with competitive and individualistic ones, result in more positive interpersonal relationships characterized by mutual liking, positive attitudes toward each other, mutual concern, friendliness, attentiveness, feelings of obligation to other students, and a desire to win the respect of other students (Johnson & R. Johnson, 1975, 1978). There is evidence that cooperative learning experiences, compared with individualistic ones, promote more positive attitudes toward heterogeneity among peers (Johnson, Johnson, & Scott, 1978), and that cooperativeness is related to liking peers who are smarter or less smart than oneself (Johnson & Ahlgren, 1976; Johnson, Johnson, & Anderson, 1978). In studies involving students from different ethnic groups, handicapped and nonhandicapped students, and male and female junior high school students, the evidence indicates that cooperative learning experiences, compared with competitive and individualistic ones, promotes more positive attitudes among heterogeneous students (Armstrong, Johnson, & Balow, 1980; Cook, 1978; Cooper, Johnson, Johnson, & Wilderson, 1980; DeVries & Slavin, 1978; Johnson, Rynders, Johnson, Schmidt, & Haider, 1979; Rynders, Johnson, Johnson, & Schmidt, in press; Slavin, 1978).

Liking for school personnel   The more favorable students' attitudes toward cooperation, the more they believe that teachers, teacher aides, counselors, and principals are important and positive; that teachers care about and want to increase students' learning; that teachers like and accept students as individuals; and that teachers and principals want to be friends with students (Gunderson & Johnson, 1980; Johnson & Ahlgren, 1976; Johnson, Johnson, & Anderson, 1978). Moreover, these findings hold in elementary, junior high, and senior high schools in rural, suburban, and urban school districts. In suburban junior and senior high schools, student competitiveness becomes positively related to perceptions of being liked and supported personally and academically by teachers. Individualistic attitudes are consistently unrelated to attitudes toward school personnel. There are also several field experimental studies that demonstrate that students experiencing cooperative instruction like the teacher better and perceive the teacher as being more supportive and accepting, academically and personally, than do students experiencing competitive and individualistic instruction (Gunderson & Johnson, 1980; Johnson, Johnson, Johnson, & Anderson, 1976; Johnson, Johnson, & Scott, 1978; Johnson, Johnson, & Tauer, 1979; Tjosvold, Marino, & Johnson, 1977; Wheeler & Ryan, 1973).

SUMMARY

Perhaps the most important aspect of group dynamics a teacher can control is the way in which learning goals are structured. The structure of the learning goals controls how students interact with each other which, in turn, greatly affects the cognitive and affective outcomes of instruction. When teachers wish to promote positive interaction among students (characterized by peer acceptance, support, and liking; student-student exchange of information; motivation to learn; and emotional involvement in learning), a cooperative goal structure should be used and competitive and individualistic goal structures should be avoided. The emphasis on positive goal interdependence among students not only will create the supportive, accepting, and caring relationships vital for socialization but will also promote achievement, perspective-taking ability, self-esteem, psychological health, liking for peers, and positive attitudes toward school personnel. . . .

REFERENCES

Ames, C., Ames, R., & Felker, D. Informational and dispositional determinants of children's achievement attributions. *Journal of Educational Psychology*, 1977, *68*, 63–69.

Armstrong, B., Johnson, D. W., & Balow, B. Cooperative goal structure as a means of integrating learning-disabled with normal-progress elementary pupils. *Contemporary Educational Psychology*, in press, 1980.

Barnett, M., Matthews, K., & Howard, J. Relationship between competitiveness and empathy in 6- and 7-year-olds. *Developmental Psychology*, 1979, *15*, 221–222.

Blake, R. R., & Mouton, J. S. Comprehension of own and outgroup positions under intergroup competition. *Journal of Conflict Resolution*, 1961, *5*, 304–310.

Blaney, N., Stephen, C., Rosenfield, D., Aronson, E., & Sikes, J. Inter-dependence in the classroom: A field study. *Journal of Educational Psychology*, 1977, 69, 139–146.

Bower, S. *Early identification of emotionally handicapped children in school*. Springfield, Illinois: Thomas, 1960.

Bridgeman, D. *Cooperative, interdependent learning and its enhancement of role-taking in fifth grade students*. Paper presented at the meeting of the American Psychological Association, San Francisco, August, 1977.

Cook, S. Interpersonal and attitudinal outcomes in cooperating interracial groups. *Journal of Research and Development in Education*, 1978, *12*, 97–113.

Cooper, L., Johnson, D. W., Johnson, R., & Wilderson, F. The effects of cooperation, competition, and individualization on cross-ethnic, cross-sex, and cross-ability friendships. *Journal of Social Psychology*, 1980.

Crawford, J., & Haaland, G. Predecisional information seeking and subsequent conformity in the social influence process. *Journal of Personality and Social Psychology*, 1972, *23*, 112–119.

Deutsch, M. Cooperation and trust: Some theoretical notes. In M. R. Jones (Ed.), *Nebraska symposium on motivation*. Lincoln, Nebraska: University of Nebraska Press, 1962, 275–320.

DeVries, D., & Slavin, R. Teams-games-tournaments: Review of ten classroom experiments. *Journal of Research and Development in Education*, 1978, *12*, 28–38.

Furman, W. *Friendship selections and individual peer interactions: A new approach to sociometric research*. Paper presented at biennial meetings of the Society for Research in Child Development, New Orleans, 1977.

Garibaldi, A. *Cooperation, competition, and locus of control in Afro-American students*. Unpublished doctoral dissertation, University of Minnesota, 1976.

Geffner, R. *The effects of interdependent learning on self-esteem, interethnic relations, and intraethnic attitudes of elementary school children: A field experiment*. Unpublished doctoral dissertation, University of California at Santa Cruz, 1978.

Gronlund, N. *Sociometry in the classroom*. New York: Harper, 1959.

Gunderson, B., & Johnson, D. W. Promoting positive attitudes toward learning a foreign language by using cooperative learning groups. *Foreign Language Annals*, 1980, *13*, 39–46.

Hartup, W., Glazer, J., & Charlesworth, R. Peer reinforcement and sociometric status. *Child Development*, 1967, *38*, 1017–1024.

Horowitz, F. The relationship of anxiety, self-concept, and sociometric status among 4th, 5th, and 6th grade children. *Journal of Abnormal and Social Psychology*, 1962, *65*, 212–214.

Johnson, D. W. Communication and the inducement of cooperative behavior in conflicts: A critical review. *Speech Monographs*, 1974, *41*, 64–78.

Johnson, D. W. Constructive peer relationships, social development, and cooperative learning experiences: Implications for the prevention of drug abuse. *Journal of Drug Education*, 1980, *10*, 7–24.

Johnson, D. W., & Ahlgren, A. Relationship between student attitudes about cooperation and competition and attitudes toward schooling. *Journal of Educational Psychology*, 1976, *68*, 92–102.

Johnson, D. W., & Johnson, R. *Learning together and alone: Cooperation, competition, and individualization*. Englewood Cliffs, New Jersey: Prentice-Hall, 1975.

Johnson, D. W., & Johnson, R. (Eds.). Social interdependence within instruction. *Journal of Research and Development in Education*, 1978, *12*(1).

Johnson, D. W., Johnson, R., & Anderson, D. Relationship between student cooperative, competitive, and individualistic attitudes and attitudes toward schooling. *Journal of Psychology*, 1978, *100*, 183–199.

Johnson, D. W., Johnson, R., Johnson, J., & Anderson, D. The effects of cooperative vs. individualized instruction on student prosocial behavior, attitudes toward learning, and achievement. *Journal of Educational Psychology*, 1976, *68*, 446–452.

Johnson, D. W., Johnson, R., & Scott, L. The effects of cooperative and individualized instruction on student attitudes and achievement. *Journal of Social Psychology*, 1978, *104*, 207–216.

Johnson, D. W., Johnson, R., & Skon, L. Student achievement on different types of tasks under cooperative, competitive, and individualistic conditions. *Contemporary Educational Psychology*, 1979, *4*, 99–106.

Johnson, D. W., & Matross, R. The interpersonal influence of the psychotherapist. In A. Gurman & A. Razin (Eds.), *The effective therapist: A handbook.* Elmsford, New York: Pergamon Press, 1977.

Johnson, D. W., & Norem-Hebeisen, A. Attitudes toward interdependence among persons and psychological health. *Psychological Reports,* 1977, *40,* 843–850.

Johnson, D. W., Maruyama, G., Johnson, R., Nelson, D., & Skon, L. The effects of cooperative, competitive, and individualistic goal structures on achievement: A meta-analysis. University of Minnesota, *Psychological Bulletin,* 1980.

Johnson, R., & Johnson, D. W. Type of task and student achievement and attitudes in interpersonal cooperation, competition, and individualization. *Journal of Social Psychology,* 1979, *108,* 37–48.

Johnson, R., Johnson, D. W., & Tauer, M. Effects of cooperative, competitive, and individualistic goal structures on students' achievement and attitudes. *Journal of Psychology,* 1979, *102,* 191–198.

Johnson, R., Rynders, J., Johnson, D. W., Schmidt, B., & Haider, S. Producing positive interaction between handicapped and nonhandicapped teenagers through cooperative goal structuring: Implications for mainstreaming. *American Educational Research Journal,* 1979, *16,* 161–168.

Laughlin, P., & McGlynn, R. Cooperative versus competitive concept attainment as a function of sex and stimulus display. *Journal of Personality and Social Psychology,* 1967, *7,* 398–402.

Mensh, I., & Glidewell, J. Children's perceptions of relationships among their family and friends. *Journal of Experimental Education,* 1958, *27,* 23–39.

Norem-Hebeisen, A., & Johnson, D. W. The relationship between cooperative, competitive, and individualistic attitudes and differentiated aspects of self-esteem. University of Minnesota, mimeographed report, submitted for publication, 1980.

Rynders, J., Johnson, R., Johnson, D. W., & Schmidt, B. Effects of cooperative goal structuring in producing positive interaction between Down's Syndrome and nonhandicapped teenagers: Implications for mainstreaming. *American Journal of Mental Deficiencies,* in press.

Schmuck, R. Some relationships of peer liking patterns in the classroom to pupil attitudes and achievement. *School Review,* 1963, *71,* 337–359.

Schmuck, R. Some aspects of classroom social climate. *Psychology in the School,* 1966, *3,* 59–65.

Slavin, R. Students teams and achievement divisions. *Journal of Research and Development in Education,* 1978, *12.*

Tjosvold, D., Marino, P., & Johnson, D. W. Cooperation and competition and student acceptance of inquiry and didactic teaching. *Journal of Research in Science Teaching,* 1977, *14,* 281–288.

Van Egmond, E. *Social interrelationship skills and effective utilization of intelligence in the classroom.* Unpublished doctoral dissertation, University of Minnesota, 1960.

Wheeler, R., & Ryan, F. Effects of cooperative and competitive classroom environments on the attitudes and achievement of elementary school students engaged in social studies inquiry activities. *Journal of Educational Psychology,* 1973, *65,* 402–407.

THEODORE C. WAGENAAR

High School Seniors' Views of Themselves and Their Schools: A Trend Analysis

Questions to think about

1 *What changes in students' views occurred between 1972 and 1980? What do you think accounted for these changes?*

2 *How are students' views of themselves and of their schools shaped by their experiences in the bureaucracy? Refer to related articles such as the one by David W. Johnson.*

3 *To what extent are the changes outlined here a product of the larger societal system or environment outside the school, as opposed to the school experience?*

4 *How do these findings compare with your own attitudes and experiences in high school?*

A great many changes in society and in the schools occurred during the Seventies. At the beginning of the decade high school students faced the realities of Vietnam, the Kent State shootings, widespread student activism, the draft, the coalescence of the women's movement, a growing economy, a deemphasis on academics, and a landing on the moon. By the end of the decade a great deal had changed. Military service was voluntary; the economy was stagnating; energy had become scarce and costly. Although the women's movement continued to expand, a move to the political right was under way, and, in education, the rallying cry was "back to basics."

Such momentous changes should be reflected in the experiences and attitudes of high school students, but documenting these effects has generally been difficult. The completion of two nationwide studies of high

From the *Phi Delta Kappan* (September 1981):29–31. Reprinted by permission of the author.

school students—one undertaken near the beginning of the decade (1972), the other at the end (1980)—makes possible a trend analysis of the views of high school seniors toward themselves and their schools.

Both studies were sponsored by the National Center for Education Statistics, employed longitudinal design, and made use of large stratified random samples, which make it possible to draw conclusions about the entire population of seniors at the beginning and at the end of the 1970s. (All reported values are weighted.)

The *National Longitudinal Study* of the high school class of 1972 was completed by the Research Triangle Institute. Base-year data were gathered from seniors in the spring of 1972, and follow-up surveys were administered in the autumns of 1973, 1974, 1976, and 1979. The base-year questionnaire, which provided the data I used in this study, was administered to 16,683 students in 1,062 schools (typically 18 per school).[1]

The *High School and Beyond Study* of 1980 high school seniors and sophomores was completed by the National Opinion Research Center. Base-year data were gathered in the spring of 1980 from 30,030 sophomores and 28,240 seniors in 1,015 high schools (typically 36 seniors and 36 sophomores per school). I used only the seniors in my analysis.[2]

ACADEMIC ISSUES

Data are available on several aspects of seniors' academic achievements and orientations. The data on standardized test scores show a negligible decline in mathematics scores (from a mean of 12.9 items correct out of 25 possible in 1972 to 12.6 in 1980) and modest declines in vocabulary scores (6.4 to 5.7, out of 15 possible) and reading scores (9.7 to 8.8, out of 20 possible). These figures confirm previous findings regarding a general, if modest, decline in test scores.

If test scores have declined and if teachers are still applying similar standards, we would expect a corresponding decline in grades. But such is not the case. The proportion of students receiving grades of B or better increased slightly between 1972 and 1980 (from 29% to 33%), while the proportions receiving grades ranging from B to C and from C to D declined slightly (from 50% to 47% and from 21% to 19% respectively). The proportion receiving mostly D's or lower remained constant at 1%. Females typically receive higher grades than do males. This finding is curious, given the negligible sex differences in the vocabulary and reading test scores and the small edge for males in mathematics.

Perhaps students in 1980 are receiving higher grades than students in 1972 because they are doing more homework. The data do not support this explanation, however. Although the proportions of students with no homework assigned and of those who do not do their homework declined slightly (from 4% to 3% and from 7% to 4% respectively), the proportion doing fewer than five hours per week increased dramatically, from 54% to 68%. Meanwhile, the proportion doing five to 10 hours per week declined from 30% in 1972 to 18% in 1980, and the proportion doing more than 10 hours per week remained stable at about 6%.

Males are almost twice as likely as females to report that no homework was assigned and nearly four times as likely to refuse to do assigned homework. For both variables, however, the percentages were low. Females, on the other hand, are much more likely than males to do more than five hours of homework per week. Hence females are more likely to complete homework assignments, and this may explain their tendency to earn higher grades than males.

Perhaps students in 1980 received higher grades, despite doing less homework, because their study habits improved over the decade. But both males and females reported substantially higher levels of difficulty with study habits in 1980 than in 1972. In 1972, 65% of the males and 50% of the females noted that poor study habits had interfered with their education; in 1980 the respective proportions were 76% and 66%. Although males reported more difficulties than females in both years, the increase over the decade was considerably greater for females. Increased difficulties with studying may stem from a wide range of factors: less adequate instruction in study habits in the elementary and junior high grades, less homework assigned, less support for doing homework from teachers and parents, reduced ability to do homework, and reduced availability of a specific place to study at home. With respect to this last item, the data show a decline over the decade from 59% to 49% of students having a specific place to study.

The data presented above clearly reflect grade inflation. One of the dangers during a period of grade inflation is that students may develop inaccurate assessments of their abilities. Too high grades may engender a false sense of academic security. In fact, the proportion of seniors stating that they definitely have the ability to complete college rose from 42% in 1972 to 48% in 1980.

FUTURE EXPECTATIONS

Seniors' expectations for the future are typically focused on education and employment. In terms of the former, students look forward to higher levels of education in 1980 than they did in 1972. The proportion of seniors anticipating some postgraduate education rose from 13% in 1972 to 21%

in 1980. The substantial difference that was evident in 1972 between men and women anticipating graduate study (17% and 9% respectively) disappeared by 1980. Thus the increase in the proportion of women anticipating graduate study was considerably greater than that for men.

The proportion of seniors not expecting to graduate from high school dropped from 2% to nearly zero. However, these figures do not reflect the actual incidence of dropping out, since all of those surveyed were already seniors. The proportion of seniors planning some type of vocational, technical, or business education as their highest level of academic attainment remained constant at about 18%, but the proportion planning on two- or four-year college declined from 51% to 41%. This decline is largely made up by the increase among those anticipating postgraduate education.

Several shifts occurred in the selection of a college major among those planning to attend college. Among the majors that more high school seniors preferred in 1980 than in 1972 were: business (13% to 22%), engineering (5% to 9%), and computer and information sciences (2% to 4%). Majors exhibiting the greatest decrease in student selection included social sciences (17% to 7%) and education (12% to 6%). A number of other majors selected by fewer than 5% of students in 1972 did even less well in 1980: English, ethnic studies, foreign languages, interdisciplinary studies, mathematics, music, philosophy or religion, and physical science. Seniors' choices are clearly moving from education, social sciences, and several liberal arts categories to business and the technical fields of engineering and computer sciences. Undoubtedly, part of the shift can be attributed to greater job opportunities in these technical fields. The data also show that women are increasingly selecting majors formerly dominated by males, especially business, communications, engineering, and mathematics.

The most striking feature of the job expectations of high school seniors is the similarity between the occupational choices in the two years. Nearly half the students in both years plan a professional career (46% in 1972 and 44% in 1980). The second most frequently selected occupational category is clerical, although fewer students selected this category in 1980 (10%) than in 1972 (14%). Although still relatively small, the proportion of students selecting the manager/administrator category has more than doubled (3% to 7%), as has the proportion selecting the proprietor/owner category (less than 2% to 4%). Most of the remaining occupational categories were each selected by fewer than 5% of the seniors in both years, and none of the differences between the two years exceeded 1%. The categories that increased most were business-related—a finding that parallels the increased selection of business as a college major.

All categories except sales were selected predominantly by one sex, and this pattern is found in both years. However, some of the disparity between males and females has been reduced. The largest change has occurred in the proportion of females selecting the clerical category (25% in 1972 and 17% in 1980). In short, the pattern of sex differences in occupational selection is similar in both years, but fewer women are selecting clerical occupations and more are choosing professional and business occupations.

For the year immediately following high school, women increasingly select attendance at an academic college, and men increasingly select full-time work. The proportion of males planning to attend an academic college declined slightly between 1972 and 1980 (from 46% to 44%), while the number planning to work full time increased from 25% to 32%. Women who were planning to attend an academic college increased from 44% to 49%, while the number who planned to work full time remained constant at 27%. In short, the predominant choice for the immediate future continues to be attendance at an academic college; working full time remains a distant second choice.

VALUES

Several significant shifts in the values held by seniors occurred during the Seventies. Six factors affecting seniors' occupational expectations for themselves at age 30 were examined (see Table 1). In both years the rank ordering of the six factors was as follows (highest to lowest): important and interesting work, meeting friendly people, freedom to make decisions, job security, good income, and previous work experience in the area. However, considerably greater proportions of seniors in 1980 rated *each* of these factors as "very important" than did their counterparts in 1972. This suggests that seniors today are more concerned about these basic factors than they were nearly 10 years ago. (Perhaps in 1972 other factors not included in this list, such as the social relevance of a particular occupation, were judged more important.) The greatest increases were found for freedom to make decisions, job security, and good income; undoubtedly the stagnating economy contributed to these changes.

In addition, several sex differences emerged. In both years females were much more likely than males to stress the importance of meeting and working with friendly people; they were somewhat more likely to stress the role of important and interesting work. Males were more likely in both years to stress the importance of good income, but women are narrowing the gap. While men were more likely to stress the importance of job security in 1972, no difference existed in 1980. And while men were more likely than women to emphasize autonomy in 1972, in 1980 the reverse was true.

T A B L E 1
Choice of Occupation Factors, by Year and Sex*

	1972			1980		
% Rating factor very important	Males %*	Females %*	Total %*	Males %*	Females %*	Total %*
Prior experience	19.3	19.3	19.3	29.6	31.7	30.7
Good income	35.8	26.5	31.1	48.3	43.4	45.7
Job security	43.4	37.9	40.6	57.8	58.1	58.0
Important work	75.5	82.8	79.2	81.4	89.4	85.6
Freedom to make decisions	46.4	40.0	43.2	60.6	63.0	61.8
Meet /work with friendly people	47.2	67.5	57.4	58.4	72.6	65.9

*Percentages reported for "very important" category only.

Seniors were asked to rate several work-related values in terms of importance in their lives as a whole. Table 2, part A, displays these data. Being successful in their work was rated very important by more than 80% of seniors in both years. Having lots of money was seen as very important by only 18% of seniors in 1972 but by 31% in 1980. While the increase occurred for both men and women, more men continued to regard money as very important than do women. The proportion noting steady work as very important rose slightly. Both men and women attached more importance to income and job security in 1980—a finding that may reflect their coming of age during a period of economic decline.

Parts B, C, and D of Table 2 display data for family, community, and other values in terms of the importance seniors attach to them. A happy family was rated very important by more than 80% of seniors in both years; the slightly higher proportion of women attaching importance to a happy family was constant from 1972 to 1980. Two-thirds of men and of women in both years rated better opportunities for their children very important. The proportion who rated living close to parents and relatives as very important nearly doubled (8% to 14%) between 1972 and 1980. Thus family values still constitute an important part of the lives of high school seniors.

Being a leader in the community was very important to only about 10% of the seniors in both years. Men were more likely to rate this value highly and women to rate happy family life highly, suggesting continued

T A B L E   2
"Very Important" Life Values, by Year and Sex *

	1972			1980		
	Males %	Females %	Total %	Males %	Females %	Total %
A. Work						
1. Being successful in work	86.1	82.7	84.4	89.1	87.8	88.4
2. Having lots of money	25.9	9.7	17.8	40.5	23.1	31.4
3. Finding steady work	81.9	73.2	77.6	85.8	83.0	84.3
B. Family						
1. Happy family life	78.5	84.9	81.7	78.0	83.4	81.0
2. Giving kids better opportunities	66.5	66.4	66.5	67.3	66.5	66.9
3. Living close to parents/relatives	7.1	8.3	7.7	13.0	14.8	14.0
C. Community/Society						
1. Being leader in community	14.7	8.1	11.3	12.3	7.4	9.7
2. Helping correct inequalities	22.4	31.3	26.9	12.3	13.6	13.0
D. Other						
1. Having strong friendships	80.5	78.3	79.4	81.2	81.8	81.5
2. Moving away from area	14.5	14.6	14.6	14.7	14.0	14.3

* Percentages reported for "very important" category only.

sex-role socialization. Seniors rated working to correct social and economic inequalities much less important in 1980 than in 1972 (27% to 13%); this decline was particularly pronounced among women. Strong friendships continued to be very important to about four-fifths of both men and women in both years. Moving to a new area was not very important in either year.

The values held by seniors have changed little between 1972 and 1980. Seniors continue to stress successful and steady work, a happy family life, and strong friendships. But seniors of the early 1980s are clearly less concerned with remedying social inequalities and more concerned with financial security than were their 1972 counterparts.

THE SCHOOLS

Thus far we have seen how seniors feel about themselves, their achievements, and their futures. What of the changes in curriculum and instruction within the high schools themselves? What of changes in facilities and programs?

I found a high degree of similarity between 1972 and 1980 in both the frequency with which students mentioned certain instructional techniques and in the proportions of seniors noting frequent exposure to them. Lecturing is by far the most frequently used technique. More than 80% of both males and females in both years report often or frequent exposure to lectures. Writing and discussion are the next most commonly employed techniques. A clear majority of students in both years experienced both discussion and writing (59% and 64% respectively). In both years, women noted more frequent exposure to discussion and writing than did men (about six percentage points difference for each year). Women may be more likely to take English and other courses in which discussion and writing frequently occur, while men may be more likely to take mathematics and science courses, where discussion and writing occur less frequently.

Somewhat less than half the seniors frequently worked on projects or in a laboratory—a figure that declined slightly between 1972 and 1980 (from 49% to 44%). About a fourth of the seniors noted frequent use of individualized instruction in both years, with the proportion of women slightly higher than men. While computers and teaching machines were more frequently used in 1980, the increase is not as substantial (from 12% to 16%) as might have been predicted.

In short, instructional techniques do not seem to be changing very dramatically in response to societal events. The proliferation of computers in society might be expected to have filtered down to the high schools. I would also have expected increased emphasis on writing, given the prominence of the back-to-basics movement and college instructors' complaints about poor writing. But the reports of the students in the 1980 survey differ only slightly from those of their counterparts nearly a decade earlier.

Table 3 reports the ratings given by seniors to various aspects of their high schools. Students were asked if they felt that their high school should have placed more emphasis on academic subjects. While half agreed in 1972, nearly three-fourths agreed in 1980. This finding is particularly interesting when compared with the previously noted decline in test scores, decline in the amount of homework done, and modest increase in study habit problems. Table 3 also shows that nearly half the seniors reported that the difficulty of some courses has interfered with their education. Thus

T A B L E   3
Characteristics of High School, by Year and Sex

	1972			1980		
Agreeing*	Males %	Females %	Total %	Males %	Females %	Total %
1. School should have placed more emphasis on academics.	49.4	50.6	50.1	70.6	72.7	71.7
2. School should have placed more emphasis on vocations.	69.7	72.3	71.1	76.0	74.5	75.2
3. School did not offer enough practical work experience.	69.4	65.3	67.4	65.8	62.5	64.1
4. School provided counseling to help continue education.	62.6	62.7	62.7	66.9	64.9	65.8
5. School provided counseling to help find employment.	35.0	40.0	37.6	50.2	48.3	49.2
Rating as good or excellent †						
1. Condition of buildings and classrooms	70.4	68.1	69.2	65.6	61.9	63.7
2. Library facilities	65.0	62.9	64.0	68.5	67.4	67.9
3. Quality of academic instruction	66.1	67.6	66.8	65.8	63.1	64.4
4. Reputation in community	74.6	75.7	75.1	69.3	68.6	68.9
5. Teacher interest in students	51.1	52.3	51.7	56.6	54.1	55.3
Noting that the following interfered with their education						
1. Courses too hard	43.3	41.0	42.1	49.0	49.2	49.1
2. School routine	28.3	20.0	24.1	34.4	25.6	29.8
3. Poor teaching	50.1	50.5	50.3	59.7	60.8	60.3

*Those to whom the question did not apply were deleted from the base.
†Those responding "don't know" were deleted from the base.

seniors in 1980 seem to be responding to factors other than grades (which have improved) in their desire for more emphasis on academic subjects.

Perhaps seniors hold teachers partly responsible for their difficulties. The percentage of students rating the quality of academic instruction as good or excellent is fairly high, but it has declined slightly since 1972 (67% to 64%). In addition, the proportion of seniors noting that poor teaching has interfered with their education has risen from 50% to 60%, despite the fact that the rating given teacher interest in students has increased slightly. Seniors in 1980 apparently have mixed reactions to teachers and their teaching. On the one hand, more students in 1980 sense teacher interest; on the other hand, more of these same students say they have been hindered to a degree by poor teaching.

Nearly three-fourths of seniors in both years felt that their high schools should have placed more emphasis on vocational and technical programs, and about two-thirds noted that their schools did not offer enough practical work experience. Whereas their concern with academics is relatively recent, students have felt the desire for more emphasis on vocational and technical programs throughout the decade. Taken together, these desires pose a difficult problem for curriculum planners. It will be interesting to see how they respond to the large proportion of students desiring increased emphasis on *both* academic courses and vocational/technical courses.

Nevertheless, high school personnel *do* seem to be giving more attention to the vocational needs of their students. Whereas 38% of the seniors in 1972 noted that their high schools provided them with employment counseling, by 1980 that figure had risen to 49%. This increase may be due in part to greater federal funding for vocational education activities. However, many students continue to see the counselor's role as primarily focused on postsecondary education. Nearly two-thirds in each year agreed that their high schools provided them with this type of counseling.

Students were also asked to rate their high school's facilities and its reputation in the community. The proportion of students who rated the condition of buildings and classrooms as good or excellent fell slightly, while the proportion giving a good or excellent rating to the library facilities rose slightly. Ratings given to the reputation of the school in the community also showed a small decline. The reported decline in the condition of buildings may stem from reduced budgets for maintenance and new construction. The decline in reputation may be associated with increased public concern for discipline and declining achievement.

Only one item surveys the effects of bureaucratization on the high school experiences of seniors: The percentage noting serious difficulty adjusting to school routine rose from 24% in 1972 to 30% in 1980. In both years males were more likely to report such problems.

MAJOR TRENDS

At least three major trends emerge from the comparison of the experiences and attitudes of high school seniors in 1972 with those of seniors in 1980.

The first of these trends is that seniors at the end of the decade show an increased emphasis on the importance of academics. This is especially interesting in light of the fact that at the end of the decade they are experiencing more study-habit problems and doing less homework. Nevertheless, the greatest change among all the variables I examined was the increase in the proportion of seniors indicating that their high school should have placed more emphasis on academics. Seniors also increasingly reported that poor teaching had interfered with their education. Perhaps the heightened attention of the media and such developments as minimum competency testing have combined to sensitize today's students to the widespread societal concern for falling academic achievement.

The second major trend is reflected in the realm of student values. Seniors today show a heightened awareness of economic problems, which is reflected in the increased importance they attach to high income and job security. Although the grim realities of the job market have caused seniors today to attach more importance to all work-related values and less importance to correcting social inequities than did seniors in 1972, a striking consistency also characterizes the things they value. Seniors today continue to stress the importance of success at work, of a happy family life, and of strong friendships. They value these goals even more highly than they do job security and high income.

The growth of the women's movement has been a major development during the past decade, and its influence accounts for the third major trend in the data: The expectations for education and employment of men and women are more similar in 1980 than they were in 1972. Although many significant sex differences still exist, the data reflect a lessening of the effects of traditional sex-role socialization. For example, the discrepancies between the sexes in time spent on homework and study-habit difficulties have diminished. The plans for postgraduate education of men and women are now virtually identical, and females are now more likely than males to plan to attend college. In addition, the percentage of females selecting clerical occupations is smaller in 1980 than in 1972. Across the board the expectations and aspirations of young men and women are becoming more alike. Similar reductions in sex differences have occurred in such life values as the importance of money, of steady work, and of correcting social inequalities. All of these developments took place during a time of growing acceptance of the women's movement and may plausibly reflect the impact of this significant social change.

These three trends in the data show evidence of both consistency and change in the attitudes of seniors during the Seventies. Moreover, the reciprocal relationship between society and education emerges most clearly where attitudes have changed most significantly: in lessening of sex-related differences, in increased stress on work-related values, and especially in the renewed emphasis on academics.

NOTES

1. Jay Levinsohn et al., *National Longitudinal Study Base-Year, First, Second, and Third Follow-up Data File Users Manual* (Washington, D.C.: National Center for Education Statistics, 1978).
2. *High School and Beyond: Information for Users* (Chicago: National Opinion Research Center, 1980).

DAN LORTIE

The Partial Professionalization of Elementary Teaching

Questions to think about

1 *What is the process by which teachers learn their roles? Why could teachers be called semiprofessionals or partial professionals?*

2 *Using your knowledge of teacher roles, how do teachers differ from other professionals? What would have to happen to change their status?*

3 *Where do teachers fit in the overall educational system? Diagram teachers' reciprocal relations with others in their role set within the open system.*

4 *Design a research project to study the teacher role. Indicate questions you would ask and methods you would use.*

ELEMENTARY TEACHING AND THE ESTABLISHED PROFESSIONS

Although sociologists have not achieved consensus on a single set of criteria for the identification of professions, there is general agreement that a few fields clearly belong within the category. Examples are medicine, law, and architecture. But such fields are fee-for-service professions where the practitioner renders service to an aggregate of clients. The problem is to find organizational characteristics peculiar to professions which can, with equal facility, be applied to salaried occupations. Direct

From *The Semi-Professions and Their Organization,* edited by Amitai Etzioni. Copyright © 1969 by The Free Press. Reprinted by permission of Macmillan, Inc.

and concrete applications of fee-for-service categories create confusion. (Who is the client of the elementary teacher: students? parents? taxpayers? the school system?) We can, however, locate certain issues which must be resolved in all occupations, and, noting the peculiar resolution employed in clearly established professions, test individual fields in terms of the proximity of their resolutions to professional ones. We use four such issues here:

1. How the individual relates to the market.
2. The nature of knowledge and skill possessed by members of the occupation.
3. The relation established to the polity.
4. The extent to which those performing similar activities influence the careers of members of the occupation.

The established practitioner in a well-established profession occupies a favored position in the market.[1] He can assert himself vis-à-vis a single client without serious economic risk, for the multiplicity of his clientele and their lack of organization reduces his economic dependence upon any single individual. This economic independence provides him with a basis for professional autonomy; he can choose to act in ways congruent with professional norms when the latter collide with the wishes of a client. He can withstand pressures which he considers contrary to his professional principles or interests.

Elementary teachers receive their income from "one big client." But is it not true that tenure arrangements serve to balance the exchange and give the teacher an autonomy similar to that enjoyed by the professional practitioner? There are differences between the functions served by multiple clienteles and tenure; tenure protects the individual in his position only within a given school district. It is difficult for elementary teachers to build a reputation which transcends their local area; teaching, even superb teaching, throws a short shadow. Since mechanisms for broadcasting one's competence are limited, the teacher cannot be entirely unconcerned with her employer's goodwill. Since employment elsewhere can be threatened by negative recommendations, the teacher is wise to avoid actions which would antagonize her "one big client."

The knowledge and skill possessed by those practicing established professions are recognized both as vital to individual and social welfare and as esoteric in nature. The layman experiences here his vulnerable status—he knows he needs the professional's service and lacks the professional's knowledge and skill. The critical point is that of evaluation by relevant publics; whatever the actual state of professional knowledge in scientific terms, the relevant publics (clients, political agencies, and the like) *believe* that knowledge to be both essential and restricted to members of the professional group. The possession of esoteric knowledge over a period of time strengthens those within the profession vis-à-vis the public in *general* terms. There are indications that protracted occupancy of professional status permits an occupation to play an important role in defining the very nature of the service it will provide. Thus, lawyers have influenced the meaning and substance of justice, and, in some respects, doctors have defined the essential characteristics of health and illness.

"No one ever died of a split infinitive" is a quip which throws the less-than-vital nature of teaching knowledge into relief. Nor can elementary teachers point to an arcane body of substantive or technical knowledge to assert professional status vis-à-vis the school board or the public-at-large. That which is taught in elementary school is presumed to be known by almost all adults, and teachers have not been able to convince many critics— and more importantly, legislatures—that "methods courses" constitute a truly distinct and impressive body of knowledge.[2] The subjects teachers themselves believe useful in teaching (e.g., child psychology) are primarily the property of others. Lacking the clear autonomy which leads to the assurance that professional knowledge will provide the basis of action, teachers have not developed codified and systematic bodies of professional knowledge; lacking that knowledge, their stance vis-à-vis laymen is, in turn, weakened.

The state can ill-afford to ignore well-established professions and the claims of persons to their powers, for, since the service is presumed to be vital, the charlatan can threaten the welfare of citizens. Complex licensure arrangements develop which are mainly delegated by political authorities to members of the profession who implement them. Such delegation is not, however, a formal abrogation of powers: there is the implied threat to reclaim the government of affairs by political officials should the profession lose their confidence.

The situation in licensing elementary teachers is somewhat quixotic. A complex and elaborate procedure exists which, as Conant indicates, is by-passed by thousands of teachers.[3] Lieberman points out that educational licensing boards are *not* controlled by members of the teaching profession.[4] Further confusion is evident when we observe that some high-status schools, such as private preparatory schools, employ teachers without regard to such certification specifics where they can do so.

Those outside a well-established profession, acknowledging their ignorance of its special knowledge, are inclined to delegate much of its governance to members of the professions. It makes sense to conceptualize this process as one of exchange by means of which the profession can retain its self-governing perquisites as long as it retains the trust of political authorities. Professions possess and use complex formal machinery for the discipline of errant members who threaten that exchange. But what is less widely realized is that in important sectors of the professions, senior colleagues hold enormous and sustained power over the careers of those aspiring to full recognition.[5] Informal referral systems in medicine and partnership probation periods in law and architecture enable senior practitioners to undertake protracted testing of the technical competence and normative integrity of aspirants.

The ambiguity of colleague group boundaries makes it difficult for an observer to decide whether teachers are subjected to collegial scrutiny in their career progression. The tenure promotion, for example, is assessed by administrative superiors (the principal and superintendent normally recommend candidates to the board) but not by fellow teachers. It is a curious fact, unexplained by Sharma, that teachers in his national sample did not wish to participate in personnel decisions about other teachers.[6]

This review of four issues reveals as much dissimilarity as similarity to professional modes of resolution. We encounter serious ambiguities on each count; the role of the elementary teacher differs significantly from that found in situations where professional status is uncontested.

THE INCOMPLETE SUBCULTURE

The controls one finds in well-established professions are more than external mechanisms for rewarding the faithful and punishing the deviants. Members of a profession are supposed to internalize the standards of their profession—they talk of "professional conscience." But the inculcation of such standards requires an elaborate subculture buttressed by complex machinery for its transmission to neophytes.[7] Witness, for example, the protracted socialization we find in medicine with its pre-medical curriculum, its four years of specialized schooling, its complex internship and residency arrangements. Established professions take few chances with newcomers—the neophyte is subjected to years of scrutiny and indoctrination by professors and members of the profession.

Elementary teaching represents, at best, a faint replica of such inculcation of technical and moral practices. Although inquiry into teacher socialization is still very limited, it is possible to note some important ways in which teaching, as a subculture, differs from what is associated with a high degree of professionalization.

Entrants to most professions are, as materials for professional socialization, largely unformed. Few students entering law or medicine or architecture are intimately familiar with the working round of practitioners or feel qualified to make judgments about professional performances. Teaching, on the other hand, is well known to entrants, and they have already formed opinions about what constitutes an effective teaching performance. Teachers interviewed by the author were able to describe their outstanding public school teachers in considerable detail, and some volunteered the information that they currently employ techniques learned as young students.[8] Those seeking to socialize their students into a particular conception of teaching must overcome such preexisting attitudes and values. It is noteworthy that the same teachers who found it easy to describe their former teachers had difficulty in describing colleagues of outstanding competence; their replies frequently contained the phrase "we never see each other at work." These data suggest that the flow of influence from generation to generation encounters less influence from colleagues than we associate with professional fields and may, in fact, account for the conservatism ascribed to school people by Waller and Durkheim.[9]

We have noted that the public school network, as a series of linked organizations, can eliminate those who, as students or beginning teachers, fail to show the appropriate characteristics and attitudes. To test for *general* acceptability, however, is not the same process as indoctrinating beginners with a set of clear, precise, and usable specifications for the performance of the occupation's tasks. The role of college preparation for teaching is not well understood at the present time, but it appears that its potency, in confronting students with extended prior exposure to teaching, is limited. Teachers themselves tend to discount the contribution of pre-service courses in influencing their current work habits and choices.[10] Some studies point to a shift in teacher attitudes as they move from professional training courses to actual classroom confrontation.[11] One study indicates that actual experience in teaching tends to "wash out" earlier differences associated with attendance at different types of undergraduate colleges.[12] There is no evidence that pre-service experiences provide those exposed to them with a significant body of directives for teaching or affect their work values in lasting fashion.

There is indication that work socialization occurs primarily during the beginner's actual confrontation with responsibility in performing occupational tasks.[13] Elementary teachers acquire their substantive knowledge through sixteen years of studentship, but what of the core interpersonal skills involved in their craft? Learning to control a class of thirty students, determining appropriate levels of vocabulary and effective sequences of presentation, realizing variations in individual potentials for learning— these are complex accomplishments requiring immersion in actual teaching. Elementary teachers usually undergo a period of practice teaching before assignment to a regular class and one study shows that the tutelage of the supervising teacher has an important influence.[14] But it is significant to observe that the first year of actual teaching experience—the point of full involvement in accountable teaching responsibility—is generally not accompanied by regular or intensive contact with senior colleagues. The beginning elementary teacher is, of course, "visited" by the principal and probably a central office supervisor, but the fraction of working time which is supervised is very small. (Twelve visits of two hours' duration each would be high and would consist of less than 3 per cent of the teacher's first year, estimated at thirty-eight weeks of thirty hours each.) Where obvious trouble arises with a beginning teacher, special attention will be paid; otherwise, she may be left almost entirely to her own resources in mastering her new role. Other teachers have little time available, for they too are caught in the time and space economy of elementary schools which permits them little time away from students. The system of supervising beginning teachers is compatible with the exercise of gross control and of centering on trouble points; it does *not* suggest a precise instrument of work socialization through which the organization or professional colleagues engage in on-the-spot assistance to the newcomer. Elementary teachers learn their core skills in isolation from other adults.

Occupational cultures, no less than other types, grow through protracted interaction and communication among members of the group. Teaching, as an activity involving contact with students, is carried on by individuals whose contacts with one another are essentially at the periphery of the central transactions. Such conditions are neither likely to produce a culture marked by rich, specific, and detailed technical terms and procedures nor calculated to develop norms which operationalize values. We can see this in the state of practical knowledge about teaching, for, in addition to the private nature of this activity, there are no regular mechanisms for overcoming its evanescent qualities. Teaching techniques are developed and used by thousands of individuals in restricted contact with one another; there are no general expectations that individual teachers should record their experiences in such a way that it becomes the general property of the professional group. No provisions are made in the daily schedule of the teacher for such activity. Yet we note that physicians since Galen (with important historical gaps) have identified and described syndromes and have tested and recorded alternative therapies and their effects. Law, through its elaborate, refined procedures for recording the deliberations and decisions of courts, represents the distillation of generations of practitioner effort. The successes and failures of architects are recorded in stone, wood, and steel. Experience in these professions has a cumulative quality; what teachers learn is largely lost. It is not possible for the professor of education to gain ready access to decades of "cases" for critical review and scientific testing; nor is it easy for the beginning teacher to get the feeling that she begins where predecessors left off.

The absence of a refined technical culture is evident in the talk of elementary school teachers. Analysis of long, somewhat "open" interviews with teachers reveals little by way of a special rhetoric to delineate the essence of their daily grappling with interpersonal and learning problems. The language one finds, as might be expected from the foregoing paragraph, is the language of persons of their general educational and class background.[15] Where trade jargon is used, it is frequently characterized by various meanings among different speakers (e.g., "growth" is advanced performance on achievement tests for one, the overcoming of shyness for another). Isolation and evanescence seem to have had the expected effects.

The general status of teaching, the teacher's role and the condition and transmission arrangements of its subculture point to truncated rather than fully realized professionalization. The ideology of professionalism among elementary teachers has yet to result in the structural characteristics or collegial assertiveness found in clearly established professions. It appears that considerable militancy and knowledge-building must occur if teachers are to acquire the work arrangements and technical apparatus associated with high-prestige professions.

In view of the truncated nature of professionalization among elementary teachers, it seems highly unlikely that collegial ties play a major part in reducing the potency of hierarchical authority. It may be, of course, that board members and administrators occasionally restrain their assertions of authority in deference to the attributed expertise of teachers. But professional ways of organizing work have yet to be institutionalized in the public schools. The absence of such institutionalization suggests skepticism rather than credulity on the count of teacher professionalization, and this skepticism should, in the writer's opinion, extend to ruling out *a priori* formulations which grant professional controls a major part in containing administrative authority. The autonomy possessed by elementary teachers is not the collectively shared right of recognized professionals.

NOTES

I wish to thank Mrs. Carol Kronus for her assistance in the preparation of this chapter. I am also indebted to Former Dean Francis Keppel, Harvard Graduate School of Education; Dean Ronald Campbell, Department of Education, University of Chicago; Donald Mitchell and the New England School Development Council for support which underlies the larger research from which this paper is drawn.

1. Dan C. Lortie, "The Striving Young Lawyer: A Study of Early Career Differentiation in the Chicago Bar," unpublished Ph.D. dissertation (Chicago: Department of Sociology, University of Chicago, 1958), p. 182.

2. The legislatures of California and New York have recently augmented the discipline-based study required of all elementary teachers.

3. James B. Conant, *The Education of American Teachers* (New York: McGraw-Hill, 1963), Appendix G (pp. 242–46).

4. Myron Lieberman, *Education as a Profession* (Englewood Cliffs, N.J.: Prentice-Hall, 1956), pp. 91–97.

5. Oswald Hall, "Stages of a Medical Career," *American Journal of Sociology*, 53 (1948), pp. 327–36; Dan C. Lortie, "Laymen to Lawmen: Law School, Careers and Socialization," *Harvard Educational Review*, 29 (1959), pp. 352–69.

6. Chiranji La. Sharma, "Practices in Decision-Making as Related to Satisfaction in Teaching," unpublished Ph.D. dissertation (Department of Education, University of Chicago, 1955).

7. Everett C. Hughes, *Men and Their Work* (New York: Free Press, 1958), ch. 9.

8. The interviews referred to were part of the Boston Area Study.

9. Emile Durkheim, *Education and Sociology* (New York: Free Press, 1956); Willard Waller, *The Sociology of Teaching* (New York: John Wiley & Sons, Inc., Science Editions, 1965).

10. Teachers dismiss most of their courses as "too theoretical." It seems that they are referring less to an inappropriate level of generalization than to overly idealistic depictions of what it is possible to attain in classrooms.

11. J. W. Getzels and P. W. Jackson, "The Teacher's Personality and Characteristics," in N. L. Gage (ed.), *Handbook of Research on Teaching* (Chicago: Rand McNally & Co., 1963), p. 574.

12. Egon G. Guba, Philip W. Jackson, and Charles E. Bidwell, "Occupational Choice and the Teaching Career," *Educational Research Bulletin*, 38 (1959), pp. 1–12.

13. Lortie, "Laymen to Lawmen," in *Challenge and Change in American Education*, ed. Seymour Harris (Berkeley: McCutchan, 1965), pp. 149–56.

14. Laurence Iannoccone and H. Warren Button, *Functions of Student Teaching: Attitude Formation and Initiation on Elementary School Teaching*, Cooperative Research Project No. 1026 (St. Louis: Graduate Institute of Education, Washington University, 1964).

15. Emil Haller, in the course of research on teacher socialization, sampled conversation from the author's tape-recorded interviews with elementary teachers and compared it with the Thorndike-Lorge Word Test.

Teachers Are in Trouble

Questions to think about

1 *What problems and frustrations face teachers today?
What changes in school structures or administrative
hierarchies might alleviate these problems?*

2 *How does learning the teacher role differ from learning
other adult professional roles? Compare this article with
the Lortie discussion of professionalism.*

3 *What are a teacher's reciprocal roles? How do these
relate to teacher problems and frustrations? How do
you predict the teacher role will change in the next few
years, especially in relation to changes in the student
role?*

In the end, it comes down to one teacher facing a
classroom full of kids. After all the arguments over money, all the talk of
educational theories, all the debate over brains vs. bricks and new math
and decentralization and open classrooms, those kids have to learn from
that teacher. It isn't easy.

Take it from Baltimore County junior-high teacher Calvin Wood, who
speaks of a former job as "baby-sitting classes of 35 to 40 students who
didn't want to be there, who didn't like each other, didn't like me, didn't
like their homes, didn't like anything." Or from Seattle's Sue Byers, who
quit full-time teaching after ten years because "I was overwhelmed with
the problems and needs of my students. There was no way I could meet
them all. I started to hate teaching. I wanted to clean motels, anything
that you could leave at the end of the day." Or from Nancy Hunt of Los
Angeles, who says she was so seldom gratified by teaching that "I got in
the habit of not talking about it. There's no glamour in being a teacher.
We've become the new secretaries."

Teachers are in trouble. While it is the children who ultimately suffer from shortcomings in the educational system, it is the teachers who catch the heat. They are guilty victims, blamed for all that's wrong with the schools: unruly kids, uncaring administrators, addlebrained educational philosophies, straitjackets of red tape. They are criticized for their teaching when many have never been properly taught themselves. They are asked to mold young minds for wages that others wouldn't take to mold bathroom fixtures. And they are held accountable for the decision of everyone from the Supreme Court to unfit mothers. "There is a certain unfairness about it," says former Federal education official Mary Berry. "Learning is a shared experience among parents, students, administrators, and teachers. It is something the teacher alone is not responsible for. But teachers are not in vogue at the moment."

Teaching has never been a highly valued or a highly skilled job. People who took it traded a decent wage for the psychic income of a special calling; they were commended for their idealism and pitied for their hardship. Until not so long ago, they were at least thought to be smarter—in a general, impractical sort of way—than almost everybody else. But today, says American Federation of Teachers president Albert Shanker, "we have a public which is as well educated or more educated than the teachers. Instead of looking up at teachers, they can look straight at them or down on them. Teachers are surrounded by parents who feel they could do as good a job teaching their children if they weren't too busy making more money."

That shifting perception has seriously compromised the attitude teachers have toward their job and their students. Never mind the apple: all they want is a little respect, and if they can't have that, they'll settle for a raise and a clause that says they don't have to monitor the lunchroom. They are fed up with a public that howls for accountability at the same time it begs them virtually to raise their children. Many younger teachers are dropping out as fast as they can—to the cheers of their colleagues left behind. Many older ones are doing a slow burn, scheming for extended leaves and marking the days to retirement.

Meanwhile, they complain. Brooklyn first-grade teacher Ellen Richardson charges that most of her training was "just garbage" that left her unprepared for the classroom and "on the verge of hysteria" when she began. Gerald Kobata of Los Angeles is more wistful. "You see kids striving for bigger and better things," he says. "They've gone up and left you on the bottom. You're still teaching with no place to go." John Oliver, a burly Miami phys-ed teacher, shrugs off the chest pains brought on by the pressure and begins each year hoping it will be better—but knowing it won't. "I wouldn't be a teacher all over again," he says. "I'm just trying to make the best of a bad situation."

Lately, more and more teachers have been taking their grievances to the picket lines. But while unions have helped turn teachers into a political force, no amount of organizing can make teaching pleasant or create jobs where there are none. Twenty years ago one-third of all the bachelor's degrees were in education. Demand continued to climb through the 1960s as the baby-boomers toddled through school; then it dropped precipitously through the '70s. Fewer than half the prospective teachers who graduated in 1979 landed teaching jobs, a trend that was not lost on incoming freshmen the following year. Just 6 percent of them said they planned to teach, compared with 25 percent in 1968. A NEWSWEEK Poll conducted by the Gallup Organization shows that 68 percent of American adults think teaching is not an attractive career for young people.

As enrollment in education programs plummeted—it has fallen by half since 1973—colleges and universities began to lower their standards to stay in business. "Professors would rather have poor students than no students," says W. Timothy Weaver, associate professor at Boston University. Prospective public-school teachers are not the worst and the dumbest, but with a national average salary of only $17,264 awaiting them, they are hardly the cream of the crop. SAT scores of 1980 high-school seniors who planned to major in education were 48 points below the national average in math and 35 points below in the verbal component. What helps bring down the curve is the defection of able young women who were once relegated to teaching but who can now claim much higher salaries—and status—as doctors or lawyers or business executives. "American public education owes much of its success to the exploitation of prominent women," says Lyn Gubser of the National Council for Accreditation of Teacher Education in Washington, D.C. The exodus of bright women leaves education now in a situation similar to that at the end of the Depression, when the teaching profession stopped getting the talented people who had turned to it for security in the absence of job prospects in other fields.

A good many people have come to believe that the teaching ranks are filled with outright incompetents—illiterates who can't read or write and emotional cripples who can't relate to kids. That clearly overstates the problem; for every really bad teacher who stumbles over Shakespeare, there is another truly gifted one who inspires kids to memorize Shelley. Yet even professional educators acknowledge that far too many teachers are mediocre at best. Graham Down of the Council for Basic Education says the majority of teachers are only marginally competent. The best teaching, he says, is done in elementary schools and the worst in junior highs. Reading is taught as well today as it was twenty years ago, he believes, but writing, math, science and languages have suffered. "If you could measure competency on a thermometer," says Gubser, "I think we've gone from 80 degrees down to 60 degrees."

Some teachers have slipped even lower. Aniese Boyd, a fifth-grade teacher in South Carolina's Batesburg-Leesville Middle School, has been in the classroom since 1952. In 1979 a new principal assigned her to different classes, including one filled with higher achievers than any of Boyd's present or former students. She was observed several times that year and cautioned to improve her grammar, her lesson plans and her teaching techniques. At the end of the year, when the school did not renew her contract, Boyd decided to fight. At her hearing she was given a ten-word vocabulary test. She could not pronounce or define "agrarian." She correctly pronounced "suffrage" but defined it as "people suffering for some reason or another." She defined ratify as "to get rid of something." Her attorney argued that she had never been challenged as long as she was teaching black kids, "but that as soon as she got [white] students, things changed." "I'm not saying I was the best," Boyd says, "but I don't think I did more harm than anyone else." The school board ruled that the teacher's contract should not be renewed, but a judge ordered that she be rehired. He also pointed out that her dismissal notice contained a misspelled word, that the principal used faulty grammar in his deposition and that the official school-district policy manual had 77 grammatical errors in the first 82 pages.

And faulty grammar may be a comparatively venial sin. One Salt Lake City junior-high science teacher rarely wrote lesson plans, failed to correct homework papers promptly, confused her students by jumping from subject to subject, and very nearly beat her class out the door at the final bell. The students knew she didn't care and so they didn't, either. During class they opened windows and threw things out. They stacked chairs. They drowned a guinea pig. Last month, when the teacher didn't show up at an evening school fair, they ransacked the classroom and glued her books to her desk. The next day she walked out at noon and never came back.

Some of the teachers' problems are developed after years of bad habits, and others can be traced to the nation's schools of education. The teachers colleges frequently grew from normal schools that turned out yesteryear's well-meaning schoolmarms and are now full-fledged state colleges or universities. A few large private universities get into the act as well, but the emphasis there is more often on research. Education professors who actually train students to teach have second-class status. "It's a circle which doesn't touch the orbit of the public-school planet," says Nancy Hunt, a graduate student in educational psychology at the University of Southern California.

As the SAT scores suggest, it's not hard to get in. California State University, Los Angeles, considered a good teaching school, is not atypical in turning away only 5 percent of its applicants. It's almost as easy to stay in. "You have to try to flunk out," confesses one recent graduate of the highly regarded program at Ball State University in Indiana. A California graduate student who grades the papers of education majors is distressed at how badly they write. "They don't know how to organize or present an idea, so you can't figure out whether they don't know the subject or are just plain dumb," she says. Yet she gives them all A's and B's: "It's mandatory. The school needs students so badly it will take anybody, and it has to keep everybody."

The course work is generally a hodgepodge of academic work, fieldwork and methodology—which can be helpful tricks of the trade or irrelevant nonsense. "We were taught how to write instructional objectives and how to order materials," says Fred Gardaphe, a University of Wisconsin graduate who now teaches English in Chicago. Some believe that students spend too much time on theory and not enough learning the subjects they mean to teach. "If you know your field you'll find a way to get it across," insists Chicago teacher Leroy Lovelace. Others maintain that all the knowledge in the world won't help 21-year-olds crossing the threshold of their own classrooms. "It can be a tremendous shock when they arrive starry-eyed, with idealized memories of the fourth-grade teacher they had more than a decade ago," says former Ball State associate dean Leslie Mauth.

That's just the sort of problem Robert Kitchen ran into in Mt. Orab, Ohio. As part of his training at Miami University, he did sixteen weeks of student teaching in a Cincinnati suburb. But when he got to the rural community where he now teaches high-school English, he wasn't ready. Truancy and apathy were commonplace and, for all his enthusiasm, Kitchen, 24, found he couldn't do anything about it. "My expectations were misguided as to what I thought teaching was going to be," he says. "If only one person in school had given me any forewarning at all about the kind of things you can expect, it might not have been so bad." His career plans shattered along with his preconceptions; Kitchen is quitting after three years.

For better or worse, schools of education are literally the last word in teaching; in most states, teachers are certified solely on the basis of having graduated from a college program approved by the state board or department of education. "Almost anybody can get certified somewhere," gripes Gubser. "Some states have more requirements for getting a driver's license than for teaching school." Nearly 90 percent of the respondents in the NEWSWEEK Poll think teachers should be required to pass a competency test before they are hired, and some revisions are in the works. Georgia, for example, has pioneered a certification exam that includes a three-and-one-half-hour written test and an on-the-job assessment that a teacher has three years to pass.

Even those modest efforts at reform are proving to be controversial. In Arizona, a push for a statewide teacher-proficiency exam has produced a sample test that state Rep. Jim Skelly says will "make the state the laughingstock of the country." One example: "How many words should be capitalized in the following sentence? we live in the sunny state of arizona." Skelly says he gave the 25-question test to his paperboy, who passed easily. "If somebody fails that, he's in pretty bad shape," Skelly scoffs. "He shouldn't have been let out of first grade."

The National Education Association opposes teacher tests, maintaining that they are unfair to students who might fail after investing heavily in college training. In 1979, six months after Louisiana began using the National Teacher Examination (NTE) to screen applicants, 33 percent failed. In 1978, 47 percent of Louisiana's teaching applicants failed, even though the cutoff point was roughly the 25th percentile. At two of the state's black colleges, the failure rate was 95 percent. In South Carolina, 56 percent of the state's teaching applicants have failed the NTE since 1976. Despite this record, the country's other major teachers' union, the American Federation of Teachers, favors testing for new teachers. "It won't tell you if a person is going to be a good teacher," says Shanker, "but it will tell you pretty quickly if they're illiterate."

Testing aside, the unions are the source of considerable friction within and without the profession. Some critics believe that they have given teachers an unseemly blue-collar image. It's the strikes, more than anything else, that seem to gall the public. The longest teachers' strike in the nation's history ended just last week in Ravenna, Ohio—a bitter five-month contract dispute. But John Ryor, former president of the NEA, bristles at the notion that bargaining for better pay and working conditions is a process demeaning to the profession: "For years teachers were kept on a moral pedestal and in an economic bargain basement." Strong unions, he says, have rid teachers of images that were "debilitating and humiliating." Not all teachers agree with Ryor. "It used to be a profession, but thanks to the union now it's just a job," says Seattle teacher Audrey Ireland. "The union will support me no matter how bad or good I am as a teacher."

In many cities, strong unions assure that weak teachers stay on and on and on. Few incompetents are ever fired. Instead, says Chicago District 13 Superintendent Alice Blair, "We give them an unsatisfactory rating and transfer them to another school." Salt Lake City has a different way of cracking down on teachers who can't teach. Since 1974, it has allowed parents, students, principals or even other teachers to request a "review of services" when they have a complaint about a teacher. If an impartial review panel determines that the accusations are serious and valid, the teacher can be placed on a five-month "remediation review." Four people work with the teacher to correct the problem: the principal, a learning specialist and two colleagues, one of whom helps protect the teacher's due-process rights.

Fifty-two teachers have been placed on remediation in the past six years; 29 quit or were fired, twenty are still teaching and three remain under review. The system obviously holds the potential for abuse: some teachers complain that it is used to harass them because they are unpopular, not incompetent. But a majority are happy with the process, and teachers who survive it are sometimes better for it. Third-grade teacher Lynda Brown recalls an older colleague who was challenged a few years ago because his students were falling behind on achievement-test scores. She and the other review members helped him develop stimulating new techniques and showed him how to use them. Two months later, he was taken off re-mediation. "He's still doing fine," Brown reports. "It was a breath of fresh air to him."

Teacher centers—demilitarized zones where the battle-weary meet to trade ideas, confess their failings without fear of rebuke and freshen up their skills—have turned out to be another way to keep the fires burning. As of last year there were about 90 government-funded centers scattered around the country and about 200 more independent ones. "We help teachers to see things anew, try to get them intensely amazed and thrilled, to build from a kid's perception," says Lillian Weber, director of the Work-shop Center for Open Education in New York City. Ann Sabatini, who runs a center in Brooklyn's P.S. 179, recently spent six weeks remaking a classroom—and its teacher. Sabatini helped reorganize the teacher's lesson plans, changed the way she asked questions and found more appropriate teaching materials. "I thought it was a waste of time," says Rita Leanza, an eighteen-year veteran who has been helped by Sabatini's center. "Now I see it's a terrifically useful thing."

Every teacher occasionally needs some kind of help, even if it's only a few kind words and a sympathetic ear. There are thousands who make do without much more. John Farmer is one, a man who nourishes his obsession for teaching in his chemistry classes at Broken Arrow Senior High School near Tulsa, Oklahoma. Farmer, 35, has been teaching for twelve years. "I don't talk about gas laws but about Robert Boyle and other scientists—who they were, what they sacrificed, why they loved science," he says. He adds new approaches to his subject and drops stale ones. He leads discussions about ozone and acid rain that relate chemistry to the real world. "The kids get excited," he says. "They ask questions and do their own research and start contributing."

There is only one problem. With a master's degree, Farmer earns a bit less than $17,000—about par for all teachers but half of what the average family in Broken Arrow makes. He could probably make a lot more at one of the big chemical factories nearby. Instead, he works four nights a week at the local supermarket. "There's nothing wrong with being a grocer," he says proudly. "I'm a damn good one." He's also considered a damn good teacher, one who stays in touch with former students and commands the respect of his community. Just by telling his students that a recent plan to fluoridate the town's water was not cost-efficient, he unwittingly helped defeat the measure. Farmer says that he comes home some days and kicks the mailbox out of frustration. "But for the most part I'm very happy. Besides, I just got a nice big fat raise from Safeway."

Farmer may be exceptional, but he is surely not unique. Teachers as a whole are still a remarkably dedicated lot. But the job is not what it used to be, and dedication, though necessary, is not enough. More bright people should be recruited as teachers, to begin with. Then they should be told what they're getting into, taught what to do, allowed to do it—and appreciated for their accomplishments. The rest of us, meanwhile, might do well to remember that the teachers we once had are as obsolete as the children we once were.

CHAPTER 5

The Informal System and the Hidden Curriculum

In schools we learn two systems—one formal and one informal. Many of the tasks we must accomplish are written out, and the rules that guide our behavior are based on clearly stated school goals. Alongside this manifest curriculum, however, is what some have called the *hidden curriculum;* within every formal school system is a coexistent informal system. In his book *The Hidden Curriculum* (New York: Knopf, 1971), Benson Snyder defines this system as "implicit demands (as opposed to the explicit obligations of the visible curriculum) that are found in every learning institution and which students have to find out and respond to in order to survive within it." The three Rs of the hidden curriculum are "rules, regulations and routines." These unwritten regulations determine how we learn to cope; feelings we have about school; the classroom atmosphere, which some call "climate"; and power relationships within the school. All are less obvious parts of our educational experience, yet we cannot fully understand the educational system without paying them heed. Thus this informal system has come to occupy the research efforts of a growing number of sociologists.

In the educational open systems model we have constructed so far, the formal system consists of school and classroom structure, formal goals and curriculum, and participant roles. Processes carried out by role holders are the action part of the system; you might recall in the discussion of stratification that unwritten factors affect how a student achieves in school. For instance, a student's dress, mannerisms, speech, and even name can influence a teacher's response; in turn, the student develops attitudes about school and the chances of success in school. Just as the formal educational system made up of structure and roles is influenced by what happens in the school environment, the informal system is similarly affected.

The articles in this chapter examine such areas as the formal school system as contrasted with the informal system; the educational and value climate; the effect of teacher expectations on students; an example of the effects of the informal system; and some theoretical implications of the informal system.

Life in Classrooms is something we have all experienced with mixed emotions. Masterfully, sometimes humorously, but with the insight of sociological interpretation, Philip Jackson describes the everyday experiences of classrooms. In the brief excerpt from his book given here, Jackson describes the hidden curriculum, contrasts it with the formal or official curriculum of the school, and discusses the relationship between the two. Success in school requires mastery of both systems even while inherent contradictions exist between them. While intellectual mastery, requiring curiosity and individual expression, is a formal goal of the official system, the informal system with its hidden curriculum requires compliance. Some students, according to Jackson, seem to be able to balance both systems, but this is a task not mastered by many who have problems in school.

The educational climate of the school and classroom can involve everything from the school's architecture and surroundings to its method of grouping students and interactions among role holders in the system. Climate exerts an important influence on students' levels of achievement and aspiration. We know, for instance, that the expectations teachers have for a group of students influence their subsequent achievement; we also know that the value climate of a school affects self-concept and achievement. A number of researchers have studied the relationships between such variables.

In an article based on work in progress, Edsel L. Erickson, Wilbur B. Brookover, Robert Bilby, Alan McEvoy, and Kathryn Johnson present a model of sources and functions of self-conceptions. They explain the difference between intrinsic and instrumental values to self for learning and how knowledge of a student's self-concept can help us enhance learning outcomes.

The majority of schools have some system, called tracking or streaming, for grouping students. The processes of tracking and labeling begin as early as kindergarten. How and where a student is placed in this process has an impact on their concept of what they are capable of doing. Students also find coping mechanisms for dealing with the informal labels that teachers and other students place on them. You might remember from your classrooms the teacher's pet, the clown, the brain, the troublemaker, and the recluse. These are learned roles, coping mechanisms in the informal system that arise in response to experiences such as tracking in the formal system. Student strategies for dealing with the school system vary depending on demands and labels placed upon them. When a child is labeled as a problem child or troublemaker, the teacher's interactions with and attention given that child are shown to reflect the label. P. S. Fry's study points out the effect of classroom environments and teacher interactions on children and raises the question: do problem children reflect true behavior problems, or are teacher attitudes a crucial variable in defining and even creating problem children?

Since researchers have now been working on the informal system and hidden curriculum concepts for some time, D. Hargreaves, a British sociologist, argues that we should rename the concept the *paracurriculum*, or subject matter that is taught and learned alongside the formal or official curriculum. Hargreaves points out the range of theoretical perspectives that have been brought to bear on this topic. Jackson, for instance, as well as Robert Dreeben (Chapter 7), and Talcott Parsons (Chapter 3) assume a more conservative approach, trying to understand schools through use of functional analysis. Writers such as Samuel Bowles and Herbert Gintis (Chapter 6), who write from a conflict theory perspective, as well as Ivan Illich and other educators who propose reforming the schools, advocate change, in part because of the influences the informal system exerts on student learning. This second group of writers express anger at the coerciveness of school systems and identify coping strategies developed by students to deal with the system. Through the informal system schools instill in students habits such as respect for authority, punctuality, responsibility, and obedience, which conflict theorists argue are important in perpetuating the capitalistic system. Recall the article by Randall Collins in Chapter 2, which discussed the different approaches of the functionalists and conflict theorists toward understanding and interpreting stratification in schools and society.

Environment influences the workings of both the formal system, consisting of structure and roles, and the informal system, consisting of the hidden curriculum, school climate, and expectations. Chapter 7 will examine environment as it affects both systems.

PHILIP W. JACKSON

Life in Classrooms

Questions to think about

1 *What two curricula are discussed by Jackson? What is their importance for success in school?*

2 *Relate Jackson's comments about the informal life of classrooms to self-concept, achievement, and social class in schools—topics discussed in the other articles in Section Two.*

3 *Where does the hidden curriculum fit into the open systems framework? How does it relate to other parts of the system?*

4 *How would you describe the hidden curriculum in your own classes?*

The crowds, the praise, and the power that combine to give a distinctive flavor to classroom life collectively form a hidden curriculum which each student (and teacher) must master if he is to make his way satisfactorily through the school. The demands created by these features of classroom life may be contrasted with the academic demands—the "official" curriculum, so to speak—to which educators traditionally have paid the most attention. As might be expected, the two curriculums are related to each other in several important ways.

As has already been suggested in the discussion of praise in the classroom, the reward system of the school is linked to success in both curriculums. Indeed, many of the rewards and punishments that sound as if they are being dispensed on the basis of academic success and failure are really more closely related to the mastery of the hidden curriculum. Consider, as an instance, the common teaching practice of giving a student credit for trying. What do teachers mean when they say a student tries to do his

work? They mean, in essence, that he complies with the procedural expectations of the institution. He does his homework (though incorrectly),
he raises his hand during class discussion (though he usually comes up
with the wrong answer), he keeps his nose in his book during free study
period (though he doesn't turn the page very often). He is, in other words,
a "model" student, though not necessarily a good one.

It is difficult to imagine any of today's teachers, particularly those in
elementary schools, failing a student who tries, even though his mastery
of course content is slight. Indeed, even at higher levels of education rewards sometimes go to the meek as well as the mighty. It is certainly
possible that many of our valedictorians and presidents of our honor societies owe their success as much to institutional conformity as to intellectual prowess. Although it offends our sensibilities to admit it, no doubt
that bright-eyed little girl who stands trembling before the principal on
graduation day arrived there at least in part because she typed her weekly
themes neatly and handed her homework in on time.

This manner of talking about educational affairs may sound cynical
and may be interpreted as a criticism of teachers or as an attempt to subvert
the virtues of neatness, punctuality, and courteous conduct in general. But
nothing of that kind is intended. The point is simply that in schools, as in
prisons, good behavior pays off.

Just as conformity to institutional expectations can lead to praise, so
can the lack of it lead to trouble. As a matter of fact, the relationship of
the hidden curriculum to student difficulties is even more striking than is
its relationship to student success. As an instance, consider the conditions
leading to disciplinary action in the classroom. Why do teachers scold
students? Because the student has given a wrong answer? Because, try as
he might, he fails to grasp the intricacies of long division? Not usually.
Rather, students are commonly scolded for coming into the room late or
for making too much noise or for not listening to the teacher's directions
or for pushing while in line. The teacher's wrath, in other words, is more
frequently triggered by violations of institutional regulations and routines
than by signs of his students' intellectual deficiencies.

Even when we consider the more serious difficulties that clearly entail
academic failure, the demands of the hidden curriculum lurk in the background. When Johnny's parents are called in to school because their son
is not doing too well in arithmetic, what explanation is given for their
son's poor performance? Typically, blame is placed on motivational deficiencies in Johnny rather than on his intellectual shortcomings. The teacher
may even go so far as to say that Johnny is *un*motivated during arithmetic
period. But what does this mean? It means, in essence, that Johnny does
not even try. And not trying, as we have seen, usually boils down to a

failure to comply with institutional expectations, a failure to master the hidden curriculum.

Testmakers describe a person as "test-wise" when he has caught on to the tricks of test construction sufficiently well to answer questions correctly even though he does not know the material on which he is being examined. In the same way one might think of students as becoming "school-wise" or "teacher-wise" when they have discovered how to respond with a minimum amount of pain and discomfort to the demands, both official and unofficial, of classroom life. Schools, like test items, have rules and traditions of their own that can only be mastered through successive exposure. But with schools as with tests all students are not equally adroit. All are asked to respond but not everyone catches on to the rules of the game.

If it is useful to think of there being two curriculums in the classroom, a natural question to ask about the relationship between them is whether their joint mastery calls for compatible or contradictory personal qualities. That is, do the same strengths that contribute to intellectual achievement also contribute to the student's success in conformity to institutional expectations? This question likely has no definite answer, but it is thought-provoking and even a brief consideration of it leads into a thicket of educational and psychological issues.

It is probably safe to predict that general ability, or intelligence, would be an asset in meeting all of the demands of school life, whether academic or institutional. The child's ability to understand causal relationships, as an instance, would seem to be of as much service as he tries to come to grips with the rules and regulations of classroom life as when he grapples with the rudiments of plant chemistry. His verbal fluency can be put to use as easily in "snowing" the teacher as in writing a short story. Thus, to the extent that the demands of classroom life call for rational thought, the student with superior intellectual ability would seem to be at an advantage.

But more than ability is involved in adapting to complex situations. Much also depends upon attitudes, values, and life style—upon all those qualities commonly grouped under the term: *personality*. When the contribution of personality to adaptive strategy is considered, the old adage of "the more, the better," which works so well for general ability, does not suffice. Personal qualities that are beneficial in one setting may be detrimental in another. Indeed, even a single setting may make demands that call upon competing or conflicting tendencies in a person's makeup.

We have already seen that many features of classroom life call for patience, at best, and resignation, at worst. As he learns to live in school our student learns to subjugate his own desires to the will of the teacher and to subdue his own actions in the interest of the common good. He learns to be passive and to acquiesce to the network of rules, regulations, and routines in which he is embedded. He learns to tolerate petty frustrations and accept the plans and policies of higher authorities, even when their rationale is unexplained and their meaning unclear. Like the inhabitants of most other institutions, he learns how to shrug and say, "That's the way the ball bounces."

But the personal qualities that play a role in intellectual mastery are very different from those that characterize the Company Man. Curiosity, as an instance, that most fundamental of all scholarly traits, is of little value in responding to the demands of conformity. The curious person typically engages in a kind of probing, poking, and exploring that is almost antithetical to the attitude of the passive conformist. The scholar must develop the habit of challenging authority and of questioning the value of tradition. He must insist on explanations for things that are unclear. Scholarship requires discipline, to be sure, but this discipline serves the demands of scholarship rather than the wishes and desires of other people. In short, intellectual mastery calls for sublimated forms of aggression rather than for submission to constraints.

This brief discussion likely exaggerates the real differences between the demands of institutional conformity and the demands of scholarship, but it does serve to call attention to points of possible conflict. How incompatible are these two sets of demands? Can both be mastered by the same person? Apparently so. Certainly not all of our student council presidents and valedictorians can be dismissed as weak-willed teacher's pets, as academic Uriah Heeps. Many students clearly manage to maintain their intellectual aggressiveness while at the same time acquiescing to the laws that govern the social traffic of our schools. Apparently it *is* possible, under certain conditions, to breed "docile scholars," even though the expression seems to be a contradiction in terms. Indeed, certain forms of scholarship have been known to flourish in monastic settings, where the demands for institutional conformity are extreme.

Unfortunately, no one seems to know how these balances are maintained, nor even how to establish them in the first place. But even more unfortunate is the fact that few if any school people are giving the matter serious thought. As institutional settings multiply and become for more and more people the areas in which a significant portion of their life is enacted, we will need to know much more than we do at present about how to achieve a reasonable synthesis between the forces that drive a person to seek individual expression and those that drive him to comply with the wishes of others. Presumably what goes on in classrooms contributes significantly to this synthesis. The school is the first major institution, outside the family, in which almost all of us are immersed. From kindergarten onward, the student begins to learn what life is really like in The Company.

The demands of classroom life discussed in this chapter pose problems for students and teachers alike. As we have seen, there are many methods for coping with these demands and for solving the problems they create. Moreover, each major adaptive strategy is subtly transformed and given a unique expression as a result of the idiosyncratic characteristics of the student employing it. Thus, the total picture of adjustment to school becomes infinitely complex as it is manifested in the behavior of individual students.

Yet certain commonalities do exist beneath all the complexity created by the uniqueness of individuals. No matter what the demand or the personal resources of the person facing it there is at least one strategy open to all. This is the strategy of psychological withdrawal, of gradually reducing personal concern and involvement to a point where neither the demand nor one's success or failure in coping with it is sharply felt.

EDSEL L. ERICKSON,
WILBUR B. BROOKOVER,
ROBERT BILBY, ALAN McEVOY,
and KATHRYN JOHNSON

Self-Conceptions
and Learning

Questions to think about

1 *What factors affect students' attitudes toward learning
specific subjects?*

2 *Explain the difference between intrinsic and
instrumental values to self. How does each influence
learning?*

3 *How can knowledge of self-concept help us modify
learning situations to enhance learning outcomes?*

Learning has traditionally been defined as the acquisition of new behavioral patterns. For example, when a student who
does not appropriately calculate square roots begins to calculate them
correctly, we say he or she has learned this mathematical skill. As one
might guess, learning specialists have drawn numerous distinctions among
types of learning. Some distinguish between cognitive learning and motor
learning, between rote memory and the acquisition of principles, and so
forth.

Adapted by permission of the publishers and authors from "The Development and Functions
of Self-Concepts" in *The Sociology of Education* by Wilbur B. Brookover and Edsel L. Erickson
(Homewood, Ill.: Dorsey Press, 1975), pp. 267–282; from Robert Bilby, Edsel L. Erickson,
and Wilbur B. Brookover, "Characterizations of Self and Student Decision Making," *Review
of Educational Research* 42: 4 (1972): 505–524; and from a more detailed treatment of self-
concept in *Human Abilities, Social Forces, and Learning: A Micro-Macro Interactionist Analysis* by
Edsel L. Erickson, Wilbur B. Brookover, Kathryn Johnson, Robert Bilby, and Alan McEvoy,
forthcoming. All rights reserved by the authors.

250

In addition to learning the academic skills that are so often the focal point of debate over education and schools, students also learn aversions and attractions to academic and social objects while at school, in the family, at work or play, and in other social settings. They acquire ideological values about politics, sex, clothes, school—and virtually everything else in their world. They may even acquire such behavioral patterns as stuttering, flinching, withdrawing, fantasizing, or being aggressive toward their teachers or peers. Students may learn to discard their previously learned racial or ethnic prejudices, or such attitudes may be reinforced.

The point is that what is learned in the family, in school, and elsewhere is considerable and varied. Few fail to learn anything at all. Some may not learn their prescribed arithmetic lessons, but odds are they will learn something. Wise parents and teachers recognize this. They recognize that what students learn is as often by accident as it is intention. We all learn things that neither we nor our teachers anticipated. And, of course, one of the tricks of the trade for effective teachers at school, home, or work is occasionally to cause others to learn what they had no intention of learning in the first place.

In this discussion, we focus our attention on that learning which is, in part, a function of how individuals see themselves: the reality they create about themselves. We believe that all social learning is partially a consequence of the learner's interpretations of him or herself—their constructions of reality. For example, we believe that when students construct a reality that they can, should, and will learn mathematics, they are much more likely to learn mathematics than when they are convinced that they are unable to do so. Conversely, we maintain that when students believe or decide, for whatever reason, they are not going to learn to square numbers, they usually will not.

Many types of learning require the cooperation of learners. We believe the academic subjects as currently taught in our colleges and schools are clearly of this sort. We do not, however, mean to suggest that the beliefs and decisions of students about themselves alone determine their academic performance. As shown in Table 1, many conditions determine the final learning outcome. People often decide on courses of action that result in failure. Even so, students seldom learn the prescribed academic behaviors unless such learning is also consistent with their decisions. As every effective teacher knows, the learner's cooperation must be gained for the desired results to be maximized. Furthermore, when students decide to learn something, many of the otherwise mitigating conditions are often lessened by the student's actions. Therefore, our focus in this discussion is on explaining what shapes the views of students about themselves that affects their learning.

TABLE 1
Schematic Representation of Sources and Functions of Self-Conceptions

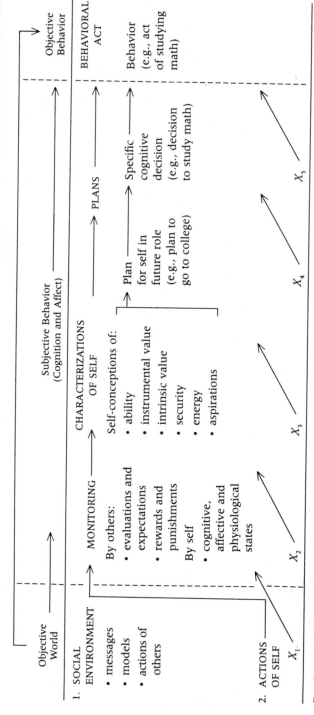

X_1 = Represents other sets of unspecified objective variables that impinge on monitoring (e.g. hereditary factors, nutritional variables, physical conditions, etc.).

X_2 = Represents all other monitorings of self and world that impinge on characterizations of self (e.g., monitoring of health state).

X_3 = Represents all other sets of unspecified self-conceptions that impinge on plans (e.g. self-assessments of likelihood of being present at some future time).

X_4 = Represents all other plans for self in related roles that impinge on decisions (e.g., plans to be a spouse, parent, worker, etc.).

X_5 = Represents all other unspecified decisions that impinge on objective behavioral outcomes.

We will show that we do not think of the self-concept as a trait one has or possesses, but as a *defining behavioral process*. The self-concept, from our perspective, is a cognitive behavior. Put another way, people do not *have* self-concepts in the same sense as they have a nose or a mouth; rather *they engage in self-conceptualizing behavior,* defining themselves in the same way that they engage in other linguistic behaviors.

Rather than viewing the self as an immutable structure, we contend that self-conceptualization represents a series of cognitive acts organized into identities that involve purposes. These identifications direct much of our other behaviors. We believe that the self in this sense provides a cognitive frame of reference for the individual to make four interrelated types of interpretations: (1) interpreting the expectations that others hold for us in our roles; (2) interpreting our own plans of action; (3) interpreting our actual behavior; and (4) interpreting the reactions of others in response to that behavior.

SELF-CONCEPTUALIZING BEHAVIOR*

In order to explain the academic decisions of students and thereby account more effectively for their academic performance, it may be helpful to ask the basic question: What is the best way to make sense out of the many ways people talk about themselves? People say many different things about themselves, and they often behave quite differently from one situation to another. The ways people think of themselves are not equally relevant in all situations. If we wished to account for the behaviors of a student in two or more different roles in school, what kinds of self-concept data would be most relevant and helpful? A man in a statistics class, for example, might say and believe that he is loved by his friends, that he is handsome, that his teachers and friends like him, that he is generally happy with his life, but that he is "dumb" in statistics. To account effectively for this student's behavior in statistics, we would need to focus on those self-conceptions directly related to the particular role in question, probably what he says about his ability to learn statistics. Our problem, then, is how to organize the role characterizations students have for themselves in each role we wish to explain and how these role characterizations impact on student performance levels.

*We are indebted to a number of our associates for helping us to clarify our thoughts on the self-conceptualizing process. We are particularly indebted to Lee M. Joiner, Shailer Thomas, and Ann Patterson. Many others have also contributed to a test of our ideas and will be reported elsewhere.

Students might make such diverse statements as: "I hate statistics." "I'm dumb in statistics." "This statistics test is keeping me from going on a date." "My dad does not care whether I learn statistics or not." "The statistics teacher is a bore." In the following set of theoretical propositions we present a model for grouping these kinds of statements.

Even so, there is still the task of determining the relevance of people with whom the students interact; this in turn shapes their views about themselves. We need a model that will help us understand students in terms of their positions in social psychological and cultural contexts where their behavior is the outcome of their symbolic interactions with self (i.e., internal conversations) and their symbolic interactions with others. The following theoretical scheme presents our view of the process by which individuals interact with others to develop their self-conceptualizing behaviors, which in turn help shape their decisions. These decisions, of course, reciprocally shape their interactions with others and the cycle is endlessly repeated.

SELF-CONCEPT: A THEORETICAL SCHEME

As can be seen in Table 2, a person's self-conceptualizing behavior can be divided for analytical purposes into eight major role categories:

1. Role requirements for self:
   a. In the specific role in question
   b. In more general roles in the setting
   c. In other roles currently engaged in and anticipated
2. Self-conception of ability to carry out role requirements
3. The intrinsic value to self of role performance
4. The instrumental value to self of role performance
5. Self-conceptions of security
6. Self-conceptions of health
7. Plans for self in role
8. Aspirations for self in role

Obviously, the many statements that a person makes can fall into more than one category. We believe, however, that there is predictive and explanatory value in recognizing each category. Although an extensive analysis of these assumptions is beyond the scope of this discussion, several hypotheses can be derived from this framework. First, the greater the functional consistency among these various analytic categories of self-conceptions, the greater the likelihood that the behavioral outcomes (learning)

T A B L E 2
Illustrative Determinants of Academic Decisions

Inputs	Output
Monitoring of Self; The Self-Concept Structure	Volitional Behavior

1. Appropriateness of Role Act
   a. *To classroom role:*
      "Is this the kind of thing I should be learning in this class?"
   b. *To general student role:*
      "Do I need French to graduate?"
   c. *To other roles:*
      "Will I use French in college?"
      "Do my friends expect me to learn French?"
      "Will I ever need to know French?"

2. Ability to Carry Out Role Act
   "I can't learn French."
   "Foreign languages are easy for me."
   "I don't know if I can learn French or not."

3. Intrinsic Value of Role Act
   "I hate French."
   "I think French is fun."
   "I couldn't care less, one way or the other."
   "A good person should know French."

4. Instrumental Value of Role Act
   "My father will give me a new bike if I take French."
   "If I take French, I can't go out for golf, which I really want to do."
   "I won't get into college unless I take a foreign language, and French is easiest for me."

5. Self-Conceptions of Security
   "Taking a course in French is a lot less dangerous than . . . "
   "I do not want to stay after school for the required French club. I would have to go home alone."

6. Self-Conceptions of Energy
   "I'm too tired to study French now."
   "Taking French will be easy."

7. Aspirations for Self
   "I would like to learn French but I would rather take another course."
   "I would rather learn French than anything else in school."
   "I don't want to learn French."

Decision to Study (e.g., to learn a French exercise)

will be consistent with the goals explicit and implicit in these self-conceptions. In other words, when a person's many cognitions of what "I am," what "I will do," and what "I want" are all congruent, learning in accord with these self-cognitions is much more likely. Of course, self-conceptions (including plans and aspirations) in other roles, as well as other constraints, may operate to influence learning.

Role Requirements for Self

We determine what we think are the appropriate behaviors for ourselves in each of our roles, and we can generally state these requirements. For example, a person may identify his or her role by saying: "I am a teacher of the emotionally impaired in elementary school X." This teacher will attach certain meanings to the role of a teacher of the emotionally impaired, including norms for what he or she should or should not do in varying situations, e.g., "It would be wrong for me to hit my pupils," or "I should spank them when they get too disobedient." Persons who see themselves as students could make various kinds of statements, for example, from "It is important for me to get all A's" to "All I need to do is get good enough grades to stay in school"; from "The teacher knows what he is talking about" to "Ms. Jones is a communist and I don't trust her"; or from "It is important for me to learn how to read French" to "French isn't relevant." Each of these statements represents ways individuals conceptualize themselves in their roles. In other words, role expectations or prescriptions for self constitute one category of self-conceptions. Social scientists have gone on to analyze ways of organizing these kinds of self-assessments which each of us makes in each of our roles. The following types of self-assessments have their origins in such analyses.

Self-Conception of Ability

Some years ago, one of the authors of this article elaborated a notion of *self-conception of ability,* or SCA (Brookover, 1975). This idea has many parallels in the social sciences. In psychology, the expectancy theories of J. W. Atkinson (1969) and J. Rotter are similar, as are the alienation concepts of power and powerlessness (Rotter, Seeman and Liverent, 1975; Seeman, 1959).

What we mean by self-conception of ability in the performance of a role task is the individual's assessment of his or her competency to carry out the behaviors appropriate for the role. A self-conception of ability develops as one defines his or her ability in a role. This self-conception functions as a threshold variable; i.e., before an individual will attempt to carry out certain role behaviors, he or she must assume some probability of being successful at some minimal level. Individuals will not make parachute jumps out of airplanes or attempt to learn Spanish unless they feel there is some possibility that they can succeed in their aims. If individuals have a high degree of confidence in their ability to accomplish role tasks, then their self-conception of ability is not functioning to impede their efforts.

Simply because one believes that he or she is able to perform a task, however, does not imply that he or she will attempt to carry out the task. In other words, students with high self-concepts of academic ability will not necessarily be high achievers. However, unless they believe they are able to be high achievers, they will not try to be high achievers. This is why we refer to self-conception of ability as a functionally limiting threshold condition. It functions to set minimal limits on what we decide to do. One's self-conceptions of ability in regard to various academic areas set limits on the kinds of subjects in which one chooses to enroll, and on the decisions one makes to study.

It should be noted that some evaluations of the environment are similar in idea to self-concept of ability and have been demonstrated to have a related but separate function, i.e., one's "sense of futility" in a situation (Brookover et al., 1979; Brookover et al., 1983). One may feel personally able while also believing that the environment will make all effort futile. This is only one type of environment assessment that is also important for learning.

Instrumental Values to Self

A second analytic category of self-assessment involves cognitions or assessments of the rewards and costs to self associated with a given performance in a particular role. The individual imaginatively "completes the act" of role performance and weighs the costs or rewards associated with the act. The use of this idea of instrumental value to self follows from a recognition of the fruitfulness of reinforcement notions employed by Homans (1961), Skinner (1953), and others. The costs and rewards considered may take the form of valued tokens (such as money or grades), social approval, or achieving and maintaining desired relationships with others.

Intrinsic Values to Self

By *intrinsic value to self* we refer to two distinct yet related types of cognitions. The first set of intrinsic values reflects an individual's cognitions about the worth, pleasure, or value he or she places on the accomplishment of some act regardless of any payoff from others. If we desire to increase our ability to predict or modify learning, we need to note the way people place value on, are neutral about, or reject doing things associated with certain roles. The second type of intrinsic value to self has a moral connotation; that is, beliefs about the quality or type of person who would or would not engage in a particular behavior. Regardless of the payoff, individuals often take into account what they consider to be the "proper" or ethically correct action. Indeed, some people may experience guilt in a role even though it gives pleasure, while others experience feelings of pride.

Our emphasis on the importance we attach to each role we play is distinct at any given time from the instrumental rewards and costs we associated with our behaviors. It should be remembered that this does not disallow the possibility that over time, instrumental values can influence our intrinsic values.

Self-Conceptions of Security

Whatever the social context, an individual's sense of safety or freedom from impending physical or psychological harm is a fundamental prerequisite for learning. In the absence of a feeling of security, the individual's sense of anxiety, fear, distrust, and the like is likely to inhibit learning. Certainly the family, school, peer group, and work situation represent primary contexts for addressing the security needs of learners. Furthermore, one's sense of security is likely to enhance the social bond between people through a process of attachment (Hirschi, 1969). For example, research on children who are abused and neglected—environments where security messages are not communicated—suggests a negative impact on cognitive and affective learning.

Self-Conceptions of Health/Energy

Self-conceptions of health and energy levels are our beliefs about such things as our vitality, the presence or absence of disease, our tensions, and all other cognitions about our state of physical and mental well-being. Our beliefs about our own energy levels and health, however, do not necessarily correspond exactly to, nor are they completely determined by, our physiological conditions. Yet our conceptions of health/energy play a role in learning, especially intended learning.

At this point, there is not enough information available on which to base precise statements of how self-conceptions of health/energy relate to learning. Perhaps our self-conceptions of health/energy operate much like self-conceptions of ability as a threshold variable. That is, if we define our current health or available physical/mental energy below a certain level, we will not attempt to learn some task. On the other hand, if we do not indicate to ourselves that we are sick, tired, or inordinately tense or anxious, then we are not likely to make the effort to learn.

Self-Concept: Theoretical Propositions

Although an extensive analysis of these propositions is beyond the scope of this discussion, several hypotheses can be derived from this framework. First, the greater the consistency among these various analytic categories of self-conception, the greater the likelihood that the learning outcomes will be consistent with the goals explicit and implicit in these self-conceptions. To further explicate how self-assessments function, a series of examples in Table 3 shows how students are likely to behave if they exhibit certain patterns of self-assessment. For purposes of example, we will use only three types of self-assessment. As will be noted, individuals could have a high self-concept of ability in a task that they value doing and that they think will have valued social consequences for them. For example, a mathematics student might feel that he is able to learn mathematics easily, that he values being a mathematician, and that others will reward him well for learning mathematics. In contrast, another mathematics student might feel that he cannot learn mathematics very well, that he hates the thought of working with numbers, and that others will penalize him if he does not learn mathematics. The reader should find it easy to project different outcomes for our two examples in a mathematics class. This is what we have done in Table 3. So far, we have specified the major components of self-concept assessment. But we have not presented a set of explicit ideas about how the parts of our model function together to affect learning.

Our theory of self-conception is different from the traditional idea that people possess a self-concept in the same way that they possess green or blue eyes. People engage in the behavioral act of conceptualizing about themselves, and it is this behavioral process we are analyzing here. A considerable amount of research has demonstrated the limited utility of attempting to measure self-concept as if it were a unitary phenomenon. Every global test of students' self-concept known to us groups all kinds of self-assessment information as if such diverse assessments referred to one self-concept, but such global measures, when analyzed, have been shown to consist of multiple factors. Second, when used as a composite score,

TABLE 3
Illustrative Hypotheses about How Students May Behave on the Basis of Their Profiles of Self-Assessments

Self-concept of academic ability A	Intrinsic value of student role for self B	Instrumental value of student role for self C	Illustrative hypotheses: Predicted outcomes
1. Positive	Positive	Positive	These students will attempt to carry out the behavior they think is appropriate for themselves as a student. They will attempt to have their performance under the surveillance of others who are also perceived to value student role and/or who are perceived to reward appropriate student behavior. However, inasmuch as carrying out the student role has intrinsic value for self (i.e., student's performance is reinforcing) surveillance and reinforcement by others is not essential for performances. Probably not many students like this.
2. Positive	Neutral	Positive	These students will carry out their roles only to the extent they think others will provide "rewards" or sanctions. Hence, perceived surveillance by others who are in a position to reinforce student behavior is crucial. Students in this category are not likely to attempt academic achievements unless there is a "payoff" from others. This type of student is probably more typical in many of our high schools and colleges.
3. Positive	Negative	Positive	This type of student will exhibit considerable tension as a result of role conflict. An example of this type would be a biology student who feels he should not learn the "theory of evolution because it is evil," but perceives high reward in doing so or considerable punishment should he fail to learn his biology lessons. Such a student will attempt to cope with the situation by becoming neutral about the value of being a biology learner or by removing himself from the surveillance of others in a position to reinforce his behavior (the latter coping behavior seems most likely). This profile is likely to be rare in most schools.

4. Positive	Positive	Neutral	Will attempt to carry out student role without concern for surveillance of others. This type of student is very rare in our society which usually emphasizes learning as a means to achieve other values and not to be valued in itself.
5. Positive	Positive	Negative	Will attempt to remove one's self in the performance of student role from the surveillance of others who are perceived to negatively sanction student behaviors he or she values for self. These students will attempt to be under the surveillance of persons who are perceived to value student achievement. If this is not possible, they are likely to devalue student role for self. A rare profile.
6. Neutral	Positive	Positive	Will not stay in these profiles long and, when they are, they will be very sensitive to cues indicating competency or incompetency to carry out appropriate student behaviors. However, neutrality about one's competency as a student is very rare in our society since most of us are taught early and regularly to accept some definition of competency in academic matters.
7. Neutral	Neutral	Positive	
8. Negative	Positive	Positive	Will attempt to devalue or modify student role for self and remove one's self from student role or from surveillance of student role. If cues are provided that the person is competent they are likely to reinforce self-competency in student role. Generally, however, the basis for others reinforcing incompetency is likely to be present so this is not too likely. Such a student will perform at low levels and will stay in student role only insofar as it is forced upon him by others. He will drop out of school at the first opportune time.
9. Negative	Neutral	Positive	

these global self-concept measures are not nearly as predictive of later achievements or performance as are the more task-specific self-concept instruments (Piers and Harris, 1964; Nash, 1964; Wylie, 1963).

The implications of this finding are several. First, it is simply inappropriate and inefficient to say that a student has a low or high self-concept. Students conceptualize about themselves in many different areas, and it is important to specify which categories of self-conceptions are being referred to and to determine whether these self-conceptions are relevant for the learning in question.

Second, it is important to note that, like other behaviors, verbal behaviors by which people define themselves are subject to change. If the situation is appropriate, students can be taught and can teach themselves to view themselves as highly able in mathematics or as incompetent.

A third implication is that self-conceptions regarding any task may vary from morning to night, from day to day, or from one situation to another. Gergen (1972) summarizes several studies that show how situational factors influence what people think and say about themselves. However, the self-conceptions of individuals tend to be repeated given similar stimuli, i.e., these are about as stable as most other behavioral habits, and of course, some cognitions about self are more resistant to change than others. Individuals who assert a belief tend to assert their belief over time unless extinction or new learning takes place. It is also true that many of our beliefs about ourselves are made with a great deal of resistance to change, while other beliefs about ourselves are more readily modified.

A fourth implication is that what one believes about oneself does not have to fit with objective facts any more than do one's beliefs about the world. One may think the world is flat or that he or she cannot learn French and be wrong on both counts. As far as that person is concerned, however, he or she is likely neither to venture forth around the world, as did Columbus, unless placed in irons (as were many of Columbus' crew) nor to attempt to learn French.

The utility of these theoretical implications can best be demonstrated by turning to empirical evidence. Research by the authors and their associates show that self-concept of academic ability is significantly correlated with academic performance (Brookover and Erickson, 1975). Measurements of students' self-conceptions of academic ability were found to account for a significant proportion of academic achievement when the analysis controlled for social class conditions and measured intelligence, the normative expectations of family, friends, and teachers, and past achievement levels. This research followed an entire class of approximately 1500 students from junior high school through three years after high school. The major finding was that changes in self-conception of ability were followed by changes in academic achievement.

This finding has been verified in many situations in North America, Europe, and Asia (Brookover et al., 1962; 1967). Several studies of the effects of self-conception of ability among retarded children have been conducted with the same results (Towne and Joiner, 1966). Similar findings have been found with male and female entry into science and mathematics (Kaminski et al., 1976; Kaminski, 1978), delinquent institutionalized youth (Haarer, 1969), deaf and blind students (Joiner and Erickson, 1967), school dropouts (Harding, 1969), black and white student entry into science (Bowe, 1977), and junior college students (Sproull, 1969). An independent national study by Edgar G. Epps (1969) of the achievement effects of self-conception of ability and other correlates among black students provides another set of interesting results. Epps concluded that self-conception of academic ability and conformity are among the most powerful predictors of academic achievement. This conclusion is in accord with the earlier findings of Morse (1963), who compared white and black eighth-grade students in Michigan and the later findings of Bowe (1977), who forecast which black and white students would enter science based upon self-conceptions of science ability.

In related research, Wamhoff (1969) found that indicators of one's vocational conceptions of ability obtained during the senior year in high school were related to vocational decisions two years later. Gabel (1970), in a study of college plans among high school students in a small Western community, obtained similar findings. Of 247 seniors who planned to go to a four-year college or university, Gabel found that only 31 percent had medium to low self-conceptions of academic ability. On the other hand, of 44 seniors who planned to go only to junior college, 82 percent had medium to low self-conceptions of academic ability. Interestingly, Gabel did not find a significant correlation between a global measure of self-concept and college plans. Only the self-concept measure that focused on the student role was predictive of plans for the student role.

Cross-cultural research also has been conducted demonstrating the relationship of self-conception of academic ability to achievement. In studies conducted in Germany by Votruba (1970) and Auer (1971) of students in three different types of schools—the *Gymnasium,* the *Mitteschule,* and the *Volkschule*—self-conception of academic ability was found to be clearly related to achievement when social class background and type of school were controlled. Sidawi (1970) in a study of Lebanese students also found self-conception of academic ability to be related to achievement. In a study of students in Thailand and the United States, Subhadhira (1979) found that social class background and sex were important variables in the origins of self-concept and this was further verified in studies of Nigerian and U.S. students by Ate (1980). Kaminski et al. (1976), however, showed that the critical factor was how parents responded to their children and that many parents overcame most problems of learning that tend to be associated with social class and sex by instilling high self-conceptions in their children. In summary, the importance of self-conception of academic ability has been well substantiated.

The other components of our model, however, have not been so comprehensively demonstrated to have utility in accounting for student behavior. Only recently has research been initiated that simultaneously takes into account all dimensions of self-assessment included in our scheme. It has been found that the instrumental and intrinsic self-assessments attached to the role of student contributed to our ability to predict student decisions concerning their career programs (Bilby, Erickson and Brookover, 1972). Of course, it takes years to develop powerful and valid instruments, and perhaps these conclusions are premature. As it stands, however, the limited evidence available to date is in accord with our scheme of the organization of the self-conceptions of individuals.

SOCIAL AND EDUCATIONAL IMPLICATIONS

The evidence relating self-conceptions to the influence of others contains a number of implications for educational practice. The following questions highlight some of them:

1. Do we as teachers or professors sometimes (perhaps inadvertently) emphasize or reinforce instrumental values of the student role while ignoring the development of intrinsic values of student achievement? What strategies, experiences, or modeling would be most effective for creating positive assessments of self in the student role? What strategies are likely to be self-defeating?

2. Can we make academic achievement its own reward or must we be totally dependent upon the "carrot" approach to school achievement?

3. Should parents be enlisted in educational programs to affect students' cognitions about their academic competencies and the instrumental and intrinsic values of student achievement? If so, how should the parents be guided? What should be avoided?

4. How can we as professors or teachers most effectively help students to achieve desired self-conceptions of ability? Are there behaviors we sometimes engage in which inadvertently lead to low self-conceptions of ability on the part of our students?

5. Are there organizational or other features in our schools and colleges that, in spite of their goals, lead to students' devaluing their student role or their abilities? What is the impact of certain grouping procedures and the labels commonly given to students in these groups?

We suggest that our characterization of self functions as a selective mechanism in processing information, that we actively seek messages from the environment, and that we adjust our behavior according to how this information is internally represented. Rogers (1951) argued that we reference or organize information in relation to the self, and that the self is the initial cognitive structure to be set in motion when processing information. We would reformulate this by contending that the self is not a structure in the sense of a building but rather is an organization of cognitive processes that mediate between the message environment and role behavior. Furthermore, we believe that the process of self-conceptualizing involves attributing different meanings to different messages as they relate to self. The adjudication of these messages is at least partially contingent upon their instrumental or their intrinsic value for self in a given role. Finally, changes in self-conceptions will reflect changes in the message environment and will in turn function to direct changes in role behavior. This relationship among the message environment, self-conceptions, and role behavior assumes added importance when considering the nature and consequences of human learning.

On the basis of our assumptions about ourselves in relation to our environment, we take certain postures toward our world. These assumptions about self provide a frame of reference for anticipating and evaluating new experiences. Individuals tend to behave in terms of how they think things really are. People also tend to behave in terms of how they think things should be. And in addition, people tend to behave in terms of how they think things *could* be. In essence, then, our lifestyles are partly a function of our frames of reference, which are basically our assumptions about self in relation to our environment. The student's self-conceptions, therefore, influence his or her "style of behavior" as a student.

REFERENCES

Ate, Julius A. (1980) A Comparison of the Relationships Between Self-Concept of Intellectual Ability and Self-Esteem, in Nigeria. Unpublished master's thesis, Western Michigan University.

Atkinson, J. W. (1969) *An Introduction to Motivation.* Princeton, N.J.: D. Van-Nostrand.

Auer, Michael (1971) Self-Concept of Academic Ability of West German Eighth-Grade Students. Doctoral dissertation, Michigan State University.

Bilby, Robert W., Edsel L. Erickson, and Wilbur B. Brookover (1972) "Characterizations of Self and Student Decision Making." *Review of Educational Research,* Vol. 42, No. 4, pp. 505–524.

Bowe, Willard (1977) "The Development of Scientific Careers among Black and White Students: A Longitudinal Study." Unpublished master's thesis, Western Michigan University, Kalamazoo, Michigan.

Blumer, Herbert (1969) *Symbolic Interactionism, Perspective and Method.* Englewood Cliffs, N.J.: Prentice-Hall.

Brookover, W. B. (1959) "A Social Psychological Conception of Learning." *School and Society,* vol. 87, pp. 84–87.

Brookover, W. B., and Edsel L. Erickson (1975) *Sociology of Education.* Homewood, Ill.: Dorsey Press.

Brookover, W. B., Ann Patterson, and Shailer Thomas (1962) *Self-Concept of Ability and School Achievement:* I. Cooperative Research Project no. 845. East Lansing: Educational Publication Services, Michigan State University.

Brookover, W. B., Jean M. LePere, Don E. Hamacheck, Shailer Thomas, and Edsel L. Erickson (1965) *Self-Concept of Ability and School Achievement:* II. Cooperative Research Project no. 1636. East Lansing: Bureau of Educational Research Services, College of Education, Michigan State University.

Brookover, W. B., E. L. Erickson, and L. M. Joiner (1967a) *Self-Concept of Ability and School Achievement:* III. Cooperative Research Project no. 2831. East Lansing: Educational Publication Services, Michigan State University.

(1967b) "Educational Aspirations and Plans in Relation to School Achievement and Socio-Economic Status." *School Review,* Vol. 75, No. 4, pp. 392–400.

Brookover, W. B., Richard J. Gigliotti, Ronald P. Henderson and Jeffrey M. Schneider (1979) *Elementary School Social Environments and Achievement.* East Lansing: College of Urban Development, Michigan State University.

Brookover, W. B., Lawrence Beamer, Helen Efthim, Douglas Hathaway, Lawrence Lezotte, Stephen Miller, Joseph Passalaequa, and Louis Tornatsky (1983) *Creating Effective Schools.* Holmes Beach, Florida: Learning Publications, Inc.

Bryan, Clifford, and Edsel Erickson (1970) "Forecasting Student Dropout." *Education and Urban Society,* Vol. 3, No. 3, pp. 443–458.

Bryan, Clifford E., Edsel L. Erickson, and Lee M. Joiner (1970) "Forecasting Student Dropout Using Social-Psychological Data." Research paper presented to American Educational Research Association, Minneapolis, Minnesota.

Coleman, James C. (1960) *Personality Dynamics and Effective Behavior.* Chicago: Scott, Foresman, p. 58.

Combs, Arthur W., and Donald Snygg (1959) *Individual Behavior.* New York: Harper and Brothers.

Epps, Edgar G. (1969) "Correlates of Academic Achievement Among Northern and Southern Urban Negro Students." *Journal of Social Issues,* Vol. 25, No. 3, pp. 55–70.

Gabel, Peter (1970) "A Study of the Self-Concepts of High School Seniors and Their Post High School Plans." Unpublished doctoral dissertation, University of Colorado.

Gecas, Victor (1982) "The Self-Concept." *Annual Review of Sociology* 8:1–33.

Gergen, Kenneth J. (1972) "Multiple Identity: The Healthy, Happy Human Being Wears Many Masks." *Psychology Today*, May, pp. 31–35.

Haarer, David (1969) "A Comparative Study of Self-Concept of Ability Between Institutionalized Delinquent Boys and Non-Delinquent Boys Enrolled in Public Schools." Unpublished doctoral dissertation, Michigan State University.

Harding, Kenneth (1969) "A Comparative Study of Caucasian Male High School Students Who Stay in School and Those Who Drop Out." Unpublished doctoral dissertation, Michigan State University.

Hirschi, Travis (1969) *Causes of Delinquency*. Berkeley: University of California Press.

Homans, George (1961) *Social Behavior: Its Elementary Forms*. New York: Harcourt Brace.

Joiner, Lee M., and Edsel L. Erickson (1967) *Scales and Procedures for Assessing Social-Psychological Characteristics of Visually Impaired and Hearing Impaired Students*. U.S. Office of Education Cooperative Research Project No. 6-8720. Washington, D.C.: U.S. Government Printing Office.

Joiner, Lee M., Edsel L. Erickson, Jerry B. Crittenden, and Vivian M. Stevenson (1969) "Predicting the Academic Achievement of the Acoustically Impaired Using Intelligence and Self-Concept of Academic Ability." *Journal of Special Education*, Vol. 3, No. 4, pp. 425–431.

Kaminski, Donna M. (1975) "The Effects of Perceived Parental Evaluations on Skills Development in Mathematics." Unpublished master's thesis, Western Michigan University.
(1978) "Entry into Science: The Effect of Parental Evaluations on Sons and Daughters." Unpublished doctoral dissertation, Western Michigan University.

Kaminski, Donna M., and Edsel L. Erickson (1978) "Parents' Role in Their Daughters' Mathematical Development." Paper presented at the Midwest Sociological Society Meeting, Omaha.
(1980) "Science: Where Are the Women? Influence of Parents During Early Adolescence." *Michigan Sociological Review*.

Kaminski, Donna M., Edsel L. Erickson, M. Ross, and L. Bradfield (1976) "Why Females Don't Like Mathematics: The Effect of Parental Expectations." Paper presented at the American Sociological Association Meeting, New York.

Kaminski, Donna, M., R. M. Franklin, and V. Fish. (1977) "The Influence of Parents on Their Daughters' Self-Concept of Mathematics Ability." In *The Effects of Schooling and Culture on Dissaffiliation Career Development and Achievement*. Grand Rapids, Michigan: Center for Educational Studies, pp. 49–54.

Manning, Peter K., and Martin Zuker (1976) *The Sociology of Mental Health and Illness*. Indianapolis: Bobbs-Merrill.

Maslow, Abraham (1954) *Motivation and Learning*. New York: Harper and Brothers.

Mead, George Herbert (1934) *Mind, Self and Society*. Chicago: University of Chicago Press.

Morse, Richard J. (1963) "Self-Concept of Ability, Significant Others and School Achievement of Eighth Grade Students: A Comparative Analysis." Unpublished master's thesis, Michigan State University.

Nash, Ralph J. (1964) "A Study of Particular Self-Perceptions as Related to Scholastic Achievement." *Dissertation Abstracts*, Vol. 24, pp. 3837–3838.

Piers, Ellen V., and Dale B. Harris (1964) "Age and Other Correlates of Self-Concept in Children." *Journal of Educational Psychology*, Vol. 55, No. 2, pp. 91–95.

Rogers, Carl (1951) *Client Centered Therapy*. Boston: Houghton Mifflin.

Rotter, J., M. Seeman, and S. Liverent (1975) "Internal and External Control of the Environment, A Major Variable in Behavior Theory." In N. F. Washburn (ed.), *Decisions, Values and Groups*, Vol. 2. London: Paragon Press.

Scott, R. A., and A. Howard (1970) "Models of Stress." In S. Levine and N. Scott (eds.), *Social Stress*. Chicago: Aldine Publishing Co., pp. 259–278.

Schurr, Kenton T., and Wilbur B. Brookover (1967) "The Effect of Special Class Placement on the Self-Concept of Ability of the Educable Mentally Retarded Child." East Lansing: Educational Publication Services, College of Education, Michigan State University.

Seeman, Melvin (1959) "On the Meaning of Alienation." *American Sociology Review*, Vol. 24, pp. 783–791.

Sidawi, Ahmad (1970) "Self-Concept of Ability and School Achievement in Lebanon." Unpublished doctoral dissertation, Michigan State University.

Skinner, B. F. (1953) *Science and Human Behavior*. Glencoe, Ill.: The Free Press.

Sproull, Kenneth (1969) "The Relationship Between High School Self-Concept of Academic Ability and Subsequent Academic Achievement at the Community College." Unpublished dissertation, Michigan State University.

Subhadhira, S. (1979) "A Cross-Cultural Comparison of Correlation of Self-Concept of Academic Ability and Self-Esteem." Unpublished doctoral dissertation, Western Michigan University.

Towne, Richard E., and Lee M. Joiner (1966) "The Effect of Special Class Placement on the Self-Concept of Ability of the Educable Mentally Retarded Child." Report on U.S. Office of Education grant 32-32-0410-6001. East Lansing: College of Education, Michigan State University.

Votruba, James Charles (1970) "A Comparative Analysis of a Social-Psychological Theory of School Achievement." Unpublished master's thesis, Michigan State University.

Wamhoff, Carroll H. (1969) "Self-Concept of a Vocational Ability: Its Relation to Selected Factors in Career Development." Unpublished doctoral dissertation, Michigan State University.

Wylie, Ruth (1963) "Children's Estimates of Their Schoolwork Ability as a Function of Sex, Race and Socio-Economic Level." *Journal of Personality*, Vol. 31, No. 2, pp. 203–224.

P. S. FRY

Process Measures of Problem and Non-Problem Children's Classroom Behavior: The Influence of Teacher Behavior Variables

Questions to think about

1 *What factors enter into the difference between problem and non-problem children's classroom behavior?*

2 *How might classroom structure and organization relate to teacher-pupil interactions discussed here?*

3 *What environmental factors influence both the teacher-pupil interactions discussed here and the labeling process?*

4 *Are problem children necessarily problems? Explain and give examples from your own experience.*

INTRODUCTION

Most findings about teacher-pupil interactional processes (e.g., Flanders et al., 1968; Brophy and Good, 1970; Eshel and Klein, 1978) are determined from means of scores of events summed across classroom situations and reported as aggregated means developed over the course of months and years. The usual procedure is that students with *varying* levels of ability and emotional make-up are observed as one group,

From *British Journal of Educational Psychology* 53 (1983):79–88. Reprinted with permission of the author and Scottish Academic Press (Journals) Limited.

and interpretations of student behaviors and teacher interactions are based upon aggregates of student data.

The present study was designed along a somewhat different line. The purpose was to examine teacher interactions with "problem children" and "non-problem children" and to study similarities and differences in measures of teacher classroom behaviors towards these two groups of students. The long-term objective was to identify any systematic changes that might develop in measures of classroom behavior of teachers towards "problem" and "non-problem" children over a period of four months. The purpose also was to determine whether any changes are reflected in the "problem" and "non-problem" children's "pupil-to-pupil interactions."

The study was based upon the assumption that teachers' views and attitudes towards children objectively labelled "problem children" are intrinsically different from the view they hold about non-problem children. Since problem children as a group are recognized to have a genuinely different effect upon other normal populations (Zubin, 1967; Cromwell et al., 1975; Peterson and Hart, 1979; McDermott, 1980), for purposes of the present study, it was hypothesized that teachers' implicit views about problem children would influence their behavioral interactions with them in a manner quantitatively different from their interactions with non-problem children. The present study was designed to assess salient differences in *teacher interactions* with problem and non-problem children over a period of four months. Differences in pupils' reactions were also studied but to a limited extent only.

Very few previous studies have attempted to examine the differences and similarities in teacher relationships with problem and non-problem children. It was hoped that such information might suggest hypotheses concerning influential factors in pupil-teacher interactions. The present study hypothesized that over a period of a four-month school term there is a systematic variation in teacher-pupil interactions and that this variation is more pronounced in the case of teacher interactions with problem pupils.

METHOD

Observation data were collected for 30 teachers each teaching two classes in English and/or Social Studies. These classes were selected because "problem children" were present in the classrooms. For each of the 30 teachers' grade five and grade six classes, observational data were sorted out by the month and four means were computed for each of the 12 variables of interest. Thirty fifth- and sixth-grade teachers were observed in classes by trained observers over a period of four months. Each class was observed an average of once a week for 60 minutes. A select list of teacher and pupil behaviors were observed on a standardized form. These data were used as predictors to describe relations between teacher behaviors and problem and non-problem children's interactions with the teachers. Some observations were also made of pupil-to-pupil interactions.

Data were obtained for 30 teachers and 30 classes in each of which 10 problem and 10 non-problem children were observed. The two groups of children were matched in terms of ability and socio-economic status. Thus a total of 600 pupils were initially selected for the study. However, five classes which were involved in the study were later dropped from the sample because of attrition in the number of problem children who remained in the classes during the period of November 1979 and January 1980. Average class size of the classes selected for study was 28 children.

Identification of Criterion Groups of Students

In November 1980 teachers in the 45 classes initially selected for the study were requested to provide ratings on the Behavior Problem Checklist (Quay and Peterson, 1979) for each child. It was assumed that the teachers had become familiar with their pupils in the four months preceding the time of this study and that they would be able to rate their pupils objectively. Teachers were naive as to the overall purpose of the study and how the pupil categories of problem and non-problem children fitted into the broad design of the investigation. However, teachers were requested to follow the procedures of Galvin and Annesley (1971) in rating pupils in the Behavior Problem Checklist and thus to identify the problem and non-problem children. According to procedures outlined by Galvin and Annesley problem and non-problem children were defined by the teachers as follows:

Problem Group

Pupils were considered conduct problems if (a) they received a score of nine or higher in the Conduct Problem section of the Behavior Problem Checklist, and (b) a score of five or higher in the Personality Problem category of the checklist.

Non-Problem Group

Pupils in this category scored low in all areas of the Behavior Problem Checklist, indicating that their teachers viewed them as not displaying behavioral difficulties.

Pupils who met one of the criteria for the problem group and not both were regarded to be in the mixed group and were not used as subjects in this study.

Once identification of problem children was made within each class, the problem children were matched with non-problem counterparts on the two dimensions of ability and socio-economic status of subjects. Ability matching in each class was done on the basis of the results in the Primary Mental Abilities Test (Thurstone, 1962) which were obtained from the individual pupil's file. Matching for socio-economic status was done on the basis of the Blishen Index (Blishen, 1967).

The total sample consisted of 150 low performing problem children matched with 150 low performing non-problem children. One hundred and fifty high performing children were matched with 150 high performing non-problem children. Distribution of high and low ability pupils was not equalized across classes. Within each classroom, however, problem and non-problem children were matched on the dimension of ability. Matching on the dimension of socio-economic status was a relatively less difficult task. All four schools that provided the classes and subjects for the study served predominantly lower middle-class communities. Therefore homogeneity of subjects' socio-economic background was assured.

Raters

Raters were 15 male graduate students who were selected on the basis of previous experience that they had in coding behavioral observations (e.g., see Fry and Coe, 1980; Fry and Grover, 1981). They received a total of 20 hours of training for coding observations on 12 variables of major interest in the study. Two master trainers prepared five 60-minute videotapes of sample teacher-pupil interactions in classes that were not used in the study. These videotapes were used for training the raters. Training continued for each individual rater until a minimum of 85 percent was achieved between pairs of master-trainers that the rater was coding according to criteria. Each rater's performance was judged on a 120-minute videotape recording; percentage of agreement between the pair of master trainers for the 15 individual raters ranged between 85 percent and 97 percent. Checks on raters' coding were conducted by master trainers three times later during the course of the study (i.e., in February, March and April). The reliability of the coding system was ascertained by calculating the percentage agreement between pairs of coders who classified three 30-minute videotapes. The percentage of agreement between pairs of coders and/or master trainers ranged between 87 and 100 percent.

Teachers

The 30 teachers who were finally selected to serve as subjects in the study were all trained teachers holding a minimum of a bachelor's degree in education and two years of teaching experience in the elementary grades. Teachers were naive as to the specific purpose of the study (i.e., to observe teachers' differential interactions with problem and non-problem children) but were told generally that the study involved an examination of the naturalistic environment of the classroom. Teachers were given assurance that any observations of individual teachers or pupils that were made in the study would be kept completely confidential from school authorities and that the researchers were only interested in gathering and reporting group data.

Procedure

As mentioned before, each class was observed by trained observers an average of 15 times, for 60 minutes, over a four-month period. Visits by observers were determined by a randomly selected predetermined schedule. With the permission of the teacher, a fixed pupil seating arrangement was required. A predetermined coding sheet was drawn up for each class. The raters were unaware of the problem or non-problem condition of the subjects and were not informed about the purpose or hypotheses of the study.

Data reported in this study were based upon ratings of 15 variables of interest adapted from Evertson et al. (1979). Ratings on each of the 15 variables were filled out at least once for each class period.

Teacher Behaviors

(a) Positive affect: Teacher behaviors that show support or positive regard for pupils and their behavior, including such behavior as smiling, joking, reinforcement and praise.
(b) Negative affect: Verbal or non-verbal behaviors reflecting hostility or negative feelings of the teacher. This category includes negative teacher evaluation of student behavior, expressing anger or criticism.
(c) Social contacts: Contacts that are non-academic in nature but initiated by the teacher as a means of exchanging greetings or conveying some personal message.

(d) Teacher-initiated problem solving: The degree to which the teacher addresses questions and problems to the individual pupil. This category includes high level synthesis questions requiring reasoning, interpretation of materials or abstract thinking on the part of the pupil.

(e) Random, memory or fact questions: Questions requiring brief factual answers. The pupil responds from rote memory.

(f) Convergent-evaluative interaction: Teacher behavior in this category is directed towards obtaining a correct answer, with little or no attempt to follow up on the contact once the response has been made.

(g) Sustaining feedback: This category includes several sequences of events in which the teacher provides sustained response opportunity to the pupil if the first response is not correct, or incomplete or unclear.

(h) Personal questioning in which pupils are required to give their personal views and preferences.

Pupil Behaviors

(i) Level of sustained attention or absence of attention: This category rates the overall quality of orientation towards the teacher or the task at hand.

(j) Call-outs: Response opportunities created by pupils calling out answers or questions without getting teacher's permission.

(k) Mild misbehavior: Behavior judged to be inappropriate but not disruptive; behaviors that involve pupils talking to or visiting each other.

(l) Serious misbehavior: Pupils' behaviors that are inappropriate and very disruptive to the class.

The 15 variables (see Table 1 for full list) were selected because they represent the dimensions that are most relevant to the hypotheses that were being tested in the study. They were also behaviors that had higher probability of occurrence during each hour of observation and therefore would allow the raters to aggregate the scores at the end of the month. Mean rate measures were computed in each class for teacher behaviors vis-à-vis problem and non-problem children. Aggregate scores for each month were converted to aggregates over a four-month period.

Data Analysis

For each of the 15 dependent variables a one-between (Problem–Nonproblem), one-within (4 months) fixed effects analysis of variance was

TABLE 1
Results of Analyses of Variance for Problem and Non-problem Children

Variable	Number of pupils		Probability		
	Problem	Non-problem	Pupil differences Problem–Non-problem	Months	Pupils × Months
Teacher Behaviors					
1. Positive affect	69	121	0.001	0.001	<0.01
2. Negative affect	94	44	0.0011	0.001	<0.05
3. Social contacts	11	71	0.0001	0.05	NS
4. Teacher-initiated problem solving	63	131	0.001	NS	NS
5. Random memory or fact questions	111	71	0.01	NS	NS
6. Convergent-evaluative interaction	127	84	0.001	0.05	<0.05
7. Sustaining feedback	41	109	0.0001	0.05	<0.01
8. Personal questions	62	82	0.05	NS	NS
9. Sustained attention	34	105	0.0001	0.01	<0.01
Student Behaviors					
10. Call-outs	78	83	NS	NS	<0.02
11. Mild misbehaviors	110	97	NS	NS	NS
12. Serious misbehaviors	167	11	0.0001	0.01	<0.01
13. Student-initiated questions	64	59	NS	NS	NS
14. Pupil-to-pupil interaction	79	71	NS	NS	NS
15. Passive pupil behavior	89	53	0.01	0.05	NS

computed. By April 1981, data were available on 28 teachers and 400 pupils. Some of the classes were not observed as frequently as planned in the four months and some ratings were omitted occasionally. The available N for analysis was less than complete for all 15 variables.

RESULTS

Reported in Table 1 are the probability values for the two main effects (Problem–Non-problem children and time of the year) and the interaction in each of the 15 analyses of variance. Table 2 contains means for the months' main effect. Cell means for significant interaction effects are reported in Table 3. Since the available N for analysis was less than complete for all variables, the results can be examined and interpreted only in terms of *trends*. These trends were inferred from inspection of the means. No specific statistical tests were conducted for linear or quadratic components of the variation in the months.

Ratings reported in Table 1 show that 11 out of 15 variables yielded significant differences for the problem–non-problem children's main effect.

Problem and Non-Problem Children's Differences

A. Teacher behaviors An examination of teacher behavior variables indicated that problem children received more negative affect from teachers, obtained fewer social contacts with them and were asked less frequently by their teachers to express their personal views and preferences on academic and class-related issues.

By comparison, non-problem children received greater positive affect from teachers and obtained more sustained feedback on their responses and task preference.

Ratings of teacher behaviors also suggested that non-problem children were receiving from teachers a more positive orientation to their intellectual capabilities. Ratings of specific variables suggested that non-problem children were asked more complex higher level cognitive questions by their teachers in contrast to problem children who were asked more factual questions involving more rote memory and less use for reasoning, interpretation or abstract thinking.

Non-problem children were involved in more sustained intellectual questions from their teachers while problem children were confronted with convergent-evaluative questions from their teachers. Such questions were coded as teacher attempts to obtain correct answers without a subsequent need to maintain sustained contact with the child.

TABLE 2
Main Effects for Months

	Months							
	January		February		March		April	
Variables	Problem	Non-problem	Problem	Non-problem	Problem	Non-problem	Problem	Non-problem
Teacher Behaviors								
1. Positive affect	23	49	19	34	16	20	11	19
2. Negative affect	11	9	22	10	19	10	39	15
3. Social contacts	5	28	4	20	1	13	1	11
4. Teacher-initiated problem solving	21	49	18	38	14	26	10	18
5. Random memory or fact questions	22	10	28	15	26	20	31	30
6. Convergent-evaluative interaction	19	14	27	10	31	24	50	26
7. Sustaining feedback	17	38	13	27	5	24	6	20
8. Personal questions	20	21	16	22	16	19	10	20
9. Sustained attention	14	38	10	34	4	26	6	17
Student Behaviors								
10. Call-outs	21	20	19	22	18	20	20	20
11. Mild misbehaviors	20	18	26	24	28	26	6	29
12. Serious misbehaviors	11	1	14	2	16	3	26	5
13. Student-initiated questions	22	18	20	119	12	12	10	10
14. Pupil-to-pupil interaction	14	12	18	14	20	19	27	26
15. Passive pupil behavior	14	6	15	12	31	16	29	19

T A B L E 3
Cell Means for Significant Interactions between Months and
Problem–Non-problem Children

		Months			
Variable	Children	January	February	March	April
Positive affect	Problem	2.62	2.21	2.01	1.98
	Non-problem	2.98	2.81	3.03	3.00
Negative affect	Problem	1.85	2.48	2.55	2.87
	Non-problem	1.46	1.35	1.40	1.67
Convergent-evaluative	Problem	2.03	2.27	2.81	3.01
interaction	Non-problem	1.87	1.61	1.67	1.92
Sustaining feedback	Problem	1.31	1.26	1.12	1.08
	Non-problem	2.05	2.51	2.64	2.59
Sustained attention	Problem	2.01	2.29	1.67	1.29
	Non-problem	2.87	2.75	2.79	2.91
Call-outs	Problem	2.03	2.47	2.87	3.89
	Non-problem	1.87	1.75	1.70	1.64
Serious misbehaviors	Problem	1.01	1.71	2.70	3.09
	Non-problem	1.10	1.05	1.61	1.59

B. Pupil behaviors   An examination of the student behavior variables
showed some significant differences between problem and non-problem
children: problem children engaged in greater frequency of serious misbehaviors, had fewer instances of sustained attention in the task on hand,
and showed more passive, withdrawal behaviors (e.g., visual wandering,
doodling).

No significant differences were observed between the two groups on
other variables of pupil behavior such as pupil-to-pupil interaction, mild
misbehaviors and pupil-initiated questions.

Change over Four Months

Nine teacher behaviors and two pupil behaviors showed significant main
effects for the four months. (See Table 1). Fluctuations in ratings for these
variables are reported in Table 2 with variations shown separately for
problem and non-problem children (see also Table 3).

Teacher behaviors   Positive affect was at its peak in January and gradually declined reaching a significant low in April. Although this effect occurred for both problem and non-problem children, the decrease was much more pronounced for problem children.

Similar variations are apparent for negative affect and convergent-evaluative interactions towards pupils. These effects are low in January but climb to a significant high peak in April. Although this effect occurred for both problem and non-problem children, the incidence of increase in teacher negative affect and convergent-evaluative interactions was more pronounced for problem children over the four-month period. These trends are the most pronounced of any of the teacher behaviors and suggest that as the winter session drew to a close teachers' reactions became more negative, and interactions with pupils became more superficial and evaluative than sustaining. Similarly, and perhaps because their patience had worn thin, there was a gradual decline in the number of social contacts that teachers made and in the sustaining feedback they provided to pupils. Frequency of sustained feedback behaviors and number of social contacts that teachers provided were at their highest in January (particularly vis-à-vis non-problem children) and gradually declined by April. This decline is more pronounced for the problem children group.

More high cognitive level questioning and problem solving characterized teacher behaviors towards both problem and non-problem children in the month of January compared to other months. There was a gradual decline in the more complex type of intellectual activity initiated by the teacher and the decline was most pronounced for the problem children group in April. These findings suggest that, for whatever the reason, teachers were shifting to other types of activity involving more rote-memory, factual information (random, memory or fact questions) by the time that April came along; activities requiring pupils to think and analyze declined correspondingly. It may be that for both teacher and pupil, fatigue sets in by the end of the winter term and teachers find that the pupils are too slow in responding to complex questions and discussion issues. Although these effects occurred for both problem and non-problem children, the trend was stronger and most pronounced for problem children in the month of April. It is possible that problem children who are generally assumed to become more easily frustrated and less cooperative with time, were treated differently by their teachers. Table 2 suggests a sharp increase in teachers' convergent evaluative interactions towards problem children in the month of April. There was also a sharp decrease in the sustained feedback which problem children, compared to non-problem children, received from their teachers in the months of March and April (compared to January and February).

Pupil behaviors   The apparent steady decline in teacher involvement in problem children appears to be accompanied by significantly greater passivity in children and a sharp decline in the incidence of problem children's serious misbehaviors. The incidence of pupil misbehaviors is different from problem and non-problem children. Non-problem children engaged in mild misbehaviors such as visual wandering, inattention, passing notes to their peers, whispering and feeble giggling. By contrast, problem students' misdemeanors were more serious and included behaviors such as disruptive comments that students may call out of context during classroom discussion, loud and angry negative comments about teachers or criticism about peers, loud chatting with peers not in response to teacher-posed questions and disruptive noise caused by banging of doors and desk covers, shuffling of chairs and wilful throwing of heavy objects. These trends were most pronounced for problem children. Problem children engaged in serious misdemeanors much more frequently than non-problem children throughout the four-month period but by April problem children's serious misbehaviors increased from one instance per hour to almost 2.8 instances per hour. This may not seem on the surface to be an important change but, taken together with other findings showing changes in teachers' process behaviors towards problem children, it adds to the general picture of teachers' declining involvement with problem children and problem children's increase in misdemeanors.

Mild misdemeanors and "call-outs" have no differential effects for problem and non-problem children.

Both groups of pupils showed an increase in pupil-to-pupil interaction which includes pupils making substantive utterances and responses directly to other pupils without the mediation of the teacher.

Sustained attention on the part of pupils also showed a significant differential effect for problem and non-problem children categories, with the sustained attention declining for both groups over the four-month period but the effect being more pronounced during each month for the problem children.

DISCUSSION

The results suggest that for problem children, more so than non-problem children, behaviors may be largely determined by the immediate classroom environment and the teachers' daily positive or negative interactions. When problem and non-problem children's behaviors were compared more closely (in terms of the four-month trend and the significant interactions for months and subjects), the problem children's sustained attentions or disruptive behaviors appeared to be more closely tied in to differences in treatment by the teachers. Sustained feedback or loss of involvement, positive or negative affect and social contacts on the part of the teacher had a more direct influence on problem pupils' sustained attentions.

Overall, the results verify some commonsense expectations. Teachers and other educators are generally aware that there is a significant loss in positive attitude towards pupils during the latter part of the school term (see Evertson and Veldman, 1981). In the present study, however, the results suggest that this loss in positive attitude of teachers is more closely related to the "problem children" categorization of pupils. It may be that teachers find that providing sustained feedback to problem children, whose sustained attentions are assumed to be more limited, is a slow and time-consuming process and is less likely to hold general class attention. Nevertheless, it is very important that teachers become more aware of their interactions with the problem children. It may be that problem children, compared to non-problem children, are in greater need of the teacher's nurturance, and it is conceivable that as the school year progresses children *become* more problems because of a greater than average need for nurturance from the teacher.

While no strong assertions about causality can be made from the data, the indications are that problem children's mild and serious misdemeanors were greater and their sustained attention was lower when teachers showed a decline in positive affect, social contact and sustained feedback towards the pupils. These findings suggest that while the functioning of all pupils may have been affected by teacher behaviors, problem children in particular appeared to be more sensitive to the teacher's social and affective orientation. Taken together with the findings of previous research (e.g., Flanders et al., 1968; Garner and Brig, 1973; Rosenshine, 1973; Evertson and Veldman, 1981) the present results confirm the importance of investigating trends in teacher-pupil interactions such as those reported here.

Further research is needed to assess whether the findings reporting monthly trends were specific to the four months under scrutiny in the present study or whether they represent ongoing trends in the relationship between teacher behavior variables and pupil reactions.

The determinants of disruptive behaviors and problem behaviors in the classroom vary widely and the precipitators of teachers' negative affect in the classroom remain relatively unknown. The results of the present study, tentative as they are, suggest that problem children's disruptive behaviors and decline in sustained attention may not necessarily reflect true problem behaviors. It is quite likely that they are mediated more often than we suspect by the prevailing attitudes and orientations of the teacher.

The limitations of the current study should be noted. The lack of objective information about the reasons and motivations that entered into teacher behaviors precluded an investigation of those specific teacher-pupil interactions that were designed and intended by teachers to have a positive or negative effect on pupils. Future research of a longitudinal nature should address the question of teacher assumptions and presumptions and limitations regarding their daily interactions with the children.

REFERENCES

Blishen, B. R. (1967). A socioeconomic index of occupations in Canada. *Can. Rev. Sociol. Anthropol.*, 4, 41–53.

Brophy, J., and Good, T. (1970). Brophy-Good system (teacher-child interaction). In Simon, A. and Boyer, E. (Eds.), *Mirrors for Behavior: An Anthology of Observation Instruments. Continued* 1970 *supplement, Vol. A.* Philadelphia: Research for Better Schools.

Cromwell, R. L., Blashfield, R. K., and Strauss, J. S. (1975). Criteria for classification systems. In Hobbs, N. (Ed.), *Issues in the Classification of Children, Vol. 1.* San Francisco: Jossey Bass.

Eshel, Y., and Klein, Z. (1978). The effects of integration and open education on mathematics achievement in the early primary grades. *Am. Educ. Res. J.*, 15, 319–323.

Evertson, C. M., Anderson, L. M., and Brophy, J. E. (1979). Texas Junior High School Study: final report of process-outcome relationships (R. & D. Rep. No. 4061). Austin: Research and Development Center for Teacher Education, University of Texas.

Evertson, C. M., and Veldman, D. J. (1981). Changes over time in process measures of classroom behavior. *J. Educ. Psychol.*, 73, 156–163.

Flanders, N.A., Morrison, B. M., and Brode, E. L. (1968). Changes in pupil attitudes during the school year. *J. Educ. Psychol.*, 50, 334–338.

Fry, P. S., and Coe, K. J. (1980). Interactions among dimensions of academic motivation and classroom social climate: a study of the perceptions of junior high and high school pupils. *Br. J. Educ. Psychol.*, 50, 33–42.

Fry, P. S., and Grover, S. (1981). Problem and nonproblem children's causal explanations of success and failure in primary school settings. *Br. J. Soc. Psychol.*, (in press).

Galvin, J. P., and Annesley, F. R. (1971). Reading and arithmetic correlates of conduct-problem and withdrawn children. *J. Special Educ.*, 5, 213–219.

Garner, J., and Brig, M. (1973). Inequalities of teacher-pupil contacts. *Br. J. Educ. Psychol.*, 43, 234–243.

McDermott, P. A. (1980). Congruence and typology of diagnosis in school psychology: an empirical study. *Psychol. in Schools*, 7, 12–24.

Peterson, C. R., and Hart, D. H. (1979). Factor structure of the WISC-R for a clinic-referred population and specific subgroups. *J. Consult. Clin. Psychol.*, 47, 643–645.

Quay, H. C., and Peterson, D. R. (1979). *Manual for the Behavior Problem Checklist.* New Brunswick, N.J.: School of Professional Psychology, Busch Campus, Rutgers State University.

Rosenshine, B. (1973). Teacher behavior and student attitudes revisited. *J. Educ. Psychol.*, 65, 117–180.

Thurstone, T. G. (1962). *Primary Mental Abilities*. Palo Alto, Calif.: Science Research Associates.

Zubin, J. (1967). Classification of the behavior disorders. In Farnsworth, P. R., McNemar, O., and McNemar, Q. (Eds.), *Annual Rev. Psychol.* (Vol. 18). Palo Alto, Calif.: Annual Reviews.

What Is the Relationship Between Educational Systems and Society?

What takes place within educational systems is in part a result of external forces. The first two sections focused on approaches to studying and understanding educational systems and on internal dynamics of schools. Section Three incorporates two purposes: First, it discusses two major processes affecting educational systems from within and without—stratification and change. Second, it examines two types of educational systems as specific examples—higher education and cross-cultural systems. The first discussion is useful in illustrating the parts of a system as they fit together into a whole working model. The second presents the world as a system with education as one part of this system; the world systems models presented are related to conflict theory discussed in Section One in that the model divides nations into haves and have-nots, powerful and peripheral.

All systems, including education, incorporate constant change, and education will continue to be a challenging field of study because it will always be developing new dynamics for us to understand.

CHAPTER 6

Education and the Process of Stratification: Are Some More Equal than Others?

Schools are scapegoats for societal ills. Because we expect schools to provide equal opportunity, solve societal inequalities, and reduce discrimination, we feel frustrated when schools fail to accomplish these goals. Schools are particularly vulnerable to criticism and pressure from the environment because of the tradition of lay control. Parents and community members sometimes feel that schools are a doorstep on which to lay frustrations that go beyond schools into other areas of social life.

Education is seen as an important determinant of a person's occupation and income, although many other variables such as sex, race, and family background are also important. Although educational opportunities are expanding, employment and income differentials between groups continue to grow even wider. The belief that a good education and hard work will get us ahead has not proven true for many people.

The process of stratification determines the location of individuals in the strata or layers of society; determinants of position include wealth, income, occupation, education, prestige, and other factors. Stratification is interwoven into the whole societal fabric. If we viewed education as an isolated institution, we could not understand the phenomenon of stratification. From our open systems perspective, however, we see that the process of stratification in society as a whole is reflected in the institution of education, a relationship that will become clear in the articles dealing with issues in stratification.

We have all heard the term *equality of educational opportunity*. What it really means, however, is a matter for debate. According to Coleman,[1] the concept has been used to refer to everything from availability of free education and a common curriculum to guaranteeing that children from diverse backgrounds attend the same school.

It is generally agreed that the concept does include provision of equal facilities, finances for schools, and availability of schooling. But conflicts arise over whether schools should be expected to narrow income and occupational gaps between groups in the adult world. This applies particularly to race, class, and gender lines. Several articles in this chapter address the differences in school experiences resulting from these variables.

Two major perspectives have dominated sociological explanations of stratification. Recall the discussion by Randall Collins in Chapter 2. The functionalist perspective argues that some members of society will inevitably receive more education and higher positions than others, thus resulting in a stratification system. There are many positions to be filled; some members of society will train long years to fill important niches. Because of the sacrifice in time and money they make to train and because of the importance of their positions to society, these individuals will receive more money and prestige. Each individual plays a role in the interdependent structure of society; those who come closest to meeting needs and values generally perceived as important in society will be accorded higher status. Inequality, therefore, is inevitable. The question is *how much* inequality is necessary.

Those holding the conflict perspective see inequities in society resulting from conflicts between those who hold power and wealth and those who do not. Those in power positions control access to high positions and to education necessary for such positions. Thus, inequalities in the educational system reflect inequality in society. By controlling the type of education and knowledge available to various groups in society, the dominant group can maintain its position of power and perpetuate inequality. That the origins of inequality in education are to be found in the class structure is a view delineated in the article by Samuel Bowles and Herbert Gintis.

The articles in Chapter 6 all deal with aspects of stratification, including integration, educational choice, achievement, attainment, and the role of education. The first three articles look at whether education can make a difference in equal opportunity. The fourth presents recent findings on achievement in private schools, and the last three deal with stratification issues affecting specific groups—minorities, women, and working class.

Can education compensate for societal inequality? This question has occupied the research efforts of many sociologists. The hopes that educational expansion of the 1950s and 1960s would reduce social inequality came to a halt in the late 1960s; the high expectations, many feel, were met by low performance of schools. Early poor evaluations of innovative programs for compensatory education caused the programs to be questioned and funding cut.

A. H. Halsey, a noted British sociologist, looks at the results of studies on compensatory education and points out that to drop programs like Headstart is to ignore the fact that educational deficits of children are in part socially created and can be socially remedied. In an extensive follow-up study of Headstart participants, he showed that preschool experience has lasting effects, both academic and attitudinal, on children. Halsey argues that preschool programs are a sound economic investment.

Another important question is whether changes in the educational system can reduce inequality. We have tried "open" classrooms. We have tried stressing the basics. We have tried compensatory education, busing, and many other supposed remedies. Yet schools are still under fire, and reduction in educational inequality remains an illusive goal.

Samuel Bowles and Herbert Gintis, writing from a Marxist conflict theoretical perspective, argue that unequal education will persist so long as capitalism survives as the dominant political-economic system. When one group has power over others and the others have no power in the division of labor, class cultures will be perpetuated in school and society, resulting in inequality. Yankelovich's review of Christopher Jencks' book, *Who Gets Ahead*, illustrates the importance of environmental factors such as family background, income, and race for school and job attainment. All these factors influence students' success in school and later life.

Much debate has been generated by James Coleman's recent study on achievement levels of public and private school students. Coleman's findings indicate that racially mixed groups of students at Catholic and other private schools achieve at a higher level in vocabulary and mathematics than students in public schools. Private schools, according to Coleman, seem to provide safer, more disciplined, and more controlled environments than public schools. But the report has created controversy because of its implications for federal support of private schools, and because of some methodological questions. For our purposes, the impact on the stratification system is the crucial issue. Coleman assumes public support would make private schools more accessible to minorities, but opponents argue that federal support of private schools would support religious educational institutions and increase segregation because many minorities would not be able to attend private schools.

When sociologists speak of stratification and educational opportunity, they generally refer to specific groups that are adversely influenced by educational programs and policy. The last three articles in Chapter 6 discuss issues of stratification for three groups: Desegregation by means of busing has been a controversial policy for racial integration of schools; gender differences in school achievement have shown females to be underachievers in math and science; and social class background can determine attitude and even success in school.

The real issues in busing for desegregation are the topic of Rist's article. In 1954, the Supreme Court ruled in the case of *Brown* v. *Board of Education* that separate is not equal and that the problem of separate schools should be corrected with all due speed. Segregated schools were judged to provide unequal education. Desegregation through busing was a major plan to achieve racial balance in schools. After considerable delays and court cases, desegregation through busing occurred in many locations, mostly southern, between 1968 and 1971. Then school districts received mixed messages from the courts and there was a lull in new busing orders; while some districts have been ordered to desegregate or come up with acceptable alternative plans, Washington has not played an active enforcement role, allowing districts to ignore or tone down efforts to integrate schools.

Girls tend to show high academic achievement up through and including high school; boys, however, are taking more math and science courses by the time they reach high school as preparation for entering a wide range of college majors and career choices. Young women select fewer courses in these areas, limiting their later options. Donna Kaminski explores reasons for the differences in math and science achievement between boys and girls. The problems resulting from these different school experiences are summed up in later life opportunities: options for specialty fields, career options, and promotions. Although educational experiences influence sex inequality, the systems perspective implies that changes are needed in the whole societal system to rectify inequality based on sex, race, or class.

The last article on the process of stratification, based on a British study of working-class youth and their fathers by Paul Willis, depicts the process of reproducing the class structure. In interviews with working-class fathers and their sons and studies of the working-class youth countercultures in school, attitudes toward work and the role of education for different social classes are explored. This study gained attention because of its comprehensive look into how social class is perpetuated by peer groups in schools and by families.

Each article in this chapter examines a complex topic within the area of stratification; in most cases there are other viewpoints or interpretations as well, not all of which could be included here. Anticipate this omission and imagine what these other perspectives might be as you read the articles in this chapter.

REFERENCE

Coleman, James S., "The Concept of Equality of Educational Opportunity." *Harvard Educational Review* 38 (1968):7–22.

A. H. HALSEY

Education Can Compensate

Questions to think about

1 *What does the study of long-term effects of early education programs show?*
2 *For what differing reasons did both liberals and conservatives give up on preschool education?*
3 *Why does Halsey believe education can compensate? Do you agree?*
4 *What do you feel are the political implications of Halsey's conclusions?*

Educational budgets are now under siege all over the western world. Ministries of Education have been dominated by optimism for a century. They pursued policies of expansion in the belief that national wealth, and the reduction of social inequality, would inevitably follow.

The official ideology of liberal progress was never undisputed, but it was dominant. The consensual political middle trudged on in Britain, through the 1870, 1902 and 1944 Education Acts, slowly developing a state system of common schooling from infancy to adolescence, topped by selective and voluntary education beyond school.

Optimism reached its apogee in the easy affluence of the 1950s and early 1960s, with education steadily increasing its share of both the gross domestic product and the public purse, until at the end of the sixties it was halted. Schools and colleges now stand in the shadows, convicted of high promises and low performance.

Professor Jensen convinced many Americans that the intelligence of black children could not be boosted by pre-school programs. In Britain this abrupt reversal of fortune was rationalized mainly by the Black Paper pessimism of the right, compounded by economic depression and now by

From *New Society* (January 24, 1980), pp. 172–173. Reprinted with permission.

a monetarist government bent on cutting public expenditure. Nursery education—formerly and ironically a darling of Margaret Thatcher when Secretary of State—is now a prime target.

But the defenses of the educational expansionists were also undermined from the left. Christopher Jencks' *Inequality* (published in 1972) was a powerful American blow against what he took to be the misguided faith of the schoolmaster turned President in Lyndon Johnson's Washington:

"As long as egalitarians assume that public policy cannot contribute to economic equality directly but must proceed by ingenious manipulations of marginal institutions like the schools, progress will remain glacial. If we want to move beyond this tradition, we will have to establish political control over the economic institutions that shape our society. That is what other countries usually call socialism. Anything less will end in the same disappointment as the reforms of the 1960s."

The most publicized "ingenious manipulations of marginal institutions" in America in the 1960s was Headstart—a program of pre-schooling. Disappointment with Headstart's early results were the starting point of Jensen's researches. All the more interesting, then, to have a study published a decade later by the American Department of Health, Education and Welfare, in which the question is elaborately asked whether there have in fact been *Lasting Effects After Pre-School* from the euphoric educational reforms of the "war on poverty."

In Britain, pre-schooling developed skeptically and tentatively (in the wake of Headstart) within the action research programs of Education Priority Areas. It was greeted with hostility from both left and right. "A research smokescreen," declared John Barron Mays, Professor of Sociology at Liverpool. "Nursery education has been tried in America and doesn't work," was the crude opinion of a high-ranking Tory minister. Moreover, and unhappily, one of the most influential and deservedly respected sociologists of education, Professor Basil Bernstein, could also be invoked in opposition to the Headstart idea. He entitled an influential *New Society* article "Education cannot compensate for society" (February 26, 1970); warned against treating children as "deficit systems"; against distracting attention from the reform of schools on to the shortcomings of parents and families; and against the sanctifying of concepts like "cultural deprivation" as labels which would add further to the burdens of the children made to wear them.

Bernstein's were humane cautions linked to sophisticated argument. But they were easily and fatally assimilated to the holy proletarianism of a then-fashionable left, with its ideologically *a priori* rejection of the possibility that anything could be wrong with a working class child.

How Many Under-achieving Students Did Better After Headstart

Headstart project	Failure rate of project children (%)	Failure rate of control children (%)	Reduction in failure by attending project (%)	Total (No.)
Good experimental design				
Gordon	39.1	61.5	36.0	82
Gray	55.6	73.7	24.6	55
Palmer	24.1	44.7	46.1	221
Weikart	17.2	38.5	55.3	123
median	31.6	53.1	41.1	481
Quasi-experimental design				
Beller	48.6	53.1	8.5	69
Levenstein	22.1	43.5	49.2	127
Miller	20.6	11.1	—	125
Zigler	26.6	32.3	17.6	144
Overall median	25.4	44.1	36.4	920

NB: "Failure" is defined as being placed in special education classes, and/or retained in grade, and/or dropped out of school. "Reduction" is % control minus % project, divided by % control. Children's data were collected in different grades. The design of the Miller project permits no "reduction" conclusion. The numbers in the total are of project children plus control children.

Those who were more concerned with practical reform than with ideological purity preferred to notice that "deficit" could be socially created. They inferred that it could therefore be socially remedied. But, as has so often happened with Bernstein's research, the message was vulgarized by others. In the popular and political mind what stuck was his:

> We should stop thinking in terms of "compensatory education"

and not the rest of the sentence, which read:

> but consider, instead, most seriously and systematically the conditions and contexts of the educational environment.

The Education Priority Area projects in London, Liverpool, Birmingham and the West Riding were well described by the neglected half of Bernstein's sentence. They also, however, contained crucial elements of "compensatory" (even though the participants preferred to call it "complementary") education. More precisely, the EPA researchers had been impressed by the principle of positive discrimination, put forward in the Plowden report of 1967.

They tried, with resources that have to be described as miniscule by comparison with the American program, to apply positive discrimination to the educational environment of slum children. The EPA projects—which were directed from Oxford—began when and because Anthony Crosland was Secretary of State at the Department of Education and Science, and Michael Young was chairman of the Social Science Research Council. They ended and reported when Mrs. Thatcher was established at the DES and Sir Keith Joseph at the DHSS. Most precisely they recommended positive discrimination in pre-schooling.

The experience of three years in four districts had led to the conclusion "that pre-schooling is *par excellence* a point of entry into the development of the community school as we conceive of it. It is the point at which properly understood, the networks of family and formal education can most easily be linked." And three years of action research supported the contention "that pre-schooling is the most effective educational instrument for applying the principle of positive discrimination and this conviction rests partly on the theory that primary and secondary educational attainment has its social foundations in the child's experience in the pre-school years, and partly on the evidence that positive discrimination at the pre-school level can have a multiplier effect on the overwhelmingly important educative influence of the family and the peer group to which the child belongs."

We can now go some way further towards testing the validity of an adherence to optimism, retained in the teeth of opposition both then and since. The new American study has been produced by a consortium of twelve research groups, carrying out studies of the *long-run* effects of the early education programs of the 1960s. The group was led by Irving Lazar and Richard Darlington. Having pooled the data from their originally independent experiments, they collected common follow-up data in 1976–77. In this way they have assembled records of the experience and performance of 3,000 children, mostly black and all poor, who were involved in early education programs in the 1960s, either as "experimental" or "control" subjects, and who by 1976–77 were between 9 and 19 years old.

This is valuable and rare evidence. It would take another 15 years and millions of dollars to re-create it. Of course, it has its imperfections, quite apart from the dangers of any transatlantic passage. The original Headstart experiments were not designed to collect common information. They varied in size, starting point and content; they were, to varying degrees, experimental; and there has been a lot of attrition. Moreover, those in the Lazar-Darlington study are not just any old Headstart projects, but ones which are usable because they were properly designed and recorded. They include, for instance, the famous projects by Susan Gray in Tennessee, and by Deutsch in New York. Nevertheless, remarkable trouble has been taken in producing the final sample, and measuring its relation to the original population. Exceptionally rigorous rules have governed the testing for the long-term effects. It is, in short, an evaluation done with meticulous care.

The upshot is that the Lazar-Darlington consortium has established the existence of lasting effects from pre-schooling (i.e., nursery schooling) in four main ways.

First, they show that the beneficiaries are less likely to be assigned later to special or remedial classes. This effect of pre-schooling was shown to be there for children of the same initial IQ, sex, ethnicity, and family background. It persisted even when the comparison was controlled for IQ scores at age six.

Second, there has been the same lasting effect with respect to drop-out from school, and what the Americans call "retention in grade"—i.e., being held back to repeat a year's work because of poor performance. According to the evidence of the eight projects which had collected the relevant data, early educational experience protects against these failures. The protection holds for all poor children regardless of sex, ethnic backgrounds, early IQ and family circumstances.

Third, achievement in mathematics at age ten (fourth grade) is significantly improved by pre-schooling. The evidence also suggests a trend to better scores on reading tests at the same age.

Fourth, children from poor families who went to pre-school programs scored higher than the "control" children on the Stanford Binet IQ test for up to three years afterwards. In some projects, this superiority was maintained, but not among those who were aged 13 or over.

Finally, it has emerged that pre-school children retain more "achievement orientation," and their mothers tend to develop higher vocational aspirations for them than they have for themselves—a discrepancy not found among "control" children.

The first and second effects are shown in the table. Those who had the "treatment"—i.e., went to one of these well-planned programs—are compared with a control group of socially and racially matched children who did not. The table tells us that, ordinarily, 44 percent of children from disadvantaged homes have had to be given special remedial education, or are made to repeat a year, or have dropped out from school: but among those given pre-school education of a certain kind the proportion is reduced to 25 percent. Altogether, if you send children to a good nursery school, they are twice as likely afterwards to stay above the minimum level of school success as a similar group of children denied the opportunity.

It is true, as I have noted, that these impressive findings come from high-quality pre-school arrangements, and not from a random sample of Headstart programs. It is true, too, that to use avoidance of remedial classes and "grade failure" as measures of effectiveness is to focus on the minimal aspirations of a school's work. On the other hand, these are appropriate measures from two points of view. They point to characteristic failures of the children for whom the pre-school programs were designed—typically, the black child from a poor family. And they are measures of actual educational experience, rather than abstractions like measured intelligence, which may or may not issue in practical performance.

Educational policy makers on either side of the Atlantic may be justifiably disappointed that research has still failed to discern any particular feature of pre-schooling which accounted for success: for example, age of entry, parental involvement, type of teacher or type of teaching. The programs varied in all these respects. What they had in common was enthusiastic and careful organization. These qualities also made them usable for comparative and retrospective research.

But what Headstart and the EPA experience do show is that a pre-school program, properly devised, can be a most economical investment for a government wishing to save money on schools. And for a government determined to relieve the handicaps of those who come from poor families, a pre-school program discriminating in their favor seems to be one of the crucial weapons in the armory. In that way, education *can* compensate for society.

SAMUEL BOWLES and
HERBERT GINTIS

Education, Inequality, and the Meritocracy

Questions to think about

1 *Explain how Bowles and Gintis view education as perpetuating inequality in society. Give examples.*
2 *Interpret the other issues in this chapter—compensatory education, busing, public versus private schools, and sex-role socialization in schools—from the viewpoint expressed by Bowles and Gintis.*
3 *What are the parallels between the open systems framework (i.e., interdependence, environment) and the thesis advanced by Bowles and Gintis?*
4 *Do you see evidence for Bowles and Gintis's comments concerning meritocracy?*

The humanity of a nation, it is said, can be gauged by the character of its prisons. No less can its humanity be inferred from the quality of its educational processes. In the initiation of youth, a society reveals its highest aspirations, tempered less by the weight of tradition than by the limits to which the social relationships of adult life can be pushed. We believe that in the contemporary United States, these limits are sufficiently narrow to preclude the educational system from simultaneously integrating youth into adult society and contributing significantly to economic equality. In promoting what John Dewey once called the "social continuity of life," by integrating new generations into the social order, the schools are constrained to justify and reproduce inequality rather than correct it. . . .

From Samuel Bowles and Herbert Gintis, *Schooling in Capitalist America.* Copyright © 1976 by Basic Books, Inc., Publishers. Reprinted by permission of the publisher.

The pattern of economic inequality is predominantly "set" in the economy itself—via market and property institutions which dictate wide inequalities in income from property, in the basic social relations of corporate enterprises, and in the tendency toward uneven development, which leads to regional, sectional, racial, sexual, and ethnic disparities. But the "legitimation hypothesis" which we hope to substantiate in this chapter goes considerably beyond this level of analysis. For it suggests that a major element in the integrative function of education is the legitimation of preexisting economic disparities. Thus efforts to realize egalitarian objectives are not simply weak; they are also, as we shall demonstrate, in substantial conflict with the integrative function of education.

The educational system legitimates economic inequality by providing an open, objective, and ostensibly meritocratic mechanism for assigning individuals to unequal economic positions. The educational system fosters and reinforces the belief that economic success depends essentially on the possession of technical and cognitive skills—skills which it is organized to provide in an efficient, equitable, and unbiased manner on the basis of meritocratic principle.

Of course the use of the educational system to legitimize inequality is not without its own problems. Ideologies and structures which serve to hide and preserve one form of injustice often provide the basis of an assault on another. The ideology of equal educational opportunity and meritocracy is precisely such a contradictory mechanism.

We shall argue that beneath the facade of meritocracy lies the reality of an educational system geared toward the reproduction of economic relations only partially explicable in terms of technical requirements and efficiency standards. Thus we shall first suggest that educational tracking based on competitive grading and objective test scores is only tangentially related to social efficiency. Then we shall confront the technocratic-meritocratic ideology head on by showing that the association between length of education and economic success cannot be accounted for in terms of the cognitive achievements of students. Thus the yardstick of the educational meritocracy—test scores—contributes surprisingly little to individual economic success. The educational meritocracy is largely symbolic.

Clearly, though, this symbolism is deeply etched in the American consciousness. Nothing exhibits this more clearly than the recent "IQ debate," where it has been generally assumed that IQ and other measures of cognitive performance are important indicators of economic success. Only the genetic or environmental determinants of IQ have been questioned. Yet we will argue that social class or racial differences in IQ are nearly irrelevant to the process of intergenerational status transmission.

THE LEGITIMATION OF INEQUALITY

Throughout history, patterns of privilege have been justified by elaborate facades. Dominant classes seeking a stable social order have consistently nurtured and underwritten these ideological facades and, insofar as their power permitted, blocked the emergence of alternatives. This is what we mean by "legitimation": the fostering of a generalized consciousness among individuals which prevents the formation of the social bonds and critical understanding whereby existing social conditions might be transformed. Legitimation may be based on feelings of inevitability ("death and taxes") or moral desirability ("everyone gets what they deserve"). When the issue is that of social justice, these feelings are both present, with a dose of "custom" and "resignation" as well.

In U.S. economic life, legitimation has been intimately bound up with the technocratic-meritocratic ideology. . . . Several related aspects of the social relations of production are legitimized, in part, by the meritocratic ideology. To begin with, there are the overall characteristics of work in advanced U.S. capitalism: bureaucratic organization, hierarchical lines of authority, job fragmentation, and unequal pay. It is essential that the individual accept and, indeed, come to see as natural, these undemocratic and unequal aspects of the workaday world. Moreover, the staffing of these positions must appear egalitarian in process and just in outcome, parallel to the formal principle of "equality of all before the law" in a liberal democracy.

This legitimation of capitalism as a social system has its counterpart in the individual's personal life. Thus, just as individuals must come to accept the overall social relations of production, so workers must respect the authority and competence of their own "supervisors" to direct their activities, and justify their own authority (however extensive or minimal) over others. That workers be resigned to their position in production is perhaps sufficient; that they be reconciled to their fate is even preferable.

The hallmark of the meritocratic perspective is its reduction of a complex web of social relationships in production to a few rules of technological efficiency. In this view, the hierarchical division of labor arises from its natural superiority as a device to coordinate collective activity and nurture expertise. To motivate the most able individuals to undertake the necessary training and preparation for occupational roles, salaries and status must be clearly associated with level in the work hierarchy. Thus Davis and Moore, in their highly influential "functional theory of stratification," locate the "determinants of differential reward" in "differential functional importance" and "differential scarcity of personnel." "Social inequality," they conclude, "is thus an unconsciously evolved device by which societies insure that the most important positions are conscientiously filled by the most qualified persons."[1]

This meritocratic ideology has remained a dominant theme of the mainstream of social science since the rise of the factory system in the United States.[2] The robustness of this perspective (even those who reject it have nagging doubts) is due, in no small part, to its incorporation in major social institutions—factories, offices, government bureaus, and schools. For the technocratic justification of the hierarchical division of labor leads smoothly to a meritocratic view of the process whereby individuals are matched to jobs. An efficient and impersonal bureaucracy, so the story goes, assesses the individual purely in terms of his or her expected contribution to production. And the main determinants of job fitness are seen to be those cognitive and psychomotor capacities relevant to the worker's technical ability to do the job. The technocratic view of production, together with the meritocratic view of hiring, provides the strongest form of legitimation of alienated work and social stratification in capitalist society. Not only does it strongly reinforce the notion that the hierarchical division of labor is technically necessary (albeit politically totalitarian), but it also justifies the view that job assignment is objective and efficient and, therefore, just and egalitarian (albeit severely unequal). Moreover, the individual is resigned to, if not satisfied with, his or her own position in the hierarchy of production. The legitimacy of the authority of superiors flows not from social contrivance but from Science and Reason.

That this view does not strain the credulity of well-paid intellectuals is perhaps not surprising. But the meritocratic perspective would not be of much use in justifying the hierarchical division of labor if it counted among its adherents only the university elite and the technical and professional experts. But such is not the case. Despite the extensive evidence that IQ is not an important determinant of individual economic success, and despite the absence of evidence that technical skills have an important causal relationship to income inequality or intergenerational status transmission, the nearly exclusive importance of IQ and skills has captured the public mind. Numerous attitude surveys exhibit this fact.[3]

The linking of technical skills to economic success indirectly via the educational system strengthens rather than weakens the legitimation process. First, the day-to-day contact of parents and children with the competitive, cognitively oriented school environment, with clear connections to the economy, buttresses, in a very immediate and concrete way, the technocratic perspective on economic organization, to a degree that a sporadic and impersonal testing process divorced from the school environment could not accomplish. Second, by rendering the outcome (educational attainment) dependent not only on ability but also on motivation, drive to achieve, perseverance, and sacrifice, the status allocation mechanism acquires heightened legitimacy. Moreover, such personal attributes are tested and developed over a long period of time, underlining the apparent objectivity and achievement orientation of the stratification system. Third, frequent failures play an important role in gradually bringing a student's aspirations into line with his or her probable career opportunities. By the time most students terminate schooling, they have been put down enough to convince them of their inability to succeed at the next highest level. Through competition, success, and defeat in the classroom, students are reconciled to their social positions.[4]

So the objective educational system has etched the meritocratic perspective deeply into both popular culture and social science methodology. Nowhere is this seen more clearly than in the recent controversy over "open admissions" in colleges and universities. Open enrollment has been called on by militant minority groups to counteract the impediments of community deprivation, discrimination, and poor secondary education.[5] Both proponents and opponents of open admission have nearly uniformly assumed that the admission of students to higher education irrespective of IQ, test scores, or grades runs counter to efficiency and educational rationality.[6] Must not the principle of meritocracy in schools be efficient? Should not the most "able" be granted the right to further educational resources, since they will be the most capable of benefiting themselves and society? So goes the argument. But if social efficiency is the objective, the justification for a meritocratic admissions policy must rest on the assertion that "smart" people benefit more from college than those with lower test scores and grades. Stated more technically, the return from higher education, namely its impact on the individual's cognitive capacities, earning abilities, or productivity, must be positively related to prior test scores: The higher the test score the greater the expected return. If this is not the case, if low test scorers get as much out of college as high scorers, the argument that the policy of admitting the smartest must be maintained in the interest of social efficiency falls apart. And the evidence generally supports the view that the return from higher education is independent of prior test scores.

In a study exploring the cognitive "value added" in higher education, Alexander Astin, Director of the American Council on Education, found that there is no evidence that smart high-school seniors learn more in college, despite the fact that they tend to go to "better" institutions.[7] That is, education is something like physical exercise: Some people are more talented than others, but all benefit about equally from athletic involvement and instruction. But the more important question for our purposes is the way in which test scores affect the economic productivity of education, and, particularly, the predominant contemporary "sorting mechanism," higher education. The fact that for the past half century people have simply assumed the economic rationality of sorting by IQ and test scores in education speaks highly for the persuasiveness of the meritocratic perspective. Yet available evidence by no means substantiates this view. Of the six statistical studies which address this question, four indicate that schooling is *not* more productive for the higher-IQ individual; one produced mixed results; and only one supported the traditional view.[8]

For instance, Daniel C. Rogers[9] investigated the lifetime earnings of 1,827 males who were in the eighth or ninth grades in 1935, in various cities of Connecticut and Massachusetts, and who took an IQ test in that year. Rogers found that the economic productivity of a year of schooling is the same at all levels of IQ: The rate of return on the individual's "investment," including tuition and supply, costs as well as foregone earnings, toward attaining a higher degree, is more or less equal across a broad spectrum of IQ levels. At least from an economic point of view, higher education benefits all ability levels fairly equally, so the usual justification for selective enrollment is quite dubious.

But we do not propose to justify open admissions on grounds of pure economics or social efficiency. Rather, we wish to emphasize that the meritocratic orientation of higher education, far from serving "economic rationality," is actually a facade that facilitates the stratification of the labor force. Open admissions threatens this legitimation mechanism by rendering school success a less important factor in the opportunity to obtain higher education.

Experience with open enrollment seems to support our assertion that the ostensibly meritocratic and objective nature of selective admissions serves mainly the reproduction of the labor force through legitimation. The City College of New York, which began an extensive program of open enrollment in 1970, asked Astin and his associates at the American Council on Education to evaluate its first year of operation. They found that regular and open-enrollment students improved their test scores at the same rate, and there was no evidence that academic standards were lower in the first year. Of course, the test scores of open-enrollment students were initially lower than those of regulars (by the end of the freshman year, the test scores of open-enrollment students had attained the level of entering regular students). Nonetheless, while 50 percent of the open-enrollment students progressed at the normal rate (i.e., had earned twenty-four college credits), the proportion of regular students who did so was only slightly higher than 60 percent. In their interim report, Astin and Rossman conclude:

> Whether a student was regularly admitted or was an open-
> admissions student proved relatively unimportant in predicting his

or her success in the first year. Although the two groups did indeed differ in many ways, it is clear that open-admissions students brought a number of personal characteristics besides past achievements that proved to be important for college.[10]

In summary, the ostensibly objective and meritocratic selection and reward system of U.S. education corresponds not to some abstract notion of efficiency, rationality, and equity, but to the legitimization of economic inequality and the smooth staffing of unequal work roles. Every society must and will reward some individual excellences. But which ones they reward, in what manner, to what extent, and through what social process depend critically on how economic life is organized. The predatory, competitive, and personally destructive way in which intellectual achievement is rewarded in U.S. schools and colleges is a monument not to creative rationality, but to the need of a privileged class to justify an irrational, exploitative, and undemocratic system.

EDUCATION, INCOME, AND COGNITIVE ATTAINMENT

Why does education increase people's income? The traditional explanation—which we have labeled the technocratic-meritocratic perspective—presents a simple and compelling answer. Earnings reflect economic productivity. In a technologically advanced society, an individual's economic productivity depends partly on the level of the cognitive skills he or she has attained. Each year of education increases cognitive skill levels, thus indirectly leading to higher income.

Were this view correct, our heavy emphasis on the legitimating role of education would be more than a little misleading. In that case, the competitive educational system would be a meritocratic "game" in which the stakes (economic success) would be directly related to the criteria (cognitive attainment) of winning or losing in a very rational and even technological way.[11] Again, were this view correct, it would be difficult to argue that there are fundamental contradictions among the integrative, egalitarian, and personal development functions of education in capitalist society. Education could be as egalitarian as people's innate biological capacities allowed—which would be pretty far. Moreover, were the technocratic-meritocratic perspective correct, the persistence of repressive education—in the face of alternatives which appear to offer both a more democratic and participatory environment and a more effective vehicle for the transmission of cognitive skills—would merely reflect an irrational institutional inertia on the part of the school system. If schools could be made more humane and more efficient producers of intellectual skills, why have not all parties concerned—educators, students, employers, parents, workers, school boards, everybody—celebrated the opportunity? The answer, we believe, lies in a simple, but often overlooked, fact: The role of schools in promoting cognitive growth by no means exhausts their social functions. Indeed, while skills are developed in schools and a skilled labor force is necessary in a technologically advanced society, a cognitive approach to the educational system which focuses on the production of mental skills cannot provide the basis for understanding the link between schools and the economy.

In particular, we shall demonstrate that although higher levels of schooling and economic success tend to go together, the intellectual abilities developed or certified in school make little *causal* contribution to getting ahead economically. Only a minor portion of the substantial statistical association between schooling and economic success can be accounted for by the school's role in producing or screening cognitive skills. The economic function of schools is thus not limited to the development or identification of these skills.

This assertion may strike some as curious. Many commentators on the educational scene—social scientists, educators, and employers among them—have mistakenly attributed overarching importance to the intellectual role of schooling. A mid-nineteenth century industrialist, for example, wrote:

> Whenever a mill or a room should fail to give the proper amount of work, my first inquiry . . . would be as to the character of the help, and if the deficiency remained any great length of time, I am sure I should find many who had made marks upon the payroll, being unable to write their names.[12]

Interestingly, the records of a mill virtually identical to that owned by this industrialist have been preserved, and a careful study of the number of pieces produced by each worker (paid according to piece rates) revealed absolutely no statistical relationship between worker productivity and literacy, as measured by the marking of the payroll receipt book with an "X" or a written signature.*

While our more general claim—that the primary economic function of schooling is not the production or selection of intellectual skills—can be verified through a wide variety of data sources,[13] our major illustration will be drawn from an extensive sample which we have subjected to close statistical analysis.[14]

*Hal Luft, "New England Textile Labor in the 1840's: From Yankee Farmgirl to Irish Immigrant," unpublished, Harvard University, January 1971.

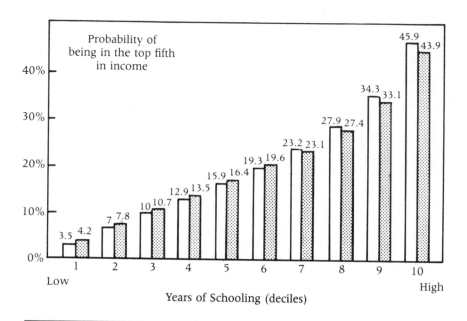

F I G U R E   1

Differences in Cognitive Test Scores Do Not Explain the Association Between Years of Schooling and Economic Success

Notes: The left-hand bar of each pair shows the estimated probability that a man is in the top fifth of the income distribution if he is in the given decile of education. The right-hand bar of each pair shows the estimated probability that a man is in the top fifth of the income distribution if he has an average adult cognitive test score and is in the given decile of education.

Note that the bars of any given pair are nearly the same height, showing that the income-education relationship is almost the same for individuals with the identical cognitive attainments as for all individuals.[18]

Sample: Non-Negro males of nonfarm background, 1962, aged 35–44 years.

Source: Samuel Bowles and Valerie Nelson, "The 'Inheritance of IQ' and the Intergenerational Transmission of Economic Inequality," *The Review of Economics and Statistics*, Vol. 56, No. 1, February 1974.

We must first choose a convenient way to represent the statistical association between level of educational attainment in years and earnings in dollars. While our results are clearly independent of any particular representation, some representations can be more easily interpreted than others. We have chosen the top-quintile-by-decile method. . . .[15] We first order all individuals from lowest to highest in terms of level of educational attainment in years, dividing them into ten equal parts ("deciles"). We then determine the percentage of individuals in each decile who are in the top fifth of the sample (the "top quintile") in income. We thus find the probability that an individual with a given level of education has of attaining the top 20 percent of the income distribution.[16]

For instance, the left-hand bars in Figure 1 illustrate that an individual in the ninth (next to highest) education decile has a 34.3 percent chance of attaining a position in the top fifth of income earners, while an individual in the bottom decile in education has only a 3.5 percent chance. This illustrates the well-known importance of education in achieving economic success.

Just as the technocratic-meritocratic theory asserts, education is also closely associated with cognitive attainments. For instance, if the probability of attaining the top fifth in adult IQ is plotted against educational level, we find that a person in the top decile in education has a 57.7 percent chance of falling in the top fifth in cognitive scores, while a person in the bottom decile in education has less than a 1 percent chance.[17]

But is the higher average cognitive attainment of the more highly educated the *cause* of their greater likelihood of achieving economic success? This, of course, is the crucial question. If the cognitive theory is correct, two individuals with the same test scores but different levels of education should have, on the average, exactly the same expected incomes, and conversely people with different test scores but similar levels of education should on the average exhibit different incomes. Thus, if we restrict our observation to individuals with the same test scores, at whatever level, the association exhibited in the left-hand bars of Figure 1 should disappear—i.e., they should all have the same height at the 20-percent mark on the vertical scale.

To address this problem we will need to go beyond simple statistical associations and construct a causal model explaining the independent direct and indirect contribution of each important variable to individual economic success. Our model is illustrated in Figure 2. According to this figure, among individuals of similar age, race, and sex, differences in income are caused by differences in adult IQ, schooling, and socioeconomic background, as well as by other unmeasured differences. Differences in adult IQ and schooling are likewise due to the effects of the causally prior variables, socio-economic background and childhood IQ. Differences in childhood IQ are caused by differences in genetic inheritance, in socioeconomic background and their interaction. In the model, socioeconomic background influences income directly (arrow b) and indirectly through its effect both on educational attainments (arrows c and d; arrows e, g, and d) and on adult IQ (arrows e, j, and i; arrows e, g, j, and i; and arrows e, h, and i). Schooling influences income both directly (arrow d) and indirectly through its effect on adult IQ (arrows j and i). The direct and indirect effects of genetic inheritance may likewise be traced.

Our statistical technique for the estimation of these statistical relationships will be that of linear regression analysis. This technique allows us to

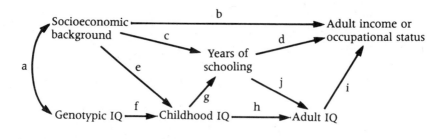

FIGURE 2
Causal Model of IQ, Socioeconomic Background,
Schooling and Economic Success

Notes: The model applies to people of the same sex, race, and roughly the same age. Additional variables would be required to take account of these important aspects of the income determination process. Arrows indicate the assumed direction of causation. The one double-headed arrow represents statistical association with no implied causation. For a fuller discussion of the model, see Bowles and Nelson, "The 'Inheritance of IQ' and the Intergenerational Transmission of Economic Inequality," op. cit., 1974.

derive numerical estimates of the independent contribution of each of the separate but correlated influences (socioeconomic background, childhood IQ, years of schooling, adult cognitive attainment) on economic success, by answering the question: What is the magnitude of the association between any one of these influences among individuals who are equal with respect to some or all the others? Equivalently, it answers the question: What are the probabilities of attaining particular levels of economic success among individuals who are in the same decile in some or all of the above influences but one, and in varying deciles in this one variable alone?

The results of "holding constant" IQ at a particular level (e.g., average level) is exhibited in the right-hand bars of Figure 1.[18] Rather than being of equal height, the right-hand bars are only slightly different from the left. For instance, in general a person from the ninth decile in education is nearly ten times as likely to be in the top quintile in income as is a person in the bottom education decile; but among people with identical adult cognitive test scores, the former is still eight times more likely to be in the top income quintile than the latter. Holding cognitive attainments constant barely changes the education-income relationship. Hardly comforting for those who assert the economic importance of mental skills in explaining inequality.[19]

Since the association between level of economic success and years of schooling is reduced only slightly when we look at individuals with the same level of adult cognitive skills, the association of schooling and economic success is largely unrelated to the differences in cognitive skills observed between workers with differing levels of education. Numerous other studies support these conclusions. . . .[20]

The reader may find our argument, despite its wide statistical support, not only counterintuitive, but actually incredible. For the figures seem to refute the manifest observation that the economy could not operate without the cognitive skills of workers, and these skills are acquired in school. This observation is eminently correct, and by no means contradicted by our data. What our argument suggests is merely that the mental-skill demands of work are sufficiently limited, the skills produced by our educational system sufficiently varied, and the possibilities for acquiring additional skills on the job sufficiently great so that skill differences among individuals who are acceptable for a given job on the basis of other criteria including race, sex, personality, and credentials are of little economic import. At most levels in the occupational hierarchy mental skills are productive, but are not scarce, and hence do not bear a direct monetary return. Indeed, we have suggested that the educational system serves to produce surpluses of skilled labor, thereby increasing the power of employers over workers. Thus the statistical evidence, far from being a striking curiosity, is an expected reflection of the class nature of the production process. Workers' skills are an absolutely fundamental element in economic growth, but skill differences do not explain the lack of progress toward social justice.

In sum, the available evidence seems to support our legitimization hypothesis. The meritocratic orientation of the educational system promotes not its egalitarian function, but rather its integrative role. Education reproduces inequality by justifying privilege and attributing poverty to personal failure.

IQism; OR "IF YOU'RE SO SMART, WHY AREN'T YOU RICH?"

The technocratic-meritocratic ideology is also at the root of the currently popular "the poor-are-dumb" theories of inequality. The notion that economic inequality is rooted in genetically determined differences in IQ has never lacked advocates. Yet the fortunes of this idea exhibit a curious ebb and flow; the economic and social importance of genetic differences never appears more obvious than in the aftermath of a series of unsuccessful liberal reforms. On the other hand, the three major periods of liberal educational reform—the two decades prior to the Civil War, the Progressive Era, and the 1960s—were all marked by a lack of concern with genetically inherited characteristics and a profound optimism concerning the malleability, even the perfectability, of youth. The main problem for reformers was to structure an environment in which individual development would be promoted rather than retarded. Not surprisingly, liberals have concentrated on those aspects of nurture which appeared susceptible to social intervention: schools, housing, medical care, and the like. Yet the demise of each liberal reform movement has been greeted by a genetic backlash: If improving the school environment does not achieve its elevated objectives, there must be something wrong with the kids. In the late 1960s, with the War on Poverty losing momentum and the dismal evaluation of the compensatory education programs accumulating, the historian Michael Katz predicted a counterattack by those who locate the roots of inequality in nature and, particularly, in genetically determined differences in IQ.[21]

The predicted reaction has since gathered force: The genetic interpretation of inequality had regained much of its tarnished academic respectability and has come to command the attention of social scientists and policymakers alike. The first major shot was Arthur Jensen's argument in the *Harvard Educational Review* that the failure of compensatory education to raise scholastic achievement levels must be attributed to the heritability of IQ.[22] Jensen's survey of the heredity research of Burtt and others was embraced and extended by Harvard psychologist Richard Herrnstein. The distribution of wealth, privilege, and social status, asserted Herrnstein, is determined to a major and increasing extent by the distribution of IQ. Because IQ is highly heritable, economic and social status is passed on within families from one generation to the next.[23]

These assertions by Jensen, Herrnstein, and others constituted a fundamental attack on the liberal reformist position. Yet the liberal defense has been curiously superficial. The putative economic importance of IQ has remained undocumented by the genetic school and unchallenged by their critics. Amidst a hundred-page statistical barrage relating to the genetic and environmental components of intelligence, Jensen saw fit to devote only three sparse and ambiguous pages to this issue. Later advocates of the "genetic school" have considered this "elemental fact," if anything, even less necessary of support.[24] Nor has their choice of battleground proved injudicious; to our knowledge, not one of their environmentalist critics has taken the economic importance of IQ any less for granted.[25]

This glaring lapse in the liberal defense is itself instructive. "The most important thing . . . that we can know about a man," says Louis Wirth, "is what he takes for granted, and the most elemental and important facts about a society are those that are seldom debated and generally regarded as settled." We are questioning here the undisputed assumption underlying both sides of the recently revived IQ controversy: that the distribution of IQ is a basic determinant of the structure of privilege.[26]

Our empirical results will reinforce our contention that the emphasis on IQ as the basis for economic success serves to legitimate an authoritarian, hierarchical, stratified, and unequal economic system, and to reconcile individuals to their objective position within this system. Legitimation is enhanced when people merely believe in the intrinsic importance of IQ. This belief is facilitated by the strong associations among all the economically desirable attributes—social class, education, cognitive skills, occupational status, and income—and is integrated into a pervasive ideological perspective. That IQ is not a major determinant of the social class structure also supports our argument . . . that access to a particular job depends on the individual's pattern of noncognitive personality traits (motivation, orientation to authority, discipline, internalization of work norms), as well as on such personal attributes as sex, race, age, and educational credentials. These personality traits and personal attributes aid in legitimating and stabilizing the structure of authority in the modern enterprise itself. Thus, primarily because of the central economic role of the school system, the production of adequate intellectual skills becomes a spin-off, a by-product of a stratification mechanism grounded in the supply, demand, production, and certification of an entirely different set of personal attributes.

We must begin a discussion of genetic transmission of economic status by asking what "heritability" means. That IQ is highly heritable is merely to say that individuals with similar genes will exhibit similar IQs independent of differences in the social environments they might experience during their mental development. The main support for the genetic school are several studies of individuals with precisely the same genes (identical twins) raised in different environments (i.e., separated at birth and reared in different families). Their IQs tend to be fairly similar.[27] In addition, there are studies of individuals with no common genes (unrelated individuals) raised in the same environment (e.g., the same family) as well as studies of individuals with varying genetic similarities (e.g., fraternal twins, siblings, fathers and sons, aunts and nieces) and varying environments (e.g., siblings raised apart, cousins raised in their respective homes). The difference in IQs for these groups conform roughly to the genetic inheritance model suggested by the identical twin and unrelated individual studies.[28]

Leon Kamin recently presented extensive evidence casting strong doubt on the genetic position.[29] But by and large, environmentalists have been unable to convincingly disprove the central proposition of the genetic school. But then, they have emphasized that it bears no important social implications. They have argued, for example, that the genetic theory says nothing about the "necessary" degree of racial inequality or the limits of compensatory education.[30] First, environmentalists deny that there is any evidence that the average IQ difference between black and whites (amounting to about fifteen IQ points) is genetic in origin,[31] and second, they deny that any estimate of heritability tells us much about the capacity of enriched environments to lessen IQ differentials, either within or between racial groups.[32]

But the environmentalists' defense strategy has been costly. In their egalitarian zeal vis-à-vis racial differences, the environmentalists have sacrificed the modern liberal interpretation of social inequality. The modern liberal approach is to attribute social class differences to unequal opportunity. That is, while the criteria for economic success are objective and achievement-oriented, the failures and successes of parents are passed onto their children via distinct learning and cultural environments. From this it follows that the achievement of a more equal society merely requires that all youth be afforded the educational and other social conditions of the best and most successful.[33] But the liberal counterattack against the genetic position represented a significant retreat, for it did not successfully challenge the proposition that IQ differences among whites of differing social class backgrounds are rooted in differences in genetic endowments. Indeed, the genetic school's data come precisely from observed differences in the IQ of whites across socioeconomic levels! The liberal failure to question the causal role of IQ in getting ahead economically completes the rout. The fundamental tenet of modern liberal social theory—that progressive social welfare programs can gradually reduce and eliminate social class differences, cultures of poverty and affluence, and inequalities of opportunity—has been done in to a major extent by its erstwhile advocates. So the old belief—adhered to by present-day conservatives and liberals of past generations—that social classes sort themselves out on the basis of innate individual capacity to cope successfully in the social environment, and hence tend to reproduce themselves from generation to generation, has been restored.[34]

The vigor of their reaction to Jensen's argument reflects the liberals' agreement that IQ is a basic determinant (at least ideally) of occupational status and intergenerational mobility. Indeed, the conceptual framework of the testers themselves would appear to insure this result. Jensen is thus merely stating what the testers had taken for granted: ". . . Psychologists' concept of the 'intelligence demands' of an occupation . . . is very much like the general public's concept of the prestige or 'social standing' of an occupation, and both are closely related to an independent measure of . . . occupational status."[35] Jensen continues, quoting the sociologist O. D. Duncan: ". . . 'Intelligence' . . . is not essentially different from that of achievement or status in the occupational sphere. . . . What we now mean by intelligence is something like the probability of acceptable performance [given the opportunity] in occupations varying in social status."[36] Moreover, Jensen argues that the purported trend toward making intelligence a requirement for occupational achievement will continue to grow.[37] This emphasis on intelligence as explaining social stratification is set even more clearly by Carl Bereiter: "The prospect is of a meritocratic caste system, based . . . on the natural consequences of inherited difference in intellectual potential. . . . It would tend to persist even though everyone at all levels of the hierarchy considered it a bad thing."[38]

Jensen and his associates cannot be accused of employing an overly complicated social theory. Thus Jensen's reason for the "inevitable" association of status and intelligence is that society "rewards talent and merit." And Herrnstein adds that:

> If virtually anyone is smart enough to be a ditch digger, and only half the people are smart enough to be engineers, then society is, in effect, husbanding its intellectual resources by holding engineers in greater esteem and paying them more. . . . [S]ociety [thus] expresses its recognition, however imprecise, of the importance and scarcity of intellectual ability.[39]

Finally, according to Herrnstein, each generation is further refined into social strata on the basis of IQ:

> New gains of wealth . . . will increase the IQ gap between upper and lower classes, making the social ladder even steeper for those left at the bottom.

Herrnstein then proceeds to turn liberal social policy directly against itself, noting that the heritability of IQ and hence the pervasiveness of social stratification will increase, as our social policies become more progressive:

> The growth of a virtually hereditary meritocracy will arise out of the successful realization of contemporary political and social goals . . . as the environment becomes more favorable for the development of intelligence, its heritability will increase. . . .[40]

Similarly, the more we break down discriminatory and ascriptive criteria for hiring, the stronger will become the link between IQ and occupational success. And the development of modern technology, adds Herrnstein, can only quicken this process.

That such statements should be made by the "conservative" genetic school is hardly surprising. But why should liberals, who have contested the genetic hypothesis in the minutest detail, have so blindly accepted the genetic school's description of the social function of intelligence? The widespread assumption among all parties to the debate that IQ is an important determinant of economic success does not rest on compelling empirical evidence. Quite the contrary.

The most immediate support for the IQ theory of social inequality—which we will call "IQism"—flows from two substantial relationships. The first is the significant association between socioeconomic background and childhood IQ. Thus, according to our research, having a parent in the top decile in socioeconomic status gives a child a 42 percent chance of being in the top fifth in IQ, while having a parent in the bottom socioeconomic status decile gives him only a 4.9 percent chance.[41] The second is the important association between childhood IQ and later economic success: An individual in the top childhood IQ decile is nearly four times as likely to achieve the highest income quintile as an individual from the bottom IQ decile.[42]

The proponent of IQism argues that higher social class leads to higher IQ, which, in turn, leads to a greater chance of economic success. We shall show, however, that this inference is simply erroneous. Specifically, we will demonstrate the truth of the following proposition, which constitutes the empirical basis of our thesis: the fact that economic success tends to run in the family arises almost completely independently from any inheritance of IQ, whether it be genetic or environmental. Thus, while one's economic status tends to resemble that of one's parents, only a minor portion of this association can be attributed to social class differences in childhood IQ, and a virtually negligible portion to social class differences in genetic endowments even if one were to accept the Jensen estimates of heritability. Thus a perfect (obviously hypothetical) equalization of IQs among individuals of differing social backgrounds would reduce the intergenerational transmission of economic status by only a negligible amount. We conclude that a family's position in the class structure is reproduced primarily by mechanisms operating *independently* of the inheritance, production, and certification of intellectual skills.

How are we to support this proposition? The correct way of posing the question is to ask the following: To what extent is the statistical association between socioeconomic background and economic success reduced when childhood IQ is held constant? If the proponents of IQism are correct, the reduction should be substantial. If the only source of intergenerational status transmission were the inheritance of IQ, there should be no relationship whatever between family background and economic success among individuals with the same IQ. The way to test this is again to use linear regression analysis on our basic data set. The left-hand bars in Figure 3 show the overall association between socioeconomic background and economic success. The results of holding constant IQ by linear regression, indicated in the right-hand bars of Figure 3, shows that the

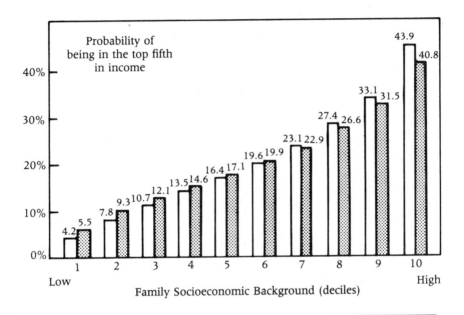

FIGURE 3
Relationship Between Income and Inherited Social Status
Cannot Be Accounted for by Differences in IQ

Notes: The left-hand bar of each pair shows the estimated probability that a man is in the top fifth of the income distribution if he is in a given decile of socioeconomic background. The right-hand bar shows the estimated probability that a man is in the top fifth of the income distribution if he has average childhood IQ and is in a given decile of socioeconomic background.

Note that the bars of any given pair are very close, showing that the income/socioeconomic background relationship is almost the same for individuals with identical IQs as for all individuals.

Sample: Non-Negro males of nonfarm background, 1962, aged 35–44 years.

Source: Samuel Bowles and Valerie Nelson, "The 'Inheritance of IQ' and the Intergenerational Transmission of Economic Inequality," *The Review of Economics and Statistics,* Vol. 56, No. 1, February 1974.

actual reduction in the relationship is practically nil.[43] Evidently, IQ—whether inherited or not—plays a negligible role in passing economic status from parent to child.

The unimportance of the specifically genetic mechanism operating via IQ in the intergenerational reproduction of economic inequality is even more striking. Figure 4 exhibits the degree of association between socioeconomic background and income which can be attributed to the genetic inheritance of IQ alone. This figure assumes that all direct influences of socioeconomic background upon income have been eliminated. On the other hand, it assumes Jensen's estimate for the degree of heritability of IQ. A glance at Figure 4 shows that the resulting level of intergenerational

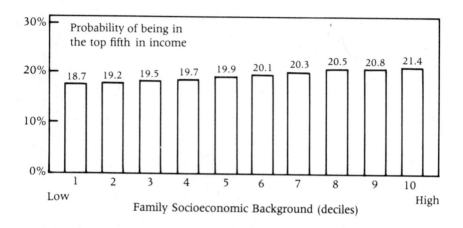

FIGURE 4
Family Background and Economic Success in the Hypothetical Meritocracy with Inheritable IQ

Notes: Each bar shows the estimated probability that a man would be in the top fifth of the income distribution if he is in the given decile of socioeconomic background and the entire relationship between background and economic success worked through the genetic inheritance of IQ, so that no other sources of social inequality existed. All bars are close to the "random" probability of 20%.

Sample: Non-Negro, nonfarm males, aged 35–44 years.

Source: Samuel Bowles and Valerie Nelson, "The 'Inheritance of IQ' and the Intergenerational Transmission of Economic Inequality," *The Review of Economics and Statistics,* Vol. 56, No. 1, February 1974 (Table 3).

inequality in this highly hypothetical example would be negligible,[44] and contrasts sharply with the actual degree of inequality exhibited in the left-hand bars of Figure 3.

Our proposition is thus supported: The intergenerational transmission of social and economic status operates primarily via noncognitive mechanisms, despite the fact that the school system rewards higher IQ, an attribute significantly associated with higher socioeconomic background.

The unimportance of IQ in explaining the relationship between socioeconomic background and economic success, together with the fact that most of the association between IQ and income can be accounted for by the common association of these variables with education and socioeconomic background, support our major assertion: IQ is not an important criterion for economic success. Our data thus hardly lends credence to Duncan's assertion that ". . . 'intelligence' . . . is not essentially different from that of achievement or status in the occupational sphere, . . ."[45] nor to Jensen's belief in the "inevitable" association of status and intelligence, based on society's "rewarding talent and merit,"[46] nor to Herrnstein's dismal prognostication of a virtually hereditary meritocracy as the fruit of successful liberal reform in an advanced industrial society.[47]

The power and privilege of the capitalist class are often inherited, but not through superior genes. (Try asking David Rockefeller to hand over his capital in return for thirty more IQ points!) Differences in IQ, even were they genetically inherited, could not explain the historical pattern of economic and educational inequalities. The intractability of inequality of income and of economic opportunity cannot be attributed to genetically inherited differences in IQ. The disappointing results of the "War on Poverty" cannot be blamed on the genes of the poor. The failure of egalitarian school reforms reflects the fact that inequality under capitalism is rooted not in individual deficiencies, but in the structure of production and property relations.

In this chapter, we have suggested that education should be viewed as reproducing inequality by legitimating the allocation of individuals to economic positions on the basis of ostensibly objective merit. Moreover, the basis for assessing merit—competitive academic performance—is only weakly associated with the personal attributes indicative of individual success in economic life. Thus the legitimation process in education assumes a largely symbolic form.

This legitimation process, however, is fraught with its own contradictions. For the technocratic-meritocratic ideology progressively undermines the overt forms of discrimination which divide the work force into racially, sexually, and ethnically distinct segments. Ironically, the partial success of the meritocratic ideology has helped to create a political basis for working class unity. With the irrationality of these forms of discrimination increasingly exposed, the justification of inequality must increasingly rely on educational inequalities and IQism. Yet workers, minorities, and others have fought hard and to some extent successfully to reduce educational inequality, with little effect on economic inequality itself. This has tended to increase conflicts within education, to cast further doubt on the fairness of the income distribution process, and at the same time undercut traditional educational philosophy. Thus even the symbolism of meritocracy is threatened in the contemporary period.

NOTES

1. K. Davis and W. E. Moore, "Some Principles of Stratification," *American Sociological Review*, Vol. 10, No. 2, 1945, pp. 242–249.
2. See Leon J. Kamin, *The Science and Politics of IQ* (Potomac, Md.: Erlbaum Associates, 1974), p. 8.
3. Orville Brim, *American Beliefs and Attitudes about Intelligence* (New York: Russell Sage Foundation, 1969).

4. Recent studies indeed indicate a lack of social class or racial bias in school grading. Given a student's cognitive attainment, his or her grades seem not to be significantly affected by class or racial origins, at least on the high-school level. See Robert Hauser, "Schools and the Stratification Process," *American Journal of Sociology,* Vol. 74, May 1969, pp. 587–611; Barbara Heyns, "Curriculum Assignment and Tracking Policies in 48 Urban Public High Schools," unpublished Ph.D. dissertation for the University of Chicago, 1971; and Christopher Jencks et al., *Inequality: A Reassessment of the Effects of Family and Schooling in America* (New York: Basic Books, 1972).

5. For an extended treatment, see Jerome Karabel, "Community Colleges and Social Stratification," *Harvard Educational Review,* Vo. 424, No. 42, November 1972, and references therein.

6. Daniel Bell, *The Coming of Post-Industrial Society* (New York: Basic Books, 1973), Coda, Part 3.

7. Alexander W. Astin, "Undergraduate Achievement and Institutional 'Excellence,'" *Science,* Vol. 161, August 1968.

8. Christopher Jencks, "The Effects of Worker Characteristics on Economic Success: An Inquiry into Nonlinearities, Interactions, and Unmeasured Variables Using the NORC Veterans' Sample" (Cambridge, Mass.: Center for Educational Policy Research, July 1973), using the NORC Veterans Survey of 2,672 males, aged 25–34, enumerated in the May 1964 Current Population Survey, finds that the rate of return to college education is lower for individuals with high test scores (AFQT). . . .

9. Daniel C. Rogers, "Private Rates of Return to Education in the U.S., A Case Study," *Yale Economic Essays,* Spring 1969.

10. Alexander Astin and Jack Rossman, "The Case for Open Admissions: A Status Report," in *Change,* Vol. 5, No. 6, Summer 1973.

11. Even in this case, the institutional arrangements would not satisfy the elementary dictates of justice and equity. See Noam Chomsky, "Psychology and Ideology," *Cognition,* Vol. 1, No. 1, 1972.

12. Quoted by Michael Katz, *Class, Bureaucracy and Schools* (New York: Praeger Publishers, 1971), p. 146.

13. See Herbert Gintis, "Education, Technology, and the Characteristics of Worker Productivity," *American Economic Review,* May 1971; and Ivar Berg, *Education and Jobs: The Great Training Robbery* (Boston: Beacon Press, 1971).

14. Samuel Bowles and Valerie Nelson, "The 'Inheritance of IQ' and the Intergenerational Reproduction of Economic Inequality," *The Review of Economics and Statistics,* Vol. 56, No. 1, February 1974; Samuel Bowles and Herbert Gintis, "IQ in the U.S. Class Structure" in *Social Policy,* November–December 1972 and January–February 1973. . . .

15. Most popular discussions of the relationship of IQ and economic success (e.g., Arthur A. Jensen, "How Much Can We Boost IQ and Scholastic Achievement?" *Harvard Educational Review,* Vol. 39, No. 1, 1969; Richard Herrnstein, "IQ," *Atlantic Monthly,* Vol. 228, No. 3, September 1971; Jencks [1972]) presents statistical material in terms of "correlation coefficients" and "contribution to explained variance." . . .

16. . . . These general issues are discussed in Jencks (1972); and, with respect to our data, in Bowles (1972), *op. cit.;* and Gintis (1971), *op. cit.* . . .

17. Cognitive test scores are measured by a form of the Armed Forces Qualification Test, which is strongly affected both by childhood IQ and by years of schooling, and, hence, can be considered a measure of adult cognitive achievement.

18. Figure 1 is calculated from data reported in Bowles and Nelson (1974), *loc. cit.* . . .

19. The method of linear regression analysis, as its name implies, assumes that the level at which cognitive scores are held constant is irrelevant, as all effects are linear and additive. We have set this level at the average for the sample to render the education-income associations, before and after holding cognitive skills constant, closely comparable. Changing the level of cognitive scores merely moves this curve up or down. The assumption of linearity is, moreover, a good approximation to reality. See Jencks (1973), *op. cit.*; and Rogers (1969), *op. cit.*

20. [A reference to Table A-2 has been deleted from the text of this article. Table A-2 appears in Appendix A of the original article but not in this reprinted version.]

21. Katz (1971), *op. cit.*

22. Arthur R. Jensen (1969), *op. cit.*

23. Herrnstein (1971), *op. cit.*

24. J. Eysenck, *The IQ Argument* (New York: Library Press, 1971); and Herrnstein (1971), *op. cit.*

25. For a representative sampling of the criticism, see the issues of the *Harvard Educational Review* which follow the Jensen essay of 1969.

26. By IQ, we mean—here and throughout—those cognitive capacities which are measured in IQ tests. We have avoided the use of the word "intelligence" as, in its common usage, it ordinarily connotes a broader range of capacities.

27. Jensen (1969), *op. cit.*

28. Jensen (1969), *op. cit.*; Jencks (1972), *op. cit.*

29. Kamin (1974), *op. cit.*

30. Jerome S. Kagan, "Inadequate Evidence and Illogical Conclusions," *Harvard Educational Review*, Reprint Series, No. 2, 1969; J. McI. Hunt, "Has Compensatory Education Failed?" *Harvard Educational Review*, Reprint Series, No. 2, 1969; and Kamin (1974), *op. cit.*

31. Does the fact that a large component of the differences in IQ among whites is genetic mean that a similar component of the differences in IQ between blacks and whites is determined by the former's inferior gene pool? Clearly not. First of all, the degree of heritability is an *average*, even among whites. For any two individuals, and *a fortiori*, any two groups of individuals, observed IQ differences may be due to any proportion in genes and environment—it is required only that they average properly over the entire population. For instance, *all* of the difference in IQ between identical twins is environmental, and presumably, a great deal of the difference between adopted brothers is genetic. Similarly, we cannot say whether the average difference in IQ between Irish and Puerto Ricans is genetic or environmental. In the case of blacks, however, the genetic school's inference is even more tenuous. R. Light and P. Smith, "Social Allocation Models of Intelligence: A Methodological Inquiry," *Harvard Educational Review*, 39, 3 (August 1969), have shown that even accepting Jensen's estimates of the heritability of IQ, the black-white IQ difference could easily be explained by the average environmental differences between the races. Recourse to further experimental investigations will not resolve this issue, for the "conceptual experimental" which would determine the genetic component of black-white differences cannot be performed. Could we take a pair of black identical twins and place them in random environments? Clearly not. Placing a black child in a white home, in an overtly racist society, will not provide the same environment as placing a white child in that house. Similarly, looking at the difference in IQs of unrelated black and white children raised in the same home (whether black or white, or mixed) will not tell us the extent of genetic differences, since such children cannot be treated equally, and environmental differences must continue to persist. (Of course, if, in these cases, differences in IQ disappear, the environmentalist case would be supported. But if they do not, no inference can be made.)

32. Most environmentalists do not dispute Jensen's assertion that existing large-scale compensatory programs have produced dismal results (Jensen [1969], *op. cit.*; and Harvey Averch *et al.*, "How Effective Is Schooling: A Critical Review and Synthesis of Research Findings" (Santa Monica: The Rand Corporation, 1972). But this does not bear on the genetic hypothesis. As Jensen himself notes, the degree of genetic transmission of any trait depends on the various alternative environments which individuals experience. Jensen's estimates of heritability rest squarely on the existing array of educational processes and technologies. Any introduction of new social processes of mental development will change the average unstandardized level of IQ, as well as its degree of heritability. For instance, the almost perfect heritability of height is well documented. Yet the average heights of Americans have risen dramatically over the years, due clearly to changes in the overall environment. Similarly, whatever the heritability of IQ, the average unstandardized test scores rose 83 percent between 1917 and 1943 (Jencks [1972], *op. cit.*). But compensatory programs are obviously an attempt to change the total array of environments open to children through "educational innovation." While existing large-scale programs appear to have failed to produce significant gains in scholastic achievement, many more innovative small-scale programs have succeeded. (Carl Bereiter, "The Future of Individual Differences," *Harvard Educational Review,* Reprint Series, No. 2, 1969; Silberman [1971], *op. cit.*; and Averch [1972], *op. cit.*). Moreover, even accepting the genetic position should not hinder us from seeking new environmental innovation—indeed it should spur us to further creative activities in this direction. Thus, the initial thrust of the genetic school can be at least partially repulsed: There is no reliable evidence either that long-term contact of blacks with existing white environments would not close the black-white IQ gap, or that innovative compensatory programs (i.e., programs unlike existing white child-rearing or education environments) might not attenuate or eliminate IQ differences which are indeed genetic.

33. James S. Coleman et al., *Equality of Educational Opportunity* (Washington, D.C.: U.S. Government Printing Office, 1966).

34. E.g., Ross, as quoted in Clarence Karier, "Ideology and Evaluation: In Quest of Meritocracy," Wisconsin Conference on Education and Evaluation at Madison, April 1973; Lewis M. Terman, *Intelligence Tests and School Reorganization* (New York: World Books, 1923); and Joseph Schumpeter, *Imperialism and Social Classes* (New York: Kelley, 1951).

This is not to imply that all liberal social theorists hold the IQ ideology. See also David McClelland, *Achieving Society* (New York: The Free Press, 1967); and Oscar Lewis, "The Culture of Poverty," *Scientific American,* Vol. 215, October 1966, who, among others, explicitly reject IQ as an important determinant of social stratification.

35. Jensen (1969), p. 14, *op. cit.*

36. O. D. Duncan, "Properties and Characteristics of the Socio-economic Index," and "A Socio-economic Index for All Occupations," in Albert J. Reiss, ed., *Occupations and Social Status* (New York: The Free Press, 1961), pp. 90–91.

37. Jensen (1969), p. 19, *op. cit.*

38. Bereiter (1969), p. 166, *op. cit.*

39. Herrnstein (1971), *op. cit.*, p. 51.

40. *Ibid.*, p. 63.

41. Socioeconomic background is measured here by a weighted sum of parents' income, father's occupational status, and father's education. Childhood IQ is measured by the Stanford-

Binet Test or its equivalent. These statistics are computed from an estimated zero-order correlation coefficient of .399 between socioeconomic background and early childhood IQ, as reported in Bowles and Nelson (1974), *op. cit.* The relationship is slightly stronger for men of other age groups than for the ages of 35–44 used in this figure: .410 for ages 25–34; .410 for ages 45–54; and .426 for ages 55–64 years.

42. These figures are based on an estimated correlation coefficient between IQ and income of .28 for non-Negro, nonfarm males, aged 35–44 years. The coefficient is also .28 for the age group 25–34; .29 for ages 45–54; and .27 for ages 55–64 years.

43. These relationships are based on an estimated correlation coefficient between socioeconomic background and income of .43 for non-Negro, nonfarm males, aged 35–44 years. The coefficient for other age groups is .32 for ages 25–34; .46 for ages 45–54; and .31 for ages 55–64 years. The relationship between socioeconomic background and income for men with the same IQ is based on estimated normalized regression coefficient of .38 on background in an equation using background and early childhood IQ to predict income, for the same age group. The coefficient for the other age groups is .25 for ages 25–34; .41 for ages 45–54; and .24 for ages 55–64 years.

44. This figure is based on the correlation between socioeconomic background and income via the genetic inheritance of IQ alone. The correlation was computed by the path model presented in Bowles and Nelson (1974), *loc. cit.* . . .

45. O. D. Duncan (1961), *op. cit.*, p. 90.

46. Jensen (1969), *op. cit.*, p. 73.

47. Herrnstein (1971), *op. cit.*, p. 63.

DANIEL YANKELOVICH

Who Gets Ahead
in America

Questions to think about

1 *According to Jencks's study, who gets ahead in America and why?*
2 *Discuss the relationship between schools and stratification as reviewed in this article.*
3 *Using the open systems model, how would you describe the parts of the system that interrelate in Jencks's study?*
4 *Do you see evidence for Jencks's findings in your schools and community?*

Seven years ago, Christopher Jencks unsettled many believers in traditional American values with his book, *Inequality: A Reassessment of the Effect of Family and Schooling in America.* What Jencks and several colleagues found, by examining the body of research material then available, was that neither family background nor education could account for all the variations in income and status among Americans. Economic success, he concluded, was explained not as much by birth, or striving, or "competence" as by a number of other unmeasured variables, which he described collectively as "luck."

Even though it discounted the importance of family advantage, Jencks's analysis upset liberals by downplaying the value of education and special compensatory programs—which educational reformers and antipoverty warriors believed would eventually narrow the income gap between the rich and the poor. As Jencks saw it, the only real way to achieve economic equality in America was some form of income redistribution that would

Reprinted from *Psychology Today* Magazine, July 1979. Copyright © 1979 by the American Psychological Association.

remove inequities through the tax system or through government subsidies.

Now, Jencks and 11 colleagues at the Harvard Center for Educational Policy Research have published a new report that analyzes a broader range of studies covering a number of new variables. In *Who Gets Ahead?—The Determinants of Economic Success in America,* Jencks abandons the conclusion that "luck" is the most critical factor in economic success. He and his colleagues report a host of other findings that appear, on the surface, to be less controversial, but may turn out to be more so.

The investigators examined five large-scale national surveys of men, covering a 12-year span, along with six special-purpose surveys, four of which had never been previously analyzed. They worked during a five-year period, with research costs estimated at $400,000 (most of it from the U.S. Department of Health, Education, and Welfare and from private foundations).

The portrait drawn by Jencks and his colleagues is of a classridden America in which being born into the "right" family looms large. It is a rigid America, in which a man's academic test scores in the sixth grade shape his own expectations and those of others toward him. The men who were studied (none of the 11 surveys included women, a serious drawback) seem to be divided at an early stage of their lives into two fixed groups: those with promise and those without. Those with promise finish college, the gateway to success.

Who Gets Ahead? also depicts a superficial America, in which surface characteristics, such as college credentials or the color of a man's skin, count so heavily that what he is really worth as a person, his moral character, what he knows, what he can do, how hard he tries, hardly seem to count at all. Finally, although Jencks's group would acknowledge it was concerned with just one important set of values—economic success—their report furthers the impression of a unidimensional America, in which only making money and achieving occupational success seem to count in life. I recognize Jencks's America as one might recognize a friend whose features suddenly appear abstract, contorted, remote. I know the image from my own surveys—yet something is amiss.

Jencks's report contains many important findings, but we cannot draw valid prescriptions for action from them unless we see the work in a broader social context. For several powerful reasons, we must exercise extreme caution in accepting its messages at face value. . . .

The Jencks team tried to determine the degree to which four sets of factors studied in the surveys were associated with success. They were: family background; cognitive ability, as reflected in scores on academic tests in primary and secondary school; personality traits and behavior in high school, as described by the subjects themselves and their teachers;

and number of years of school completed. A rough breakdown of the amount of influence attributed to the various factors is shown in the [accompanying] box.

Through statistical analysis, an effort was made to isolate how much of the variation in men's later economic success was attributable to each of those variables when considered independently of the others. Since the four sets of factors interact with one another in complex fashion, pulling them apart to assess the contribution of each was not easy. It involved some deft statistical footwork, especially since complete data for all four sets of factors were not available for any of the respondents.

The breakdown shows that some factors contributed more to occupational status than to earnings. If all other factors were ignored, for example, the years of schooling men completed would have accounted for 45 to 55 percent of the variations in occupational status, but only 15 to 20 percent of variations in earnings. Family background was reckoned to account for 45 to 50 percent of the variation in occupational status, but apparently for only about 15 to 35 percent of variations in men's incomes.

Of the 13 demographic specifics that came under the heading of "family background," not all have equal weight. One of the 13, "father's occupation," by itself accounts for about one-third of the influence attributed to family background; another third is accounted for by a cluster of variables that included father's and mother's education, parental income, family size, and race.

Another group of variables appears to have a weight equal to each of the others. That is the group of "unmeasured variables," which were part of what Jencks in his first study referred to as "luck," . . .

One difficulty in discerning relative influences on economic success stems from the fact that everything seems to be related to everything else. If you come from the right family background, you are more likely to finish college, to have high academic test scores, and to have the personality traits associated with economic success. But the correlations are far from perfect. In fact . . . 52 percent of the variations in occupational status come from factors other than family background.

The most important of those is educational attainment: the number of years of schooling completed. One of the most interesting findings shows how important the last year of college is, relative to other years. What counts is *finishing* college and getting credentials, rather than what one might learn in the last year, or any year. Besides family background, the single most important factor contributing to a man's economic success is finishing college. Of course, academic promise, motivation, and other personality characteristics may help a man graduate. But if you don't translate promising academic ability into college credentials, you gain precious little economic advantage.

INFLUENCES ON SUCCESS

Factors affecting differences in earnings and occupational status (men, 25 to 65 years old, as of the early 1970s)

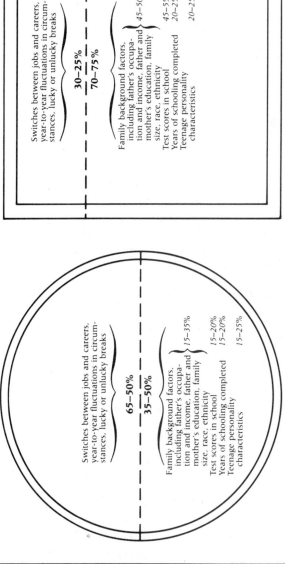

Earnings

Switches between jobs and careers, year-to-year fluctuations in circumstances, lucky or unlucky breaks — **65–50%**

35–50%

Family background factors, including father's occupation and income, father and mother's education, family size, race, ethnicity — 15–35%

Test scores in school — 15–20%
Years of schooling completed — 15–20%
Teenage personality characteristics — 15–25%

Occupational status

Switches between jobs and careers, year-to-year fluctuations in circumstances, lucky or unlucky breaks — **30–25%**

70–75%

Family background factors, including father's occupation and income, father and mother's education, family size, race, ethnicity — 45–50%

Test scores in school — 45–55%
Years of schooling completed — 20–25%
Teenage personality characteristics — 20–25%

Family background factors contribute less to earnings than to status. Percentages in italic show the weight each factor would have in determining either occupational status or earning levels if all other factors were ignored. Percentages in bold show the combined effect of all factors together.

Because different factors overlap and influence one another, their combined importance is smaller than the sum of their separate weights. (Figures extrapolated by Christopher Jencks for *Psychology Today*.)

For men coming from the same types of homes and having similar test scores, the earnings advantage of completing only high school is not great, especially for nonwhites. Completing college, on the other hand, brings considerable economic advantage. Completing high school gives whites a 15 to 25 percent future earnings advantage over those not completing high school (the figure is smaller for blacks). But completing college gives whites a whopping 49 percent advantage over those who do not—the percentage is even larger for blacks. This income advantage derives primarily from the fact that those who finish college have won the credential needed for entering higher-status occupations. "Unless high school attendance is followed by a college education," the researchers conclude, "its economic value appears quite modest"—especially for blacks.

The results of academic tests in the sixth grade can predict future success, as can scores on tests taken in later years. The ability to predict from early performance is attributed to the presence of stable motivational attitudes in the person being tested. The researchers point out that this pattern has remained fairly constant since the turn of the century. They underscore the point, frequently made, that those with academic ability succeed because they are selectively encouraged to have higher aspirations and to attend school for longer periods. The researchers emphasize that the mere ability to remain in school is more important than the results of academic test scores. "A man's ability in the sixth to 11th grade has important effects on his later occupational status," they say, "but 60 to 80 percent of the effect is explained by the *amount of schooling he gets*" (italics added).

The data on racial factors in success are more clear-cut. Given the same test scores and years of schooling, blacks have fewer opportunities to get ahead than whites do. The researchers state: "A strong prima facie case can be made for assuming . . . that despite affirmative action, nonwhites suffer from discrimination." Discrimination appears to operate less for those who graduate from college than for those who attain lower levels of education, the investigators conclude.

But they also found a significant general decrease in racial discrimination in the period covered by the surveys. In 1961, the researchers maintain, 60 percent of the income gap between blacks and whites was due to "constants" (which they assume to have been made up largely of racial discrimination). By 1971, they say, only 35 to 45 percent of the gap was due to similar factors. "We believe this represents a sharp decrease in direct earnings discrimination," the researchers conclude.

In a chapter on race, Joseph Schwartz and Jill Williams, two of Jencks's coauthors, suggest that the change in racial prejudice from the early 1960s to the early 1970s might have been qualitative as well as quantitative. Polls taken in the past several years by the New York Times/CBS Survey, by Louis Harris, and by my own firm, Yankelovich, Skelly and White, all confirm a significant diminution in the intensity and spread of overt racist attitudes. Trend data show a marked reduction in white animosity toward nonwhite neighbors, friends, and business associates. Americans seem more willing now than they were a decade ago to give the disadvantaged an extra measure of help to create real equality of opportunity—as long as reverse discrimination does not result.

If we are not to be misled by literal interpretations of the analysis, . . . we must keep in mind the limited scope of the data. Jencks's report excludes women. Several of the studies it examines focus solely on a man's characteristics when he *first* enters the labor market and how those match up with both initial and subsequent earnings; none takes into account changes in skill, competence, and emotional growth after he is launched on his career, and how those factors affect earnings. (I have no quarrel with the conclusion that traits measured in the sixth and 10th grades may have an important bearing on eventual occupational success or failure. I have more difficulty in believing that changes occurring in those factors during a man's career have *no* bearing on subsequent earnings and status.) And, perhaps most seriously of all, there is virtually no data later than 1973. Jencks and his associates are forthcoming in acknowledging the limitations in the scope of their study, but they do not tell us how to adjust for them. . . .

. . . Jencks and his colleagues have taken long strides in developing techniques to study the enigma of economic success in America. But even after this excellent and thorough study, we must assume that the present state of the investigative art does not yet tell us why some people achieve success while others do not. We may know more now than we did before, but not enough to allow us to build public policy on the results with any confidence.

Eventually, effective bridges may be built between scientific study and public policy. But they have not yet been built, and, in the end, studies such as this one will always be haunted by philosophical questions that have not yet been resolved: Can we ever understand complex human behavior by preselecting all the relevant variables and measures (thereby excluding other, perhaps more elusive, influences)? Will this approach ever bring us deeper knowledge of human behavior than more direct, insightful approaches? In its present form, social science forces us to choose between, on the one hand, *a priori* statistical models of human behavior and, on the other, understanding based on intuition, experience, insight, judgment, and observation—all of which pose serious difficulties of their own. Until the two paths of study are integrated and understood, as many uneasy questions must be raised about computer-based models as about intuitive judgment. Calling one "science" and the other "intuition" does not prove the superiority or inadequacy of either method . . .

Even with all its drawbacks, the Jencks report, properly understood, can be of considerable value. One of the most provocative suggestions in the book, for instance, is that the nature of racial prejudice in America may be changing in significant ways. I believe that it is. In earlier years, racial discrimination was due more to the kinds of gross disenfranchisement that could be combated by legal action and legislative mandate. More recently, it seems to be based mainly on stereotype and "image" factors, some of which operate subliminally.

These stereotypes serve, in much the same way as the presence or absence of academic credentials do, to close the door to minority groups, whose cultural styles and mannerisms are different from those of the white majority. They are quick, mindless methods of communicating information about people, much of which may not be germane to questions of competence or employability.

Many blacks mistrust survey findings that show a lessening of prejudice, believing they are meaningless when evidence shows that the economic situation of blacks has, in fact, grown worse in recent years. This is a complex and distressing situation, and I believe Jencks's findings suggest a number of constructive approaches to the problem.

The psychological aspects of the problem, though intangible, may be even more important for individual blacks. To blacks, there may be little difference between being blocked from advancement by a "real prejudice" and being blocked by a "negative stereotype." Such fine distinctions may seem like hair-splitting—evidence of obtuseness or bad faith. Perhaps the fault lies in our language.

Deeply rooted racial prejudice is difficult to extirpate. To do so requires all the authority, even the coerciveness, of the law. But the kind of stereotypes that appear to exist today may be easier to get around. For example, the Jencks findings show that where a negative black stereotype is upheld (the black-as-high-school-dropout, for instance), blacks fare worse economically than comparable white high school dropouts. But when the black stereotype is broken (the black-as-college-graduate), blacks do *better* than white counterparts when other variables are controlled. The black who finishes college makes two significant breakthroughs: he measurably improves his occupational and employment position, and he breaks the stereotype for himself and for others. If social and economic stereotypes can be broken by education, then they are not totally racial (based on skin color alone), but at least partly a matter of social-class prejudice and mental laziness . . .

If *Who Gets Ahead?* provides clues on how to undermine the social damage done by racism, prejudice, and excessive credentialism, then that alone makes it a major contribution to American society. But if implications for educational, governmental, and familial behavior are plucked prematurely and indelicately from the study's regression equations, the good work done by Jencks and his colleagues will become part of the problem rather than part of the solution.

RAY C. RIST

Sorting Out the Issues
and Trends of
School Desegregation

Questions to think about

1 *What issues does Rist argue are not issues in
desegregation through busing? What are the real
issues? Why?*

2 *How does the busing issue and arguments surrounding
it relate to stratification in society? What are the effects
of busing on students?*

3 *How do issues of busing relate to the rest of the
educational system and society?*

4 *Compare Rist's points about busing with what is
happening to busing in your area.*

Few debates related to domestic social policy have
more intensely challenged the viability of the U.S. as a democratic, diverse,
and responsive society than has that surrounding the desegregation of our
educational systems. The emotions generated by such terms as "forced
busing," "the destruction of the neighborhood school," "whites have rights,"
and "community control" have tended to blur our focus, but the central
pivot must remain the interrelations of education, race, and equality. It is
only in such a context that discussion of school desegregation becomes
meaningful. Otherwise, one is left to first reify and then parcel out frag-
ments of what is, in fact, a complex mix of law, politics, pedagogics, and
cultural values.

In one form or another, the matter of school desegregation has been
on the national agenda for more than two decades. The *Brown* v. *Board of*

Reprinted from *USA Today*, November 1978. Copyright 1978 by the Society for the Advancement of Education.

Education of Topeka, Kansas decision of 1954 has been the touchstone from which our society has been grappling with this matter in the courtrooms, the classrooms, the political arenas, and the streets. To mention only Federal troops at Little Rock in the 1950s or the events in Boston and Louisville in the 1970s is to gloss over a generation of conflict. Even so, the direction in which we are headed appears irreversible. The question now is how quickly and in what manner shall we achieve the objectives of constitutional protections and quality educational environments?

It is merely a restating of the obvious to note that there are many misconceptions and misunderstandings regarding school desegregation efforts in the U.S. Further, the infusion of these misconceptions into our national dialogue and policy-making efforts inhibits informed discussion and thwarts successful implementation.

WHAT THE ISSUE IS NOT

The issue is not that of busing *per se*. Of the nearly 42,000,000 children in public elementary and secondary schools, more than 50% (21,800,000) ride buses to school. Of these, an estimated 7% (1,500,000) are bused for reasons of desegregation. Stated differently, participation in a desegregation program through the riding of a bus impacts on three or four of each 100 children in the public schools. Furthermore, when one surveys busing programs across the country, noting the disproportional numbers and years of black children who are bused, the number of white children being bused for any reason related to desegregation may be no more than one in 100.

The issue is not that of *de facto* segregation in either the North or the South. Every standing court order related to school desegregation has been issued on the grounds of *de jure* segregation. In each case where court orders have been issued, the courts have found that the local school districts—and occasionally, the state educational agencies as well—have systematically carried out policies that led to segregation between black and white students. The stance of the courts, embodied in a massive amount of litigation since the *Brown* decision, has consistently been that *there is no essential difference* in the reasons for ordering system-wide desegregation in either Northern or Southern cities.

The issue is not one of school achievement. Numerous data-collection endeavors provide no uniformity of opinion that desegregation efforts are harmful to student achievement. Rather, it is more realistic to assume that there are specific instances where achievement is hindered, but these are offset by other specific instances where there is no change or academic performance rises.

The issue is not a rejection of the principle of desegregation. Indeed, most Americans say they believe in school desegregation. The percentages have held relatively stable now for more than a decade, in spite of the media sharing few success stories and each and every difficulty. The acceptance among white Americans of multiracial schools as a place for their own children has also been growing. Recent national public opinion data indicates that a majority of white American parents would now be willing to have their children attend a majority black school.

This issue is not that school desegregation can not go smoothly. In the period from 1968 to 1971, a large portion of the South underwent massive desegregation and little was heard about it. Likewise, in the North, Wichita, Las Vegas, Stockton, Providence, Waukegan, Berkeley, Riverside, Portland (Ore.), Racine, Minneapolis, Ann Arbor, and many others have desegregated, mostly on a voluntary basis, and little has been heard. Even in places such as Little Rock and Pontiac, where there was initial violence and controversy, education is now occurring in a calm and non-hostile setting. Recent estimates are that some form of school desegregation has been effected in approximately 3,000 of the nearly 17,000 school districts in the country. Boston and Louisville comprise .0006% of that total. We are enmeshed in selective perception on a national scale.

WHAT THE ISSUE IS

The issue is the apparent randomness of desegregation efforts, leading some to believe that they have been unfairly singled out by the courts or Federal government. The matter of "fairness," of comparing one city's treatment versus another, raises the question of distributive justice. If the resolution of school segregation in Atlanta is vastly different from that in Boston, or Indianapolis from Denver, doubts can justifiably begin to arise. If Atlanta is allowed to retain several all-black schools, why must Boston eliminate each and every one of theirs? The moral force of the law exists only so long as those to whom it applies believe that they have been justly treated. When they believe they have not, the willingness to comply diminishes.

The issue is that the continued exodus of whites from the cities into suburban areas has created a situation where many of the large cities are increasingly, if not predominantly, black. So long as the suburbs are excluded from desegregation plans in these circumstances, substantial desegregation can not occur. If the only required integration is within district, present demographic trends will produce a thorough resegregation of black students in many of the nation's largest cities. The suburbs appear content to have it so. In addition, what such population shifts have created are not only divisions of race, but also of social class. As in Boston, the poor whites and poor blacks are left to be integrated among each other.

The issue is the resistance to Federal intervention and control. Court orders and HEW regulations take options away from local communities to effect their own educational policies. While there has been clear justification for such intervention on the part of the Federal government when the dimensions of school segregation were stark and readily visible, the matter at present is more obscure. Not the least of the reasons for this is the lack of an unambiguous position on the part of the Federal government. The failure of the Executive and Legislative branches to take responsible and articulated stands has left the matter entirely in the laps of the courts— and the courts are not the most appropriate places from which to educate people as to their legal and civic responsibilities. The consequence—apparent to state and local officials as well as to laypersons—is that the Executive branch holds one position, the Legislative another, and the courts yet a third. While the first two are seemingly content to make political gain from opposing the rulings of the third, local folks feel they are being pushed about.

The issue is that, even though the courts and educational officials alike have sought to implement integration plans that would provide creative and imaginative additions to the educational system, they have not been able to persuade the communities that desegregation will enhance the quality of their schools. In fact, the opposite is generally believed to be more nearly the truth. While the evidence continues to accumulate that desegregation provides a more equal distribution of educational resources and creates learning opportunities not otherwise available, the white community in particular continues to define school desegregation as little more than the creation of educational disaster zones.

The issue is that the signals from the black community as to the desirability of further school desegregation are increasingly mixed. What in the past gave clear moral legitimation to the desegregation effort was the black community's near unanimity that segregated schools be abolished post haste. (So far as I know, not a single court case pressing for school desegregation has ever been instigated by the white community anywhere in the country.) At present, however, there are an increasing number of persons in the black community willing to trade off desegregation for "community control" of all- or predominantly black schools. This growing diversity of opinion on school desegregation has had the effect of neutralizing large portions of the white liberal community, thus weakening the alliance which was so potent in the 1960s and early 1970s.

SORTING OUT THE TRENDS

For the past decade, primary governmental responsibility for issues of race and schooling has been lodged in the Federal courts. The identification of school desegregation as a judicial matter has by now become so automatic that one has to strain to remember that, during the mid-1960s, it was Congress and the Executive branches of government—not the courts— that exercised leadership in this area. As the policy problem changed its character, becoming national in scope and more politically menacing in form, the coordinate branches of government initially withdrew, then sought to undermine what had become an almost exclusively judicial effort.

The recent public record concerning school desegregation is not a particularly felicitous one, from almost anyone's point of view. The vigor of court action has outstripped the judiciary's willingness—or capacity—to inform the rest of us concerning its justifications for those actions. As a consequence, the great constitutional principles that underlie *Brown* seem destined to be forgotten amidst the tangle of legalisms that have emerged as ostensible elaborations of the Equal Protection Clause. At the Federal level, Congress and the Executive seem capable of expounding only what they oppose—the busing of school children. What they support, what political meanings they would attribute to the phrases "racial justice" and "equal educational opportunity," has to be reckoned a great unknown.

The present flight from responsibility is an altogether unfortunate state of affairs. Questions of race, schooling, and equality have political and moral, as well as constitutional, dimensions. To structure a viable approach for taking on these interrelations, much less assume one can "solve" them, requires different levels to assume responsibility. If the country is to do better in the near future than it has done in the near past, the critical question may be simply stated: Can the non-judicial branches of government at both the state and Federal levels make useful policy and programatic contributions? The possibility for such a response does exist.

Recent judicial decisions also point to another important trend—the inclusion of state educational agencies as parties to the litigation. This is something of a dramatic shift for, heretofore, the litigation was local citizens or the Justice Department versus the local school board and perhaps the superintendent of schools. Now, the state educational authorities are increasingly being brought into the suits, most often in the role of co-defendant with local educational authorities. Key cases to cite in this regard would include, among others, *Milliken* v. *Bradley* in Detroit, *Arthur* v. *Nyquist* in Buffalo, *Evans* v. *Buchanan* in Wilmington, *U.S.* v. *State of Missouri* in St. Louis County, and *Crawford* v. *Board of Education* in Los Angeles.

As these and other suits have proceeded through the courts, their final adjudications would suggest the following trends with respect to state level involvement in school desegregation. What underlies all these cases, although each was unique, was that the state educational agencies were held responsible for segregatory action and were ordered to be a party to the remedies. To summarize the trends, consider the following:

> Where states can be shown to be a party, by acts of either omission or commission, to intentional discrimination in the schools, the courts will order them to participate in the remedies.
>
> Where states accept a responsibility, through either enactment of a state law or passage of a resolution by a state agency, to end discrimination in the schools, the courts will require them to fulfill that responsibility.
>
> Federal courts will not order interdistrict remedies unless each district involved can be found to have *intentionally* taken segregatory actions with interdistrict effects. However, states with enabling legislation may, on their own initiative, merge districts, change school boundaries, order interdistrict transfers, or take other steps to end segregation in their schools without court order.[1]

FURTHER DECLINES IN SCHOOL SEGREGATION

Progress is being made in the desegregation of public schools in the South, but the picture is not as positive in the North and West. In fact, in some parts of these latter two regions, schools are becoming more intensely segregated. Recently published HEW data indicate, for example, that, in 1970, 74% of all black children in the public schools in Chicago were in schools with 99–100% minority enrollment. In 1974, the comparable figure was 80%. In Los Angeles, the figures for the same years are 55 and 62%, respectively; for Detroit, 36 and 50%, respectively. It should be remembered that these data are for the extreme—99–100% minority enrollments. The same picture is emerging for Hispanic children. Nearly two-thirds of all Spanish-surnamed students in the New York City schools were in schools with 99–100% minority student enrollments. In fact, on a national average, Hispanic children are now as concentrated in schools with more than 70% minority enrollment as are black students.

In spite of these increased concentrations in various sectors of the country, the national average shows a decline in the levels of school segregation. Whether such a decline will continue depends upon several critical factors. First among these is the matter of how the courts and Federal agencies define *de jure* segregation in areas where schools have never been segregated by law. While there have been individual instances where desegregation efforts have been set back because of judicial rulings that schools are not required to alleviate racial imbalances they did not cause, the more general stance of the courts has been oriented differently. Desegregation has been ordered where school officials were able to maintain segregation by arbitrarily drawing attendance zones, by selectively erecting new schools, and by the assignment of black teachers to black schools. If the courts continue to see such action as having the *intent* to segregate, these actions will be remedied under current statutes governing *de jure* segregation.

A second factor concerns what remedies for segregation will be invoked by governmental agencies and courts. While such efforts as magnet schools, the pairing of schools, and the altering of attendance zones may mitigate segregation, the evidence is overwhelming that the greatest decreases in segregation have come in those districts where students were bused to achieve desegregation. There is little doubt that, if busing as a tool of desegregation is limited or banned, urban areas would revert to having largely segregated schools due to neighborhood patterns.

A third factor, and one related to the second, concerns the future for interdistrict desegregation. If the only required integration in many of our urban areas is that of within-district, present demographic trends will produce a thorough *re*segregation for hundreds of thousands of black students. The reality is that within-district desegregation is simply not possible in many of our large cities. While desegregation can continue to proceed apace in many of our medium and smaller cities and towns, it is increasingly possible in the larger areas only when initiated on a metropolitan basis.

FUTURE IMPLEMENTATION

The matter of school desegregation is likely to be with us for years to come. Despite substantial desegregation in Southern and Border states in recent years, more than half of the black children in these areas are in majority black schools. In the North and West, the figures are even higher. In these regions, more than 80% of all black students are in majority black schools. Similarly, in states where there is a sizable Hispano-American school population, less than half of these students attend majority white schools— and the proportion who do so is generally declining. That so much of the task of desegregation still lies before us, coupled with the realization that desegregation has not fulfilled the expectations many have had, suggests it is time for a reconsideration of the basic and underlying assumptions influencing the present approaches.

Such a period of reevaluation is necessary if the desegregation process is to proceed in such a manner as to maximize the probabilities that the ultimate goals of this major effort at social change will be achieved. While most people sympathetic to these goals will have little quarrel with this admonition in principle, the implications may be less widely accepted.

In order to respond to the conditions listed at the beginning of this article that make school desegregation an "issue," remedies and new initiatives would have to move in ways different than at present. Further, strategies that are at present rejected out of hand—for example, partial desegregation, the preservation of one-race schools, different strategies in different parts of the school district, etc.—may have to be reconsidered. Strategies of school desegregation—be they at the local, state, or Federal levels—can not proceed as if the schools existed in a political and cultural vacuum.

If there is indeed to be future school desegregation in the U.S., the present pattern of sporadic efforts by the courts does not appear to be an effective instrument for achieving it. The more the task of desegregation has fallen to the courts alone, the less systematic, comprehensive, and acceptable the process has become. This is not the fault of the courts, but possibly, just possibly, those who have defaulted will be sufficiently disenchanted with the current state of affairs to reenter the fray and seek new and sensible initiatives. What is lacking at present is not the expertise, not the accumulated wisdom of the past two decades, and not those with leadership skills to see the process through. Rather, what we face is the absence of political will.

NOTE

1. Bert Mogin, *The State Role in School Desegregation* (Menlo Park, Calif.: Stanford Research Institute, 1977).

JAMES S. COLEMAN

Public Schools, Private Schools, and the Public Interest

Questions to think about

1 *Explain the differences the Coleman study found between public and private schools.*
2 *What are the implications of Coleman's findings for stratification and opportunity in schools and society? Why are Coleman's findings controversial?*
3 *What aspects of the open systems framework are reflected in Coleman's discussion?*
4 *Write a critique of the implications of Coleman's study for public and private schools. Cover such issues as separation of church and state, implications for the stratification system, and consequences of tuition tax credits.*

There is not *one* private school policy issue today, there are *two*. Certain proposed policies would expand the role of private schools in American education or at least make it easier to attend them; other policies would inhibit their use. Thus, there is the unusual situation in which conflict is so strong that support exists for policies that would go in exactly opposite directions. The principal examples of policies that would aid private schooling are tuition tax-credit legislation at the federal level, such as the Moynihan-Packwood bill . . . and tuition vouchers at the state level, such as the proposal designed for California by John Coons, Professor of Law at Berkeley. The principal examples of policies that would restrict private schooling are attempts by the Internal Revenue Service to impose

From *The Public Interest* 64 (Summer 1981), 19–30. Copyright © 1983 by National Affairs, Inc. Reprinted by permission of the author.

some form of racial-balance criterion on private schools in order for them to maintain tax-exempt status. Opponents of the first set of policies argue that those policies would destroy the public school system; opponents of the second set argue that those other policies would destroy the private school alternative to the public system.

Another unusual aspect of the private-public education conflict, especially in its voucher incarnation, is that it cuts across traditional liberal-conservative lines. John Coons, for instance, was also the principal moving force behind the Serrano case in California, which brought equal financing to schools in California and elsewhere. Vouchers have been supported or proposed by conservatives like Milton Friedman and liberals like Christopher Jencks. Still another curious aspect is that the conflict separates action from advocacy for a number of persons: There are many who vigorously oppose making private school attendance easier and at the same time have their own children enrolled in private schools; and there are many who support private schools and still have their children in public schools.

The principal arguments of those who favor aid to private schools are that: (a) private schools provide better education; (b) attendance at private schools is available only to those who can afford it; therefore, (c) reducing costs of private schooling will make the better education of private schools more equally available to families of different incomes. What may be questioned in this argument is the assumption that private schools provide a better education. This assumption is one of the two central questions studied in the research to be summarized here.

The principal argument of those who support constraints upon private schooling, or oppose making it easier to attend them, is that private schools segregate different segments of the population, due to the "self-selective" character of these schools. The specific arguments differ. One, the oldest, is that private schools draw off the most economically affluent from the public school system, and then engage in further economic stratification among schools within the private sector, resulting in economic elitism in the schools. Another argument, the most recent, is that private schools segregate racially by drawing off whites from the public sector, and then further segregate among schools within the private sector as whites choose certain schools and blacks others. The only solution is for students to be assigned to particular private schools, as is ordinarily done in the public sector. One final argument is somewhat different. This argument says that assisting private schooling, by any public means, constitutes "establishment" of a church and thereby violates the church-state separation provision of the Constitution.

What is subject to test in these arguments, except the last, is the fundamental assumption that private schools do segregate different segments of the population. The truth of this assumption appears at first self-evident, but the matter turns out to be more complex: Public schools are themselves not perfectly integrated on these economic and racial dimensions, and there is already social self-selection within the public sector when people choose where to live. The question is whether the education system as it now stands, containing private schools, is more segregated along income, racial, or religious grounds than would be a system without private schools. Or to put it differently: Does the choice which results from the existence of private schools lead to greater segregation than the choice that exists within the public sector?

A STUDY OF SCHOOL DIFFERENCES

To help address these important questions about private-public school differences, the National Center for Education Statistics held a conference in April 1981 at which the first reports of its "High School and Beyond" study of high school sophomores and seniors were presented and criticized. Both analyses had to do with comparisons of public and private schools, but the first one, conducted by Andrew Greeley, was focused mainly on the role of Catholic schools in the education of blacks and Hispanics. The second analysis ranged more broadly over the issues of achievement and segregation that I discussed above, and was conducted by Thomas Hoffer, Sally Kilgore, and me.[1]

As has become evident from the intensity of the response to these reports, the issues they addressed touched some very sensitive points— more sensitive than was anticipated by any of the authors, and certainly more than was anticipated when the reports were initially planned in the spring of 1980. For this reason, it is useful to briefly review the results of the Coleman-Hoffer-Kilgore report here—an action which may also help to dispel the confusion created by what has appeared in the media—and to suggest something about the deeper and more sensitive questions which this report touched.

First of all, it is useful to give a sense of how schools in the public and private sectors differ. Public high schools (grades nine through twelve) enroll over 90 percent of the total high school population and have an average of 750 students, while the Catholic schools enroll about 6 percent and average about 500 students, and the other private schools enroll between 3 and 4 percent and average only about 150 students. The pupil-teacher ratios in Catholic and public schools are very similar but in the other private schools they are less than half as large.

Students and principals in Catholic schools are much more likely than students and principals in public schools to report that their schools have rules about student dress and that students are held responsible for damage to school property; students and principals in the other private schools report this more frequently than in public schools but less than in Catholic schools. Students in Catholic schools are much more likely than public school students to report that discipline in their school is effective, with the other private schools again in between. And both Catholic and the other private school students are somewhat more likely than public schools students to say that school discipline is fair. Overall, *the evidence shows that discipline in the Catholic and other private schools is both stronger and fairer than in the public schools,* with discipline in the Catholic schools being strongest, and that in the other private schools more (as perceived by the students).

Students in Catholic schools are much less likely to be absent or to cut classes than are those in public schools (again with the other private schools in between and closer to the Catholic schools) and public school principals are much more likely to report that absenteeism constitutes a problem in their school than are either Catholic or other private school principals. On other measures of student behavior as well, *students in the Catholic and the other private schools show far fewer "problems"—as reported either by the students themselves or the principals—than do those in the public schools.* Catholic school students do about half again as much homework as do public school students, and students in the other private schools do even more.

In all these respects, Catholic schools are the most homogeneous, differing least from one another, while the other private schools are most heterogeneous, showing greatest variation in discipline and student behavior.

ACHIEVEMENT—PUBLIC AND PRIVATE

This sketch of the differences between schools in the public, Catholic, and other-private sectors gives an indication of how these schools differ in their everyday activities. But it says nothing about the central policy questions. The question of whether there is higher average achievement in the private sector than in the public sector is answered very simply through a comparison of scores on standardized tests in the two sectors. The answer is that in the areas in which both sophomores and seniors were tested (in reading, vocabulary, and mathematics), students in Catholic schools and students in other private schools scored about two grade-levels higher than did students in the public sector. But this is not the question asked by the parent choosing between a public and private school, or legislators deciding whether to support a bill assisting attendance at private schools. They ask a question asked of me by a colleague shortly after the report had been released. He asked, "How can you determine whether the *same* child would achieve more highly in the private school? Couldn't the achievement difference be solely due to selection?"

This question—which asks whether the school itself really makes a difference, and if so, how much—is as difficult to answer as the first one is simple. But it is not impossible. An extreme way would be illustrated by pairs of identical twins with one twin from each pair assigned to School A, and the other to School B. If the achievement of the twin assigned to School A was consistently higher, this would be strong evidence that School A brings about greater achievement.

A study of identical twins assigned to different schools, or even a study of non-twins assigned randomly to different schools, could test the effect of the schools on achievement. With random assignment of non-twins, a larger number of children would be necessary for statistical reasons—but the conclusions could be just as strong. Absent this kind of evidence—a problem which is characteristic of research in the social sciences because of ethical constraints on "arbitrary" assignment (and random assignment is certainly arbitrary) to different settings which might have long-term consequences—other methods must be used to separate the effects of selection from the effects of the school itself.

We used three methods in our study. The first was to "control" the background characteristics of students through multiple regression analysis, in effect comparing achievement for students who have similar background characteristics. Seventeen background characteristics were used (including some which might be consequences rather than causes of achievement) in order to control as fully as possible, even to the extent of overcompensating, for selection into the schools. These background characteristics ranged from things like family income, to each parent's education, to ownership of a pocket calculator, to each parent's aspirations for the child's education. The result of this analysis showed that about half of the original difference in achievement is due to selection, and about half the original difference remains. Less remains in reading and more in mathematics, and slightly less remains in the other private schools than in the Catholic schools.

A second method of analysis examined differences between the sophomore and senior groups (adjusting for dropouts) and used the two groups to measure gains and learning rates between sophomore and senior year.

This method showed higher learning rates in the other private schools than in public schools in all three achievement areas, higher rates in the Catholic schools than in the public schools in vocabulary and mathematics, and equal Catholic and public rates in reading comprehension. Learning rates in the other private schools were higher than those in Catholic schools in reading comprehension and mathematics, but the two sectors were alike in vocabulary.

This second method roughly confirms the public-private differences in the first analysis, though it shows achievement growth in the other private schools to be somewhat higher than that in the Catholic schools, while the first analysis showed the sophomore achievement levels to be slightly higher in the Catholic schools.

BETTER SCHOOLS DO BETTER

Both of these methods for discovering differences among schools in their effects on achievement contain a potential flaw: There may be some *other* uncontrolled background factor which determines whether, even among students alike in all the characteristics that are statistically controlled, the better-performing students are selected into the private sector and the less-well-performing students remain in the public sector. This seems possible or even likely for those private schools which select entrants using admissions tests, but these constitute only a handful of schools, a tiny fraction of the more than 6,000 private schools with secondary grades in the country. It seems less likely for the vast majority of private schools in which admission depends on the parents' ability to pay.

Despite the improbability of selection accounting for the remaining differences, we carried out a third analysis. And it is this analysis which carries special implications for public education. The argument is as follows: *If* Catholic or other private schools bring about higher achievement for comparable students, and *if* they do so through those attributes measured in the research which distinguish Catholic and other private schools from public schools, *then* we should find achievement differences among schools within any sector, public or private. In other words, those schools within any sector which are like the Catholic and other private schools should have students performing at levels comparable to those in the Catholic and other private schools, while those schools in any sector that are like the public schools should have students performing at the public school levels.

The major measured differences between the public and private sectors, other than size, are those described earlier: differences in disciplinary climate, in academic demands, and in student behavior. Further, even when the backgrounds of students are statistically controlled, much of these differences remains—differences in homework, in student attendance and in-school behavior, and differences in the disciplinary climate perceived by students. These differences can reasonably be attributed to differences in school policy rather than student background.

When we examined, wholly within the public sector, the performance of students similar to the average public school sophomore, but with the levels of homework and attendance attributable to school policy in the Catholic or other private schools, and those levels of disciplinary climate and student behavior attributable to school policy in the Catholic or other private schools, the levels of achievement are approximately the same as those found in the Catholic and other private sectors.

The first implication of these results is that they strongly confirm the school-effect results found by the other two methods. For the selection hypothesis necessary to account for these differences must be especially tortured, operating not only between sectors but also to the same degree within sectors, and operating to select students, on the behavior variables indicated above, into schools with particular disciplinary climates. Thus, the validity of the private-sector effects is strongly confirmed by these results.

A broader implication holds as well: that *these attributes described above are in fact those which make a difference in achievement in all American high schools no matter what sector they are in.* Schools which impose strong academic demands, schools which make demands on attendance and on behavior of students while they are in school are, according to these results, schools which bring about higher achievement. This is not to say that such policies are easy to institute in all schools. Public schools have greater constraints on suspending or expelling students than do private schools, for example, and quite beyond that, a public school principal may have less autonomy from the district in establishing a particular educational and disciplinary philosophy than does a private school principal. Rather, it may be said that in those schools where these policies *do* exist, students achieve more on average than in schools where these policies do not exist.[2]

Besides the overall difference between the public sector and the private sector in effects on achievement, there is another strong achievement-related difference—this time between the Catholic schools on the one hand, and the public schools and other private schools on the other. This is in the *homogeneity* of achievement: Catholic schoolchildren of college-educated and high-school-only parents achieve about the same, as do whites and blacks in those schools, even after other background characteristics are statistically controlled. This means that Catholic schools in general do less for students from the most advantaged backgrounds, and more for students from the most disadvantaged backgrounds, than do schools in the other-private sector. In both the public sector and the other-private sector there is a wide range of schools from the benighted to the elite; there is far less variance in the Catholic sector.

DO THE PRIVATE SCHOOLS SEGREGATE?

The second major policy-relevant question examined in the report is whether private schools increase segregation. Segregation operates as the consequence of two different mechanisms: first, the segregation *between* sectors (that is, through high-income or white students going to the private sector), and second, through internal segregation within each sector. The segregation in American secondary education as a whole is a result of both between-sector and within-sector segregation.

As it turns out, the impact of the private sector on segregation differs in the religious, economic, and racial dimensions. Examining only segregation between Catholics and non-Catholics, the proportion of Catholics is, of course, sharply different in the Catholic, public, and other-private sectors—about 90, 30, and 17 percent, respectively. This means that the between-sector segregation is very high. Within each of the three sectors, *given* the proportion of Catholics in the sector, the within-sector segregation is quite low. Taking together the high between-sector segregation and the low within-sector segregation, *the overall effect of the private sector is to increase somewhat the degree of religious segregation in American secondary schools,* relative to that which would exist if Catholic and non-Catholic students from the private sector were distributed into the public schools as Catholics and non-Catholics are now distributed in those schools.[3]

The impact of the private sector on economic segregation is somewhat different. Both the Catholic and other private schools have somewhat higher proportions of high-income students than do the public schools, and smaller proportions of the lowest-income students. The economic differences between sectors are not, however, especially high, with median incomes reported as $18,200 in the public sector, $22,700 in the Catholic sector, and $24,300 in the other-private sector. The economic segregation within each sector is also low, though there is more economic segregation in the public sector than in either of the private sectors or in both taken together. *The combined result of the between-sector and within-sector economic segregation is to give a degree of overall economic segregation that is not high, but is slightly higher than is found in the public sector.* In other words, it is slightly higher than would exist if private school students were redistributed among the public schools.

The impact of the private sector on black-white segregation is still different.[4] There is a substantial difference between the proportion of blacks in the public sector, the Catholic sector, and the other-private sector: about 14, 6, and 3 percent, respectively. *Within* the public sector, segregation is much higher than the black-white segregation in either of the private sectors or in the total private sector combined. *The joint result of the substantial between-sector segregation and the substantially lower private within-sector segregation is that there is no overall impact of the private sector on black-white segregation.* If whites and blacks now in private schools were redistributed into the public sector in just the way whites and blacks are now distributed in that sector, there would be no greater and no less segregation than currently exists. This result may go against intuition, which sees the private sector as a haven used by whites when desegregation rulings are passed; but intuition overlooks the fact that suburban schools within the public sector are used as a haven to a much greater extent than is the private sector. Eliminating the private sector would hardly deposit whites back in the public schools they were attending, even those who had used a private school as a haven in the first place. It is probably less true to say that private schools increase the degree of racial segregation in education than to say that private schools permit a greater degree of residential integration by race than would exist in their absence.

TUITION AS "TARIFF"

The results of this report, as I have described them above, are generally favorable to private schools. Further results in the report not described here are also generally favorable to private schools. A common response of some people, when confronted with these results, is the question, "But is the public interest served by assisting enrollment at private schools?" This is a question that merits serious attention, for private schooling on its face negates the classic American ideal of the public school.

I believe the matter can be usefully examined by viewing private school tuition as a protective tariff relative to tax support for free public schools. Just as a protective tariff on automobiles would protect the American automobile industry from foreign competition, private school tuition, measured against the free tuition at public schools, protects the public schools from competition by private schools. As students in first-year economics have learned, protective tariffs are generally inimical to the public interest. They benefit producers at the expense of consumers, but the producers they benefit most are those that would fail without the tariff—that is, the least efficient firms and industries. Protective tariffs keep resources employed inefficiently, lowering the general level of welfare, and opposing the general public interest. Furthermore, protective tariffs harm the interests of the least well-off, for the increase in prices relative to incomes (which is what protective tariffs bring about) hurts most those with the fewest dollars.

The effect of private school tuition and other barriers to attendance at private schools is very much the same. It protects the public schools to which students are assigned, and it protects most the worst public schools, those public schools that would be most depopulated by families' freedom to choose. It harms the consumers of education (the children and their families) and it harms most those to whom the price of tuition or the choice of school by moving residence is the greatest barrier—that is, the low-income family that is least able to leave a bad public school, and the black family that confronts the greatest barriers to moving elsewhere. (The evidence that this has occurred in American high schools is most fully seen in Greeley's report, which I have not discussed here.)[5]

There are some conditions under which protective tariffs can be beneficial to the public interest—though as economists are quick to point out, these are rare, far less numerous than the arguments of certain producers would lead one to believe. In the same way that one must be suspicious of these arguments, one should be suspicious of public school arguments for maintaining their protective tariff. The most frequent condition under which protection is beneficial is when "infant industries" need a period of protection to get started.

Public schooling is not an infant industry, but a somewhat different argument could be made: There is a public interest (or perhaps a community interest or a national interest) in broad participation in common institutions. The same kind of argument could be (and sometimes is) made for the military draft, or for non-military national service. The same kind of argument could be made against "private schools in the public sector"— that is, homogenous elite public schools in homogenous suburbs. But there are two points of importance about this argument as it applies to private schools. One is that the public schools are no longer a "common" institution. Residential mobility has brought about a high degree of racial segregation in education, as well as segregation by income. The second point is that the public interest in common institutions is not an *overriding* public interest. It is a relatively weak public interest when measured against the public interest in helping all children, particularly those of the disadvantaged, receive a better education. It is a relatively weak public interest when measured against the interests of children who are being directly and manifestly harmed by the school environment in which they find themselves, but who are unable to escape that environment. That plight is a poor family's plight, not one that policy-makers find themselves in. It takes sympathetic identification beyond their own experience to recognize this plight.

Some part of the plight is of very recent origin, for it is only very recently that control of a community's schools has been taken largely out of the community's hands by federal (and to a lesser extent, state) intervention. Public schools have become an overregulated industry, with regulations and mandates ranging from draconian desegregation to mainstreaming of emotionally disturbed children, to athletic activities that are blind to sex differences. It is in part these regulations, imposed on the community and the school, which are responsible for the slackening of academic demands and the breakdown of disciplinary climate that many public schools have experienced in recent years. And it is the disadvantaged who are least able to select a school, in the public or private sector, that continues to function reasonably well.

There may be a rationale for some protective barriers to encourage participation in the public schools, but certainly not those that exist now, which harm most the interests of those least well-off and protect most those public schools that are worst. In short, the tuition barrier to private schooling as it exists now is almost certainly harmful to the public interest, and especially harmful to the interests of those least well-off.

NOTES

1. The Coleman-Hoffer-Kilgore report was written in August 1980, and initially planned for release in the fall of 1980. However, delays in the reviewing-and-revision process led NCES to defer its release until April 1981. The Greeley report was written in early fall 1980, and was also initially intended to be released in fall 1980. A fuller outline of overall study is given in the research note at the end of this article.

2. Nor is this to imply that the same factors would be critical in other settings or at other times in American schools when discipline would be taken as given. Results of the sort discussed here, while they point to factors that affect achievement in a given population of schools, will not hold in a population of schools which varies much less on the factors found to be important, or more on others. Twenty-five years ago, when discipline in American public schools was far less problematic than it is now, the results found here might very well not hold.

3. The results of such a "redistribution" are obtained very simply, merely by assuming that the public sector was expanded to cover all students, maintaining the same level of religious segregation now found in the public sector.

4. There is no effect on the Hispanic/non-Hispanic segregation because the private sector has about the same proportion of Hispanics as does the public sector, and the degree of segregation within public and private sectors is about the same.

5. An interesting proposal that would give tuition vouchers, but only to children who do badly for a period of time in public schools, has recently been made by Barbara Lerner in *Minimum Competence, Maximum Choice: Second Chance Legislation*. This would eliminate the tuition tariff barrier in those schools which are doing the worst for those students who are most harmed by the barrier.

RESEARCH NOTE

The study from which these data were taken, titled "High School and Beyond," is designed as a longitudinal study of a national sample of high school seniors and sophomores of 1980. The study is sponsored by the National Center for Education Statistics of the U.S. Department of Education, and has been conducted by the National Opinion Research Center of the University of Chicago. The first wave of data, on which the results described in the article are based, was collected in the spring of 1980. The sample of schools consists of 1,015 high schools, the sample of seniors in these schools (randomly drawn from the list of seniors in each school) consists of 28,465 students, and the sample of sophomores, drawn in the same way, consists of 30,263 students. The study is designed for examining a number of policy questions, perhaps the most central of which are those involving the transition of youth from secondary education to a variety of post-secondary activities and into adulthood. The data set, which will be augmented by subsequent waves of questionnaires at approximately two-year intervals, is publicly available for analysis from NCES. The two reports which have been released to date are "Minority Students in Catholic Secondary Schools" by Professor Andrew Greeley of the University of Arizona and NORC, and "Public and Private Schools" by James Coleman, Thomas Hoffer, and Sally Kilgore at the University of Chicago and NORC.

DONNA M. KAMINSKI

Where Are the Female Einsteins? The Gender Stratification of Math and Science

Questions to think about

1 *What are the differences in men's and women's experiences with math and science? Why do those differences occur?*

2 *How would functionalists deal with male and female differences in experience with math and science? How would conflict theorists (as discussed in the Bowles and Gintis and the Collins selections) deal with them?*

3 *What other parts of the open system would have to be involved to bring about change in men's and women's experiences?*

4 *What long-term effect do differences in math and science experiences have on women's life opportunities? Do you see any of these effects in your life or in the lives of those close to you?*

Sociologists have long been interested in the stratification of society, particularly the social and economic inequalities related to social class and race and ethnic group. Researchers in sociology of education have studied how educational inequities relate to these variables, both as cause and consequence. Only recently, however, have social scientists begun to consider the relationship between gender-based economic stratification and education in terms of sex differences in occupations.

The majority of "working" women (i.e., working for pay outside the home) are clustered in a very limited range of occupations, primarily teaching, nursing, social work, and clerical jobs. These are all fields made up of a very high proportion of women—and are relatively poorly paid. On the other hand, the math/science/engineering/computer/technical areas are some of the more highly paid occupations today and have considerably greater employment and mobility potential. But women make up less than 10 percent of these workers.

Indeed, across all occupations, women are less likely to be working in math-related areas—e.g., the high school science teacher, the sociologist specializing in quantitative research, the accountant or economist in business. One can notice a similar underrepresentation of women (and other minorities) majoring in these fields in college. In fact, this pattern is apparent as early as high school, where two to three times as many males as females take physics, chemistry, and advanced math.

Is this a problem? If so, for whom? Women? Society? Can something be done about it? Why are there so few women in the sciences? Is it because they aren't able to, aren't allowed to, or don't want to achieve in sciences?

Many questions center on biological differences and whether these affect abilities. Do the different sex hormones facilitate different intellectual skills? Are males' and females' brains different? (Do they show left/right brain differences?) Is the observed discrepancy due to different rates of early physiological development? A noted psychologist has done an extensive review of the studies on this topic. Sherman (1976) concludes from this review that there does not appear to be a natural ability difference between females and males that could explain much (if any) of the observed difference in areas such as math behavior.

Looking further, one begins to note other evidence contradicting a "biological difference" explanation. For example, most studies find that girls and boys do about equally well on math/science ability tests up through junior high school; only then do girls seem to fall behind, at a time when gender roles and gender-appropriate behavior suddenly becomes increasingly important to students. And if one examines actual academic performance, girls consistently earn better grades than boys all through the school years—including math and science marks. Studies today have also begun to take into account the important variable "number of previous math courses taken" when comparing overall male and female test scores. Most of the difference in scores disappears when similarly prepared students are compared. Also, some females do successfully study and enter careers in the sciences, and their numbers are growing. These may eventually match the proportions of women scientists found in Eastern European countries, where females and males are much more equally represented.

The evidence makes it difficult to assume an innate sex difference; instead it suggests an examination of social, cultural, and educational causes.

Researchers have done considerable study in this area since the early 1970s. (For good summaries, see Chinn, 1980; Fox, 1976; Fennema, 1976; Kaminski, 1978, 1982). A major focus has been on trying to explain why there is such a gender gap in the number of students studying math and science in high school. This factor, more than ability or performance differences, appears to be the critical filter differentiating men's and women's career options.

But why do so many fewer young women than men take elective math, science, mechanical drawing, and computer courses in high school? Given our culture's current definitions of sex roles, young women are likely to lack both the pushes and the pulls to science areas. Consider gender socialization. Studies show that girls get less experience and encouragement to be independent, curious, active experimenters and manipulators of the physical and abstract world by being socialized into the traditional female role. For example, families are less likely to give girls chemistry or erector sets, telescopes and microscopes, science books and math puzzles. Teachers are less likely to ask girls to run machinery (e.g., movie projectors), demonstrate science experiments, or to fix broken things. The peer group gives girls fewer opportunities to play computer games, which not only develop certain skills, but also foster favorable attitudes toward space and computers (as well as conquering and aggression!). Children also see relatively few role models of women as scientists or as competent in math. Consider images in children's science textbooks, toy packaging, TV advertising of science-related toys and games, books on famous scientists, and children's books showing adult occupations. Other questions arise: Are parents likely to help with math homework or a science project? What are the high school science teacher's attitudes toward female students? Studies show that even by junior high school, attitudes, interests, and career plans toward or away from the sciences are being formed.

Commonly held gender stereotypes about women and girls hold that they aren't logical; aren't good with figures; can't think abstractly; don't do well in math; don't like computers; aren't inventors, experimenters, tinkerers, constructors, adventurers, or puzzle solvers—all skills related to being a scientist. Studies show that comedians think so, textbook publishers seem to think so (there are three to four times as many pictures of boys as girls in science books), toy manufacturers appear to believe it (note the advertising and packaging of chemistry sets, erector sets, computer games), elementary school teachers expect it (expectations are that girls will like spelling and reading, boys will like math and science), high school counselors give advice on courses and careers based on the stereotypes, parents are likely to accept the idea that daughters are more likely than sons to be "forgiven" for doing poorly in math and science*—even females themselves believe it.

Is this ideology based on fact? Statistics do support this to an extent. As mentioned, males are much more likely to choose courses and careers in the sciences. Boys use more books, toys, and games related to computers and science. Boys are more likely to be involved in programs for the mathematically gifted. Men also score higher than women on the math section of the SAT test, Graduate Record Examination, civil service tests, and various math/science ability tests.

This lack of support for girls is manifested directly in math and science schoolwork. Teachers hold lower expectations for girls' performance in these areas, parents are more likely to allow girls to do poorly in math and opt out when it becomes elective ("Oh, your mother was never good in math, either"), counselors are less likely to push girls toward taking optional advanced courses ("What will you ever use it for?" or "Physics will only hurt your good GPA"), and peers don't provide much support to young women for being a "brain" or taking "male subjects." All this feedback operates to lower girls' self-confidence in their math/science/technical abilities and becomes a self-fulfilling prophecy. By early high school, girls are already much more likely than boys to rate their math/science ability as "just average," as opposed to "above average" or "among the best"—in spite of their earning better grades in these subjects. Young women are likewise much more likely to develop mathophobia—a fear of math.

Another important obstacle to women's entry into science-related courses and careers is our cultural stereotypes of science and the scientist—some perhaps accurate, some not so. First of all, science is seen as largely a male endeavor—as embodied in famous scientists; high school and college teachers; the majority of students taking advanced math and science courses in high school; math/science/computer/engineering majors in college; students participating in science fairs, accelerated programs, and computer workshops; and so on. Thus females making a commitment to such a field are seen as deviant and may lack peer reinforcement. Some young women obviously do overcome this label barrier—and as more and more do so, the field will become less restricted. For example, studies of all-female high schools show young women's course taking and ability in math and science are much higher than for those in mixed-sex schools.

A second important stereotype of science and the scientist that inhibits

---

*Henceforth, the term *science* will be used to refer to the natural and physical sciences and will also include the related areas of mathematics, computer science, and engineering. The social sciences are not included because women are more equally represented in these fields and because career development patterns are different in these sciences.

women's (and perhaps some men's) entry into the science field is the negative picture of what scientists and their jobs are like. High school women perceive the scientist to be quiet, unpopular, unsociable, not good looking, head in the clouds, not "with it"; the woman scientist is a large, manly, rumpled old spinster. The job is seen to involve extra time and hard work in training, working all alone in a laboratory, putting in long hours, working on something impersonal which has little direct relevance to humans. These characteristics are especially at odds with the traditional female role, particularly as it is defined by adolescents. Young women are more likely to want a job working with people rather than things, to be concerned with positive physical, psychological, and social charcteristics and to deal more directly with human concerns. Given the realities of women's continued respnsibility for home and family, women are less likely to look toward careers rather than jobs, the extra years of schooling in preparation, or the long work hours. And whether or not these stereotypes are accurate, students' (especially females') perceptions contribute to their decision to close off these career options in mid-adolescence.

This leads to a final important barrier—young women's perceptions of the lack of future usefulness of math, science, and computer courses. As adolescents, young women are less concerned with occupational plans; many still view wife/mother/homemaker as the major female role. Many also see their job or career as supplemental, temporary, combined with raising a family, and secondary to their husbands' career. So why take hard courses if they're not seen as necessary for adult life? Studies show that high school students rate physics, chemistry, and advanced math as the hardest in high school. Why prepare for a career in science when another occupation may take less schooling, work, and commitment? Why be concerned with the pay and long-term employment potential of a field when your job is supplemental? Isn't it better to be able to choose something you like, working with people, as a tradeoff for pay, security, and advancement? These are the views of many adolescent women, but not exactly an accurate picture of many adult women's lives today.

The majority of women work many years of their lives; many have preschool children. Nearly half the labor force is women, and increasing with the rapidly rising divorce rate; many women are the sole support of themselves and their families. On the average, female college graduates earn less than male high school dropouts. This is in part due to the different fields women and men choose to enter (e.g., teaching versus computer science)—decisions influenced by courses taken or not taken in high school. Unlike fields such as psychology, elementary education, or social work where students may postpone commitment decisions until mid-college, the math and science areas generally require adequate foundations in high school coursework. Thus, not studying chemistry in high school virtually closes off the chemistry career option by mid-adolescence.

The potential benefits from an emphasis on greater involvement by women in science can be viewed from several value perspectives. Conflict theorists contend that alteration of the education system alone will not affect the opportunity structure for women. Economic, political, and family institutions must also alter to bring about meaningful change. It would certainly seem to be in the interest of society as a whole to increase the number of possible scientists and the potential for scientific contributions to society. The value of greater involvement for women seems particularly important as it could increase women's career options, open up higher paying, higher status jobs to women, and counteract current gender-based occupational segregation and its many consequences. Besides improving and enlarging the future potential pool of scientists, increasing the number of young women taking elective science courses has the potential for contributing to a more knowledgeable and scientifically aware future adult population of nonscientists. For example, in dealing with issues such as energy conservation and environmental pollution, in maintaining technological conveniences, in dealing with an increasingly computerized society, a more scientifically informed citizenry seems desirable. Women stand to benefit from improved investigative, mechanical, analytic, and problem-solving skills (in which they have traditionally been weak) by increasing their training in science and laboratory work.

One could also argue for greater math preparation because of its benefits in nonmath-related jobs. For example, screening tests for entry into college, graduate school and civil service jobs as well as many job aptitude tests include a significant portion covering math-related skills. Also, many fields today such as education, sociology, business, and psychology are requiring greater quantitative, computer, and experimental skills. Largely female occupations—clerical jobs, library work, teaching—are moving in this direction as computers are incorporated into their everyday work worlds. And in spite of a current overall surplus of teachers, there is a shortage of qualified science and math teachers; the entry of more women into these fields might help solve this problem if women continue to choose the teaching profession and can provide role models for young women.

And lastly, our society should try to eliminate the barrier to females' entry into science because of its potential intrinsic interest for women—as great as for men. Must sex role stereotypes and the accompanying socialization discourage the next generation from choosing a field they might find interesting, challenging, and rewarding?

REFERENCES

Chinn, Phyllis (1980) *Women in Science and Mathematics Bibliography.* Arcata, Calif.: Mathematics Department, Humboldt State University.

Fennema, Elizabeth (1976) *Influences of Selected Cognitive, Affective, and Educational Variables on Sex-Related Differences in Mathematics Learning and Studying.* Washington, D.C.: National Institute of Education.

Fox, Lynn (1976) *The Effects of Sex-Role Socialization on Mathematics Participation and Achievement.* Washington, D.C.: National Institute of Education.

Fox, Lynn, Linda Brody, and Dianne Tobin (eds.) (1981) *Women and the Mathematical Mystique.* Baltimore: Johns Hopkins University Press.

Kaminski, Donna (1978) "Entry into Science: The Effect of Parental Evaluations on Sons and Daughters," Ph.D. dissertation, Kalamazoo, Mich.: Western Michigan University.

Kaminski, Donna (1982) "Girls and Mathematics and Science: An Annotated Bibliography of British Work (1970–1981)." *Studies in Science Education* 9 (1982):81–108.

Sherman, Julia (1976) *Effects of Biological Factors on Sex-Related Differences in Mathematics Achievement.* Washington, D.C.: National Institute of Education.

PAUL WILLIS

Class and Institutional
Forms of Culture

Questions to think about

1 *What are some characteristics of "the lads"? How do cliques of kids in school teach and reinforce role preparation for the adult years?*
2 *How does the school counterculture influence a student's experience in school and life changes after school? Relate this culture to self-concept as discussed in Erickson's article in Chapter 5.*
3 *Discuss and compare the internal school stratification system described here with the external stratification system.*
4 *What differences in terminology and structure do you notice between English and American schools?*

CLASS FORM

. . . It is now time to contextualize the counter-school culture. Its points of contact with the wider working class culture are not accidental, nor its style quite independent, nor its cultural skills unique or special. Though the achievements of counter-school culture are specific, they must be set against the larger pattern of working class culture in order for us to understand their true nature and significance. This section is based on fieldwork carried out in the factories where "the lads" get jobs after leaving school, and on interviews with their parents at home.

Reprinted from Paul Willis, *Learning to Labor: How Working Class Kids Get Working Class Jobs* (New York: Columbia University Press, 1981), pp. 52–59.

In particular, counter-school culture has many profound similarities with the culture its members are mostly destined for—shopfloor culture. Though one must always take account of regional and occupational variations, the central thing about the working class culture of the shopfloor is that, despite harsh conditions and external direction, people do look for meaning and impose frameworks. They exercise their abilities and seek enjoyment in activity, even where most controlled by others. Paradoxically, they thread through the dead experience of work a living culture which is far from a simple reflex of defeat. This is the same fundamental taking hold of an alienating situation that one finds in counter-school culture and its attempt to weave a tapestry of interest and diversion through the dry institutional text. These cultures are not simply layers of padding between human beings and unpleasantness. They are appropriations in their own right, exercises of skill, motions, activities applied towards particular ends.

The credentials for entry into shopfloor culture proper, as into the counter-school culture, are far from being merely one of the defeated. They are credentials of skill, dexterity and confidence and, above all, a kind of presence which adds to, more than it subtracts from, a living social force. A force which is *on the move,* not supported, structured and organized by a formal named institution, to which one may apply by written application.

The masculinity and toughness of counter-school culture reflects one of the central locating themes of shopfloor culture—a form of masculine chauvinism. The pin-ups with their enormous soft breasts plastered over hard, oily machinery are examples of a direct sexism but the shopfloor is suffused with masculinity in more generalized and symbolic ways too. Here is a foundryman, Joey's father, talking at home about his work. In an inarticulate way, but perhaps all the more convincingly for that, he attests to that elemental, in our culture essentially masculine, self-esteem of doing a hard job well—and being known for it:

> I work in a foundry . . . you know, drop forging . . . do you know anything about it . . . no . . . well you have the factory down in Bethnal St with the noise . . . you can hear it in the street . . . I work there on the big hammer . . . it's a six tonner. I've worked there twenty-four years now. It's bloody noisy, but I've got used to it now . . . and it's hot . . . I don't get bored . . . there's always new lines coming and you have to work out the best way of doing it . . . You have to keep going . . . and it's heavy work, the managers couldn't do it, there's not many strong enough to keep lifting the metal . . . I earn eighty, ninety pounds a week, and that's not bad, is it? . . . It ain't easy like . . . you can definitely say that I earn every penny of it . . . you have to keep it up you know. And the managing director, I'd say 'hello' to him you know, and the progress

> manager . . . they'll come around and I'll go . . . 'Alright' [thumbs
> up] . . . and they know you, you know . . . a group standing there
> watching you . . . working . . . I like that . . . there's something
> there . . . watching you like . . . working . . . like that . . . you have
> to keep going to get enough out.

The distinctive complex of chauvinism, toughness and machismo on
the shopfloor is not anachronistic, neither is it bound to die away as the
pattern of industrial work changes. Rough, unpleasant, demanding jobs
which such attitudes seem most to be associated with still exist in considerable numbers. A whole range of jobs from building work to furnace work
to deep sea fishing still involve a primitive confrontation with exacting
physical tasks. The basic attitudes and values most associated with such
jobs are anyway still widely current in the general working class culture,
and particularly in the culture of the shopfloor. The ubiquity and strength
of such attitudes is vastly out of proportion to the number of people actually
involved in heavy work. Even in so-called light industries, or in highly
mechanized factories where the awkwardness of the physical task has long
since been reduced, the metaphoric figures of strength, masculinity and
reputation still move beneath the more varied and visible forms of workplace culture. Despite the increasing numbers of women employed, the
most fundamental ethos of the factory is still profoundly masculine.

Another main theme of shopfloor culture—at least as I observed and
recorded it in the manufacturing industries of the Midlands—is the massive
attempt to gain informal control of the work process. Limitation of output
or "systematic soldiering" and "gold bricking" have been observed from
the particular perspective of management from Taylor onwards, but there
is evidence now of a much more concerted—though still informal—
attempt to gain control. It sometimes happens now that the men themselves
to all intents and purposes actually control at least manning and the speed
of production. Again this is effectively mirrored for us by working class
kids' attempts, with the aid of the resources of their culture, to take control
of classes, substitute their own unofficial timetables, and control their own
routines and life spaces. Of course the limit to this similarity is that where
"the lads" can escape entirely, "work" is done in the factory—at least to
the extent of the production of the cost of subsistence of the worker—and
a certain level of activity is seen as necessary and justified. Here is the
father of one of "the lads," a factory hand on a track producing car engines,
talking at home:

> Actually the foreman, the gaffer, don't run the place, the men run
> the place. See, I mean you get one of the chaps says, 'Alright,
> you'm on so and so today.' You can't argue with him. The gaffer

don't give you the job, they swop each other about, tek it in turns. Ah, but I mean the job's done. If the gaffer had gi'd you the job you would . . . They tried to do it one morning, gi'd a chap a job you know, but he's been on it, you know, I think he'd been on all week, and they just downed tools [. . .] There's four hard jobs on the track and there's dozens that's . . . you know, a child of five could do it, quite honestly, but everybody has their turn. That's organized by the men.

Shopfloor culture also rests on the same fundamental organizational unit as counter-school culture. The informal group locates and makes possible all its other elements. It is the zone where strategies for wresting control of symbolic and real space from official authority are generated and disseminated. It is the massive presence of this informal organization which most decisively marks off shopfloor culture from middle class cultures of work.

Among workers it is also the basis for extensive bartering, arranging "foreigners" and "fiddling." These are expanded forms of the same thing which take place in school among "the lads."

The informal group on the shopfloor also shows the same attitude to conformists and informers as do "the lads." "Winning" things is as widespread on the shopfloor as theft is among the lads, and is similarly endorsed by implicit informal criteria. Ostracism is the punishment for not maintaining the integrity of the world in which this is possible against the persistent intrusions of the formal. . . .

The distinctive form of language and highly developed intimidatory humor of the shopfloor is also very reminiscent of counter-school culture. Many verbal exchanges on the shopfloor are not serious or about work activities. They are jokes, or "pisstakes," or "kiddings" or "windups." There is a real skill in being able to use this language with fluency: to identify the points on which you are being "kidded" and to have appropriate responses ready in order to avoid further baiting. . . .

Associated with this concrete and expressive verbal humor is a well-developed physical humor: essentially the practical joke. These jokes are vigorous, sharp, sometimes cruel, and often hinged around prime tenets of the culture such as disruption of production or subversion of the boss's authority and status. . . .

It is also interesting that, as in the counter-school culture, many of the jokes circle around the concept of authority itself and around its informal complement, "grassing." . . .

The rejection of school work by "the lads" and the omnipresent feeling that they know better is also paralleled by a massive feeling on the shopfloor, and in the working class generally, that practice is more important than theory. As a big handwritten sign, borrowed from the back of a matchbox and put up by one of the workers, announces on one shopfloor: "An ounce of keenness is worth a whole library of certificates." The shopfloor abounds with apocryphal stories about the idiocy of purely theoretical knowledge. Practical ability always comes first and is a *condition* of other kinds of knowledge. Whereas in middle class culture knowledge and qualifications are seen as a way of shifting upwards the whole mode of practical alternatives open to an individual, in working class eyes theory is riveted to particular productive practices. If it cannot earn its keep there, it is to be rejected. . . .

. . . The working class view would be the rational one were it not located in class society, i.e., that theory is only useful insofar as it really does help to do things, to accomplish practical tasks and change nature. Theory is asked to be in a close dialectic with the material world. For the middle class, more aware of its position in a class society, however, theory is seen partly in its social guise of qualifications as the power to move up the social scale. In this sense theory is well worth having even if it is never applied to nature. It serves its purpose as the *means* to decide precisely which bit of nature one wants to apply it to, or even to choose not to apply it at all. Paradoxically, the working class distrust and rejection of theory comes partly from a kind of recognition, even in the moment that it oppresses, of the hollowness of theory in its social guise.

Even the non-conformists in the high status grammar school in the most exclusive part of the larger conurbation recognize the *social* essence of theory as it is articulated with practice in our society. For them, qualification is choice and mobility in a class society. It is not simply the ability to do the job better. It is this central realization, in fact, which characteristically limits their anti-school feeling:

Larry   . . . What I want to do, I want to get me "A" levels [he had only just finished his "O" levels and decided to carry on to "A" level] and then go touring the world, then OK, live it fairly rough for a few years, just dossing around, then I'll carry on, but at least then I've got the choice of whether I want to carry on, whether I want to go back and get a decent job. If you've got qualifications, then you can choose what you want to do: if you want to drop out, or whether you want to carry on being part of the system. But if you haven't got, you know . . . if I didn't have the qualifications, I don't know what I'd do, this is all according if I get them, but if I do get them, at least I'll know I'll have a choice of whether I want to get a steady job and you know pension scheme, car, two kids and wife and house mortgage and everything like, or whether I just want to roam the world.

It is, of course, the larger class dimension which gives the working class counter-school culture its special edge and resonance in terms of style, its particular force of opposition and its importance as an experiential preparation for entry into working class jobs. Although all forms of institution are likely to breed their own informal accretions, and although all schools of whatever class always create oppositional cultures, it is the crucial conjunction of institutional opposition with a working class context and mode which gives the special character and significance to "the lads'" culture. Institutional opposition has a different meaning according to its class location and expression. The non-conformists in the high status grammar school, although sharing similar attitudes to school, know that they are different from the Hammertown lads. They cannot through institutional means alone transcend their class location. Ultimately, they have not only a different attitude to qualifications but also an inevitable sense of different social position.

Larry   A lot of kids that you've been talking to [in Hammertown], they'd regard us as poufs, 'cos we go to a grammar school. Not only 'cos we go to a grammar school, but because we're from here in the first place which is regarded as a snob area.

Some of the non-conformist group in the grammar school are, in fact, from working class families. Despite even their origins and anti-school attitude, the lack of a dominant working class ethos within their school culture profoundly separates their experience from "the lads." It can also lead to artificial attempts to demonstrate solidarity on the street and with street contacts. That the working class cultural forms of school opposition are creative, specific, borne and reproduced by particular individuals and groups from afresh and in particular contexts—though always within a class mode—is shown by the cultural awkwardness and separation of such lads. The lack of the collective school based and generated form of the class culture, even despite a working class background and an inclination to oppositional values, considerably weakens their working class identity. . . .

It could be suggested that what non-conformists in middle class schools—no matter what their individual origins—are struggling for is some kind of conversion of their institutional opposition into a more resonant working class form. Insofar as they succeed and become influenced by various processes . . . so does their future "suffer." Insofar as they fail, or insofar as, for instance, conformist working class boys in a working class school are insulated from working class culture, and become free from its processes, so they are likely to "succeed." . . .

INSTITUTIONAL FORM

No matter how hard the creation, self-making and winning of counter-school culture, it must, then, be placed within a larger pattern of working class culture. This should not lead us, however, to think that this culture is all of a piece, undifferentiated or composed of standard clonal culture modules spontaneously reproducing themselves in an inevitable pattern.

Class cultures are created specifically, concretely in determinate conditions, and in particular oppositions. They arise through definite struggles over time with other groups, institutions and tendencies. Particular manifestations of the culture arise in particular circumstances with their own form of marshalling and developing of familiar themes. The themes are *shared* between particular manifestations because all locations at the same level in a class society share similar basic structural properties, and the working class people there face similar problems and are subject to similar ideological constructions. In addition, the class culture is supported by massive webs of informal groupings and countless overlappings of experience, so that central themes and ideas can develop and be influential in practical situations where their direct logic may not be the most appropriate. A pool of styles, meanings and possibilities are continuously reproduced and always available for those who turn in some way from the formalized and official accounts of their position and look for more realistic interpretations of, or relationship to, their domination. As these themes are taken up and recreated in concrete settings, they are reproduced and strengthened and made further available as resources for others in similar structural situations.

CHAPTER 7

Educational Systems and Their Environments

No educational system exists in a vacuum. Feedback from the environment is essential to schools, enabling them to absorb change and meet new needs. Note in our open systems model the many environmental factors affecting a school's day-to-day operation, and sometimes its survival. Each participant in the school brings in influences from the world outside; community composition, political decisions, economics, and family all affect decision making in schools, which in turn are dependent on their environments for funds, new knowledge, technology, materials, and even clients. Some parts of the environment are more important for schools than others, and this importance changes over time. Today testing and accountability may be major issues, tomorrow multicultural curriculum may be critical. How much schools must change to adapt to environmental pressures depends on those school needs that must be met by the environment. The readings in this chapter examine examples of environmental influences on classrooms and schools.

Schools are vulnerable to environmental pressures because they are held accountable for children's achievement, because they are asked to provide equal opportunities and a better chance for economic success in life, and because they are expected to provide training that will lead to jobs, including those in newly developed high technology fields. When people are dissatisfied with school performance or other aspects of their lives, their frustration is most easily vented on schools because the latter are controlled by lay boards and are located in the community. The irate parent who demands to know why Johnny isn't reading; the conservative group of community members who insist on changes in the curriculum; innovations in the field of education that require new materials and equipment such as computers; failed levies that cause financial pressure and require cutbacks in staff and program—all represent environmental pressures brought to bear on schools. Sometimes these pressures conflict—for example, in demands to include programs for the handicapped and gifted and cut expenditures at the same time. The Kanawha County textbook controversy discussed in Chapter 10 is a further example of environmental pressure.

Environments vary in importance depending on their salience to parts of the educational system. In the first article, Robert Dreeben discusses the immediate external environment surrounding classroom teachers and schools which is made up of system administrators who concern themselves with resources and policy. Though these role holders may not influence or be present in the daily lives of teachers, their decisions affect the classroom structure and process, long-range planning, class size, curriculum, and other factors that have a bearing on classroom life. Dreeben also points out community influences on schools: organizations such as the PTA and teacher unions, the children served and community in which the school exists, population shifts, and new educational ideas and technology.

As any teacher or school administrator can testify, the influence of community members on schools is significant. Communities vote on school levies. Parents hold schools accountable for their children's learning and success. Therefore, the attitudes held by members of the community are another important environmental influence on what happens within the school and classroom. Because of traditional lay control of these factors, monies available, curriculum, school policies and programs, and enrollments depend on community support and receive community input whether school personnel want it or not.

Every year since 1970, George Gallup has conducted an opinion poll for *Phi Delta Kappan* magazine. The 1983 poll included here shows what the public considers major problems in schools. Over the years discipline, along with funding and curriculum issues, has consistently ranked high among major concerns facing schools.

A third type of environmental influence on schools is represented in the article by Wynn DeBevoise. As our society becomes increasingly technological, schools experience pressure to respond and to be leaders in the changes. This implies incorporation of technology in classrooms—for example, use of microcomputers in teaching. Changes require recognition of new societal demands in the workforce and home, as well as leadership from educational institutions at all levels to deal with both skill training and issues brought about by changing lifestyles. DeBevoise identifies both the changes that are taking place and the controversies over how educational systems should deal with these changes in order to prepare young people for the society of the future.

All these environmental examples illustrate the interdependence of educational systems with other parts of the larger societal system. To some extent, adaptation and change occurs in every system in response to environmental feedback. As you read Chapter 8, which discusses the system of higher education, keep in mind the importance of the environment for the survival of institutions of higher education, especially in funding and in attracting students.

ROBERT DREEBEN

The School as a Workplace

Questions to think about

1 *How can we rate the importance to schools of various parts of the environment? Give some examples.*

2 *Name some environmental influences on individual classroom teachers. What effects might these influences have on the functioning of the classroom?*

3 *How do parts of the school system relate to the environment? Give several examples (e.g., influence of home environment on students; teachers' unions).*

In a strict sense the central administration of a school system represents the immediate external environment of schools within the system: the hierarchy of general policy-makers and supervisors éxtending between the levels of system superintendent and school principal. Fundamental decisions about the allocation of the budget, hiring policies, building plans, negotiations with a variety of trade unions (including those of teachers), contractual arrangements with suppliers, political relationships with the relevant units of municipal, state and federal government, codes governing internal operations, relationships with organized and unorganized community groups, and general educational policy making all fall within the jurisdiction of the system-wide administration. Except in the smallest school systems, members of the top administrative echelon have little *direct* contact with teachers and little *direct* influence on the style and content of their daily work activities. School system administrators, like the managers of other kinds of large-scale organizations, in other words, concern themselves primarily with matters pertaining to the acquisition of resources, their internal allocation, and the setting of general

From *Second Handbook of Research on Teaching,* edited by M. W. Travers (Chicago: Rand-McNally, 1973), pp. 451–453. Copyright 1973 by the American Educational Research Association, Washington, D. C.

lines of policy, but not with the day-to-day direction of the activities of workers (Parsons, 1963, pp. 59–96).

That the conduct of central office administrators does not directly influence the daily activities of teachers does not mean that administrative action has no effect on their work; quite the contrary is true. To the extent, for example, that significant portions of the budget are allocated to hiring more teachers to reduce class size, for providing special ancillary services, for modernizing buildings, and the like, the teachers' working conditions can be made more palatable. Similarly indirect is the nature of the relationships that school administrations strike with organized parents and political groups (Rogers, 1968) whose support, indifference or hostility can determine whether particular schools will be viable or strife-torn institutions: whether teaching and learning activities can occur, or whether chaos and hostility will prevail.

It is only in a narrow range of areas—not trivial ones by any means— that the direct impact of administrative action can be traced in the work of teachers: in matters pertaining to remuneration, to the selection and purchase of books and materials, to the assignment of pupils to classrooms and to the inclusion of particular courses in the curriculum. (This, of course, is an illustrative, not an exhaustive, list.)

That school systems are bureaucratically organized in many respects (Weber, 1947, pp. 329–333) is unmistakable; but it would be a gross distortion to regard school systems (and particularly schools) as bureaucratic in the same way, for example, that certain government agencies, certain parts of the military, and certain commercial and industrial organizations in which workers are ranked hierarchically to facilitate the "rational" accomplishment of routine and repetitive tasks for the production of tangible, measurable goods and services are considered bureaucratic. Certainly schools and school systems are bureaucratically organized in many important respects: they are hierarchical and governed by rules; workers are appointed to "offices" (or positions) according to criteria of merit, and the sequence of positions that workers occupy can constitute a career (actually several different careers). But the work of teachers can be properly understood only if the nonbureaucratic elements of schools are also identified. Among the most important of these nonbureaucratic elements is the teacher's immediate work site—the classroom, a setting subject to administrative direction (at least within the school hierarchy and under the authority of the principal) and yet significantly independent of such direction (Bidwell, 1965, pp. 1014–1016).

The term *nonbureaucratic* is residual and therefore cannot as such denote specific aspects of the external environment having consequences for the work of teachers. Accordingly, it is important to identify some of those aspects. First, the school system hierarchy does not serve as a direct transmission line for the communication of policy decisions designed to influence teachers' classroom activities or for the close supervision of those activities to gauge the accomplishment of school system goals, even though a school system can be viewed as an arrangement of hierarchical positions. This is not to deny that some policy decisions pass down the line, nor to deny that supervision occurs. Rather, the statement indicates that the central *classroom* activities of teachers—instruction and classroom management—are not *primarily* determined by high level policy decisions; they cannot be viewed as "following orders," and the reasons are not hard to find. The educational goals of school systems tend to be vaguely defined and refer to present and future outcomes that defy easy measurement and specification into readily identifiable goal-directed activities. Much of the teacher's work, in short, derives its character from the exigencies of classroom, school and community events (Jackson, 1968), not from administrative directives.

Second, teaching activities tend not to be defined in terms of conformity to system-wide rules (though clearly certain types of teacher conduct have their origins in rules, e.g., taking attendance, monitoring students in public gatherings and the like). The reasons for the relative absence of rule domination are similar to those described above: activities difficult to codify in terms of sequences of means and ends are also difficult to subsume under general rules. That is, where work situations contain many unknowns and unpredictable exigencies, and where work entails significant loyalties to the needs of clients, work activities will be governed to a substantial degree according to the judgment of workers under the constraints of immediate situational demands (Gouldner, 1954, pp. 105–180; Perrow, 1970, pp. 75–89; Stinchcombe, 1959).

Third, the "quality control" function, to use a term with industrial overtones, tends to be highly attenuated in school systems. If, in fact, it is difficult to define educational goals, and to design a "technology" to effect them, then the meaning of the supervisory rating of workers becomes difficult to interpret and not terribly instructive as far as the overall management of a school system is concerned. Thus, although the rhetoric of supervision has great currency in the vocabulary of school administrators, the practice of supervision and the definition of what it entails continue to be ill defined (Dreeben, 1970, pp. 42–50). In sum, the facts that the administrative hierarchy does not serve primarily as a "line" for transmitting and effecting policy decisions, the relative unimportance of administrative rules for the classroom activities of teachers, and the attenuated nature of supervision constitute the more important nonbureaucratic elements that affect teaching.

One should not conclude from these assertions that teachers are essentially autonomous workers whose dealings with administrators are minimal and whose work is largely free of the conflicts usually engendered by hierarchical arrangements. Conflicts between teachers and administrators are legion and arise over such issues as the participation of teachers in the governance of schools and school systems, academic freedom, disciplinary policies, teacher ratings, closeness of supervision, red tape, the assignment of pupils and many more (Corwin, 1970, pp. 105–171). While the fact remains that the character of teachers' work in the classroom is not mainly determined through a bureaucratic apparatus, conflicts with the administration develop to a large extent from the ambiguous position of teaching as an occupation—it is not an autonomous profession nor is it a bureaucratized occupation; the prevailing conflicts frequently develop between the vaguely defined jurisdictional lines separating teachers and administrators.

The administrative hierarchy of a school system is not the totality of the teacher's external environment. It is perfectly obvious that in the American educational system, whose primary political units are states, municipalities, and other local units of government, the characteristics of communities and the problems they engender are likely to affect the work of teachers directly. Moreover, the recent growth of teachers' unions and the continuing activity of the National Education Association (NEA) more than likely influence teachers' work activities. The difficulty with the general proposition that the characteristics of the surrounding environment affect the work of teachers is that very little systematic knowledge is available about the nature of community influence. Suggestive, though hardly systematic, evidence exists that some teachers have difficulty managing the disciplinary problems that arise in schools serving working class populations (Becker, 1952), though comparatively less has been said about disciplinary problems in middle-class schools. More important for this discussion, however, is the fact that classroom difficulties that supposedly originate in communities have been studied more in terms of teacher job satisfaction and propensity to transfer than in terms of work activities designed to cope with classroom problems. An important exception to this statement, however, is Kounin's work on disciplinary strategies (Kounin, 1970).

In recent years a great deal has been written, much of it in the public prints, union newspapers, and in books about education directed toward popular audiences, illustrating the problems posed by children from disadvantaged backgrounds and the frustrations experienced by the teachers of these children; but we are not yet able to disentangle the relative contributions of the children, the teachers, and the process of schooling itself to the creation of these problems nor to the ways in which teachers cope with them. In fact, strategies for coping with classroom problems have yet to be characterized in terms of general formulations of teachers' work.

The advent of teachers' unions (accompanied somewhat later and more slowly by the increasingly aggressive and militant action of the NEA) has led to changes in the economic circumstances of teachers and in their working conditions: the reduction of class size, the introduction of para- professionals, the release of teachers from onerous clerical obligations, and the introduction of grievance procedures have been some of the main areas of concern. And though it is not too much to surmise that the lot of teachers has improved—particularly economically—it is not yet possible to ascertain what impact these changes have had on the *character* of teach- ers' work: whether reductions in class size, for example, are related to changes in instructional and disciplinary strategies, to the reduction or change of characteristic classroom problems, to changes in work satisfac- tion; whether the introduction of paraprofessionals has in fact relieved teachers from tasks readily assumed by less skilled workers (and to what effect); or whether new patterns of classroom conduct have appeared among teachers and pupils with more than one adult present in classrooms at the same time. . . . On the other hand, schools appear to be among the most conservative and unbending of institutions, maintaining traditional ways of doing things in the face of intense pressures to change. Both contentions have important elements of truth, but no one can yet identify the conditions under which they are true.

REFERENCES

Becker, H. S. The career of the Chicago public schoolteacher. *American Journal of Sociology,* 1952, 57(5), 470–477.

Bidwell, C. E. The school as a formal organization. In J. G. March (Ed.), *Handbook of orga- nizations.* Chicago: Rand McNally, 1965, pp. 972–1022.

Corwin, R. G. *Militant professionalism.* New York: Appleton-Century-Crofts, 1970.

Dreeben, R. *The nature of teaching.* Glenview, Ill.: Scott, Foresman, 1970.

Gouldner, A. W. *Patterns of industrial bureaucracy.* Glencoe, Ill.: Free Press, 1954.

Kounin, J. *Discipline and group management in classrooms.* New York: Holt, Rinehart & Winston, 1970.

Parsons, T. *Structure and process in modern societies.* Glencoe, Ill.: Free Press, 1963.

Perrow, C. *Organizational analysis: A sociological view.* London: Tavistock Press, 1970.

Rogers, D. *110 Livingston Street.* New York: Random House, 1968.

Stinchcombe, A. L. Bureaucratic and craft administration of production: A comparative study. *Administrative Science Quarterly,* 1959, 4(2), 168–187.

Weber, M. *The theory of social and economic organization.* Translated by A. M. Henderson, & T. Parsons. Glencoe, Ill.: Free Press, 1947.

GEORGE H. GALLUP

Gallup Poll of the Public's Attitudes Toward the Public Schools

Questions to think about

1 *What are the major concerns of the public about schools? How does your ranking compare with the poll findings?*
2 *What effects might public attitudes have on schools?*
3 *Within the open systems model, do public attitudes fall into the immediate or secondary environment, or both? Explain.*
4 *What is the overall "grade" given schools in the 1983 Gallup poll? How does your grade compare? How do these grades differ by sex, by parents, and by nonparents?*

PURPOSE OF THE STUDY

This survey, which measures the attitudes of Americans toward their public schools, is the 15th annual survey in this series. Funding for this survey was provided by Phi Delta Kappa, Inc. Each year the poll attempts to deal with issues of greatest concern both to educators and to the public. New as well as trend questions are included in this and every survey.

To be sure that the survey would embrace the most important issues in the field of education, Phi Delta Kappa organized a meeting of various

Reprinted from George H. Gallup, "The 15th Annual Gallup Poll of the Public's Attitudes Toward the Public Schools," *Phi Delta Kappan* 65 (September 1983):33–47. Copyright © 1983 by Phi Delta Kappa, Inc.

leaders in the field of education to discuss their ideas, evaluate proposed questions, and suggest new questions for the survey.

We wish to thank all those who contributed their ideas to this survey.

RESEARCH PROCEDURE

The Sample. The sample used in this survey embraced a total of 1,540 adults (18 years of age and older). It is described as a modified probability sample of the United States. Personal, in-home interviewing was conducted in all areas of the U.S. and in all types of communities. A description of the sample can be found at the end of this report.

Time of Interviewing. The fieldwork for this study was carried out during the period of 13–22 May 1983.

The Report. In the tables that follow, the heading "Nonpublic School Parents" includes parents of students who attend parochial schools and parents of students who attend private or independent schools.

Due allowance must be made for statistical variation, especially in the case of findings for small groups in which relatively few respondents were interviewed, e.g., nonpublic school parents.

The findings of this report apply only to the U.S. as a whole and not to individual communities. Local surveys, using the same questions, can be conducted to determine how local areas compare with the national norm.

IMPACT OF THE REPORT OF THE PRESIDENT'S COMMISSION ON EXCELLENCE IN EDUCATION

This year's survey was conducted shortly after the report of the National Commission on Excellence in Education was released. Thus it was possible to obtain some indication of the initial reaction of the public to the report.

The survey results reflect only the first reactions of the public, however. The debate over the Commission's findings is sure to continue and may become part of the campaign rhetoric in the 1984 Presidential race.

At the time this survey was conducted, the Commission report was only two weeks old. At that time only 28% of those interviewed in the national sample had heard or read about the report. Of those, 79% could cite some of the facts and conclusions of the report. In short, at the time of the survey, the report had reached an audience of approximately one person in five in the U.S. adult population.

Examination of the survey results indicates that the Commission report had not substantially changed the views of the public about public edu-

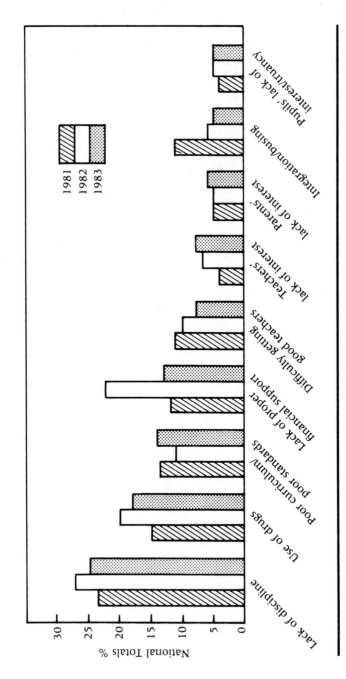

FIGURE 1
Major Problems Confronting the Public Schools, 1981, 1982, 1983

cation. One reason, perhaps, is that the public already agreed with many of the Commission's main conclusions.

The survey results that follow will point out how the views of those familiar with the report differ from the views of other groups in those instances in which the Commission report deals with issues covered in this survey.

MAJOR PROBLEMS CONFRONTING THE PUBLIC SCHOOLS IN 1983

When respondents in this year's survey were asked to name the biggest problems facing their local public schools, the answers were quite similar to those recorded in earlier surveys. The top four problems cited continue to be "discipline," "use of drugs," "poor curriculum/poor standards," and "lack of proper financial support." Parents who have children now attending public schools cite the same four problems and in the same order as the public at large.

Although discipline continues to be regarded as the number one problem, the frequency with which other problems or concerns have been recorded has changed. For example, "integration/busing" and "lack of proper facilities" were named frequently in earlier surveys; they are now far down the list of major concerns.

Because discipline is so frequently cited as a major problem in the public schools, this year's survey has sought to shed further light on underlying causes that may contribute to the perceived lack of discipline. These will be described later in this report.

Here is the question:

What do you think are the biggest problems with which the *public* schools in this community must deal?

	National totals %	No children in school %	Public school parents %	Nonpublic school parents %
Lack of discipline	25	23	29	31
Use of drugs	18	17	20	16
Poor curriculum/poor standards	14	14	14	19
Lack of proper financial support	13	12	17	8

(Figures add to more than 100% because of multiple answers.)

continued

Table continued

	National totals %	No children in school %	Public school parents %	Nonpublic school parents %
Difficulty getting good teachers	8	8	9	7
Teachers' lack of interest	8	9	6	9
Parents' lack of interest	6	6	9	5
Integration/busing	5	6	8	4
Pupils' lack of interest/truancy	5	6	4	1
Moral standards	4	4	4	6
Drinking/alcoholism	3	3	4	5
Large schools/overcrowding	3	2	5	6
Lack of respect for teachers/ other students	3	3	2	6
Mismanagement of funds	2	2	1	1
Problems with administration	1	2	1	—
Crime/vandalism	1	1	1	—
Teachers' strikes	1	1	1	6
Communication problems	1	1	2	1
Lack of proper facilities	1	1	1	3
Parental involvement with school activities	1	1	1	1
Lack of needed teachers	1	1	2	1
Fighting	1	1	*	1
Non-English-speaking students	1	1	1	—
Government interference	1	1	*	1
There are no problems	1	1	3	1
Miscellaneous	2	2	3	3
Don't know/no answer	16	19	7	15

*Less than one-half of 1%.

1983 RATING OF THE PUBLIC SCHOOLS

The public's rating of the local public schools in 1983 follows the downward trend reported in the years since 1974, when this question was instituted. In 1974, 48% gave local public schools a rating of A or B. This year, the comparable figure is 31%. (The 1974 ratings were: A, 18%; B, 30%; C, 21%; D, 6%; FAIL, 5%; and Don't know, 20%.)

More significant, perhaps, is the rating given their local public schools by parents with children attending public schools. In 1974, 64% of the parents gave the schools their children attended an A or B rating. This year, the comparable figure is 42%.

The question:

Students are often given the grades A, B, C, D, and FAIL to denote the quality of their work. Suppose the *public* schools themselves, in this community, were graded in the same way. What grade would you give the public schools here—A, B, C, D, or FAIL?

Ratings given the local public schools	National totals								
	1983 %	1982 %	1981 %	1980 %	1979 %	1978 %	1977 %	1976 %	1975 %
A rating	6	8	9	10	8	9	11	13	13
B rating	25	29	27	25	26	27	26	29	30
C rating	32	33	34	29	30	30	28	28	28
D rating	13	14	13	12	11	11	11	10	9
FAIL	7	5	7	6	7	8	5	6	7
Don't know	17	11	10	18	18	15	19	14	13

	Rating of the local public schools					
	A %	B %	C %	D %	FAIL %	Don't know %
By adults with:						
Children in public schools	11	31	36	10	7	5
Children in nonpublic schools	5	22	24	23	9	17
No children in school	5	23	31	13	6	22

Further breakdowns:

	Rating of the local public schools					
	A %	B %	C %	D %	FAIL %	Don't know %
National Totals	6	25	32	13	7	17
Sex						
Men	7	26	33	13	7	14
Women	6	24	31	14	6	19
Race						
White	7	26	33	12	6	16
Nonwhite	4	16	29	19	9	23
Age						
18–29 years	3	24	40	18	6	9
30–49 years	7	26	34	14	8	11
50 and over	9	24	24	9	5	29

continued

Table continued

	Rating of the local public schools					
	A %	B %	C %	D %	FAIL %	Don't know %
Community Size						
1 million and over	5	20	36	15	7	17
500,000–999,999	10	20	29	17	6	18
50,000–499,999	7	25	30	15	8	15
2,500–49,999	8	29	34	6	5	18
Under 2,500	5	27	32	12	6	18
Central city	5	20	32	16	10	17
Education						
Grade school	6	28	16	5	7	38
High school	8	21	36	14	7	14
College	5	28	33	15	6	13
Region						
East	7	24	30	13	8	18
Midwest	9	27	34	11	5	14
South	7	25	30	12	6	20
West	2	21	36	18	8	15

WHY IS THERE A DISCIPLINE PROBLEM?

The problem of discipline continues to loom large in the public's mind. Thus, this year we attempted to find out who or what is chiefly to blame for the lack of discipline that the public says is a major problem in the local public schools. A card listing 11 reasons for a lack of discipline was handed to each respondent included in the survey.

The question:

Many people say that discipline is one of the major problems of the public schools today. Would you please look over this list and tell me which reasons you think are most important to explain why there is a discipline problem?

Those identified with the public schools can take comfort from the fact that the chief blame is laid on the home, with disrespect for law and order throughout society ranking second in frequency of mention.

The percentage of votes given each of the 11 statements are as follows, listed according to frequency of mention:

1. Lack of discipline in the home (72%)
2. Lack of respect for law and authority throughout society (54%)

3. Students who are constant troublemakers often can't be removed from school (42%)
4. Some teachers are not properly trained to deal with discipline problems (42%)
5. The courts have made school administrators so cautious that they don't deal severely with students misbehavior (41%)
6. Viewing television programs that emphasize crime and violence (39%)
7. Punishment is too lenient (39%)
8. Decline in the teaching of good manners (37%)
9. Teachers themselves do not command respect (36%)
10. Failure on the part of teachers to make classroom work more interesting (31%)
11. One-parent families (26%)

VOTING ON TAX INCREASES

Although only a minority of the respondents (39%) say that they would vote to raise school taxes at this time, the report of the National Commission may help persuade more citizens to favor a tax increase. Those familiar with the report favor raising taxes by a margin of 48% to 46%.

The question:

Suppose the local public schools said they needed much more money. As you feel at this time, would you vote to raise taxes for this purpose, or would you vote against raising taxes for this purpose?

| | Financial support of the public schools | | |
National Results	Favor raising taxes %	Opposed to raising taxes %	Don't know %
1983 survey	39	52	9
1981 survey	30	60	10
1972 survey	36	56	8
1971 survey	40	52	8
1970 survey	37	56	7
1969 survey	45	49	6
1983 Survey			
Parents of children attending public school	48	45	7

continued

Table continued

	Financial support of the public schools		
1983 Survey	Favor raising taxes %	Opposed to raising taxes %	Don't know %
Parents of children attending nonpublic school	40	55	5
Adults with no children in school	36	53	11

Further breakdowns:

	Favor raising taxes %	Opposed to raising taxes %	Don't know %
National Totals	39	52	9
Sex			
Men	40	51	9
Women	37	53	10
Race			
White	37	54	9
Nonwhite	50	40	10
Age			
18–29 years	46	44	10
30–49 years	44	48	8
50 and over	28	62	10
Community Size			
1 million and over	38	51	11
500,000–999,999	50	42	8
50,000–499,999	44	48	8
2,500–49,999	31	59	10
Under 2,500	33	57	10
Central city	44	48	8
Education			
Grade school	24	70	6
High school	35	55	10
College	49	41	10

	Favor raising taxes %	Opposed to raising taxes %	Don't know %
Region			
East	31	60	9
Midwest	35	57	8
South	40	48	12
West	53	39	8

THE VOUCHER SYSTEM

The idea of the voucher system—a plan whereby the federal government allots a certain amount of money for the education of each child, regardless of whether the child attends a public, parochial, or independent school—is favored today by a clear majority of the public (51% to 38%). Significantly, public school parents favor the voucher system by a margin of 48% to 41%.

The current support for the voucher system represents a substantial shift in the public's attitude. Between 1970 (when the question was first asked) and 1981, the idea elicited a mixed reception. In 1970 a slightly higher percentage opposed the idea than favored it. This was also true in 1971. In the 1981 survey those in favor held a slight majority over those opposed.

The question:

> In some nations, the government allots a certain amount of money for each child for his or her education. The parents can then send the child to any public, parochial, or private school they choose. This is called the "voucher system." Would you like to see such an idea adopted in this country?

	National totals %	No children in school %	Public school parents %	Nonpublic school parents %
Favor voucher system	51	51	48	64
Oppose voucher system	38	37	41	30
No opinion	11	12	11	6

continued

Table continued

National Totals	Favor %	Oppose %	No opinion %
1970 survey	43	46	11
1971 survey	38	44	18
1981 survey	43	41	16
1983 survey	51	38	11

PROMOTION BASED ON EXAMINATIONS

Promotion from grade to grade based on examinations and not "social" promotion is favored by a substantial majority of the survey respondents. This view is shared by parents of schoolchildren and by those who have no children in school—and by almost the same percentages.

The question:

In your opinion, should children be promoted from grade to grade only if they can pass examinations?

	National totals %	No children in school %	Public school parents %	Nonpublic school parents %
Yes	75	75	73	71
No	20	19	23	27
Don't know	5	6	4	2

National Totals	1983 %	1978 %
Yes	75	68
No	20	27
Don't know	5	5

NATIONAL TEST SCORES USED FOR COMPARISON PURPOSES

The results of the question about the use of national tests as a way of judging the local schools reveals the public's faith in tests and, at the same time, the public's desire to have another measure of the quality of education in their own local schools.

One important provision should be added, however. Earlier survey reports have pointed out that comparisons should take full account of the composition of the school population. Comparisons are only valid if the local school population reflects the national population. Schools that draw students from poor neighborhoods where parents have had little education and where language barriers exist obviously cannot be expected to achieve the same levels of test scores as schools in high-income communities.

The question:

Would you like to see the students in the local schools be given national tests, so that their educational achievement could be compared with students in other communities?

	National totals %	No children in school %	Public school parents %	Nonpublic school parents %
Yes	75	72	80	79
No	17	17	16	18
Don't know	8	11	4	3

National Totals	1983 %	1971 %	1970 %
Yes	75	70	75
No	17	21	16
Don't know	8	9	9

TOO MUCH OR TOO LITTLE SCHOOLWORK FOR STUDENTS?

Are students in elementary schools or high schools made to work too hard? Widespread agreement exists on this issue among parents of schoolchildren and those without children in the public schools.

Two-thirds of all respondents, in both the case of elementary school children and of high school students, agree that the workload given students is too light. An earlier survey of students found that students themselves say that they are not given enough homework.

A significant change has been recorded since the 1975 survey when the same questions were asked of the public. At that time 49% said that students in elementary school were not required to work hard enough. In this year's survey the percentage has increased to 61%. In 1975, 54% said that high school students were not required to work hard enough; now that percentage is 65%.

The 1983 survey includes another question related to this issue. When respondents were asked if they thought that what is now covered in the first two years of college could be covered before graduation from high school, a total of 65% predicted that this would happen by the year 2000.
The question:

In general, do you think *elementary* school children in the public schools here are made to work too hard in school and on homework, or not hard enough?

	National totals %	No children in school %	Public school parents %	Nonpublic school parents %
Too hard	4	3	6	4
Not hard enough	61	62	60	70
About right amount	19	15	27	16
Don't know	16	20	7	10

National Totals	1983 %	1975 %
Too hard	4	5
Not hard enough	61	49
About right amount	19	28
Don't know	16	18

Further breakdowns:

	Too hard %	Not hard enough %	About right amount %	Don't know %
National Totals	4	61	19	16
Sex				
Men	3	64	17	16
Women	5	58	20	17
Race				
White	4	60	19	17
Nonwhite	4	71	12	13
Age				
18–29 years	6	61	22	11
30–49 years	4	62	21	13
50 and over	3	60	14	23

	Too Hard %	Not hard enough %	About right amount %	Don't know %
Community Size				
1 million and over	2	65	20	13
500,000–999,999	4	68	14	14
50,000–499,999	2	66	16	16
2,500–49,999	6	54	19	21
Under 2,500	7	54	22	17
Central city	1	66	16	17
Education				
Grade school	6	49	17	28
High school	5	59	22	14
College	2	69	15	14
Region				
East	3	60	22	15
Midwest	6	64	16	14
South	3	52	22	23
West	4	72	12	12

The question:

What about students in the public high school here—in general, are they required to work too hard or not hard enough?

	National totals %	No children in school %	Public school parents %	Nonpublic school parents %
Too hard	3	3	4	—
Not hard enough	65	66	63	69
About right amount	12	11	14	9
Don't know	20	20	19	22

National Totals	1983 %	1975 %
Too hard	3	3
Not hard enough	65	54
About right amount	12	22
Don't know	20	21

Further breakdowns:

	Too hard %	Not hard enough %	About right amount %	Don't know %
National Totals	3	65	12	20
Sex				
Men	2	69	11	18
Women	3	63	13	21
Race				
White	3	65	12	20
Nonwhite	3	71	8	18
Age				
18–29 years	6	67	15	12
30–49 years	3	65	11	21
50 and over	1	66	10	23
Community Size				
1 million and over	1	70	14	15
500,000–999,999	2	71	9	18
50,000–499,999	3	67	12	18
2,500–49,999	5	60	11	24
Under 2,500	4	60	13	23
Central city	2	69	11	18
Education				
Grade school	2	55	13	30
High school	4	64	13	19
College	1	71	11	17
Region				
East	3	65	14	18
Midwest	3	68	11	18
South	3	55	15	27
West	3	77	6	14

INCREASING THE LENGTH OF THE SCHOOL YEAR

Although more individuals oppose than approve increasing the length of the school year in their communities by one month, more respondents favor a 10-month school year in this year's survey than in last year's. Moreover, those who were familiar with the report of the National Commission on Excellence in Education are strongly in favor of such a change.

More of those parents with children in nonpublic schools approve than disapprove of extending the school year. Individuals who have no children attending school show the least enthusiasm for increasing the school year from the present 180 days.

The question:

> In some nations, students attend school as many as 240 days a year as compared to about 180 days in the U.S. How do you feel about extending the public school year in this community by 30 days, making the school year about 210 days or 10 months long? Do you favor or oppose this idea?

	National totals %	No children in school %	Public school parents %	Nonpublic school parents %
Favor	40	39	43	50
Oppose	49	47	52	44
Don't know	11	14	5	6

National Totals	1983 %	1982 %
Favor	40	37
Oppose	49	53
Don't know	11	10

Further breakdowns:

	Favor %	Oppose %	Don't know %
National Totals	40	49	11
Sex			
Men	40	48	12
Women	41	49	10
Race			
White	39	50	11
Nonwhite	51	35	14
Age			
18–29 years	37	55	8
30–49 years	40	52	8
50 and over	42	41	17

continued

Table continued

	Favor %	Oppose %	Don't know %
Community Size			
1 million and over	52	37	11
500,000–999,999	45	44	11
50,000–499,999	47	44	9
2,500–49,999	31	56	13
Under 2,500	28	59	13
Central city	50	38	12
Education			
Grade school	32	45	23
High school	36	53	11
College	50	43	7
Region			
East	41	49	10
Midwest	36	52	12
South	35	50	15
West	54	38	8

SATISFACTION OF PARENTS WITH SUBJECTS TAUGHT

Parents who are sending their children to nonpublic schools are more satisfied with the learning that takes place there—and with the general curriculum—than are parents who are sending their children to the public schools. The difference is not great, however, and a high degree of satisfaction is found among both groups. Both groups have registered some decline in satisfaction with the general curriculum since 1973.

The question:

Do you think your child is learning the things you believe he or she should be learning?

	Public school parents %	Nonpublic school parents %
Yes	74	82
No	20	9
Don't know	6	9

	Public school parents	
	1983 %	1973 %
Yes	74	81
No	20	14
Don't know	6	5

SUBJECTS THE PUBLIC WOULD REQUIRE IN HIGH SCHOOL

A majority of the American public would require high school courses in mathematics and English, regardless of whether students plan to continue their education in college or to get jobs following graduation. For those students who plan to go on to college, the public would require courses in history/U.S. government, science, business, and foreign language. For those who plan to end their education with high school, the public would require vocational training, business, history/U.S. government, and science.

Those respondents who would require a foreign language were asked, Which foreign language(s)? The preferred language, by a large margin, is Spanish, followed by French and German, in that order. A surprising number of parents with children in school (12%) would require that the Russian language be taught.

The question:

Would you look over this card which lists high school subjects. If you were the one to decide, what subjects would you require every public high school student who *plans to go on to college* to take?

	1983 %	1981 %
Mathematics	92	94
English	88	91
History/U.S. government	78	83
Science	76	76
Business	55	60
Foreign language	50	54
Health education	43	47
Physical education	41	44
Vocational training	32	34
Art	19	28
Music	18	26

(Figures add to more than 100% because of multiple responses.)

The question:

What about those public high school students who do *not plan to go to college* when they graduate? Which courses would you require them to take?

	1983 %	1981 %
Mathematics	87	91
English	83	89
Vocational training	74	64
Business	65	75
History/U.S. government	63	71
Science	53	58
Health education	42	46
Physical education	40	43
Foreign language	19	21
Art	16	20
Music	16	20

(Figures add to more than 100% because of multiple responses.)

The question (asked of those who would require foreign language for high school graduates):

What foreign language or languages should be required?

	National totals %	No children in school %	Public school parents %	Nonpublic school parents %
Spanish	56	58	54	44
French	34	35	32	34
German	16	16	14	20
Latin	8	6	11	12
Russian	8	7	12	7
Japanese	6	6	5	7
Other	4	4	5	10
Don't Know	24	23	21	30

(Figures add to more than 100% because of multiple responses.)

INSTRUCTION IN SPECIAL AREAS

In addition to traditional school subjects, the public would like the schools to give special instruction in many other fields, presumably because other institutions, including the home, have not been notably successful in dealing with these areas of instruction. This is especially true in the case of education about the abuse of drugs and alcohol.

More than seven in 10 adults would require driver education. A majority would also require instruction in the use of computers, as well as training in parenting.

This year's survey included several additional subject areas; all of these except the dangers of nuclear war were approved by a slight majority.

The question:

In addition to regular courses, high schools offer instruction in other areas. As I read off these areas, one at a time, would you tell me whether you feel this instruction should be required or should not be required for all high school students?

	Should be required %	Should not be required %	No opinion %
Drug abuse	81	14	5
Alcohol abuse	76	18	6
Driver education	72	23	5
Computer training	72	21	7
Parenting/parent training	58	32	10
Dangers of nuclear waste*	56	33	11
Race relations*	56	33	11
Communism/socialism*	51	38	11
Dangers of nuclear war*	46	42	12

*These topics were not included in the 1981 survey.

	Should Be Required	
	1983 %	1981 %
Drug abuse	81	82
Alcohol abuse	76	78
Driver education	72	71
Computer training	72	43
Parenting/parent training	58	64

IMPORTANCE OF A COLLEGE EDUCATION

It will come as good news to college administrators that in the last five years the public has changed markedly in its view about the importance of a college education. Since a question about the importance of a college education was first asked (1978), the percentage of individuals who say that a college education is "very important" has increased from 36% to 58%. Those with children now attending school are even more convinced of the importance of a college education.

The question:

How important is a college education today—very important, fairly important, or not too important?

	National totals %	No children in school %	Public school parents %	Nonpublic school parents %
Very important	58	57	60	60
Fairly important	31	31	32	30
Not too important	8	8	7	6
Don't know	3	4	1	4

National Totals	1983 %	1978 %
Very important	58	36
Fairly important	31	46
Not too important	8	16
Don't know	3	2

Further breakdowns:

	Importance of College			
	Very important %	Fairly important %	Not too important %	Don't know %
National Totals	58	31	8	3
Sex				
Men	57	31	9	3
Women	60	30	7	3

	Importance of College			
	Very important %	Fairly important %	Not too important %	Don't know %
Race				
White	56	32	9	3
Nonwhite	68	24	5	3
Age				
18–29 years	53	34	11	2
30–49 years	60	31	7	2
50 and over	60	28	7	5
Community Size				
1 million and over	64	28	6	2
500,000–999,999	63	26	6	5
50,000–499,999	59	30	8	3
2,500–49,999	54	34	10	2
Under 2,500	52	34	10	4
Central city	64	25	7	4
Education				
Grade school	61	24	9	6
High school	54	33	10	3
College	63	29	5	3
Region				
East	61	29	7	3
Midwest	50	37	10	3
South	63	28	7	2
West	58	28	10	4

TEACHING AS A CAREER

In five surveys, beginning in 1969, respondents have been asked if they would like a child of theirs to take up teaching as a career. This year, substantially more respondents were undecided than in earlier years when the same question was asked. The percentage giving a definite yes answer this year is slightly lower than in 1981 and substantially lower than in 1969, when 75% of all respondents said that they would like a child of theirs to take up teaching in the public schools as a career. The comparable figure today is 45%.

To help explain this marked change, respondents were asked why they would, or would not, like a child of theirs to become a public school teacher.

The answers to this question from those who said no, listed in order of frequency of mention, are: 1) low pay; 2) discipline problems; 3) unrewarding, thankless work; and 4) low prestige of teaching as a profession. Those who said that they would like a child of theirs to enter the teaching profession said that teaching: 1) is a worthwhile profession, 2) contributes to society, 3) is a challenging job, and 4) can make a real difference in a child's life.

The question:

Would you like to have a child of yours take up teaching in the public schools as a career?

		National totals %	No children in school %	Public school parents %	Nonpublic school parents %
Yes		45	42	51	40
No		33	33	33	39
Don't know		22	25	16	21
	1983 %	1981 %	1980 %	1972 %	1969 %
Yes	45	46	48	67	75
No	33	43	40	22	15
Don't know	22	11	12	11	10

PERSONAL QUALITIES MOST DESIRED IN TEACHERS

When respondents were asked in an "open" question about the personal qualities they would look for if they could choose their child's teacher, their responses indicate that they would seek a model of perfection—someone who is understanding, patient, friendly, intelligent, and who has a sense of humor and high moral character. Farther down the list the public would seek out a person who has the ability to motivate and inspire children and possesses enthusiasm for the subject being taught.

The question:

Suppose you could choose your child's teachers. Assuming they had all had about the same experiences and training, what *personal* qualities would you look for?

The qualities respondents named most often, in order of mention:

1. Ability to communicate, to understand, to relate
2. Patience
3. Ability to discipline, to be firm and fair
4. High moral character
5. Friendliness, good personality, sense of humor
6. Dedication to teaching profession, enthusiasm
7. Ability to inspire, motivate students
8. Intelligence
9. Caring about students

MORE PAY FOR MATH AND SCIENCE TEACHERS

The public is evenly divided on the question of giving higher wages to math and science teachers and to those who teach technical and vocational subjects than to teachers of other subjects because of the present shortage of teachers in these fields. When those who have "no opinion" are eliminated, however, more respondents say that they favor paying these teachers higher wages than that they would oppose such a move. Widespread agreement on this question exists among those with children now attending public and nonpublic schools and those who have no children in school.

The question:

Today there is a shortage of teachers in science, math, technical subjects, and vocational subjects. If your local public schools needed teachers in these subjects, would you favor or oppose paying them higher wages than teachers of other subjects?

	National totals %	No children in school %	Public school parents %	Nonpublic school parents %
Favor paying them higher wages	50	50	49	45
Oppose	35	34	41	38
Don't know	15	16	10	17

MERIT PAY FOR TEACHERS

The public votes nearly two-to-one in favor of merit pay for teachers. The percentage favoring merit pay has increased slightly since 1970, when the same question was asked of a similar cross section of U.S. adults. In 1970, 58% of the public favored merit pay and 36% favored a standard scale. Today, the comparable percentages are 61% and 31%.

Parents of schoolchildren favor merit pay by almost the same margin as the general public. Those who were familiar with the report of the President's Commission are more strongly in favor of merit pay, voting 71% to 25% in favor of it.

The question:

Should each teacher be paid on the basis of the quality of his or her work, or should all teachers be paid on a standard-scale basis?

	National totals %	No children in school %	Public school parents %	Nonpublic school parents %
Quality of work	61	61	61	64
Standard scale	31	30	34	30
Don't know	8	9	5	6

National Totals	1983 %	1970 %
Quality of work	61	58
Standard scale	31	36
Don't know	8	6

EARLY REACTIONS TO THE REPORT OF THE PRESIDENT'S COMMISSION ON EXCELLENCE IN EDUCATION

Only 28% of the respondents included in this year's survey had heard or read about the report of the National Commission on Excellence in Education at the time of this survey. Those who said that they had heard or read about it were asked to state the overall findings of the report, as evidence that they had given it some attention. This "informed" group was then asked, if, in general, they agreed or disagreed with the conclusions of the report. Among this informed group, nearly nine in 10 agreed with the findings of the Commission.

To obtain some indication of whether those who had *not* read the report would agree with its conclusions, they were asked whether they agreed or disagreed with the finding that "the quality of education in the U.S. public schools is only fair and not improving." This group, as in the case of the informed group, expressed overwhelming agreement with the conclusion.

The question:

Have you heard or read anything about the recent report of the President's National Commission on Excellence in Education?

	National totals %	No children in school %	Public school parents %	Nonpublic school parents %
Yes	28	27	31	29
No	68	69	65	69
Don't know	4	4	4	2

The question (informed group *only*):

In general, do you agree or disagree with the report's conclusions?

	National totals %	No children in school %	Public school parents %	Nonpublic school parents %
Agree	87	87	84	90
Disagree	8	8	9	10
Don't know	5	5	7	—

The question (uninformed group *only*):

The Commission concluded that the quality of education in the U.S. public schools is only fair and not improving. Do you agree with this opinion or disagree?

	National totals %	No children in school %	Public school parents %	Nonpublic school parents %
Agree	74	74	77	77
Disagree	13	12	15	10
No opinion	13	14	8	13

LOOKING AHEAD TO THE YEAR 2000:
CHANGES THAT THE PUBLIC FORESEES
IN THE EDUCATIONAL SYSTEM

Many suggestions for improving the educational system were presented to respondents to determine what chance they think these suggestions have of being carried out between now and the year 2000.

Those respondents who were familiar with the report of the President's Commission differ little in their views from those who now have children attending the public and nonpublic schools.

The question:

As you look ahead to the year 2000 (that's 17 years from now), what do you think the schools will be doing then to educate students?

	National totals %	No children in school %	Public school parents %	Nonpublic school parents %
Do you think that all students will have access to a computer and be trained in its use?				
Yes	86	84	92	90
No	6	6	5	7
Don't know	8	10	3	3
Do you think that more importance will be given to vocational training in high school?				
Yes	76	76	77	69
No	11	11	13	19
Don't know	13	13	10	12
Do you think that more attention will be given to teaching students how to think?				
Yes	70	68	73	72
No	16	16	17	15
Don't know	14	16	10	13

	National totals %	No children in school %	Public school parents %	Nonpublic school parents %
Do you think that what is now covered in the first two years of college will be covered before graduation from high school?				
Yes	65	62	71	67
No	19	20	19	23
Don't know	16	18	10	10
Do you think that more attention will be given to individual instruction?				
Yes	53	53	51	59
No	32	31	37	28
Don't know	15	16	12	13
Do you think children will start school at an earlier age—such as 3 or 4 years old?				
Yes	51	49	52	55
No	37	37	38	37
Don't know	12	14	10	8
Do you think that taxpayers will be willing to vote more favorably on bond issues and give more financial support to the schools?				
Yes	45	44	47	49
No	36	35	37	38
Don't know	19	21	16	13
Do you think that the school program will cover 12 months of the year—with less time for holidays?				
Yes	33	30	38	40
No	53	53	54	53
Don't know	14	17	8	7

COMPOSITION OF THE SAMPLE

Analysis of Respondents

Adults	%	Political affiliation	%
No children in schools	68	Republican	24
Public school parents	27*	Democrat	41
Nonpublic school parents	6*	Independent	30
		Other	5

*Total for both starred categories exceeds 32% because some parents have children attending more than one kind of school.

Sex	%	Income	%
		$40,000 and over	11
		$30,000–$39,999	10
Men	48	$20,000–$29,999	19
Women	52	$10,000–$19,999	30
		$9,999 and under	24
Race	%	Undesignated	6
White	86		
Nonwhite	14	Region	%
		East	28
Religion	%	Midwest	27
Protestant	54	South	27
Catholic	30	West	18
Jewish	3		
Other	13	Community size	%
		1 million and over	20
Age	%	500,000–999,999	13
18–29 years	27	50,000–499,999	26
30–49 years	36	2,500–49,999	14
50 and over	37	Under 2,500	27
Occupation	%	Education	%
Business/professional	26	College	30
Clerical/sales	6	High school	56
Manual labor	38	Grade school	14
Non-labor force	19		
Farm	3		
Undesignated	8		

WYNN DeBEVOISE

Education and Technology: Predicting the Needs of the Future

Questions to think about

1 *What are the effects of technology on various aspects of education, including skills, math, science, and vocational training?*

2 *What is the relationship between technological advances in society and their impact on the schools?*

3 *How is the process of change in the open systems model affected by technological changes in the school's environment?*

4 *What is your opinion of the level of skill needed for economic productivity and human skills needed for future survival? What should education's role be in providing these skills?*

Our perceptions of education seem to be tracing a path similar to that of a pendulum. In times of prosperity and national preeminence, we laud education, broaden our educational offerings, and focus our attention on educational access. During periods of economic distress and national embarrassment, we denigrate our institutions of learning, narrow program options, and concentrate on excellence rather than access.

Because of the current economic decline and the fear that America may be losing its position of technological superiority, much has been written about the need to reshape our educational system to better meet the needs of business and high technology. Representatives of industry,

From *R & D Perspectives* (Fall 1982), a publication of the Center for Educational Policy and Management at the University of Oregon. Reprinted by permission of the author.

government, and schools warn of the inadequate pool of workers skilled enough to contribute to our technological advancement.

Some find the answer to the problem in the increased allocation of resources to vocational education, career education, studies in science and math, work/study programs, or courses in the use of microcomputers. These answers tend to lead down the path of increasing specialization.

Others argue the merits of a liberal course of study that prepares students to adapt to a rapidly changing society by imparting general skills. Those defending a general curriculum envision the mission of education as offering, in the words of Ted Mills, "a taste of human wisdom, an understanding of inner human needs, the meaning of self-worth." In some cases, the humanist perceives education as compensating for the rigor, tedium, and dissatisfaction characterizing many jobs.

In fact, the desires of proponents of a liberal education and those who argue the advantages of an education more relevant to the workplace need not be mutually exclusive. The differentiated needs of students suggest that the curriculum should be both broad and specialized. In reviewing research on the effects of technology on skill requirements, this article attempts to identify those skills needed generally and those that are peculiar to higher level jobs. It then suggests implications for curricular programs based on these needs.

THE EFFECTS OF TECHNOLOGY

Technology is substantially altering our lives, especially through the expanding application of microcomputers to all phases of human activity. It would seem reasonable to conclude, then, that school curricula will inevitably need to accommodate demands for increased knowledge and skills necessary for the design and use of new technology.

Some social scientists, such as Peter Blau, Wilbert Moore, and Wickham Skinner, have argued that new technology increases the differentiation and specialization of labor and affords workers higher levels of responsibility and skill. Concurring with this judgment are certain economists who point out that the differences in wages for skilled and unskilled workers have narrowed with increasing technology, an indication that technological advancement has upgraded unskilled jobs.

Lynn Grover Gisi and Roy Forbes of the Education Commission of the States have recently completed an evaluation of skills needed for our modern society. Based on their study, they have compiled a list of the "basics" that should be mastered by future workers:

- Evaluative and analytical skills
- Critical thinking
- Problem-solving
- Organizational and reference skills
- Synthesis
- Application
- Creativity
- Decision-making (with incomplete information)
- Communication skills (using a variety of modes)

In contrast to the argument that technology raises skill levels, Harry Braverman, Ivar Berg, and others contend that technology may actually lower the skills required in most work. Berg examined the educational requirements for about 4,000 jobs for which educational and training requirements were estimated first in 1957 and then again in 1965. By adjusting these data so that they could be correlated with census reports on the educational achievements of the work force by occupation, he was able to calculate the approximate relationship of educational requirements for jobs to the educational achievements of the American labor force. He concluded that "since 'achievements' appear to have exceeded requirements in most job categories, it cannot be argued helpfully that technological and related changes attending most jobs account for the pattern whereby better-educated personnel are 'required' and utilized by managers."

Braverman argues that, in the capitalist system, managers find it expedient and cost-effective to fragment and routinize jobs over time, irrespective of the skills workers possess. In fact, Braverman finds that the changing conditions of industrial and office work result in a polarization of the skills possessed by managers and those possessed by workers. It is the managers and engineers who gain upgraded skills and are able to manipulate new technology. Meanwhile, at the other end,

> the more science is incorporated into the labor process, the less the worker understands of the process; the more sophisticated an intellectual product the machine becomes, the less control and comprehension of the machine the worker has. In other words, the more the worker needs to know in order to remain a human being at work, the less does he or she know.

Braverman's concern for the worker as human being raises the issue of job satisfaction and self-concept. Training students for the workplace is not simply a matter of matching skills to jobs.

In many cases, technology has transformed skilled workers into intelligent machine tenders. An example of this transformation is afforded by Western Electric Company's manufacturing plant in Allentown, Pennsylvania. According to a report in *Newsweek*, the plant once housed 700 women who manually assembled transistors in old, airy rooms. Today, workers monitor computer consoles in "clean cells that filter out dust and humidity." In the same article, Robert Lund, assistant director of the Center for Policy Alternatives at the Massachusetts Institute of Technology, observed that as a result of installing automated equipment in one firm, "the skills required went down, but the pay went up." In this case, the salary was determined by the need to attract responsible workers to a boring job rather than by the skills required for performing the work.

In examining a more pervasive innovation, three scholars in Great Britain, Erik Arnold, Lynda Birke, and Wendy Faulkner, have defined the ways in which word processing deskills the job of typing:

> Even typing itself involves varied tasks at present: changing paper, typing, arithmetic for text centering, page layout and so on. Word processors deskill typing tasks by means of such facilities as easy correction, automatic text centering and automatic layout. Thus, while still requiring some basic ability to operate a standard keyboard, word processors dispense with the need for layout skills and high levels of keystroke accuracy.

If technology has the effect of making certain jobs less challenging and more tedious, education may have an important role to play apart from the teaching of basic skills. When work is not satisfying, avocational interests assume greater significance. A broader, more adaptive view of life (the result, many argue, of a liberal education) may provide workers in jobs deskilled by technology with the ability to find other meaning in life.

How do we reconcile, then, the two seemingly opposing views of the skills needed for work in the world of high technology? Both perceptions— that technology requires a higher level of skills and that technology deskills many jobs—seem to be at least partially accurate.

Certainly those who are responsible for the design of technological innovations and those who manage the production of goods and services need to understand and be able to control the machines that are daily changing our lives. And even the average worker in the service-producing industries will need skills that may not be currently required, such as the ability to think critically and manipulate data. The skilled or semi-skilled worker in the goods-producing sector, on the other hand, would seem to require fewer of the skills of craftsmanship that characterize the accomplishment of labor-intensive work. Rather, employers expect these workers to have a well-developed sense of responsibility and the inclination to follow very specific instructions in tending the machinery of capital-intensive production processes.

SKILL REQUIREMENTS

The review of the literature for this article revealed over and over that employers, in discussing the needs of modern business and industry, are actually emphasizing the need for basic skills, rather than highly specialized or technical skills. When interviewed by Thomas Toch for *Education Week,* Sol Hurwitz, senior vice president of the Committee for Economic Development (a public-policy organization representing 200 major corporations), spoke of employers' concerns about the preparation of students in schools: "There's a widespread feeling within the business community that the schools have failed to produce students who can communicate, who can listen and think, and who can work with other people." Moreover, a report in *School Business Affairs* on a word-processing program offered at a Milwaukee (Wisconsin) high school indicates that students enrolling in the program lacked basic skills required for word processing, such as the ability to spell and punctuate properly, knowledge of proper sentence construction, and the use of correct grammar.

Additionally, in a recent analysis of the impact of new electronic technology on jobs, Richard Riche suggested that the emphasis now is on formal knowledge, precision, and perceptual attitudes. These skills rely on the ability to read and write on a functional level in order to interpret the operating manuals of complex equipment and to facilitate retraining in new skills.

Generally, then, the skills described by these writers, and echoed by business leaders generally, should be mastered at the secondary level. If, indeed, students are graduating from high schools without these skills, the answer would seem to lie in the restructuring of secondary education. In fact, high schools are already under pressure to raise their standards for student promotion and graduation as colleges nationwide consider stiffening entrance requirements.

At the same time that high schools strengthen their basic curriculum, however, they will also need to ensure that highly specialized and technical courses are available for those who need them. Training in such fields as higher math and science, electronics, and advanced computer programming is essential to the preparation of those seeking to become researchers, designers, and managers of technological systems.

The provision of "elite" classes is perennially at odds with our concept of equity. To prevent the further polarization of skills between workers and managers described by Braverman, careful consideration will have to be given to the question of access to and sequential tracking for these highly specialized classes. In addition, some adjustments will need to be made in the workplace to avoid widespread alienation and dissatisfaction among those in routinized jobs.

SCIENCE AND MATH

Present educational planning attempts to look ahead and evaluate the effects of the computer and other technology on the symbiotic relationship between education and work. Attention has focused on the need for more and better instruction in math and the sciences as a foundation for understanding and using the sophisticated tools of the future. In addition, a smaller, less strident voice is being raised in support of increased foreign language requirements and international studies programs to facilitate two-way communication with a world no longer content to consider English as the only language of diplomacy and commerce. And not least of the needs spawned by the technological revolution is the ability to locate, evaluate, and adapt information to specific purposes. These skills, say many, are imparted through a broad rather than a technical curriculum.

A cursory look at any newspaper or popular magazine today is all that is needed to show that the educational and business establishments and the federal government are concerned about the shortage of graduates in science and math. Of special concern is the need for elementary and secondary teachers trained in these disciplines, particularly in higher math and the physical sciences.

This concern was manifested and given nationwide publicity during the National Academy of Science's National Convocation on Precollege Education in Science and Mathematics held in Washington, D.C., May 12–13, 1982. In his address, which has been quoted repeatedly, Paul Hurd of Stanford University deplored the failure of Americans to appreciate the importance of science and math to economic and cultural progress. He stated that other nations, such as the Soviet Union, East Germany, and Japan, offer specialized instruction in science and math beginning in the fourth grade. Students in those countries spend up to three times as many class hours on the two disciplines as American students.

An analysis of survey results on the knowledge and skills of American 17-year-old students by the National Assessment of Educational Progress (NAEP) reveals some specific weaknesses in the mathematical ability of the nation's youth. According to authors Gisi and Forbes, from 1973 to

1978 students declined in their demonstration of mathematical understanding, their use of mathematical applications, and their ability to complete multistep math problems. In general, the NAEP surveys suggest that "students have acquired very few skills for examining ideas. Many are capable of preliminary interpretations, but few are taught to move on to extended comprehensive and evaluative skills."

The NAEP results and the higher-level thinking skills required by a technological society that is increasingly devoted to the processing of information point inevitably to needed curriculum reforms. Gisi and Forbes argue that "with technological devices pervading everyday lifestyles, students who are not planning a technical career will need an understanding of the basic principles underlying their operations." By the same token, the thinking, evaluative, and comprehension skills needed for future work are not necessarily covered in a technical course of study. Future workers at all levels will need to understand the workings of entire systems, not just of their specific duties. The increasing interdependency of technology and communications demands that workers approach their work with a sense of perspective and avoid giving too much importance to any one set of responsibilities.

These overlapping needs suggest the efficacy of providing a basic core curriculum for all students. The emphasis should be on the interrelated nature of multidisciplinary skills. James O'Toole sees a continued, if not more pressing, need for broadly educated workers:

> The problems most people face at work are complex, interdependent, and above all have to do with working with people cooperatively and ethically. Most of the really tough problems that people encounter at work are not technical—the computer can be made to solve those. Indeed, the toughest questions are not problems at all, if a problem is defined as having a single solution. For there are no solutions to the tough policy and organizational problems of work—there is only a spectrum of alternative responses . . . It is such problems that a broadly educated, truly enculturated worker is best equipped to handle.

A BROAD-BASED CURRICULUM

It is a temptation, in time of crisis or substantial change, to concentrate on one answer to a problem, even in answer to those problems that, according to O'Toole, do not have a solution. Consequently, during the current preoccupation with technology and specialization, it is important to be reminded of those skills found to be productive that are not part of any one discipline.

Gisi and Forbes, O'Toole, Sol Hurwitz, Richard Riche and others previously cited in this paper have reiterated the need for critical thinking skills in workers of the future. Many employers talk in abstract terms about the poor problem-solving capacities of young workers. O'Toole makes an important distinction between problem-solving as we have visualized it in the past and problem-solving as it will be required in the future. He foresees that workers trained in unidimensional problem-solving methods, such as cost-benefit analysis and statistical regression, will become anachronistic as computers take over routine problems treatable by formulaic solutions. Instead of finding tidy answers to recurrent problems, O'Toole envisions future workers facing "intransigent systemic" problems—energy, food availability, unemployment, urban decay—that "cannot be solved by empirical trial and error or reduced to mathematical precision . . . Perhaps it is not problem solving at all that is needed in business, government, and academia, but problem identification and definition."

An important attribute identified with a broad education is the ability to adapt to change. Often, the narrowly trained specialist finds such adjustments more difficult than does the more generally trained worker. O'Toole reports,

> Significantly it is starting to dawn on corporate leaders that they need broadly and liberally educated employees. In the last two decades, corporate recruiters and personnel managers have been hiring narrowly trained specialists to fill lower-level openings. While these new hires meet the immediate needs of a firm, as time goes along it becomes clear that they are not promotable. Thus American corporations now are being forced to spend hundreds of millions of dollars on employee education in a not terribly successful effort to prepare lower- and middle-level employees to assume greater responsibility.

Industrialist William Agee has also articulated the need for a wide range of abilities to function competently in the business world. In an address to a national meeting of business educators, he remarked, "I would hope that you are working hard at producing more than a student of business. Clearly, managers of the eighties must be political animals . . . The business of business today is the whole sociopolitical economy."

THE ROLE OF VOCATIONAL EDUCATION

During the current recession, marked by declining productivity growth and unprecedentedly high levels of unemployment, interest has grown in the roles vocational education and other alternatives can play in reversing both of these trends. Gene Bottoms, executive director of the American Vocational Association, sees the new Job Training Partnership Act as giving added support to vocational education. The resources of local vocational programs, he contends, are the "logical choice for serving the economically disadvantaged," who comprise a disproportionate share of the unskilled and unemployed labor pool.

Support for the status quo in vocational and career education programs, however, will not be sufficient. Several researchers have questioned the effectiveness of vocational programs and others have detected socioeconomic repercussions that operate counter to the goals of educational equity.

Shortcomings in vocational education as currently conceived include its often narrow focus on training in specific skills and the frequent neglect of affective and thinking skills valued by most employers. In *Work in America*, written by O'Toole and others, Beatrice Reubens reported the results of an evaluation showing that the initial employment record of vocational graduates—in terms of income, job status, turnover, upward mobility, unemployment rates, and job satisfaction—is no better than that of students graduating from academic programs. This may partially be explained by the argument that skills taught in vocational programs are not general enough for use in a rapidly changing world and are often obsolete before the students secure their first jobs.

Additionally, O'Toole has found that vocationally trained workers have difficulty adapting to the more democratic forms of self-management that are expected to pervade American industry in the future. He sees an inadequacy on the part of these workers in dealing with nonroutine conditions and contends that employers will require more "analytical and entrepreneurial skills, people who know how to solve problems, and people who will not panic when something untoward starts to occur at places like Three-Mile Island." Moreover, he continues, "People who are vocationally trained to unquestioningly perform a single task are manifestly unprepared to design their own work, participate in decision making, assume control over their own working conditions, work as members of a community of equals, or take responsibility for the quantity and quality of their own work when a boss is not looking over their shoulders."

Approaching the subject of vocational education from another perspective, John Goodlad, dean of the UCLA Graduate School of Education, has studied the distribution of secondary curricular opportunities compared to the distribution of teachers by specialty. His findings, to be published at the end of February 1983 in a book entitled *A Place Called School*, indicate that there is enormous variability in the assignment of teachers and that vocational education teachers comprise a disproportionate share of the teaching force—24 percent in senior high schools. In some schools, vocational education teachers constitute over 40 percent of the teaching force.

According to Goodlad, vocational education enjoys curricular luxury as a result of this distribution. Vocational teachers teach their specialty while English, math, and social studies teachers are "spread all over the place." He attributes the inconsistent allocation of the teaching force to the fault of omission rather than to conscious design.

In response to this forceful indictment, others suggest that vocational education, offered as a choice rather than a necessity, may help to keep students who are not academically inclined from dropping out of school. Concurrently, they express the need for a *modern* program of vocational education to provide skills for those having little interest in or aptitude for academic work. And although Russell Rumberger of Stanford University has found that for students who do not attend college, differences in high school curriculum appear to have little effect on employment opportunities, he did determine that there were payoffs to certain specific vocational programs when the training was actually utilized in later jobs, especially in programs training for office occupations. He concludes, therefore, that both vocational and academic curricula show positive results in specific circumstances.

The National Center for Research in Vocational Education at Ohio State University has investigated the effects of participating in a vocational curriculum. In 1981, research staff at the center examined almost 1,500 studies covering such topics as earnings, employee satisfaction, academic achievement, and basic skills attainment. The literature surveyed indicated that a majority of vocational education graduates found employment related to their technical training, particularly in the fields of business, office, and health education. In addition, vocational graduates were found to be confident in their skills.

There is also evidence that vocational educators are interested in incorporating more general skills, such as those O'Toole emphasizes, into their programs. Stuart Rosenfeld, director of research and programs for the Southern Growth Policies Board in Research Triangle Park (North Carolina) refers to a "generic" approach to vocational education that results in a closer connection to the regular secondary program. According to Rosenfeld, vocational agriculture exemplifies for some a successful model encompassing less specialized and more integrated training. He states that by "combining farming, business, and problem-solving skills with strong leadership training, vocational agriculture has contributed to large gains in productivity."

CONCLUSION

Technology has substantially affected our perceptions of how much education is desirable or required to keep pace with current and forecasted changes. Some researchers suggest that skill levels are rising and will need to continue doing so. Others argue that the actual skill levels required for technological work are lower than those required for manual work. Both arguments support the notion that human knowledge and skills are important determinants of economic productivity, but they differ over the types of skills that should be stressed in schools.

Those who believe there is a shortage of job-specific or highly specialized skills give impetus to the movement toward more vocational training in the schools. On the other hand, those who believe that work in general is becoming deskilled emphasize the importance of a broad course of studies to develop the potential of the whole person. They see vocational training as a way of narrowing student competencies and lowering expectations, in other words, of tailoring the skills of workers to the requirements of the workplace without concern for other human needs.

The evidence presented here is not intended to suggest that every student should become a generalist. What it does indicate is a pressing need to evaluate the type of curriculum that will best prepare students not for specific jobs but for a range of tasks that will be required by society and industry in the near future.

Adaptability to change appears to be one essential quality demanded by rapid technological change. Educators must consider to what degree a curriculum that is becoming increasingly specialized at the secondary and postsecondary levels will produce workers who are flexible and able to adjust to continuing transformation in the tools and conditions of work.

The other skills identified as important to modern society—analysis and critical thinking, organizational and reference skills, creativity, and the ability to communicate interpersonally and internationally—call for general training in addition to specialized training. The former should furnish a foundation for the latter. Therefore, the core curriculum that is designed to provide this general foundation should be emphasized in the formative elementary and secondary years and protected from encroachment by peripheral studies. At the same time, high schools will need to prepare a sufficient cadre of highly skilled students in technical fields who are college bound, for our society requires not only competent users of technology, but also technological innovators at ease with complex systems.

REFERENCES

Agee, William M. "An Agenda for the U.S. Economy." *Business Education Forum* (October 1979): 11–15.

Arnold, Erik; Birke, Lynda; and Faulkner, Wendy. "Women and Microelectronics: The Case of Word Processors." *Women's Studies International Quarterly* 4 (1981): 321–40.

Berg, Ivar. *Education and Jobs: The Great Training Robbery.* Boston: Beacon Press, 1971.

Braverman, Harry. *Labor and Monopoly Capital.* New York: Monthly Review Press, 1974.

Gisi, Lynn Grover, and Forbes, Roy H. "The Information Society: Are High School Graduates Ready?" Denver, Colorado: Education Commission of the States, 1982.

Hunt, James B., Jr. "The Year of the Public Schools." *State Education Leader* (Education Commission of States) 1 (Fall 1982): 1–2.

Newsweek. "Jobs. Putting America Back to Work." Oct. 18, 1982, pp. 78–84.

O'Toole, James, and others. *Work in America.* Cambridge: Massachusetts Institute of Technology Press, 1972.

O'Toole, James. "Education in Education, and Work in Work—Shall Ever the Twain Meet?" *Teachers College Record* 81 (Fall 1979): 5–21.

Riche, Richard W. "Impact of New Electronic Technology." *Monthly Labor Review* 105 (March 1982): 37–39.

Rumberger, Russell W., and Daymont, Thomas N. "The Economic Value of Academic and Vocational Training Acquired in High School." Paper presented at the annual meeting of the American Educational Research Association, 19–23 March 1982, in New York City.

Toch, Thomas. "New Activism Marks Corporate Role in Schools." *Education Week,* November 10, 1982.

CHAPTER 8

The Higher Education System

We share something in common—we are all participants in the system of higher education. Unlike attendance in primary and secondary schools, however, our attendance and involvement in higher education is voluntary. Most discussions up to this point have referred, implicitly or explicitly, to primary or secondary education. The organization of institutions of higher education—their structure, professional roles of the faculty, and atmosphere—give higher education some of its distinctive features. This chapter will review some of these features as well as some issues facing institutions of higher education today.

Higher education is a term encompassing institutions with varying sponsorship—public and private; varying student composition (male and/or female, age differentials, minority groups, foreigners, members of different social classes); and varying types of programs (two-year, four-year, graduate, and professional schools). These structural differences have implications for the education system. For instance, with an increasingly older student body and many more women attending institutions of higher education, student services and educational offerings may change to meet new demands.

Using our open systems framework, higher education can be viewed as an example of a total system with some unique structural features, role relations, informal system dynamics, and environmental stresses and strains; it also has many features in common with other systems (see Figure 1).

Higher education has been studied from each major theoretical perspective. For instance, functionalists interpreted the rapid growth of higher

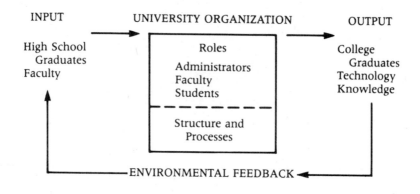

FIGURE 1
University Systems Model

education as resulting from improved opportunity structure in society and the necessity for more education to meet the needs of an increasingly technological world. Higher education, in this view, prepares individuals to fill these roles. Conflict theorists interpret the growth in higher education as directly related to changes in the needs of the capitalist economic system, structured to perpetuate the advantaged position of the elite. Higher education, just like primary and secondary schools, is built around a series of tracks including two-year institutions, four-year institutions, and graduate training.

Over the years, moods and movements in society have influenced the direction of change in higher education. The role of higher education institutions, especially universities, has changed and expanded. Universities in earlier times had teaching as the primary function; in recent years the function of research, or purposefully expanding knowledge, has been added. Finally, the latest function is that of service, providing expertise to the community in the form of publications, media, teaching, lecturing, and consulting.

The excerpt from Joseph Ben-David's book *American Higher Education* describes the rapid growth of the American system and distinguishes it from its international counterparts by discussing three unique characteristics: differentiation, or the degree structure; standardization, or the comparability and similarities between institutions in American higher education; and integration, the extension of standardization that allows for interchangeability and transfer among systems. His comparative discussion of the structure of American higher education provides a fresh new perspective. Note also how this compares with the discussion of worldwide education in Chapter 9.

As society becomes increasingly complex, we seek new ways to sort people into appropriate slots. Conflict theorists argue that tests used as group measures to sort people discriminate against those who do not come from the dominant group in society, because these tests are based on knowledge deemed important and passed on by the powerful and educated as written by their representatives. Tests used for tracking students in school, gaining acceptance into college, and placing individuals in jobs are seen as unfair by the conflict theorists. The issue of testing has implications for who gains entry into elite institutions, and how they succeed in doing so. College entrance exams are required for getting into many colleges, yet questions have been raised as to their real value in determining a student's chances in college, as well as their possible bias against students from less achievement-oriented high schools. Christopher Jencks, presenting findings from a study of the Scholastic Aptitude Test, points out that students with the best chances to be received by the Ivy League are those from the best high schools and high socioeconomic level. The question of "coachability" for tests is addressed in a brief insert on the Federal Trade Commission's report on the testing industry.

Burton Clark looks at the functions of another institutional structure in higher education—the two-year college. He argues that these colleges serve to "cool out" students who want to go on for higher education but do not qualify for a university. Some might succeed in transferring to four-year colleges, but many will end with a two-year degree. Clark points out what he sees as functions of this cooling-out process for higher education and for society. Some conflict theorists argue that two-year colleges are filters and dead ends for those who do not make it into the elite system. And to some extent they act as a pacifier to give limited opportunity to many.

Two significant trends have affected higher education in the past decade. First, what had been a rapidly growing market as described by Ben-David went bust. Fewer students were enrolling in college for several reasons—the dropping birth rate, which resulted in a reduced pool of available students; the withering job market; and widespread questioning of the value and effects of receiving a college degree. Howard R. Bowen reviews some of the benefits that higher education offers for society and individuals: the payoff of investments in higher education and its impact on family, health, political activities, economic productivity, general knowledge, and attitudes toward future education. Clark's findings support his contention that the return on investment is well worth the cost.

The Carnegie Council on Policy Studies in Higher Education recently issued a study on trends and changes in higher education. This excellent review identifies, among other trends, the rise of public institutions, more government regulation, dependence on public sources of funding, and changing faculty and student populations. Higher education is in a continuing process of change to adapt to environmental demands. Additional issues related to change in educational systems will be discussed in Chapter 10.

JOSEPH BEN-DAVID

Distinguishing Characteristics of the United States System of Higher Education

Questions to think about

1 *How does the U.S. system of higher education differ from that of most other countries? What is the significance of these differences?*

2 *What changes do you observe between what Ben-David reports and the current state of higher education as described by other articles in this chapter?*

3 *What factors in American society may have caused America's higher education system to develop differently from the systems in many other countries?*

4 *In your opinion, have the factors that distinguish American higher education helped or hindered development of the system?*

The most conspicuous characteristic of the United States system of higher education is its size. In 1968, 6,928,000 students, constituting 43 percent of the 18–21 age group, were enrolled in institutions of higher education (American Council on Education [ACE], 1970, No. 1, pp. 60.5, 70.6). This is a much higher percentage than in any other country. The difference between the United States and other systems of higher education is not a recent phenomenon that can be attributed to a passing constellation of conditions, but a phenomenon that has existed

From *American Higher Education* (1972), pp. 1–9. Copyright © by The Carnegie Foundation for the Advancement of Teaching. Reprinted with permission.

since the beginning of this century (Ben-David, 1963–64, p. 263). The position on the percentage scale of all other countries with respect to attendance at higher educational institutions has changed. While today the United States is followed by Japan, Canada, Australia, New Zealand, and the U.S.S.R., earlier in this century it was followed by the countries of Western Europe. However, the position of the United States itself has remained unchanged (ibid.).

Furthermore, as pointed out by Sir Eric Ashby, this growth has been continuous. From 1870 until the 1950s, enrollment doubled about every 15 years with a regularity practically unaffected by anything (Ashby, 1971, p. 4). Since 1955, however, there has been a noticeable acceleration. Enrollments grew from 2,660,000 in fall 1955, to 5,526,000 in fall 1965, to 6,928,000 in fall 1968, which is more than a 100 percent growth rate per 10 years (ACE, 1970, No. 1, p. 70.5).

A similar pattern emerges if, instead of total enrollment, one looks at graduate enrollment. On the average, the latter doubled every 10 years after 1899–1900, when it amounted to a mere 5,800, and reached the figure of 250,000 in 1955. Since then, however, a further acceleration occurred, and graduate enrollment increased to 582,000 by fall 1965, and 758,000 by 1968 (ibid., p. 70.5).

This change becomes even more dramatic when one looks at the percentage of students who graduate from college in a given year and who then enter graduate school the following year. Of the 1951 cohort of graduates, 13.8 percent continued to study as full-time students in 1952. The percentage increased to 28.6 percent in 1960 (cohort of 1959 graduates) and to 41.4 percent (50.3 percent among male and 30.4 percent among female students in 1965 [cohort of 1964 graduates (Folger, Astin, & Bayer, 1970, pp. 182–183)]. This again shows a regular growth until the fifties, and an acceleration since then.

This sustained growth in the quantity and level of education was not accompanied by any decline in quality, at least not as far as the early 1960s. The scientific reputation of American institutions of higher education rose all the time. Their share in the world production of scientific papers, or in such honors as Nobel prizes, reached an all-time high after World War II (Ben-David, 1968, p. 107). And in the 1950s, United States institutions of higher education became the principal center for advanced study and research for students and scientists from all over the world (UNESCO, 1966, pp. 34, 72, 1351–1352).

It is often asserted that this growth of research and advanced study has resulted in a diminishing devotion of the professors to their teaching duties. The only evidence for this is that the required teaching load has decreased through time in most institutions. This, however, is very inconclusive evidence, since classroom hours per teacher are a poor index of the quality and effectiveness of the education received by students. Other evidence points in the opposite direction. The academic requirements in the liberal arts program were strengthened between 1957 and 1967 (Spurr, 1970, pp. 54–55). The Academic Aptitude Tests show no lowering of standards (Folger, 1970, pp. 158–159). Further evidence that indicates no decline in the effectiveness of college education is the stability of the dropout rate, which has been about 40 percent for the last 40 years. It is unlikely that the average level of intelligence of college students did not somewhat decline during this period, since the percentage of the age group attending college rose from 7.88 percent in 1919–20 to 31.15 percent in 1959–60, and to 43 percent in 1968 [Department of Health, Education and Welfare (HEW), 1969, p. 65, table 86]. Therefore, it can be concluded that increased emphasis on research, whatever effects it may have had on other aspects of life at college, did not lead to a decline in the effectiveness of college study. If anything, the change has probably been for the better.[1]

Another characteristic of the United States system has been its equalitarianism. This may seem a surprising statement to readers who are reminded everyday of the social injustices generated by the United States "capitalist system," and in particular of the racial discrimination practiced by the "system." But at least in higher education these charges are without foundation. Socioeconomic status has an effect on educational progress and success, but probably much less than anywhere else in the world; the percentage of high school graduates in 1960 who went to college the following year was 24 percent among boys from the lowest quintile of socioeconomic background and 81 percent among those from the highest quintile. The corresponding percentages among girls were 15 percent and 75 percent. A great part of this difference is, however, due to differences in the academic aptitude of the different socioeconomic groups. When those are held constant, the difference decreases, especially in the higher aptitude groups. Thus, in the highest aptitude quintile, 69 percent of the boys and 52 percent of the girls from the lowest socioeconomic quintile went to college as compared with 91 and 90 percent from the highest socioeconomic groups (Folger et al., 1970, p. 310). If the influence of socioeconomic differences were eliminated, then, with ability held constant, this would add only 60,000–75,000 to the number of bachelor's degrees, an increase of 2.5–3.0 percent per year (Folger et al., 1970, p. 324).

Every applicant for higher education finds a place in college, and once he has entered the system, even if only in a junior college, there are numerous possibilities of transfer. Transfers depend on academic aptitude, and socioeconomic status has little effect on the chances of graduation (Folger et al., 1970, pp. 194, 216, 320).

All this is not to say that there is no room for improvement, but (a) improvement probably has to take place first and foremost at the lower levels of education, and/or in the home; (b) the existing system of higher education, including such aspects as selection and transfer, has been effective in the absorption and education of students from all socioeconomic backgrounds; and (c) probably the only step which can be effectively taken at present toward further equalization at the higher education level *alone* is an increase in scholarship aid which covers so far only about half of the students from the lowest socioeconomic groups. Surveys indicate that if such aid were provided, a considerable fraction of the able students from low socioeconomic background, who do not at present attend college, might do so in the future (Folger et al., 1970, pp. 311–312).[2]

These conclusions are corroborated by comparisons with other systems of education. Such comparisons have been made with all the important Western European countries, and they all show that there is, and for some time in the past has been, less class discrimination in education in the United States than in the other countries, including socialist countries (Poignant, 1969, pp. 79, 195–202; Ben-David, 1963–64, pp. 284–291).

As to race, recent data show that, if anything, there is discrimination in favor of black students in the educational system. Everything else being equal, nonwhite students are slightly, but consistently, favored in placement at high school as well as college (Heyns, 1970, pp. 6–7; Folger et al., 1970, pp. 156–157). This again is no reason for complacency, but it may indicate that the main problem today does not lie within the domain of the higher educational system. Or if it does, it is not something that can be solved by further "equalization" of placement, but by qualitative improvements and innovations in education, probably more at the lower than at the higher levels.

This comprehensiveness of American higher education has been due to its willingness to cater to a great diversity of demands, and its initiative in offering educational innovations of all kinds. . . . But an idea of the magnitude of the differences between the United States and the European systems of higher education (with the exception of the U.S.S.R. system) can be obtained from the constant changes that took place in the United States in the distribution of students studying for degrees in different fields, as compared with the stability in the distribution of the degrees in different fields in Europe. At the beginning of this century the situation in the United States was similar to that in Europe. This was the time when United States colleges and universities were still in the process of imitating the European, or more specifically the German, model. Thus the distribution of students studying for a first-level degree (and there were very few who studied for higher degrees) among the fields of study in the United States in 1901–1905 was very similar to that in Germany. The exceptions were engineering, which, at that time, was still studied mainly by apprenticeship in the United States, and the beginning of such new fields of academic study in the United States as the social sciences and business which did not have academic recognition in Germany. By the 1930s, however, the situation had completely changed. In the United States the percentage of students in the old professional fields of law and medicine declined, while in the newer professional fields, such as education and business, it increased; and, a similar decline took place in science and arts scholarship as a result of the rise of the newer social sciences (Ben-David, 1963–64, pp. 268–272). It must be noted, of course, that this change did not take place through a redistribution of the same number of students, since rapid growth of the whole system allowed the redistribution of the proportions to take place without an actual reduction of the size of any of the fields.

However, what is most striking is the fact that the proportions in Europe remained unchanged through this whole period of time, in spite of the changes that occurred in the economy as well as in science and scholarship. Obviously, a system that was willing to adjust itself to the changes in the demand for different types of education was in a better position to expand than one that resisted change and adjustment. One must understand what the structural differences were between the United States and the other systems in order to understand what made this greater flexibility possible.

The structural characteristics which set the United States system of higher education apart from other systems are a combination of differentiation, standardization, and integration. By differentiation, I refer to the degree structure which is divided into three levels, each with distinct contents and functions. The first is a bachelor's degree. In the majority of the cases, it is nonspecialized and emphasizes breadth of education rather than expertise; in the minority of cases, it is a low-level, specialized professional degree (Poignant, 1969, pp. 154–155). The second is a master's degree, where emphasis is reversed, and which usually aims at training students for professional work, such as teaching, engineering, social work, and business, in a fairly practical and specialized manner [this was the case in about 70 percent of such degrees granted in 1967 (U.S. Bureau of Foreign Trade, 1968, p. 129)]. But again, there is a minority of master's degrees that are only a less than half completed Ph.D. degree. The third level of degree structure, the Ph.D. level, has as its purpose the training of researchers, implemented by courses designed to explore a field in depth and by the preparation of an advanced piece of research. The existence of these last two functions also involves the establishment by the university of a great variety of basic and applied research facilities.

In addition, there is a fourth, or rather a pre-first degree, the "associate degree," granted by the two-year junior (or community) colleges. Similar to the bachelor's degree, it is in most cases a diploma in nonspecialized general education, equivalent to a less than half completed bachelor's degree; but in other cases, it indicates the completion of a subprofessional course in technology, agriculture, nursing, commerce, etc. (Spurr, 1970, pp. 41–48).

The deviations from this scheme are few. There is the M.D. degree, which is a professional degree of a somewhat more advanced level than the master's degree; there are bachelor's degrees in law and theology, which are high-level professional second degrees; and there are five-year professional bachelor's degrees, which are equivalent, as far as requirements go, to a master's degree. These are minor deviations from the general scheme. They do not fit the standardized cutting points of the scheme, but they are consistent with its rationale, as the four-year professional bachelor's course only represents a lower, and the M.D., second law, and theological degrees only slightly higher cutting points that are nonetheless in the same dimension as the professional master's course.

The institutions that provide all or some of these degrees vary in their quality a great deal, since each institution is differently funded and differently staffed and since there is no central body to ensure uniformity. Nevertheless, the conception of what constitutes a degree course of a certain kind (professional, general, etc.) at a certain level is fairly standardized throughout the whole system; the contents of the individual courses in a given field are also standardized to a considerable extent, partly as a result of the effectiveness of the textbook publishing industry. And accreditation boards have had some success in establishing minimum standards. Hence the difference in quality of the institutions manifests itself, above all, in the range and types of courses taught, in the degrees conferred, and in the quality of the teachers and the students rather than in the formal contents of the courses.[3]

This standardization makes possible the integration of the system. There are practically no blind alleys in it. One can always transfer from one level to another, and it is easy to transfer from one institution to another, especially between degrees. In practice, these possibilities are limited by the evaluation of the qualities of the different colleges, but there are, nevertheless, cases of transfer from practically any type of accredited institution to any other type (Folger et al., 1970, pp. 172–175).

The most controversial aspect of this scheme is that part of the associate and part of the master's degrees are, in effect, consolation prizes for students not capable of completing the B.A. or the Ph.D. programs, respectively. As long, however, as everyone can easily tell which of these degrees are, and which are not, consolation prizes, this does not seem to be a major problem. A problem does exist, however, in that as a result of this practice there does not exist in the basic arts and sciences a high-level degree suitable for the training of advanced high school and college teachers below the Ph.D. level. As a result, such teachers are compelled to engage in research that does not suit either their talents or their tastes and does not constitute a contribution to knowledge.

This differentiation of levels of study, and their standardization—which makes the whole system integrated so that the student can move with relative ease from level to level and from one part of the system to another (such as from liberal arts college to a professional school)—is unique to the United States. Until the 1950s or 1960s, other systems of higher education had provided systematic education practically only on a single level, which was roughly equivalent to the United States second-level degree (Poignant, 1969, p. 15). There were no academic degrees lower than this, and formal training for the third-level degree was either very unsystematic or nonexistent. The doctorate, or its equivalent, was conferred upon graduates after the completion of a thesis written with more or less supervision by a single teacher.

It was therefore extremely difficult to change one's field of study after the first year at the university, and it was practically impossible for people with different types and degrees of interests in the same field to find the course of study which suited them. The universities offered one kind of course at a single and rather specialized level in each field that was taught. Those for whom this was more than what they wanted had to study up to the standard level. In practice, many of the recipients of degrees barely scraped through the examinations and never acquired a real competence in their chosen field of study. Those for whom this was less than enough, or who were interested in unusual combinations of fields, could try to complement the curriculum by private effort. This, however, was satisfactory only for the energetic and highly talented few, provided that they were also wealthy enough to be able to afford several years of apparently "aimless" study.

Only since the 1950s have other countries started to develop their graduate schools following, as a rule, the United States model (Bowles, 1963, pp. 153–154). Similarly, only since then have some universities outside the United States taken up the idea of a nonspecialized first degree, similar to a United States liberal arts degree. Such a degree had not existed on the continent of Europe since the beginning of the nineteenth century. It had existed in England and Scotland, but in England was gradually eliminated during this century. Only in Scotland did this type of degree survive until the present. But the Scottish example had little impact on any other country (including England), and the recent experiments were inspired by the example of the United States. In any case, compared to the

United States, differentiation by levels of study is still in its beginnings in most of the other countries.

There are also differences between the United States and other countries in the standardization and integration of their respective systems of higher education. Everywhere outside the United States, many of the professional studies are taught in specialized nonuniversity institutions which grant diplomas of their own. In some places, such as France and Germany, there is a considerable confusion, even in degrees of approximately the same level (Spurr, 1970, pp. 174–179). All these differences make transfers complicated. In its conception, the nearest analogue to the United States higher education system today is that of Japan, which after World War II was deliberately reformed according to the United States model. But that system has never attained anything like the degree of integration of the United States higher education system. There is practically no transfer there from one type of institution to another type, and hardly any from one institution to another. Furthermore, neither the college of general studies nor the graduate school has developed in Japan satisfactorily.

The diversification of the system described in this chapter was made possible by the combination of differentiation, standardization, and integration. The existence of different levels made possible the assimilation of new contents within the system and the construction of programs of study for a variety of purposes. If a field of study did not seem academically respectable, there would be a reluctance to grant a Ph.D. in it, but a first or a second professional degree could be granted without the implication that the field was deemed intellectually equal to the more established and/or intellectually more developed fields. It was also possible to institute second- and third-level professional degrees by changing the description of the title, such as in M.B.A. or D.Ed.

The standardization of the degrees of different levels, and the incorporation of different professional degrees into the general three-level degree structure, eliminated many of the invidious distinctions between different types of study which persisted in Europe. This made educational mobility easier. Thus new fields and educational experiments had a better chance than in Europe, since those participating were not threatened with entering an academic blind alley or with being labeled for life as inferior by the monopolists of academic prestige.

NOTES

1. Why "more" did not, in the majority of institutions, mean "worse" has been explained by Martin Trow (1962, 241–246). The constantly growing pool of applicants allowed the colleges to raise requirements and standards, and the growing importance to employers of the student's academic record provided increased motivation among the students to learn.

2. Of course, it is a serious question whether higher education should be subsidized at all, and if the answer is yes, whether this should be done through personal scholarships. But this is a question that needs separate treatment.

3. My guess would be that there is a greater standardization of the contents of the courses in the United States than in other countries outside the Communist bloc.

REFERENCES

American Council on Education: *Factbook on Higher Education*, nos. 1, 5, and 6, Washington, D.C., 1970.

Ashby, Eric: *Any Person, Any Study: An Essay on Higher Education in the United States*, McGraw-Hill Book Company, New York, 1971.

Ben-David, Joseph: "Professions in the Class System of Present Day Societies," *Current Sociology*, vol. 12, no. 3, 1963–64.

Ben-David, Joseph: *Fundamental Research and the Universities*, Organization for Economic Co-operation and Development, Paris, 1968.

Bowles, Frank: *Access to Higher Education I*, UNESCO, Paris, 1963.

Folger, John K., Helen S. Astin, and Alan E. Bayer: *Human Resources and Higher Education: Staff Report of the Commission on Human Resources and Advanced Education*, Russell Sage Foundation, New York, 1970.

Heyns, Barbara: *Curriculum Assignment in Teaching Policies in Public High Schools*, Ph.D. dissertation abstract, University of Chicago, Dept. of Sociology, August 1970.

Poignant, Raymond: *Education and Development in Western Europe, The United States, and the U.S.S.R.*, Teachers College Press, Columbia University, New York, 1969.

Spurr, Stephen H.: *Academic Degree Structures: Innovative Approaches*, McGraw-Hill Book Company, New York, 1970.

Trow, Martin: "The Democratization of Higher Education in America," *The European Journal of Sociology*, vol. 3, no. 2, pp. 231–262, 1962.

UNESCO: *World Survey of Education IV*, Paris, 1966.

U.S. Bureau of Foreign Trade and Commerce: *Statistical Abstract*, U.S. Bureau of the Census, Washington, D.C., 1968.

U.S. Department of Health, Education and Welfare: *Digest of Educational Statistics*, U.S. Office of Education, Washington, D.C., 1969.

The SAT Controversy: When an Aptitude Is Coachable

Questions to think about

1 *What issues underlie the controversy over the SATs?*

2 *How do SAT test scores relate to issues of stratification discussed in Chapter 2?*

3 *Who is most likely to benefit from the idea of "coaching"? Who might be penalized?*

The most common outgrowths of the "intelligence" test are the Scholastic Aptitude Tests (SATs) taken every year by nearly 1.5 million college-bound high school students. "Aptitude" is an ill-defined term to start with, and students and their parents have long suspected that the scores that come back are not such accurate indicators of it as they seem. Recently, a study by the Federal Trade Commission's Bureau of Consumer Protection backed up those suspicions and shook the testing industry. The study showed that special coaching can improve SAT scores by an average of 25 points out of 800. Such a difference can matter. College admissions offices weigh SAT scores along with school records, individual achievements, recommendations, and interviews. But many colleges set minimum SAT scores for making their first cut. When other factors are equal, they generally choose the applicant with the higher score. They do so because the SAT has proven over the years to be a relatively good predictor of academic performance in college—although that performance is often measured, of course, by similar exams.

The Educational Testing Service (ETS), which administers the tests for the College Entrance Examination Board, has long issued warnings against making any admissions decision on the basis of the SAT score alone. Because of luck, motivation, and other external factors, the ETS says, an individual's score can vary from one occasion to another on the same SAT by plus or minus 30 to 35 points. That adds up to a spread of 60 to 70 points in which any test-taker's "true" score might lie. Beyond that range, however, the ETS maintains that the tests measure basic abilities acquired over a student's lifetime and therefore supposedly immune to any attempt at special preparation or last-minute cramming.

A $10-million-a-year coaching industry has mushroomed in the last decade, based on exactly the opposite premise. The coaching schools offer to train students for their first or repeat attempts at the SAT or other aptitude tests, like the Graduate Record Exam and the Law School Admissions Test. The schools use a variety of methods: practicing on actual tests, cramming the material to be tested, using behavior modification techniques and biofeedback exercises to reduce test anxiety. Stanley H. Kaplan, who operates a nationwide chain of more than 80 schools that tutored 30,000 students last year, charges $275 for a 10-week SAT course of classroom sessions and homework assignments. He claims the course can improve scores by up to 100 points.

To the extent that such claims are true, they imply that the SAT does not measure some relatively fixed ability, but a combination of knowledge and test-taking skill—both teachable. Many satisfied graduates of coaching schools who did poorly on their first try at the SAT say they did much better after taking the course. Nevertheless, the College Board and ETS have insisted that the tests are "coach-proof," and that coaching sessions amount to a waste of students' time and money. The test-makers also argue that those who attend coaching schools may do better on the SAT because they are a self-selected sample of students more motivated than average to improve their scores, and more confident that a little coaching will help.

The report of the Federal Trade Commission's investigation of several SAT coaching schools, released last May, rejected accusations that the coaching schools were engaging in false advertising. Despite numerous qualifications, the report found that some commercial coaching courses can indeed raise SAT scores significantly, regardless of the normal range of error: an average of 25 points on both the verbal and math sections. (The ETS accused the FTC of propagating "erroneous conclusions based on poorly designed research," but did concede that students with low levels of achievement might improve more after coaching than other groups.)

If a 10-week coaching course can significantly improve a student's score on the test, then the test's validity as a measure of aptitude becomes dubious. In addition, the FTC study raises the troubling question of whether college admission should partly depend on a skill gained by those who can afford a coaching course.

CHRISTOPHER JENCKS and
JAMES CROUSE

Should We Relabel the
SAT . . . or Replace It?

Questions to think about

1 *What are the implications for high schools and colleges
of using SAT/ACTs or other achievement tests?*
2 *What impact does testing have on individuals, on
organizations of higher education, and on the
stratification system?*
3 *Do all students have an equal chance to do well on
SATs and on achievement tests? How can you explain
the differences, using the open systems framework?*
4 *Interview several students on their experiences with the
SATs. What factors do they mention as influencing
performance?*

The idea that colleges should choose among appli-
cants on the basis of their academic ability appeals to both educators and
the public. But "ability" has two distinct meanings, which imply different
admissions policies.

In one usage, academic ability means an *existing* capacity to do academic work. In the other usage, academic ability means a *potential* capacity
to do such work. To say that an applicant "has the ability to do differential
calculus," for example, can mean either that the applicant can already do
differential calculus or that the applicant could learn to do it, given opportunity and motivation. To avoid this ambiguity, psychometricians usually call potential ability "aptitude" and existing ability "achievement."

From *New Directions for Testing and Measurement* (March 1982). Reprinted by permission of
Jossey-Bass, Inc.

When colleges say that they wish to select the "ablest" applicants, they almost always mean the applicants with the greatest academic aptitude, not those with the highest current levels of academic achievement. Yet, so far as we know, the U.S. is the only major industrial nation in which more than 90% of colleges and universities use so-called aptitude tests to help them make admissions decisions. Most U.S. colleges and universities require the College Entrance Examination Board's Scholastic Aptitude Test (SAT), designed by the Educational Testing Service (ETS). Almost all the rest require the American College Testing Program's ACT, which is similar to the SAT but shorter.

This does not mean that universities in Britain, France, Germany, Japan, and the Soviet Union are indifferent to aptitude as we have defined it. But educators in these countries assume that the best single predictor of how much a student will learn from studying something in a university is how much he or she learned from studying something similar in secondary school. Therefore, they rely on what psychometricians call achievement tests, rather than on so-called aptitude tests, to help them make admissions decisions.

U.S. colleges and universities made the same assumption until well into the 20th century. In the 19th century most American colleges were so eager for students that they admitted virtually anyone who applied. Only a handful of elite institutions—mostly private colleges in the Northeast—tried to screen out unpromising students. They did this primarily by relying on grades and on letters of recommendation from secondary schools with which they had ongoing relationships. A number of selective private colleges also gave their own admissions tests, largely to determine whether students who did not come recommended by established secondary schools could do college-level work. But the growth of public secondary education in the late 19th century caused students from far more secondary schools to begin applying to selective colleges, and the burden on these colleges of administering their own admissions tests multiplied. So in 1900 several selective private colleges established the College Entrance Examination Board (CEEB) to administer a single set of admissions tests to all applicants.

Like the exams they replaced, the new College Board tests measured mastery of the subjects that academically oriented secondary schools had traditionally taught: ancient and modern languages, history, mathematics, and science. But many of the new public high schools did not teach these subjects or offered less than four years of instruction in them. For applicants from such schools, poor performance on the College Board exams did not necessarily predict poor performance in college. What the colleges needed, therefore, was a test that would identify "diamonds in the rough"—students who could be expected to overcome poor preparation and learn a lot if admitted. What they needed, in other words, was a measure of academic aptitude.

The College Board administered its first SAT in 1926. Although it described the new test as a measure of aptitude rather than intelligence, most people used the two terms almost interchangeably at the time and still do so today. Both aptitude and intelligence are supposed to be stable traits that influence behavior throughout life. By calling the SAT an "aptitude" test, therefore, its designers were encouraging users to assume that it was insensitive to the quality of an individual's previous schooling.[1] They were also implicitly claiming that the SAT would predict college success more accurately than existing achievement tests. Had they not believed this, of course, they would not have developed and marketed the test in the first place.

To make the SAT insensitive to high school quality, its designers tried to measure skills and information that were taught either in all schools or in none. Virtually all elementary schools taught reading and arithmetic, for example, so the SAT included questions that tried to measure reading comprehension and arithmetic reasoning. Almost all secondary schools taught elementary algebra, so this too seemed a "fair" test of academic aptitude. And although good secondary schools tended to assign books that employed a larger vocabulary than the books assigned in mediocre schools, students from mediocre schools often acquired large vocabularies from parents, friends, and extracurricular reading. The SAT therefore placed considerable emphasis on vocabulary and verbal fluency.

As time went on, colleges placed more emphasis on the SAT and less on the College Board's traditional achievement tests. Eventually, many colleges stopped requiring applicants to take the achievement tests at all. And when colleges that had previously relied entirely on high school grades for screening applicants began requiring applicants to take standardized tests as well, as many did in the 1960s and 1970s, almost all of them required a test like the SAT, not achievement tests. The College Board still offers multiple-choice achievement tests in 14 subjects, but only 20% of those who take the SAT take even one achievement test.

ETS and the College Board have played a critical role in the shift from achievement tests to so-called aptitude tests. College admissions officers seldom have either the resources or the technical skills to make independent judgments about the merits of different kinds of tests. They rely on ETS and the College Board to do this for them. They emphasize the SAT because it purports to measure aptitude, which is what they wish to measure. They believe—wrongly, as it turns out—that the SAT predicts future academic success more accurately than achievement tests do, and they think—again wrongly, as far as we can tell—that the quality of an applicant's secondary school preparation has less effect on SAT scores than on traditional achievement scores.

Until the 1960s ETS also seems to have believed that the SAT measured a stable underlying trait of the kind that the label "aptitude" implied. In 1959, for example, ETS published a booklet by Martin Katz titled *You: Today and Tomorrow,* which was supposed to help 10-year-olds interpret their aptitude test scores. "In making their decisions," this booklet suggested, "the first questions that John, Andy, Betsy, and Bill have to ask themselves are these: How much general scholastic ability have I? What special abilities have I?"[2] Later it explained, "Your scholastic ability is like an engine. It is the source of your power and speed in school: It tells you how fast and how far you *can* go."[3] Clearly, ETS thought that scores on those tests that purported to measure scholastic ability were, in fact, like horsepower ratings on an engine.

ETS does not make such claims today. A great deal of evidence has now accumulated indicating that scores on such tests as the SAT are not, in fact, stable. Not only do scores change over time, but these changes also grow larger as the interval between tests lengthens, suggesting that the trends are real. Moreover, scores on "aptitude" tests are no more stable than scores on conventional "achievement" tests.[4] The idea that so-called aptitude tests measure stable traits better than so-called achievement tests is therefore in disrepute among psychologists. Nonetheless, ETS and the College Board continue to call the SAT an "aptitude" test, and most people take this to mean that the SAT measures a stable trait.

Rex Jackson formulates the ETS rationale for calling the SAT an "aptitude" test as follows. The SAT, he says, "measures intellectual skills learned through both formal and informal educational experiences—skills that are exercised and further developed through application to school work in a wide variety of academic subjects and through experiences outside of school."[5] Note that this formulation implies that school quality is likely to affect SAT scores. Nonetheless, Jackson offers two rationales for calling the SAT an "aptitude" test. First, "it is not tied to a particular course of study." Second, "it is designed to assist in predicting future academic performance."[6]

Jackson's claim that SAT scores do not depend on "a particular course of study" is hard to reconcile with his assertion that they depend on "educational experiences"unless the relevant educational experiences do not vary from one course of study to another. This seems unlikely. Knowing the meanings of particular vocabulary words, for example, depends largely on having seen these words in context and having either inferred or investigated their meanings. A course of study that involves reading books written for adults is therefore likely to result in higher SAT scores than a course of study that relies on textbooks purged of unfamiliar terms. In fact, there is as much school-to-school variation in vocabulary, reading comprehension, and arithmetic reasoning scores as in scores on conventional secondary school achievement tests.

Jackson's argument that the SAT is an "aptitude" test because colleges use it to predict future academic performance is even less persuasive. Colleges use the results of all the tests they give applicants for either admissions or placement decisions. In either case, the tests are supposed to predict future performance. If this makes the SAT an "aptitude" test, it makes achievement tests in French and physics "aptitude" tests too. In one sense, of course, all of these tests do measure aptitude. But if this is the only sense in which the SAT measures aptitude, the label is surely misleading.

If one defines aptitude as the capacity to master something, given opportunity and incentives, and achievement as having already mastered it, then almost every achievement test is also an aptitude test, and almost every aptitude test is also an achievement test. If everyone taking an "achievement" test has had equal opportunities and incentives to master the material the test covers, those who interpret the test can assume that it measures "aptitude" as well as "achievement." But we cannot even approximate these conditions outside laboratory settings. College applicants have never had either equal opportunities or equal incentives to master anything. A "pure" measure of aptitude for higher education is therefore unattainable.

So why do ETS and other testing organizations persist in claiming that certain tests measure "aptitude"? Why not just say that the SAT measures vocabulary, reading comprehension, and quantitative reasoning? One possible answer is economic. Colleges *want* a measure of academic "aptitude" as distinct from "achievement." ETS is not in business to make money, but it must still worry about supporting its staff. If ETS were to give a vocabulary test, a reading comprehension test, and a basic mathematics test, scores on these tests would probably seem less significant than SAT scores to some college admissions offices, and some colleges might stop requiring applicants to take the tests. Yet it is hard to believe that this would happen on a large scale.

The main reason the SAT's label remains unchanged, despite all the recent changes in psychometric opinion about "aptitude," is probably institutional inertia. Why change the name of a product that is in such demand? Yet continuing to call the SAT a measure of "aptitude" involves significant risks. ETS is under increasing criticism from a variety of groups. Some of this criticism is mindless, but its pervasiveness means that ETS and other test designers must be extremely careful to maintain their credibility among expert observers and test users. Claiming more for one's products than they can accomplish is a sure way to lose credibility and invite legal restrictions on the use of these products. The issue is not what ETS writes about the SAT in technical manuals or what ETS employees say about the SAT in academic journals. The name of a test has more influence on how both educators and students interpret the results than technical manuals and scholarly articles can ever have. As long as ETS and the College Board call the SAT an "aptitude" test, people will assume that it tries to measure "aptitude" in the traditional sense, and they will be understandably angry if they find that it does not really do this.

Reporting SAT scores as vocabulary, reading comprehension, and basic mathematics scores would not, of course, tell colleges whether to base their admissions policies on these scores or on a mastery of history, literature, physics, biology, and other secondary school subjects. In making this decision most colleges are likely to ask two questions: Which tests best predict college success? And which tests minimize the tendency of all admissions systems to favor white, middle-class applicants from elite schools? Let us look, then, at the predictive powers of various kinds of tests.

Freshman grades. As far as we know, the College Board did not investigate whether the SAT predicted college grades more or less accurately than traditional achievement tests when it first introduced the SAT in the 1920s. Since then there have been a number of studies in specific colleges, but results differ from college to college, and as far as we can discover there has been no study covering a large representative sample of college applicants. The best data we have found are from a study ETS conducted in 1979 of 22 highly selective colleges and universities. Seventy-eight percent of the freshmen in these colleges had taken at least one achievement test. The data show that, in the typical highly selective college, SAT and achievement scores predict freshman grades equally well. In most of the 22 colleges, scores on ETS achievement tests were almost interchangeable with SAT scores.[7] This suggests that colleges should choose between the two kinds of tests on grounds other than their ability to predict freshman grades.[8] Colleges committed to predicting applicants' grades as accurately as possible, regardless of the cost to the applicants, obviously should require both sorts of tests.

College completion. As far as we know, ETS has not investigated whether its traditional achievement tests predict college completion better or worse than the SAT does. But some relevant evidence on this question comes from Project Talent, which surveyed a representative national sample of students who were in grades 9 through 12 of a public or private secondary school in 1960 and followed them up 11 years after their expected high school graduation, when they were around 29 years of age. We analyzed data on a representative subsample of those who had attended college.[9] To estimate college applicants' "aptitude" scores, we summed their scores on the Talent tests of vocabulary, reading comprehension, and arithmetic reasoning.[10] To estimate their overall "achievement" scores, we summed their standardized scores on the Talent tests covering English, history and social studies, mathematics, and natural sciences.[11] When we correlated the Talent "aptitude" and "achievement" composites, the number of years of higher education that college entrants completed, and whether they earned a bachelor's degree, our results suggested that, at least in the 1960s, selective colleges could probably have reduced their attrition rates slightly if they had substituted a battery of achievement tests for the SAT.[12] The reduction would not have been great, however, since the Talent aptitude and achievement composites correlated .82 among 12th-graders who attended college.

Economic success.   Although colleges usually claim that their admissions policies are designed primarily to identify applicants who will do high-quality academic work, many are also concerned with selecting applicants who will eventually be able to support the college financially. This concern is especially strong among highly selective private colleges, where alumni contributions play a major economic role. As far as we know, ETS has not examined the relationship of its achievement tests to adult economic success. We have shown, however, that the Talent "aptitude" and "achievement" composites we have just described predict adult economic success equally well.[13] If this were true for ETS achievement tests as well, colleges could substitute conventional achievement tests for the SAT without any loss of information about applicants' future economic prospects.

Although the SAT was originally supposed to help colleges identify able students from mediocre secondary schools, we have not been able to discover any research on whether it does this more effectively than achievement tests do. If the SAT were less sensitive than traditional achievement tests to variations in secondary school quality, schools' mean SAT scores should vary less relative to individual scores than schools' mean achievement test scores do. Indeed, if the SAT were truly insensitive to the quality of the schools an individual had attended, schools' mean SAT scores should not vary at all once we controlled the characteristics of entering students.

Although ETS has not investigated the sensitivity of the SAT to school quality, it has conducted research that bears on the issue. The 1965 Equality of Educational Opportunity Survey (EEOS) administered tests of verbal ability, nonverbal ability, reading comprehension, and math achievement to about 100,000 12th-graders in more than 800 public high schools. ETS designed the EEOS tests of verbal ability and reading comprehension, and many of the items were similar to those in the verbal section of the SAT. ETS also designed the math achievement test, using items from the mathematical achievement tests in its Sequential Tests of Educational Progress (STEP) series. Since the EEOS did not collect data on changes in individuals' test performances between ninth and 12th grades, it does not provide direct evidence regarding the relative impact of high school quality on these tests. It does, however, provide some indirect evidence. The well-known Coleman report stated that schools' mean math achievement scores varied less relative to individual scores than schools' mean verbal ability or mean reading comprehension scores. This suggests, though it certainly does not suffice to prove, that variations in the quality of public high schools have less impact on math achievement than on verbal ability and reading comprehension.

Somewhat more satisfactory evidence regarding the relative impact of school quality on different sorts of tests comes from the longitudinal testing program carried out by Project Talent. In 1963 Talent retested about 7,000 12th-graders whom it had initially tested as ninth-graders in 1960. After controlling ninth-grade test scores, family background, and college plans, Christopher Jencks and Marsha Brown found that students who had said they were in a college preparatory curriculum in 1960 ended up with higher scores on Talent's 12-grade test of social studies and history information than otherwise comparable students who had said they were in a noncollege curriculum.[14] The difference was about .11 standard deviations. But in similar comparisons using Talent's tests of vocabulary, reading comprehension, arithmetic reasoning, and abstract reasoning—all of which contain questions similar to the SAT—12th-graders who had been in the college preparatory curriculum averaged only .03 standard deviations above initially similar students who had been in some other curriculum. These results support Jackson's claim that so-called aptitude tests are less "tied to a particular course of study" than are achievement tests.

The fact that being in a college preparatory curriculum has less effect on "aptitude" than on "achievement" scores is not of much practical importance, however, since virtually all applicants to selective colleges have been in a college preparatory curriculum. From the college's viewpoint, the important question is whether school-to-school differences in the quality of college preparatory programs have more effect on "achievement" tests than on "aptitude" tests. Jencks and Brown found that, after controlling the characteristics of entering ninth-graders, variation in schools' mean achievement accounted for between 1% and 3.4% of the total variance in individual 12th-graders' vocabulary, reading comprehension, arithmetic reasoning, and abstract reasoning scores. The analogous figure for social studies and history information was 2.9%. This does not suggest that conventional achievement tests are any more sensitive to variations in high school quality than are so-called aptitude tests.

Both Coleman's findings and those of Jencks and Brown raise serious doubts about the College Board's traditional assumption that the SAT places applicants from secondary schools of varying quality on a more equal footing than do achievement tests. This assumption may have been correct half a century ago, when the SAT was developed, and it may still be correct today if one compares the SAT to achievement tests in subjects that are only taught in a limited number of secondary schools. But as far as we can tell from the limited evidence available, it is not likely to be true for achievement tests in subjects such as mathematics and social studies that are taught, albeit in very diverse ways, in all secondary schools.

As far as we can discover, ETS has not investigated whether race and socioeconomic status (SES) affect scores on conventional achievement tests as strongly as they affect SAT scores. Barbara Heyns's book, *Summer Learning,* suggests that both race and SES have more impact on what students learn outside the classroom than inside it. Thus, if the SAT were less tied to classroom learning than are conventional achievement tests, we would expect race and SES to have more impact on SAT scores than on conventional achievement test scores. But, as we have seen, the SAT may in fact be just as tied to classroom learning as are conventional achievement tests. Here as elsewhere, we need evidence to choose between the plethora of potentially plausible theories.

The Academic Growth Study (AGS), conducted by ETS, surveyed ninth-graders in 1965 and followed them up in 11th and 12th grades. The AGS gave ninth-graders both "aptitude" and "achievement" tests, gave 11th-graders a battery of achievement tests, and gave 12th-graders either the SAT or the Preliminary Scholastic Aptitude Test (PSAT). Unpublished correlations indicate that the AGS "aptitude" and "achievement" scores correlate .87 in ninth grade and .84 in 11th and 12th grades.[15] Father's education, father's occupation, and mother's education have mean correlations of .234 with the two "aptitude" scores and of .236 with the two "achievement" scores. The mean correlations for race are .255 and .267. These figures suggest that, for those concerned with equality of opportunity, the choice between so-called aptitude tests and conventional achievement tests is a toss-up.

The evidence we have just reviewed indicates that tests such as the SAT do not measure what we normally mean by "aptitude" any better than do conventional achievement tests. SAT scores appear to be just as dependent on home environment and school quality as are scores on conventional achievement tests. And conventional achievement tests predict success in college and adult life just as well as do the SAT or other "aptitude" tests. Many at ETS conclude from this that, although the SAT is no better than conventional achievement tests, it also is no worse. We disagree. We believe that emphasizing tests such as the SAT for college admissions undermines efforts to improve secondary education.

Both college teachers and the general public have become increasingly concerned in recent years over the fact that college freshmen know less than they used to. The decline in mean SAT scores is the most publicized symptom of this problem, but other testing programs have found the same trend. The problem is not that primary school children aren't mastering the three R's as well as they used to. If anything, they are doing better. But teenagers are not moving as far beyond the three R's as they used to.[16]

Talking to high school students, teachers, and parents, one gets the strong impression that high school students do less academic work today than they did 20 years ago. Yet their grades are higher than they were 20 years ago. This means that a clever student can earn A's without learning much. Such students know that, if they earn A's in high school and do well on the SAT, they will be able to get into a top college. And they assume—erroneously, in many cases—that, because they earned A's without doing much work, they must be "smart" and therefore likely to do well on the SAT. If they then do badly, they often blame the test rather than their school.

Although we have no quantitative data on the number of hours secondary school students in different countries spend studying, most observers agree that U.S. high school students do less academic work than their counterparts in Europe or Japan. Most observers also agree that one crucial thing—perhaps *the* crucial thing—that motivates European and Japanese teenagers to study hard is that they must take achievement tests at the end of secondary school, and their scores on these tests largely determine whether and where they will be allowed to obtain higher education.

We would not wish to see U.S. teenagers become as preoccupied with academic success and exams as, say, Japanese teenagers are, but this is not a real danger. We *would* like to see U.S. teenagers do more academic work than they now do. If selective colleges were to base admission on high school grades and tests that measure mastery of the secondary school curriculum (instead of basing it on grades and tests that measure vocabulary, reading comprehension, and basic mathematics), high school students who wish to attend selective colleges might take their academic work more seriously.

Emphasizing mastery of the secondary school curriculum would have other benefits as well. First, it would help to reinforce the traditional American notion that effort will be rewarded. Emphasizing the SAT, in contrast, reinforces the notions that working harder won't help much and that success depends on such factors as "smarts" over which individuals have no control. As we have seen, these notions are probably mistaken, since the SAT is also an achievement test. But neither students nor teachers fully realize this fact. If we want high school students to believe that hard work pays off, colleges must not only reward applicants who have worked hard, but also do so in an obvious way.

Emphasizing tests that measure mastery of secondary school subjects would also encourage secondary schools to offer more demanding academic courses. One should not, of course, exaggerate the potential impact of college admissions tests on high school curricula. Only about half of U.S. high school graduates attend college, and only a handful even apply to selective colleges where test scores play a major role in admissions decisions.[17] This minority does, however, influence the overall character of secondary education disproportionately to its numbers.

Those who attend selective colleges often come from influential families, and many educators judge their school's overall success by such students' accomplishments. Furthermore, although such students are not always social leaders in their schools, they typically exert more overall influence on their peers than their peers exert on them. Changes in college admissions policies that affect these students therefore tend to have ripple effects on secondary schools as a whole.

The effect of substituting conventional achievement tests for the SAT would depend, of course, on how the new system worked. If all colleges were to require conventional achievement tests, more secondary schools would feel obliged to offer courses explicitly tailored to such tests. Those who oppose such exams usually point with horror to their consequences in France; those who favor them usually point to England, where national exams have produced more curricular uniformity than in the U.S. but far less than in France. Given the small proportion of U.S. students applying to selective colleges, national exams would probably have even less impact here than in England. Furthermore, if our concern is with maintaining diversity, it would be easy to establish a set of achievement tests more flexible than those used in either France or England.

The College Board now offers achievement tests in 14 subjects. If more colleges were concerned with measuring achievement, ETS could easily double or triple this number, even giving several types of tests in the most popular subjects. If the College Board allowed students to take as many tests as they wished and to report only their highest scores, students could take a variety of unorthodox courses without jeopardizing their admissions prospects. Such a system would still reward "smarts," as the SAT does, but it would also require and reward sustained application in at least a few areas, which the present system does not.

Since our argument up to this point has been somewhat convoluted, it may help if we recapitulate. Most discussions of college admissions policies focus on distributive justice, asking whether the existing system admits the students somebody thinks selective colleges "ought" to admit. If we apply criteria of this kind, the choice between the SAT and conventional achievement tests appears, on present evidence, to be a toss-up. Both are equally helpful in identifying applicants who will earn above-average grades, who will finish college rather than drop out, and who will be more successful than average after they graduate. Both pose comparable obstacles to blacks, working-class whites, and applicants from second-rate high schools.

But we must also ask how college admissions policies affect the behavior of secondary school students, teachers, and administrators. Because this issue is harder to quantify, experts tend to ignore it. But in the long run it may be even more important than the question of distributive justice. A good college admissions system should encourage diligence rather than sloth and seriousness rather than frivolity among secondary school students. The present system does not seem to us to do this. Selective colleges today base their admissions decisions largely on grades and SAT scores. Some high schools distribute grades in such a way as to promote diligence and seriousness, but many do not. Because of both its content and its name, the SAT does not appear to reward diligence. Furthermore, by emphasizing skills that secondary schools do not explicitly teach, at least after 10th grade, the SAT implicitly tells secondary schools that most of what they do teach does not really matter.

It is always hard to defend a curriculum concerned with what Matthew Arnold called the best that has been known and said. Lacking external support, U.S. secondary schools have largely stopped trying. The time has come for colleges to give them some help.

NOTES

1. For critical assessments of the ideas about testing held by the creators of mental testing, the founders of ETS, and the designers of the SAT, see Leon J. Kamin, *The Science and Politics of I.Q.* (Potomac, Md.: Erlbaum, 1974); and Allan Nairn and Associates, *The Reign of ETS: The Corporation That Makes Up Minds* (Washington, D.C.: Ralph Nader, 1980).

2. Martin R. Katz, *You: Today and Tomorrow* (Princeton, N.J.: Cooperative Test Division, Educational Testing Service, 1959), p. 14.

3. Ibid., p. 30.

4. See, for example, Marion Shaycoft, *The High School Years: Growth in Cognitive Skills* (Pittsburgh: Project Talent, 1967). See also the correlations that Karl L. Alexander, Martha Cook, and Edward L. McDill used in "Curriculum Tracking and Educational Stratification," *American Sociological Review*, February 1978, pp. 47–66.

5. Rex Jackson, "The Scholastic Aptitude Test: A Response to Slack and Porter's Critical Appraisal," *Harvard Educational Review,* August 1980, pp. 382–91.

6. Samuel Messick and Ann Jungeblut formulate the ETS position in similar terms in "Time and Method in Coaching for the SAT," *Psychological Bulletin,* 1981, pp. 191–216.

7. See Christopher Jencks and James Crouse in William Schrader, ed., *New Directions for Testing and Measurement: Measurement, Guidance, and Program Improvement,* No. 13 (San Francisco: Jossey-Bass, 1982), Table 1, p. 40.

8. Because these colleges did not admit many students with low SAT scores, SAT scores do not explain as much of the variation in freshman grades at these colleges as they do at less selective colleges. The admissions process probably restricts the range of SAT scores more than the range of achievement test scores, although the high correlation between SAT and achievement test scores means that the difference is not likely to be appreciable. On the other hand, selective test taking may restrict the range of achievement test scores relative to SAT scores. Furthermore, the fact that some students took only one or two achievement tests may make achievement test scores less reliable than SAT scores in this sample. Thus achievement test scores might predict freshman grades either slightly better or slightly worse than SAT scores, if we had equally reliable scores on samples with equally restricted ranges.

9. About a quarter of the initial sample returned a mail follow-up. Talent drew 3% to 4% subsamples of nonrespondents each year and followed them up intensively, obtaining data from 80% to 85% of these individuals. Our sample includes 3% to 4% of the initial mail respondents and all those in the subsample that was followed up intensively. The effective response rate is thus about 87%.

10. Because the reading comprehension test is longer than the other two and has a larger standard deviation, it dominates the aptitude composite. We have shown, however, that this fact does not account for the weak relationship of the aptitude composite to educational attainment (Christopher Jencks, James Crouse, and Peter Mueser, "The Wisconsin Model of Status Attainment: A National Replication with Improved Measure of Ability and Aspiration," *Sociology of Education,* forthcoming).

11. Our "English" score includes not only knowledge of English literature but mastery of "proper" English, measured by tests of punctuation, capitalization, usage, and the like. Dropping the "proper" English component of the composite slightly increases its correlation with eventual educational attainment among 11th-graders. Jencks, Crouse, and Mueser give additional details on the construction of the composites and their correlations with other variables in "The Wisconsin Model of Status Attainment. . . ."

12. See Jencks and Crouse, *New Directions for Testing and Measurement . . . ,* p. 40 and Table 2, p. 41.

13. Jencks, Crouse, and Mueser, "The Wisconsin Model of Status Attainment. . . .".

14. Christopher Jencks and Marsha Brown, "The Effects of High Schools on Their Students," *Harvard Educational Review,* August 1975, pp. 273–324.

15. From Alexander, Cook, and McDill, "Curriculum Tracking and Educational Stratification."

16. Christopher Jencks, "Declining Test Scores: An Assessment of Six Alternative Explanations," *Sociological Spectrum,* December 1980, pp. 1–15.

17. From a sample survey of 200 four-year colleges, Rodney T. Hartnett and Robert A. Feldmesser estimate that one-third of all four-year colleges admit more than 90% of their applicants, slightly more than half admit more than 80%, four-fifths admit more than 70%, and nine-tenths admit more than 50% ("College Admissions Testing and the Myth of Selectivity," *AAHE Bulletin,* March 1980, pp. 3–6). We know of only six private colleges that admitted fewer than 25% of their applicants in 1979: Amherst (14%); Harvard-Radcliffe (18%); Princeton, Stanford, and Williams (23% each); and Yale (24%).

BURTON R. CLARK

The "Cooling-Out" Function in Higher Education

Questions to think about

1 *How does the process of cooling out work? What are the results of cooling out?*

2 *How would the functional and conflict theorists explain the process of cooling out?*

3 *How does cooling out relate to the open systems framework?*

4 *Do you feel the cooling-out process is necessary or good for the system of higher education and for society? Explain.*

A major problem of democratic society is inconsistency between encouragement to achieve and the realities of limited opportunity. Democracy asks individuals to act as if social mobility were universally possible; status is to be won by individual effort, and rewards are to accrue to those who try. But democratic societies also need selective training institutions, and hierarchical work organizations permit increasingly fewer persons to succeed to ascending levels. Situations of opportunity are also situations of denial and failure. Thus democratic societies need not only to motivate achievement but also to mollify those denied it in order to sustain motivation in the face of disappointment and to deflect resentment. In the modern mass democracy, with its large-scale organization, elaborated ideologies of equal access and participation, and minimal commitment to social origin as a basis for status, the task becomes critical.

The problem of blocked opportunity has been approached sociologically through means-ends analysis. Merton and others have called attention to the phenomenon of dissociation between culturally instilled goals and

From *The American Journal of Sociology* 65 (May 1960), pp. 569–575. Copyright © 1960 by the University of Chicago. Reprinted by permission of the University of Chicago Press.

institutionally provided means of realization; discrepancy between ends and means is seen as a basic social source of individual frustration and recalcitrance.[1] We shall here extend means-ends analysis in another direction, to the responses of organized groups to means-ends disparities, in particular focusing attention on ameliorative processes that lessen the strains of dissociation. We shall do so by analyzing the most prevalent type of dissociation between aspirations and avenues in American education, specifying the structure and processes that reduce the stress of structural disparity and individual denial. Certain components of American higher education perform what may be called the cooling-out function,[2] and it is to these that attention will be drawn.

THE ENDS-MEANS DISJUNCTURE

In American higher education the aspirations of the multitude are encouraged by "open-door" admission to public-supported colleges. The means of moving upward in status and of maintaining high status now include some years in college, and a college education is a prerequisite of the better positions in business and the professions. The trend is toward an ever tighter connection between higher education and higher occupations, as increased specialization and professionalization insure that more persons will need more preparation. The high-school graduate, seeing college as essential to success, will seek to enter some college, regardless of his record in high school.

A second and allied source of public interest in unlimited entry into college is the ideology of equal opportunity.[3] Strictly interpreted, equality of opportunity means selection according to ability, without regard to extraneous considerations. Popularly interpreted, however, equal opportunity in obtaining a college education is widely taken to mean unlimited access to some form of college: in California, for example, state educational authorities maintain that high school graduates who cannot qualify for the state university or state college should still have the "opportunity of attending a publicly supported institution of higher education," this being "an essential part of the state's goal of guaranteeing equal educational opportunities to all its citizens."[4] To deny access to college is then to deny equal opportunity. Higher education should make a seat available without judgment on past performance.

Many other features of current American life encourage college-going. School officials are reluctant to establish early critical hurdles for the young, as is done in Europe. With little enforced screening in the pre-college years, vocational choice and educational selection are postponed to the college years or later. In addition, the United States, a wealthy country, is readily supporting a large complex of colleges, and its expanding economy requires more specialists. Recently, a national concern that manpower be fully utilized has encouraged the extending of college training to more and different kinds of students. Going to college is also in some segments of society the thing to do; as a last resort, it is more attractive than the army or a job. Thus ethical and practical urges together encourage the high-school graduate to believe that college is both a necessity and a right; similarly, parents and elected officials incline toward legislation and ad-mission practices that insure entry for large numbers; and educational authorities find the need and justification for easy admission.

Even where pressures have been decisive in widening admission policy, however, the system of higher education has continued to be shaped partly by other interests. The practices of public colleges are influenced by the academic personnel, the organizational requirements of colleges, and ex-ternal pressures other than those behind the open door. Standards of per-formance and graduation are maintained. A commitment to standards is encouraged by a set of values in which the status of a college, as defined by academicians and a large body of educated laymen, is closely linked to the perceived quality of faculty, student body, and curriculum. The raising of standards is supported by the faculty's desire to work with promising students and to enjoy membership in an enterprise of reputed quality— college authorities find low standards and poor students a handicap in competing with other colleges for such resources as able faculty as well as for academic status. The wish is widespread that college education be of the highest quality for the preparation of leaders in public affairs, business, and the professions. In brief, the institutional means of the students' prog-ress toward college graduation and subsequent goals are shaped in large part by a commitment to quality embodied in college staffs, traditions, and images.

The conflict between open-door admission and performance of high quality often means a wide discrepancy between the hopes of entering students and the means of their realization. Students who pursue ends for which a college education is required but who have little academic ability gain admission into colleges only to encounter standards of performance they cannot meet. As a result, while some students of low promise are successful, for large numbers failure is inevitable and *structured*. The denial is delayed, taking place within the college instead of at the edge of the system. It requires that many colleges handle the student who intends to complete college and has been allowed to become involved but whose destiny is to fail.

RESPONSES TO DISJUNCTURE

What is done with the student whose destiny will normally be early termination? One answer is unequivocal dismissal. This "hard" response is found in the state university that bows to pressure for broad admission but then protects standards by heavy dropout. In the first year it weeds out many of the incompetent, who may number a third or more of the entering class.[5] The response of the college is hard in that failure is clearly defined as such. Failure is public; the student often returns home. This abrupt change in status and in access to the means of achievement may occur simultaneously in a large college or university for hundreds, and sometimes thousands, of students after the first semester and at the end of the freshman year. The delayed denial is often viewed on the outside as heartless, a slaughter of the innocents.[6] This excites public pressure and anxiety, and apparently the practice cannot be extended indefinitely as the demand for admission to college increases.

A second answer is to sidetrack unpromising students rather than have them fail. This is the "soft" response: never to dismiss a student but to provide him with an alternative. One form of it in some state universities is the detour to an extension division or a general college, which has the advantage of appearing not very different from the main road. Sometimes "easy" fields of study, such as education, business administration, and social science, are used as alternatives to dismissal.[7] The major form of the soft response is not found in the four-year college or university, however, but in the college that specializes in handling students who will soon be leaving—typically, the two-year public junior college.

In most states where the two-year college is a part of higher education, the students likely to be caught in the means-ends disjuncture are assigned to it in large numbers. In California, where there are over sixty public two-year colleges in a diversified system that includes the state university and numerous four-year state colleges, the junior college is unselective in admissions and by law, custom, and self-conception accepts all who wish to enter.[8] It is tuition-free, local, and under local control. Most of its entering students want to try for the baccalaureate degree, transferring to a "senior" college after one or two years. About two-thirds of the students in the junior colleges of the state are in programs that permit transferring; but, of these, only about one-third actually transfer to a four-year college.[9] The remainder, or two out of three of the professed transfer students, are "latent terminal students": their announced intention and program of study entails four years of college, but in reality their work terminates in the junior college. Constituting about half of all the students in the California junior colleges, and somewhere between one-third and one-half of junior college students nationally,[10] these students cannot be ignored by the colleges. Understanding their careers is important to understanding modern higher education.

THE REORIENTING PROCESS

This type of student in the junior college is handled by being moved out of a transfer major to a one- or two-year program of vocational, business, or semiprofessional training. This calls for the relinquishing of his original intention, and he is induced to accept a substitute that has lower status in both the college and society in general.

In one junior college[11] the initial move in a cooling-out process is pre-entrance testing: low scores on achievement tests lead poorly qualified students into remedial classes. Assignment to remedial work casts doubt and slows the student's movement into bona fide transfer courses. The remedial courses are, in effect, a subcollege. The student's achievement scores are made part of a counseling folder that will become increasingly significant to him. An objective record of ability and performance begins to accumulate.

A second step is a counseling interview before the beginning of the first semester, and before all subsequent semesters for returning students. "At this interview the counselor assists the student to choose the proper courses in light of his objective, his test scores, the high school record and test records from his previous schools."[12] Assistance in choosing "the proper courses" is gentle at first. Of the common case of the student who wants to be an engineer but who is not a promising candidate, a counselor said: "I never openly countermand his choice, but edge him toward a terminal program by gradually laying out the facts of life." Counselors may become more severe later when grades provide a talking point and when the student knows that he is in trouble. In the earlier counseling the desire of the student has much weight; the counselor limits himself to giving advice and stating the probability of success. The advice is entered in the counseling record that shadows the student.

A third and major step in reorienting the latent terminal student is a special course entitled "Orientation to College," mandatory for entering students. All sections of it are taught by teacher-counselors who comprise the counseling staff, and one of its purposes is "to assist students in evaluating their own abilities, interests, and aptitudes; in assaying their vocational choices in light of this evaluation; and in making educational plans to implement their choices." A major section of it takes up vocational planning; vocational tests are given at a time when opportunities and requirements in various fields of work are discussed. The tests include the "Lee Thorpe Interest Inventory" ("given to all students for motivating a self-appraisal of vocational choice") and the "Strong Interest Inventory" ("for all who are undecided about choice or who show disparity between accomplishment and vocational choice"). Mechanical and clerical aptitude tests are taken by all. The aptitudes are directly related to the college's terminal programs, with special tests, such as a pre-engineering ability test, being given according to need. Then an "occupational paper is required of all students for their chosen occupation"; in it the student writes on the required training and education and makes a "self-appraisal of fitness."

Tests and papers are then used in class discussion and counseling interviews, in which the students themselves arrange and work with a counselor's folder and a student test profile and, in so doing, are repeatedly confronted by the accumulating evidence—the test scores, course grades, recommendations of teachers and counselors. This procedure is intended to heighten self-awareness of capacity in relation to choice and hence to strike particularly at the latent terminal student. The teacher-counselors are urged constantly to "be alert to the problem of unrealistic vocational goals" and to "help students to accept their limitations and strive for success in other worthwhile objectives that are within their grasp." The orientation class was considered a good place "to talk tough," to explain in an *impersonal* way the facts of life for the overambitious student. Talking tough to a whole group is part of a soft treatment of the individual.

Following the vocational counseling, the orientation course turns to "building an educational program," to study of the requirements for graduation of the college in transfer and terminal cirriculum, and to planning of a four-semester program. The students also become acquainted with the requirements of the college to which they hope to transfer, here contemplating additional hurdles such as the entrance examinations of other colleges. Again, the hard facts of the road ahead are brought to bear on self-appraisal.

If he wishes, the latent terminal student may ignore the counselor's advice and the test scores. While in the counseling class, he is also in other courses, and he can wait to see what happens. Adverse counseling advice and poor test scores may not shut off his hope of completing college; when this is the case, the deterrent will be encountered in the regular classes. Here the student is divested of expectations, lingering from high school, that he will automatically pass and, hopefully, automatically be transferred. Then, receiving low grades, he is thrown back into the counseling orbit, a fourth step in his reorientation and a move justified by his actual accomplishment. The following indicates the nature of the referral system:

Need for Improvement Notices are issued by instructors to students who are doing unsatisfactory work. The carbon copy of the notice is given to the counselor who will be available for conference with the student. The responsibility lies with the student to see his counselor. However, experience shows that some counselees are unable to be sufficiently self-directive to seek aid. The counselor should, in such cases, send for the student, using the Request for Conference blank. If the student fails to respond to the Request for Conference slip, this may become a disciplinary matter and should be referred to the deans.

After a conference has been held, the Need for Improvement notices are filed in the student's folder. *This may be important* in case of a complaint concerning the fairness of a final grade.[13]

This directs the student to more advice and self-assessment, as soon and as often as he has classroom difficulty. The carbon-copy routine makes it certain that, if he does not seek advice, advice will seek him. The paper work and bureaucratic procedure have the purpose of recording referral and advice in black and white, where they may later be appealed to impersonally. As put in an unpublished report of the college, the overaspiring student and the one who seems to be in the wrong program require "skillful and delicate handling. An accumulation of pertinent factual information may serve to fortify the objectivity of the student-counselor relationship." While the counselor advises delicately and patiently, but persistently, the student is confronted with the record with increasing frequency.

A fifth step, one necessary for many in the throes of discouragement, is probation: "Students [whose] grade-point averages fall below 2.0 [C] in any semester will, upon recommendation by the Scholarship Committee, be placed on probationary standing." A second failure places the student on second probation, and a third may mean that he will be advised to withdraw from the college altogether. The procedure is not designed to rid the college of a large number of students, for they may continue on probation for three consecutive semesters; its purpose is not to provide a status halfway out of the college but to "assist the student to seek an objective (major field) at a level on which he can succeed."[14] An important effect of probation is its slow killing-off of the lingering hopes of the most stubborn latent terminal students. A "transfer student" must have a C average to receive the Associate in Arts (a two-year degree) offered by the junior college, but no minimum average is set for terminal students. More important, four-year colleges require a C average or higher for the transfer student. Thus probationary status is the final blow to hopes of transferring and, indeed, even to graduating from the junior college under a transfer-student label. The point is reached where the student must permit himself to be reclassified or else drop out. In this college, 30 per cent of the students enrolled at the end of the spring semester, 1955–56, who returned the following fall were on probation; three out of four of these were transfer students in name.[15]

This sequence of procedures is a specific process of cooling-out;[16] its effect, at the best, is to let down hopes gently and unexplosively. Through it students who are failing or barely passing find their occupational and academic future being redefined. Along the way, teacher-counselors urge the latent terminal student to give up his plan of transferring and stand ready to console him in accepting a terminal curriculum. The drawn-out denial when it is effective is in place of a personal, hard "No"; instead, the student is brought to realize, finally, that it is best to ease himself out of the competition to transfer.

COOLING-OUT FEATURES

In the cooling-out process in the junior college are several features which are likely to be found in other settings where failure or denial is the effect of a structured discrepancy between ends and means, the responsible operatives or "coolers" cannot leave the scene or hide their identities, and the disappointment is threatening in some way to those responsible for it. At work and in training institutions this is common. The features are:

1. *Alternative Achievement.*   Substitute avenues may be made to appear not too different from what is given up, particularly as to status. The person destined to be denied or who fails is invited to interpret the second effort as more appropriate to his particular talent and is made to see that it will be the less frustrating. Here one does not fail but rectifies a mistake. The substitute status reflects less unfavorably on personal capacity than does being dismissed and forced to leave the scene. The terminal student in the junior college may appear not very different from the transfer student— an "engineering aide," for example, instead of an "engineer"—and to be proceeding to something with a status of its own. Failure in college can be treated as if it did not happen; so, too, can poor performance in industry.[17]

2. *Gradual Disengagement.*   By a gradual series of steps, movement to a goal may be stalled, self-assessment encouraged, and evidence produced of performance. This leads toward the available alternatives at little cost. It also keeps the person in a counseling milieu in which advice is furnished, whether actively sought or not. Compared with the original hopes, however, it is a deteriorating situation. If the individual does not give up peacefully, he will be in trouble.

3. Objective Denial. Reorientation is, finally, confrontation by the facts. A record of poor performance helps to detach the organization and its agents from the emotional aspects of the cooling-out work. In a sense, the overaspiring student in the junior college confronts himself, as he lives with the accumulating evidence, instead of the organization. The college offers opportunity; it is the record that forces denial. Record-keeping and other bureaucratic procedures appeal to universal criteria and reduce the influence of personal ties, and the personnel are thereby protected. Modern personnel record-keeping, in general, has the function of documenting denial.

4. Agents of Consolation. Counselors are available who are patient with the overambitious and who work to change their intentions. They believe in the value of the alternative careers, though of lower social status, and are practiced in consoling. In college and in other settings counseling is to reduce aspiration as well as to define and to help fulfill it. The teacher-counselor in the "soft" junior college is in contrast to the scholar in the "hard" college who simply gives a low grade to the failing student.

5. Avoidance of Standards. A cooling-out process avoids appealing to standards that are ambiguous to begin with. While a "hard" attitude toward failure generally allows a single set of criteria, a "soft" treatment assumes that many kinds of ability are valuable, each in its place. Proper classification and placement are then paramount, while standards become relative.

IMPORTANCE OF CONCEALMENT

For an organization and its agents one dilemma of a cooling-out role is that it must be kept reasonably away from public scrutiny and not clearly perceived or understood by prospective clientele. Should it become obvious, the organization's ability to perform it would be impaired. If high school seniors and their families were to define the junior college as a place which diverts college-bound students, a probable consequence would be a turning-away from the junior college and increased pressure for admission to the four-year colleges and universities that are otherwise protected to some degree. This would, of course, render superfluous the part now played by the junior college in the division of labor among colleges.

The cooling-out function of the junior college is kept hidden, for one thing, as other functions are highlighted. The junior college stresses "the transfer function," "the terminal function," etc., not that of transforming transfer into terminal students; indeed, it is widely identified as principally a transfer station. The other side of cooling-out is the successful performance in junior college of students who did poorly in high school or who have overcome socioeconomic handicaps, for they are drawn into higher education rather than taken out of it. Advocates of the junior college point to this salvaging of talented manpower, otherwise lost to the community and nation. It is indeed a function of the open door to let hidden talent be uncovered.

Then, too, cooling-out itself is reinterpreted so as to appeal widely. The junior college may be viewed as a place where all high-school graduates have the opportunity to explore possible careers and find the type of education appropriate to their individual ability; in short, as a place where everyone is admitted and everyone succeeds. As described by the former president of the University of California:

> A prime virtue of the junior college, I think, is that most of its students succeed in what they set out to accomplish, and cross the finish line before they grow weary of the race. After two years in a course that they have chosen, they can go out prepared for activities that satisfy them, instead of being branded as failures. Thus the broadest possible opportunity may be provided for the largest number to make an honest try at further education with some possibility of success and with no route to a desired goal completely barred to them.[18]

The students themselves help to keep this function concealed by wishful unawareness. Those who cannot enter other colleges but still hope to complete four years will be motivated at first not to admit the cooling-out process to consciousness. Once exposed to it, they again will be led not to acknowledge it, and so they are saved insult to their self-image.

In summary, the cooling-out process in higher education is one whereby systematic discrepancy between aspiration and avenue is covered over and stress for the individual and the system is minimized. The provision of readily available alternative achievements in itself is an important device for alleviating the stress consequent on failure and so preventing anomic and deviant behavior. The general result of cooling-out processes is that society can continue to encourage maximum effort without major disturbance from unfulfilled promises and expectations.

NOTES

This article is a revised and extended version of a paper read at the Fifty-Fourth Annual Meeting of the American Sociological Association, Chicago, September 3–5, 1959. The author is indebted to Erving Goffman and Martin A. Trow for criticism and to Sheldon Messinger for extended conceptual and editorial comment.

1. "Aberrant behavior may be regarded sociologically as a symptom of dissociation between culturally prescribed aspirations and socially structured avenues for realizing these aspirations" (Robert K. Merton, "Social Structure and Anomie," in *Social Theory and Social Structure* [rev. ed.; Glencoe, Ill.: The Free Press, 1957], p. 134). See also Herbert H. Hyman, "The Value Systems of Different Classes: A Social Psychological Contribution to the Analysis of Stratification," in Reinhard Bendix and Seymour M. Lipset (eds.), *Class, Status and Power: A Reader in Social Stratification* (Glencoe, Ill,: The Free Press, 1953), pp. 426–42; and the papers by Robert Dubin, Richard A. Cloward, Robert K. Merton, and Dorothy L. Meier, and Wendell Bell, in *American Sociological Review,* 24 (April, 1959).

2. I am indebted to Erving Goffman's original statement of the cooling-out conception. See his "Cooling the Mark Out: Some Aspects of Adaptation to Failure," *Psychiatry,* 15 (November, 1952), 451–63. Sheldon Messinger called the relevance of this concept to my attention.

3. Seymour Martin Lipset and Reinhard Bendix, *Social Mobility in Industrial Society* (Berkeley: University of California Press, 1959), pp. 78–101.

4. *A Study of the Need for Additional Centers of Public Higher Education in California* (Sacramento: California State Department of Education, 1957), p. 128. For somewhat similar interpretations by educators and laymen nationally see Francis J. Brown (ed.), *Approaching Equality of Opportunity in Higher Education* (Washington, D.C.: American Council on Education, 1955), and the President's Committee on Education beyond the High School, *Second Report to the President* (Washington, D.C.: Government Printing Office, 1957).

5. One national report showed that one out of eight entering students (12.5 per cent) in publicly controlled colleges does not remain beyond the first term or semester; one out of three (31 per cent) is out by the end of the first year; and about one out of two (46.6 per cent) leaves within the first two years. In state universities alone, about one out of four withdraws in the first year and 40 per cent in two years (Robert E. Iffert, *Retention and Withdrawal of College Students* [Washington, D.C.: Department of Health, Education, and Welfare, 1958], pp. 15–20). Students withdraw for many reasons, but scholastic aptitude is related to their staying power: "A sizable number of students of medium ability enter college, but . . . few if any of them remain longer than two years" (*A Restudy of the Needs of California in Higher Education* [Sacramento: California State Department of Education, 1955], p. 120).

6. Robert L. Kelly, *The American Colleges and the Social Order* (New York: Macmillan, 1940), pp. 220–21.

7. One study has noted that on many campuses the business school serves "as a dumping ground for students who cannot make the grade in engineering or some branch of liberal arts," this being a consequence of lower promotion standards than are found in most branches of the university (Frank C. Pierson, *The Education of American Businessmen* [New York: McGraw-Hill, 1959], p. 63). Pierson also summarizes data on intelligence of students by field of study which indicate that education, business, and social science rank near the bottom in quality of students (*ibid.,* pp. 65–72).

8. Burton R. Clark, *The Open Door College: A Case Study* (New York: McGraw-Hill, 1960), pp. 44–45.

9. *Ibid.,* p. 116.

10. Leland L. Medsker, *The Junior College: Progress and Prospect* (New York: McGraw-Hill, 1960), Chapter IV.

11. San Jose City College, San Jose, Calif. For the larger study see Clark, *op. cit.*

12. San Jose Junior College, Handbook for Counselors, 1957–58, p. 2. Statements in quotation marks in the next few paragraphs are cited from this.

13. *Ibid.*, p. 20.

14. Statement taken from unpublished material.

15. San Jose Junior College, "Digest of Analysis of the Records of 468 Students Placed on Probation for the Fall Semester, 1956," September 3, 1956.

16. Goffman's original statement of the concept of cooling-out referred to how the disappointing of expectations is handled by the disappointed person and especially by those responsible for the disappointment. Although his main illustration was the confidence game, where facts and potential achievement are deliberately misrepresented to the "mark" (the victim) by operators of the game, Goffman also applied the concept to failure in which those responsible act in good faith (*op. cit., passim*). "Cooling-out" is a widely useful idea when used to refer to a function that may vary in deliberateness.

17. *Ibid.*, p. 457; cf. Perrin Stryker, "How To Fire an Executive," *Fortune*, 50 (October, 1954), 116–17 and 178–92.

18. Robert Gordon Sproul, "Many Millions More," *Educational Record*, 39 (April, 1958), 102.

HOWARD R. BOWEN

The Effects of
Going to College

Questions to think about

1 *Why does Bowen argue that individuals and society are getting their money's worth from investment in higher education?*

2 *Considered from an open systems framework, how does higher education contribute to society and to other institutions?*

3 *Compare Bowen's major findings with relevant articles in other chapters concerning learning.*

I. THE EFFECTS OF GOING TO COLLEGE

A college education appears to have profound effects upon traditional sex roles, marital relationships, divorce, family planning, rearing of children, and other family relationships.

Curiously, the literature on the outcomes of higher education has tended to minimize or even overlook those effects.

In the many studies in which students or alumni have been asked to rank the various goals of college education, the rank order given to preparation for marriage and the family has been uniformly low. Faculty members and administrative leaders also seem to ignore the importance of college education for the family—at least judging by their rhetoric.

It could be that one of the most important outcomes of higher education is attained without the participants being aware that it is happening.

Reprinted from Howard R. Bowen, *The Chronicle of Higher Education* (October 31, November 7, November 14, and November 21, 1977).

453

Traditional Sex Roles

College education is associated with a perceptible narrowing of traditional differences between the sexes in interests, attitudes, and behavior patterns.

A study in 1974 found that college women are less inclined than noncollege young women to demand or expect traditionally "masculine" behavior of men. A survey in 1975 of college students of both sexes reported that seniors were somewhat more favorable to women's liberation than freshmen.

Studies directed to the entire adult population also reveal differences between college alumni and others in attitudes toward sex roles.

College-educated women are more likely to be in the labor force than other women. Moreover, college alumni are more likely than others to approve of women working and participating in public affairs.

College-educated men are somewhat more likely to share with their wives in housework, care of children, and companionship with children than are noncollege men.

Higher education is associated with a preference on the part of both men and women for role-sharing in marriage; that is, for husband and wife roles that are not strongly differentiated.

Marriage

College education affects attitudes and behavior toward marriage in several ways.

- It has a significant influence on choice of marriage partners. College-educated people are likely to marry persons of similar educational levels. For example, in one survey of high-school graduates, 70 per cent of the fathers who were college graduates were married to women who had achieved education beyond high school. Indeed, one study of alumni found that a quarter of the respondents had attended the same college as their wives or husbands.
- College-educated people marry at a somewhat older age than other persons.
- Some older studies have suggested that marital happiness is greater among college-educated people than among other groups. Recent surveys have conveyed the good news that previous differences in the degree of marital happiness between the two groups have been narrowed and also that both groups are experiencing greater marital happiness than had been indicated in a comparable study made in 1960.

Divorce

A comparison of the educational levels of divorced persons with those of the entire population 20 to 54 years old suggests that the divorce rate is slightly lower among college-educated people than among persons with a high-school education. For different reasons, the divorce rate is also low among those with only an elementary-school education.

Family Planning

Education has historically been inversely related to the number of children in a family. However, such radical changes in the birth rate have occurred in recent years among persons of all levels of education that generalizations from the past may not hold in the present or future.

Recent surveys of the general population have found that college-educated people favored slightly smaller families than persons with less education. All available evidence, however, suggests that there is little support for childlessness or even for families with only one child.

A 1970 survey of unwanted fertility indicated that unplanned, unwanted, and actual births are all inversely related to education.

The Rearing of Children

College education of parents is highly favorable to the careful rearing of children. It encourages the parents' expenditure of thought, time, and money on behalf of their children, with the effect of improving the children's characteristics and achievements.

College-educated parents devote more time to their children than other parents do. A 1975 study found that college-educated wives devoted about 25 per cent more time than other women to child care, and also that the husbands of college-educated women spent about 30 to 40 per cent more time in child care than other husbands.

The same study found that although college-educated women were more likely to be in the labor force than other women, they were less likely to be working when there were children of preschool or school age in the family.

College-educated parents also spend relatively more of their money in ways that foster the personal development of their children than do other parents.

For example, college graduates spend a substantially higher proportion of their incomes for education (not all of it for children) than do persons of less education, and this holds at every income level. They also spend more for books, magazines, and other reading materials.

An abundance of evidence based on major national studies with huge samples indicates a very strong and positive relationship between the education of parents and the measured intelligence, academic achievement, and extracurricular participation of children in school or college. The education of parents is strongly and positively correlated with children's attendance at nursery school and at college.

A study in 1972 found that the education of parents was a better predictor of college attendance than parental income.

The conclusion is almost certain that one of the most important outcomes of higher education is the favorable effect of parents' education on the intelligence and achievement of children.

That effect, moreover, may be transmitted through many generations—though probably with declining impact on each successive generation. Indeed, this intergenerational effect may be the most important single consequence of higher education.

When higher education adds to the ability and motivation of parents, it enhances the life chances—the opportunities for economic success and personal happiness—of their children and, through them, influences the life chances of succeeding generations. The effect of education is thus multiplied as it is transmitted over the generations.

The intergenerational consequences of higher education may also be considered in reverse.

In most studies of educational outcomes, much attention is given to distinguishing the effects of the current generation's education from the effects of their socio-economic background. But when socio-economic background is seen as partly the effect of education received in the past by parents, grandparents, and even more distant ancestors, then some part of socio-economic background must be ascribed to education.

When socio-economic background is not properly taken into account, the error is not necessarily overstating the effect of education, but rather failing to distinguish between education that occurred earlier and education that occurred later.

Any estimate of outcomes that is limited to a single generation is bound to understate the total impact.

Other Family Relationships

The evidence is scant, but it is probable that the experiences of young people in college affect the opinions, attitudes, and behavior of their parents, other members of their families, and indeed of their friends and associates as well.

It is sometimes asserted that college education alienates sons and daughters from their parents. A 1975 study casts doubt on this matter. It found that attitudes of college students toward their parents were overwhelmingly favorable and did not change over the four years of college.

Consumer Behavior

We tend to view economic efficiency and progress in terms of the amount of goods and services produced. We often overlook the possibility of achieving our goals more fully through greater efficiency in consumption—better values and better allocation of expenditures in achieving those values.

Data from a government study in 1966 show that college-educated people, as compared with other people of equal income, spend a considerably smaller percentage of their income on food, tobacco, alcoholic beverages, and automotive and other transportation.

College-educated people also spend less on clothing and personal care, although they spend about the same percentage of their income on medical care and recreation. They spend a considerably larger percentage on housing, reading, and education.

The evidence strongly suggests that higher education tends to orient the values of consumers toward the home, intellectual and cultural interests, and the nurture of children.

College-educated people save more than others, relative to incomes, and that saving tends to be more largely directed toward the advancement and welfare of children than toward emergencies and provisions for old age.

They seem to be more sophisticated in their investment and financial behavior than less-educated people.

College education probably helps people to deal with legal red tape and bureaucracies, to assert their rights, and to thread their way through complicated procedures, although there is little evidence on these matters.

Leisure

College-educated people receive greater satisfaction from their work, work longer hours, and are inclined to retire later. Thus, they have less nonworking time than other people.

In their use of discretionary, nonworking time, they tend to be less addicted to television than others and more selective in the programs they watch. They are more inclined to read, engage in adult education, attend cultural events, and participate in the arts.

They are more likely to take part in community and civic affairs, and they are more likely to take vacations.

Despite the long historical association of education and sports, we have found little specific information about the effects of physical education on character, on lifelong interest and participation in physical activities, on physical fitness, or on general well-being.

Health

Education exerts a positive influence on health. The causal connections are not wholly understood.

Education may affect the use of health services, and it may be conducive to a way of life favorable to good health. Whatever the causal connections, educated people are, on the average, more healthy than other people.

Educated people visit physicians and dentists more frequently than others, even when compared with others of equal income.

The older people who are the majority of the less-educated population are presumably subject to more illness than the better-educated young, yet they utilize health services less.

Limited evidence suggests that education is to some extent correlated with ways of life that are believed to be healthful. A survey in 1973 suggested that quality of diet may be positively related to education. The smoking of tobacco may be somewhat less prevalent among educated persons than among others.

Disability and Mortality

Many studies show that persons of more education suffer less disability or enjoy better health than those of less education.

Relatively more of those persons who attended college report that they are in excellent health—and fewer that they are in poor health—than those who did not attend.

A study in 1975 found that education had a "positive and statistically significant effect on current health" and that the evidence favored "a causal relationship that runs from schooling to current health."

The same study concluded that a "one-year increase in schooling lowers the probability of death by four-tenths of a percentage point."

Other investigators have found that education is perhaps the most important correlate of good health. Some have suggested that to reduce mortality, investment in general education would be more effective than investment in improved medical care.

II. THE LIBERALIZING ROLE OF COLLEGE

Most studies of college students' attitudes indicate that during the college years they veer toward liberal, as distinct from conservative, views.

On specific issues, most studies find that seniors are more likely than freshmen:

- To favor civil liberties, individual autonomy, and freedom of choice in personal conduct.
- To oppose discrimination on grounds of race, age, sex, religion, and national origin, and to favor racial integration.
- To oppose economic growth and growth of population.
- To favor conservation of natural resources and environmental protection.
- To be concerned about foreign affairs, to favor international understanding and world government, and to lean toward pacifist views.
- To have opposed the Vietnam War.
- To have a low regard for conventional patriotism.
- To be tolerant of activism and disorderly political activity.
- To hold somewhat tolerant views toward Communism, foreign and domestic.
- To hold mildly unfavorable views toward business and labor unions.
- To be suspicious of the political establishment and big government.

Observers will, of course, differ in their evaluation of these results, but the great bulk of evidence suggests that seniors are generally more liberal in political attitudes than freshmen.

College seniors and graduate students are considerably to the left of college freshmen. College alumni are to the right of college seniors—perhaps simply because they are older—but college alumni are to the left of other adults.

In recent college generations, higher education has had a perceptible impact on the political interest of students.

The evidence overwhelmingly indicates that college alumni are more interested and involved in community and political affairs than non-college people.

Party Affiliation

A study in 1975 indicated that seniors were less likely than freshmen to call themselves Republicans and more likely to call themselves Democrats, but the differences were slight.

A more important finding of the study was that 50 per cent of all college students regarded themselves as independents. That percentage is far higher than that for the population generally and raises the possibility that the spread of higher education may be a factor in the pronounced trend in the general population toward independent status.

On the other hand, two studies on the comparative political party preferences of college and non-college youth showed that the differences were slight and the influence of college appeared to be small.

Voting and Community Participation

College-educated people are more likely to vote than other persons. The higher voting rates of college alumni are clearly evident, even when compared with non-college persons of the same income, sex, and race.

College education appears to exert a minor influence toward participation in community affairs during the college years but seems to be a significant influence in adult life.

One study found that education was among the most important factors related to voluntary contributions of time to serve people and organizations outside the family. College alumni are more likely than other adults to belong to political clubs, service clubs, P.T.A.'s and other school organizations, and church-affiliated groups.

The evidence scarcely justifies the assertion that higher education discourages antisocial or illegal behavior. It is plausible, however, to conclude that, to the extent that education at both the high-school and college levels produces jobs, it could inhibit the kind of violent crime that flourishes in conditions of economic desperation.

Economic Productivity

The linkages between education and economic productivity are not precisely known, and they are subject to controversy.

Nevertheless, there is evidence on the matter, and it is obvious that some of the known effects of higher education on its students do contribute to their productive powers.

The impact of higher education on productivity is due partly to broad, general traits that it helps its students to acquire, and it is due partly to specific skills or knowledge—some derived from general education and some from professional or vocational education.

The results from vocational training should not, however, be exaggerated. The theory that workers acquire their skills through formal education and then bring those skills to the labor market is only partially valid.

Investigators in a 1976 study found that most college graduates had not selected their careers during the college years: Two-thirds of the men and half the women had made their career choices afterward.

The same study found that the great majority of those who were holding jobs unrelated to their college majors were doing so voluntarily, that most of this group were satisfied with their jobs, and that the difference in job satisfaction between those with jobs related to their college major and others was slight.

A large survey in 1976 of college graduates who had entered college in 1961 found that college education had been useful to them in many ways in which specific job skills were of secondary importance.

Another well-established effect of college education is that it increases the capacity of individuals to benefit from on-the-job training, other adult education, and experience.

Unemployment

Since most men are in the labor force between the age of leaving school and the age of retirement, level of education is a weak influence on participation.

For older men, however, level of education appears to be a potent influence. This may be explained in part by the dropping out of those with less education for reasons of health, low earnings, unattractiveness of available jobs, and inability to find work.

A study in 1976 of persons now working found less preference for early retirement among those with more education than among those with less education.

For women, labor-force participation is strongly and positively affected by level of education. The percentage of women in the labor force is steadily rising, and the effect of educational attainment on participation may be expected to diminish and eventually to approximate that for men.

A public-opinion survey in 1974 found college alumni were considerably more favorable than other adults to wives' working.

The evidence is overwhelming that, for both men and women, unemployment varies inversely with the level of education.

That has long been true and continues to hold today, despite the widespread (but erroneous) belief that the rate of unemployment is higher among college-educated people than among other groups.

Even among young people, unemployment rates for college students and college graduates are far below those for groups of less education. One study concluded that education factors alone accounted for between three-fifths and three-quarters of the higher unemployment among blacks as compared with whites in 1960 and 1970.

Working Hours

Education appears to encourage longer working hours. An important study in 1962 found that each additional year of education added about one hour to the average weekly working time.

The explanation may be that successful work in technical, professional, and managerial occupations requires long hours; that their high rates of compensation reward them for long hours; that people in those occupations enjoy their work; that education conditions people to work long hours; that educated people have exceptional energy; or that people who are destined to work long hours are the very ones who choose to become well educated.

Grading and Labeling

College plays a significant role in the labor market by "grading and labeling" its students, providing various formal credentials, such as transcripts, certificates, and degrees, and conferring honors and awards.

Two criticisms of higher education's role in the career placement of its students are:

- That higher education is oriented unduly toward supplying the manpower needs of the economy and maintaining the class structure of the economy, rather than toward the optimum development of its students as persons.
- That the higher earnings of college-educated people as compared with those of less education are due largely to grading and labeling rather than to differences in actual productivity.

Except in a few fields (the most notable being medicine), American higher education has not rationed places in various fields of study but has permitted students to choose freely among many major fields.

In any event, it is no crime to prepare young people for careers, so long as that single objective is not allowed to overwhelm other important goals relating to personal development and to preparation for nonvocational aspects of life.

Nor is it a disservice to the society or to young people to help them locate jobs within their chosen vocations.

It must be conceded that grading and labeling might give college-educated people an advantage in the labor market that is not always based on superior productivity. It may endow college people to some extent with a partial monopoly position. However, the amount of the advantage can easily be exaggerated. The real problem is to provide comparable facilities to help non-college people find their identity and to assist them in selecting appropriate careers and finding jobs.

Job Satisfaction

If one looks at the matter historically and from a broad social point of view, it is almost certain that higher education has had a favorable influence on the instrinsic rewards from work.

College-educated people gain more satisfaction from their work than others, but the difference is small, partly because job satisfaction is high among all groups.

Rates of Return

Literally hundreds of studies have been made, especially during the past two decades, on the "rates of return" on "investments" in higher education.

They do not produce a simple and clear-cut conclusion about the effects of higher education on future income, but virtually all studies report positive private and social returns, usually in the range of 8 to 15 per cent.

From the point of view of students and their families, the alternative investments (savings accounts, stocks, bonds, and houses) yield from 5 to 8 per cent. Business investments in capital equipment, on the other hand, may yield from 10 to 15 or even 20 per cent, depending on the risk involved.

Though the studies vary in reliability and plausibility, they show overwhelmingly that higher-education investments produce substantial and positive returns.

Since they admittedly leave out the many valuable returns that are not reflected in augmented money income, the rates of return estimated by economists may be regarded as a kind of lower boundary to the range of possible "true" rates of return.

Economic Growth

A leading study among those that have attempted to trace the influence of education on growth of the total national economy, or gross national product, indicates that perhaps 3.5 per cent of total economic growth between 1929 and 1969 might be attributed to higher education. Thus, for 1969 alone, the direct contribution to economic growth by higher education, excluding academic research and public service, could be estimated at $15.3-billion. This is an exceedingly rough and probably low estimate, but it may give some idea of the magnitude involved.

III. THE RESIDUE OF ACADEMIC LEARNING

Everyone knows that the half-life of memorized details from academic learning is short unless the information is used frequently. What we do not know, and should investigate, is the residue of academic learning after the details have been lost.

The residue may take the form of verbal facility, broad general principles, ways of looking at the world, and improvement in the ability to learn, instead of retained knowledge and information.

Verbal and Quantitative Skills

Available data indicate that students do make significant gains during the college years in verbal and quantitative skills. We found no substantial evidence to the contrary.

A study that compared sophomore and senior test scores in spelling, grammar, punctuation, vocabulary, and mathematics for 2,830 college students during 1930 and 1932 reported gains for all of the subjects except mathematics. In mathematics, the average remained virtually unchanged, reflecting the fact that students who do not take mathematics or mathematically related subjects in college tend to lose ground in that field.

More recently, the steady fall in average scores on the Scholastic Aptitude Tests for college admission suggests that those skills, as measured at the end of high school, are declining for the entire population of college-bound students.

Colleges cannot be held directly responsible for changes occurring in high school, but the rising chorus of complaints of college professors and of employers about the apparent decline in the ability of college students and graduates to read and write raises questions about the effectiveness of colleges in imparting skill in verbal communications.

However, popular complaints about the alleged inability of college graduates to speak and write effectively and correctly are not new. They have been voiced frequently over many decades.

Substantive Knowledge

The overwhelming weight of evidence is that, on the average, students make gains in substantive knowledge during the college years. A study in 1938 comparing sophomores and seniors found moderate gains in literature, foreign literature, fine arts, history and social sciences, and general science. Very large gains were found in a series of studies during the 1950's of scores of freshmen, sophomores, juniors, and seniors on area tests of the Graduate Record Examination.

Studies that asked students and alumni to assess college education's impact upon them found that virtually all in each group rated college as useful in adding to their general knowledge.

Rationality

Studies of the effects of college on ability to think logically, critically, and independently suggest that, on the average, students do make gains but that the amount of those gains is modest. In 16 such studies, gains were found in seven, losses in five, and no change in four.

In other studies, measuring interest in academic activities, abstract thought, and the broad range of ideas typically expressed in literature, art, and philosophy, those who attended college generally made greater gains than those who were employed or became homemakers.

For that type of thinking, homemaking apparently had a strongly negative impact upon young women. The gains for men were greater for those of low ability and low socio-economic status than for those of high ability and high socio-economic status.

Nearly all studies using self-assessments from students and alumni indicate that an overwhelming majority believe they achieved considerable progress in intellectual interests and rationality during college. These studies suffer from the subjectivity inherent in the method, but they provide evidence to reinforce other data.

Aesthetics and Creativeness

From the many studies reviewed, we may conclude that college does, on the average, raise perception or appreciation of the fine arts and literature. We found no evidence on the effect of college on appreciation of natural beauty.

The evidence on creativeness is so scanty and so nebulous that educators should be cautious in making claims about the effect of college in enhancing that quality in its students. It should be added that the sources and conditions of true creativeness are so little understood that its appearance—often in unexpected circumstances—appears more as an act of God than as an outcome of educational technique.

Intellectual Tolerance

In studies of students' intellectual tolerance, seniors tend to be less authoritarian, less dogmatic, and less prejudiced than freshmen; more open to new ideas; and more able to deal with complexity and ambiguity.

Studies of differences by academic fields show gains in intellectual tolerance are greater among students of the arts and sciences than among those in such professional fields as business and engineering.

Cultural Activities

A study in 1968 compared cultural activities of high-school graduates who had attended college four years and those who had been employed for four years.

The college group was more likely to browse in a bookstore and attend dramatic performances, concerts, public lectures, and art exhibits.

Even comparing persons of equal ability and socio-economic status, the differences between the two groups were marked. The results were undoubtedly influenced by the greater accessibility of bookstores and cultural events to college students than to working young people.

The study found that the college group's interest had shifted slightly toward cultural magazines and significantly toward news magazines but that "as manifested by their reading habits, the college students did not appear to have increased markedly in intellectual interests more than employed youth."

Several studies at various colleges indicate that college seniors are more likely than freshmen to be regular readers of newspapers, news magazines, and literary periodicals.

The authors of another study that produced similar results commented that the college graduates who have acquired a taste for serious reading will make up "the 'attentive audience' for serious political and cultural discussion, the large and growing audience of educated men.

"This is not the least important effect of mass higher education: not that it creates an educated cultural elite (which other, more selective systems of higher education perhaps do more effectively), but that it raises the standard of mass entertainment and information by creating an audience for more serious popular journals and magazines."

Lifelong Learning

Most studies show that 50 to 80 per cent of what is learned in courses is lost within one year. One must be leery of easy generalization about the residue of college education: No one remembers everything—or forgets everything.

While exact chemical formulas and equations, the details of political life in the era of Charlemagne, the conjugation of Latin verbs, or the kinky demand curve as understood by economists may be retained by some, they tend to slip away if not used in later life.

It is, therefore, unreasonable to judge the results of higher education on the basis of retained data; it is inevitable that much of the detail will vanish or prove useless.

The important *substantive* aims of higher education lie in the realm of residues.

The residues include the general knowledge and perspectives that enable students to participate in the general culture—for example, to read significant literature, to understand and appreciate the arts, to converse with educated people about matters of importance, to comprehend the news in historical, geographic, and social perspective, to have some basic understanding of science and technology, and to be at home with religious and philosophical issues.

Future Learning Encouraged

Perhaps most important of all, the residues may include the tendencies, triggered by college, that encourage future exploration and learning.

In a survey of a large sample of college alumni from the class of 1950 more than 20 years after their graduation, roughly two-thirds said they felt they had received lasting benefits from their college education: 64 per cent in terms of background for further education in some specialized field;

62 per cent in broadened literary appreciation; 64 per cent in awareness of different philosophies and ways of life; 54 per cent in appreciation of science and technology; 79 per cent in vocabulary, terminology, and facts in various fields of knowledge.

Obsolescence of Knowledge

A study in 1975, designed to measure the obsolescence of knowledge, found that college graduates are either "more efficient users of prior knowledge in acquiring more knowledge" than high school graduates, or, alternatively, that high-school graduates are subject to greater rates of depreciation and obsolescence of knowledge than college graduates.

Many public-opinion polls have tested the general public's knowledge of prominent public figures and events, popular culture, sports, history, geography, and so on.

In virtually all questions in those areas, correct responses are closely related with level of education; the differences between college graduates and high-school graduates are substantial.

However, the questions refer to discrete facts rather than broad principles, and require no reasoning, analysis, synthesis, judgment, or critical thinking. Since they may be related more closely to information acquired through the media of mass communications than to what is learned through education, they may merely reflect the tendency of education to encourage media use.

Alumni Reading Habits

There is abundant evidence that college alumni read more than high-school graduates.

They buy, own, and read more books. They read more magazines of all types, particularly more magazines devoted to news and analytic commentary. Though they do not spend much more time with newspapers, they pay more attention to serious content, such as national and international news and editorials.

These differences in reading habits persist in comparison between groups with equal income or social background.

College alumni are less addicted to television than other people. When television was first introduced, they lagged behind the rest of the population in purchasing sets. Though they eventually acquired sets, alumni now spend less time as viewers, and their viewing is weighted more heavily toward news, documentaries, and programs of educational stations.

The percentage of college-educated people attending motion pictures is higher than for the rest of the population.

College-educated people are more likely than others to be engaged in adult education courses or self-study.

Alumni Interest in the Arts

A few pertinent public-opinion polls show that substantial percentages of alumni take an interest in the arts.

They engage in such activities as listening to classical music, reading poetry, attending concerts and plays, visiting museums, playing musical instruments, and painting. Their participation is significantly higher than for the rest of the population, even when the comparisons are between persons of equal income.

All this evidence from studies of alumni behavior as it relates to the goal of "desire and ability for lifelong cognitive development" resists definitive appraisal. Most of the data do not provide adequate controls to allow isolation of the effects of college from many other effects.

Our judgment is that the goal is attained to a moderate degree.

IV. COLLEGE HELPS PEOPLE DISCOVER THEMSELVES

There is an abundance of evidence about personal self-discovery during college and related changes in values, attitudes, and life choices.

Between one-third and two-thirds of all students significantly alter their choices of major fields or careers during the college years, but personal self-discovery goes beyond the choice of a major field and of a career.

The evidence, though largely based on subjective reports, supports the view that a major outcome of higher education is to facilitate the search of each student for his identity—for discovery of his talents, interests, values, and aspirations.

It may well be that this is one of the more important services that higher education can render for its students.

Moreover, this outcome inevitably has a bearing on the "placement" of students, not only in their careers but also in their roles as participants in family life, religious organizations, political activities, recreation, and cultural pursuits.

Social Poise

A number of miscellaneous studies comparing freshmen and seniors show gains in such traits as social poise, self-assurance, imperturbability, self-sufficiency, and leadership, although the degree of change was not striking.

Public-opinion surveys have indicated only a slight difference in favor of the college-educated over others in reported degree of happiness, especially when income differences are taken into account.

Data on admissions to public mental hospitals show sharply lower rates of admission for college-educated people than for others. But the data on admissions to public and private outpatient psychiatric services are less clear.

For younger age groups, the admission rate for college-educated people is greater than that for high-school graduates, whereas for older age groups the reverse is true.

These data are doubtless affected by the greater awareness of and access to psychiatric services on the part of college-educated people.

A study in 1964 concluded that the higher the social class and level of education, the better the chances that people will finish psychotherapy and benefit from it.

A study in 1970 of symptoms of psychological distress, such as headaches, dizziness, and nervousness, found a definite trend of higher symptom rates for the less-educated compared with more-educated groups. Only nervousness showed a counter pattern, with lower rates for the less-educated than for the more-educated.

The incidence of nervous breakdowns, however, was always lower for the better-educated, for each sex, at all age levels.

Emotional Support

A number of psychologists have expressed the view that college provides needed emotional support for students who are passing through several critical stages of development on their way from adolescence to maturity.

Most studies find that college-educated people are more tolerant and less prejudiced toward different races, nationalities, and religions, and toward women's liberation.

The majority of alumni and upperclassmen report that college helped them to become more tolerant and understanding of others and more skilled in interpersonal relations.

Indeed, most students and alumni report that getting along with people is one of the most significant results of their college education.

No Impact on Altruism

On the other hand, college seemingly does not have a marked impact on attitudes of altruism and philanthropy leading to kindness, sympathy, unselfishness, sociability, or friendliness toward other individuals.

These results may mean that college reduces prejudice toward groups of people on the basis of their race or sex or nationality without greatly affecting their one-to-one human relationships.

An obvious warning against too-easy acceptance of college influence as favorable to the development of sound values is that academic cheating, shoplifting, and vandalism have been on the increase on most campuses in the past decade.

The revelations about misconduct in the higher reaches of business and government—where virtually all of the persons involved are college-educated—surely implies that the spread of college education has not brought on a great moral renaissance. Some observers who are concerned about the allegedly slack moral condition of American society hold college and university educators primarily responsible.

Tolerance Imparted

Insights into the effects of college on certain aspects of morality may be derived from surveys of attitudes toward specific kinds of personal behavior.

These surveys suggest strongly that higher education has tended, at least in recent years, to impart greater flexibility, tolerance, permissiveness, and individual choice in matters of personal behavior.

Higher education appears to have been near the vanguard in the decline of Puritan values in our society.

This appears to be true whether one compares seniors with freshmen, college students with other young people of comparable age groups, college alumni with non-college adults, or trends over time in the attitudes of college students.

Non-college youths have been following college students—with a lag of only a few years—in the espousal of new attitudes that place an emphasis on individual freedom and choice in personal behavior and that deny conventional values.

The experience of the late 1960's, when student unrest was at its height, may also shed some light on the question of values.

That episode was a sudden mobilization of values long latent in the college population, against such acute social problems as racial and sexual injustice, deterioration of the environment, rampant population growth, paternalism on campus and, in particular, the Vietnam war and the draft.

The student movement, built around humanistic conceptions, sought an egalitarian and person-centered society and opposed material values, bureaucratic organizations, nationalism, militarism, and individual conformity.

Latent Values

The implicit values were akin to those often prized within the academic community and which in one form or another are part of the teachings of liberal education.

In one possible interpretation, the experience of the turbulent 1960's may be construed to mean that college transmits values to some of its students, that these values may be latent much of the time, and that under certain stimuli they can erupt into overt social action.

One of the embarrassments to educators dealing with the student protests was that on the whole they were sympathetic to some of the demands of students and the value-premises on which these demands were based, while being shocked and revolted by the tactics employed.

Current critics of higher education seem to hit the mark by stressing a breakdown of conventional standards of personal morality on the campus.

It is clear that in the late 1970's colleges and universities are far from being bulwarks of *conventional* morality, though some would argue that the new campus morality has more depth and less hypocrisy than the traditional brand.

The effect of college on religious attitudes and religious observance has been investigated in great detail.

A number of studies indicate that the relative strength of religious values declines during college.

Less Favorable Toward the Church

A series of rather specific studies between 1929 and 1960 indicated, with few exceptions, that students become less favorable toward the church, less convinced of the reality of God, less favorable toward observance of the Sabbath, less accepting of religious dogma, less fundamentalistic, less conservative, less orthodox, and more religiously liberal.

Moreover, the degree of change varies with the major fields of students, the greatest change occurring for those in the liberal arts, and the least for those in professional fields.

A public-opinion poll in 1975 suggests that the changes may be of modest proportions, but that the direction of change is clearly toward less orthodoxy and less affiliation with formal religious organization.

Formal religious observance, as measured by church attendance, drops off during the college years.

More Interest in Religion

Church attendance, however, is not the only vehicle that college offers for formal religious expression. Another is the formal study of philosophy and religion.

The number of courses offered and the enrollment in them have increased greatly over the past two decades. These courses may be taking the place of the more traditional activities associated with the college chapel.

Departments of religion now exist in many public as well as private institutions, and enrollments have been growing steadily. For example, the number of students enrolled for advanced degrees in religion (not counting those seeking professional degrees in theology) increased from 5,314 in 1960 to 15,431 in 1974. The number of undergraduate enrollments in religion also is known to have increased.

A recent poll of college students inquiring about the subjects of study that had most changed their outlook on life revealed that philosophy and religion were among the leading fields, along with psychology and sociology.

Resurgence of Evangelism

Perhaps more important, most of the available data on the religious outcomes of college antedate the current resurgence of evangelical or fundamentalist religious thought and practice, both on and off the campus, and the more publicized (though less widespread) vogues for various Far Eastern forms of religious thought and expression.

The relatively rapid growth of private colleges affiliated with conservative or fundamentalist sects also is worth noting.

In view of these cross-currents, we should be wary of concluding that the higher-education experience as a whole lessens lifelong interest in religious thought and practice or discourages the quest for the meaning of human existence.

CHAPTER 9

Education Around the World: Cross-Cultural Models for the Study of Educational Systems

At this moment children sit in classsrooms around the world, but their experiences differ greatly. In some poor Third World countries, children attend school erratically and often only until the third grade; they are functionally illiterate. The agricultural life in developing countries, however, demands many hands, and schooling is a luxury. A few may go on, but this may require money for clothing, shoes, books, transportation, and perhaps room and board. Even when education is free, other expenses are always involved.

In many countries all children are expected, even required, to attend school until a certain age, usually around 16, but the schooling received by different children in the same country may vary widely. In England, for instance, all children must attend school until age 17, but children from higher socioeconomic levels often have access to elite schools, better education, and more opportunity for elite university training leading to responsible jobs. Paul Willis has given an excellent description of perpetuation of class differences,[1] showing how kids learn very early where they fit into the educational system and what it can do for them. The "lads" in the English system, referred to in Chapter 6, see little value in education. They feel they are going to work in the factory just as their fathers and grandfathers did before them. Essentially they are just putting in time in school, and their attitudes and behaviors reflect this feeling. These working-class youths especially resented the "'ear 'oles," those mostly middle-class students who accept the formal goals of the school and strive for success within the system.

Using the open systems framework, we can consider the world as the environment within which individual countries or even regions are influenced by political and economic forces. One approach divides the world into *peripheral areas* and developed *center areas.* International forces and networks controlled by center areas influence and even dictate educational system policies in peripheral areas, some of which may not be suited to the educational needs of peripheral countries. Thus we see a worldwide system not only of elite and poor within countries, but also rich and poor countries and regions.

Bill Williamson, a British sociologist of education, presents a typology of educational systems related to political and economic systems and level of development in societies.[2] His typology includes four sectors into which most of the world's societies can be placed. Williamson argues that the economic development of a society, along with its ideology, is an important determinant of the type of education system that evolves. This theme is elaborated by the authors included in this chapter, especially Ramirez and Boli-Bennett.

Until recently, comparative education has focused on descriptions or case studies of individual educational systems. Cross-cultural studies have attempted to compare specific aspects of educational systems such as quality and quantity, internal structures, differentiation of students within systems, goals, materials and resources, teaching techniques, and curricula. Now there is a movement among sociologists to go beyond descriptive studies to model building and problem solving. Some studies focus on the large picture of macro-level analysis, using nation-states and world systems for cross-cultural study. You are encouraged to read further about individual education systems and apply these models to your findings. (One source for descriptions of national educational systems is UNESCO's *Country Education Profiles.*)

In our first article, Clark Kerr presents five models of educational systems, pointing out that what works in one nation may be dysfunctional for another. His models, diagrammed and discussed with specific country examples, exemplify the range of structures, goals, country needs, and motives behind educational systems.

On another level of analysis that focuses on the world system, Francisco Ramirez and John Boli-Bennett examine the expansion of the world education system and the interconnections among nation-states. Their findings indicate that two poles operate, one related to societal development and the other to individual meaning, in setting transnational educational norms.

Finally, Judith Barnet presents a summary of results from the study *No Limits to Learning: Bridging the Human Gap*, sponsored by the Club of Rome. Educational systems have developed as adaptive, cybernetic systems, reacting to changing world environments rather than actively embracing anticipatory and participatory learning in preparing for the future. Barnet indicates changes that would move education toward goals of a humanistic world educational system. Some of these recommendations for change include movement to forms of alternative education, a topic to be discussed in Chapter 10.

NOTES

1. Paul Willis, *Learning to Labor: How Working Class Kids Get Working Class Jobs* (New York: Columbia University Press, 1981).

2. Bill Williamson, *Education, Social Structure, and Development* (London: Macmillan, 1979).

CLARK KERR

Five Strategies for Education and Their Major Variants

Questions to think about

1 *Match the models of educational systems discussed in Kerr's article with educational systems in several countries. What is the rationale behind their development?*

2 *Compare similarities and differences in Kerr's model and those of the other authors in this chapter. How complete are Kerr's models? Can you think of any other models?*

3 *Within the open systems framework, how do educational strategies correspond to political strategies?*

4 *Which of Kerr's models depicts your educational experience? Explain. What are the implications of Kerr's models for the day-to-day school experiences of children?*

Education takes many forms in many places. It is not one, but many things. One errs in talking about *the* contribution of education to national development without specifying what kind of education, for whom, at what stage of development, and where. Some kinds of education for certain kinds of people under one set of circumstances may be very helpful; and the same kind for different people under other circumstances may be equally harmful. Western models do not work equally well in Africa or Asia. Education is a multiform, not a uniform, phenomenon.

Comparative Education Review (June 1979), pp. 171–182. Copyright © 1979 by the Comparative and International Education Society. Reprinted by permission of the University of Chicago Press.

MODEL I. ELITE-ORIENTED EDUCATION

One strategy for education is to consider it as serving a small elite only. This elite may be defined by birth—an aristocracy, or by demonstrated talent—a meritocracy, or by some combination of both. The difference between definition by birth and by talent, however, is a substantial one. The persons chosen will be quite different because talent does not uniformly follow family origin. The method of selection is quite easy when based on birth and quite difficult when based on talent. The latter basis requires much better primary and secondary schools that are widely distributed and better methods of examination. The tone of the educational process varies also, from a leisurely one when based on birth to a highly competitive one when based on talent.

Yet there are substantial similarities in education serving elites defined by birth or by talent. In each case, small numbers are involved. The curriculum tends to be of the classical type: all students receive much the same background in terms of the central content of the curriculum and the style of approach in residential living and codes of personal conduct. Once a student is on the ladder, the effort of the system is expended on his or her support as an individual and on the student's preservation within the elite group. Graduates enter into a distinct class status raised far above that of nongraduates. The quality of academic degrees is held, wherever possible, to a single "Gold Standard." A degree has a certain value for all holders regardless of what field they study or their personal performance. Graduates have an assured status.

The British system of higher education until the middle of the nineteenth century was elitist, and largely hereditary elitist. Entry into Oxford and Cambridge was limited by rule to males who were members of the Anglican church and by fact mostly to sons of the gentry and the upper middle classes. During the next century, reliance gradually was placed more on talent and less on heredity. Good preparatory schools based on talent were developed, and effective sorting examinations were devised. Harvard, in the United States, followed a somewhat similar historical course. The Scottish universities were always more open to talent. Sub-Sahara Africa with its missionary schools and French lycées followed the meritocratic elite system then in effect in Britain and France. China had such a system to prepare its mandarins for 2,000 years.

Higher education in Latin America, by and large, has not yet given up selection on the basis of family position in favor of selection based on talent. One reason for this is that the good secondary schools are almost universally private and costly, although higher education is generally tuition free. Thus only the children of the wealthier families can qualify for

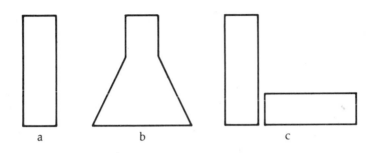

FIGURE 1
*(a) Hereditary Elitist; (b) Meritocratic Elitist; (c) Hereditary Elitist
with Separate Mass Elementary System*

the university through prior attendance at the better secondary schools.
And, once they arrive at the universities, they are often but not always
heavily subsidized from the public purse. A largely unconnected mass
elementary system of low quality exists for the children of peasants and
workers. There is almost no way for talent to rise through the formal system
of education. It is more likely to emerge through the military forces. Much
of the Moslem world parallels the pattern found in Latin America. Ancient
Rome also had an elitist system for children of the upper class based on
tutors and private schools and a large-scale elementary system for the
masses.

There are, then, at least three major elitist approaches: (1) The hereditary elitist which may be visualized as a ladder that leads from entry almost
automatically to exit. (2) The meritocratic elitist which has a broader base:
able young persons are sought more widely than in the wealthy classes
alone and are subject, in the early stages of education, to intense competition through which some are eliminated. (3) The hereditary elitist with
a separate, largely unconnected, low-level egalitarian system at the primary
level, looking like a disconnected figure L (see fig. 1).

MODEL II. PRODUCTION-ORIENTED EDUCATION

The University of London, which was founded in 1836 with a different
orientation than that of Oxford and Cambridge, was much more open to
bright young people drawn from the total population and not only trained
them to be scholars and gentlemen, but also prepared them for a much

broader variety of professions. A great system of training for the health professions was developed there long before Oxford and Cambridge took any broad interest in such training. The redbrick universities in England followed London's lead.

The most dramatic step toward the occupational orientation of higher education took place in the United States with the founding of the land-grant universities at the time of President Lincoln. These institutions aimed to serve the children of farmers and workers. They turned their backs on the classical curriculum of the day and, instead, sought to fill the needs of developing industry and agriculture for managers and technical experts. They were not at all oriented toward class status but clearly toward productive effort.

Russia, after 1917, moved in the same general direction, but with more ideological content, more centralized control, and even more emphasis on technocratic aspects. The purpose in Russia, as in the United States, was to aid the economic growth of an advancing society and, simultaneously, to open up new opportunities for more of the youthful population.

Japan, since World War II, has enormously expanded and diversified its national system of higher education. Adopting a production-oriented approach to education, Japan has put less emphasis on university-based research than either the United States or Russia. Applied research in Japan has been left principally to large private industry, and basic research, until recently, has been comparatively neglected.

The tendency in all production-oriented systems is to concentrate at first on high-level manpower and then, more gradually, on paraprofessional manpower. This development reflects three factors. First, full recognition of how many paraprofessionals are needed to make good use of the highly skilled professional is usually not forthcoming. Second, for educating paraprofessionals, to the extent that they are used, reliance is initially placed on secondary schools and on on-the-job training. Later, provision of some formal training at the postsecondary level as well is usually found desirable. Third, paraprofessional training has lower status and is avoided by students if they have the alternative of professional training. As industrial growth proceeds, however, this impediment is less effective, and paraprofessional training becomes more common. Policy conclusions based on these three considerations have contributed to the rise of community colleges with 2-year programs in the United States. They are now, in enrollment, the largest single element of American higher education. In Canada, community colleges and comparable institutions more than doubled in size in the 1960s. The British government recently has particularly aided the polytechnics, and Australia has done the same for the institutions of technical and further education.

A modified occupation-oriented approach is the civil-servant approach: education, particularly secondary and higher education, is designed to turn out civil servants rather than the whole range of professionals and paraprofessionals required by an industrializing or industrialized nation. This narrower concentration has marked France, India, and much of Africa until very recent times. Napoleon in France and the British colonial authorities in India both concentrated on the need of the state for well-trained civil servants. In both countries today teachers are included in the class of civil servants.

Another variation of the production-, or occupation-oriented, model entails preservation of elements of the older classical system reformed to include a meritocratic base and the addition of a newer technocratic system. The land-grant universities were founded while the older liberal-arts colleges continued to thrive in the United States; the redbricks were added on to Oxford and Cambridge; the technical universities to the Humboldt-type universities in Germany; and now, in Latin America, new technical universities are being started while older universities, such as San Marcos, remain largely unchanged. Over a period of time, classical institutions, in competition for funds and students, begin to look more like the newer, technocratic institutions. There is a movement of the classical institution toward the production-oriented institution, and the civil-servant institution begins to train for a wider range of careers—thus also merging toward the dominant modern type.

The pyramidal model may change shape, as in the United States, when more jobs require more training and more persons can afford more education. The sides will slope less steeply as more people stay in school for a longer period of time, and the apex will be rounded off as many more positions require training at quite advanced levels. The shape becomes that of a haystack.

There are, then, at least five major production-oriented approaches: (1) The pure pyramid, which is closely tied to manpower planning, with a universal base of literacy, topped by successively smaller components of training for clerks and technicians, advanced technicians, scientists, scholars, and advanced professionals. Within higher education in Russia, only 10 percent of the students are in universities; 90 percent are in technical colleges. The United States demonstrates a more varied approach because dynamics of the labor market, rather than manpower planning, fit education to jobs, and because the system responds to student demand for education beyond the needs of industrial production. (2) The truncated pyramid, or partially truncated pyramid, as in Japan, where great emphasis is placed on primary and secondary education and less (until the postwar period) on higher education. (As a corollary, the universities are weak in

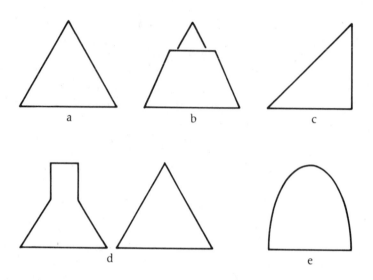

FIGURE 2
(a) Pure Pyramid; (b) Truncated Pyramid with Reduced Emphasis upon Higher Education, Including Research; (c) Half Pyramid Directed Toward Civil-Service Occupations; (d) Pyramid Arising Alongside an Older Elitist System; (e) Advanced-Stage Pyramid

basic research.) This pyramid has a reduced apex. (3) The half pyramid, found historically in France and India, with emphasis on training for the public civil service rather than for private industry and commerce. (4) The pyramid rising alongside an older elite system, as in England where until recently the redbricks drew heavily on the public grammar schools while Oxbridge continued to draw substantially on private schools, like Eton and Harrow. (5) The advanced-stage pyramid with a more rounded top, when more and more occupations require more and more training (see fig. 2).

One may note that the pyramidal approach applies within higher education, as well as to the totality of education, and results within higher education in an emphasis on differentiation of functions—some elements have higher academic value and some, lower. Thus the binary system in England; the universities versus the technical institutes in Russia; the tripartite system of community colleges, state colleges, and universities in California; the institutions of technical and further education, the colleges of advanced education, and the universities in Australia; and so forth. There is no Gold Standard. There is instead a diversity of programs, standards, and status. In all pyramidal systems the emphasis is on identifying and eliminating the less able individual and on preserving within the system only the most able. Less able students drop off as the slopes rise higher.

MODEL III. UNIVERSAL ACCESS EDUCATION

A third approach is universal schooling and open enrollment in higher education, which is open to all persons 18 years of age and over. California (1960) and New York City (1970) are examples in the United States, and within the foreseeable future, 95 percent of all Americans will be within commuting distance of an open-access college. The first community college in the United States was founded in 1902, and the University of Chicago opened its adult extension division in 1892. Community colleges and adult extension are the two great devices tried in the United States to date to achieve universal open access.

As other examples, Britain has now established (1970) the Open University; Japan has begun (1971) the "University of the Air"; Sweden is establishing regional centers attached to its universities; Spain is planning an "open university"; the University of Nairobi has a "Mature-Age Entry Scheme."

The open-access approach to higher education in industrialized nations follows four developments: first, the prior creation of universal primary and secondary education; second, the continuing need by employed persons for technical retraining in the midst of dynamic technological changes; third, the widely held view that education should be a continuing part of the lives of all people who wish it for whatever purpose; and fourth, the new electronic technology which makes an open-access approach possible.

Open access to higher education relates to a basic question: Does education exist for the sake of an elite in a class society, for the sake of productive efficiency in an industrial society, or for all people throughout their lives in a populist-oriented society? Given the financial resources and necessary levels of prior education, the concept of open access to higher education demands that education be available to all who wish it. The courses taught will cover many more subject areas than either elitist or production-oriented higher education. Many courses, for example, will be oriented toward consumption activities. An elitist curriculum is more directed toward development of political leadership; a production-oriented curriculum, toward the needs of the labor market; and the open access curriculum, toward the interests of daily life. Academic standards will be lower, on the average, in an open-access system and may even disappear in some areas in favor of mere attendance. Remedial work for adults will be a major component. Relevance is not defined as what a highly educated person should know, nor as what an expert must know, but, rather, as what any person may want to know for whatever reason.

Open access may extend to college-age youth only, or to persons of all ages.

The open-access approach may not only develop in wealthy industrial, fully modernized, societies but also in largely rural societies with a low level of per capita wealth. Gandhi, for example, wanted to make "basic education" available to all the people living in a village to assist them in all aspects of their lives. Tanzania has advocated "education for self-reliance" for its entire population. Modern China has instituted literacy training and basic education throughout its vast country. A century ago, Denmark began its rural folk schools. "Store front" schools, in a few American ghettos, follow the same general pattern. An industrializing nation may adopt a form of open access at some level, or levels, of education based on an egalitarian ideological drive, or as a way of letting everybody in— for political reasons—on some of the improvements in society, or as a way of keeping people in rural areas so that they will not swamp the modern sector.

Open access may be developed as a pure system, standing by itself, as Gandhi essentially wanted since he did not favor industrialization. Or it may be added onto a production-oriented system serving modern industry and government.

There are, thus, at least two major forms of open access: (1) The pure type with equal educational opportunity for all citizens. (2) The alternative type where an open access system of education stands as an alternative to the meritocratic system (see fig. 3).

Of course, comparatively heavy emphasis in the second type may be found on the pyramid (as in the United States), or heavy emphasis may be placed on the circle (as in Tanzania).

In any event, open access can arise under quite diverse circumstances: as a chosen instrument in a progressive, egalitarian, largely rural society; as an adjunct to the modernizing sector of society—perhaps as part of a rural development program; or as a supplement to the meritocratic educational system of a highly industrialized society with populist tendencies. An open-access approach may be combined in various ways, and for various reasons, with a pyramidal system. Open access, however, is essentially incompatible with an elitist—particularly a hereditary elitist—approach. Egalitarianism and hereditary elitism make strange bedfellows in education, as in society as a whole.

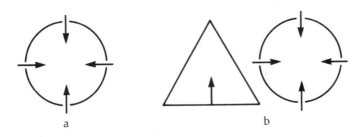

FIGURE 3
(a) Pure Open Access; (b) Open Access as an Alternative

MODEL IV. HORIZONTAL EDUCATION

Recently, the suggestion has been made that education, which has historically been vertical in the effect on social stratifications, be laid on its side horizontally. The "knowledge commune" has been posited as a central aspect of "horizontal collectivism."[1] In a society fitting such a model there would be no highly trained experts; people would rotate from job to job as they saw fit. There would be equality among teachers and students in the knowledge commune—no "chair" professors, no assistants, no subservient students. No one would be allowed to rise above a certain fixed level. Society, as well as the education system, would have a flat profile when projected graphically. Education would be an instrument of leveling conformity.

This model may be visualized as a horizontal line or, perhaps better, as a wide room with a low ceiling (see fig. 4a).

This is a vision that is beautiful to some but one that I do not believe realistic. Some experts, meritocratically selected and trained, are needed to make an atom bomb, even in Maoist China. The little Red Book does not suffice in this case, nor in the provision of surgical care or the building of bridges and dams. No modernized or modernizing system can get along without technical experts and the necessarily pyramidal educational structure to train them. Modernization is not a necessity, but a pyramidal structure of education is essential if modernization is undertaken.

Horizontal equalization of all citizens in all aspects of their lives engenders enormous pressures for conformity, and these pressures require a supreme charismatic personality or a strong bureaucratic hierarchy—or both—to give inspiration and to assure control of the masses. The greatest

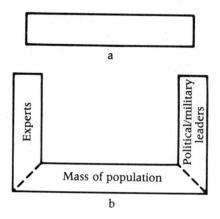

FIGURE 4
(a) Horizontal-Egalitarian; (b) Modified Horizontal Approach
with Elite Groups

personality cult in the world today is that surrounding Mao Tse-tung who during his lifetime had the backing of an all pervasive military establishment. Furthermore, different people have different tastes, interests, and abilities, and it would be both unwise and impossible to confine them all on a horizontal level forever. The leveling of humanity to one universal standard is inconsistent with both human nature and the realities of the modern world.

Nevertheless, the horizontal approach has been tried recently in a modified form in China during the cultural revolution. A political and military elite remained, however, above the mass of the people, as well as a small technological elite with an educational background. The experience of China may be termed a modified horizontal approach with two small elite classes rising above the horizontal mass—one raised through on-the-job training and selection (political and military leaders) and the other through formal education (technical experts) (see fig. 4*b*). This approach, in fact, looks something like that found in Latin America, but it is quite different because the Chinese elite groups were chosen on the basis of ideology and merit, not heredity, and through on-the-job selection and training as well as education. The mass of the population was held to low levels of education, not as a result of poverty but as the consequence of an ideology emphasizing the interchangeability of man in the essential roles of soldier-peasant-worker. Enforced homogenization, politically determined, was the force at work in China rather than socially and economically determined neglect.

The horizontal approach is quite different from open access. The open-access approach allows an individual to obtain whatever education he wants, at any time and at any level. The horizontal approach not only sets a ceiling on individual aspirations but also prescribes a set curriculum for everyone regardless of individual interests. The curriculum is heavily oriented toward literacy, ideology, vocational skills, and "coping" skills in health, nutrition, etc.

MODEL V. ATOMISTIC EDUCATION

This may be viewed as the oldest, or the newest, or the most constant form of education: oldest because education began informally in the family and on the job, newest because of recent proposals for the "deschooling of society,"[2] and most constant because education always takes place informally as well as formally—in the home, on the job, in the library, beside the radio, in front of the TV screen. The emphasis in atomistic education is on the individual being educated as a by-product of some other activity or on his own, but not through a system of formal education. Atomistic education might be represented by a series of random dots (see fig. 5). Such a system can coexist with any of the other systems we have discussed, but it is most consistent with the open-access approach. The atomistic system if dominant will supplant all other systems; its central theme is ultimately incompatible with the organized character of the other models.[3]

Current interest in atomistic education comes from philosophical anarchist sources. Proponents argue that most, or at least many, people in the world are not now receiving formal education and that universal formal education is too expensive to attempt to realize; that formal education unwisely elevates some people above others and does more harm than good by smothering interest in learning and alienating youth from manual labor; and that schools serve to perpetuate the status quo against the real interests of the people by teaching them to be passive consumers of whatever the society offers. Apprenticeship training and informal learning centers, which people can enter and leave when they wish, are favored instead of formal schools. The argument calls for the abolition of all compulsory attendance in education and of all degrees and certificates.[4] The content of individual learning programs would be highly idiosyncratic.

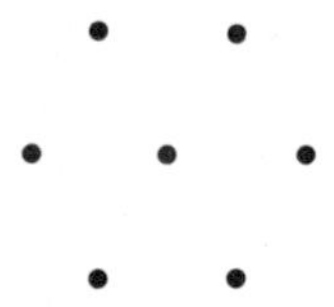

FIGURE 5
Atomistic Education

CONCLUSION

The five pure models of educational systems I have presented vary from a vertical line to a pyramid, a circle, a horizontal line, and a series of dots.

I have set forth these several strategic approaches to education first to reinforce the point that education is many different things and must be looked at in its specific forms rather than as a single form, and second to emphasize the range of strategic choices that individuals have and may choose among.

The elitist approach responds to social class in a stratified society. All persons who step on the lowest rung of the ladder are expected to climb on the top, and most do so. Dropout rates are low. Emphasis is on the selection and training of political leaders.

The occupational approach to structuring education responds to dramatic insistence on national economic growth, to skill needs in a production- and service-oriented society. Students drop out when they face increasingly difficult competition or when they choose to withdraw. Emphasis is on the selection and training of experts for industry, commerce, and the professions, on the skills related to the production of goods and services.

The open-access approach responds to populist pressures, to the interests of all the people all the time. The circle is open to them at any time and contains any subject they may want to study. Sir Eric Ashby has written about this, in the American context, as "any person, any study."[5] Nobody drops out by definition. Some persons may choose to stop out, however, precisely as they may choose to stop in. The emphasis is on everybody and free choice.

The horizontal approach is grounded in an egalitarian ideology that emphasizes the homogenization of the masses who have no free choice. The atomistic approach turns its back on all formal schooling as not only unproductive but even counterproductive. The elite approach fits best a nation under either dynastic or colonial leadership; and the occupational model fits an industrializing society with middle-class or nationalistic, socialistic, or communistic leadership.[6] The open-access approach best fits an egalitarian rural society, or serves as an adjunct to the modernizing sector of a developing nation, or stands as an alternative and supplement to the meritocratic structure in a modernized society. The horizontal approach is found, in modified form, in an ideologically managed political and military dictatorship. The atomistic approach is connected with anarchistic thought and the socioeconomic conditions of primitive society.

NOTES

1. Johan Galtung, "Social Structure, Education Structure and Life Long Education," mimeographed (Paris: OECD, November 1970).

2. Ivan Illich, *Deschooling Society* (New York: Harper & Row, 1971). Also see Paul Goodman, *Compulsory Miseducation* (New York: Horizon, 1964), and his essay in *Summerhill: For and Against* (New York: Hart, 1970), pp. 205–22.

3. While atomistic education is not a viable total approach to education in industrialized and industrializing societies, proponents of atomistic education have added impetus to some developments which have been taking place for other reasons, such as (1) more efforts to find talent throughout all elements of the population, (2) more attention to lifelong learning opportunities, (3) more active participation by learners in the educational process, (4) more acceptance of individualized learning programs, and (5) more use of noneducational institutions for educational purposes.

4. See Everett Reimer, *School Is Dead: Alternatives in Education* (Garden City, N.Y.: Doubleday, 1971).

5. Eric Ashby, *Any Person, Any Study: An Essay on Higher Education in the United States* (New York: McGraw-Hill, 1971).

6. For a discussion of the various elite groups that lead the industrialization process and their several strategies, see Clark Kerr, John T. Dunlop, Frederick H. Harbison, and Charles A. Myers, *Industrialism and Industrial Man: The Problems of Labor and Management in Economic Growth* (Cambridge, Mass.: Harvard University Press, 1960).

FRANCISCO O. RAMIREZ and
JOHN BOLI-BENNETT

Global Patterns of
Educational
Institutionalization

Questions to think about

1 *How does the world system operate to influence
national education systems, and what is the outcome?
Give specific examples.*
2 *What are the two dialectic poles discussed in this
article, and what are their influences on the world
educational system?*
3 *Using the open systems framework, diagram and
explain the world system of education discussed in this
article.*
4 *Where does the United States fit into discussions of
world systems of education, and what are implications
for its educational system?*

Since World War II there has been an extraordinary
expansion of educational systems throughout the world. A striking degree
of convergence in the organizational structure and ideological charters of
these systems has also occurred. These developments are of such generality
and uniformity that they cannot be explained by standard comparative
education discussions that treat national systems as essentially autonomous
units developing in accordance with endogenous social, political, and economic forces. We offer, instead, a global perspective that focuses on the

increasingly integrated and influential transnational social structure and
its effects on nation-states as subunits of that structure.[1] We seek, therefore,
not to identify national characteristics that make countries more or less
likely to structure their educational systems in common ways, but to discuss
the world system's ideological elements and organizational constraints concerning education and to show how these factors account for the post-war
educational "revolution."[2]

THE EXPANSION OF EDUCATION

We begin with a discussion of the universality and uniformity of the expansion of education in the past three decades. Table 1 shows the growth
of national primary, secondary, and higher educational enrollment ratios.
These ratios are taken from the UNESCO *Statistical Yearbook*[3] and measure
school enrollments as proportions of standardized age-specific populations.
The ratios are computed for every five years from 1950 to 1975 and are
averaged across all countries with adequate information at each time period, yielding mean country scores for each date. Separate mean enrollment
ratios are computed for subsamples of richer and poorer countries. Table
1 enables us to gauge the overall pattern of educational change and allows
us to compare the growth pattern characteristic of the richer nations (the
top one-third) with that of the poorer ones (the bottom two-thirds).

The overall pattern of educational change is clear. The average primary
enrollment ratio in 1950 was 59.9 per cent; by 1975 this figure had soared
to 86.5 per cent. Secondary and higher educational enrollment ratios expanded in a similar fashion: from 11.5 per cent to 40.7 per cent for the
secondary educational level and from 1.3 per cent to 9.8 per cent for higher
education. Consider what these percentages mean from the perspective of
computing the average national proportion of children and youth that fell
outside the educational system. Only three decades ago, on the average,
nearly four out of every ten primary-age children were not enrolled in
school; but, by 1975, the educational web included on the average nearly
nine out of ten such children. In 1950 the doors of higher education were
closed to a national average of virtually ninety-nine out of every hundred
youth; but, by 1975, nearly one out of ten young adults was absorbed in
some institution of higher learning.

This overall pattern of educational growth does not merely reflect
enrollment increases among the rich countries. The rich/poor country comparison shows that their secondary and tertiary educational growth patterns between 1950 and 1975 were quite similar. Poor countries also
expanded their primary school systems; the pattern for rich countries was

T A B L E 1

Educational Enrollment Ratios, 1950–1975*
(Mean percentages; number of cases in parentheses)

Educational level	1950	1955	1960	1965	1970	1975
A. Primary						
All countries	59.9	65.9	72.0	79.9	83.7	86.5
	(128)	(130)	(137)	(142)	(140)	(132)
Richer countries	103.1	104.7	104.4	104.2	106.8	100.3
	(35)	(34)	(38)	(43)	(49)	(42)
Poorer countries	43.7	52.1	59.6	69.4	71.3	80.1
	(93)	(96)	(99)	(99)	(91)	(90)
B. Secondary						
All countries	11.5	15.7	21.3	27.3	33.3	40.7
	(120)	(119)	(147)	(147)	(146)	(127)
Richer countries	26.7	37.4	44.1	52.2	59.2	66.9
	(35)	(34)	(43)	(44)	(51)	(48)
Poorer countries	5.3	7.0	11.8)	16.6	19.4	24.7
	(85)	(85)	(104)	(103)	(95)	(79)
C. Tertiary (higher)						
All countries	1.3	1.8	4.4	6.0	7.1	9.8
	(125)	(122)	(114)	(125)	(133)	(124)
Richer countries	3.7	4.7	8.4	12.1	13.6	18.9
	(30)	(31)	(42)	(43)	(48)	(46)
Poorer countries	0.6	0.8	2.1	2.7	3.4	4.5
	(95)	(91)	(72)	(82)	(85)	(78)

*Ratios are calculated as enrollments divided by the appropriate age group populations and may exceed 100.0. Richer countries are those in the top third ranked by GNP/capita.
Source: UNESCO, *Statistical Yearbook* (Louvain, Belgium: UNESCO, 1965–1979).

different only because the latter had already attained nearly universal primary enrollments by 1950 (changes from 1950 to 1975 mainly reflect measurement error). The principal inference derived from the rich/poor comparisons is that both their educational systems expanded rapidly during this era.

Extensive multivariate panel analyses of educational expansion during the latter period show that most of the increase took place independent of variations in the internal economic, political, and social structures of national societies.[4] The models used in these earlier analyses included one term depicting educational growth as a "built-in" expansionary force inherent in each national system and another term capturing the idea that educational expansion resulted from a global thrust toward educational expansion exogenous to national societies and located in the world system itself. These two terms accounted for much of the educational growth observed in the period, and additional terms employing measures of varying national characteristics had at best small and negligible effects.[5] In particular, developmentalist or modernization explanations of educational growth[6] were not supported by these analyses. Nor were the theories that interpret this expansion as the outcome of competition or conflict among classes or status groups seeking to maximize the educational resources ("human capital") of their members.[7] These analyses also failed to support the argument that certain kinds of states or regimes expand education (especially at the lower levels) to create the illusion of equality and help maintain the existing status hierarchy.[8]

These analyses suggest, instead, that all of these theories have failed to address the fundamental issue: Why has education become the most legitimated cultural capital in country after country in the present world system? To raise this question is to remind ourselves that competing groups have not always demanded more schooling for themselves or their children. Nor have central political authorities always vigorously imposed more schooling on greater numbers within their territorial domains. The rush for schooling is a relatively recent historical phenomenon. The extensiveness of the linkages between national states and educational systems is also not an historical constant, but, rather, has dramatically increased in recent years. Neither developmentalist nor conflict arguments have come to terms with the fact that states, groups, and individuals act as if education were an inevitable system of socialization, certification, and legitimation without which social life itself would not be possible. Neither developmentalist nor conflict arguments recognize the degree to which educational institutionalization (the taken-for-granted character and uses of education) has become an important mechanism everywhere for coping with the collective/individual dialectic, the topic to which we now turn.

EDUCATIONAL IDEOLOGY AND STRUCTURE IN THE WORLD SOCIAL SYSTEM

Table 1 and the analyses referred to in Meyer et al.[9] suggest that national educational systems are all marching to the beat of a common transnational drummer. What is the message of this marching song?

The world social system, as it has crystallized in the postwar era, contains a powerful dialectic whose twin poles are continually undergoing elaboration in all national societies. One pole is the ideology of the state as the primary locus of social organization and vehicle of societal development; the other is the ideology of the individual as the basic unit of social action, the ultimate source of value, and the locus of social meaning.[10] These poles are united in the ideology of citizenship, in which the individual is seen as both a contributor to the national development project (as a producer and as a loyal supporter of state programs, laws, and regulations) and as a beneficiary of state organizational action (as a consumer and as a citizen in the pure sense who enjoys certain protections and guarantees underwritten by the state).

This dialectic has clear implications for the meaning and structure of education in the world system. The ideology of the individual rests in part on the theory that new members of society (children) are essentially unformed beings requiring comprehensive initiation and socialization. Education is the means to achieve this end, and it does so with two purposes: to integrate individuals into the social structure so that their participation in the structure will be unproblematic; and to provide individuals with the means to carry out their own, self-directed personal development ("lifelong learning," as college bulletins are likely to describe their adult education programs).

But to this point there is no compelling reason for education to be state-directed and formalized. Why cannot parents provide the right sort of education for their children? Here the ideology of the state comes into play. Children are to be initiated not merely into society but, in the twentieth-century world system, into the *national* society. The state organizes society; therefore, the individual must be an effective agent of the state if the social structure is to function well. That is, the individual must be a citizen who learns to identify (however begrudgingly, and with however many protestations) with the national symbols and programs so as to help ensure the success of state action. And this is not a purely insidious Machiavellianism—the state demands citizen support not merely for its own good but also, from the state's point of view, for the good of the citizen himself. Citizenship, as noted, not only imposes duties on the citizen—it also offers civil rights protection, health and welfare guarantees, and much more.

Further, all of this takes place in the context of the world system's dedication to the myth of progress. In saying that the state has assumed responsibility for organizing national development, we are implicitly recognizing the strong link that has been forged over the past several decades between the state and the myth of progress. Here a basic alteration has occurred in the nineteenth century's doctrine of unrestricted capitalism as the guarantor of progress: Smith's "invisible hand" is now seen as a guarantor of inequality, institutionalized poverty, and antidemocratic concentration of power. All of these effects of capitalist development in the absence of a strong state are precisely contrary to the revised version of the ideology of progress, contradicting as they do the universalism and basic equality inherent in the doctrine of individualism.

The current doctrine of progress declares that only the state can be counted on to bring about the equality of individuals and ensure the basic integrity of each societal member.[11] And, of course, the technical necessity of state control and coordination of the national economy and polity is universally accepted across a broad range of domains, in order to ensure orderly economic growth, rising per capita income, adequate health care to all sectors of the population, and so on.[12] These things are the very essence of progress in the contemporary world, and it is worth noting that one of the most visible functions of the state is the compilation and dissemination of statistics that monitor the degree of progress achieved by the national society: gross national product, infant mortality rates, disposable income, television sets per capita, and so on.

The myth of state-directed progress further cements the relationship between education and the individual. Education is seen as a major source of value in that it creates "cultural capital" that individuals can use to further societal progress, and certain analyses go so far as to assign primary importance to this mythical construct in the generation of economic growth.[13] Education is also seen as contributing to other forms of progress: literacy, newspaper readership, environmental awareness, racial tolerance, and self-actualization, to give but a few examples. This entire ideological structure views progress as the summation of the actions and efforts of discrete individual citizens working in harmony under the overall planning and guidance of the national state.

Our view is that this elaborate dialectical construct has been increasingly and strongly institutionalized in the transnational social system over the past century, despite the fact that there is no correspondingly powerful transnational organizational apparatus to implement it. Implementation has been carried out, instead, by the various nation-states, all responding to a fairly uniform institutional environment as to the role of education in the state/individual relationship.[14] It is for this reason that the expansion of education shown in Table 1 is so universal and is not subject to the influences of varying national characteristics. States are operating under the imperatives of a common global social system and, like individuals immersed in their native social environment, states seek to make actual the structures of the larger social system almost unquestioningly. In other words, everybody *knows* that education is good for both the national society and the individual citizen; and everybody knows that no self-respecting (or respectable) country can be satisfied with only 60, 70, or even 80 percent of its primary-age children in school.

Although it seems clear that transnational ideology is more powerfully institutionalized than the transnational organizational apparatus that might implement it, the organizational constraints of the world system are not to be dismissed. On the one hand, there are the constraints of historical example and analysis: There is widespread agreement that education has been a key factor in national development, particularly in the industrialized countries, and academic literature is replete with detailed, highly technical studies purporting to show the great benefits obtained by the establishment and expansion of educational systems over the past century. The link between education and development is so strongly established that Julius Nyerere of Tanzania has been led to say, "If I leave to others the building of our elementary school system, they (the people) will abandon me as their responsible national leader."[15]

On the other hand, the actual mechanisms of development in the world system generally favor educational expansion. Many of the transnational funding programs for development tend to look most favorably at proposals that offer educational solutions to development problems (World Bank, 1980). Similarly, bilateral aid programs between richer and poorer countries very often support the establishment of schools, supply of study materials, or training of teachers (for example, Sweden, noted for devoting an exceptionally large percentage of national product to foreign aid, allocated 18 per cent of its aid between 1969–1970 and 1971–1972 directly to education).[16] Another such form of aid is the granting of scholarships or stipendia to students from developing countries for study in Europe or North America; the assumption is that a formally educated elite will be better equipped to organize development. And, of course, there is the whole panoply of development experts—national consulting firms, academicians, United Nations organs and commissions, and so on—who are thoroughly imbued with the ideology of education and whose advice and proposals reflect the felt imperative of a developed educational system for every country. Although the formal authority and power of all these mechanisms vis-à-vis particular countries is relatively weak, they nevertheless help implement educational ideology very effectively in the world system as a whole.

NOTES

1. Earlier formulations of the theory of education underlying this paper are found in John W. Meyer, "The Functions of Education as an Institution," *American Journal of Sociology,* **83** (September 1977), pp. 340–363, and Francisco O. Ramirez and John W. Meyer, "Comparative Education: The Social Construction of the Modern World System," *Annual Review of Soci-*

ology, **6** (Palo Alto: Annual Reviews, Inc., 1980), pp. 369–399. This paper was supported by funds from the Organizational Training Program of Stanford University (Grant No. HSMA 2T32 MH 15149–03) and by funds from the Boys Town Center for Youth Development, Stanford University. Only the authors are responsible for the opinions expressed herein.

2. John W. Meyer, Francisco O. Ramirez, Richard Rubinson, and John Boli-Bennett, "The World Educational Revolution, 1950–1970," *Sociology of Education,* **50** (Fall 1977), pp. 242–258.

3. UNESCO, *Statistical Yearbook* (Louvain, Belgium: UNESCO, 1965–1979).

4. Meyer et al., op. cit.

5. The only exception was the significant effect of economic development on secondary school expansion, a reasonable substantive finding.

6. For example, Fritz Machlup, *Education and Economic Growth* (Lincoln, Neb.: University of Nebraska Press, 1970); Mark Blaug, Ed., *Economics of Education,* Vols. I and II (Baltimore: Penguin Press, 1968–1969).

7. Randall Collins, *The Credential Society: A Historical Sociology of Education and Stratification* (New York: Academic Press, 1979).

8. Martin Carnoy, "Marxian Approaches to Education," IFG Progress Report 80–B13 (Stanford: School of Education, 1980).

9. Meyer et al., op. cit.

10. See the discussions in John Boli-Bennett and John W. Meyer, "The Ideology of Childhood and the State: Rules Distinguishing Children in National Constitutions, 1870–1970," *American Sociological Review,* **43** (December), pp. 797–812; John W. Meyer, "The World Polity and the Authority of the Nation-State," in Albert Bergesen, Ed., *Studies of the Modern World-System* (New York: Academic Press, 1980); Francisco O. Ramirez and George M. Thomas, "Structural Antecedents and Consequences of Statism: Synthesis and Agenda," to be published in Richard Rubinson, Ed., *Dynamics of World Development,* Political Economy of World System Annuals, Vol. 4 (Beverly Hills: Sage Publications, 1981).

11. Herein, of course, lies what has come to be seen as the basic dilemma facing the Western democracies: recognizing that unbridled capitalism tramples the lower classes, the strong and expanding state is a necessity; but how is total state dominance and its eventual curtailment of all individual liberty (meaning, here, freedom of choice) to be avoided? See the articles in *Daedalus,* special issue on "The State," Fall 1979.

12. Jacques Ellul, *The Technological Society* (New York: Knopf, 1962).

13. E. F. Denison, *The Sources of Economic Growth in the U.S. and the Alternatives Before Us* (New York: Committee for Economic Development, 1962).

14. See John W. Meyer and Brian Rowan, "Institutionalized Organizations: Formal Structure as Myth and Ceremony," *American Journal of Sociology,* **83** (1977), pp. 340–363.

15. Quoted in Kenneth Thompson, "Universities and the Developing World," in S. Kertesz, Ed., *The Task of Universities in a Changing World* (South Bend, Ind.: University of Notre Dame Press, 1971).

16. Klas Markensten, "Swedish Foreign Assistance," *Cooperation and Conflict,* **4** (2, 1970), pp. 95–101.

JUDITH M. BARNET

Learning: In Crisis
the World Over

Questions to think about

1 *What does the author consider to be major problems in education worldwide? How might these problems be tackled?*

2 *How are the education systems of countries around the world interrelated? What common problems do they face?*

3 *Considering the Club of Rome report, what might be done to improve education around the world and in the United States specifically?*

4 *What are some implications of the report for the day-to-day school experiences of children?*

What does Saudi Arabia's "temporary step-up" of oil production in July 1979 have to do with human learning? What does a worker-owned, cooperatively managed printing company in Clinton, Massachusetts, have to do with teacher education? Is it possible that the way we learn, and teach others to learn, creates, aggravates, and perpetuates the critical social/economic/political malaise currently being experienced worldwide? Could innovative learning help resolve—even avert—that malaise? Answers to those puzzles underlie the critique and the accompanying proposals of *No Limits to Learning: Bridging the Human Gap,*[1] the newest study commissioned by the Club of Rome.

Followers of the Club of Rome will hear in that title an echo of *The Limits to Growth,* the 1972 report that ended an era of belief in limitless resources, the capacity of the biosphere to reprocess everything we chose

From *Phi Delta Kappan* (October 1979), pp. 112–114. Reprinted by permission of the author.

to dump into it, and the promise of the trickle-down distribution system to meet the basic needs of poor people and poor nations. Now a team of educators has proposed that not material resources but the human learning system lies at the heart of the trouble *and* at the heart of the answer. Educators at *all* levels, formal and informal, should join the debate over *No Limits to Learning,* for it explores far beyond traditional educational systems into the learning process, into misapplications of power (the arms race), into wasted potential (television, underemployed women and minorities)—indeed, across the full agenda of modern societies.

No Limits uses the term "learning"

> in a broad sense, [going] beyond what conventional terms like education and schooling imply. . . . [L]earning means an approach, both to knowledge and to life, that emphasizes human initiative. It encompasses the acquisition and practice of new methodologies, new skills, new attitudes, and new values necessary to live in a world of change. Learning is the process of preparing to deal with new situations.[2]

No Limits argues that modern learning has been shaped by two wrong models. The biological model, which we initially greeted as a welcome injection of life after the mechanistic nineteenth century, views learning as the process of adapting to changing circumstances, past experience, and other influences. The key factor is adaptation. But purely adaptive learning is reactive; it fails to train us to shape our own futures.

Therein lies the answer to the first question posed in this article. Our habits of adaptation make it highly likely, speculates *Business Week's* special report on energy (30 July 1979), that the oil surplus expected on the market this fall, resulting from the combination of expanded production, conservation, and the effect of recession on demand, will lull Americans back into the conviction that the oil shortage is a trumped-up corporate conspiracy. We act only on the latest news. Each time the shock of shortage occurs, we adapt to the immediate circumstances but we rarely face an issue as a whole and design a responsible, long-term response.

Instead of continuing to learn by shock, say the authors of *No Limits,* we ought to be developing *anticipatory learning,* teaching the capacity to invent the future rather than merely acting frantically to cope with changing circumstances.

The second false paradigm that shapes learning is the cybernetic model. In this model, once a problem is stated as a "given set," all eyes focus on solution. Engineering or management formulas for problem solving employ this approach: Fix the objectives, marshal the available resources, initiate methods to use the resources.

The Club of Rome report would have us pause longer over the first step in that process. How certain are we that we have correctly identified the problem? *No Limits* calls for greater reliance on participation, seen as not just the formal sharing of decisions but rather "an attitude characterized by cooperation, dialogue, and empathy," so that "solutions become almost self-evident, are better supported, can be more readily implemented, and are less likely to generate unwanted repercussions (including conflict)."[3]

Unlike the cybernetic model, which reflects but does not question a set of values, *participatory learning* acknowledges the interplay of values, images, and human relations as essentials of the learning process. It should be invited into every classroom, faculty meeting, task force session, or cabinet meeting—in short, any problem-solving, management, or human relations context.

But it is a fundamental tenet of *No Limits* that neither anticipatory nor participatory learning alone adds up to the learning reform we need. For truly innovative learning, both must occur simultaneously.

For example, "participation without anticipation can be counterproductive or misguided, leading to paralysis (where countervailing forces preclude action) or to counteraction (where there is backlash or when rights are asserted without the acceptance of responsibilities)."[4] As an instance of the latter, consider the problems that would have resulted if the worker-buyers of the Clinton Colonial Press had set up a cooperatively managed business without foreseeing the need for the skills that custom assigns to white-collar rather than blue-collar workers. But because they were anticipatory as well as participatory, the employee-owners studied owner management with a group of organizers, economists, and financial experts who help workers, union representatives, and plant owners retain local control over industry. With that guidance the company's new owners set up a structure requiring a system of weekly education meetings in which one worker, designated to continue formal studies, both collects and responds to questions and concerns from the others. He serves his companions by learning and teaching at the same time—surely a description of an ideal teacher.

Here, then, is the answer to the second query that opened this article. Education, sought as needed, adds management tools and imagination to the vocational skills and commitment already possessed by the workers. Without education, a key factor in anticipation, despite all the participation in the world, the Colonial Cooperative Press would not exist.[5]

Critics of this report have already begun attacking it, claiming that it offers nothing new and that its proposals are too general. The authors defuse the first criticism by admitting that there is nothing novel about calling for participatory or innovative learning (anticipatory learning is a little newer but still familiar). And, after all, what is so virtuous about novelty? Novelty is a young and comparatively hollow mistress; nobody faults Shakespeare for using old plots. Why demand that we move on to something new when we have yet to assimilate the old? Many of our oldest educational theories are good ideas that have never really been tried. Better to admit that we flee to novelty upon discovering that the current issue is harder than we thought. That faint-hearted and undisciplined response may explain why education has grasped at so many highly touted innovations of late.

But we are prompted to question whether "innovative learning" is the best term for the reforms *No Limits* suggests. Most likely we are dealing here with a language problem. The report was produced by scholars from the U.S., Morocco, and Romania, for whom proper terminology constituted a major stumbling block on several occasions. After much futile exploration, including considering coining new words, the authors settled on "innovative" with some trepidation.

The second criticism—that the report is too general—is less easily dispatched. If the focus of the debate over *No Limits* is to be on solutions rather than on an endless recital of problems, "innovative learning" needs to be much more precisely defined, delineated, and exemplified than it is in this report. Educators brought by the Club of Rome to Salzburg in June to critique the report asked for precise definition and were consistently urged to supply definitions appropriate to their own cultures. Aurelio Peccei, the Club of Rome's founder and guiding spirit, pleaded with conference participants to use the report as a detonator, important more for its consequences than for itself. This answer, like the report's broad language, serves to defer rather than to focus debate and may limit application of the ideas.

Let me suggest some applications that *might* have been included. I shall confine my suggestions to the role of educators. (Note that, according to *No Limits*, the ranks of educators include, in addition to members of the education establishment, community institutions such as museums, the media, and practitioners.) What are some of the issues that educators of all sorts might address if they were to try to apply some of the precepts in *No Limits*, if they were to try to initiate or promote innovative learning?

Let's start with the schools. According to *No Limits*, which ties the purpose of learning to the resolution of global issues, higher education will participate much more effectively in the pursuit of that goal "when the chauvinism, nationalism, and sovereignty of academic disciplines yields to a transdisciplinary basis" of organization.

Some reorganization of academic and administrative structures should be reconsidered to combine university departments according to issues rather than only and always according to disciplines. These newly constituted groupings could be considered as task forces, to be dissolved once their original objective is attained and to be recombined when new objectives are sought. Teaching as well as research work could then be organized around broad themes, . . . reducing the present segmentation and sectorialization of the curricula. Such a focus would bring the university closer to the basic concerns of society. It would . . . introduce some vital issues currently underemphasized on the university agenda—such as rural development, malnutrition, unemployment, illiteracy, housing, and juvenile delinquency. These are but a few of the areas which require research and practical action and where the university population of students and teachers alike could be of great significance.[6]

The renowned Swedish educator Torsten Husen lists specialization, fragmentation, the rigidities of big school units, and hierarchical administrative decision making as some of the impediments to innovative learning. Those inflated structures beg to be broken into smaller units organized on the principle that individuals participate most meaningfully in wholes rather than only in parts. To meet this objective we need a fresh definition of efficiency—one that subordinates short-term cost-effectiveness to the desirability of educating more happily, more profoundly, more humanely, and more effectively. As John Goodlad points out, this sort of appeal—radical a few years ago—is now verging on an idea whose time has come. Everywhere, his own articles included, one begins to find compelling descriptions of the humane school that sets its standards on formulas other than those dictated by short-term economic thinking.[7]

An Austrian school director attending the Salzburg meeting described his 20 years of success in a highly participatory small school. Many private and alternative schools in the U.S. believe in human scale and integrated curricula; the principal stumbling block in the U.S. is the large, publicly supported school system. Public education is experiencing some changes, however; see the list of contacts and breakthroughs I have included.[8]

Many more restructuring (not deschooling) possibilities lie untapped. *No Limits to Learning* deplores the artificial separation of schooling and life so common in formal education. That "impermeable boundary" takes different forms in different societies. In India, study is seen as a way to escape "toil on the soil"; in many former colonial nations an education modeled after that of the former overlord results in alienation from one's own culture. If reintegration of school and work is valued, says Husen, why do Americans not reconsider keeping children in school full time from age 5?

Harold Shane has designed an elegant, full-blown lifelong alternative plan, which he calls the "paracurriculum," in *The Educational Significance of the Future* (Bloomington, Ind.: Phi Delta Kappa Educational Foundation, 1973). Has it been attempted?

Let me suggest one final scheme to promote innovative learning, based on my own experience as a teacher. The pressure under which conscientious teachers labor precludes their having time and energy to learn anything new, much less form new attitudes. Why not divide classroom teachers' time in two segments, half devoted to teaching, half to restoking their own furnaces? The schedule I have in mind is two to three days of teaching and two to three of learning. Summers and sabbaticals do not work; they are too far off. Continuous refreshment, restimulation, updating, and opportunity to try out new ideas could have unprecedented effects on productivity.

Again, of course, we need to be governed by something other than a bottom-line mentality, because this program could require communities to employ almost double the current number of teachers.[9] But consider the impact of such a policy on unemployment. (The fact that the local community does not pay the direct costs of unemployment does not eliminate them; they are merely paid by another level of government, which indirectly extracts them from local taxes. Does it not make sense to pay people for constructive work rather than in unemployment compensation, probably accompanied by added costs of physical and mental ill health?)

In the area of *content* of schooling, multicultural experiences—as a means of coping with our ever-increasing global interdependence—are a pressing need. For instance, more than 50% of the business of Midwestern farmers is export-related. Japan has 400 international salespeople, all of whom speak English; the U.S. has 1,000 international salespeople, none of whom speaks Japanese. Who do you suppose drives the better bargain? According to Edwin O. Reischauer, the U.S. is already getting third-rate service from its solely English-speaking diplomatic corps.

All of this indicates that innovative learning in today's schools must be widely multicultural if a nation is to participate effectively in the world. We must revive our dying foreign language programs. We must expand our travel and exchange programs and make study *in* another culture a requirement for graduation, certainly from college, possibly even from secondary school. We must integrate area centers into the central disciplines of the universities and the communities in which they are located. We must encourage imagination in the interweaving of technical and cultural learning—for example, by using conversion to foreign currencies in the teaching of elementary arithmetic. What steppingstones from a drachma to applied multiplication to Keats's "Ode on a Grecian Urn"!

I have saved for last an item of major importance and of maximum challenge to leaders in education. The education system—not just in the U.S., but worldwide—has its priorities backwards in allocating resources to higher versus primary education. Everywhere it is acknowledged that the education of primary students has greater import for the future of the society than university education. Tunisians, Indians, and Sri Lankans, among others, contributed statistics to the Salzburg discussion confirming the fact that infinitesimal proportions of their societies take part in secondary, to say nothing of higher, education. In Sri Lanka, for example, only 10% of the age cohort reaches grade 8, and 10% of that number gets to the university. The entire Sri Lankan education system is organized for 1% of the population.

Perhaps Tunisia is more representative of the world situation: The state uses 32% of its budget for the 20% of pupils who proceed to secondary school. Yet the greatest proportion of resources, rewards, and prestige are reserved for higher education, if not in the Third World then at least in the First, where universities are 50 times more expensive per unit than primary schools.

Clearly this is an issue for the sociopolitical agenda. But advocates of education cannot continue supporting the existing imbalance. Systematic reform of the reward structure is the obvious need.

Space permits only a cursory listing of specific projects that might be undertaken by academic disciplines to encourage innovative learning. The political sciences (including secondary school social studies departments) might respond to the integrated curriculum challenge by exploring UNCTAD V as an example of the failure of societal learning.[10] Or they might develop scenarios for a successor to the nation-state, something more suited to the twenty-first century. Both of these suggestions were made at Salzburg by Morocco's Mahdi Elmandjra, a co-author of No Limits.

The education and philosophy disciplines might seek models for learning better suited to social needs than the biological or cybernetic models. One prerequisite of a new model must be techniques for maximizing the learning of details when the scope of a course is multidisciplinary. Or the obverse: techniques for gaining perspective without sacrificing specificity. Another element in this inquiry relates to the imponderables of commitment. Where do multiculturally educated students place their loyalty? Can love of the world ignite the same patriotic fervor that love of country has traditionally engendered?

The arts and humanities have at least two formidable challenges. First, there is work to be done in creating a humanities agenda for the sustainable society, comparable to the agenda being developed by economists and sociologists. (See the publications from the Woodlands Alternatives to

Growth conferences.[11]) Second, although this is probably an item on the aforementioned agenda, the arts need to revive the age-old discussion of how they can function as a social instrument, a means of correcting social ills. I hasten to point out that the arts need not serve the state to be socially useful; in fact, they are most useful when criticizing the state.

For truly innovative learning, all the academic disciplines could address themselves to the proposition that since behavioral change often precedes consciousness change (e.g., the civil rights laws), social activism is an educative tool par excellence. Enter a natural connection between school and community!

Similar exciting opportunities for initiating innovative learning exist outside formal education, in non-school settings. They include a formidable challenge to industry to take greater responsibility for education (not just for on-the-job training or the inculcation of free-enterprise values). Perhaps most crucial is the role of the communications media in enhancing rather than deadening learning. All of these, however vital, are only hints and demand more extensive treatment.

One final observation: It must be evident that *No Limits to Learning* is idealistic, intensely humanistic, and in many respects not practical in the world as it operates today. But that is exactly the point. *No Limits* has no intention of settling for our present perilous situation; it intends to join its voice to the many rescue propositions being articulated daily. Perhaps, as the global predicament continues to worsen, we shall see the rightness and the inevitability of translating some of these propositions into efforts supported by community resources and commitments. Only then can we claim to have done our best.

NOTES

1. James W. Botkin, Mahdi Elmandjra, and Mircea Malitza, co-authors. Publication was expected in August/September 1979 by Pergamon Press, London.

2. *No Limits to Learning: Bridging the Human Gap* carried the working title at conference time of *The Human Gap: The Learning Report to the Club of Rome.* Page references in this article, written before publication of *No Limits*, are to that earlier version. Page 11.

3. *The Human Gap*, p. 41.

4. Ibid., pp. 18, 19.

5. See Patricia Greene, "Visions of Economic Democracy: Workers 'Press' Cooperation," *New Roots*, May/June 1979.

6. *The Human Gap*, p. 123.

7. "Can Our Schools Get Better?," *Phi Delta Kappan*, January 1979, p. 342.

8. The following are only a few members of a widening network compiling successful records at integrating curriculum and willing to share materials and experiences:

Sara P. Boucher, Florida Junior College at Jacksonville, North Campus, Jacksonville, FL 32218. Ref: integrating humanities with law, medical ethics.

Don Bragaw, Chief, Bureau of Social Studies Education, New York State Department of Education, Albany, NY 12224. Ref: social studies curriculum.

Geoffrey F. Fletcher, Milford Junior-Senior High School, 5733-5 Pleasant Hill Rd., Milford, OH 45150. Ref: Milford Futurology Program.

Virginia Graham, Social Studies Department, East Junior High School, Watertown, MA 02172.

Francis Grose, Humanities Department, Billerica Public Schools, Billerica, MA 01821.

National Association of Alternative Community Schools, c/o Lucia Rogers Vorys, Jefferson Center, Columbus, Ohio.

David T. Nelson, Assoc. Prof. of Finance, Ball State University, Muncie, IN 47306. Ref: Gened 230: Colloquium on the Future.

Ann Roelofs, The New School, Utica, NY 13502. Ref: umbrella theme program description.

See also the options plans in Minneapolis and Indianapolis described in "If Not Public Choice, Then Private Escape," by Evans Clinchy and Elisabeth Allen Cody, *Phi Delta Kappan*, December 1978, p. 270 ff.

9. Much of the teacher released time could probably be absorbed by a combination of teacher aides and student self-management programs. See Frank Hunnes, "The Kelloggsville Story," *Phi Delta Kappan*, December 1978, p. 283.

10. The Fifth United Nations Conference on Trade and Development, held in Manila in the spring of 1979, was widely considered a major setback to the North-South dialogue. Besides standard periodicals, see "In and Around the U.N.," the June 1979 newsletter of the Quaker Office at the United Nations, 777 U.N. Plaza, New York, NY 10017, or 13 Avenue du Mervelet, 1209 Geneva.

11. Dennis I. Meadows, ed., *Alternatives to Growth—I: A Search for Sustainable Futures* (Cambridge, Mass.: Ballinger, 1977). The papers of the 1977 conference are in press.

CHAPTER 10

Educational Movements, Alternatives, and Trends: Change and the Future

Change falls in the same category as taxes and death—we cannot escape it! Sometimes it is positive, sometimes negative, but as an integral feature of the open systems framework it is ever-present. This final chapter considers change that has been brought about by educational movements, trends in education, and predictions for educational systems of the future.

We have tried all sorts of ideas! Progressive education, free and alternative schools, open classrooms, back-to-basics, competency-based education, and the New Right are passwords for a few educational movements of recent years. There is seldom a time when all the people are satisfied with the educational system; educational movements, reflecting some of these discontents, can have a significant impact on its structure and processes. Generally only small numbers are initially involved in each movement, but their impact can be disproportionate to their numbers. In this chapter we look at two examples of recent educational movements.

Movements are part of the educational system's environment and cannot be ignored; they keep the system adapted to pressures and trends in society. In fact, the open systems model is clearly illustrated by the impact of societal movements on educational systems. Movements alert power structures to discontents within society. Where the system is being challenged, decision makers may attempt to squelch the discontent or to heed its warning, depending on the salience of that part of the environment for the survival of the educational system.

Some social movements stem from societal discontents and reach into all sectors of society, including education. The civil rights movement was instrumental in the integration of schools and classrooms. The women's movement has stimulated challenges to the male power structure in education, sexism in curricular materials, and support for girls' athletics. Change in one part of the societal system will affect other parts of the system.

Consider the educational movements just listed. Within the past two decades, each has had its share of proponents, righteously adamant in their respective positions. A group's strength, in terms of resources they can muster (votes, money, influence), will determine its success in achieving goals. Once an educational movement gains momentum and adherents, it can prove to be a powerful force in bringing about change. Such change may involve structure, curriculum, materials, and teaching staff.

Educational movements have differing purposes; some reflect conservative moods or trends in society, others liberal ones. Regressive movements aim to "set the clock back" to a former, presumably better, state of affairs; the back-to-basics movement is an example. Reform movements, on the other hand, attempt to alter the existing system and bring it into line with goals of society; integration/desegregation efforts stemming from the civil rights movement exemplify this type. Utopian movements attempt to construct the perfect state of affairs; free school advocates moved outside the existing system and attempted to construct ideal schools. The "deschooling" movement contains elements of utopianism, too. Educational movements throughout the twentieth century show a pendulum swing from conservative to progressive, with a counterreaction to conservative, back to liberal, and so on. Reflecting this pendulum swing, the following articles focus on several examples of recent and current educational movements.

Some citizens and educators argue that the innovations of the alternative school movements of the 1960s and early 1970s led to lower academic standards. The Council on Basic Education and other leaders advocating conservative policies toward schools argue that schools need to eliminate the frills and get back to basics. The back-to-basics emphasis has given rise to an influential group now referred to as the "New Right." The New Right is composed of disaffected citizens concerned with such issues as busing, prayer in schools, vouchers and tax credits, and private school aid. The movement has been powerful enough that the federal government responded to its concerns by appointing and funding the National Commission on Excellence in Education to study the status of education in the United States. In May 1983, the commission released its findings and recommendations, which are reported here. The swing of the pendulum toward "basics" thus seems assured for the next few years, and some recommendations may become institutionalized as permanent additions to schools.

A nation's diversity is reflected in its educational movements because groups of people have differing beliefs about the role of education and what it can do to meet their needs. Movements in education often serve to voice the frustrations of groups with a broad range of concerns about society. In the United States education is an institution vulnerable to attack because it is controlled by lay boards elected by the public and because it is locally situated and available to scrutiny. Ann Page and Donald Clelland analyze a movement that typically represents issues more complex than the immediate issue around which controversy centered. Using the sociological perspective, they discuss what they call "politics of life style concern." Differences in belief systems, ways of life, and social class underlie basic lifestyle differences that led to conflict in Kanawha County and other districts around the country.

Movements in education bring about change. Some change occurs gradually, even imperceptibly. At times, however, change is dramatic and disruptive. Educational systems may plan for change or it may be imposed upon them from outside by legislation, teacher strikes, community pressures, or a number of other external *stresses*. These stresses stem from new knowledge and technology; changes in school staff and student composition; changes in environmental needs and demands; changes in the population; and even changes in the natural environment such as fuel shortages.

Internal *strains* also bring about change in the structure and functioning of organizations. For instance, goals of different system members may be in conflict; we see this daily in the struggle between the teacher who is trying to keep the class's attention and students who sabotage the system with an ingenious array of techniques.

Functional theorists see change as an adaptive, balancing process allowing for schools or other organizations to adjust to demands without major disruption. They allow for disequilibrium or imbalance in the system, and suggest that the system attempts to realign itself and establish balance. Functional theorists also recognize that some parts of the internal or external environment may be dysfunctional for the system. This model, however, does not deal effectively with the fact that there may be sudden, revolutionary changes. Conflict theorists see some degree of change as inevitable, part of the nature of things. Conflicts between competing interest groups in society provide the setting for constant tension that may erupt in radical change. The idea of feedback from the open system's environment suggests that much change will be anticipated and dealt with before it reaches crisis proportions, but the possibility of disruptive change is not discounted.

Most educational systems plan for change. Initiative comes from administrators, teachers, school boards, and students. Clearly those individuals with most power in the system have the best chance of implementing or preventing change, but any change is difficult if the key players are not involved and in agreement. Numerous "great" ideas have been proposed by administrators, only to flop because teachers did not find it in their interest to implement these ideas at the classroom level.

Sociologists of education have been involved in the educational change process at every level of the system. In major court cases on desegregation, sociologists have testified. In helping school districts plan for dropping enrollments, sociologists have conducted demographic studies and made policy recommendations. In teaching students about the structure, functions, and processes of educational systems, sociologists have played a major role. In studying the dynamics of classroom interaction, sociologists have contributed to our understanding of the processes operating in schools to help or hinder student learning.

The final articles, focusing on trends and change in education, deal with what has happened and what futurists predict will take place. As you read the comments of these educators, keep in mind the constraints that exist whenever new change is proposed, and evaluate how feasible and realistic some of the changes are.

The article by David Tyack and his colleagues reviews past eras in education; drawing lessons from history, they suggest strategies for the 1980s. The authors single out key innovations in education that have been tried and, more important, have lasted: innovations that have had structural impact, have been easily monitored, and have been responsive to new educational needs. The authors stress the need for loyalty to public education as a promoter of participation in governance and democracy.

One recent suggestion for educational reform—*The Paideia Proposal: An Educational Manifesto*—has received some attention. Written by a philosopher, Mortimer Adler, the model is based on the assumption that all children deserve the same quality of education. Adler argues for a single-track system with no electives or vocational training. Education, he believes, should be composed of three elements: fundamental knowledge, basic intellectual skills, and enlargement of understanding. Though all educators will not agree on a single plan and many other plans have been proposed, Adler's proposal is an example of the type of thinking that stimulates discussion on the direction education should take in the future.

The last article of our book focuses on the future of education in the United States. Harold G. Shane discusses challenges of rapid change and how schools must adapt. The electronic environment presents both benefits and challenges, and schools should be at the forefront of technological and value changes. New knowledge will be necessary for an individual to be a literate, functioning member of society in the future.

Our open systems perspective tells us that change is inevitable. The articles in this chapter tell us further that we had better anticipate coming educational directions and plan for them. Change won't wait for us, so we'd better not wait for it!

NATIONAL COMMISSION ON
EXCELLENCE IN EDUCATION

A Nation at Risk: The Imperative for Educational Reform

Questions to think about

1 *Why is our nation at risk, and who says so? What are major weaknesses in the educational system?*
2 *Considering what you know about educational movements, what factors led to the formation of this commission?*
3 *How does a weakness in one part of the open system affect other parts?*
4 *Which parts of these proposals might easily be implemented? Which parts are more difficult to implement and why?*

Our Nation is at risk. Our once unchallenged preeminence in commerce, industry, science, and technological innovation is being overtaken by competitors throughout the world. This report is concerned with only one of the many causes and dimensions of the problem, but it is the one that undergirds American prosperity, security, and civility. We report to the American people that while we can take justifiable pride in what our schools and colleges have historically accomplished and contributed to the United States and the well-being of its people, the educational foundations of our society are presently being eroded by a rising tide of mediocrity that threatens our very future as a Nation and a people. What was unimaginable a generation ago has begun to occur—others are matching and surpassing our educational attainments.

Reprinted from a report published by the U.S. Government Printing Office, April 1983.

If an unfriendly foreign power had attempted to impose on America the mediocre educational performance that exists today, we might well have viewed it as an act of war. As it stands, we have allowed this to happen to ourselves. We have even squandered the gains in student achievement made in the wake of the Sputnik challenge. Moreover, we have dismantled essential support systems which helped make those gains possible. We have, in effect, been committing an act of unthinking, unilateral educational disarmament.

Our society and its educational institutions seem to have lost sight of the basic purposes of schooling, and of the high expectations and disciplined effort needed to attain them. This report, the result of 18 months of study, seeks to generate reform of our educational system in fundamental ways and to renew the Nation's commitment to schools and colleges of high quality throughout the length and breadth of our land.

That we have compromised this commitment is, upon reflection, hardly surprising, given the multitude of often conflicting demands we have placed on our Nation's schools and colleges. They are routinely called on to provide solutions to personal, social, and political problems that the home and other institutions either will not or cannot resolve. We must understand that these demands on our schools and colleges often exact an educational cost as well as a financial one.

FINDINGS

We conclude that declines in educational performance are in large part the result of disturbing inadequacies in the way the educational process itself is often conducted. The findings that follow, culled from a much more extensive list, reflect four important aspects of the educational process: content, expectations, time, and teaching.

Findings Regarding Content

By content we mean the very "stuff" of education, the curriculum. Because of our concern about the curriculum, the Commission examined patterns of courses high school students took in 1964–69 compared with course patterns in 1976–81. On the basis of these analyses we conclude:

- Secondary school curricula have been homogenized, diluted, and diffused to the point that they no longer have a central purpose. In effect, we have a cafeteria-style curriculum in which the appetizers and desserts can easily be mistaken for the main courses. Students have migrated from vocational and college preparatory programs to "general track" courses in large numbers. The proportion of students taking a general program of study has increased from 12 percent in 1964 to 42 percent in 1979.

- This curricular smorgasbord, combined with extensive student choice, explains a great deal about where we find ourselves today. We offer intermediate algebra, but only 31 percent of our recent high school graduates complete it; we offer French I, but only 13 percent complete it; and we offer geography, but only 16 percent complete it. Calculus is available in schools enrolling about 60 percent of all students, but only 6 percent of all students complete it.

- Twenty-five percent of the credits earned by general track high school students are in physical and health education, work experience outside the school, remedial English and mathematics, and personal service and development courses, such as training for adulthood and marriage.

Findings Regarding Expectations

We define expectations in terms of the level of knowledge, abilities, and skills school and college graduates should possess. They also refer to the time, hard work, behavior, self-discipline, and motivation that are essential for high student achievement. Such expectations are expressed to students in several different ways:

- by grades, which reflect the degree to which students demonstrate their mastery of subject matter;
- through high school and college graduation requirements, which tell students which subjects are most important;
- by the presence or absence of rigorous examinations requiring students to demonstrate their mastery of content and skill before receiving a diploma or a degree;
- by college admissions requirements, which reinforce high school standards; and
- by the difficulty of the subject matter students confront in their texts and assigned readings.

Our analyses in each of these areas indicate notable deficiencies:

- The amount of homework for high school seniors has decreased (two-thirds report less than 1 hour a night) and grades have risen as average student achievement has been declining.

- In many other industrialized nations, courses in mathematics (other than arithmetic or general mathematics), biology, chemistry, physics, and geography start in grade 6 and are required of *all* students. The time spent on these subjects, based on class hours, is about three times that spent by even the most science-oriented U.S. students, i.e., those who select 4 years of science and mathematics in secondary school.
- A 1980 State-by-State survey of high school diploma requirements reveals that only eight States require high schools to offer foreign language instruction, but none requires students to take the courses. Thirty-five States require only 1 year of mathematics, and 36 require only 1 year of science for a diploma.
- In 13 States, 50 percent or more of the units required for high school graduation may be electives chosen by the student. Given this freedom to choose the substance of half or more of their education, many students opt for less demanding personal service courses, such as bachelor living.
- "Minimum competency" examinations (now required in 37 States) fall short of what is needed, as the "minimum" tends to become the "maximum," thus lowering educational standards for all.
- One-fifth of all 4-year public colleges in the United States must accept every high school graduate within the State regardless of program followed or grades, thereby serving notice to high school students that they can expect to attend college even if they do not follow a demanding course of study in high school or perform well.
- About 23 percent of our more selective colleges and universities reported that their general level of selectivity declined during the 1970s, and 29 percent reported reducing the number of specific high school courses required for admission (usually by dropping foreign language requirements, which are now specified as a condition for admission by only one-fifth of our institutions of higher education).
- Too few experienced teachers and scholars are involved in writing textbooks. During the past decade or so a large number of texts have been "written down" by their publishers to ever-lower reading levels in response to perceived market demands.
- A recent study by Education Products Information Exchange revealed that a majority of students were able to master 80 percent of the material in some of their subject-matter texts before they had even opened the books. Many books do not challenge the students to whom they are assigned.

- Expenditures for textbooks and other instructional materials have declined by 50 percent over the past 17 years. While some recommend a level of spending on texts of between 5 and 10 percent of the operating costs of schools, the budgets for basal texts and related materials have been dropping during the past decade and a half to only 0.7 percent today.

Findings Regarding Time

Evidence presented to the Commission demonstrates three disturbing facts about the use that American schools and students make of time: (1) compared to other nations, American students spend much less time on school work; (2) time spent in the classroom and on homework is often used ineffectively; and (3) schools are not doing enough to help students develop either the study skills required to use time well or the willingness to spend more time on school work.

- In England and other industrialized countries, it is not unusual for academic high school students to spend 8 hours a day at school, 220 days per year. In the United States, by contrast, the typical school day lasts 6 hours and the school year is 180 days.
- In many schools, the time spent learning how to cook and drive counts as much toward a high school diploma as the time spent studying mathematics, English, chemistry, U.S. history, or biology.
- A study of the school week in the United States found that some schools provided students only 17 hours of academic instruction during the week, and the average school provided about 22.
- A California study of individual classrooms found that because of poor management of classroom time, some elementary students received only one-fifth of the instruction others received in reading comprehension.
- In most schools, the teaching of study skills is haphazard and unplanned. Consequently, many students complete high school and enter college without disciplined and systematic study habits.

Findings Regarding Teaching

The Commission found that not enough of the academically able students are being attracted to teaching; that teacher preparation programs need substantial improvement; that the professional working life of teachers is on the whole unacceptable; and that a serious shortage of teachers exists in key fields.

- Too many teachers are being drawn from the bottom quarter of graduating high school and college students.
- The teacher preparation curriculum is weighted heavily with courses in "educational methods" at the expense of courses in subjects to be taught. A survey of 1,350 institutions training teachers indicated that 41 percent of the time of elementary school teacher candidates is spent in education courses, which reduces the amount of time available for subject matter courses.
- The average salary after 12 years of teaching is only $17,000 per year, and many teachers are required to supplement their income with part-time and summer employment. In addition, individual teachers have little influence in such critical professional decisions as, for example, textbook selection.
- Despite widespread publicity about an overpopulation of teachers, severe shortages of certain kinds of teachers exist: in the fields of mathematics, science, and foreign languages; and among specialists in education for gifted and talented, language minority, and handicapped students.
- The shortage of teachers in mathematics and science is particularly severe. A 1981 survey of 45 States revealed shortages of mathematics teachers in 43 States, critical shortages of earth sciences teachers in 33 States, and of physics teachers everywhere.
- Half of the newly employed mathematics, science, and English teachers are not qualified to teach these subjects; fewer than one-third of U.S. high schools offer physics taught by qualified teachers.

RECOMMENDATIONS

In light of the urgent need for improvement, both immediate and long term, this Commission has agreed on a set of recommendations that the American people can begin to act on now, that can be implemented over the next several years, and that promise lasting reform. The topics are familiar; there is little mystery about what we believe must be done. Many schools, districts, and States are already giving serious and constructive attention to these matters, even though their plans may differ from our recommendations in some details.

We wish to note that we refer to public, private, and parochial schools and colleges alike. All are valuable national resources. Examples of actions similar to those recommended below can be found in each of them.

We must emphasize that the variety of student aspirations, abilities, and preparation requires that appropriate content be available to satisfy needs. Attention must be directed to both the nature of the content available and to the needs of particular learners. The most gifted students, for example, may need a curriculum enriched and accelerated beyond even the needs of other students of high ability. Similarly, educationally disadvantaged students may require special curriculum materials, smaller classes, or individual tutoring to help them master the material presented. Nevertheless, there remains a common expectation: We must demand the best effort and performance from all students, whether they are gifted or less able, affluent or disadvantaged, whether destined for college, the farm, or industry.

Our recommendations are based on the beliefs that everyone can learn, that everyone is born with an *urge* to learn which can be nurtured, that a solid high school education is within the reach of virtually all, and that life-long learning will equip people with the skills required for new careers and for citizenship.

RECOMMENDATION A: CONTENT

We recommend that State and local high school graduation requirements be strengthened and that, at a minimum, all students seeking a diploma be required to lay the foundations in the Five New Basics by taking the following curriculum during their 4 years of high school: (a) 4 years of English; (b) 3 years of mathematics; (c) 3 years of science; (d) 3 years of social studies; and (e) one-half year of computer science. For the college-bound, 2 years of foreign language in high school are strongly recommended in addition to those taken earlier.

Whatever the student's educational or work objectives, knowledge of the New Basics is the foundation of success for the after-school years and, therefore, forms the core of the modern curriculum. A high level of shared education in these Basics, together with work in the fine and performing arts and foreign languages, constitutes the mind and spirit of our culture. The following Implementing Recommendations are intended as illustrative descriptions. They are included here to clarify what we mean by the essentials of a strong curriculum.

Implementing Recommendations

1. The teaching of *English* in high school should equip graduates to:
   (a) comprehend, interpret, evaluate, and use what they read; (b) write well-organized, effective papers; (c) listen effectively and dis-

cuss ideas intelligently; and (d) know our literary heritage and how it enhances imagination and ethical understanding, and how it relates to the customs, ideas, and values of today's life and culture.

2. The teaching of *mathematics* in high school should equip graduates to: (a) understand geometric and algebraic concepts; (b) understand elementary probability and statistics; (c) apply mathematics in everyday situations; and (d) estimate, approximate, measure, and test the accuracy of their calculations. In addition to the traditional sequence of studies available for college-bound students, new, equally demanding mathematics curricula need to be developed for those who do not plan to continue their formal education immediately.

3. The teaching of *science* in high school should provide graduates with an introduction to: (a) the concepts, laws, and processes of the physical and biological sciences; (b) the methods of scientific inquiry and reasoning; (c) the application of scientific knowledge to everyday life; and (d) the social and environmental implications of scientific and technological development. Science courses must be revised and updated for both the college-bound and those not intending to go to college. An example of such work is the American Chemical Society's "Chemistry in the Community" program.

4. The teaching of *social studies* in high school should be designed to: (a) enable students to fix their places and possibilities within the larger social and cultural structure; (b) understand the broad sweep of both ancient and contemporary ideas that have shaped our world; and (c) understand the fundamentals of how our economic system works and how our political system functions; and (d) grasp the difference between free and repressive societies. An understanding of each of these areas is requisite to the informed and committed exercise of citizenship in our free society.

5. The teaching of *computer science* in high school should equip graduates to: (a) understand the computer as an information, computation, and communication device; (b) use the computer in the study of the other Basics and for personal and work-related purposes; and (c) understand the world of computers, electronics, and related technologies.

In addition to the New Basics, other important curriculum matters must be addressed.

6. Achieving proficiency in a *foreign languge* ordinarily requires from 4 to 6 years of study and should, therefore, be started in the elementary grades. We believe it is desirable that students achieve

such proficiency because study of a foreign language introduces students to non-English-speaking cultures, heightens awareness and comprehension of one's native tongue, and serves the Nation's needs in commerce, diplomacy, defense, and education.

7. The high school curriculum should also provide students with programs requiring rigorous effort in subjects that advance students' personal, educational, and occupational goals, such as the fine and performing arts and vocational education. These areas complement the New Basics, and they should demand the same level of performance as the Basics.

8. The curriculum in the crucial eight grades leading to the high school years should be specifically designed to provide a sound base for study in those and later years in such areas as English language development and writing, computational and problem solving skills, science, social studies, foreign language, and the arts. These years should foster an enthusiasm for learning and the development of the individual's gifts and talents.

9. We encourage the continuation of efforts by groups such as the American Chemical Society, the American Association for the Advancement of Science, the Modern Language Association, and the National Councils of Teachers of English and Teachers of Mathematics, to revise, update, improve, and make available new and more diverse curricular materials. We applaud the consortia of educators and scientific, industrial, and scholarly societies that cooperate to improve the school curriculum.

RECOMMENDATION B: STANDARDS AND EXPECTATIONS

We recommend that schools, colleges, and universities adopt more rigorous and measurable standards, and higher expectations, for academic performance and student conduct, and that 4-year colleges and universities raise their requirements for admission. This will help students do their best educationally with challenging materials in an environment that supports learning and authentic accomplishment.

Implementing Recommendations

1. Grades should be indicators of academic achievement so they can be relied on as evidence of a student's readiness for further study.

2. Four-year colleges and universities should raise their admissions requirements and advise all potential applicants of the standards for admission in terms of specific courses required, performance in these areas, and levels of achievement on standardized achievement

tests in each of the five Basics and, where applicable, foreign languages.

3. Standardized tests of achievement (not to be confused with aptitude tests) should be administered at major transition points from one level of schooling to another and particularly from high school to college or work. The purposes of these tests would be to: (a) certify the student's credentials; (b) identify the need for remedial intervention; and (c) identify the opportunity for advanced or accelerated work. The tests should be administered as part of a nationwide (but not Federal) system of State and local standardized tests. This system should include other diagnostic procedures that assist teachers and students to evaluate student progress.

4. Textbooks and other tools of learning and teaching should be upgraded and updated to assure more rigorous content. We call upon university scientists, scholars, and members of professional societies, in collaboration with master teachers, to help in this task, as they did in the post-Sputnik era. They should assist willing publishers in developing the products or publish their own alternatives where there are persistent inadequacies.

5. In considering textbooks for adoption, States and school districts should: (a) evaluate texts and other materials on their ability to present rigorous and challenging material clearly; and (b) require publishers to furnish evaluation data on the material's effectiveness.

6. Because no textbook in any subject can be geared to the needs of all students, funds should be made available to support text development in "thin-market" areas, such as those for disadvantaged students, the learning disabled, and the gifted and talented.

7. To assure quality, all publishers should furnish evidence of the quality and appropriateness of textbooks, based on results from field trials and credible evaluations. In view of the enormous numbers and varieties of texts available, more widespread consumer information services for purchasers are badly needed.

8. New instructional materials should reflect the most current applications of technology in appropriate curriculum areas, the best scholarship in each discipline, and research in learning and teaching.

RECOMMENDATION C: TIME

We recommend that significantly more time be devoted to learning the New Basics. This will require more effective use of the existing school day, a longer school day, or a lengthened school year.

Implementing Recommendations

1. Students in high schools should be assigned far more homework than is now the case.

2. Instruction in effective study and work skills, which are essential if school and independent time is to be used efficiently, should be introduced in the early grades and continued throughout the student's schooling.

3. School districts and State legislatures should strongly consider 7-hour school days, as well as a 200- to 220-day school year.

4. The time available for learning should be expanded through better classroom management and organization of the school day. If necessary, additional time should be found to meet the special needs of slow learners, the gifted, and others who need more instructional diversity than can be accommodated during a conventional school day or school year.

5. The burden on teachers for maintaining discipline should be reduced through the development of firm and fair codes of student conduct that are enforced consistently, and by considering alternative classrooms, programs, and schools to meet the needs of continually disruptive students.

6. Attendance policies with clear incentives and sanctions should be used to reduce the amount of time lost through student absenteeism and tardiness.

7. Administrative burdens on the teacher and related intrusions into the school day should be reduced to add time for teaching and learning.

8. Placement and grouping of students, as well as promotion and graduation policies, should be guided by the academic progress of students and their instructional needs, rather than by rigid adherence to age.

RECOMMENDATION D: TEACHING

This recommendation consists of seven parts. Each is intended to improve the preparation of teachers or to make teaching a more rewarding and respected profession. Each of the seven stands on its own and should not be considered solely as an implementing recommendation.

1. Persons preparing to teach should be required to meet high educational standards, to demonstrate an aptitude for teaching, and to

demonstrate competence in an academic discipline. Colleges and universities offering teacher preparation programs should be judged by how well their graduates meet these criteria.

2. Salaries for the teaching profession should be increased and should be professionally competitive, market-sensitive, and performance-based. Salary, promotion, tenure, and retention decisions should be tied to an effective evaluation system that includes peer review so that superior teachers can be rewarded, average ones encouraged, and poor ones either improved or terminated.

3. School boards should adopt an 11-month contract for teachers. This would ensure time for curriculum and professional development, programs for students with special needs, and a more adequate level of teacher compensation.

4. School boards, administrators, and teachers should cooperate to develop career ladders for teachers that distinguish among the beginning instructor, the experienced teacher, and the master teacher.

5. Substantial nonschool personnel resources should be employed to help solve the immediate problem of the shortage of mathematics and science teachers. Qualified individuals including recent graduates with mathematics and science degrees, graduate students, and industrial and retired scientists could, with appropriate preparation, immediately begin teaching in these fields. A number of our leading science centers have the capacity to begin educating and retraining teachers immediately. Other areas of critical teacher need, such as English, must also be addressed.

6. Incentives, such as grants and loans, should be made available to attract outstanding students to the teaching profession, particularly in those areas of critical shortage.

7. Master teachers should be involved in designing teacher preparation programs and in supervising teachers during their probationary years.

RECOMMENDATION E: LEADERSHIP AND FISCAL SUPPORT

We recommend that citizens across the Nation hold educators and elected officials responsible for providing the leadership necessary to achieve these reforms, and that citizens provide the fiscal support and stability required to bring about the reforms we propose.

Implementing Recommendations

1. Principals and superintendents must play a crucial leadership role in developing school and community support for the reforms we propose, and school boards must provide them with the professional development and other support required to carry out their leadership role effectively. The Commission stresses the distinction between leadership skills involving persuasion, setting goals and developing community consensus behind them, and managerial and supervisory skills. Although the latter are necessary, we believe that school boards must consciously develop leadership skills at the school and district levels if the reforms we propose are to be achieved.

2. State and local officials, including school board members, governors, and legislators, have *the primary responsibility* for financing and governing the schools, and should incorporate the reforms we propose in their educational policies and fiscal planning.

3. The Federal Government, in cooperation with States and localities, should help meet the needs of key groups of students such as the gifted and talented, the socioeconomically disadvantaged, minority and language minority students, and the handicapped. In combination these groups include both national resources and the Nation's youth who are most at risk.

4. In addition, we believe the Federal Government's role includes several functions of national consequence that States and localities alone are unlikely to be able to meet: protecting constitutional and civil rights for students and school personnel; collecting data, statistics, and information about education generally; supporting curriculum improvement and research on teaching, learning, and the management of schools; supporting teacher training in areas of critical shortage of key national needs; and providing student financial assistance and research and graduate training. We believe the assistance of the Federal Government should be provided with a minimum of administrative burden and intrusiveness.

5. The Federal Government has *the primary responsibility* to identify the national interest in education. It should also help fund and support efforts to protect and promote that interest. It must provide the national leadership to ensure that the Nation's public and private resources are marshaled to address the issues discussed in this report.

6. This Commission calls upon educators, parents, and public officials at all levels to assist in bringing about the educational reform pro-

posed in this report. We also call upon citizens to provide the financial support necessary to accomplish these purposes. Excellence costs. But in the long run mediocrity costs far more.

AMERICA CAN DO IT

Despite the obstacles and difficulties that inhibit the pursuit of superior educational attainment, we are confident, with history as our guide, that we can meet our goal. The American educational system has responded to previous challenges with remarkable success.

ANN L. PAGE and
DONALD A. CLELLAND

The Kanawha County Textbook Controversy: A Study of the Politics of Life Style Concern

Questions to think about

1 *How does the "politics of life style" theory help explain textbook controversies in Kanawha County and other communities?*
2 *Discuss the similarities between this article and "A Nation at Risk."*
3 *How do environmental factors, including social movements, interrelate to influence schools in controversy such as this one?*
4 *What are some school controversies in your own community? Can this theory help explain them?*

Since the 1950s, when Hofstadter (b) introduced the term "status politics" to explain the rise of the radical right, it has enjoyed a modicum of popularity as a useful analytic tool for understanding a variety of political movements. Well-known examples of the use of the concept include the analysis of the temperance movement by Gusfield and a study of antipornography campaigns by Zurcher and his associates. But the fact that "status politics" has never really caught hold as a fundamental analytic concept is indicated by its relative neglect in recent texts in political sociology and social movements. Yet status politics provides one of the fundamental approaches of political sociology. Its relevance has been obscured by a misleading narrowing of focus. As pointed out in an earlier

Reprinted from *Social Forces* 57: 1 (September 1978), 265–281. Copyright © by The University of North Carolina Press.

paper (Clelland and Guess), previous work has been marred by: (1) a confusion of prestige and life style as the basis of status politics; (2) the confusion of individual and group bases of status; and the assumptions that status politics is (3) abnormal; (4) irrational; and (5) tends toward merely symbolic victories (see also, Brandmeyer and Denisoff). We believe that these problems can be avoided by recasting the approach to focus on life style rather than on prestige loss. Thus we will replace the term "status politics" with the phrase "politics of life style concern."

ANALYTIC FRAMEWORK

The basis for the misconception of the essence of status politics is to be found in the misreading of the source concept of "status" as found in the works of Weber (esp. 302–7, 901–40). The idea that stratification is multi-dimensional has become a sociological cliche. But most sociologists have grossly misread Weber in their use of his basic concepts.[1] In his life-long dialog with the ghost of Marx, Weber was interested in designating the basic structural conflict groups and quasi-groups in addition to, and cross-cutting, economic classes. The categories which Weber added were status groups (*Stände*) and parties. If economic classes may be defined by their relations to the means of production (doing), status groups may be defined in terms of the ends of existence (being). That is, status groups are defined by a common life style (*Lebensführung*), which is more than a set of stylish characteristics which set a social tone and maintain boundaries between prestige groupings. Rather, a status group stands for a way of life; and such groups are consequently involved in constant struggles for control of the means of symbolic production through which their reality is constructed. Such struggles are the essence of status politics.

Since it is much more difficult to monopolize control of symbolic than of material production, status groups, unlike classes, may proliferate. And although they are engaged in constant claims for social honor, they are not neatly ordered in any hierarchy because there can be no full consensus across groups concerning the basis for such a hierarchy (cf. Stone and Form). They are not, in essence, prestige groups; and status politics is not, in essence, the attempt to defend against declining prestige but the attempt to defend a way of life. As such, it is a group phenomenon; it is part and parcel of the politics of everyday life, engaged in by nearly all status groups. The politics of life style concern is the politics of the propagation of arational goals; but the means of pursuing these goals, the strategy and tactics are, in general, as rational as the politics of economic interests. The intent is the establishment of symbolic systems for defining reality, but the adherents of the politics of life style concern are, in general, no more or less likely to be satisfied with purely symbolic victories than are the adherents of economic interests. The politics of life style concern often stresses symbolic issues in another sense, that of seizing on narrow issues which stand for a larger whole. But it is not clear that status politics is uniquely symbolic in this sense, since the selection of such issues is also common in the politics of economic interests.

Previous research has accounted for a wide variety of minority social movements in terms of status politics, including rural populism, Know-Nothingism and Progressivism (Hofstadter, a), Prohibitionism (Gusfield; Mennell), right-wing extremism (Bell; Hofstadter, b; Lipset, a; Lipset and Raab; McEvoy), anti-pornography campaigns (Zurcher et al.), student politics (Braungart; Westby and Braungart), and intellectual liberalism (Lipset, b). Such applications of the concept are both too narrow and too wide. The application of the concept to rural populism and to much of right-wing extremism is probably too loose, because these movements often can be better understood as the political expressions of commodity classes (Wiley) and small business classes. The application of the concept has been too narrow, first, in the sense that the emphasis has been placed on declining prestige and resulting status frustration. Second, the concept has been used primarily to explain political deviance.

We believe that the politics of life style concern is the master concept which should be applied to all struggles involving noneconomic belief systems. Such struggles are not always reducible to economic conflict but are central to everyday politics for the simple reason that humans are symbolic animals who organize the world in symbolic terms. A style of life can be maintained or propagated only to the extent that its adherents exercise some control over the means of socialization and social intercourse. Life style concern is most clearly evident when fading majorities come to recognize the eclipse of their way of life through loss of such control. But rising minorities also engage in these struggles for cultural protection and dominance.

This essay is intended as an example of social analysis. The textbook dispute in Kanawha County, West Virginia, is an intellectual puzzle that challenges the sociological imagination. Although it is more than an isolated episode, neither sophisticated journalism (Cowan; Humphreys; Kaufman) nor accepted sociological paradigms provide wholly satisfactory explanations. Our aims are modest. Although the analysis is based on the available data which do not allow a conclusive test of our ideas, we will try to demonstrate that our reformulation of the status politics paradigm provides a direct and parsimonious "explanation sketch" (Hempel, 465) of the events of Kanawha County. We will argue that the textbook controversy should be interpreted as a life style issue because participants on both sides view it as a conflict over beliefs and ways of life and because neither economic nor prestige issues are major elements in the conflict. We will argue that the protest movement is an indicator of developing status group consciousness representing a "vertical cleavage in the status arrangement" (Stone and Form, 155) between "cultural fundamentalists" and "cultural modernists" (Gusfield, 140), which cuts across economic and educational class or strata lines.[2]

THE SETTING, THE CONTROVERSY AND ITS PARTICIPANTS

The Setting

Kanawha County, West Virginia (907 square miles) is an area of small communities with one major population concentration centering around the state capital of Charleston. Approximately 229,500 people reside in the county, 71,500 within the city limits of Charleston. Several smaller urban areas (combined populations—65,000) are contiguous to the city of Charleston and stretch westward down the Kanawha Valley. The rest of the population (93,000) lives in small mining towns or are scattered throughout the rural areas of the county (U.S. Bureau of the Census, b: 22). The population is distinctly non-ethnic and Protestant. Less than 1 percent of the population is nonwhite and only 2.9 percent are first or second generation foreign-born (U.S. Bureau of the Census, a: 126). Most of the county's workers are employed in coal mining and in large absentee-owned chemical and glass manufacturing plants. The county, then, is heavily industrialized, but it draws many of its workers from rural areas and contains a sizeable small town and rural nonfarm population.

The Kanawha County school district encompasses the whole county, one of the largest school districts in the United States. The school board has five members, elected at large. During recent years, the county school board has suffered much resentment because of school consolidation (National Education Association, 37). (Opposition to busing, in this case, is independent of protest against forced desegregation.) But the conflict on which we focus here centers on the content of 325 language arts textbooks (English, Composition, Journalism, Speech). It is the cultural relativism of these books which lies at the heart of the controversy.

A Brief Summary of the Controversy

The conflict was instigated by a single member of the school board, the articulate wife of a fundamentalist minister. At the April 11, 1974 meeting of the school board, this member objected to the method of textbook selection, saying that the "board should have stronger control over selection." At the June 2 meeting, she again objected to the new books: "the books lack taste, serve no real purpose, and denounce traditional institutions." On June 23, she spoke in opposition to the books to the congregation of a local Baptist Church. Offensive excerpts were distributed to the congregation and petitions against the books circulated. All of these events were duly covered by the news media. On June 27, over 1,000 anti-textbook protestors appeared at the regularly scheduled school board meeting. However, after hours of testimony, the board voted formally to adopt the disputed books. This final vote appeared to be the precipitating factor for the movement (*Charleston-Gazette*, 11-1-1974:4D).

During July and August of 1974, the anti-textbook protestors organized their ranks and developed strategy. They held marches, rallies, circulated petitions, appealed to elected officials, and planned a boycott of the school system for September. On September 3, the new school term started for some 45,000 students. Protesting parents withheld their children from the schools (10,000 by school board estimates), picketed businesses and mines throughout the county, and prevented school and city buses from operating. On September 12, the county school board closed the schools for a three-day period. The controversial textbooks were removed from the classrooms pending their review by a special citizens committee (*Charleston-Gazette*, 11-1-1974:4D).

During this so-called cooling-off period, violence escalated. Random sniping was reported; vandalism of school property was commonplace; two schools were fire-bombed; and a picketing protestor was shot. The protestors demanded that the county school board and superintendent resign and that the offensive books be banned permanently. The special citizens review committee split into two factions, one favoring the books, the other opposing. On October 28, the majority review committee recommended that all but 35 of the 325 books be returned to the classrooms. Two days later, the minority committee issued a report recommending that 180 of the books be permanently banned. During the night of October 30, the county board of education building was dynamited and partially destroyed. On November 9, the school board voted (4-1) to return most of the books to the classrooms. The 35 most controversial books were to be placed in school libraries to be read only by students with parental permission (*Charleston-Gazette*, 11-1-1974:4D).

The November 9 board vote to reintroduce the textbooks was a severe blow to the protestors' hopes. They responded by having the school superintendent and four board members arrested on November 15 for "contributing to the delinquency of minors" (*Charleston-Gazette*, 11-16-1974). Many parents continued to withhold their children from the public schools, while other students attended newly created private Christian schools. On November 27, several mayors representing Upper Kanawha Valley towns proposed a plan for the secession of their part of the county. From the beginning of the controversy, the Upper Kanawha Valley had been "the hotbed" of anti-textbook protest. The primary purpose of the secession plan was the establishment of a more responsive county school system. The proposal proved to be unworkable because of the lack of an adequate tax base, but it did draw attention to the area of protest concentration.

By the end of 1974, the protestors appeared to win a number of major concessions from the county school board. As a response to the protestors' objections, the board issued strict new guidelines for textbook selection and content. In addition, parents were to be placed on text selection committees. However, these new guidelines were declared illegal by the State Superintendent of Schools. The school board also planned to have a number of "alternative" elementary schools in operation by Fall of 1975. These schools were to take a more "conservative" approach to education (*Charleston-Gazette*, 12-11-1974:2A; 1-20-1975; 1-31-1975). In the meantime, a number of private Christian schools were organized and managed to enroll nearly two thousand students by the beginning of the 1975 school year. This siphoning off of much of the core of the protest movement diminished the demand for public alternative schools so that the latter were never put into operation. The existence of these private schools within the county has resulted in a type of self-imposed segregation.

More recently, in the 1976 West Virginia primary election, several textbook protest leaders who were candidates for state and national offices were defeated, but the dissident school board member was reelected by a landslide margin (*Charleston-Gazette*, 5-13-1976:2B). The protestors then began organizing to defeat the next Kanawha school bond issue. A protest spokesman stated their position: "We can't see the need for more schools and facilities when what's being taught isn't right" (*Charleston-Gazette*, 8-19-1976). Although the vehemence of the protest has subsided, the anger lingers on.

The Participants in the Conflict

There are several identifiable protest organizations within the anti-textbook movement. The Concerned Citizens of Kanawha County is a large, loosely organized coalition of church organizations. The recognized spokesmen for the group are three fundamentalist ministers. Coalition activity has been based within a number of church buildings where information centers and telephone answering services have been established. Much of the mass protest activity which has occurred in Kanawha County may be attributed to this group. Many of its members have been arrested while demonstrating or picketing, including the three ministers mentioned above (*Charleston-Gazette*, 11-1-1974:5D, 7D).

A second goup is the Businessman and Professional People's Alliance for Better Textbooks. The Alliance is a well-organized protest group with elected officers, membership dues, and an official headquarters. The founder and current president is a wealthy businessman. As the title suggests, this is a middle-class group composed mainly of businessmen, teachers, and other professionals. To date, the Alliance has sponsored public meetings, arranged textbook presentations, and lobbied for favorable legislation, but it has not engaged in more militant activities such as picketing or demonstrations. The existence of this organization demonstrates that the protest cannot be characterized simply as a fundamentalist working-class or rural-based movement. The leader of the organization places a greater emphasis on the need to teach economic individualism than do other movement spokesmen.

A third group, the Christian American Parents, is the smallest and least vocal of the anti-text groups. There are no accounts of persons claiming membership in this group having engaged in instances of protest violence. The founder and informal leader is an ordained minister.

A fourth organization, the Non-Christian American Parents, was in existence for several months before being disbanded by its leader, a supreme kleagle in the Ku Klux Klan of West Virginia. During its existence, the group arranged a number of rallies for national Klan figures who appeared in the Charleston area on behalf of the text protestors. Little is really known about the membership of this group, other than the fact that they were not necessarily "born-again" Christians (hence the name Non-Christian). The N.C.A.P. is suspected of having been responsible for some of the more violent activities of this protest.

The Citizens for Quality Education has been the only pro-text organization to appear during the controversy. The group has held public meetings, issued position statements, and provided speakers for television programs. The spokesman for this group and the most outspoken critic of the protest is a local Episcopalian rector. He has since come to be known as "Lucifer" to the protestors (*Charleston-Gazette*, 11-1-1974:5D, 7D). Further support for the books has come from the A.C.L.U., the N.A.A.C.P. and from teachers and school administrators.

Some major characteristics of the leaders in the dispute are shown in Table 1. The two groupings are similar in age and male dominance. It is perhaps of some interest that the traditionalist leaders are younger. At first glance, the two groupings appear quite similar in occupational distribution. However, the classification by primary source of income disguises the fact

T A B L E   1
Characteristics of Kanawha County
Textbook Dispute Leaders

	Anti	Pro
Mean age	41	45
Sex		
Male	8	7
Female	1	1
Occupation		
Minister	0 (6)	1
Professional	1 (0)	3
Proprietor-manager	5 (2)	4
Working class	2 (1)	0
Housewife	1 (0)	0
Education		
College graduate	2	7
Some college	3	1
High school	2	0
Less than high school	1	0
Not available	1	0

Source: *Charleston-Gazette*, 11–1–74:5D, 7D and 1–11–1975.
The numbers in parentheses show the occupational distribution after all lay ministers have been reclassified and the housewife classified by her husband's occupation.

that five of the opposition leaders are lay ministers and that the housewife is married to a minister. All of the ministers lead fundamentalist congregations, which provide them with an organizational base. Clearly, the leadership reflects the strong traditional religious base of the movement. On the other hand, the pro-textbook minister is Episcopalian and all of the leaders hold middle to upper prestige level occupations. The social background differences between the two sets of leaders are even more distinctly illustrated in their educational level. Four of the textbook defenders have graduate degrees and all have at least attended college; at least three of the protest leaders have not attended college.

More can be learned about the social base of the movement by analysis of the demographic characteristics of the portion of the county which had threatened secession over the issue. The Upper Kanawha Valley contains a scattering of small mining communities and most of the rural population of the county (approximately 41,500). This demographic fact suggests that the textbook controversy is partially a rural-urban schism. However, the

T A B L E 2
Comparison of Characteristics of the Protest Region and
the Rest of Kanawha County

	Proposed new county	Rest of county
% families below poverty level	16.6	12.2
% families on public assistance	5.0	3.8
Median family income	$7632	$ 8897
Mean family income	$7842	$10016
4 years high school	26.6	34.0
1–3 years college	5.7	11.2
4 years or more college	3.4	11.4
% high school graduates	35.7	56.6
% families on social security	26.3	19.8

Source: 1970 Census data—quoted in *Charleston-Gazette,* 12-7-74.

comparisons shown in Table 2 demonstrate that the protest region is not
an area of extreme poverty. It is primarily an area of solid working-class
people. The difference in median family income between the two sections
is not remarkably great. But the mean income figures demonstrate that
the protest region has many fewer wealthy residents. A more significant
source of variation is the level of education; nearly two-thirds of the protest
region residents did not complete high school. That this region has a disproportionate aged population is indicated by the social security figure.
Such structural characteristics as rurality, low education, and age provide
strong clues to the basis of the conflict but hardly a satisfactory explanation.

The relevance and ambiguity of the educational figure can be illustrated
from the data in Table 3. Letters-to-the-editor on the textbook controversy
published in the *Charleston-Gazette* between October 31, 1974 and September 25, 1975 were analyzed, using the Gunning Fog Readability Index
(Lesikar, 165–67).[3] This index provides an estimate of the educational level
of the writer on the basis of the use of difficult words (meaning words of
three or more syllables). Clearly, the anti-textbook letter writers demonstrate a lower level of education, but letter writers on both sides show a
wide range of educational levels. More importantly, there is no significant
difference in the mean educational level of the male anti-textbook corre-
spondents and the female defenders of the texts. This finding casts doubt
on the hypothesis that the conflict is simply a dispute between members
of educational strata. More probably, schooling is only one of a number
of factors which determines the position taken. But if traditional measures

TABLE 3
Mean Grade Level (Gunning Fog Readability Index) and Range Values for Textbook Controversy Letter Writers by Position Taken and Sex

	Antibook		Probook	
	$\overline{X}$	Range	$\overline{X}$	Range
Total	10.9	5.2–18.4	14.2	8.4–21.6
Females	9.9	5.2–13.6	12.3	8.4–17.6
Males	11.9	8.0–18.4	16.0	11.2–21.6

of occupational and educational levels provide only an incomplete and not wholly satisfactory explanation of the dispute, perhaps more can be gained from a close examination of the issues involved.

THE ISSUES AT HAND

The Kanawha County textbook conflict is a struggle over words. If sticks and stones have been used in the battle, it is because of the belief of some that words have and will hurt them. In explaining such symbolic conflicts, it is our methodological assumption that the expressed concerns of the participants should be given analytic priority. An examination of the published statements and pamphlets of protest leaders and of letters-to-the-editor reveals four basic thematic complaints: (1) disrespect for traditional orthodox conceptions of God and the Bible; (2) use of profanity and vulgar language; (3) disrespect for authority; and (4) advocacy of moral relativism. In general, these four themes can be viewed as objections to an ideology of secular humanism as a substitute for a preferred authoritarian theocentrism. As such, they are statements of concern about the destruction of a style of life.

The following excerpts from a speech by one of the protest leaders illustrate all four of the fundamental themes.

> The textbooks from the first to the sixth grade teach God to be a myth. They teach our children to rebel against authority and also to rebel against their parents. The Bible teaches the children to 'obey their parents that their days may be long upon the earth.' The Bible also teaches that we should obey authorized authority as long as man's law doesn't prevail against God's law.

. . . . We just can't afford to lose one child by this corruption
that the majority of the board of education has put in our schools.

. . . . We stand to lose the respect of our children and suffer the
loss of the parent-child relationship. The books are filled with
profanity. . . . The books teach permissiveness that the Bible doesn't
teach.

. . . . Stand together and preserve the sanity and respect and
love, the morals, ideals, principles and righteousness that God has
given us in order to make the nation the greatest nation under
God. . . . (*Charleston-Gazette*, 11-1-1974:2A).

Specific examples of textbook offerings which are said to represent
disrespect for Christian orthodoxy include stories by Dylan Thomas and
Mark Twain which belittle the religion of their childhood and an assignment which asks fifth graders to invent a myth, including making up "some
unusual gods for characters." In general, the protestors find little in the
texts which support a traditional conception of God, the Bible, and religion.
The arguments are sometimes focused on a lack of religious neutrality
rather than on a demand for support of a theocentric world-view. This
view was expressed by a local teenager.

I can expect someone who doesn't believe in God not to see
anything wrong with the textbooks. But they can at least respect
our rights since it (the books) does say something about our God.
We're not asking that they teach Christianity in the schools. We're
just asking that they don't insult our faith (quoted in Cowan, 22).

Although the profanity used in the textbooks is no doubt mild by usual
conversational standards, its appearance in official textbooks carries a peculiar symbolic charge. Followers who may not be sufficiently theologically
astute to recognize the examples of "humanism" and "situation ethics"
decried by the ministers can readily agree on language which has traditionally been proscribed from print by local standards. Examples of such
"profane" or "crude" language include: "by God," "good Lord," "for Chris-
sake," "ass-whipping," and "poor bastards."

Less than total respect for authority is implied in a series of textbook
exercises which ask the student to question institutionalized practices, quite
often those of the school system itself. The writings of Shaw, Twain, Mailer,
Heller, Cleaver, and Gregory, among others, are somehow not considered
supportive of the established order. The difficulties of pursuing this line of
protest are illustrated by the objection of one leader to an exercise which
asks students to consider whether "school authorities should make rules
about symbols," such as dress codes proscribing blue jeans. The paradox

that the protestors, on the one hand, desire to eliminate such exercises on the grounds that they engender disrespect for authority but, on the other hand are themselves disrespectfully protesting against the exercise as a symbol of the ideology of authorities, seems not to have been recognized. Nevertheless, this paradox provides an important clue as to why traditionalist protests against school authorities are not even more widespread.

In objecting to moral relativism, a number of the protest leaders commonly refer to "situation ethics." An example of the source of their concern is an exercise in which pupils are asked to consider whether there is ever a time when cheating might be right. More generally, the protestors object to the whole spirit of the new texts which presents a variety of life styles (e.g., ghetto, ethnic) in a neutral manner as equally valid.

Interwoven among the major objectives are a number of subsidiary themes: concerns about lack of patriotism, leftist political values, neutral treatment of immoral sex, drinking and violence, violations of privacy, and evolutionism. These also may be regarded as important elements of status concern, particularly in the light of previous studies which indicate that under different circumstances alcohol use (Gusfield), sexual morality (Rodgers; Zurcher et al.) and evolutionism (Wade) have become the central foci of status politics.

All of these concerns are elements of a way of life which has been under attack for generations and increasingly so today. We designate the world-view as "cultural fundamentalism" and view its adherents as members of a status group. The status group is defined by its way of life. It has structural roots within the old entrepreneurial middle class, subsistence farming, and the "secondary market" working class (Gordon). But it is only one possible response to such objective structural conditions and is not totally defined by them. It cuts across economic classes and is not a prestige class. There is little, if any, evidence in the large number of public expressions by textbook protestors which we have reviewed which would indicate that their real concerns are a sublimated response to status frustration stemming from slippage in a hierarchical social order. Such explanations, common in the literature on status politics, are the sociological equivalent of sexual frustration theories in psychology; since they are based on a minimum of evidence and depend on the extrapolation of hidden motives, they are irrefutable. The central concern of status group members is the viability of their way of life. It is, therefore, no accident that the politics of life style concern should so often center on the school system, one of the major means of production of ways of living. The recognition of the importance of control of the socialization process is illustrated in the two following comments by protestors.

The textbooks are just a subliminal method of injecting anti-American, antireligious thoughts into the formulative (sic) minds of American children—our future leaders; just as the pornographic studios and bookstores, and just as a baby doctor's permissive training was and is (*Charleston-Gazette*, 12-10-1974).

It's an insidious attempt to replace our periods with their question marks (Cowan, 20).

Cultural fundamentalism was once the dominant life style in the United States. Its strength has been eroded by such master trends as urban heterogeneity, consumer-oriented affluence, and the pervasive drive of rationalization in all spheres of life. These trends and others have given rise to a multiplicity of competing status groups (Miller and Sjoberg). The control of the schools is now primarily in the hands of these other status groups and that is what the fight in Kanawha County is all about.

Historically, the election of school boards has been marked by many instances of rancorous conflict between life style groups (Ravitch) and educational practices constantly have been reshaped as a consequence of ideological disputes over the goals of education (Bernier and Williams). Usually, however, school board elections and the establishment of educational policy, including textbook selection, are nonissues in the realm of routine politics (National Educational Association). The fact that this is so is a measure of the cultural hegemony of the educational strata and the economic elites which largely have set public school policy since the foundation of the republic (Spring) and, particularly, to the "depoliticalization" of school politics during the Progressive Era through the techniques of centralization, professionalization and non-partisanship (Ravitch). This political structure has allowed a "cultural minority" (Litt) of "cosmopolitans" (Gans; Ladd) to exert disproportionate influence in setting school policy. Such cultural modernists can be elected in issueless school board contests on the basis of their skilled use of such resources as time, community prestige, and verbal and organizational abilities. They can then, without conflict and even without self-consciousness, "subvert" or change educational policy (expropriate the means of symbolic production) in order to socialize youth to their own construction of social reality, that is, to their own life style. This style of life is largely an adaptation to affluence, rational large-scale organization, and a service economy. Among other characteristics, it inculcates reality testing (thus stimulating the questioning of accepted norms and authority), cultural relativity (thus teaching the tolerance of a variety of life styles), the segmentation of religion from other spheres of life (thus replacing traditional views of God with personal morality), rationality, creativity, moderate consummatory hedonism (including alcohol use and sexual practices) and, in general, "the tradition of the new" (Rosenberg). This is a life style which gains support from at least a large minority of teachers and, especially, from the university-based elite of the educational profession (Bernier and Williams). It is furthered by the politics of state and federal requirements which set standards for textbooks. In the present instance, the disputed textbooks were selected to reflect federal requirements for a multiethnic and multicultural approach to the subject matter (National Educational Association, 1).

Because the pro-textbook side in the Kanawha County dispute had previously been successful in the issueless arena of normal politics, they had never had to formulate a statement of their goals. As a cultural minority, it hardly would have been good tactics to do so in the midst of the dispute.[4] Thus, the previous description of the life style concerns of cultural modernists, which forms the basis of their educational politics, is necessarily even more inferential than the analysis of the cultural fundamentalist life style concerns.

Textbook defenders have cast the issue in terms of censorship and academic freedom. A main line of defense emphasizing the dangers of a narrow world-view as opposed to rational, creative reality-testing can be seen in the following statements.

> . . . is it so wrong to teach our children how other people think, act, and believe? Do you not feel that it would be better for our children to know all possible ways of thought, so that they might one day decide for themselves which path they might take in life. One can not keep his children enclosed in a protective environment all their long and natural life. Would it be fair to your children to know only your small world? (*Charleston-Gazette,* 11-2-1974).
>
> We know of no way to stimulate the growth of our youth if we insulate them from the real issues. We feel this program will help our students to think intelligently about their lives and our society. We do not believe that citizens of Kanawha County are ready to settle for anything less than a complete education with the use of the most modern texts available, nor do we think the best interests of this community are being served by stirring the emotions and raising hysteria in our midst (Excerpt from petition sent to board of education by 10 ministers representing different denominations, quoted in National Educational Association report, 15).

A more effective strategy of the proponents was an emphasis on the emotional and authoritarian style of their opponents. The escalation of violence enabled the two local newspapers and the television stations to support the pro-text book side by decrying violence and protest activity.

The violence was a serious embarrassment to the protesting traditionalists and helped to stymie their cause. But the protestors did manage to win some minor victories, such as agreements from the school board to remove a number of the texts from the classroom to the library. They also gained considerable national publicity for their struggle and established ties with a number of outside groups and leaders involved in similar life style conflicts. It is not at all clear that the protestors will be satisfied with a token symbolic victory in this clash over cultural symbols.

DISCUSSION

The question still remains as to why this movement arose where and when it did, since neither the loss of control of the means of socialization by the cultural fundamentalists, nor its reflection in the changing content of school texts, is a sudden development. A number of elements of structural conduciveness (Smelser) may be noted. First, the conflicting status groups are ecologically and organizationally segmented so that in-depth contact between members is hindered. Second, the ecological base of the protestors in the Upper Kanawha Valley is relatively homogeneous in occupation, religion, and culture, allowing for the development of a sense of status community or common life style consciousness. Third, the county is a single school district so that the establishment of school policy is more of a conflict-inducing zero-sum game than is common elsewhere.

Another important factor in the development of the protest was the presence of a charismatic leader who, to her supporters, literally bore the grace of God and who said, in effect, "It is written (in the state law)—but I (from God) say unto you . . . !" She also carried the charisma of office as a member of the school board, which allowed for the critique of authority from a position of authority. Her background in the Church of Christ, a denomination more theologically oriented than most fundamentalist churches, probably aided her in her ability to shape a rather consistent ideological position on a variety of issues.

Still another factor in the generation of the movement may have been the recent successes of two economic class movements, the Miners for Democracy and the Black Lung Movement. Charleston, as the state capital, had been the site of a number of Black Lung Movement demonstrations and other protests by miners. If the textbook demonstrators had not been participants, they had at least been witnesses of these events.

Finally, despite their influence, the power base of the cosmopolitans of Charleston should not be exaggerated. Although they possess leadership skills and administrative positions, they are small in numbers. They are not the economic dominants. Contrary to a vulgar Marxist interpretation, the controllers of the means of production do not necessarily even wish to control all elements of the local superstructure, especially when they are located hundreds of miles distant. Since large portions of the middle strata are neither cultural fundamentalists nor cultural cosmopolitans, but bystanders, the small number of the cosmopolitans, who can operate successfully in the realm of routine politics, are vulnerable to the demands of mass protest politics.

We should also note two factors which are apparently unimportant. First, poverty seems not to have been a factor. Kanawha County is not a poverty area by state standards, and the poor were not the core of the movement. Second, the movement was not a substitute for class action on the part of the working class. A major coal strike took place in the midst of the textbook protest. If anything, the protest was used by local miners for economic purposes. When miners went out on a massive wildcat strike in support of the anti-textbook protest, it had the effect of reducing the stockpiles which the mine operators had built up in anticipation of the contract strike.

CONCLUSIONS

The Kanawha County textbook dispute is a case study in the politics of life style concern. We believe that the protestors are adherents of a life style and world view which are under threat from a variety of sources— the educational system, the mass media, the churches—fundamentally from every socialization agency beyond their immediate control which impinges on their lives. It would be easy to dismiss this spontaneous movement as the last gasp of a dying subculture on the margin of the mass society. But we believe that the Kanawha County dispute is the excrescence of a larger revitalization movement (Wallace) which elsewhere centers on sex education, pornography, evolution, busing and "decency." These are not simply examples of irrational, displaced aggression in response to a economic deprivation or some general undefined frustration. Rather, they are attempts to build and sustain moral orders which provide basic meaning for human lives.

History is a graveyard of status groups but the death throes are often long and painful. And the forces which have led to the rise of alternative, counter-cultural life styles may be conducive to the resurgence of cultural fundamentalism as another alternative. Our prognosis for this apparently dying subculture is a long life of continued ill health.

NOTES

We are grateful to John Pease, Patricia Yancey Martin, and Michael Bremseth for their helpful comments and corrections. An earlier version of this paper was presented at the annual meeting of the S.S.S., 1976.

1. There are important exceptions, especially in British sociology. A valuable explication of Weber's stratification concepts is found in Giddens (163–168). Gusfield presents a fundamentally sound Weberian interpretation of status politics on which we have drawn heavily. But we differ with Gusfield on a number of basic points, most particularly, in his emphasis on the prestige factor. A more complete explication of problems in interpreting Weber and a broadened analytic framework for the study of status politics are found in Clelland.

2. We assume that in modern industrial societies, status group consciousness, like class consciousness, is *not*, typically, fully developed. As Weber says, *Stände* are often groups "of an amorphous kind" (932). We prefer Gusfield's designation of conflicting life styles to the more commonly used local-cosmopolitan distinction because of their implied emphasis on manner of living (*Lebensführung*) rather than on type of participation or attachment to community. The growing conceptual and operational diversity in the definitions of localism and cosmopolitanism (the latter was used by Stone and Form in reference to a life style) have fragmented the concepts, possibly beyond recovery (but cf. Thielbar).

3. All letters on the issue except those in the Sunday edition of the paper were examined, a total of 325. In order to be scaled for readability, each letter had to have at least 100 words. All others were excluded. Writers of more than one letter were represented in the analysis by their first letter of more than 100 words. Subsequent letters by the same author were excluded. The first twelve letters in each of the four categories shown in Table 3 were then categorized by grade level. This analysis was carried out by Michael Morris.

4. A survey by the Kanawha County Board of Education reveals the weakness of support for the disputed texts. Students in all sixty-nine neighborhood elementary schools were given request forms, to be filled out by their parents, which would allow the children to use the disputed texts. A majority of parents requested such use in only seventeen of the schools (i.e., a majority of the parents from fifty-two of the schools rejected the texts or did not return the request forms). Majority support was found in *none* of the eighteen nonurban neighborhood schools.

REFERENCES

Bell, D. 1960. "Status Politics and New Anxieties: on the 'Radical Right' and the Ideologies of the Fifties." In *The End of Ideology*. New York: Free Press.

Bernier, Normand R., and Jack E. Williams. 1973. *Beyond Beliefs: Ideological Foundations of American Education*. Englewood Cliffs: Prentice-Hall.

Brandmeyer, G. A., and R. S. Denisoff. 1969. "Status Politics: An Appraisal of the Application of a Concept." *Pacific Sociological Review* 12(Spring):5811.

Braungart, R. G. 1971. "Status Politics and Student Politics: an Analysis of Left- and Right-wing Student Activists." *Youth and Society* 3(December):195–209.

Charleston-Gazette. Charleston, West Virginia. Issues from October 31, 1974 to August 16, 1976.

Clelland, D. A. 1976. "On the Theory of Status Politics: A Critique and an Extension." Paper presented at the annual meetings of the Society for the Study of Social Problems.

Clelland, D. A., and L. L. Guess. 1975. "The Politics of Life Style Concern: a Review of the Literature on Status Politics." Paper presented at the annual meeting of the S.S.S.

Cowan, P. 1974. "A Fight over America's Future." In *The Village Voice* (December 9):19–23.

Gans, Herbert J. 1967. *The Levittowners.* New York: Pantheon.

Giddens, Anthony. 1971. *Capitalism and Modern Social Theory.* Cambridge: Cambridge University.

Gordon, David M. 1972. *Theories of Poverty and Unemployment.* Lexington, Mass.: Heath.

Gusfield, Joseph R. 1963. *Symbolic Crusade: Status Politics and the American Temperance Movement.* Urbana: University of Illinois.

Hempel, C. G. 1949. "The Function of General Laws in History." In Herbert Feigl and Wilfred Sellers (eds.), *Readings in Philosophical Analysis.* New York: Appleton-Century-Crofts.

Hofstadter, Richard. a:1955. *The Age of Reform.* New York: Knopf.

————. b:1955. "The Pseudo-Conservative Revolt." In Daniel Bell (ed.), *The New American Right.* New York: Criterion.

Humphreys, J. 1976. "Textbook War in West Virginia." *Dissent* 23(Spring):164–70.

Kaufman, P. J. 1975. "Alice's Wonderland." *Appalachian Journal* 2(Spring):162–66.

Ladd, Everett Carll, Jr. 1966. *Ideology in America: Change and Response in a City, a Suburb, and a Small Town.* Ithaca: Cornell University Press.

Lesikar, Raymond V. 1961. *Report Writing for Business.* Homewood, Ill.: Irwin.

Lipset, Seymour Martin. 1955. "The Sources of the 'Radical Right'." In Daniel Bell (ed.), *The New American Right.* New York: Criterion.

————. 1960. "American Intellectuals: Their Politics and Status." In *Political Man.* New York: Doubleday.

Lipset, Seymour Martin, and Earl Raab. 1970. *The Politics of Unreason: Right Wing Extremism in America, 1790–1970.* New York: Harper & Row.

Litt, E. 1966. "The Politics of a Cultural Minority." In M. Kent Jennings and L. Harmon Zeigler (eds.), *The Electoral Process.* Englewood Cliffs: Prentice-Hall.

McEvoy, James, III. 1971. *Radicals or Conservatives? The Contemporary American Right.* Chicago: Rand McNally.

Mennell, S. J. 1973. "Prohibition: a Sociological View." *American Studies* 3:159–75.

Miller, P. J. and G. Sjoberg. 1973. "Urban Middle-Class Life Styles in Transition." *Journal of Applied Behavioral Science* 9:144–62.

National Educational Association. 1975. *Kanawha County, West Virginia: A Textbook Study in Cultural Conflict.* Washington: N.E.A.

Ravitch, Diane. 1974. *The Great School Wars: New York City 1805–1973.* New York: Basic Books.

Rodgers, H. R., Jr. 1975. "Prelude to Conflict: The Evolution of Censorship Campaigns." *Pacific Sociological Review* 18(April):194–205.

Rosenberg, Harold. 1959. *The Traditional of the New.* New York: Horizon.

Smelser, Neil J. 1962. *Theory of Collective Behavior.* New York: Free Press.

Spring, Joel H. 1972. *Education and the Rise of the Corporate State.* Boston: Beacon.

Stone, G. P., and W. H. Form. 1953. "Instabilities in Status: The Problem of Hierarchy in the Community Study of Status Arrangements." *American Sociological Review* 18(April): 149–62.

Thielbar, G. W. 1970. "On Locals and Cosmopolitans." In Geogory P. Stone and Harvey A. Faberman (eds.), *Social Psychology Through Symbolic Interaction*. Boston: Blaidell.

U.S. Bureau of the Census. a:1970. *General Social and Economic Characteristics: West Virginia, PC (1)–C50 WVa*. Washington: Government Printing Office.

—————— . b:1970. *Number of Inhabitants: West Virginia, PC (1)–A50 WVa*. Washington: Government Printing Office.

Wade, N. 1972. "Creationists and Evolutionists: Confrontation in California." *Science* 178 (November 17):724–29.

Wallace, A. F. C. 1956. "Revitalization Movements." *American Anthropologist* 58:264–81.

Weber, Max. 1968. *Economy and Society*. New York: Bedminster.

Westby, D. L., and R. C. Braungart. 1970. "The Alienation of Generations and Status Politics: Alternative Explanations of Student Political Activism." In Roberta S. Sigel (ed.), *Learning About Politics*. New York: Random House.

Wiley, N. 1967. "America's Unique Class Politics: The Interplay of the Labor, Credit, and Commodity Markets." *American Sociological Review* 32(August):529–41.

Zurcher, L. A., Jr., R. G. Kirkpatrick, R. G. Cushing, and C. K. Bowman. 1971. "The Anti-Pornography Campaign: a Symbolic Crusade." *Social Problems* 19(Fall):217–38.

DAVID B. TYACK, MICHAEL W. KIRST,
and ELISABETH HANSOT

Educational Reform:
Retrospect and Prospect

Questions to think about

1 *How are changes and specific characteristics of a given time reflected in its schools?*

2 *Compare this discussion of past eras with discussions of the future in the last two articles. What areas of change will predominate?*

3 *Discuss the change described in this article in terms of the open systems framework. For instance, what environmental factors might have brought about change in different eras?*

4 *In the light of current events, draw on the authors' analyses of previous times to suggest how you think schools will change in the future.*

Observers sometimes lament that educational reform is an institutional Bermuda Triangle. Intrepid change agents go out to the schools and never surface again. Whatever *did* happen to performance contracting, or airborne television instruction, or Program, Planning, Budgeting System?[1] We admit that many educational panaceas have been abortive, but we argue that there is a long history of important changes in *educational programs,* in *governance,* and in *beliefs* about education. In this article we examine what some of these reforms were and why they persisted. We look at the diversity of attempted changes from Sputnik to the mid-seventies. We suggest some strategies that may be learned from this history.

From *Teachers College Record* 81: 3 (Spring 1980), 253–269. Reprinted with permission.

But we start with a caution: There is good reason to suppose that educational reform in the 1980s may be quite different from most educational change thus far. The reason is that many parts of the nation now face conditions unprecedented in educational history, except perhaps for the depression of the 1930s, for now we have declining enrollments, tax revolts, and shaky public support. Although public education has historically been an expanding and optimistic enterprise, today it is contracting. Morale is low in many districts as staff debate who is to walk the plank next. It is quite possible that present adversarial relationships between professionals and between educators and the public will grow worse, not better.[2]

Decisions to cut back or eliminate existing programs collide with conflicting goals and interests. It is much easier to be tolerant of differences when new functions are added than when they are swept away. It is one thing to disagree about where to place a new elementary school and quite another to decide which one to close. While reform by accretion often brings good feeling, retrenchment tends to produce accusations and hand-wringing. Fear and anxiety rarely prompt creative solutions to problems.[3]

Most ominous today for people who believe in public education—as we do—are signs of a declining loyalty to the ideology and institution of the "common school," the old term for public education. Like others, we have spent much of our professional lives criticizing the gap between the ideal and the actuality of public education. Now we are coming to feel rather like the railroad buff who complains about dirty cars, poor food, and bumpy roadbeds on Amtrak only to find others nodding and suggesting that passenger trains be abolished.[4]

Today there may be declining consensus that public education is a public good and an increasing tendency to see education as a consumer good to be purchased in the market. If the people most attuned to quality in schooling and most capable of acting on their choices begin to find alternatives like private schools and vouchers attractive, a danger exists that (in Albert Hirschman's terms) *exit* from the system of public schools rather than *voice* to improve it will become increasingly common.[5] Thus it is imperative, we feel, to revive the sense of public education as a public good and to renegotiate the ideological contract Americans made long ago to use the common school to realize democracy. This will be no easy task, for school people in many parts of the nation today are in a state of shock, conflict, and overload, and citizens lack the kind of leadership that once gave focus and resonance to the aspirations of public education.

We begin this article with a discussion of reform waves from the 1840s to Sputnik, briefly analyzing changes in governance, in ideology, and in growth of programs by accretion. We argue that the common school of the nineteenth century was the product of a widely based social movement that shared a similar ideology. During the progressive era at the turn of the twentieth century, subtle and important changes began to take place both in decision making and in the normative bases for those decisions. School people and lay allies pressed for a centralization of power that increasingly turned over leadership to professionals who sought to elaborate and differentiate systems of public schools. Still talking about democracy, they redefined it to mean that public education was for the people but that it was best run by experts who could adapt the schools to the different needs and destinies of pupils in a complex industrial society. In recent years many new actors who have been skeptical about the wisdom of such established experts have entered the politics of education. Time has altered the balance of power in public schooling. In recent years several competing ideologies and programs have emerged as the earlier consensus eroded.

Over the decades the innovations in programs that have lasted were mostly structural in nature, were easily monitored, and responded to or created new constituencies. Examples of such changes include school lunches, vocational tracks, or classes for handicapped pupils. It was easy to monitor the existence of such structural reforms and to identify the people who had strong motives for retaining them. By contrast, reforms calling for new skills or added efforts on the part of existing staff have had a more checkered fate. Team teaching and the core curriculum are cases in point.[6]

The history of programmatic change in education is thus an ambiguous legacy for the present for several reasons. One is that it is precisely structural add-ons that will be unlikely during the next decade, while new efforts and new skills on the part of existing teachers could make a difference even in hard times. A second is that the creation of a fractionated system of specialized groups has clouded much of the older sense of common purpose and increased the possibility of internecine conflict over scarce resources. In addition, the erosion of a sense of a common ideology of public education and bitter conflicts over the governance of the system have made it difficult to recapture a sense of common purpose, of morale, and of loyalty to the common school as a public good.

REFORM MOVEMENTS, 1840–1958

Cheerful amnesia and lack of balance have often characterized educational reformers. Those with longer memories have often commented on the cyclical pattern of attempted changes in education, however. Periodically, people discover with alarm problems that have been with us for decades if not centuries: poverty, wayward youth, inadequate preparation for work, and rigid schools. Specific solutions are proposed with all the hype that advertisers invest in the "new" Old Dutch Cleanser, yet often these are recycled solutions from earlier eras: accountability and business efficiency, the career motive in education, or teaching the "whole child."[7] When the difficulty of actually changing schooling becomes apparent, when the costs in effort and money become onerous, panaceas often fade, and little changes behind the classroom door.

Reaction to overpromising often brings unintended consequences. Some observers begin to find genetic explanations of "failure" convenient or persuasive. Others of more radical persuasion argue that only changes in the basic social and economic system can bring about lasting educational change. Both arguments undercut the case for gradual improvement of schools.[8]

As we have said, we believe that waves of reform do leave lasting deposits when they pass through the educational system, although not always the ones most desired. These deposits are legacies of what many historians see as three major periods of educational reform: the common school movement of the mid-nineteenth century, the progressive era in the early twentieth, and the great ferment of the last generation, which as yet has no generally agreed-upon name (though by the year 2000 historians will no doubt have found a label).

Viewed over a long time perspective, these three periods share certain common features. Each brought subtle and pervasive changes in the belief system that supported citizens' loyalty to public education; each questioned and altered existing patterns of educational governance; and each brought in its train substantial changes in the educational program.

THE COMMON SCHOOL MOVEMENT OF THE MID-NINETEENTH CENTURY

The common school of the nineteenth century was the product of a vast social movement that spread a basically similar institution from coast to coast across a sparsely settled continent. In 1860, 80 percent of Americans lived in rural areas. There was at that time no United States Office of Education and only the tiniest beginnings of state educational bureaucracies (indeed, as late as 1890, the median size of state departments of education was two, including the superintendent). It was largely lay people who built and supervised the public schools and young, untrained teachers who instructed the pupils. Yet by the Civil War a pattern institution had emerged—the common school—that was already the mainstream of schooling in the United States. As advocated by Horace Mann and other school promoters, the common school was to be public in political control and economic support, was to include the children of all classes, sects, and ethnic groups, and existed to produce literate, numerate, and moral citizens. While theoretically nonsectarian and nonpartisan in politics, the common school often had a pan-Protestant and conservative slant, but apart from Catholics, most citizens found its teachings nonoffensive. Unlike the situation in other English-speaking countries, Protestants joined to support the public school and political parties did not differ in their educational programs to any significant degree.[9]

The creation of such a system was a reform of immense magnitude—indeed, the greatest institution-building success in American history. It is hard today, when public education is so familiar a part of our lives, to recapture the ambience of the pre-Civil War era when the common school was still a tenuous experiment. Prior to the movement, Americans supported all kinds of schools with enthusiasm—private colleges and academies; charity schools; proprietary schools; schools based on class, sect, or ethnicity; and public schools.[10] But it was the genius of the common school crusaders to persuade citizens that American millennial destiny was best served by support of a common school. It was hundreds of thousands of such promoters from Maine to Oregon who accomplished this task, not a central ministry of education.

Unifying the common school movement were a basic system of similar beliefs and a common vision of their institutional embodiment. The promoters of public education were Victorian opinion-shapers, largely British-American in ethnic origins, bourgeois in economic outlook and status, and evangelical Protestant in religious orientation. They believed that a common school controlled and financed largely by local trustees and public taxation was essential to the realization of a millennial vision of a righteous republic. The Protestant-republican ideology embodied in this institution was vividly expressed by the *McGuffey Readers*, which were probably used by 200,000,000 school children of that period. The characteristic form of that institution was the one-room school of rural communities and the graded schools of towns and cities. Neither type of school was highly differentiated, and both were designed to give pupils a basic elementary education to fit them for participating in political life and for entering the world of work.[11]

THE PROGRESSIVE ERA: CENTRALIZATION OF CONTROL AND THE ELABORATION OF THE SYSTEM

At the turn of the twentieth century a new vision inspired many of the leaders of American public education. It was a time of rapid expansion and massive elaboration of the system around the central nucleus of the common school. A key political goal of educational administrators and their lay allies was to centralize control of urban schools in small boards of education elected at large, to destroy local ward boards, and to vest most decision making in appointed expert superintendents. They sought to use state legislatures and departments of education to standarize public education and to consolidate one-room schools into larger township or regional schools. Essentially they wished to "take education out of politics"—meaning, usually, away from decentralized control by lay people—and to turn "political" issues into matters for administrative discretion. In large degree they succeeded in centralizing structures of governance in cities (though the reforms did not always bring the results they hoped for) and in creating increasingly effective state regulation of schools, but it was not until after World War II that the campaign to eliminate small rural schools gained rapid momentum.[12]

These reformers were simply exchanging one form of politics for another, of course, and the changes in educational governance were part of a larger shift of power in the society as a whole from local constituencies to large national organizations and professional groups. In arguing for these changes, reformers claimed that educational leadership was becoming an expert profession that deserved to be buffered from the vagaries of locally elected officials. In practice much of the actual direction of change came from nonelected and private individuals and groups claiming special competence to judge what was in the public good. In this way, psychologists devised intelligence and achievement tests that profoundly shaped the destiny of students; university professors at leading institutions like Teachers College, Columbia, trained and placed superintendents in major cities; educators from foundations and higher education made surveys of states and cities that told citizens what was approved practice and how well their schools matched this new professional wisdom; and accreditation agencies made such standards criteria for good standing. It was a time of great confidence in a new "science of education" that would reshape schooling in such a way that public education could engineer a smoothly running, "socially efficient" society. They believed that they were discovering the means of shaping social evolution; it was a heady dream, comparable in power to the earlier millennial ideology of Horace Mann.[13]

As the progressive administrators redefined the concept of democracy, the school systems they constructed were internally hierarchical and shielded from lay influence. The new school systems stratified and differentiated public education, particularly in cities, adding new layers and functions. Secondary education grew enormously until it became a mass institution. In junior and senior high schools educators added a plethora of new subjects and services: vocational classes, health education, physical education, guidance, classes for retarded children, programs for truants and delinquents, and revised curricula in older subjects like English or history. Whereas the older common school had provided only basic education in the three Rs and civic morality, now school people increasingly believed that they should prepare students directly for specific later roles in life and that schools should sort and train the young according to their future destinies. Equality came less to mean sameness of treatment and more a specialized training adapted to different abilities and careers. As compulsory attendance laws began to bring young people into schools for a longer span of years, and as employers increasingly attended to educational attainment, schools became more important as doorways to a specialized labor market.[14]

Like many other occupational groups, educators sought to use the power of the state to strengthen their position, as in certification requirements, better state funding, and standardization of facilities and curricula. Although there were disputes within the profession over child-centered pedagogical practices and over the emphasis to be given to such innovations as vocational training, by and large there was more consensus than conflict over the elaboration of the system and the attempt to buffer school politics. One reason was that the national and state educational associations were mostly dominated by administrators trained in the new education departments and schools. In times of expansion, there was little controversy over reform by accretion, and even in the retrenchment of the Great Depression there was relatively little infighting among educators, partly because the persistence of a common value system dampened factionalism.[15]

As we shall suggest, however, many of the ideals and achievements of the progressive administrators have come under sharp attack during the last generation. The ideal of a "closed system" in equilibrium run by professional managers and their experts has been shaken by the entry of new groups into educational decision making: minorities pressing for desegregation and community control and jobs for their members; activists calling for black history or bilingual instruction; lawyers and judges demanding changes in assignment policies or student rights; state and federal legislators passing categorical programs or requiring new forms of accountability; and various other reformers both inside and outside the schools. Decentralizers in cities have sought to reinstitute something resembling the old ward boards of education abolished during the years from 1890 to 1920. Legal activists have challenged the use of an earlier reform, the IQ test. Professional associations have been torn by internal battles. Older loyalties were questioned, and the stage was set for an era when a fundamental institution was no longer seen as a self-evident public good.[16]

REFORMS FROM SPUTNIK TO THE MID-1970s: NEW VOICES AND OLD PROBLEMS

The reform generation starting with Sputnik in 1958 and lasting to the mid-1970s had no single focus but changed kaleidoscopically. The federal government's role in education grew to include sixty-six categorical programs, while California alone mounted fifty-two reform initiatives from 1958 to 1975. To mention but a few reform efforts is to suggest how diverse they were in philosophy and program: new curricula in science and mathematics aimed at gifted students; compensatory education for "disadvantaged" children; ethnic studies courses; programs to eliminate sexual bias in athletics or vocational education; desegregation; bilingual, bicultural programs; performance contracting; head-start and follow-through programs; open classrooms; team teaching; minimum competency testing; affective education and sensitivity training; creation of alternative schools; legal protection of student rights; management by objectives; provision for the handicapped; and experiments in parental choice of education through vouchers. In many cases extravagant claims were made for the efficacy of the innovations, yet as soon as one was alleged to have "failed," another panacea quickly appeared on the horizon.[17]

Why was there such a rapid succession of attempted innovations? One reason is that schools today perform a variety of functions, themselves legacies of earlier reform eras, yet innovations usually focus on only a narrow range of purposes. People want schools to:

Give children basic skills and knowledge

Sort people out for future roles by grading and testing them, thus providing an apparently fair way to ration opportunity

Encourage personal attributes such as creativity, self-reliance, or interpersonal sensitivity

Provide daytime custody for children

Socialize children to core values of the society and provide a bridge between the home and the world of work and political participation

These are explicit functions. There are, of course, a number of implicit ones as well, like giving jobs to the administrators, teachers, aides, and others who work in schools.[18]

While Americans have always argued to some degree about the purposes of education, in recent years there has been heightened factionalism over which functions are most important. At different times different weights were given to this range of purposes and this tendency has been reinforced by the "issue-attention cycle" in education, which has rapidly shifted attention from one feature to another—basic skills to creativity, for example, or the gifted to the disadvantaged.[19] People eager to enhance the standing of their particular group or identified with particular reforms often saw others as competitors for attention and funds. Few spoke and worked for balance; few worried about those who had not yet found a voice in the forum of educational politics.

Despite the many changes in educational rhetoric and the insistent claims of new squads of reformers, each with solutions ready, actual practices in the classrooms may not have changed markedly. Behind the classroom door teachers can sabotage the best-laid plans of systems analysts if they disagree with them or can unwittingly derail a reform if they are not helped to understand it. Regulations by the state, strictures of accrediting bodies, the influence of testing agencies, and garden-variety bureaucratic inertia often inhibit change. American education in recent years may thus be considered both faddish and resistant to change.[20] Patterns of governance in public education during this period became very complex and often contradictory. Rapidly the older ideal of direction by professionals buffered from the external environment gave way as new people entered educational politics. Successive groups banded together to influence the schools in a series of powerful social movements, triggered first by blacks in the civil rights movement and then joined by the women's movement, various ethnic groups, coalitions of the handicapped, and other people who believed that they had been excluded from influence. Such groups often turned to legislation and the state and federal courts to bring about changes. Certain innovations were also pushed by "professional reformers" in foundations, universities, and government who felt it their duty to represent the poor and disfranchised. A small network of lawyers and social scientists, for example, spearheaded school finance reform in many states, aided by funds and people from foundations.[21]

One result of the new politics of educational reform was greatly increased regulation of local districts. There was an explosion of litigiousness as publicly financed lawyers pressured schools to guarantee rights to an enlarging number of categories of people. In consequence, a part of the governance of education became increasingly centralized. A single federal judge could order a large city to desegregate its schools. A state legislature could mandate minimum competencies for all students. Fear of the cutoff of federal funds could impel districts to eliminate differentiation by sex in physical education or vocational classes. Courts could order educators to change their policies of tracking handicapped students.[22]

But along with centralization came new pressures for lay participation at the local level. Federal and state laws required districts to set up school site councils. Large systems experimented with decentralization and community control. And some reformers called for parental choice, whether in the form of alternative schools within the public system or vouchers.

In the meantime, within the educational profession there were similar tugs-of-war between centralization of power and factionalism. Once weak, teachers' unions grew in numbers and influence, and state teachers' associations gained much greater clout in politics. Once anathema, strikes by teachers multiplied, while collective negotiations became mandated by law in most of the populous states. As teachers banded together to press their economic and political demands, they split away from administrators; conflict rent the once-unified National Education Association, for example. Principals and other middle managers were caught in the middle in the power squeeze and sometimes formed separate bargaining units of their own. Adversarial relationships became commonplace in a profession that once had prided itself on consensus.[23]

The fate of programmatic educational reform amid this internal and external turbulence was confusing. As in prior history, the changes that were most likely to last were additive, structural, and supported by new constituencies. Thus programs in compensatory education or bilingual instruction, for example, created new positions such as coordinators of federal programs or remedial reading teachers. Many of the attempted reforms, however, were short-lived if they did not possess these characteristics. Reforms such as team teaching or the open classroom were often implemented only partially at best, and they were easy targets when the issue-attention cycle shifted "back to basics." Efforts at top-down curricular change, treating the school and the teacher as a neutral "black box," often were ignored. Federal program standards that stressed fancy business management techniques often met only symbolic compliance. Ambitious programs like President Nixon's experimental schools program that called for "comprehensive change" according to multiple, vague, and conflicting goals led to arm-wrestling matches between federal monitors and local educational agencies eager for funds. The rational model of bureaucratic change often espoused by government administrators ignored the organizational realities of actual school systems and the power of passive resistance, which teachers had mastered.[24]

The reform wave of the 1960s brought not only new programs but also important changes in governance and in attitudes toward education. New groups not previously heard in educational decision making now made their needs felt. Issues of social justice too long ignored became salient in the public mind. School people came more and more to understand that in a democratic polity, public education could never be "above politics." In important ways educators were forced by laws, by court decisions, by protest groups, and by their own changed consciousness to become more responsive to outcast groups.

But the new factionalism in school governance also had its unfortunate consequences. Amid the shock and overload of attempted reforms and new demands, the competition of new constituencies for attention, it was hard to remember that the public schools existed to serve all children, not simply those with vocal defenders. Amid the contests of single-issue reformers and special interest groups, it was easy to forget the broader purposes of the common school, the belief system that made the parts coherent.[25]

PROBLEMS OF THE LATE 1970s AND
STRATEGIES FOR THE 1980s

For all the conflict, the 1960s and early 1970s were heady years. Schools were rapidly expanding to accommodate the population bulge of pupils, funding grew at a rate unparalleled in history, and reformers found ready audiences and sponsors. In the early years of the war on poverty it seemed as if the traditional American faith in schooling had never been stronger. People talked of educational moon shots. Long-awaited reforms such as federal aid to education seemed to promise real solutions to old problems.[26]

In 1980 the educational universe looks far different. Now we confront declining enrollments and tax revolts. Some people talk of public schools as a declining industry and expect pathologies similar to those in the railroads: an aging work force, an overwhelming concern for job security and hence some featherbedding, the exit of ambitious and talented people, less willingness to take chances, a gradual deterioration of plant and equipment, and a public increasingly inclined to seek alternatives. Just as railroad passengers turned to the airlines and shippers to trucks, so some expect education-conscious parents to shift their children to private schools (a movement that would be accelerated by the California voucher initiative if it passes).

When an organization declines, people have various responses: *apathy*, as bystanders observing its demise; *exit*, the withdrawal of one's presence or support; *voice*, or the mobilization of forces to change the organization; and *loyalty*, a commitment so deep to the purposes and character of the organization that one must revitalize it and cannot contemplate alternatives.[27] We believe that loyalty is the appropriate response since public schools are major institutions for the continuous re-creation of democracy and social justice. These are freighted words not especially fashionable today. Now there is a retreat from funding of public services, a glorification of the market and individual choice, and a privatism that negates the common good. Educators, like many other civil servants, are often viewed as yet another interest group at the public trough—a perception in part magnified by infighting within the educational profession over declining resources and by the splintering of the common front of the profession during the 1960s. Today there is less optimism about education than has historically been the case. In part this may stem from real problems that people see in their communities such as violence and vandalism in the schools, and apparently dropping test scores. In part it may reflect widely publicized studies that purport to show that schools do not make much difference in the life chances of children. And some of the deflation of confidence may come from the angry and funereal tone of muckraking books like *Death at an Early Age*.[28]

So just when a traditionally expanding and optimistic enterprise—the public school—has entered an era of declining enrollments and unstable fiscal support, we face a crisis of public confidence and low morale in the profession. At such a time as this it is perhaps useful to ask if historical perspectives can give us some guidance and if we can learn from dead people as well as by experimenting on the living. We think that people can learn from the past—not specific courses of action in the present but a general knowledge of how past reforms have turned out and what those outcomes may imply for the present.

STRATEGIES ABOUT PROGRAM

It is unlikely that educational reform in the 1980s will proceed in the incremental fashion of old reforms, simply adding on new layers and functions around the existing ones. As we have seen, much of the innovation of the recent past has followed an issue-attention cycle (now the gifted, now the handicapped, now minorities, now ecology, now vocational education) that has tended to forget the need to balance the different functions of schooling and to set priorities for what schools can do well. Citizens and educators disagree about what is "basic" about education. They need to be reminded that all children need a rounded education. In addition, in order to gain attention for some favored change, reformers have often become Cassandras and snake-oil salesmen, making exaggerated laments and positive claims. In promoting a "new" reform, advocates have often forgotten what is to be learned from past similar experience or theory (the fans of open education might have read John Dewey with profit, and current promoters of accountability and management by objectives would have discovered the limits of rationalism by studying the fate of the "cult of efficiency" in the second decade of this century).[29] People are tired of overpromising, of crying with alarm. Now is a time for the balancing of functions, for realism in claims, for improving the way schools do what they can actually accomplish.

STRATEGIES ABOUT GOVERNANCE

There is a danger today that retrenchment will increase the factionalism and me-tooism that is apparent in many districts. One of the forces that makes a programmatic reform stick—the constituency it creates—could make cutbacks an intensely competitive process. It will be tempting simply to find targets of least resistance rather than to make decisions based on the interests of the children (to fire art teachers, for instance, or to close an innovative school in a low-income district rather than one in a silk-stocking district). Yet opportunistic administrative decisions belie the statesmanship required in public education, and factionalism among educators ultimately weakens the whole enterprise.

As we shall suggest later, what we most need now is a renewed sense of loyalty to the goals of public education. This is not a plea for a return to the older administrator-dominated professional associations, for their unity was often achieved at the expense of real voice for teachers and other interested people. Rather, it is a warning that factionalism could lead to the situation described by Benjamin Franklin: If people do not hang together, they will hang separately. There are signs today that educators do perceive the need for unified appeal and action.

The history of lay governance of education shows swings, both rhetorically and actually between centralization and decentralization. We have suggested that the common school originally was created and governed by broad-based lay participation, that it became increasingly insulated from such direct lay control, and that during the last generation there have been conflicting pressures toward both centralization and decentralization. Power has migrated both up and down the system. It is time, we think, to ask which kinds of decisions can best be made at which levels. Many recent discussions on this matter tend to oversimplify the normative and technical issues.[30] We believe that some questions are best decided at the federal or state levels. Constitutional issues like the separation of church and state, student rights, and racial and sexual equity cannot be left to the opinions of local board members. Fiscal equity is probably best handled through federal and state legislatures.[31]

But the history of pedagogical reforms centrally imposed on teachers has not been an encouraging one. As Arthur Wise and others have argued, we simply do not have a sufficiently solid technology of teaching to warrant the imposition of uniform methodologies or curricula.[32] The search for the one best system has proved illusory. Most of the available evidence suggests that decisions about instruction require the active involvement of the teachers if they are to be successfully implemented. Effective programs are typically well adapted to particular groups of children. We believe that federal and state funds for instructional improvement should be channeled to individual schools and allocated by committees including both staff and lay residents. Instead of giving salary increments based on university course credits, pay increases might well be tied to in-service workshops coupled to such attempts to improve teaching.[33]

Public schools have tended to respond to organized groups. This is the way politics typically operates in this country. Businessmen and unions, for example, have had impact on vocational education, patriotic groups on the teaching of history, and minority groups on the teaching of ethnic studies and hiring of staff.[34] In recent years formerly excluded groups have gained a needed voice in school affairs. But in a pluralistic society such as ours—one in which there are great differences of wealth, status, and political power—some groups or individuals will remain unrepresented. We do not advocate returning to an older paternalistic tradition in which wise experts supposedly took care of everyone—for that was a pious fraud— but we do believe that there is danger in a me-tooism in which only the loud will be heard. There is a valuable tradition in public education, and one that should not be lost, that sees teachers as the trustees of all children. And this brings us to our next and final subject.

LOYALTY

The issue of loyalty to public education as a public good is closely related to participation in governance. In a democratic polity, to be able to influence an institution helps to create loyalty to it. Loyalty without voice is blind; voice without loyalty can easily lead to premature disillusionment and exit. Exit may make sense in some markets. If a soap manufacturer refuses to make a biodegradable product, a consumer might rationally shift to another brand. But public schools are not just a consumer good.

In recent years we have seen a large number of citizens seeking particular changes—a long line of petitioners or agitators, often with little communication between them about the central goals of the institution they sought to change. Many decision makers—school board members, legislators, educational leaders—have also lacked a coherent system of beliefs about public schooling that might help them to set priorities. Reforms have come and gone, and intellectual fashions have changed. An ardent integrationist of one period has become an equally ardent advocate of parental choice, private schools, and vouchers.

We do not believe that it is possible to find one narrowly defined set of principles that should underlie loyalty to public schools. Education so deeply involves basic values in tension—liberty and order, quality and equality—that each generation must renegotiate its own educational belief system. We welcome the notion of pluralistic and decentralized participation in school decision making, for it can create loyalty through voice. But we do believe that in the historic conception of the common school is a broad justification for a loyalty that could reestablish commitment to public education. In this view the public school was common not in the sense of vulgar, but common as the air we all breathe—a public good as vital to the commonwealth as public health. As citizens we all depend on the civic competence, good will, and knowledge of others. The same is true of our economic interdependence, as the future of the social security system illustrates. It has been estimated that the ratio of workers to retired people will drop from five-to-one to three-to-one by the turn of the twenty-first century; surely those children now in school will need to be a highly trained labor force. The effective education of *all* children—not just those whose parents know how to find it—is a public good, for ultimately society pays for ignorance just as it pays for disease and crime. The fact that these are old arguments for public education does not destroy their cogency.[35]

American society has invested less than most economically advanced nations in public goods and has made relatively few commitments to all citizens. Our vast system of public education, however, is an exception. More than any other nation in the world we have made extensive free education a right of all children and youth. Even when educators have criticized the shortcomings of our educational system, we have usually done so according to what Gunnar Myrdal called an American creed—one that stressed democracy, social justice, and equality. Most of our institutions—including public education—have fallen far short of that creed. It is foolish to believe that the public schools alone can bring about social justice or guarantee precarious democratic processes, but it is hard to imagine such goals without the public schools. We need to remind ourselves and the public forcefully and repeatedly of the principles that underlie the system. It was just such a forceful and repeated statement of ideology that helped to create the system in the first place.

Educators can no longer count on reform by accretion, nor can we do much directly about birth rates, oil shortages, stagflation, or other macro forces. What educators can do, however, is to rediscover and revitalize the images of potentiality of public education. The difficulties we face today are large, but by no means more awesome than those confronted by school people at the turn of the century, who coped with masses of immigrants in overcrowded classrooms in the cities and with grossly underfinanced rural schools. But then they had a deep faith in their task, a sense of almost millennial aspiration. "The community's duty to education," wrote an educator of that time, "is . . . its paramount moral duty. By law and punishment, by social agitation and discussion, society can regulate and form itself in a more or less haphazard and chance way. But through education society can formulate its own purposes, can organize its own means and resources, and thus shape itself with definiteness and economy in the direction in which it wishes to move." Once thus aroused, he believed, the community would give educators the attention and resources they needed. The writer was John Dewey, who realized more than any other American of the last century how fully democracy and social justice need to be re-created in each generation.[36]

NOTES

We wish to acknowledge the support of the Institute for Finance and Governance at Stanford University, an agency financed by the National Institute of Education. The views expressed are of course those of the authors and not necessarily those of the sponsoring groups.

1. Franklin Parker, "Where Have All the Innovations Gone?" *Educational Studies* 7 (Fall 1976): 237–43.

2. The question of public confidence in American institutions is, of course, somewhat tricky to judge, although available evidence suggests a drop during most of the 1970s. The October issues of *Phi Delta Kappan* include an annual poll on the public rating of public education. It demonstrates a decline every year for the last five. In a 1977 Field Poll of public attitudes toward 24 major institutions, 38 percent of respondents indicated that they had "not much confidence" in the public schools, second from the bottom in the entire list (above unions with 43 percent negative opinions) (*San Francisco Chronicle*, May 12, 1977). Rates of approval of local bond levies have declined—see, for example, Philip K. Piele and John Stuart Hall, *Budget, Bonds, and Ballots* (Lexington, Mass.: Lexington Press, 1973).

3. William L. Boyd, "Retrenchment in American Education: The Politics of Efficiency," AERA address, April 9, 1979. The entire issue of *Education and Urban Society* 11, no. 3 (May 1979) is edited by Boyd on the politics and economics of enrollment decline.

4. For an analysis of the historic grounds for loyalty to the common school, see R. Freeman Butts, *Public Education in the United States: From Revolution to Reform, 1776–1976* (New York: Holt, Rinehart & Winston, 1978).

5. Albert O. Hirschman, *Exit, Voice, and Loyalty: Responses to Decline in Firms, Organizations, and States* (Cambridge: Harvard University Press, 1970).

6. Donald Orlosky and B. Othanel Smith, "Educational Change: Its Origins and Characteristics," *Phi Delta Kappan* 53 (March 1972): 412–14.

7. H. Thomas James, *The New Cult of Efficiency* (Pittsburgh: University of Pittsburgh, 1969); and Arthur G. Wirth, *Education in the Technological Society: The Vocational-Liberal Studies Controversy in the Early Twentieth Century* (Scranton, Pa.: Intext Educational Publishers, 1972).

8. Michael B. Katz has pointed out the drift to genetic explanations in *The Irony of Early School Reform: Educational Innovation in Mid-Nineteenth Century Massachusetts* (Boston: Beacon Press, 1968), pp. 216–18.

9. David Tyack, "The Spread of Schooling in Victorian America: In Search of a Reinterpretation," *History of Education* 7 (October 1978): 173–82.

10. Michael B. Katz, *Class, Bureaucracy, and Schools: The Illusion of Education Change* (New York: Praeger, 1971), chap. 1.

11. Robert Wiebe, "The Social Functions of Public Education," *American Quarterly* 21 (Summer 1969): 147–50; and Daniel Walker Howe, ed., *Victorian America* (Philadelphia: University of Pennsylvania Press, 1976), pp. 3–28.

12. David Tyack, *The One Best System: A History of American Urban Education* (Cambridge: Harvard University Press, 1974), parts 1, 4.

13. On the importance of private power, see David K. Cohen, "Reforming School Politics," *Harvard Educational Review* 48 (November 1978): 429–47.

14. Edward A. Krug, *The Shaping of the American High School* (New York: Harper & Row, 1964).

15. Edgar B. Wesley, *NEA, The First Hundred Years: The Building of a Teaching Profession* (New York: Harper and Brothers, 1957).

16. Diane Ravitch, "A Wasted Decade," *The New Republic*, November 5, 1977, pp. 11–13; and Tyack, *The One Best System*, Epilogue.

17. Dale Mann, *Making Change Happen?* (New York: Teachers College Press, 1978).

18. Stephen K. Bailey, *The Purposes of Education* (Bloomington: Phi Delta Kappan, 1976).

19. Anthony Downs, "Up and Down With Ecology—The Issue-Attention Cycle," *Public Interest* 28 (Summer 1972): 38–50.

20. William L. Boyd, "The Changing Politics of Curriculum Policy-making for American Schools," *Review of Educational Research* 48 (Fall 1978): 577–628. Also see Frederick M. Wirt and Michael Kirst, *Political and Social Foundations of Education* (Berkeley: McCutchan, 1975), chap. 10.

21. Michael W. Kirst, "The New Politics of State Education Finance," *Phi Delta Kappan* 60, no. 6 (February 1979): 427–32.

22. Arthur E. Wise, "The Hyper-Rationalization of American Education," *New York University Quarterly* 4 (Summer 1977): 2–6.

23. Lorraine H. McDonnell and Anthony Pascal, "National Trends in Collective Bargaining," *Education and Urban Society* 11, no. 2 (February 1979): 124–51.

24. Paul Berman and Milbrey W. McLaughlin, *Federal Programs Supporting Educational Change, Vol. VIII: Implementing and Sustaining Innovations* (Santa Monica, Calif.: Rand Corporation, 1978); Mann, *Making Change Happen*; and Robert Herriott and Neal Gross, *The Dynamics of Planned Educational Change* (Berkeley: McCutchan, 1979).

25. Paul E. Peterson, "The Politics of American Education," in *Review of Research in Education*, ed. Fred N. Kerlinger and John B. Carroll, vol. 2 (Itasca, Ill.: Peacock, 1974), pp. 348–89. Also see Edith K. Mosher and Jennings Wagoner, eds., *The Changing Politics of Education* (Berkeley: McCutchan, 1978).

26. See Stephen K. Bailey and Edith Mosher, *ESEA: The Office of Education Administers a Law* (Syracuse: Syracuse University Press, 1968), especially chap. 2.

27. Hirschman, *Exit, Voice, and Loyalty*. For the scenario of schools as a declining industry, see Lewis Mayhew, *Educational Leadership and Declining Enrollments* (Berkeley: McCutchan, 1974), chap. 7.

28. As a sample of the poor public press, see Connie Cronley, "Blackboard Jungle Updated," *TWA Ambassador*, September 1978, pp. 25–28, 62–64.

29. Raymond E. Callahan, *Education and the Cult of Efficiency* (Chicago: University of Chicago Press, 1962).

30. Jonathan Sher, ed., *Education in Rural America: A Reassessment of Conventional Wisdom* (Boulder, Colo.: Westview Press, 1977).

31. John C. Hogan, *The Schools, The Courts and The Public Interest* (Lexington, Mass.: D. C. Heath, 1974). See also Joel S. Berke, *Answers to Inequity* (Berkeley: McCutchan, 1974).

32. Arthur E. Wise, "Minimum Competency Testing: Another Case of Hyper-Rationalization," *Phil Delta Kappan,* May 1978, pp. 596–98; and Arthur E. Wise, "Why Educational Policies Often Fail: The Hyper-Rationalization Hypothesis," *Journal of Curriculum Studies* 9 (May 1977): 43–57.

33. Herriott and Gross, *The Dynamics of Planned Educational Change,* especially chaps. 11 and 14.

34. Boyd, "The Changing Politics of Curriculum Policy-making for American Schools." Also see Frederick M. Wirt and Michael W. Kirst, *The Political Web of American Schools* (Boston: Little, Brown, 1972).

35. Lawrence A. Cremin, *The American Common School: An Historic Conception* (New York: Bureau of Publications, Teachers College, Columbia University, 1951), part 2.

36. John Dewey, *My Pedagogic Creed* (Washington, D.C.: Progressive Education Association, 1929), p. 16.

TIME MAGAZINE

Quality, Not Just Quantity

Questions to think about

1 *What is new about the Paideia proposal? How does the Paideia proposal recommend changing schools?.*
2 *What criticisms have been directed at the proposal? How might its implementation affect minorities? Do you feel it could be effective? Why or why not?*
3 *How could the Paideia proposal be integrated into the open systems model?*
4 *With a specific school district in mind, outline a plan of action for implementing major change.*

Of his early education, Henry Adams once wrote, "It taught little and that little ill." Many of America's schools today teach precious little of what students ought to know, and that little ill. High school diplomas are routinely awarded to students who are functionally illiterate, who cannot do long division, and who have no idea what is contained in the Bill of Rights. Among educators there is a sense of desperation that America's young lack even the rudiments of learning, and a still greater feeling of despair that nothing can be done bout it. What can and should be done about it, declares Philosopher Mortimer Adler, is a radical return to an education that is both general and liberal, and equal in quality for all.

Equal quantity of schooling for all students, Adler argues, has only half fulfilled "the democratic promise of equal educational opportunity"; the deeper commitment should be for equal quality for everyone. The present multitrack system, he maintains, must therefore be completely reformed. In *The Paideia Proposal: An Educational Manifesto* (Macmillan;

$2.95), published this week, he proposes a sweeping, nationwide, twelve-year, single-track academic program with virtually no electives and no vocational training. The ringing words of the late Robert Maynard Hutchins are Adler's anthem: "The best education for the best is the best education for all."

The Paideia proposal (which takes its name from the Greek word meaning the upbringing of a child) rests on Adler's conviction that specialization is the besetting sin of our time. The program aims, he says, at "enabling the young to become better human beings and better citizens, not just better at some particular line of work." The goal is bold, perhaps utopian and typical of this tireless polymath. Adler, 79, is an encyclopedist and organizer of knowledge whose Great Books (with Hutchins) and Great Ideas volumes set out simply, and comprehensively, to make the intellectual monuments of Western civilization available to any reader.

Three years ago, Adler, director of the Chicago-based Institute for Philosophical Research, formed the Paideia Group, a panel of 22 educators and scholars who held a series of conferences seeking a new approach to public schooling. Among the participants: former Columbia University Provost Jacques Barzun, Bard College President Leon Botstein, Editor and Critic Clifton Fadiman.

The primary elements of the Paideia proposal are what Adler calls the three columns. These represent the three types of learning that should go on simultaneously throughout all twelve years as well as the styles of teaching required for each. The first consists of the acquisition of fundamental knowledge: history, literature, languages, mathematics, science and the fine arts. This material should be instilled didactically, through lectures and the like. The second column develops the basic intellectual skills of reading, writing, mathematical computation and scientific investigation: know-how as opposed to know-what. These should be taught just as physical or athletic skills are taught, through practice and coaching. The third and most innovative column refers to the enlargement of understanding: the aesthetic appreciation of works of art and the ability to think critically about ideas and values. This calls for a Socratic method of teaching, the lone requirement a large table of students where the teacher is simply the first among equals.

In addition, Adler proposes twelve years of physical education and eight years of manual arts (such as cooking, typing, automobile repair), and at least one year of instruction to help in choosing a career. Paideia thus becomes "the general learning that should be the possession of all human beings."

To Adler, Paideia is a model within reach. He is preparing a manual, to be issued next year, that will help school systems and teachers implement the proposal. One teaching experiment has already been carried out at the Skyline High School in Oakland, Calif. Seventy-five students spent one year studying 50 of Adler's Great Books, using the Socratic method of pedagogy. The results, says Principal Nicholas Caputi, were "stellar," but some 80% of the students were classified as gifted anyway. A fuller test will come in Chicago, where Superintendent Ruth Love plans a pilot school that will give the program a three-year trial run.

Some educators familiar with Paideia suggest that Adler has neglected one crucial question: Who will teach the teachers? Phil Keisling, an editor of the *Washington Monthly*, believes that "the legions of incompetent teachers is an even more distressing problem that the laxity of curricular standards." Adler acknowledges that further reforms will be necessary to retrain teachers, and he urges that teachers should receive a solid liberal arts education and "the hell with courses in pedagogy and educational philosophy."

A more serious objection being raised against Paideia is the charge that it is elitist. Harvard Sociologist David Riesman doubts that a nation as diverse as the U.S. could sustain a uniform "core" curriculum: "It could be done in Japan, it is done in France, but we're too hetergeneous in this country." Educational Historian Paul Nash of Boston University places Paideia in "the tradition of the gentleman's education." Studying such things as the *Iliad*, he contends, will serve to make the "non-gentlemen groups"—blacks, Hispanics, women, the lower class—less employable than before. Adler, however, fiercely maintains that society's low expectations of children are self-fulfilling. He affirms that "everyone is educable up to his or her capacity," precisely what Paideia is designed to do.

Adler does not deny the difficulties. He concedes that it may take 30 years for Paideia and like-minded reforms to reverse entrenched attitudes and practices. Indeed, Paideia is part of a nationwide trend toward more traditional and rigorous schooling. Ultimately, as David Riesman suggested, only by hitching the rickety wagon of American education to a star can it be made to budge an inch. Affirms Adler: "An ideal—even a difficult one— excites everyone's imagination. To say it cannot be done is to beg the question. We've got to try it."

HAROLD G. SHANE

The Silicon Age II:
Living and Learning in
an Information Epoch

Questions to think about

1 *How does Shane describe the silicon age? What are its implications for schools and individuals?*

2 *Taking into account all the articles you have read here on change and the future, which changes do you think will be the most challenging for schools?*

3 *How can schools use the concept of open systems to prepare for change and the future?*

4 *Draw up a proposal for educators, describing how to deal with change and future needs of society and individuals.*

> *What is there in the list of strange and unexpected events that has not occurred in our time? Our lives have transcended the limits of humanity; we are born to serve as the theme of incredible tales to posterity.*
> —Aeschines (389–314 B.C.)

Some years ago Daniel Bell, the Harvard sociologist, coined the term "post-industrial society" to describe an era based on services, into which our industrial age was being transformed. More recently, however, it has become clear that the post-industrial world is not just a service society; it is an "information society"—one in which knowledge and the handling of information have elbowed aside the smokestack and the assembly line as symbols of America's prowess.[1]

Reprinted from *Phi Delta Kappan* (October 1983). Copyright © 1983 by Phi Delta Kappan, Inc.

When did the U.S. enter the information epoch? John Naisbitt argues persuasively that the "megashift" from industrial to information society occurred in 1956 and 1957. In 1956 white-collar workers—managerial, technical, clerical, and professional—for the first time outnumbered blue-collar workers. And 1957 "marked the beginning of the globalization of the information revolution: The Russians launched Sputnik, the missing technological catalyst in a growing information society."[2]

The unique opportunities (and demands) that accompany the information epoch required us to explore and to understand more clearly the myriad ways in which society is being influenced by the information sciences and microtechnologies. We must determine what social inventiveness and institutional repair work may be required because of (1) the enormous impact of the microprocessor and of telecommunications networks, (2) ergonomic[3] responses to increasingly robotized workplaces and computerized homes, and (3) ubiquitous 24-hour television which, in some areas, now allows access to more than 100 channels.

LEARNING TO LIVE WITH NEW REALITIES

Change in our modern age takes place with bewildering speed. In recent decades the life sciences have produced clones of mammals, oral contraceptives, artificial life forms, heart transplants, and gene splicing. The physical sciences have given us lasers and holography, the computer, and landings on our moon and on Mars; they have even sent a probe into the infinite reaches of space that lie beyond the orbits of the outermost planets in our solar system.

One outcome of this rapid change has been social disorientation. The disorientation manifests itself in many ways—from worldwide assassinations, political kidnappings, and terrorism to alienation, drug and alcohol abuse, and teenage pregnancies and suicides. Correcting problems such as these—and a host of others—will be a prime task for humans to undertake in the information age.

Another challenge in an era of information overload or "infoglut"[4] is meeting the demands that will be placed on education. As Bentley Glass put it in 1968, "The educated man of yesterday is the maladjusted, uneducated man of today and the culturally illiterate misfit of tomorrow." Consequently, educated humans need to acquire much more knowledge than they needed to have 25 or 30 years ago. Traditional curriculum content and instructional practices are certain to change as educators begin to master the art of using knowledge to react promptly and wisely to the difficulties created by the demands that accompany an era of infoglut.

In the remainder of this article I plan to outline some of the ways in which the world community is being transmuted by the electronic environment. Since "knowledge potential" is our one infinite resource, I have also suggested some ways in which we need to modify certain personal and educational values as we use this potential to thread our way through the maze of information that Daniel Bell estimated will soon be doubling every two years.

THE ELECTRONIC ENVIRONMENT

The implications of microelectronic phenomena go far beyond the microcomputers that have captured popular attention. The steam-powered technology of the 18th and 19th centuries and the internal combustion/electrical technology that shaped the early decades of the 20th century greatly reduced the need for arduous physical labor. However, because microelectronic technology has begun to supplant both physical *and* intellectual labor in the 1980s, significant changes are taking place at all levels of society throughout the world.

The effect of the microelectronic revolution on the military, for example, is dramatic and rather alarming. On the one hand, many of the most advanced developments in microelectronics lend themselves readily to military applications. On the other hand, the rapid development in sophisticated communications and weaponry could further destabilize the nuclear arms race. Devastatingly accurate targeting, guidance, and damage assessment devices have been developed. A report from the Worldwatch Institute suggests that the new technology may make first strikes more tempting to an enemy that hopes to score a nuclear knockout.

One other factor adds a devastating element of uncertainty in a society that has begun to depend heavily on the power of microelectronics: the electromagnetic pulse (EMP) effect. Scientists believe that a nuclear device exploded over, say, Nebraska—even though detonated 250 miles above the earth's surface—would blanket the entire United States with an electromagnetic pulse that could completely paralyze much of the equipment powered by electricity—some of it permanently.[5] This EMP effect renders electronic gear—from toasters and telephones to transistors, computers, and even our airborne command posts—dysfunctional. Imagine the catastrophic effect on a society that is coming to depend ever more heavily on microelectronics of all kinds.

The changes wrought by the microelectronic revolution go far beyond the military, however; they affect all parts of society today, including the times and places where work is done, the range of foods available, the bewildering array of video- and audiocassette equipment, our increased mobility and choice of mode of transportation (more than 700 models of cars and trucks were on the U.S. market in 1982), and even new patterns of personal relationships. The microchip has created living quarters in which mail, information sources such as videotext and viewdata, security control, and the selection and ordering of goods and services are all handled electronically.

Health and longevity are also being influenced in our microelectronic epoch. Computerized prosthetic devices have already helped the paraplegic to walk, the voiceless to speak, and the brain-injured to function. It has even become technically possible to use brain-dead bodies, housed in a "neomortorium," to provide storage for living organs until they are harvested to replace the lungs, kidneys, hearts, or livers of those who need transplants.[6]

The growing use of laser-beam surgery represents yet another dramatic advance in medicine. Doctors can now snake a laser through tubing and reach organs in locations that heretofore were inoperable because they are out of the reach of traditional surgical tools and techniques.

And then there are the electronic media (particularly television)— possibly the most pervasive manifestation of the silicon age. The "tube" brings us visual mobility and instant information, as well as the phenomenon of "interactive TV," which enables viewers in some communities to express opinions on various issues and questions merely by pressing a button. TV also barrages us with manic ads, increasingly explicit sex, and gore-in-detail during the *1½ billion* hours Americans spend daily in televiewing.

Until recently, the TV programs available to European audiences were for the most part limited, and to some extent controlled, by the governments of the various countries. One cannot avoid speculating about the socioeconomic and political implications of a vastly increased public exposure to American-style TV with multiple stations and dozens of program choices. One European official, who requested anonymity, suggested that, to protect the public from garbage on TV, his government might consider forbidding the use of receiving dish antennae that pick up signals from satellites.

Charles Owen of the Illinois Institute of Technology is among a growing group who forecast the proliferation of in-the-home electronic equipment that ranges far beyond television. Among his images: robots to perform routine household chores; appliances responsive to voice commands; force fields to detect intruders; high-tech food processors to chop, mix, cook, and store victuals; and "holographic" TV to project three-dimensional scenes *outside* the confines of the tube.

Though experts disagree as to the merits and demerits of video games, it seems safe to conclude that they have pervaded our lives. In 1982 alone, 38 billion quarters clinked into coin slots, and home video vendors grossed $4.5 billion in sales. Some communities have felt obliged to set a minimum age for admission to video arcades. Others have forbidden their youths to enter such arcades during school hours, in an effort to stem absenteeism on the part of pupils who had become "video junkies." The most unusual—and alarming—information that testifies to the possible effects of "video-mania" indicates that prolonged play—five or six hours at a stretch—has triggered epileptic seizures (both grand and petit mal) in young addicts.[7]

THE CHANGING WORKPLACE

The new microelectronic age is radically changing the workplace. This transformation has implications for education that we are only now beginning to understand.

The long-term impact of rapid technological change is nearly impossible to forecast accurately. The technological changes reported almost daily tend to threaten us with technogenic unemployment even as they open new employment vistas. In July, for instance, *Robotics World* announced that scientists at the Nippon Telegraph and Telephone Public Corporation had created a robot that could read the news with 99.5% accuracy. The robot's computer (programmed with a dictionary) can scan print, check its memory banks, and deliver a properly inflected sentence. The report suggests a future for news-reading robots on the radio and for robots as telephone operators and as readers for the blind.[8] Some innovations are already creating technogenic unemployment, as when, for instance, a factory is retooled and automated. Consider this example:

> The General Electric Company is investing $316 million over
> the next three years to revitalize its locomotive plant in Erie,
> Pennsylvania. When all of the robots, computerized machine tools,
> and other automation systems are in place, the Erie "factory with
> a future" will have increased its production capacity by one-third.[9]

Obviously, such investments should strengthen the nation's economy. As far as the workforce is concerned, however, *two* workers in the future will do in 16 *hours* at General Electric what *70* employees did in 16 *days* before the plant received its electronic facelift.

Developments of this nature promise more major job-market shifts for the Eighties and Nineties. For instance, electronic mail promises to reduce the need for postal workers; linotype workers, elevator operators, and farm laborers will probably continue to dwindle in number; and our homes, as they become "electronic cottages," are likely to take less time to maintain.

On the other hand, the ranks of computer operators, office machine technicians, and tax-form specialists should swell, along with those of child-care personnel, geriatric nurses, social workers, and fast-food distributors. A volume perpared for the World Future Society forecasts a sampling of new occupations, the number of workers likely to be required, and average salaries as of 1990: energy technicians, 1.5 million at $26,000; housing rehabilitation technicians, 1.75 milion at $24,000; genetic engineering technicians, 150,000 at $30,000; holographic inspection specialists, 200,000 at $28,000; bionic-electronic technicians, 200,000 at $32,000; and many more.[10] Educators from the preschool to the graduate school will need to be increasingly alert to shifting demands posed by a rapidly changing workplace.

Automated offices and an increase in stay-at-home workers have added two new buzz words to our vocabularies: (1) *telecommuters*, to describe people who "commute" to work via TV or computer terminals, and (2) *flexiplaces*, which refers to flexibility in the sites where one earns a living. The terms also suggest that new employer/employee relationships will continue to emerge and that many of our long- and dearly held images of work are obsolete. As Alvin Toffler observes in his most recent book, *Previews and Premises*,[11] the nature of work in the emerging Third Wave information sector that is superseding the industrial society mandates enriching and enlarging jobs, increasing employee participation in policy making, devising more varied organizational approaches to the tasks performed in our workplaces, and—of particular importance to educators—graduating workers who are knowledgeable, literate, resourceful, empathic, and innovative.

The increasingly widespread deployment of industrial robots may prove to be the most important phenomenon to restructure industry since steam engine technology appeared in the 18th century. James Albus, chief of the industrial systems division at the National Bureau of Standards, estimates that, as of early 1983, there were perhaps 5,000 robots in U.S. factories and that their numbers would increase by at least 20,000 and perhaps by as many as 60,000 installations *per year* between 1990 and the year 2000 if present trends continue. Since two to four person-years of work go into the installation of a system of industrial robots, a robot/electronic economy could be a welcome source of employment. However, these "steel-collar workers" will take jobs from a substantial number of human blue-collar workers. As Vary Coates noted, "[S]ince robots have neither flexibilities nor the restrictions of humans, a work environment organized for humans is not necessarily the environment that is best for robots. . . . To use robots most efficiently, the flow of work and the factory floor may have to be completely redesigned."[12]

Consider the challenge to education presented by (1) meeting new skill requirements of workers and of managers and (2) retrofitting or retraining the personnel displaced. In fact, as Toffler sees it, educators need to begin revamping our present system of mass education:

> Today's schools are turning out still more factory-style workers for jobs that won't exist. Diversify. Individualize. Decentralize. Smaller, more local schools. More education in the home. More parental involvement. More creativity, less rote (it's the rote jobs that are disappearing the fastest).[13]

Another development that may create spectacular changes in the workplace is examined by Colin Norman in his study of science and technology in the Eighties.[14] The potential impact of microtechnology and biotechnology is so tremendous that it seems unlikely that any new industries will even begin to approach the wallop that these two fields promise to have on our lives by the end of the century. Gene splicing, for instance, permits the gene for human interferon to be fished out of a cell possessing tens of thousands of other genes. Among other possible biochem/microtech contributions to the information epoch are self-fertilizing corn and wheat that draw nitrogen from the air. Other innovations include new ways to produce drugs and chemicals at modest cost, to produce fuel from waste materials, and to produce bacteria that clean up oil spills.

Let me mention one final development of the silicon age that could soon affect all our lives. Kenneth Hanck and Keith DeArmond, chemistry professors at North Carolina State University at Raleigh, have been working for more than four years to replace microchips with individual molecules. Such molecules would be capable of storing readable, coded information in approximately *one-millionth* of the space that even today's tiny computer chips require. To date, Hanck and DeArmond have identified chemical compounds with molecules that retain six electrons potentially useful as memory devices. Computers using molecular memory devices would be incredibly more powerful, tinier, and more efficient than anything now available.

EDUCATION IN AN ELECTRONIC AGE

In recent months our entire system of education—kindergarten through college—has come under harsh scrutiny. In part, this is because governments, institutions, and individuals are discovering that dynamic developments in electronic information technologies, in biotechnologies, and in complex global communications are rapidly changing what they do, how they do it, and how they relate to one another. But the onrushing silicon age is already changing the entire landscape of education. According to the Office of Technology Assessment:

> The so-called *information revolution*, driven by rapid advances in communication and computer technology, is profoundly affecting American education. It is changing the nature of *what needs to be learned, who needs to learn it, who will provide it, and how it will be provided and paid for.*[15] (Emphasis added)

We cannot improve our schools without first determining how to cope with the silicon age: we need to develop strategies—both as professional educators and as private citizens—for living and learning in an electronic epoch, as well as future-oriented administrative policies, curriculum content, instructional practices, links with parents and community and other educational agencies—including the omnipresent TV set and its video-appendages.

ALTERNATIVES AND CONSEQUENCES

As the microelectronic boom enhances the information explosion, I see no cause for "technophobia" in public school classrooms or on the college-campus. However, we must recognize that in an information society the schools seem fated to find themselves no longer cloistered retreats but lively arenas in which an increasing array of conflicting social, economic, moral, and political ideas will collide. A good curriculum for the 1990s will be one that, among other things, helps learners understand the nature of an era of value conflicts.

Basic skills, clearly defined, are of even greater importance in the new knowledge society that we are entering. As we define "basic skills," we find that, in addition to the basic computer skills necessary to an information epoch, familiar basic elements—e.g., reading and writing, which have constituted traditional literacy—will acquire new meanings. In the language arts, for instance, an understanding of propaganda and the nature of and reasons for selected news is now basic. So is an understanding of ecological relationships, toxic waste problems, and the subtle meanings of entropy in the natural sciences. As for the social sciences (e.g., history, political science, economics, sociology, anthropology), all must acquire new meanings that will be compatible with the demands of the era in which our young learners will spend their lives.

Perhaps above all, one of the basic qualities of good schools will be their ability to teach skills that are transferable from one job to another in a rapidly changing world of work. This has become an important direction for traditional career and vocational education to take.

In addition, the "mind workers" of tomorrow—many of them already enrolled in our kindergarten-to-university continuum—must be exposed to value choices by wise and courageous teachers who are themselves aware of contemporary ideological crises and who have clarified their *own* values. Educators must understand that the nature of the world of tomorrow cannot be forecast with precision; what tomorrow brings will depend on where our insightful, humane values—or their absence—will lead us as we move into the future of the information society. This is what living and learning in a high-tech/microtech age involves.

The societal tensions generated by microtechnologies and their impact on our world will not grow less. Schools must begin living in the future now, just as their young charges will have to do. Even amid rapid and often bewildering changes, I remain optimistic. I believe we are passing the crest of our Third Wave malaise and are ready to debate and to determine what the "microkids" of today and tomorrow need to know and how U.S. schools can best educate the "microelectronic generation."

NOTES

1. See, for example, Yoseji Masuda, *The Information Society as Post-Industrial Society* (Tokyo: Institute for the Information Society, 1980).

2. John Naisbitt, *Megatrends* (New York: Warner Books, 1982), p. 12.

3. "Ergonomics" originally referred to the study of worker/machine relationships with the aim of reducing fatigue, strain, or discomfort. In the computer era, it has begun to be used to encompass psychological and social relationships. For example, the computer may begin to take the place of the imaginary playmate in the affections of some children; hence it has become the object of psychosocial analysis.

4. To the best of my knowledge, "infoglut" is a useful coinage by Michael Marien, editor of *Future Survey.*

5. For a more detailed report on EMP, see William J. Broad, "The Chaos Factor," *Science 83,* January/February 1983, pp. 41–49.

6. For compelling arguments supporting this rather unsettling proposal, see Willard Gaylin, "Harvesting the Dead," *Harper's,* September 1974, pp. 23–30.

7. T. K. Daneshmend and M. J. Campbell, "Dark Warrior Epilepsy," *British Medical Journal,* 12 June 1982, pp. 1751–52.

8. *Indianapolis Star,* 4 July 1983, p. 10–A.

9. The June 1983 issue of *Futurist,* from which this illustration is taken (p. 18), notes that further information can be obtained from the News Bureau, General Electric Company, P.O. Box 5900, Norwalk, CT 06856.

10. Marvin Cetron and Thomas O'Toole, "Careers with a Future: Where the Jobs Will Be," in Edward Cornish, ed., *Careers Tomorrow: The Outlook for Work in a Changing World* (Bethesda, Md.: World Future Society, 1983), pp. 10–18.

11. Alvin Toffler, *Previews and Premises* (New York: William Morrow, 1983).

12. Vary T. Coates, "The Potential Impact of Robotics," *Futurist,* February 1983, pp. 28–32.

13. Toffler, p. 58.

14. Colin Norman, *The God That Limps: Science and Technology in the Eighties* (New York: W. W. Norton, 1981).

15. Office of Technology Assessment, *Informational Technology and Its Impact on American Education* (Washington, D.C.: OTA, Autumn 1982), p. 3.